"Thomas and Tweeddale have brought together an impressive team of sympathetic scholars to provide us with this wonderful in-depth exposition of many important aspects of Calvin's life and teaching. The contributors to *John Calvin* not only highlight but also understand the profound contemporary relevance of his theological and pastoral emphases. Here is a genuine Calvinian treat! May it encourage twenty-first-century pastors and teachers—indeed, all serious Christians—to think, worship, serve, and live in the kind of dependence on God and confidence in his word that Calvin so courageously exhibited in his day."

    Sinclair B. Ferguson, Chancellor's Professor of Systematic Theology, Reformed Theological Seminary; Teaching Fellow, Ligonier Ministries

"If I have only one chance to influence the minds of my students with a voice from the past, I turn to John Calvin. No one marries biblical knowledge to systematic theology with an eye to Christian piety like Calvin. Unfortunately, many Christians today have never read Calvin, and their theological house is the less stable for it. Do not fear: *John Calvin: For a New Reformation* equips Christians to withstand the storms of theological compromise. By introducing Calvin's theology, this book provides the church with a biblical and theological foundation that will not be shaken. Read this book, and then run to read Calvin himself. In doing so, you will discover an exegetical ally, a theological father, and a Christian friend whose life, teachings, and ministry will guide you into Christian godliness."

    Matthew Barrett, Associate Professor of Christian Theology, Midwestern Baptist Theological Seminary; Executive Editor, Credo Magazine; editor, *Reformation Theology*

"Those who think everything about John Calvin has already been said and written will be pleasantly surprised by this great book. Complete, accessible, scholarly, and highly relevant, this fine collection makes Geneva's Reformer a companion and guide for today's church and theology."

    Herman Selderhuis, President, Theological University Apeldoorn, the Netherlands; Director, Refo500; President, Reformation Research Consortium

"Not all books on John Calvin are equally helpful, interesting, or valuable. This one ranks high in all three areas. The team of scholars and pastors that Thomas and Tweeddale have assembled is impressive; the accounting of Calvin's life, ministry, and thought is both thorough and accessible; and the overall value of the essay collection is significant. For busy pastors and church leaders who wonder what John Calvin thought or how he served, this is the place to turn. For all those of us who long for a new reformation in the global church, this is the book we can return to again and again."

    Sean Michael Lucas, Senior Pastor, Independent Presbyterian Church, Memphis, Tennessee; Chancellor's Professor of Church History, Reformed Theological Seminary

"Tweeddale, Thomas, and their team have produced a wonderful volume that will surely be a useful companion to Calvin scholars and students alike. Well-written pages rest on piles of densely packed notes, and for newcomers to Calvin, the bibliographic essay at the book's close is worth half the price of the book. Best of all, Calvin himself emerges as the careful scholar, complicated friend, severe pastor, and brilliant theologian that he really was."

Chad Van Dixhoorn, Professor of Church History, Westminster Theological Seminary; author, *Confessing the Faith* and *God's Ambassadors*

"A comprehensive and engaging survey of Calvin's life, theology, and pastoral practice that deserves to be read—and savored—again and again."

Scott M. Manetsch, Professor of Church History and the History of Christian Thought, Trinity Evangelical Divinity School; author, *Calvin's Company of Pastors*

"After five hundred years, the life, writings, and legacy of John Calvin continue to pose considerable challenges. How are we today to understand such an extraordinarily creative yet, in many ways, enigmatic figure whose influence on Christianity has been, and is still, enormous? From his own day to ours, this Frenchman has remained a profoundly controversial figure. These essays, rich in learning and thoughtful in approach, offer a sympathetic and accessible approach to Calvin as a theologian, churchman, and pastor, without avoiding the difficult questions. Readers will encounter the Reformer of Geneva in the full force of his character. The editors have brought together an important and fine collection of essays that interpret Calvin for our time."

Bruce Gordon, Titus Street Professor of Ecclesiastical History, Yale Divinity School

"*John Calvin: For a New Reformation* bears witness to the vastly significant contributions made by the famous French Reformer, pastor, and theologian. Not only have the editors assigned topics that represent the many foci of Calvin's thought—and they are great in both number and quality—but they have also chosen widely respected authorities to write on them. In addition, they have allotted to them a generous page limit to explore the topics in depth. This volume will whet the appetite of those who are in the initial stages of exploring Calvin and will also satisfy those who have long studied the legacy of Reformed thought."

W. Andrew Hoffecker, Professor of Church History Emeritus, Reformed Theological Seminary

John Calvin

John Calvin

For a New Reformation

Edited by Derek W. H. Thomas
and John W. Tweeddale

Afterword by R. C. Sproul

WHEATON, ILLINOIS

Library of Congress Cataloging-in-Publication Data

Names: Thomas, Derek W. H., 1953– editor.
Title: John Calvin : for a new Reformation / Derek W. H. Thomas and John W. Tweeddale, eds. ; afterword by R. C. Sproul.
Description: Wheaton : Crossway, 2019. | Includes bibliographical references and index.
Identifiers: LCCN 2018051977 (print) | LCCN 2019014665 (ebook) | ISBN 9781433512827 (pdf) | ISBN 9781433512834 (mobi) | ISBN 9781433523991 (epub) | ISBN 9781433512810 (hc)
Subjects: LCSH: Calvin, Jean, 1509–1564. | Calvinism.
Classification: LCC BX9424.3 (ebook) | LCC BX9424.3 .J64 2019 (print) | DDC 284/.2092—dc23
LC record available at https://lccn.loc.gov/2018051977

Contents

Preface

More than five hundred years after his birth, John Calvin (1509–1564) remains an important figure for understanding the modern world. A remarkable scholar, organizer, preacher, and churchman, Calvin emerged as a leading second-generation Reformer in the sixteenth century. While many outstanding theologians shaped the Protestant Reformation, Calvin's labors in Geneva in particular set the stage for reformation around the world. Since his death, admirers and despisers alike have reflected on his legacy. His protégé, Theodore Beza, captured this dynamic in the conclusion of his biography on Calvin: "In [Calvin] all men may see a most beautiful example of the Christian character, an example which it is as easy to slander as it is difficult to imitate."[1] To put the matter less starkly, whether as an object of criticism or as a model to follow, Calvin is a man worthy of consideration.

In this book, leading Reformed pastors and scholars reflect on the significance of the ministry and teaching of John Calvin for the church today. Part 1 focuses on "the life and work of John Calvin" and gives specific attention to his pastoral ministry. Chapters 1 and 2 sketch the contours of Calvin's biography. Michael Haykin begins by surveying the formative years of Calvin's life prior to his ministry in Geneva, concentrating on his education, conversion, and earliest publication and on the events that led to his joining the ranks of the Reformation. Steve Nichols then picks up the story with Calvin's call to Geneva and shows how he and his colleagues struggled for the cause of orthodoxy in seeking to reform the church according to the teaching of Scripture.

---

1. Theodore Beza, "Life of John Calvin," trans. Henry Beveridge, in *Tracts and Letters*, 1:c.

The next five chapters provide case studies from Calvin's life and ministry. In chapter 3, David Calhoun gives a portrait of Calvin as a pastor. Relying on an extensive cross section of sources, he shows that Calvin's primary calling in life was to serve as a "minister of the word of God in the Church of Geneva." Building on this theme, Doug Kelly makes the case in chapter 4 that Calvin viewed the Reformation primarily as a pastoral-care movement. Although we learn much from Calvin's writings, Kelly contends that we can never really know what kind of pastor he was until we study the "session minutes" of the Consistory in Geneva. Bob Godfrey reminds us in chapter 5 that the work of reforming and pastoring the church was not the work of one man or city. Godfrey demonstrates how friendship was an important way for Calvin to extend the reach of the Reformation. In chapter 6, Steve Lawson contends that Calvin was primarily a preacher. He surveys the expository method of Calvin's preaching by identifying the central theological principles that undergirded his preaching while also noting several distinctives of his pulpit ministry. Rounding out this section, Derek Thomas explains in chapter 7 why Calvin wrote the *Institutes of the Christian Religion.* He traces its development throughout Calvin's ministry, provides an overview of key themes, and gives suggestions for first-time readers of Calvin's classic work. Taken together, the chapters in part 1 provide a biographical mosaic of Calvin's life as a theologian and pastor, and chapter 7 serves as a bridge to the focus of part 2.

Part 2 considers "the teaching of John Calvin." Using the *Institutes* as a rough guide, this section incorporates analysis of Calvin's commentaries, sermons, and other writings to introduce readers to his views on theology and the Christian life.

Scott Oliphint begins this discussion by tackling the organizational rationale of Calvin's doctrine of Scripture, focusing especially on the role of the Holy Spirit. In doing so, he draws attention to the importance of Calvin's view of Scripture for the development of a Reformed apologetic. In chapter 9, John Fesko surveys the broad contours of Calvin's doctrine of creation and humanity and explores the relationship of this doctrine to related topics, such as government, natural law, science, art, and music. In particular, he explains how Calvin viewed creation as the theater of God's glory. Related to this point, Burk Parsons summarizes Calvin's teaching on the providence of God in chapter 10 by examining its place in the *Institutes* and its relationship to the doctrines of predestination and creation. He reminds us that for Calvin, the doctrine of providence leads us to worship. The following chapter, by Guy Waters, takes up Calvin's teaching on the law in relation to creation, sin, and redemptive history. He notes how the Reformer's sensitivity to the unfolding of Scripture affected his understanding of biblical law and its application to the contemporary church.

Chapter 12 covers the person and work of Christ in Calvin's thought. Paul Wells highlights the theme of mediation to reflect on Calvin's development of related topics, such as reconciliation, union with Christ, and the promise of new creation. In chapter 13, Joel Beeke addresses the topic of the Holy Spirit in Calvin's theology. He summarizes Calvin's thinking on the Spirit in relation to the Scriptures, Christ, the order of salvation, the assurance and application of redemption, and spiritual gifts. Next, Ted Donnelly introduces readers to Calvin's well-known *Golden Booklet*. He shows that for Calvin, the Christian life entails cross bearing and self-denial. Then, in chapter 15, Derek Thomas takes us deeper into Calvin's understanding of Christian living by exploring his sermons on the book of Job. Thomas connects the incomprehensibility of God, a critical theme in Calvin's theology, with Christian endurance through adversity. In chapter 16, Paul Helm outlines Calvin's view of predestination. After considering how this doctrine intersects with themes such as providence and union with Christ, Helm demonstrates that Calvin never intended for his teaching on predestination to promote speculation but rather for it to encourage us to be sure of our relation to Christ, who is the mirror of election.

The next two chapters cover aspects of Calvin's ecclesiology. In chapter 17, John Tweeddale explains that Calvin describes the church as mother in order to refine arguments of church fathers on the role of the church, promote the Reformation doctrine of salvation, develop a theological framework for the ministry in Geneva, and urge fellow Christians not to forsake the means of grace in the visible church. Then Keith Mathison situates Calvin's views on the sacraments in their historical context, probes possible influences on his doctrine, considers the relationship of the sacraments to union with Christ, and sketches the broad contours of his teaching on baptism and the Lord's Supper.

The last two chapters draw on Calvin's eschatology. In chapter 19, Robert Peterson explores the topic of God's preservation of his people in Calvin's writings. He considers how Calvin's view differed from Roman Catholic teaching, what biblical texts Calvin relied on to develop his thought, and how Calvin applied this doctrine. Finally, Cornelis Venema provides a comprehensive treatment of Calvin's eschatology. By examining topics such as the intermediate state, the signs of the times, the second advent of Christ, the antichrist, the millennium, the resurrection, and the consummation of all things, Venema shows that Calvin's teaching on the last things pervades his writings. While Calvin's theology extends beyond what is covered in this book, the chapters in part 2 give readers an overview of the scope of his biblical and theological writing.

As can be seen in this overview, the goal of this book is to encourage you to read and study Calvin. Our aim is to provide an accessible one-volume introduction to his life and teaching. We hope that these chapters will serve both as a primer for those who have never read Calvin and as a resource for students of Reformed theology. While each chapter reflects exceptional scholarship, this book is not intended for the academy but for the church. We have in mind pastors, elders, Sunday school teachers, Bible college students, seminarians, and serious lay readers who are interested in learning about Calvin and his theology. For those wanting to know more about Calvin than what is covered in the pages of this volume, we have included a bibliographic essay in the hopes of helping readers navigate the world of Calvin and his many interpreters.

We would like to express our profound thanks to the contributors of this volume, and the editors and staff at Crossway, for their hard work and uncommon patience as we sought to bring this book to completion. "Thank you" does not begin to articulate how much we appreciate each person who supported this project.

By introducing a new generation of readers to the writings of John Calvin, we want to urge Christians to continue the work of reformation today. One way we can help further the reformation is through theological education. Toward this end, all royalties from this book will be given to African Bible University in Uganda, led by Paul Chinchen as chancellor and, until recently, O. Palmer Robertson as vice-chancellor, who has returned to the United States to begin a new ministry. He has served in the role of vice-chancellor since 2004 but has been teaching in Africa since 1992. Their vision for training African leaders through a biblically based education represents the kind of work that is needed to carry out reformation in our own day. For a new reformation, we need new reformers. This is why we are especially grateful to include in this volume an afterword by R. C. Sproul. It is a fitting tribute to his ministry to have one of his last published writings serve as the final word in a book on Calvin. Few have done more in the past fifty years to rekindle the light of Reformed theology than Dr. Sproul. His closing paragraph is not only a stirring conclusion to the volume but also a powerful reminder that we stand in need of a new reformation.

Derek W. H. Thomas and John W. Tweeddale

Abbreviations

ACPQ	*American Catholic Philosophical Quarterly*
AcTS	Acta Theologica Supplementum
ARG	*Archiv für Reformationsgeschichte*
BLR	Bibliotheque litteraire de la Renaissance
BRT	*Baptist Review of Theology*
BTM	*Banner of Truth Magazine*
CH	*Church History*
ChrT	*Christianity Today*
CJJC	Collection Jésus et Jésus-Christ
CNTC	*Calvin's New Testament Commentaries*. Edited by David W. Torrance and Thomas F. Torrance. 12 vols. Grand Rapids, MI: Eerdmans, 1959–1972.
CO	*Ioannis Calvini opera quae supersunt omnia*. Edited by Guilielmus Baum, Eduardus Cunitz, and Eduardus Reuss. 59 vols. *Corpus Reformatorum 29–88*. Brunswick and Berlin: Schwetschke, 1863–1900.
Comm.	*Calvin's Commentaries*. Edited by John King et al. Edinburgh: Calvin Translation Society, 1844–1856.
ConcJ	*Concordia Journal*
CourtSRT	Courtenay Studies in Reformation Theology
CR	*Corpus Reformatorum*. Edited by C. G. Bretschneider and H. E. Bindseil. Halle and Brunswick: Schwetschke, 1834–1860.
CSRT	Columbia Series in Reformed Theology

CSSP	Calvin Studies Society Papers
CTJ	*Calvin Theological Journal*
CTQ	*Concordia Theological Quarterly*
CWS	Classics of Western Spirituality
EHP	European History in Perspective
ETR	*Etudes théologiques et religieuses*
EvQ	*Evangelical Quarterly*
FC	Fathers of the Church
FJ	*Founders Journal*
FKDG	Forschungen zur Kirchen- und Dogmengeschichte
HQ	*Hartford Quarterly*
IJST	*International Journal of Systematic Theology*
Institutes	Calvin, John. *Institutes of the Christian Religion* (1559 ed.). Edited by John T. McNeill. Translated by Ford Lewis Battles. 2 vols. Library of Christian Classics 20–21. Philadelphia: Westminster, 1960.
Institutes (1536)	Calvin, John. *Institutes of the Christian Religion* (1536 ed.). Translated by Ford Lewis Battles. H. H. Meeter Center for Calvin Studies. Grand Rapids, MI: Eerdmans, 1975.
JChSt	*Journal of Church and State*
JEH	*Journal of Ecclesiastical History*
JETS	*Journal of the Evangelical Theological Society*
JHI	*Journal of the History of Ideas*
LCC	Library of Christian Classics
LCL	Loeb Classical Library
LEH	Library of Ecclesiastical History
Letters	*Letters of John Calvin*. Edited by Jules Bonnet. 4 vols. Philadelphia: Presbyterian Board of Publication, 1858.
LQ	*Lutheran Quarterly*
MQR	*Mennonite Quarterly Review*
OiC	*One in Christ*

OER	*Oxford Encyclopedia of the Reformation.* Edited by Hans. J. Hillerbrand. 4 vols. New York: Oxford University Press, 1996.
OSHT	Oxford Studies in Historical Theology
Pneuma	*Pneuma: Journal for the Society of Pentecostal Studies*
PRCPE	*Proceedings of the Royal College of Physicians of Edinburgh*
Presb	*Presbyterion*
PRJ	*Puritan Reformed Journal*
PRR	*Presbyterian and Reformed Review*
PRRD	Muller, Richard A. *Post-Reformation Reformed Dogmatics: The Rise and Development of Reformed Orthodoxy, ca. 1520 to ca. 1725.* 4 vols. Grand Rapids, MI: Eerdmans, 2003.
PrTMS	Princeton Theological Monograph Series
R&R	*Reformation and Revival*
RefR	*Reformed Review*
Registres	*Registres du Consistoire de Genève au temps de Calvin.* Edited by Thomas Austin Lambert, Isabella M. Watt, Robert M. Kingdon, and Jeffrey R. Watt. Geneva: Librairie Droz, 2004.
RHT	Reformed Historical Theology
RRR	*Reformation and Renaissance Review*
RSHT	Rutherford Studies in Historical Theology
RTJ	*Reformed Theological Journal*
RTS	Renaissance Text Series
SBET	*Scottish Bulletin of Evangelical Theology*
SCES	Sixteenth Century Essays and Studies
SCJ	*Sixteenth Century Journal*
SDog	Studies in Dogmatics
SEMRR	Studies in Early Modern Religious Reforms
SHCT	Studies in the History of Christian Thought
SHT	Studies in Historical Theology

SJT	*Scottish Journal of Theology*
SMRT	Studies in Medieval and Reformation Thought
STJ	*Stulos Theological Journal*
TaiJT	*Taiwan Journal of Theology*
Theological Treatises	Calvin, John. *Calvin: Theological Treatises.* Translated by J. K. S. Reid. Library of Christian Classics 22. London: SCM, 1954.
ThH	Theologie Historique
THR	Travaux d'humanisme et Renaissance
ThTo	*Theology Today*
Tracts and Letters	Calvin, John. *Tracts and Letters.* Edited by Henry Beveridge and Jules Bonnet. Translated by Henry Beveridge, Jules Bonnet, David Constable, and Marcus Robert Gilchrist. 7 vols. Carlisle, PA: Banner of Truth, 2009.
Tracts and Treatises	Calvin, John. *Tracts and Treatises.* Translated by Henry Beveridge. Edited by Thomas F. Torrance. 3 vols. 1849. Reprint, Grand Rapids, MI: Eerdmans, 1958.
TSRPRT	Texts and Studies in Reformation and Post-Reformation Thought
UBCLR	*University of British Columbia Law Review*
WCF	Westminster Confession of Faith. In *Westminster Confession of Faith.* Glasgow, Scotland: Free Presbyterian Publications, 1997.
WLC	Westminster Larger Catechism. In *Westminster Confession of Faith.* Glasgow, Scotland: Free Presbyterian Publications, 1997.
WSC	Westminster Shorter Catechism. In *Westminster Confession of Faith.* Glasgow, Scotland: Free Presbyterian Publications, 1997.
WTJ	*Westminster Theological Journal*
ZKG	*Zeitschrift für Kirchengeschichte*
Zwing	*Zwingliana*
ZZ	Zeugen und Zeugnisse

PART 1

The LIFE *and* WORK *of* JOHN CALVIN

1

The Young Calvin

Michael A. G. Haykin

My ministry . . . ought to be dearer to me than my own life.
—John Calvin, preface to his *Commentary on 2 Thessalonians*[1]

"I Am Not Eager to Speak about Myself"[2]

At one point in John Calvin's earliest publication after his conversion, *Psychopannychia*, the 1534 treatise against the Anabaptist doctrine of soul sleep, the French theologian reflected on what life is like without a saving knowledge of the living God. While his comments are not autobiographical in form, they can, as Heiko Oberman has pointed out, be interpreted as a commentary on his own life prior to his conversion:

> Do you want to know what the death of the soul is? It is to be without God, to be deserted by God, to be abandoned to yourself.

1. This chapter is adapted from Michael A. G. Haykin, "The Young Calvin: Preparation for a Life of Ministry," in Joel R. Beeke, David W. Hall, and Michael A. G. Haykin, *Theology Made Practical: New Studies on John Calvin and His Legacy* (Grand Rapids, MI: Reformation Heritage Books, 2017), chap. 1. Used by permission of Reformation Heritage Books. For help with obtaining a couple of the sources used in the writing of this chapter, I am indebted to two dear friends, Dr. Monte Shanks and Dr. Ian Clary.

2. *De me non libenter loquor*. Calvin makes this remark in his *Reply to Sadoleto*, in CO, 5:389.

. . . Since there is no light outside of God who lights our darkness, when he withdraws his light then our soul is certainly blind and buried in darkness; our soul is mute because it cannot confess, and call out to embrace God. The soul is deaf because it cannot hear his voice. The soul is crippled since it does not have a hold on . . . God.[3]

It is not at all surprising that Calvin would have veiled his experience in this way, for of all the Reformers, he was the most reluctant to discuss details of his life in works destined for public consumption. As he told Cardinal Jacopo Sadoleto (1477–1547), "I am not eager to speak about myself."[4] He had, as Oberman aptly puts it, a "dislike of self-disclosure."[5] From his hand, there are really only two major sources for details about his life before his conversion, namely, sections from his *Reply to Sadoleto* (1539), which need to be used with caution since they are not explicitly autobiographical,[6] and those from the preface to his *Commentary on the Book of Psalms* (1557).[7] Occasional remarks here and there in other passages in the works of Calvin, some of which are noted below, help fill in some of the gaps of his early life,

---

3. John Calvin, "Subita Conversio: The Conversion of John Calvin," trans. Heiko A. Oberman, in *Reformiertes Erbe: Festschrift für Gottfried W. Locher zu seinem 80. Geburtstag*, ed. Heiko A. Oberman, Ernst Saxer, Alfred Schindler, and Heinzpeter Stucki, *Zwing* 19, no. 2 (Zürich: Theologischer Verlag, 1993), 2:295n4. For a translation of *Psychopannychia*, see *Tracts and Treatises*, 3:413–90. For Beveridge's rendering of the passage that Oberman has translated, see *Tracts and Treatises*, 3:454–5. For the Latin behind this translation, see CO, 5:204–5. For a study of *Psychopannychia*, see George H. Tavard, *The Starting Point of Calvin's Theology* (Grand Rapids, MI: Eerdmans, 2000). Also see Bernard Cottret, *Calvin: A Biography*, trans. M. Wallace McDonald (Grand Rapids, MI: Eerdmans, 2000), 77–82.

4. Calvin, *Reply to Sadoleto*, in CO, 5:389.

5. Heiko A. Oberman, *Initia Calvini: The Matrix of Calvin's Reformation* (Amsterdam: Koninklijke Nederlandse Akademie van Wetenschappen, 1991), 7. This article can also be found in Wilhelm H. Neuser, ed., *Calvinus Sacrae Scripturae Professor: Calvin as Confessor of Holy Scriptures* (Grand Rapids, MI: Eerdmans, 1994), 113–54. See also the comments by Bruce Gordon in his definitive biography, *Calvin* (New Haven, CT: Yale University Press, 2009), viii–x, 1, 4.

6. Thus Richard Stauffer, "Les discours à la première personnes dans les sermons de Calvin," in *Regards contemporains sur Jean Calvin: Actes du Colloque Calvin, Strasbourg 1964* (Paris: Presses Universitaires de France, 1965), 206.

7. For the relevant portion of the *Reply to Sadoleto*, I have used the translation by J. K. S. Reid in Elsie Anne McKee, ed. and trans., *John Calvin: Writings of Pastoral Piety*, CWS (Mahwah, NJ: Paulist, 2001), 41–49. Further references to the *Reply to Sadoleto* are cited as *Reply to Sadoleto* with the page number in McKee's volume. For the Latin, see CO, 5:385–416. For more detail on this work, see John C. Olin, ed., *A Reformation Debate: John Calvin and Jacopo Sadoleto* (1966; repr., Grand Rapids, MI: Baker, 1976).

For the preface to Calvin's *Commentary on the Book of Psalms*, I have used the translation of Joseph Haroutunian with Louise Pettibone Smith, *Calvin: Commentaries*, LCC 23 (Philadelphia: Westminster, n.d.), 51–57. For an older translation, see James Anderson's translation in *Comm.*, 4:xxxv–xlix. My quotations from and references to Haroutunian and Smith's translation are henceforth cited as "preface to *Commentary on the Psalms*" along with the relevant page number. For both the Latin and French versions of the preface, see CO, 31:13–36.

as does the biography of the French Reformer by his friend and ministerial colleague Theodore Beza (1519–1605). Beza wrote two lives of his friend and mentor. The first saw the light of day three months after Calvin's death in 1564.[8] The following year, one of Beza's fellow pastors, Nicolas Colladon, published a considerably enlarged life of Calvin that built on the work of Beza but incorporated new material.[9] Ten years later, after Colladon had left Geneva in 1571 for Lausanne, Beza issued a revision of his own biography but one that also made liberal use of the material in Colladon's work.[10]

"Intended . . . for Theology"

John Calvin[11] was born on July 10, 1509, in Noyon, Picardy, in northeastern France, to Gérard Cauvin (d. 1531) and his first wife, Jeanne, née le Franc (d. 1515), both of whom Beza described as "widely respected and in comfortable circumstances."[12] From a town clerk, Calvin's father had risen to occupy the position of a financial administrator in the cathedral of Noyon. A quarrel with the cathedral authorities, however, led to his excommunication, in which state he died in 1531. Calvin's mother, whom Calvin does not appear to have ever actually mentioned in print,[13] died when John was a young boy of six. It may well be the case, as some historians have argued, that his mother was steeped in the medieval Roman Catholic devotion to relics, for in Calvin's biting treatise on relics, he recalls kissing a reputed fragment of the hand of Anna, the mother of Mary, at the Church of Ourscamp, not far from Noyon, where his mother may have taken him.[14] John also had three brothers—an older brother,

---

8. CO, 21:21–50.

9. CO, 21:51–118.

10. CO, 21:119–72. It is this third edition of the life of Calvin that has been used in this chapter. For an accessible translation of this version, see Theodore Beza, *The Life of John Calvin*, trans. Henry Beveridge, in BTM 227/228, August/September 1982, 1–68. This translation is essentially that of *Tracts and Treatises*, 1:xvii–c. Quotations are from the translation as found in *Banner of Truth Magazine* and are cited as Beza, *Life*, along with the page number.

11. The French form of Calvin's name was Jean Cauvin. It became Calvin via the Latinized form that Calvin used for his surname, Calvinus.

12. Beza, *Life*, 11. For more details on the background of Calvin's family, see Cottret, *Calvin*, 8–12.

13. Allan Menzies, "The Career and Personality of Calvin," in Menzies, *A Study of Calvin and Other Papers* (London: Macmillan, 1918), 129.

14. Cottret, *Calvin*, 10. Though cf. Menzies, "Career and Personality," 129. For the recollection, see Calvin, *An Admonition, showing the Advantages which Christendom might derive from an Inventory of Relics*, in *Tracts and Treatises*, 1:329.

Charles (d. 1537), and two younger brothers, Antoine (d. 1573) and
François, the latter dying as a child—and two half sisters, daughters
of Gérard by his second wife.[15]

Given Gérard's close ties to the church, it is not surprising that he
initially desired John to study for the priesthood. In fact, Gérard also
directed John's older brother, Charles, into the priesthood, though the
latter left it in 1536.[16] "My father," Calvin recalled in the late 1550s,
"intended me as a young boy for theology."[17] So it was in 1523[18] that
young Calvin set off for Paris to study for a master of arts degree
that would eventually lead to theological studies and the priesthood.
Owing to his father's connection with the church, Calvin was able to
finance his studies from various church benefices he had been given
in childhood and his early teens—one of the abuses of the medieval
church. In Paris he initially studied for three months at the Collège
de la Marche, where he improved his skill in Latin under the superb
tutelage of Mathurin Cordier (1479–1564). Calvin later recognized his
debt to Cordier when in 1550 he dedicated his *Commentary on the
Epistles of Paul the Apostle to the Thessalonians* to his old teacher:

> It was under your guidance that I entered on a course of studies,
> and made progress at least to the extent of being some benefit to
> the Church of God. When my father sent me as a boy to Paris I had
> done only the rudiments of Latin. For a short time, however, you
> were an instructor sent to me by God to teach me the true method
> of learning, so that I might afterwards be a little more proficient.
> . . . It was my desire to testify to posterity that, if they derive any
> profit from my writings, they should know that to some extent you
> are responsible for them.[19]

After this brief time of what might be viewed as preparatory studies
at the Collège de la Marche, Calvin went on to the formidable Collège

---

15. Richard Stauffer, "Calvin," in *International Calvinism, 1541–1715*, ed. Menna Prestwich (Oxford: Clarendon, 1985), 16; "Notice littéraire," in *CO*, 21:14; Gordon, *Calvin*, 4.

16. Cottret, *Calvin*, 11.

17. Calvin, preface to *Commentary on the Psalms*, 51.

18. For the date, see Ford Lewis Battles, "Calvin's Humanistic Education," in Battles, *Interpreting John Calvin*, ed. Robert Benedetto (Grand Rapids, MI: Baker, 1996), 48; Cottret, *Calvin*, 11.

19. *CNTC*, 8:331. On Cordier, see Battles, "Calvin's Humanistic Education," 52–53; Cottret, *Calvin*, 12–16; Gordon, *Calvin*, 5–6.

de Montaigu. This institution, founded in 1314 and revived in the late fifteenth century after a period of decline, was well known for both its theological conservatism and severe discipline. Overall, the Collège de Montaigu was marked by a "narrow-minded and hair-splitting orthodoxy" that resulted in violent opposition to and persecution of nascent French Protestantism.[20] The mode of life inculcated within the college walls then is well seen in a description of the college by the Dutch humanist Desiderius Erasmus (1466/1469–1536), who, reflecting on a stay at the college in 1495, recalled the place as "filthy, bleak, inhospitable, reeking with the foulest smells, [and] clotted with dirt." As he went on, "I carried nothing away from there except a body poisoned with infected humors"![21] It is noteworthy that another key figure of this era, namely, the Counter-Reformation leader Ignatius of Loyola (1491–1556), as equally renowned as Calvin for his disciplined life, also studied at this college, though just after the Frenchman.[22]

Much has been written about the philosophical and theological influences that shaped Calvin during his time at Montaigu,[23] but the truth of the matter is that there are no documents from Calvin during this period that can accurately pinpoint the exact nature of these influences. Was Stoicism one of them, as Alexandre Ganoczy has suggested?[24] Calvin's first book *was* a commentary on a treatise by the Stoic philosopher Seneca (ca. 4 BC–AD 65), and in the sixteenth century, Seneca was viewed as a Stoic with a distinct sympathy for Christianity. Or was the Augustinian theology of Gregory of Rimini (ca. 1300–1358) a major influence, as Alister McGrath has posited?[25] To put things in perspective,

---

20. Alexandre Ganoczy, "Calvin's Life," trans. David L. Foxgrover and James Schmitt, in *The Cambridge Companion to John Calvin*, ed. Donald K. McKim (Cambridge: Cambridge University Press, 2004), 4.

21. Cited by Hans J. Hillerbrand, *The Division of Christendom: Christianity in the Sixteenth Century* (Louisville: Westminster John Knox, 2007), 296; Cottret, *Calvin*, 17. On the college, see also Battles, "Calvin's Humanistic Education," 48–49; Alister E. McGrath, *A Life of John Calvin: A Study in the Shaping of Western Culture* (Oxford: Blackwell, 1990), 27–31; Cottret, *Calvin*, 16–20.

22. Battles, "Calvin's Humanistic Education," 49. Cf. the remark by Hillerbrand about Calvin: "His temperament seems to suggest kinship with none other than Ignatius of Loyola. The second generation of the Reformation called for men of this type, brilliant, determined, cool." Hillerbrand, *Division of Christendom*, 314.

23. For an overview of these studies and a response to this method of inquiry, see Oberman, *Initia Calvini*, 10–19. See also Gordon, *Calvin*, 6–8.

24. Alexandre Ganoczy, *The Young Calvin*, trans. David Foxgrover and Wade Provo (Philadelphia: Westminster, 1987), passim; T. H. L. Parker, *John Calvin: A Biography* (Philadelphia: Westminster, 1975), 28. On Calvin's Seneca commentary, see below. See also the response of Oberman, *Initia Calvini*, 13–14, to this suggestion of the influence of Stoicism over the young Calvin.

25. McGrath, *Life of John Calvin*, 37–47, passim.

Oberman has noted that Calvin never mentioned Gregory, and even McGrath concedes that in the end, "we do not know with any certainty precisely what Calvin studied while at Montaigu; we do not know under whom he studied (with the obvious exception of Cordier), or what lectures he attended; we do not even know what books he read."[26] Such uncertainty about the ideas and books shaping Calvin during a formative period in his life does not mean Calvin is not indebted intellectually to elements of the medieval world, but it does mean that claims about such influences need to be made with great circumspection.[27]

French historian Richard Stauffer has also noted that Calvin, during his time in Paris, must have been aware to some degree of the presence of evangelicals in France. Evangelicals were martyred in 1525—for instance, Jean Châtelain, an Augustinian monk, was burned in January at Metz, and a Franciscan who had embraced Lutheran ideas, very possibly one Pierre de Sébiville, suffered and died by burning at Grenoble. And evangelicals suffered martyrdom in 1526 as well—Jacques Pauvan was killed in Paris itself at the Place-de-Grève in August of that year.[28] And in 1524, the King of France's sister, Marguerite d'Angoulême (1492–1549), the most powerful woman in France after the queen mother, published a book in which she took a decided stand for the Lutheran doctrine of justification by faith alone.[29] But there is no evidence that at this point Calvin had even a modicum of interest in joining the cause of reform.

"Called Back . . . to Learn Law"

After obtaining his arts degree in 1528, Calvin was ready to begin his formal training in theology, but it was not to be. Although his father

---

26. McGrath, *Life of John Calvin*, 36.
27. For a succinct summary of the theologians of the Patristic and medieval era to whom the mature Calvin was indebted, see Stauffer, "Calvin," 29. As Stauffer notes, "While Calvin was nurtured on the Bible, his reading of it was enriched by his astonishing knowledge of the great authors of the Christian tradition." For more detail, see Ford Lewis Battles, "The Sources of Calvin's Seneca Commentary," in Battles, *Interpreting John Calvin*, 65–89; Anthony N. S. Lane, *John Calvin: Student of the Church Fathers* (Grand Rapids, MI: Baker, 1999); Jean-François Gilmont, *John Calvin and the Printed Book*, trans. Karin Maag, SCES 72 (Kirksville, MO: Truman State University Press, 2005), 156–66.
28. Philip Edgcumbe Hughes, *Lefèvre: Pioneer of Ecclesiastical Renewal in France* (Grand Rapids, MI: Eerdmans, 1984), 147–50.
29. Stauffer, "Calvin," 16. Similarly, John T. McNeill, *The History and Character of Calvinism* (1954; repr., New York: Oxford University Press, 1967), 109. On Marguerite d'Angoulême, see George Saintsbury, "Marguerite de Valois," *The Encyclopaedia Britannica*, 11th ed. (New York: Encyclopedia Britannica, 1910), 17:706.

had all along intended his son to become a priest like his older brother, suddenly he changed his mind and instructed John to go into law and move to Orléans to study at what was then the preeminent French university for legal studies. Calvin later described this sudden change in his life thus:

> When he [i.e., Calvin's father] saw that the science of law made those who cultivate it wealthy, he was led to change his mind by the hope of material gain for me. So it happened that I was called back from the study of philosophy to learn law.[30]

Calvin studied at Orléans from 1528 to 1529 and then transferred to Bourges for two more years of legal studies, from 1529 to 1531. The central reason for this move was the coming of the famous Italian jurist Andrea Alciati (1492–1550) to the town of Bourges.[31] The legal knowledge obtained by this period of concentrated study gave Calvin an abiding interest in the nature of law and justice, the tools to create institutions in Geneva that would serve the advance of the gospel, and a mastery of how to read texts in light of their literary and linguistic contexts.[32] What is also especially important about this shift into law was the fact that one of Calvin's tutors at both Orléans and Bourges was a German scholar by the name of Melchior Wolmar (1497–1560), who was committed to the evangelical perspective of Martin Luther (1483–1546).[33] It was at Bourges that Wolmar began teaching Greek to Calvin, which would open up for the future Reformer the riches of the New Testament.[34] It is noteworthy that a number of Calvin's contemporaries regarded the study of Greek with deep misgivings. As one writer put it, "We must avoid [Greek] at all costs, for this language gives birth to heresies. Especially beware of the New Testament in Greek; it is a book full of thorns

---

30. Calvin, preface to *Commentary on the Psalms*, 51–52. See also Beza, *Life*, 11.

31. For details about these two law schools and the teachers at them under whom Calvin studied, see Battles, "Calvin's Humanistic Education," 49–50, 55–58; Cottret, *Calvin*, 20–24.

32. G. R. Potter and Mark Greengrass, *John Calvin* (New York: Saint Martin's Press, 1983), 4; McGrath, *Life of John Calvin*, 59; Oberman, *Initia Calvini*, 38; Randall C. Zachman, *John Calvin as Teacher, Pastor, and Theologian: The Shape of His Writings and Thought* (Grand Rapids, MI: Baker Academic, 2006), 16–17; Gordon, *Calvin*, 18–22.

33. On Wolmar, see Battles, "Calvin's Humanistic Education," 57–58; Helmut Feld, "Volmar (Rufus), Melchior," *Biographisch-Bibliographisches Kirchenlexikon*, ed. Friedrich Wilhelm Bautz and Traugott Bautz (Herzberg: Verlag Traugott Bautz, 1997), 12:1588–91.

34. See also Menzies, "Career and Personality," 136–37.

and prickles!"[35] In 1530 the faculty of theology in Paris went as far
as to condemn the idea that one cannot understand the Scriptures
without a knowledge of the original languages in which they were
given.[36] Calvin, on the other hand, would come to consider the study
of Greek essential for anyone wishing to be a herald of the gospel.[37]
Simon Grynaeus (1493–1541), the winsome professor of Greek at the
University of Basel, would help him personally deepen his own grasp
of Greek when Calvin resided in Basel from 1535 to 1536.[38]

   To what extent Wolmar may have shared his faith with Calvin is
not known.[39] When Calvin noted his debt to Wolmar for the rudiments
of Greek in the dedicatory preface of his *Commentary on 2 Corinthians*, he made no mention of theological matters.[40] In fact, there is clear
evidence to show that at this time Calvin was still seriously committed to the Roman church.[41] There was a deeply conservative streak
in Calvin's character. As he admitted in his reply to Sadoleto, "It was
with the greatest difficulty I was induced to confess that I had all my
life long been in ignorance and error."[42]

   After his law studies, Calvin returned to Paris, where he learned that
his father was seriously ill. He hurried to Noyon to be with him during
his final days. His father had run afoul of Roman Catholic authorities
two years earlier, in November 1528, when he refused to give the local
bishop the accounting books for the cathedral. It is not clear whether
he was guilty of a misdemeanor or whether his pride was piqued at the
questioning of his integrity.[43] He was excommunicated and thus died

---

35. Cited by Parker, *John Calvin*, 21.
36. McGrath, *Life of John Calvin*, 62.
37. See John Currid, *Calvin and the Biblical Languages* (Fearn, Ross-shire, Scotland: Mentor, 2006).
38. On Grynaeus, see Alexander Gordon, "Grynaeus, Simon," *Encyclopaedia Britannica*, 11th ed., 11:642. On Calvin's relationship with him, see also Cornelis Augustijn, Christoph Burger, and Frans P. van Stam, "Calvin in the Light of the Early Letters," in *Calvinus Praeceptor Ecclesiae: Papers of the International Congress on Calvin Research*, ed. Herman J. Selderhuis, THR 388 (Geneva: Librairie Droz, 2004), 145–47.
39. For a brief discussion of Wolmar's possible influence on Calvin's religious development, see Danièle Fischer, "Nouvelles réflexions sur la conversion de Calvin," *ETR* 58 (1983): 216–17.
40. "The first time my father sent me to study civil law, it was at your instigation and under your tuition that I also took up the study of Greek, of which you were at that time a most distinguished teacher. . . . My indebtedness to you for this is still great for you gave me a good grounding in the rudiments of the language and that was of great help to me later on." *CNTC*, 10:1.
41. Cottret, *Calvin*, 24; Ganoczy, "Calvin's Life," 5.
42. Calvin, *Reply to Sadoleto*, 48.
43. Hillerbrand, *Division of Christendom*, 296.

unreconciled to the Roman church.[44] Whether this had an effect on Calvin's thinking about the Roman church and its discipline is unknown.

The year following his father's death saw the appearance of Calvin's first publication, his *Commentary on Seneca's "De Clementia."*[45] This publication, funded out of his own pocket,[46] is a clear indication that Calvin's intellectual roots are to be found in Renaissance humanism, whose watchcry, in its desire to rejuvenate certain aspects of medieval civilization, was *ad fontes*, "back to the sources," particularly those of Western culture in the ancient Greco-Roman world.[47] Allan Menzies notes that Calvin's knowledge of the classics is abundantly evident in this first venture into the world of print culture: Calvin "shows himself acquainted with the whole of Greek and Latin classical literature, citing 155 Latin authors and 22 Greek, and citing them with understanding."[48] In the providence of God, this Renaissance passion for seeking wisdom from the past would provide invaluable direction to humanist scholars who, like Calvin, came to accept evangelical convictions: the source of church renewal could be found only at the fountainhead of the Christian faith, the Holy Scriptures. As Calvin later noted, the teaching of the Reformers went back to Christianity's "source and, as it were, clearing away the dregs, restored it to its original purity."[49]

Calvin's footsteps between the publication of his humanist treatise in April 1532 and his moving back to Paris in the late autumn of 1533 are not easy to trace. He did go back to Orléans to receive his law degree. And at some point in 1533, the greatest of all changes took place in his life when, in his words, the "Lord shone upon [him] with the brightness of [his] Spirit,"[50] and he joined the ranks of the Reformers.

"A Taste and Knowledge of True Piety"

The date of Calvin's conversion is among the most disputed topics of Reformation scholarship. When did it take place? T. H. L. Parker has

---

44. Cottret, *Calvin*, 24.
45. CO, 5:1–162. For a discussion of this work, see Gordon, *Calvin*, 22–29.
46. Calvin to Francis Daniel, May 23, 1532, in *Letters*, 1:31. See also Calvin to Francis Daniel, 1532, in *Letters*, 1:32.
47. See Alister E. McGrath, *The Intellectual Origins of the European Reformation*, 2nd ed. (Oxford: Blackwell, 2004), 125–30.
48. Menzies, "Career and Personality," 137.
49. Calvin, *Reply to Sadoleto*, 48.
50. Calvin, *Reply to Sadoleto*, 44.

argued for 1529–1530, a dating that a number of other scholars have followed, among them J. I. Packer.[51] Traditionally, though, the date that has been given is 1533, a date that still rightly commands strong scholarly support.[52] Although we do not possess irrefutable data to determine the time of Calvin's conversion, Calvin himself discussed the nature of his conversion in two places—his *Reply to Sadoleto* and his 1557 preface to his *Commentary on the Book of Psalms*—and of these, the latter is more important.[53] In his preface, after mentioning his father's desire that he become a lawyer, Calvin states,

> God, by the secret leading of his providence, turned my course another way [rather than the study of law]. First, when I was too firmly addicted to the superstitions of the Papacy to be drawn easily out of such a deep mire, by a sudden conversion God subdued and made teachable [*domta et rangea à docilité*] my mind, already more rigid than suited my age. Having therefore received a taste and knowledge of true piety, I burned with such a desire to carry my study further, that although I did not drop other subjects, I had no zeal for them. In less than a year, all who were looking for a purer doctrine began to come to learn from me, although I was a novice and a beginner.[54]

Six aspects of this concisely worded theological reflection on God's saving work in Calvin's life beg comment.

First, Calvin was indeed recounting the historical circumstances by which God brought him from a state of spiritual death to a living faith in God. Alexandre Ganoczy, though, has denied that this text should be primarily read as a historical narrative of Calvin's conversion. Rather, it must be viewed as a theological reflection from the vantage point of Calvin's mature theological thought. For example, Calvin's assertion

---

51. Parker, *John Calvin*, 22, 162–65; J. I. Packer, "John Calvin and Reformed Europe," in *Great Leaders of the Christian Church*, ed. John D. Woodbridge (Chicago: Moody Press, 1988), 206, 210.

52. Menzies, "Career and Personality," 143; François Wendel, *Calvin: Origins and Development of His Religious Thought*, trans. Philip Mairet (1963; repr., Durham, NC: Labyrinth, 1987), 37–45; Stauffer, "Calvin," 18; Oberman, trans., "Subita Conversio," 283, 283n17; Gordon, *Calvin*, 33.

53. Parker, *John Calvin*, 162.

54. Calvin, preface to *Commentary on the Psalms*, 52, altered. For the original Latin and French, see CO, 31:21–22. This translation is from the French version primarily, though in what follows I have also referred to the Latin version.

that he underwent a "sudden conversion" is a statement made for theological reasons to emphasize conversion as a divine miracle. Ganoczy believes that the primary sources for Calvin's life from the 1530s bear this out and reveal that Calvin's movement away from the Roman church was that of "a gradual spiritual development."[55] Undoubtedly, Calvin's account of his conversion is not free from theological interpretation, and as Ganoczy has argued, Calvin here included details of his conversion to help explain his call to be a minister of the word in Geneva. But none of this lessens the historicity of his conversion account.[56] Moreover, it is telling that Calvin embedded the story of his conversion within a larger block of text that details historical events and recounts how it was that Calvin became involved in the Genevan Reformation.

Second, Calvin remembered that, prior to his conversion, he was "too firmly addicted to the superstitions of the Papacy to be drawn easily out of such a deep mire." Calvin did not specify which superstitions he had in mind, but by comparing them to a bog, he was indicating that liberation from these distortions of Christian truth and "the matrix of late medieval religion" could have taken place only through an outside agency.[57] Calvin made no mention of the human instruments through whom he may have heard the gospel: possibly Wolmar; or his cousin Pierre Olivétan (1506–1538), who translated the New Testament into French and whom Beza wrongly saw as the key figure through whom Calvin became "acquainted with the reformed faith";[58] or the early Protestant martyr Étienne de la Forge, with whom Calvin lodged while in Paris.[59] Nor did he make any mention of human writings that he must have read, works by Martin

---

55. Ganoczy, *Young Calvin*, 252–66; Ganoczy, "Calvin's Life," 9–10. Similarly, James A. de Jong, "'An Anatomy of All Parts of the Soul': Insights into Calvin's Spirituality from His Psalms Commentary," in Neuser, *Calvinus Sacrae Scripturae Professor*, 3–4n7; Gilmont, *John Calvin and the Printed Book*, 9–10; McGrath, *Intellectual Origins*, 55–56.

56. See Fischer, "Nouvelles réflexions," 203–7; Cottret, *Calvin*, 68–70.

57. The quoted phrase is from McGrath, *Life of John Calvin*, 70. For a summary of what Reformed authors like Calvin considered to be distortions of Christianity, see Graeme Murdock, *Beyond Calvin: The Intellectual, Political and Cultural World of Europe's Reformed Churches, c. 1540–1620*, EHP (New York: Palgrave Macmillan, 2004), 8–15.

58. Beza, *Life*, 11–12. On Beza's error in this regard, see Menzies, "Career and Personality," 140–41.

59. Étienne de la Forge was a Waldensian merchant from Piedmont. See McNeill, *History and Character of Calvinism*, 109; O. R. Johnston, "Calvin the Man," in *Able Ministers of the New Testament: Papers Read at the Puritan and Reformed Studies Conference, December 1964* ([London]: Puritan and Reformed Studies Conference, 1964), 22; James Leo Garrett Jr., introduction to *Calvin and the Reformed Tradition*, ed. Garrett (Nashville: Broadman, 1980), 24.

Luther, for instance.[60] But this is typical of Calvin and the Reformed faith: an emphasis on the absolute sovereignty of God in salvation. Calvin could thus state in his treatise *The Eternal Election of God* (1562), "It is not within our power to convert ourselves from our evil life, unless God changes us and cleanses us by his Holy Spirit."[61] Or as he put it in his *Reply to Sadoleto*, referring to the way he came to realize that salvation was by grace alone, "You, O Lord, shone upon me with the brightness of Your Spirit."[62]

Third, the Latin behind the word "sudden," in the phrase "sudden conversion," is *subita*, which in Latin can mean "unexpected" or "unpremeditated," and this is probably the better translation. In other words, Calvin's conversion was not ultimately the result of any wish or intention of Calvin.[63] McGrath puts it well when he writes that this word "resonates with overtones of the unexpected, the unpredictable, the uncontrollable."[64] One of Calvin's natural characteristics was a resistance to change, as he indicated in this text. But God broke into his life and, as this passage intimates, brought to pass a completely unexpected upheaval that caused him to change his views of God and salvation and led him to embrace evangelical doctrine as the truth. What led him to hesitate and refuse to listen to evangelical authors, as he made clear in his *Reply to Sadoleto*, was "reverence for the church":

> But when once I opened my ears and allowed myself to be taught, I perceived that this fear of derogating from the majesty of the church was groundless. For they reminded me how great the difference is between schism from the church, and studying to correct the faults by which the church herself is contaminated. They spoke nobly of the church and showed the greatest desire to cultivate unity.[65]

60. For Luther's influence on Calvin, see McNeill, *History and Character of Calvinism*, 109–10; Ganoczy, *Young Calvin*, 137–45. Zachman believes that Calvin's "sudden conversion to teachableness" was "most likely through the writings of Martin Luther." *John Calvin as Teacher*, 17–19, quotations on 19.

61. *CO*, 8:113. See also the similar statements in Calvin's *Commentary on Jeremiah*. *CO*, 38:466, 671; cf. Ganoczy, *Young Calvin*, 251.

62. Calvin, *Reply to Sadoleto*, 44. See McNeill, *History and Character of Calvinism*, 118.

63. Parker, *John Calvin*, 163–64.

64. McGrath, *Life of John Calvin*, 72. The fact that McGrath favors Ganoczy's nonhistorical interpretation of this passage in the preface to Calvin's *Commentary on the Psalms* does not affect the point he is making about this term.

65. Calvin, preface to *Commentary on the Psalms*, 48.

Fourth, conversion for Calvin meant the formation of a teachable heart. As he asserted, "God subdued and made teachable [*domta et rangea à docilité*] my mind, already more rigid than suited my age." The verb "subdued" was associated with the taming of wild animals, specifically horses that needed bridle and bit to be ridden and direct- ed.[66] It is a frequent metaphor in Calvin's writings, an indication of the importance Calvin placed on teachableness and submissiveness to the will of God as being central to the nature of biblical Christianity, especially among those who aspire to be ministers of the word. In Cal- vin's words, taken from his comments on 1 Corinthians 14:31, "No one will ever be a good teacher, if he does not show that he himself is teachable, and always ready to learn."[67]

Fifth, as François Wendel has noted, conversion meant for Calvin "a total change of orientation" in his studies. Having had "a taste and knowledge of true piety," Calvin says, "I burned with such a desire to carry my study further, that although I did not drop other subjects, I had no zeal for them." He had lost his passion for the sort of studies that had culminated in his *Commentary on Seneca's "De Clementia."* Rather, it was the study of Scripture and evangelical theology that henceforth gripped his heart.[68] Allan Menzies captures the depth of the change when he states that Calvin now "no longer writes as a Hu- manist, but as one who is guided by the Word, and who feels the cry newly arising from the blood of the martyrs being spilt around him."[69]

Finally, the language that Calvin used here to describe the affective impact of his conversion is noteworthy. There is a strong tradition of thought about Calvin that depicts him as cold and unemotional. But this account of his conversion—especially his statement about burning with desire (*enflammé*) to grow in his knowledge of God—indicates

66. J. I. Packer, "Calvin: A Servant of the Word," in *Able Ministers of the New Testament*, 42; Parker, *John Calvin*, 163; Oberman, *Initia Calvini*, 7–8n3; Oberman, trans., "Subita Con- versio," 290.

67. Cited by Randall C. Zachman, "The Conciliating Theology of John Calvin: Dialogue among Friends," in *Conciliation and Confession: The Struggle for Unity in the Age of Reform, 1415–1648*, ed. Howard P. Louthan and Randall C. Zachman (Notre Dame, IN: University of Notre Dame Press, 2004), 94–95.

68. Wendel, *Calvin*, 44–45. See also Harro Höpfl, *The Christian Polity of John Calvin* (Cam- bridge: Cambridge University Press, 1982), 19. And among the books he definitely read were some by Luther: see Calvin's *Second Defence of the Pious and Orthodox Faith concerning the Sacraments, in answer to the Calumnies of Joachim Westphal*, in *Tracts and Treatises*, 2:253.

69. Menzies, "Career and Personality," 145.

the exact opposite and that he had an unusually ardent nature. In fact, as James A. de Jong has noted in a study of Calvin's piety as found in his *Commentary on the Psalms*, Calvin's comments on this portion of Holy Scripture help dispel "the stubborn perception of Calvin as cold, rationalistic, vindictive, and aloof." Instead, one finds "an experiential believer of considerable depth and warmth."[70] Calvin's conversion consisted not in mere enlightenment; it entailed nothing less than an "unreserved, wholehearted commitment to the living God."[71] This ardent commitment finds pictorial expression in Calvin's crest or seal, which pictures a heart on an open, outstretched hand, with a motto underneath that reads *Cor meum tibi offero Domine prompte et sincere* ("My heart I give you, Lord, eagerly and earnestly").[72]

"All Who Were Looking for a Purer Doctrine"

Calvin's giftedness as a teacher was soon being recognized. In fact, according to Calvin's own words, within a year of his conversion, those who were seeking "a purer doctrine" than that of Rome were seeking him out.[73] Calvin was not a complete novice to teaching. For instance, he had already been involved in giving a series of lectures on Seneca in the late summer or early fall of 1533.[74] He now found himself part of a movement in France that had been seeking reform within Roman Catholicism since the early 1520s. At the heart of this reform movement was the biblical scholar Jacques Lefèvre d'Etaples (ca. 1455–1536).[75]

By the 1520s, Lefèvre was famous throughout Western Europe for the depth of his learning—for many he was equal to none other than

---

70. De Jong, "Insights into Calvin's Spirituality," 4. I owe this reference to J. Nigel Westhead, "Calvin and Experimental Knowledge of God," in *Adorning the Doctrine: Papers Read at the 1995 Westminster Conference* ([London]: Westminster Conference, 1995), 16.

71. McNeill, *History and Character of Calvinism*, 116.

72. On this crest, see Herman J. Selderhuis, "Calvin as an Asylum Seeker," in *Calvin's Books: Festschrift Dedicated to Peter De Klerk on the Occasion of His Seventieth Birthday*, ed. Wilhelm H. Neuser, Herman J. Selderhuis, and Willem van 't Spijker (Heerenveen: J. J. Groen, 1997), 286.

73. Augustijn, Burger, and Stam, "Early Letters," 144.

74. For an eyewitness report of these lectures, see Oberman, *Initia Calvini*, 36n119. See also Augustijn, Burger, and Stam, "Early Letters," 141.

75. For an excellent study of Lefèvre, see Hughes, *Lefèvre*. For an overview of his career, see also Eugene F. Rice Jr., introduction to *The Prefatory Epistles of Jacques Lefèvre d'Etaples and Related Texts*, ed. Eugene F. Rice Jr. (New York: Columbia University Press, 1972), xi–xxv. For Calvin's relationship to Lefèvre, see Hermann Dörries, "Calvin und Lefèvre," *ZKG* 44 (1925): 544–81. On the early French evangelicals, see also Gordon, *Calvin*, 11–17.

that paragon of humanist scholarship Erasmus. He had spent his early career immersed in Aristotelianism and medieval mysticism, but after the appearance of his commentary on the Pauline correspondence in 1512, he was increasingly known as a theologian, even though he had never had any formal theological education.[76] Scholars are divided over whether Lefèvre anticipated the Lutheran doctrine of justification by faith alone—Philip Edgcumbe Hughes says yes; Richard Stauffer and others say no[77]—but what is clear is that Lefèvre deeply appreciated Luther's early writings. And in Lefèvre's later works, especially those after 1518, the French scholar completely rejected the cult of the saints and other aspects of what he regarded as corrupt worship present in medieval Catholicism.[78] In Beza's words, Lefèvre began "the revival of pure religion."[79] And yet, though some of Lefèvre's disciples, such as Calvin's close friend Guillaume Farel (1489–1565), would so embrace Lefèvre's critique of medieval piety as to break with Rome, others, following Lefèvre himself, did not see this issue as a just cause for separation. Nonetheless, Calvin's doctrinal convictions concerning true worship—one of the central issues of the Reformation—are definitely rooted in Lefèvre's radical critique of late medieval piety.[80]

The 1520s had seen episodes of persecution of this reform movement, some of it extremely violent—witness the martyrdom of Jacques Pauvan, one of Lefèvre's disciples, noted earlier. Another period of persecution occurred in late 1533, following an address by the rector of the University of Paris, Nicolas Cop, one of Calvin's friends, on November 1.[81] The address, by no means radical by later Protestant

---

76. Rice, introduction to *Prefatory Epistles*, xiv. For a discussion of the theological themes in Lefèvre's commentary on Paul's letters, see Hughes, *Lefèvre*, 69–99, passim.

77. Hughes, *Lefèvre*, 74–78; Richard Stauffer, "Lefèvre d'Etaples: artisan ou spectateur de la Réforme," *Bulletin de la Société de l'Histoire du Protestantisme Français* 113 (1967): 405–23.

78. See Carlos M. N. Eire, *War against the Idols: The Reformation of Worship from Erasmus to Calvin* (Cambridge: Cambridge University Press, 1986), 168–94.

79. Cited by Eire, *War against the Idols*, 193.

80. Eire, *War against the Idols*, 186.

81. For this address, see *Institutes* (1536), 364–72. According to Beza, Calvin wrote the address for Cop. *Life*, 13. This seems unlikely. See the discussion of the address and the question of Calvin's role in the writing of it in McGrath, *Life of John Calvin*, 64–66; Cottret, *Calvin*, 73–76. For a recent defense of Calvin as the author, see Joseph N. Tylenda, "Calvin's First Reformed Sermon? Nicholas Cop's Discourse—1 November 1533," in *Calvin's Early Writings and Ministry*, ed. Richard C. Gamble, Articles on Calvin and Calvinism 2 (New York: Garland, 1992), 120–38; this article first appeared in *WTJ* 38 (1976): 300–318. Augustijn, Burger, and Stam also support the case for Calvin's authorship. "Early Letters," 143.

standards—while it did contain mild overtones of Lutheranism, it also made an invocation to the Virgin Mary—rattled enough of the faculty of theology in Paris for them to issue a condemnation of it and Cop. The latter quickly left Paris for Basel, and because the authorities began to arrest those sympathetic to Lutheran ideas in the wake of Cop's address, Calvin, known to be a friend of Cop, also fled. Beza noted that Calvin's rooms were searched at the time and various papers seized, an indication that he was indeed in danger of arrest.[82] Reflecting on this time of persecution nearly thirty years later in a sermon on 2 Samuel (1562), Calvin admitted that he was terrified and in such distress that he nearly wished himself dead to escape the agony of the time.[83]

He found safety in Angoulême with a friend, Louis du Tillet, who possessed a fabulous library of several thousand volumes. Calvin probably used these works in the spring of 1534 to do some of the research that culminated in his *Psychopannychia*, which he either wrote or finished in Orléans later in the year, though publication of this work was delayed until 1542.[84] Beza noted that Calvin also found time to visit Lefèvre d'Etaples during this period. According to Beza, Lefèvre "was delighted with young Calvin, and predicted that he would prove a distinguished instrument in restoring the kingdom of heaven in France."[85] For another trip in this year of traveling, Calvin visited Noyon, his birthplace. The cathedral records there indicate that on May 4, 1534, Calvin personally resigned one of his benefices. Presumably, he gave up the others at the same time. Curiously, Beza makes no mention of this event, but it probably signaled Calvin's final break with Rome and his full-blooded commitment to the Reformation.[86] Calvin spent the months immediately following this May journey in transit: he journeyed to Nérac, where Marguerite d'Angoulême, the king's sister, held court and was ever favorable to

---

82. Beza, *Life*, 13.
83. Cited by Oberman, *Initia Calvini*, 27–28n84.
84. McGrath, *Life of John Calvin*, 72. Du Tillet acted as Calvin's patron to 1537. His subsequent return to the Roman Catholic Church severed the bond between him and Calvin. See Tavard, *Starting Point*, 140–41; Gilmont, *John Calvin and the Printed Book*, 20.
85. Beza, *Life*, 14.
86. Johnston, "Calvin the Man," 23; Stauffer, "Calvin," 18; McGrath, *Life of John Calvin*, 73–74.

evangelical views; he went back to Paris at great risk to meet Michael Servetus (1509/1511–1553), who failed to keep the appointment; and he spent some time in Orléans.

"Christ's Road Is a Thorny One"

That fall, as he was working on the finishing touches of *Psychopanny-chia*, an event took place that would push Calvin's wanderings beyond the realm of France. During the late evening of October 17, 1534, and the wee hours of the morning of October 18, posters (*placards*) were set up in various prominent places in Paris, Rouen, Orléans, and other French towns, denouncing the Mass as an abomination before God. Driving the theological perspective of the man behind the posters, Antoine Marcourt, a pastor in Neuchâtel, was the soteriology of the book of Hebrews: What need is there for the priestly mediation of the Mass when Christ offered himself up on the cross to the Father "once for all" (Heb. 7:27)? A poster was even placed on the door of King Francis I's bedchamber![87] Francis was furious. Evangelical theology was now seen as a positive danger to the state.[88] Less than four weeks later, more than two hundred had been arrested, twenty-four of whom would be burned as heretics. Among the latter was Calvin's Parisian landlord, Étienne de la Forge.

So it was that Calvin made the decision to leave France. He found refuge, like Cop had done, in the Swiss town of Basel, where he arrived in January 1535. Other French evangelicals were there, including Guillaume Farel and Pierre Viret (1511–1571), who, Swiss-born like Farel, would, along with Farel, later be numbered among Calvin's closest friends and colleagues. Powerful testimony to what Calvin called "the holy bond of friendship" between these three men, a friendship begun during this time in Basel, can be found in Calvin's dedication to them of his *Commentary on the Epistle to Titus*:

> I think there has never been in ordinary life a circle of friends so heartily bound to each other as we have been in our ministry. With both of you I discharged here [i.e., in Geneva] the office of pastor,

---

87. Cottret, *Calvin*, 82–88; Tavard, *Starting Point*, 13–17.
88. McGrath, *Life of John Calvin*, 74.

and so far from there being any appearance of rivalry, I always seemed to be of one mind with you.[89]

While in Basel, Calvin also would have had time to reflect on what had taken place in France and its implications for Christian discipleship. Years later he was able to look back and see what God was doing in his life during this time. Some words from his exposition of Matthew 8:19 ("And a scribe came up and said to him, 'Teacher, I will follow you wherever you go'") in his *Commentary on the Synoptic Gospels* well express those later thoughts about God's work in his life in the days following his conversion:

> We realize that he was a scribe, a man accustomed to a quiet and easy existence, treated with respect, who would be no match for hard words or hard times, for persecution, or the cross. He wishes to follow Christ, but he imagines to himself a soft and pleasant path, lodging with all good things provided—while Christ's road is a thorny one for his disciples; it leads through endless pains to a cross. . . . So we should learn that, in his person, we are all being told not to make wild and irresponsible claims to be Christ's disciples, without taking any thought for the cross and the hardships. . . . This is the basic training which admits us to his school, denying ourselves and lifting up our cross.[90]

Calvin was learning in the school of Christ that if he would serve the Master of the school wholeheartedly, he must walk a "thorny" road. In modern parlance, the French scholar (scribe?) was being taught the cost of discipleship and thus being prepared for his life's work in Geneva.

---

89. *CNTC*, 10:347.
90. *CNTC*, 1:254.

2

The Call to Geneva and the Struggle for Orthodoxy

Stephen J. Nichols

I am settled here [in Geneva]; may the Lord overrule it for good.
—John Calvin, letter to Guillaume Farel, September 16, 1541

Painful Change

The story is well enough known and often enough told. On a particular day in the summer of 1536, the young Reformer John Calvin passed through Geneva, an overnight stop on his way to Strasbourg. And in that young man, Geneva's Guillaume Farel (1489–1565) found the answer to his prayers. Geneva, though an ancient city, was practically an infant in the gospel, having declared itself an evangelical city just in May of that year. Farel was gifted, but he also knew his limitations. He further sensed what Calvin was capable of and what Calvin could accomplish. Now the task fell to Farel to convince Calvin to stay. The draw to Strasbourg consisted in Calvin's desire to come under the wing of Martin Bucer (1491–1551). Farel offered Calvin a draw of a different sort to remain in Geneva, namely, that Calvin would incur the judgment of God for not staying. It worked. The two struck up a friendship and were brothers-in-arms throughout their respective careers as Reformers. Though they had a falling out later in life, the "friends of happier days"—in the words of Theodore Beza—reconciled just before Calvin died in 1564. Farel passed away the next year.[1] In addition to the formidable friendship, Calvin and Farel led the city of Geneva to the forefront of the Reformation in the Swiss lands in the sixteenth century. More than that, Calvin and Farel made a lasting impact on the Christian tradition, the benefits of which continue to be reaped many generations later. If ever the ends justified the means, then Farel's presumption to know the divine mind resulted in one of the most significant and rewarding moments in the history of the Christian church.

The following chapter explores this episode, looking at this particular season in Calvin's life and at the struggles in Geneva and across the region as the Reformation took hold. In our day, change is rapid—my six-month-old laptop is already outdated. That simply is not the case for most of human history. In the previous centuries, change tended to be glacial. There are, however, exceptions; there are also those moments of rapid upheaval and paradigm shifts, surprisingly, before the twenty-first century. The latter half of the 1530s was such a time, not only for Geneva but for the whole region and also for the face of Europe. It was a necessary change to be sure. But it was also a painful change, painful for Geneva's residents and, as we will see, painful for Calvin himself.

Calvin's Journey to Geneva

The assessment of Philip Benedict in his *Christ's Churches Purely Reformed: A Social History of Calvinism* is neither wide of the mark nor rare. As Benedict has it, Calvin "unquestionably merits the leading role traditionally assigned him in the history of the Reformed tradition."[2]

---

1. Theodore Beza, *Beza's "Icones": Contemporary Portraits of Reformers of Religion and Letters* (1580; repr., London: Religious Tract Society, 1909), 150. See also Bruce Gordon, *Calvin* (New Haven, CT: Yale University Press, 2009), 281–82.
2. Philip Benedict, *Christ's Churches Purely Reformed: A Social History of Calvinism* (New Haven, CT: Yale University Press, 2002), 72.

There was a time, however, when John Calvin was not quite John Calvin. His indisputable reputation would come later, but in 1536 he was but one of any number of young gifted theologians and churchmen. To be sure, his *Institutes* appeared in its first edition in 1536. Yet while people knew of the *Institutes*, there was little knowledge of the identity of its author. Calvin made no effort to change his relative anonymity. As he recalled of his stopover in Geneva during his attempted travel from France to Strasbourg, "Nobody [in Geneva] knew that I was its author. Here, as everywhere, I made no mention of the fact, and intended to continue doing the same."[3] The intentions of Calvin were overruled by his discovery. Calvin described this unknown discoverer as someone who later "wickedly rebelled and returned to the papists." It was precisely this unnamed and, Calvin would lead us to believe, untrustworthy fellow (whom we know to be Louis du Tillet) who revealed the identity of Calvin to Farel.[4]

Farel's first attempts at trying to keep Calvin in Geneva were the basic arguments anyone might use to bend someone to his or her wishes. But those arguments proved less than compelling for Calvin. Calvin recalled, "Finding that he got nowhere with his requests," Farel upped the ante, giving "vent to an imprecation that it might please God to curse my leisure and the peace for study that I was looking for, if I went away and refused to give support and help in a situation of such great need." It was, again in Calvin's words, "not so much by advice and argument, but by a dreadful curse."[5] Calvin longed for the quieter and calmer environs of the academy at Strasbourg, the city and university where Martin Bucer held sway.[6] Calvin had preferred the academy over the church, even before he sided with the Reformation. Upon the completion of his studies at Paris and Orléans, Calvin was supposed to return to the parish ministry in Noyon. He preferred the academic halls and evidenced no intention of going back to Noyon. Once he sided with the Reformation, he intended to stay the academic course.

---

3. CO, 31:24, cited in Alister E. McGrath, *A Life of John Calvin: A Study in the Shaping of Western Culture* (Oxford: Blackwell, 1990), 95.
4. CO, 31:24, cited in McGrath, *Life of John Calvin*, 95.
5. CO, 31:24, cited in McGrath, *Life of John Calvin*, 95.
6. For more on Bucer, see D. F. Wright, ed., *Martin Bucer: Reforming Church and Community* (Cambridge: Cambridge University Press, 2002).

The Reformation and the Swiss Cities

Strasbourg would have been a great a fit for Calvin. James Kittelson observes that this city of approximately twenty-five thousand "was both the breeding and receiving grounds for nearly every cultural and religious movement of the sixteenth century."[7] Matthew Zell (1477–1548) first brought the Reformation to this city along the Rhine River in 1521. He was helped by quite a constellation of Swiss Reformers, including Wolfgang Capito (ca. 1478–1541) and Martin Bucer. Though the city experienced moments of tension, as Kittelson notes, for the most part the ecclesiastical and civil establishments in Strasbourg worked together to firmly establish the city as a leading light of the Reformation.[8] By the early 1530s, Strasbourg was firmly planted in the Reformation camp. The city would have been a good place for young Calvin, and Bucer would have been a good fit as his mentor.

Born in 1491, Bucer showed early promise as a scholar. While pursuing his doctorate at Heidelberg, Bucer embraced the Reformation by 1518, having met Luther when the German Reformer came to the city for the Heidelberg Disputation. Bucer would also later witness a defiant Luther stand before both church and emperor at the Diet of Worms in 1521.[9] Because of his commitment to Luther's Reformation, Bucer found himself increasingly unwelcome, which forced him to flee to Strasbourg in 1523 as an "excommunicated refugee."[10] Finding a home at Strasbourg, Bucer immediately set to work, penning a theology that laid out the Reformation planks. Bucer also found himself embroiled in controversy during the decade of the 1520s. First, there was the stamping out of the last vestiges of Roman Catholicism in Strasbourg. Second, and more telling, were the controversies between the Swiss Reformers and the German Reformers. More appropriately stated, it was the controversy between *the* Swiss Reformer, Huldrych Zwingli (1484–1531), and *the* German Reformer, Martin Luther (1483–1546). Bucer was in attendance at the Marburg Colloquy in 1529. This colloquy, or meeting, attempted to bring these two sides together. It worked—until, that is, they discussed the nature

---

7. James M. Kittelson, "Strasbourg," in *OER*, 4:115.
8. Kittelson, "Strasbourg," in *OER*, 4:115.
9. Beza, *Beza's "Icones,"* 83–84.
10. Martin Greschat, "Bucer, Martin," in *OER*, 1:222.

of the presence of Christ in the Lord's Supper. The two sides could not come together, and the desired union did not occur. Bucer sided more with Luther than with Zwingli over the nature of Christ's presence in the sacrament, espousing the "spiritual presence of Christ" view that Calvin would also later espouse.[11] After the Marburg Colloquy, Bucer plied his efforts to bring about union between the Swiss and German Reformers and cities. He had mixed results.

By 1536, Bucer was finishing his second decade as a leader of the Reformation, and Calvin longed to be under his influence. Luther's early rounds with the Roman church passed right by a young Calvin, then studying at Paris. The Marburg Colloquy came and went without his notice. One gets the sense, then, that when Calvin was converted in 1533, he was determined, as it were, to make up for lost time. It would not fall to Calvin, however, to enjoy the fruits of the past labors of others who had already established Strasbourg as a Reformation city. His hope was that he could move into Strasbourg and enjoy the relatively placid and stable environment. They would be hopes mostly dashed. In God's sovereignty, Calvin would eventually get to Strasbourg— ironically, he would go there after getting exiled from Geneva. Also in God's sovereignty, it would fall to Calvin, like Bucer, to help a city in its struggle for orthodoxy. The stable and placid environs would have to wait. Calvin, by staying in Geneva, would now be entering the fray.

Zurich, under the leadership of Zwingli, had embraced the Reformation, though somewhat cataclysmically, in the first years of the 1520s. Amy Nelson Burnett notes that the citizens of Basel also accepted the Reformation almost to a person also by the early 1520s. Such was the impetus of the populace that it "forced" the magistrate of the city over to the Reformation by the end of 1520s.[12] The university community at Basel had already been with the Reformers since the 1510s. It was here that Erasmus could freely work on his text of the Greek New Testament, which first rolled off the presses at Basel in 1516. The same presses also propagated the texts of Martin Luther. As noted earlier, Strasbourg, too, embraced the Reformation in the 1520s under

---

11. See Thomas J. Davis, *This Is My Body: The Presence of Christ in Reformation Thought* (Grand Rapids, MI: Baker Academic, 2008).
12. Amy Nelson Burnett, "Basel," in *OER*, 1:125.

Bucer's leadership. These three cities fall in a line as one moves south from Germany and the Luther lands. Moving farther south, out of the Rhine River Valley and slightly to the west toward France, one finds the city of Geneva. Unlike these three cities to the north, Geneva was not firmly established in the Reformation camp in the 1520s. In fact, the city was still struggling in the 1530s when Calvin's identity was revealed and Farel took it on himself to invoke the curse.

Under normal circumstances, Calvin would never have gone through Geneva to get to Strasbourg. It would have been a much easier trip if Calvin could have just headed directly east. But because the border to the north was more heavily guarded, Calvin had to travel south, exit France, then head north through the Swiss confederacy to Strasbourg. Geneva was but a convenient stopping point along the way. But then came Farel's legendary curse. Alister McGrath observes, "Precisely what Farel saw in [Calvin] we shall never know."[13] McGrath explains why by enumerating any number of factors that made Calvin a less than ideal suitor for leading the vanguard of Geneva's reformation. Calvin "totally lacked pastoral experience." He was "withdrawn in personality and intellectual in inclination," giving "little indication of being of potential value in the cut-and-thrust world of Genevan politics of the 1530s."[14] It seems that as unfit as Geneva apparently was for Calvin and his needs at the time, he, too, was apparently unfit for the city and its needs at the time. But appearances are deceiving. If Calvin's theology teaches us anything, we begin to see that there was nothing accidental or arbitrary about the journey through Geneva; neither was there anything accidental about his decision to stay. Little did Calvin know the enormous role this city would come to play in his life; little did he know how he and this city would become inextricably linked—this city that was, in his mind at the time, a mere stopover on his way to somewhere else.

Geneva in 1536

Guillaume Farel is crucial to the story of Geneva in the 1530s. Farel, like Calvin, had also studied at Paris. Once converted to the Refor-

---

13. McGrath, *Life of John Calvin*, 96.
14. McGrath, *Life of John Calvin*, 96.

mation in the early 1520s, Farel became quite the force for reform. Philip Benedict notes that Farel, a rather peripatetic Reformer, "crisscrossed the surrounding regions, absorbing numerous banishments and at least one beating while gradually gaining hearers in a number of localities."[15] Farel managed to find success in two of these localities in particular, at the small town of Aigle and at Neuchâtel. In addition to his tireless travels, Farel also tried to promote the Reformation through writing. He wrote "the first extensive statement of Reformed doctrine in French," with *Sommaire et briefve declaration* coming off the press in 1529.[16] From his post at Neuchâtel, Farel ventured into Geneva for the first time in 1532. He was not well received, and he barely escaped. Undeterred, Farel tried again in 1535, with a modicum of success. More ventures throughout 1535 and 1536 eventually resulted in the adoption of the Reformation by the ruling civil authority, the General Council of Geneva, on May 21, 1536.

The General Council had been on the ascendancy in the city of Geneva, estimated to have a population of ten thousand in the 1530s. The council, since the 1520s, was assuming more and more power from the prince-bishop, a position that had exercised power from a more centralized seat. The council's coming of age reflected the sociological moves of the day as this era witnessed the rise of the modern nation-state. As the old civil ways were crumbling and transforming, so, too, would the old ecclesiastical ways undergo change. The political revolution of the 1520s set the stage for the theological reformation of the 1530s.[17]

Farel served as the catalyst for bringing reform to Geneva, no easy task. Farel, however, knew well his limitations. If it were not for his association with Calvin, his name would be known only within the guild of Reformation scholars and largely lost to the rest of the church. Even the Schaff-Herzog Encyclopedia speaks of Farel's few publications, despite one of them being the first statement of the Reformed faith in French, as having "little importance," and it does not lament

---

15. Benedict, *Christ's Churches Purely Reformed*, 78.
16. Francis Higman, "Farel, Guillaume," in *OER*, 2:100.
17. See Benedict, *Christ's Churches Purely Reformed*, 78–82; Robert M. Kingdon, "The Calvinist Reformation in Geneva," in *The Cambridge History of Christianity*, vol. 6, *Reform and Expansion, 1500–1660*, ed. R. Po-Chia Hsia (Cambridge: Cambridge University Press, 2007), 90–103.

the fact that they have been long forgotten. Yet Farel had at least one rather admirable quality. In knowing his limitations, Farel set the stage for the world to know Calvin. Robert Kingdon observes that Farel pinned his hopes on Calvin "to explain to Genevans what the change they had voted for really meant."[18] Farel served to bring about the vote for Geneva to become Reformed; Calvin would be the one to show Geneva what a Reformed church and a Reformed city looked like. It would not, however, be all that easy for Calvin.

Ille Gallus

The Genevan Council referred to Calvin as *ille Gallus,* or "that Frenchman," in their official documents. This leads scholar Ross William Collins to conclude, "Apparently the council was at first not greatly impressed with Farel's new recruit."[19] As Richard Horcsik points out, Calvin "did not receive any compensation [from Geneva] until February 13, 1537," months after he had arrived there and had assumed the post of "Reader in Holy Scripture to the Church in Geneva."[20] Horcsik further points to Calvin's first stay in Geneva as marked not only by financial struggle but also by illness, an infection after a cold. In the first letter he wrote from his new home in Geneva, to Francis Daniel, Calvin bemoaned, "A violent cold attacked me, which afterward settled on the upper gum, so that there was scarce any relief even after nine days, and after having been twice bled, with a double dose of pills and fomentations."[21]

Calvin had to contend with one final thing in those first few months of his pastorate. Pierre Caroli (d. ca. 1550), a scholar from Sorbonne, had been a bit of a burr in the saddle of Guillaume Farel since 1534. But in the winter of 1536–1537, he stepped up his pertinacity and widened his attack to include Calvin. He attempted to slander both Farel and Calvin's character. When that did not work, he resorted to

---

18. Kingdon, "Calvinist Reformation," 92.
19. Ross William Collins, *Calvin and the Libertines of Geneva,* ed. F. D. Blackley (Toronto: Clarke, Irwin, 1968), 96.
20. Richard Horcsik, "John Calvin in Geneva, 1536–38: Some Questions about Calvin's First Stay at Geneva," in *Calvinus Sacrae Scripturae Professor: Calvin as Confessor of Holy Scriptures,* ed. Wilhelm H. Neuser (Grand Rapids, MI: Eerdmans, 1994), 161–62. See also Herman J. Selderhuis, *John Calvin: A Pilgrim's Life,* trans. Albert Gootjes (Downers Grove, IL: IVP Academic, 2009), 53–54.
21. Calvin to Francis Daniel, October 13, 1536, in *Letters,* 1:45.

accusing them both of being Arians. When that did not work, Caroli tried to paint them as Sabellians, a more subtle heresy. Calvin reported his response to these attacks:

> When we first heard, therefore, that the Arian heresy was imputed to us, and then a little afterwards the Sabellian, none of these things very much disturbed us, seeing that our ears had long since been well seasoned against such calumnies; and we entertained the assured hope that they would eventually pass away in a wreath of smoke.[22]

The charges did not go away—these were tumultuous times. Consequently, disputations were set up between Calvin and Caroli at Bern. Calvin colorfully described the outcome: "We emptied his bag, however, to such a degree, by our refutation, as not to leave even the shadow of a suspicion upon the mind of anyone present."[23] We might say today that Calvin cleaned Caroli's theological clock.

These were the realities of the first few months of Calvin's pastorate: financial struggles, illnesses, and personal attacks. Calvin indeed was laboring under a cloud. But labor he did. John Opiron, one of Calvin's correspondents from Basel, wrote to Calvin, "I hear that you lecture on the Epistles of St. Paul with great acclaim and profit."[24] Eventually, through these lectures, and also through his sermons, Calvin did grow in the estimation of the council and even began to become more widely known beyond Geneva. In a refreshing moment of candor, Calvin referred to his struggles in attacking the canon law on marriages in favor of thinking more biblically about the institution in his 1536 edition of the *Institutes*. Calvin admitted that it had been quite a struggle to "extricate ourselves from their mire," before concluding with a touch of color, "Still, I believe that I have accomplished something in that I have partly pulled the lion's skin from these asses [i.e., donkeys]."[25] This skill of pulling the lion's skin from those who

---

22. Calvin to Simon Grynee, May 1537, in *Letters*, 1:54.

23. Calvin to Simon Grynee, May 1537, in *Letters*, 1:55.

24. John Opiron to John Calvin, November 25, 1537, cited in Horcsik, "John Calvin in Geneva," 162.

25. *Institutes* (1536), in *CO*, 1:192–95, cited in John Witte Jr. and Robert M. Kingdon, *Sex, Marriage, and Family in John Calvin's Geneva*, vol. 1, *Courtship, Engagement, and Marriage* (Grand Rapids, MI: Eerdmans, 2005), 51.

did not always know what was best for them served Calvin well. It was one of his more remarkable pastoral traits.

After Farel secured Calvin for the city of Geneva, he returned to his travels, all the while keeping Geneva central to his tasks. Farel worked so tirelessly that Calvin thought they were going to lose him. Calvin sought to enlist the help of Pierre Viret to relieve Farel of some of his burden. Calvin pled for Viret to relocate to Geneva, going as far as to say that he must come, "unless we are willing to lose Farel, who is more exhausted with the great anxiety than I ever thought would be the case with one of such iron constitution."[26] Even such iron constitutions have their breaking points. Viret accepted, setting up a virtual ecclesiastical triumvirate of Farel, Viret, and Calvin—with the last taking the lead—in the reform of Geneva. Viret joined in May 1537. In January 1537, Farel and Calvin drafted their "Articles concerning the Organization of the Church and of Worship at Geneva," which they presented to the General Council of Geneva. Based on what would come to be called the "regulative principle," this text called for the radical transformation of the church service, of preaching, of the practice of the Eucharist, and of church discipline. Bard Thompson sees their plan for the church as being conceived around two foci of "the weekly celebration of the Eucharist and, inseparable from it, parish discipline, including the act of excommunication." Thompson adds that "the 'Articles' takes us very close to the crux of Calvinism."[27] In the days prior to the Reformation, there was little discussion on what constituted the true church. It was mostly a moot point, since the only church in the West was the Roman Catholic Church. The Reformation changed that, sparking what was one of the most widely discussed questions: What are the marks of the true church? This central question spawned others. What does this church do? What does it look like? And quite crucially, what constitutes membership in this true church?

Here in the "Articles," Calvin and Farel ventured that preaching, the Eucharist, and church discipline topped the list of defining the true church. From Calvin's perspective, if the churches in Geneva were

---

26. Calvin to Pierre Viret, April 23, 1537, in *Letters*, 1:53.
27. Bard Thompson, *Humanists and Reformers: A History of the Renaissance and Reformation* (Grand Rapids, MI: Eerdmans, 1996), 488.

truly to look like what they voted themselves to be, they would need to heed the teaching of the "Articles." From another perspective, the "Articles" would be the eventual unraveling of the relationship between Calvin and Farel, on the one hand, and Calvin and the General Council of Geneva, on the other. Again, Thompson informs us that while "the Genevan magistrates accepted these 'Articles,'" they did so "with serious reservations."[28] Those reservations consisted in reducing Calvin's request for the monthly practice[29] of the Lord's Supper to a quarterly practice, which followed the specifics of their treaty obligations with the city of Bern. More important, the Genevan magistrates balked at Calvin's suggestion to create a "corps of lay elders" to carry out discipline and, if need be, excommunicate the unrepentant. The magistrates had the power over excommunication, and they simply were not willing to relinquish it. From Calvin's perspective, without the power to excommunicate, the clergy would be severely limited in their God-given task to maintain the purity of the church.

This debate over the details of the "Articles" ensued throughout 1537. Tension also arose when Calvin and Farel began to require all citizens both to attend church and to sign the Confession of Faith, which they had just drawn up.[30] According to McGrath, these were rather unpopular measures, strengthening the anti-Farel and anti-Calvin factions and even straining the commitment of Farel and Calvin's supporters.[31] Foes assailed them, while friends began abandoning them. By January 1538, the General Council held firm in its decision to keep the power of excommunication to itself. Now the rift between the clergy, especially Calvin and Farel, and the city grew deep and wide, and Calvin and Farel found themselves with diminishing if

---

28. Thompson, *Humanists and Reformers*, 489.

29. While Calvin and Farel held that it was best to celebrate the Lord's Supper on a weekly basis, they did make allowance for the fact that not all the laity were so suited. Thus Thompson notes, "Considering the 'frailty' of the people, . . . Calvin and Farel conceded that for the time being the Holy Communion might be celebrated only once a month in the three principal churches, yet on a staggered schedule, allowing the city at large to have access to the sacrament more often." Thompson, *Humanists and Reformers*, 488.

30. Calvin's logic was that it was good for all to attend church so that they would be exposed to the gospel. Calvin also thought that those who attended church might view their citizenly obligation differently. Well aware that this requirement could lead to nominalism, Calvin insisted on "fencing the Table," to use the words sometimes associated with the theology of the Westminster Confession of Faith (cf. WCF 29.8). "Fencing the Table" means ensuring that only communicant members in good standing partake of Communion.

31. McGrath, *Life of John Calvin*, 99.

not largely evaporated popular support. In March all four councils that ruled Geneva (the largest and cumulative body being the General Council) accepted the Bernese articles on worship and church practice, circumventing, overriding, and ultimately undermining Calvin and Farel in the process. On Easter Sunday that year, Calvin and Farel both refused to serve Communion after their respective sermons. Thompson explains why, noting that without church discipline, there can be no Communion, adding, "The pastors had, in effect, excommunicated Geneva."[32] The city, though, would have the last word. On April 23, 1538, both Calvin and Farel were dismissed from their duties and given three days to leave the city.

Preachers or Pastors?

Unraveling what went wrong during Geneva's first pastorate and Calvin's first stay in Geneva is crucial for a number of reasons. First, we need to understand what happened. History matters, and getting the story right brings clarity to our understanding and legitimacy to our interpretations. Second, and perhaps profoundly more important, pastors and congregations today can learn a great deal concerning pastoral ministry by dissecting this episode in Calvin's life.

Earlier we drew attention to Calvin's penchant for the academic life over entering the fray of these struggles for orthodoxy in cities like Geneva. Calvin, it may be recalled, wanted to study under and serve alongside Martin Bucer and engage in his scholarly pursuits; he avoided the (nightmarish) prospects of slugging it out in Geneva, a city that David Wright points out had no university and no major printing house.[33] Lacking these necessary ingredients for a scholar, Geneva in itself had little if anything to draw Calvin. Something happened, though, in 1536–1537 to change Calvin's mind.

All the indicators of Calvin's life prior to these years have him ensconced in the cloistered halls. But in this moment of his life, he began

---

32. Thompson, *Humanists and Reformers*, 491. Thompson also explains that the elections to the councils in February 1538 saw the removal of any supporters of Farel and Calvin, while those candidates opposed to them were swept into office. The political deck was stacked against them. See also Willem van 't Spijker, *Calvin: A Brief Guide to His Life and Thought*, trans. Lyle D. Bierma (Louisville: Westminster John Knox, 2009), 47–48.

33. D. F. Wright, "Calvin, John," in *Biographical Dictionary of Evangelicals*, ed. Timothy Larsen, David Bebbington, and Mark A. Noll (Downers Grove, IL: InterVarsity Press, 2003), 110.

to sound a different note. This can be seen in his letter to his compatriot at Zurich, Heinrich Bullinger (1504–1575). Bullinger had picked up where Zwingli left off at Zurich, after Zwingli's death on the battlefield at Kappel on October 11, 1531, a battle that came about because of the tensions between the Reformed city-states and the Roman Catholic city-states. Zwingli's meteoric career as a Reformer lasted all of a decade, from the beginnings of the Reformation in 1522 until his untimely death in 1531. Bullinger took the leadership of the church and of the academy at Zurich. He also became a towering figure of the Swiss Reformation, being the main architect of the Second Helvetic Confession (1566). He and Calvin had their disagreements over the finer points of certain theological issues but remained close friends and frequent correspondents throughout their respective careers.

Little wonder that Calvin, once he became locked in the controversy with the General Council in Geneva, turned to Bullinger as a sounding board and for moral support. Calvin started his letter with a disclaimer, "Were I to describe to you at length the full narrative of our most wretched condition, a long history must be unfolded by me. . . . But because there is not enough leisure at present for explaining everything . . . I will not trouble you with a large epistle."[34] This condensed version afforded Calvin the opportunity to synthesize the controversy and offer a succinct summary, which consists in three main points. The first centers on church discipline and excommunication. The second concerns the logistics of the church in Geneva. Calvin favored breaking down the larger churches into smaller parishes, again motivated by a desire to improve pastoral care. The third and summative point is that Geneva wanted pastors but not preachers. Calvin put the first two concerns this way:

> We have not yet been able to obtain, that the faithful and holy exercise of ecclesiastical excommunication be rescued from the oblivion into which it has fallen; and that the city, which in proportion to its extent is very populous, may be distributed into parishes, as is rendered necessary by the complicated administration of the church.[35]

---

34. Calvin to Heinrich Bullinger, February 21, 1538, in *Letters*, 1:66.
35. Calvin to Heinrich Bullinger, February 21, 1538, in *Letters*, 1:66.

Then Calvin explained the third, crucial concern: "The generality of men are more ready to acknowledge us as preachers than as pastors."[36] This sentence, it might be fair to say, sums up Calvin's take on the Reformation's ultimate issue. The *raison d'être* for the Reformation was to move from a church that had nothing more than mere preachers to one that had pastors. Calvin was not concerned with the mere formality of the church service, the performance—whether it be of the Mass or of the sermon. For Calvin, the Reformation was about the gospel taking root in and transforming one's life. Further, from his perspective, the Reformation was about that transformation eventually extending to city-states like Geneva and beyond. It is likely no exaggeration that Calvin's lifelong desire was to see the Reformation that was occurring in these Swiss city-states become a reality in his native France. Pastoral care, according to Calvin's understanding of the church and of the pastoral role, was the essential element. If Geneva was content to have preachers and not pastors, then in Calvin's estimation, Geneva would never realize the identity it voted on in May 1536. Calvin desired that Geneva become what it voted to be. This is Calvin's condensed version of what went wrong in his first pastorate. It was for Calvin a hard lesson and a trying time.[37]

Calvin in his clear-eyed perspective on the situation saw that at that time, he and the council were at an impasse over these three issues. He sagaciously informed Bullinger that only the Lord himself "may open up a way."[38]

Exile and Return

The Lord eventually opened a way, just not in the manner that Calvin had likely hoped. A few months after Calvin wrote to Bullinger about the situation, the General Council promptly dismissed Calvin and Farel. These two exiles first went to Basel. Farel stayed only for a few months, moving on to Neuchâtel, where he remained, for the most part, throughout the rest of his life. He would survive Calvin

---

36. Calvin to Heinrich Bullinger, February 21, 1538, in *Letters*, 1:66.
37. For some intriguing essays on Calvin's ecclesiology, see David Foxgrover, ed., *Calvin and the Church: Papers Presented at the 13th Colloquium of the Calvin Studies Society, May 24–26, 2001* (Grand Rapids, MI: Calvin Studies Society, 2002).
38. Calvin to Heinrich Bullinger, February 21, 1538, in *Letters*, 1:67.

by just one year, dying in 1565. At seventy-six years of age, Farel was still traveling for the sake of the gospel. Along a harsh winter's journey returning from Metz to Neuchâtel, Farel contracted an illness that would take his life. Beza records that while at Metz, in the eighth decade of his life, he "preached with all his old fire and copiousness."[39]

Back in 1538, after Farel left Basel, Calvin stayed in that city. He could now engage in the quiet academic life that he longed to pursue before Farel sidetracked him by his legendary curse just two years prior. Calvin was at Basel, though, not at Strasbourg. Strasbourg's Martin Bucer was rather keen on having Calvin join him, seeing Calvin as the ideal candidate to pastor a rather large church of French refugees, numbering five hundred. Bucer began to pressure Calvin to assume the post but to no avail. Perhaps Calvin's first pastoral charge in Geneva so soured and discouraged him that he decided to head back into the academy, to pick up the pursuits he left off in 1536. What we do know for sure was that Calvin resolutely resisted Bucer's attempts to get him to resume a pastoral charge at Strasbourg.

Calvin resisted, until, that is, Bucer pulled a play from Farel. Thompson picks up the story: "Bucer finally inquired of Farel how to deal with such an obdurate human being. From Neuchâtel came the advice: pronounce the wrath of God."[40] Farel had resorted to pronouncing God's curse on Calvin to keep him from going to Strasbourg in 1536; now Bucer was doing the exact same to get him to go to Strasbourg in 1538.

Calvin's pastoral ministry to the French refugee congregation at Strasbourg was short lived but eventful. Calvin was busy corresponding and preparing works for publication, not to mention preaching. At Strasbourg, Calvin was able to establish the monthly practice of the Lord's Supper, which Geneva had denied him. Church discipline was in ecclesiastical hands, not in political hands. Calvin was in sum a pastor and not merely a preacher. While he was in Strasbourg, Calvin published two important works, his *Commentary on Romans* (1539) and his *Short Treatise on the Supper of Our Lord* (1540), the latter

---

39. Beza, *Beza's "Icones,"* 151.
40. Thompson, *Humanists and Reformers*, 491. See also Selderhuis, *John Calvin*, 85–86.

reaching Martin Luther, who upon reading it lamented that Calvin was not present back at the Marburg Colloquy in 1529. Luther with a touch of regret exclaimed that had Calvin been there, he would have gladly "entrusted the whole affair of this controversy [over the Lord's Supper] to him from the beginning."[41]

In addition, Calvin, who went to Strasbourg as a bachelor, married. Idelette de Bure was recently widowed. Calvin had debated her husband, Jean Stordeur, then an Anabaptist. In the wake of the debate, Idelette's husband converted to the Reformed position. The couple followed Calvin to Strasbourg, and after Stordeur died, Calvin married Idelette, in August 1540. In 1542, they had a son, who died in infancy. Idelette spent much of that decade weaving in and out of illnesses. She died in 1549, leaving Calvin heartbroken and bewildered but also clinging to the providence of God. If only the Lord could make a way out of the impasse in Geneva, then only the Lord could cut a clear path through Calvin's grief and disillusionment over her loss. Before she passed, however, the couple would be moved, again with Calvin under duress.[42]

In Calvin's absence, the city of Geneva left itself vulnerable to the much stronger city of Bern, which tended toward a more mediating ecclesiology between Roman Catholicism and the typically Reformed churches of the other Swiss city-states. That Bern held sway over Geneva was part of the problem that led to Calvin's ouster in the first place. With Calvin out of the way, Bern's shadow only loomed larger over the city. Further, Geneva was vulnerable to Roman Catholic pulls. While at Strasbourg, Calvin rather handily silenced Cardinal Sadoleto, who had written a lengthy letter to Geneva to convince the city to repent of its reformation vote in 1536 and return to the fold of the Roman see.[43] While defeated in his arguments, Sadoleto nevertheless continued to hassle Geneva, campaigning for its return to Rome. No one in Geneva was up to the task of refuting him. By September 1540,

---

41. Luther's comment, first reported by Philipp Melanchthon's son-in-law Christopher Pezel, is well attested and often cited. See, among others, John T. McNeill, *The History and Character of Calvinism* (New York: Oxford University Press, 1967), 153.

42. For more on Calvin's marriage, see W. Robert Godfrey, *John Calvin: Pilgrim and Pastor* (Wheaton, IL: Crossway, 2009), 46–47.

43. For the full story, see John C. Olin, ed., *A Reformation Debate: Sadoleto's Letter to the Genevans and Calvin's Reply* (New York: Fordham University Press, 2000).

the city requested that Calvin return.[44] Thompson describes Calvin's response, "Calvin began hemming and hawing, offering again his standard list of excuses."[45] Behind those excuses lies Calvin's true reason, which he himself best describes: "There is no place under heaven that I am more afraid of."[46]

Calvin had some legitimate excuses. Given his previous experience in Geneva, his ostensible reason also carried a great deal of legitimacy. Calvin also had immediate occasions that afforded him time to think over Geneva's invitation to return. In the fall of 1540, Calvin was participating in the Diet of Worms, which just two decades prior served as the backdrop for Luther's famous "Here I Stand" speech. He also had the Diet of Ratisbon on his agenda for the spring of 1541. But these obligations merely presented convenient cover for Calvin to avoid what for him was a painful decision. Calvin revealed his true feelings in a letter to Farel on October 27, 1540: "Whenever I call to mind the state of wretchedness in which my life was spent when there, how can it be otherwise but that my very soul must shudder when any proposal is made for my return?"[47] Can we blame him? Yet Calvin could not hold off the invitation. By May 1541, he had decided to return to Geneva, this most feared city under heaven. In August he began his journey, meandering a bit along the way.

By the middle of September 1541, Calvin had resettled in Geneva. Calvin's long journey to get back to Geneva left Farel with the impression that Calvin had second thoughts and decided against it. Calvin wrote to Farel, assuring him that, indeed, he was back in Geneva. Calvin's opening lines are telling, "As you wished, I am settled here; may the Lord overrule it for good."[48] This last phrase "for good" begs interpretation. Does Calvin mean "for good" in terms of ultimate duration? Or does "for good" mean beneficially? Perhaps there is ambiguity in the expression for a reason. Calvin had learned many things since 1536, perhaps chief among them was the Lord's sovereign *and good* hand over his life—a sovereignty that more often than not

---

44. Godfrey, *John Calvin*, 13–22; Gordon, *Calvin*, 96–98.
45. Thompson, *Humanists and Reformers*, 495.
46. Cited in Thompson, *Humanists and Reformers*, 496. See also Gordon, *Calvin*, 121–22; Selderhuis, *John Calvin*, 117.
47. Calvin to Guillaume Farel, October 27, 1540, in *Letters*, 1:211.
48. Calvin to Guillaume Farel, September 16, 1541, in *Letters*, 1:284.

confounded Calvin but a sovereignty that Calvin came to rest on. As Herman Selderhuis explains, "Calvin and Geneva made for an odd couple; they didn't seem able to live with or without one another. Calvin thought God would not allow him to leave Geneva, and the people of Geneva knew they could not afford to lose Calvin."[49]

Conclusion

Calvin would remain in Geneva until his death, on May 27, 1564. Those twenty-three years would contain many accomplishments, accomplishments that fill numerous biographies of this Reformer, or, as the earlier Genevan Council referred to him, *ille Gallus*. This Frenchman had finally found a home in Geneva. But of all those accomplishments, what Calvin set out to do may be summed up in that same letter to Farel dated September 16, 1541. Calvin wrote, "Immediately after I had offered my services to the Senate, I declared that a church could not hold together unless a settled government should be agreed on, *such as is prescribed us in the Word of God*, and such as was in use in the ancient church."[50] Calvin added, as if to assure Farel that the whole controversy might start up again, "Then I touched gently on certain points from whence they might understand what my wish was."[51] Calvin had the same "wishes" for Geneva in 1541 that he had in his first stay in 1536–1538. In the interim he had learned that seeing those wishes become a reality would be a process that would take time. Calvin's wish for the church in Geneva could be summed up in this: that it would be a true church as prescribed in the Bible. This was, after all, the heart of the Reformation.

Calvin was named to Geneva's Company of Pastors, becoming the titular leader before being granted the title moderator of the Company of Pastors. He also drafted "a set of ecclesiastical ordinances that provided a kind of constitution for the city's Reformed Church."[52] In short, Geneva finally wanted pastors and not just preachers. The struggle for orthodoxy in Geneva, and elsewhere for that matter, had a great deal more to it than merely leaving Roman Catholicism and

---

49. Selderhuis, *John Calvin*, 121.
50. Calvin to Guillaume Farel, September 16, 1541, in *Letters*, 1:284, italics added.
51. Calvin to Guillaume Farel, September 16, 1541, in *Letters*, 1:284.
52. Kingdon, "Calvinist Reformation," 91.

casting a vote on the side of the Reformed church. It had to do first and foremost with grasping what a "purely reformed" church looked like. It had to do second with becoming such a church. Young Calvin, at merely twenty-seven years of age when he first went to Geneva, had to learn hard lessons himself before he could teach others. Eventually, both Calvin and his adopted city of Geneva, however, learned together as pastor and congregation how to become a Reformed church.

3

Calvin the Pastor

David B. Calhoun

Here, then, is the sovereign power with which the pastors of the church . . . ought to be endowed. That is that they may dare boldly to do all things by God's Word.

—John Calvin, *Institutes of the Christian Religion*

"Minister of the Word of God in the Church of Geneva"

John Calvin is well known as a major Reformer,[1] an important theologian, a skillful biblical expositor, a sharp polemicist, and a gifted writer in both Latin and French. He is less commonly remembered as an effective preacher and a caring pastor. James Montgomery Boice asserts that "Calvin was preeminently a preacher, and as a preacher he saw himself primarily as a Bible teacher. Calvin is hardly thought of in that way today."[2] William Naphy has written, "Calvin's importance

---

1. Williston Walker called Calvin "the organiser of Reformed Protestantism." *John Calvin: The Organiser of Reformed Protestantism, 1509–1564* (New York: Putnam, 1906).
2. James Montgomery Boice, foreword to John Calvin, *Sermons on Psalm 119* (Audubon, NJ: Old Paths, 1996), viii. Two books that treat Calvin as a preacher are T. H. L. Parker, *Calvin's Preaching* (Louisville: Westminster John Knox, 1992); Steven J. Lawson, *The Expository Genius of John Calvin* (Orlando, FL: Reformation Trust, 2007).

as a great theologian and international figure has so overshadowed his role as a minister in Geneva that this aspect of his life has been allowed to remain in . . . obscurity."[3] For twenty-five years, between 1536 and his death in 1564 (except for three years as pastor of the French church in Strasbourg), Calvin was, as he is described in his last will and testament, "minister of the word of God in the Church of Geneva."[4]

Calvin was first and foremost a preacher and minister of a local church. Emile Doumergue claims that "the real and authentic Calvin, the one who explains all the others," is "the preacher of Geneva, moulding by his words the spirit of the Reformed of the sixteenth century."[5] All his accomplishments—his *Institutes*[6] and commentaries, his correspondence and counseling, his preaching and teaching—flowed out of and supported his pastoral calling.[7] John Leith has written, "Calvin's work in Geneva was that of a preacher who was concerned that Christian faith should be embodied not simply

---

3. William G. Naphy, *Calvin and the Consolidation of the Genevan Reformation* (Louisville: Westminster John Knox, 2003), 6. Jean-Daniel Benoit says, "One loves to speak of [Calvin] as the Reformer of Geneva. It would perhaps be more correct to refer to him as the pastor of Geneva, because Calvin was a pastor in his soul, and his reformatory work, in a good many respects, was only the consequence and extension of his pastoral activity." Benoit, *Calvin, directeur d'âmes: Contribution à l'histoire de la piété réformée* (Strasbourg: Editions Oberlin, 1947), 18, quoted by Richard Stauffer, *The Humanness of John Calvin*, trans. George H. Shriver (Nashville: Abingdon, 1971), 84. Chapter 3 in Stauffer's book is titled "Pastor," and the first footnote in his book gives a number of works on this subject in French and German. Elsie McKee has written that "the work of Calvin the pastor is a rich subject for investigation. Much has been learned, much remains to be done to give a complete picture of this part of the reformer's work." McKee, "Calvin and His Colleagues as Pastors: Some New Insights into the Collegial Ministry of Word and Sacraments," in *Calvinus Praeceptor Ecclesiae: Papers of the International Congress on Calvin Research, Princeton, August 20–24, 2002*, ed. Herman J. Selderhuis, THR 388 (Geneva: Librairie Droz, 2004), 9. McKee's research has led to greater appreciation and understanding of Calvin's role as pastor. She has published a major book on this topic, *The Pastoral Ministry and Worship in Calvin's Geneva*, THR 556 (Geneva: Librairie Droz, 2016). See also Ronald S. Wallace, *Calvin, Geneva and the Reformation: A Study of Calvin as Social Reformer, Churchman, Pastor and Theologian* (Grand Rapids, MI: Baker, 1988). In his foreword, Wallace writes, "For several years I read and collected material for a biographical work on Calvin. . . . Since I was in the ministry myself, I was especially interested both in the kind of ministry which Calvin set himself to fulfill in his city church . . . and in the way in which he actually succeeded in fulfilling it" (vii).

4. Calvin, "Last Will and Testament," April 25, 1564, in *Letters*, 4:365. Calvin was a pastor for twenty-seven years, exactly half his life.

5. Emile Doumergue, *Calvin, le Prédicateur de Genève: Conférence faite dans la cathédrale de Saint-Pierre, à Genève* (Lausanne: G. Bridel, 1910), 10.

6. John H. Leith claims that "the *Institutes* were written for the sake of the sermons, not the sermons for the sake of the *Institutes*." Leith, "Calvin's Doctrine of the Proclamation of the Word and Its Significance for Today," in *John Calvin and the Church: A Prism of Reform*, ed. Timothy George (Louisville: Westminster John Knox, 1990), 219.

7. T. H. L. Parker calls the basic truth of Calvin's life "the essential harmony of the man." "Within the limits of sinful mortality, the unity of his life is astounding; his thoughts, his actions and his intentions point in the same direction." Parker, *Portrait of Calvin* (London: SCM, 1954), 9.

in books, not simply in institutions, but primarily in Christian people living in the Christian community and in society."[8]

Calvin was, according to B. B. Warfield,

> the greatest exegete of the Reformation age: he was the Reformation's greatest theologian. And he was the practical genius of the Reformation. We do not say he was the practical genius of the Reformation in spite of his learned commentaries and his profound and profoundly reasoned theology. We would better say it was in large part because of them. Calvin probably never did a more practical thing than expound the Scriptures day by day with the penetrating insight and the clear, searching honesty of comment in which he is unsurpassed. And he certainly never did a more practical thing than write the *Institutes of the Christian Religion*.[9]

Elsie Anne McKee has written, "Calvin's own life was so intertwined with his ministry, whether immediately in Geneva or indirectly much farther afield, that it is difficult to speak of his personal biography apart from his office."[10] In this chapter, I survey Calvin's life and his ministry by concentrating on his own statements about both.[11]

"God by a Sudden Conversion Subdued and Brought My Mind to a Teachable Frame"[12]

John Calvin, a young Frenchman from the common people and "obstinately devoted" to the Roman Catholic Church, had completed studies in the liberal arts and law when he was suddenly converted to a different understanding of the Christian faith and to a new and

---

8. John H. Leith, *John Calvin: The Christian Life* (San Francisco: Harper & Row, 1984), x.

9. B. B. Warfield, "Calvin and the Reformation," in *Selected Shorter Writings of Benjamin B. Warfield*, ed. John E. Meeter (Nutley, NJ: Presbyterian and Reformed, 1970), 1:403.

10. Elsie Anne McKee, ed., *John Calvin: Writings on Pastoral Piety*, CWS (New York: Paulist, 2001), 18.

11. Calvin's autobiographical comments are sparse: the preface to the Psalms commentary, his *Reply to Sadoleto*, his letters, and an occasional remark in his sermons, commentaries, and treatises. Calvin's *Reply to Sadoleto* and the preface to his *Commentary on the Book of Psalms* are harmonized by Ford Lewis Battles in "Appendix 1: The Chief Lineaments of Calvin's Religious Experience," in *Interpreting John Calvin*, ed. Robert Benedetto (Grand Rapids, MI: Baker, 1996), 343–45.

12. John Calvin, *Commentary on the Book of Psalms*, trans. James Anderson (Grand Rapids, MI: Eerdmans, 1949), 1:117.

fervent dedication to God. While there were human influences behind this momentous event, Calvin, recalling much later what happened, did not name them. "God," he wrote, "by the secret guidance of his providence" turned my course in a "different direction."[13] Calvin was "immediately inflamed"[14] with an intense desire to study the "purer doctrine" that God had used to transform his life. He completed the first edition of the *Institutes of the Christian Religion* to vindicate the persecuted French Protestants by setting forth the "principal truths of the Christian religion" as held by his fellow believers.[15]

"I Felt . . . As If God Had from Heaven Laid His Mighty Hand upon Me"[16]

Calvin did not plan to be a pastor, nor, indeed, did he want to be. Aware of his "unpolished and bashful" disposition, he sought "some obscure corner" where he could study and write.[17] "Every conversion has a price," comments David Steinmetz. "Something is gained, but something is lost as well and the loss may prove to be painful."[18] Calvin's "principal ambition both before and after his conversion was to lead the quiet life of a humanist scholar, alone with his books, his commentaries, and his grammars."[19] But God had other plans. When events made it impossible for Calvin to remain safely in France, he passed through Geneva one day in July 1536 while en route to Strasbourg, where he hoped to enjoy "literary ease with something of a free and honorable station."[20] Guillaume Farel, who, Calvin wrote, "burned with an extraordinary zeal to advance the gospel," met the young man and insisted that he stay in Geneva and help him with the work of reforming the church there. When Calvin politely refused, despite further entreaties, Farel uttered his famous "imprecation that God would curse . . . the tranquility" of

---

13. Calvin, *Commentary on the Psalms*, 1:117.
14. Calvin adopted a seal and motto—a flaming heart on the extended hand with the words *Prompte et sincere in opere Domini* ("promptly and sincerely in the work of God").
15. Calvin, *Commentary on the Psalms*, 1:117–18.
16. Calvin, *Commentary on the Psalms*, 1:118.
17. Calvin, *Commentary on the Psalms*, 1:117.
18. David C. Steinmetz, "Reformation and Conversion," *ThTo* 35, no. 1 (1978): 31.
19. Steinmetz, "Reformation and Conversion," 31.
20. John Calvin and Jacopo Sadoleto, *A Reformation Debate: Sadoleto's Letter to the Genevans and Calvin's Reply*, ed. John C. Olin (New York: Harper & Row, 1966), 54.

Calvin's studies if he did not stay in Geneva when the need was "so urgent."[21] Calvin stayed!

As professor of sacred letters, Calvin began his work by lecturing on Paul's Epistles in September 1536. Early in 1537 he was admitted to the Company of Pastors, by what act or ceremony we do not know. Writing later about Valeran Poulain, whom the refugee congregation at Frankfurt was seeking to depose because he had not been properly ordained, Calvin gave his opinion that "those whose labours first planted the gospel" ought to be "received as pastors without any other ceremony."[22] He was no doubt thinking of himself. As David was taken from the sheepfold and given a great work to do, Calvin wrote, so God took me from my "obscure and humble condition" and invested me "with the honourable office of a preacher and minister of the gospel."[23]

Before his conversion to Protestantism, Calvin had become disillusioned with the models of the clergy that he found in the Catholic Church. His father and his brother Charles were both excommunicated when they quarreled with the church authorities. Calvin "experienced the inflexible conduct of clergy who were scarcely able to differentiate between worldly and spiritual power," wrote Catholic scholar Alexandre Ganoczy.[24] Among the reasons that Calvin gave to Cardinal Jacopo Sadoleto for the necessity of making "a schism in the holy Church" was that "the pastoral office [had been] subverted."[25] "They alone are good shepherds who lead men straight to Christ," Calvin wrote in his commentary on John 10. "If the so-called shepherds try to lead us away from Christ, we should flee from them, as Christ tells us, as if they were wolves or thieves; and we ought not to join or to stay in any society save that which is agreed in the pure faith of the Gospel."[26] Calvin insisted that Protestants had not deserted the church but were determined to "establish among themselves a better form of Church."[27]

---

21. Calvin, *Commentary on the Psalms*, 1:118.

22. Calvin to the church of Frankfurt, December 22, 1555, in *Letters*, 3:242.

23. Calvin, *Commentary on the Psalms*, 1:117.

24. Alexandre Ganoczy, "Calvin's Life," trans. David L. Foxgrover and James Schmitt, in *The Cambridge Companion to John Calvin*, ed. Donald K. McKim (Cambridge: Cambridge University Press, 2004), 6.

25. Calvin, *Reformation Debate*, 74–75.

26. *CNTC*, 4:259.

27. Calvin, *Reformation Debate*, 57.

"The Welfare of This Church . . . Lay So Near My Heart That for Its Sake I Would Not Have Hesitated to Lay Down My Life"[28]

When Calvin first came to the church in Geneva, "there was preaching and that was all," as he later said; "there was no reformation. Everything was in disorder."[29] Calvin moved quickly to create the resources for a renewed and reformed church: a biblical model of church polity and discipline, a form of worship with the congregational singing of Psalms, instruction for the celebration of the Lord's Supper, a confession, and a catechism for the training of children.

The Reformers, Calvin and Farel, soon clashed with the city leaders, who were concerned to keep control of the city and its religion. Calvin insisted that the church must be free not only to preach the gospel but also to control its own doctrine, discipline, and worship. Trust and respect broke down (Calvin in a sermon called the city leaders "a council of the devil"),[30] and the preachers were ordered to leave during Easter week in 1538. Calvin was both shattered and relieved. Hurt by Geneva's rejection, he concluded that he was not really fitted for the work of a pastor. In a letter to Farel five months after they were expelled, Calvin wrote that they must "acknowledge before God and his people that it is in some measure owing to [their] unskilfulness, indolence, negligence and error that the Church committed to [their] care [had] fallen into such a sad state of collapse."[31] Calvin later wrote to a friend in Geneva,

> After that calamity, when my ministry appeared to me to be disastrous and unprosperous, I made up my mind never again to enter upon any ecclesiastical charge whatever, unless the Lord himself, by a clear and manifest call, should summon me to it.[32]

He again looked forward to the quiet life of a scholar, "free from the burden and cares" of public ministry.[33]

---

28. Calvin, *Commentary on the Psalms*, 1:119.
29. Calvin, "Farewell to the Ministers of Geneva," April 28, 1564, in *Letters*, 4:373.
30. Parker, *Calvin's Preaching*, 58. This is the only glimpse we have into Calvin's preaching from his first Geneva period!
31. Calvin to Guillaume Farel, September 1538, in *Letters*, 1:81.
32. Calvin to James Bernard, March 1, 1541, in *Letters*, 1:235.
33. Calvin, *Commentary on the Psalms*, 1:119.

Calvin, however, could not forsake or forget Geneva. He had not called himself to the church in Geneva, and so he acknowledged that he could not dismiss himself. When the Genevan leaders asked Calvin to answer a learned and friendly letter from Cardinal Sadoleto inviting them to return to the Catholic fold, Calvin accepted the task. He explained to Sadoleto that although he was at present "relieved of the charge of the Church of Geneva," he still embraced it "with paternal affection," since God, when he gave it to me, "bound me to be faithful to it for ever." Therefore, wrote Calvin, "I cannot cast off that charge any more than that of my own soul."[34] On May 31, 1541, he wrote to the pastors of Zurich, who were trying to persuade him to return to Geneva, "Although it was a very troublesome province to me, yet the thought of deserting it never entered my thoughts. For I considered myself placed in that station by God, like a sentinel at his post, from which it would be impiety on my part were I to stir a single foot."[35]

"That Most Excellent Servant of Christ, Martin Bucer, . . . Drew Me Back to a New Station"[36]

While Calvin brooded over his failure in Geneva and faced a somewhat uncertain future, Martin Bucer, who had led the Reformation movement in Strasbourg, was seeking a pastor for the large French-speaking refugee community in his city. Adopting the strategy of Farel, Bucer persuaded the reluctant Calvin to come to Strasbourg by comparing him to Jonah if he should refuse! For the second time, Calvin found himself a pastor. In an organized church with the experienced and supportive Bucer, Calvin flourished. Bucer was a good mentor. His *On the True Care of Souls and the Right Pastoral Ministry* was "the most outstanding book" dealing specifically with the pastoral ministry written during the Reformation.[37] Strasbourg was the young Calvin's internship—and he made the best of it.

---

34. Calvin, *Reformation Debate*, 51. Calvin's answer to Sadoleto (forty-five pages in the English translation) cost him six days' work. See Calvin to Guillaume Farel, September 1539, in *Letters*, 1:151.

35. Calvin to the pastors of the church of Zurich, May 31, 1541, in *Letters*, 1:266.

36. Calvin, *Commentary on the Psalms*, 1:119.

37. Wilhelm Pauck, "The Ministry in the Time of the Continental Reformation," in *The Ministry in Historical Perspectives*, ed. H. Richard Niebuhr and Daniel D. Williams (New York: Harper & Row, 1956), 115.

Calvin preached, developed a Sunday liturgy and Psalter, and visited his congregation. He cared for the sick, dying, and bereaved. He invited a group of students to live in his house and met with them for instruction and prayer. And he somehow found time to write—producing a second, expanded edition of his *Institutes* and a commentary on Romans. In a letter to Farel, Calvin described how busy he was. On that day—April 20, 1539—he had about twenty pages of the revised *Institutes* to prepare for the printer. Then he had to lecture and preach, write four letters, make peace between some persons who had quarreled with each other, and "reply to more than ten interruptions in the meantime."[38] He was indeed busy but also happy—especially after he married Idelette de Bure in August 1540. Of his wife, whose good sense, courage, and warm piety he greatly valued, Calvin wrote to Pierre Viret, a short time after her death in 1549, "I have been bereaved of the best companion of my life . . . the faithful helper of my ministry."[39]

"We Are Not Our Own: Let Not Our Reason nor Our Will, Therefore, Sway Our Plans and Deeds"[40]

When a call came for Calvin to return to Geneva, he was shocked and alarmed. He wrote to Farel that he would rather "submit to death a hundred times than to that cross, on which one had to perish daily a thousand times over."[41] Seventeen months later, he had determined what he should do. Left to himself, he would not return to Geneva, he wrote to Farel, yet he added, "But when I remember that I am not my own, I offer up my heart, presented as a sacrifice to the Lord," thus putting into action the words quoted above that he had recently added to the *Institutes*.[42] Urged on by fellow ministers, Calvin had become convinced that it was God's will for him to go back to Geneva, but "with what grief, tears, great anxiety and distress I did this, the Lord is my best witness," he wrote.[43]

---

38. Calvin to Guillaume Farel, April 20, 1539, in *Letters*, 1:132.
39. Calvin to Pierre Viret, April 7, 1549, in *Letters*, 2:216.
40. *Institutes*, 3.7.1.
41. Calvin to Guillaume Farel, March 29, 1540, in *Letters*, 1:175.
42. Calvin to Guillaume Farel, August 1541, in *Letters*, 1:280–81.
43. Calvin, *Commentary on the Psalms*, 1:119.

"I Have Felt Nothing to Be of More Importance Than to Have a Regard to the Edification of the Church"[44]

Calvin left Strasbourg literally in tears and entered Geneva on September 13, 1541. The register of the Company of Pastors noted that John Calvin, "minister of the gospel," had arrived and "offered himself to be always the servant of Geneva."[45] Again, he gave himself unstintingly to lead the church in Geneva toward a renewed faith and strengthened devotion to God—in catechisms and theological writings, sermons, biblical commentaries, liturgies, psalms and prayers, pastoral instructions, and letters of counsel and consolation. McKee writes, "Work was constant: preaching and teaching, weddings and baptisms,[46] meetings of the Consistory or consultations with the city council, visits to the sick and endless correspondence, and more preaching, visits, letters."[47]

Calvin became the city's chief legal adviser in writing the new Republic's first constitution in 1542. He advised the city authorities about safety in buildings, fire protection, and cleanliness. He was concerned with labor relations and jobs for the poor. As J. Todd Billings observes, "Calvin wanted almsgiving to be connected to a weekly celebration of the Lord's Supper. That way, sharing in the body and blood of Christ must manifest itself not only in mutual love in the church, but also in love for the hungry, the stranger, and the naked."[48]

Calvin "found Protestantism a mob, and transformed it into an army," wrote B. B. Warfield.[49] Soon after he arrived back in Geneva, Calvin submitted his *Ecclesiastical Ordinances* to the city government. After lengthy negotiations and some changes, the *Ordinances* were adopted in November 1541.[50] Four church offices—pastors, teachers, elders, and deacons—were created. Pastors proclaimed "the Word

---

44. Calvin, *Commentary on the Psalms*, 1:121.
45. Quoted in David C. Steinmetz, *Calvin in Context* (New York: Oxford University Press, 1995), 17.
46. From 1550 to 1559, the years for which we have a register, Calvin took about 270 weddings and 50 baptisms; cf. Parker, *Portrait of Calvin*, 81.
47. McKee, *Writings on Pastoral Piety*, 19.
48. J. Todd Billings, "The Problem with Mere Christianity," *ChrT*, February 6, 2007, https://www.christianitytoday.com/ct/2007/february/32.46.html.
49. Warfield, "Calvin and the Reformation," 1:404.
50. According to Pauck, Calvin's church order became "the most influential of all that were produced by the Reformation." Pauck, "Time of the Continental Reformation," 130.

of God for the purpose of instructing, admonishing, exhorting, and reproving, both in public and in private," administered the sacraments, and exercised "fraternal discipline" together with the elders. As a body, pastors were constituted as the Company of Pastors. They sought to maintain high standards of conduct for one another, and in the weekly Congregation (or Bible conference), to sharpen each other in biblical exegesis and preaching. Teachers instructed "the faithful in sound doctrine" and worked to establish a college "to raise up seed for the future so that the Church is not left desolate to our children."[51] Elders (men "who fear God and possess the gift of spiritual prudence") were "to watch over the life of each person," to admonish "in a friendly manner" those at fault, and when necessary, to bring them to the Company of Pastors where they would receive "fraternal discipline." Deacons administered poor relief and benevolences of all kinds and also actually cared for the poor, sick, aged, widows, and orphans throughout the city.[52]

Calvin welcomed and assisted refugees from many lands and encouraged them to establish congregations in Geneva for services in their own languages: Italian, Spanish, and English. He urged the Genevan authorities to offer employment and other help to refugees. Geneva became for some, as it was for John Knox, "the most perfect school of Christ that ever was in the earth since the days of the Apostles."[53]

Calvin not only labored diligently in the work of the ministry but also set forth a theology of ministry in his writings and sermons and endeavored to put it into practice. "His influence was founded on the agreement of his theology with his practice," concludes Leith.[54]

---

51. "As a pastor, Calvin . . . became vividly aware of the alarming lack of well-trained pastors for the evangelical congregations, and of the need to instruct further candidates for the ministry." Randall C. Zachman, *John Calvin as Teacher, Pastor, and Theologian: The Shape of His Writings and Thought* (Grand Rapids, MI: Baker Academic, 2006), 58. The second edition of Calvin's *Institutes* (1539) took on the additional function of a training manual for pastors. Calvin made Geneva a "school for Christ" not only for the people of the city—native-born and refugees—but also for many, like John Knox, who came there to learn. Calvin planned to establish a university, which was delayed until 1558, when he helped raise funds by going door to door.

52. Philip Edgcumbe Hughes, ed., *The Register of the Company of Pastors of Geneva in the Time of Calvin* (Grand Rapids, MI: Eerdmans, 1966), 36–43.

53. John Knox, *The Works of John Knox*, ed. David Laing (New York: AMS, 1966), 4:240.

54. Leith, *John Calvin: The Christian Life*, ix.

"God Himself Is Really the Pastor"[55]

The Lord "never delivers to pastors the government of the church," Calvin wrote, "but only the care, so that His own right remains unimpaired."[56] Calvin explained that "when the word shepherd is applied to men [as in John 10], it is used . . . in a subordinate sense; and Christ so communicates His honour to His ministers that He still remains the only Shepherd of them and of the whole flock."[57] Commenting on 2 Corinthians 4:5, Calvin stated that by this passage

> all pastors of the Church are reminded of their rank and condition for, whatever title of honour they may have to distinguish them, they are nothing more than the servants of believers, for the only way to serve Christ is by serving his Church as well. This is indeed an honourable servitude and preferable to any kind of worldly dominion but it is servitude whose only care is that Christ alone should be exalted, unshadowed by any rival.[58]

"[Christ] Raises Up Faithful Shepherds for the Church, Equips Them with the Necessary Gifts, Governs Them by His Spirit and Works by Them"[59]

Summarizing Calvin, McKee writes,

> Christians need human direction in prayer and human leadership in worship; they need human instruction and example in how to live their vocations and bear their trials. They need these from one another and owe them to one another. But especially they need them from those who have been gifted by God's Spirit and called by the church to be pastors and other leaders, people who

---

55. *CNTC*, 12:317. See Brian G. Armstrong, "The Pastoral Office in Calvin and Pierre du Moulin," in *Calvin: Erbe und Auftrag; Festschrift für Wilhelm Heinrich Neuser zum 65. Geburtstag*, ed. Willem van 't Spijker (Kampen: Kok, 1991), 157–67; David Willis-Watkins, "Calvin's Theology of Pastoral Care," in *Calvin Studies VI*, ed. John H. Leith (Davidson, NC: Davidson College, 1992), 137–46.
56. *CNTC*, 12:316.
57. *CNTC*, 4:263.
58. *CNTC*, 10:56–57.
59. *CNTC*, 4:263.

are able by training and by experience to speak God's word and be God's instruments in a special way.[60]

Calvin stressed that there must be first of all a "secret call, of which each minister is conscious before God, . . . the good witness of our heart that we accept the proffered office, not with ambition or avarice, not with any other selfish desire, but with a sincere fear of God and desire to build up the church."[61] After a call to a congregation (and approval by the city council), the candidate was ordained, the pastors laying their hands on him. Calvin explained in the *Institutes* that the significance of the laying on of hands is "to warn the one ordained that he is no longer a law unto himself, but bound in servitude to God and the church."[62] Once a pastor has accepted a call, he must not leave this office "from any motive of personal convenience or advantage." If there are good reasons for him to leave, he "ought not to attempt this on his own private opinion, but be guided by public authority."[63] As we have seen, Calvin followed these principles carefully in his own call to Strasbourg and his return to Geneva.

"I Take Pains to Live in Such a Way That My Character and Conduct Do Not Conflict with What I Teach"[64]

Pastors must not only be orthodox in doctrine but also must strive to make themselves "examples to the flock," that is, Calvin explained, "They are to excel for the purpose of being eminent in holiness."[65] In his little book *Concerning Scandals*, Calvin deplored the fact that pastors, who should "surpass all others in the purity of their lives," sometimes fail to do so and thus compromise their message so that it possesses "no more truth and seriousness than if a player were acting out a tale on the stage." Some pastors, Calvin went on to say,

---

60. McKee, *Writings on Pastoral Piety*, 6.
61. *Institutes*, 4.3.11.
62. *Institutes*, 4.3.16.
63. *Institutes*, 4.3.7.
64. *CNTC*, 9:199. Calvin here is paraphrasing 1 Cor. 9:27.
65. *CNTC*, 12:314.

boldly exalt the dignity of the ministry, but it does not enter their heads that their esteem for the ministry is not accepted because they defile it by their own disgraceful conduct. Someone once truly said, "In order to be loved, be loving." In the same way those who wish to be appreciated need to gain respect by the seriousness and sanctity of their behavior.[66]

Calvin was always aware that he was preaching to himself as well as to others. "When I go up into the pulpit," he told his congregation, "it is not only to teach other men [but] the word that proceedeth out of my mouth must serve me as well as you."[67]

"I Have Endeavoured, according to the Measure of Grace [God] Has Given Me, to Teach His Word in Purity, Both in My Sermons and Writings, and to Expound Faithfully the Holy Scriptures"[68]

T. H. L. Parker begins his book *Calvin's Preaching* with this sentence: "Sunday after Sunday, day after day Calvin climbed up the steps into the pulpit. There he patiently led his congregation verse by verse through book after book of the Bible."[69] More than any other activity, preaching occupied Calvin's time and shaped his life and ministry. Twice on Sundays and daily every other week, Calvin stood before a congregation of townspeople, refugees, and visitors to preach, teach, warn, appeal, counsel, admonish, and encourage. In Ronald Wallace's opinion, "It was more through his preaching than through any other aspect of his work that he exercised the extraordinary influence everyone has acknowledged him to have had."[70]

---

66. John Calvin, *Concerning Scandals*, trans. John W. Fraser (Grand Rapids, MI: Eerdmans, 1978), 70–71. A Christian leader must labor "to obtain credit by his integrity," Calvin wrote in his commentary on Ex. 4:18. *Comm.*, 2:99.

67. John Calvin, *Sermons on Job* (Edinburgh: Banner of Truth, 1993), 446.

68. Calvin, "Last Will and Testament," April 25, 1564, in *Letters*, 4:366.

69. Parker, *Calvin's Preaching*, 1.

70. Wallace, *Calvin, Geneva and the Reformation*, 17.

"We Are . . . Ministers of the Spirit . . . Because through Us Christ Enlightens Men's Minds, Renews Their Hearts and Wholly Regenerates Them"[71]

Calvin called the preacher God's "angel" or "mouthpiece" and his "hands and instruments." Preaching is "the place where Jesus Christ resides and has his royal seat."[72] God "will not show himself to us in a visible manner," Calvin told his Geneva congregation, but he speaks to us in the preaching of the gospel through the mouths of his ministers.[73] Calvin often asserted that when the preacher speaks, his words carry the authority of God, even as the Scriptures do. But this is true, Calvin explained, only when the preacher "is instructed in the Word of God" and "proclaims sure oracles from his mouth."[74] "We admit," Calvin wrote to Sadoleto, "that ecclesiastical pastors are to be heard just like Christ Himself, but they must be pastors who execute the office entrusted to them," that is, "in good faith to deliver the oracles which they have received at the mouth of the Lord."[75] "It is because of this bond and conjunction between Christ's grace and man's work," Calvin explained elsewhere, "that a minister is often given credit for what belongs to God alone."[76] For Calvin, the pastor's work, according to Ronald Wallace, "finally must be simply a pointing away from himself to what he hopes the soul beside him will see. The voice that must be heard is not that of the pastor but that of the true Shepherd of the sheep."[77]

Calvin illustrated the centrality of the word of God in the Protestant services by

> ordering that the altars (long the center of the Latin mass) be removed from the churches and that a pulpit with a Bible upon it be placed in the center of the building. This was not to be on one side

71. *CNTC*, 10:43.
72. Calvin, *Sermons on Deuteronomy*, trans. Arthur Golding (1583; repr., Edinburgh: Banner of Truth, 1987), 93; sermon on 1 Cor. 11:4–10 (CO, 49:734–35), quoted by Robert White in John Calvin, *Sermons on the Beatitudes: Five Sermons from the 'Gospel Harmony,' Delivered in Geneva in 1560*, trans. Robert White (Edinburgh: Banner of Truth, 2006), 93n23.
73. Calvin, *Sermons on Deuteronomy*, 32.
74. *CNTC*, 12:305.
75. Calvin, *Reformation Debate*, 77.
76. *CNTC*, 10:43.
77. Wallace, *Calvin, Geneva and the Reformation*, 177.

of the room, but at the center, where every line of the architecture would carry the gaze of the worshiper to that Book.[78]

True preaching, according to Calvin, comes from the mouth of God—that is, from the Scriptures—through the voice of the preacher, whose words are energized by the Holy Spirit. "When God's ministers speak," Calvin declared, "they cast not forth a fading sound, but such a one as is matched with effect."[79] Calvin wrote to Edward Seymour, Duke of Somerset and Lord Protector of England, serving as adviser to King Edward VI, that "good and faithful ministers" must not "make a parade of rhetoric only to gain esteem for themselves," but "the Spirit of God ought to sound forth by their voice, so as to work with mighty energy."[80] The result of true preaching is that "just as Christ is present at the Supper spiritually, that is by the working of the Spirit, so he is present in the preaching spiritually—by the working of the Spirit."[81]

In preaching, Calvin attempted to declare truly and faithfully whatever the Bible set forth in the passage before him, while emphasizing and exalting its central message of God's grace in Christ. Leith asserts that Calvin

> preaches from almost every text content that does not come specifically from that text alone but from the text in the larger framework. . . . The sermons are powerful precisely because Calvin explicated and applied the scriptures word by word, verse by verse, within the framework of a vision of the Christian faith as a whole.[82]

This principle is well illustrated in Calvin's series of sermons on the Beatitudes.[83] Robert White writes in the introduction to his translation

---

78. Boice, foreword to Calvin, *Sermons on Psalm 119*, vii.

79. Calvin, *Sermons on Deuteronomy*, 93.

80. Calvin to the Protector Somerset, October 22, 1548, in *Letters*, 2:190.

81. Parker, *Calvin's Preaching*, 42. Hughes Oliphant Old calls this "the kerygmatic real presence." Old, *The Reading and Preaching of the Scriptures in the Worship of the Christian Church*, vol. 4, *The Age of the Reformation* (Grand Rapids, MI: Eerdmans, 2002), 133.

82. Leith, "Calvin's Doctrine," 220, 224. Leith adds, "The importance of this comprehensive framework must not be minimized in our day when it is so hard to come by. No vision of the Christian faith is ever adequate, but without some comprehensive statement of faith no preaching can stand in succession to Calvin" (224). To provide such a framework was one of the prime reasons for Calvin's writing the later editions of the *Institutes*.

83. *Sermons on the Beatitudes* comprises the sixty-first through the sixty-fifth sermons in Calvin's treatment of the Synoptic Gospels begun in July 1559. These five sermons, preached in

of these sermons that even though Calvin gives "great weight to the ethical demands implicit in the Beatitudes," he does not treat them "as entrance requirements to the kingdom announced by Jesus, but rather as marks whereby those who are already in the kingdom may be discerned, and God's grace to them made visible in a fallen world."[84] For Calvin the Beatitudes began with the calling of the first disciples in Mark 3:13–19 and Luke 6:12–16. White explains that by means of his first sermon in this series (the title "Called and Chosen" given by the translator), Calvin makes clear that "grace is written into the Gospel narratives before ever Jesus begins to teach."[85] This message of grace Calvin found both set forth in the first words of Genesis and continually repeated and increasingly enlarged until the end of Revelation. His preaching was therefore never finally moralistic but always grace centered. This is seen everywhere in Calvin's preaching. At the end of the first of twenty-two sermons that he preached on Psalm 119, he prayed that God would enable him and the people "not only to understand [how] to discern between good and evil, but that we may also be sure and certain of his love and good will toward us."[86]

"Paul Assigns to Teachers the Duty of Carving or Dividing the Word, Like a Father Dividing the Bread into Small Pieces to Feed His Children"[87]

Calvin described his approach to preaching in his first sermon on Psalm 119:

> For my part, because I will frame myself to that manner and order which the Holy Ghost has here set down, I shall enforce myself to follow as briefly as I can the plain and true meaning of the text

---

Geneva in 1560, were the last to be recorded by Denis Raguenier, Calvin's remarkable stenographer, who died during the winter of 1560–1561. Calvin continued preaching on the Synoptic Gospels until February 1564, when sickness forced him to cease. He died three months later. There is no record of any of Calvin's sermons following the sermons on the Beatitudes. These sermons, therefore, are especially valuable as an example of the Reformer's most mature preaching style and his last recorded words to his congregation. Hughes Oliphant Old, who analyzes four of Calvin's sermons on the Beatitudes, claims that "here we find Calvin in all his directness and all his depth." Old, *Reading and Preaching*, 4:96.

84. Calvin, *Sermons on the Beatitudes*, ix.
85. Calvin, *Sermons on the Beatitudes*, 89.
86. Calvin, *Sermons on Psalm 119*, 22.
87. *CNTC*, 10:313. The quotation comes from Calvin's *Commentary on 2 Timothy*, where he treats 2:15.

and without continuing in long exhortations. I will only do my best to mince or shred, as we say, the words of David, because we may better digest them. For performance thereof I determine by the grace of God to finish eight verses apart in every sermon, and to hold myself within such compass, as that the most ignorant shall easily acknowledge and confess that I mean nothing else but to make open and plain the simple and pure substance of the text.[88]

"I Remember That Three Years Ago We Had a Friendly Discussion about the Best Way of Interpreting Scripture. … Both of Us Felt That Lucid Brevity Constituted the Particular Virtue of an Interpreter"[89]

Faithfulness to the Bible's message and clarity, simplicity, and directness in its exposition and application were Calvin's goals in his preaching. Above all, Calvin sought to set forth clearly the intention of the authors—that is, both the Holy Spirit and the human writer. In his first book, *Commentary on Seneca's "De Clementia,"* the young Calvin faulted the Roman philosopher for lack of clarity in the "division of the work," failure to follow his own order, and fuzziness in the use of a certain word. "I prefer a man to be a teacher of real frankness rather than delude his reader with frivolous subtleties," Calvin wrote.[90] In his sermons, theological books, and biblical commentaries, Calvin attempted to be a teacher of "real frankness, deliberate and orderly in his presentation."[91] He summed up his main goal as an exegete and expositor of Scripture in the dedication to his *Commentary on Romans*: since "it is almost [the interpreter's] only task to unfold the mind of the writer he has undertaken to expound, he misses his mark, or at least strays outside his limits, by the extent to which he leads his readers away from the meaning of the author."[92]

---

88. Calvin, *Sermons on Ps. 119*, 5. Calvin's twenty-two sermons on Ps. 119 were preached on Sunday afternoons during the first half of 1553. At the same time, Calvin was preaching on Acts in the early service and on Ezekiel during the week.

89. *CNTC*, 8:1. The person Calvin was referring to was Simon Grynaeus, to whom he dedicated his *Commentary on Romans*.

90. John Calvin, *Calvin's Commentary on Seneca's "De Clementia": With Introduction, Translation, and Notes*, ed. and trans. Ford Lewis Battles and André Malan Hugo, RTS 3 (Leiden: Brill, 1969), 79.

91. Calvin, *Commentary on Seneca's "De Clementia,"* 79n26.

92. *CNTC*, 8:1.

Ford Lewis Battles states that Calvin was such a superb expositor of Scripture because he was a master of paraphrase.[93] He was able to summarize the message of a passage of Scripture with precision and clarity and put it in the language of ordinary people. This was the result not only of Calvin's training and linguistic brilliance, notes Leith, but even more of his own "spiritual and theological resonance with the text, a skill that cannot be learned in schools."[94]

Calvin prized brevity in his writings and his preaching. "By nature I love brevity," he stated in the *Institutes*.[95] Calvin was too concerned for the communication of vital truth to weaken or confuse his writing by long and unnecessary digressions, a common practice of the church fathers and many of Calvin's contemporaries. Calvin's brevity and conciseness "bring to his writing a quality of urgency," writes John McNeill.[96] The same was true of his preaching. Calvin's sermons lasted about one hour. Others preached much longer (sometimes two or three hours), a practice that Calvin criticized.

"It Is Not Enough for a Man to Be Eminent in Profound Learning If It Is Not Accompanied by a Talent for Teaching"[97]

A good preacher must not only know the word of God but must also be "in touch with ordinary people" and know how "to apply God's Word to the profit of His people." If not, he should "go and do something else," Calvin advised.[98]

Calvin was a skillful and eloquent writer of both Latin and French (he was one of the masters and molders of modern French),[99] but in his preaching "he deliberately adapt[ed] his style to the grasp of the common people in his congregation."[100] Commenting on Romans 14:1, Calvin wrote that "those who have made greater progress in Christian doctrine are to accommodate themselves to the less expe-

---

93. Battles, ed., in Calvin, *Commentary on Seneca's "De Clementia,"* 79.
94. Leith, "Calvin's Doctrine," 212.
95. *Institutes*, 3.6.1.
96. John T. McNeill, introduction to *Institutes*, 1:lxx.
97. CNTC, 10:225.
98. CNTC, 10:225.
99. One modern scholar has given Calvin credit for inventing the modern French sentence. Francis M. Higman, *The Style of John Calvin in His French Polemical Treatises*, Oxford Modern Languages and Literature Monographs (London: Oxford University Press, 1967); Higman, "Linearity in Calvin's Thought," *CTJ* 26, no. 1 (1991): 100–110.
100. Parker, *Calvin's Preaching*, 148.

rienced, and bestow their strength to sustain the weakness of these persons."[101]

Calvin was concerned that each person hear the sermon as a personal word from God to him or her. "Whenever God speaks to all his people in a body," Calvin wrote, "he addresses himself also to each of them in particular."[102] Explaining Luke's additional word in the Beatitudes ("Blessed are *you* who are poor"; "Blessed are *you* who weep," Luke 6:20–21), Calvin said, "Our Lord means us not only to understand his teaching in a collective sense, but to receive it as a word spoken to each of us individually, and to be personally appropriated."[103] Commenting on Matthew 3:7, Calvin wrote,

> Here Matthew and Luke tell how John's preaching was not repentance in a general sense, but was a call brought home to individuals. Indeed it will be an unattractive way of teaching, if the masters do not work out carefully what are the needs of the times, what suits the people concerned, for in this regard nothing is more unbalanced than absolute balance.[104]

To make the scriptural message clear and personal, Calvin developed "a familiar, homely style of preaching."[105] He often used popular proverbs, figures of speech, homespun illustrations, and pithy statements, many of which were his own creations. Preaching on God's blessing bestowed on the meek and the merciful, he paused to contrast them with those whom "this world counts as great." "Inwardly," Calvin said, "they are in a state of turmoil." Why are they like this? "It is because God brings trouble on those who bring trouble on everyone else."[106] In another sermon, Calvin stated that the Lord Jesus forbids his disciples "to seek more light than is permissible. For by such means we appear wiser than we are, deceiving some and cheating others." Christ's disciples are "people of peaceable spirit," he declared, who have "neither wit nor skill to

---

101. *CNTC*, 8:289.
102. Calvin, *Commentary on the Psalms*, 5:90.
103. Calvin, *Sermons on the Beatitudes*, 30.
104. *CNTC*, 1:119–20.
105. Parker, *Calvin's Preaching*, 140.
106. Calvin, *Sermons on the Beatitudes*, 35–36.

fish in troubled waters."[107] Calvin's illustrations were brief but numerous. In his series on Psalm 119, he often referred to animals to make his point—including apes, donkeys, bears, cows, dogs, hogs, lions, monkeys, sheep, toads, wolves, and worms![108]

On occasion Calvin connected the sermon with the psalm that had been sung or with some aspect of the liturgy, bringing together worship and preaching. James and John were called "sons of thunder," Calvin explained, "not because they spoke with the same powerful effect as thunder—as we heard a moment ago in the Psalm, where God so thunders as to cause the deer of the forest to miscarry, the trees to topple, and the mountains to shake."[109]

Calvin worked hard to apply his preaching to the everyday life of the people—a task he acknowledged as particularly challenging. Noting that David in Psalm 10:14 "descends from the general to the particular," Calvin stated that this "ought to be attentively marked." "For nothing is easier," he added, "than to acknowledge in general terms that God exercises a care about the world, and the affairs of men; but it is very difficult to apply this doctrine to its various uses in every-day life."[110] Calvin's applications—social as well as personal—are numerous and pointed. Preaching on "Blessed are the meek," Calvin began,

> God has created all of us in his own image, so that we have only to look at our neighbour to see ourselves. We are one flesh. And although appearances and attitudes are very different, it is impossible to efface the unity which God has conferred on us. If only that were firmly etched in our minds, we would all be living at peace with each other, in a kind of earthly paradise.[111]

---

107. Calvin, *Sermons on the Beatitudes*, 52.
108. See the "animals" entry in the general index in Calvin, *Sermons on Psalm 119*.
109. Calvin, *Sermons on the Beatitudes*, 11.
110. Calvin, *Commentary on the Psalms*, 1:151–52.
111. Calvin, *Sermons on the Beatitudes*, 33. Reading Calvin's *Sermons on the Beatitudes*, I was struck with how powerful Calvin's preaching was and how relevant his applications. On Good Friday, April 6, 2007, I received a call from a doctor that a recent colonoscopy and biopsy showed that my cancer had returned after three years of remission. I had just read the following words from Calvin—words that I returned to again and again the next few days. Calvin said,

> While life for believers may be easy today, they will be ready tomorrow to endure whatever afflictions God may send them. He may, perhaps, take from them the goods he has given. They are prepared to surrender them, since they know they received them on one condition—that they should hand them back whenever God should choose. The believer reasons this way: "Rich today, poor tomorrow." If God should change my

Discussing the serious consequences of the fall of a Christian leader, Calvin said that "as is often said, when a man falls from his natural height, he can get back on his feet; but if he falls from a roof or a high window, he is past all help."[112] In another sermon, Calvin told the people to properly receive and appreciate the good things that God gives them but reminded them that these good things are "but a path" to lead us to God, "not a tomb in which to bury ourselves."[113]

"I Frame Myself to That Manner and Order
Which the Holy Ghost Has . . . Set Down"[114]

In his preaching, Calvin followed the example of the fourth- and fifth-century church fathers and the earlier sixteenth-century Reformers in practicing continuous exposition (*lectio continua*). In this way, Calvin observed, the pastor does not decide what is profitable to be preached but leaves that decision to God alone to be ordered at his pleasure. He began at chapter 1, verse 1, of a book of the Bible and continued with usually six or eight verses for each sermon until he had preached through that book. Then he started another book.

The Sunday after he arrived back in Geneva, September 13, 1541, he entered the pulpit, opened the Bible at the same page of the book of Romans at which he had left off on Easter Day over three years earlier, read the next passage as his text, and preached on it as if nothing had intervened. In a letter to a friend, Calvin explained: after a few words of introduction, "I began to comment on the text at the place where I had stopped at the time of my banishment. By doing this I wanted to show that rather than having given up the teaching office, I had only been interrupted for awhile."[115] Calvin regularly followed a practice

---

circumstances so that ease gives way to suffering and laughter to tears, it is enough to know that I am still his child. He has promised to acknowledge me always as his, and in that I rest content." (78)

112. Calvin, *Sermons on the Beatitudes*, 15.
113. Calvin, *Sermons on the Beatitudes*, 78.
114. Calvin, *Sermons on Psalm 119*, 5.
115. Quoted by Stauffer, *Humanness of John Calvin*, 78. Timothy George comments, "Nothing could have been less dramatic or more effective." George, *Theology of the Reformers* (Nashville: Broadman, 1988), 185.

of beginning with a brief introduction, a summary of the main theme of the previous sermon. Then he worked through the passage, verse by verse, sentence by sentence, sometimes word by word, explaining and applying the text to the people.

Calvin usually chose a New Testament book for Sunday morning sermons and the Psalms for Sunday afternoons. On weekdays he preached on Old Testament books. He interrupted this pattern for church festivals: Christmas, Easter week, and Pentecost, when he preached on appropriate passages. Hughes Oliphant Old comments, "The thoroughness and completeness, the systematic nature, of his expository preaching is truly remarkable."[116]

Calvin prepared his sermons by carefully studying the text in the original languages. Leith has written that when "he walked to his pulpit from his study," Calvin was ready to preach "with an intensity and skill few have ever matched."[117] As Calvin himself put it,

> If I should enter the pulpit without deigning to look at a book and should frivolously think to myself, "Oh, well, when I preach, God will give me enough to say," and come here without troubling to read or think what I ought to declare, and do not carefully consider how I must apply Holy Scripture to the edification of the people, then I should be an arrogant upstart.[118]

"[Preachers Must Be Like] Good Trumpets, Which Shall Sound into the Very Depths of the Heart"[119]

In a sermon on 2 Timothy 3:16–17, Calvin asserted that not only must the preacher expound the Scripture and explain its meaning, but he must also "give vigour and power to the Word of God."[120] The goal of preaching is not to make us "eloquent and subtle and I know not what," Calvin said. "It is to reform our life, so that it is known that we desire to serve God, to give ourselves entirely to him and to conform ourselves to his good will." Teaching by itself, the mere pointing out the way, is insufficient. Also needed are the "incitements of exhorta-

---

116. Old, *Reading and Preaching*, 4:91.
117. Leith, "Calvin's Doctrine," 217.
118. Calvin, *Sermons on Deuteronomy*, 292.
119. Calvin to the Protector Somerset, October 22, 1548, in *Letters*, 2:192.
120. The entire sermon is summarized in Parker, *Calvin's Preaching*, 8–16.

tions and reproofs."[121] Calvin wrote to the Protector Somerset in 1548 that "preaching ought not to be lifeless but lively, to teach, to exhort, to reprove, as Saint Paul says."[122] For Calvin, preaching was the core of pastoral ministry. He believed that pastors' "whole task is limited to the ministry of God's word; their whole wisdom to the knowledge of his word; their whole eloquence, to its proclamation."[123] Parker aptly sums up Calvin's preaching as

> the quiet, persistent call to frame our lives according to the teaching of Holy Scripture. . . . There is no threshing himself into a fever of impatience or frustration, no holier-than-thou rebuking of the people, no begging them in terms of hyperbole to give some physical sign that the message has been accepted. It is simply one man, conscious of his sins, aware how little progress he makes and how hard it is to be a doer of the Word, sympathetically passing on to his people (whom he knows to have the same sort of problems as himself) what God has said to them and to him.[124]

"The Office of a True and Faithful Minister Is Not Only Publicly to Teach the People for Whom He Is Ordained Pastor, but Also, As Much As He Is Able, to Admonish, Exhort, Reprove and Console Each One Individually"[125]

Preaching was crucial for Calvin; no less important was pastoral care:

> Whatever others may think, we do not regard our office as bound within so narrow limits that when the sermon is delivered we may rest as if our task was done. They whose blood will be required of us if lost through our slothfulness, are to be cared for much more closely and vigilantly.[126]

---

121. *CNTC*, 10:331.
122. Calvin to the Protector Somerset, October 22, 1548, in *Letters*, 2:190.
123. *Institutes* (1536), 195.
124. Parker, *Calvin's Preaching*, 118–19.
125. The quotation is from "The visiting of the sick" in Calvin's *Form of Prayers*. Quoted in McKee, *Writings on Pastoral Piety*, 292.
126. *CNTC*, 7:174–75.

It is the pastor's duty, therefore, "both publicly and privately, to comfort the people of God by the gospel teaching."[127]

A pastor must preach the word of God "meekly and mildly and patiently,"[128] and he must rule and govern with humility and compassion, knowing that God alone is "the sole Governor of our souls" and his law "the only rule and spiritual directory for our consciences."[129] Calvin's favorite illustration of preaching, as we have seen, is that of a father breaking the bread into small pieces to feed his children. His picture of governing—or pastoral care—is that of "a mother nursing her child." She "makes no show of authority and does not stand on any dignity." Furthermore, she "reveals a wonderful and extraordinary love, because she spares no trouble or effort, avoids no care, is not wearied by their coming and going, and gladly even gives her own life to be drained."[130]

Given Calvin's self-confessed diffident and retiring personality, it must have been difficult for him to become involved in the lives of people. But Calvin did it nonetheless. Bucer wrote Calvin in 1547, "I must greatly praise you for visiting the brethren, for you know with what pain I have observed that the duty of piety and love, on the part of the clergy—to visit, warn, and comfort the people—is greatly neglected."[131]

In her research in the archives in Geneva, Jeannine Olson discovered a much more friendly and accessible Calvin than the one often pictured. He comes across, she asserts, "as humane, cordial, concerned, even warm."[132] Mary Beaty and Benjamin Farley also found a friendly, approachable, pastoral Calvin—at least as a rule—even in his handling of the complex and controversial matters of church polity and discipline. They write that "the advice contained in these pieces [collected in their book] portrays the familiar reformer whom Calvinists have come to know and expect, occasionally surprising his readers with the depth of his compassion and wit, patience

---

127. *Institutes*, 3.4.12.

128. John Calvin, *Sermons on the Epistles to Timothy and Titus* (Edinburgh: Banner of Truth, 1983), 941.

129. Calvin to the Protector Somerset, October 22, 1548, in *Letters*, 2:189.

130. *CNTC*, 8:344.

131. Wallace, *Calvin, Geneva and the Reformation*, 173n21.

132. Jeannine Olson, "Calvin as Person," *ConcJ* 17 (1991): 393.

and rigor."[133] "Countless friends and strangers made his house their hostel," comments McNeill. "One of these wrote him afterwards: 'Your hospitality in the name of Christ is not unknown to anybody in Europe.'"[134] On one occasion, the city council voted to give Calvin a larger wine allowance than provided for his fellow pastors, presumably because of the great amount of entertaining that he did.[135]

One of Calvin's colleagues in Geneva wrote,

> No words of mine can declare the fidelity and prudence with which he gave counsel. The kindness with which he received all who came to him, the clearness and promptitude with which he replied to those who asked his opinion on the most important questions, and the ability with which he disentangled the difficulties and problems which were laid before him. Nor can I express the gentleness with which he could comfort the afflicted and raise the fallen and the distressed.[136]

Calvin objected to the medieval sacrament of confession because it looked too much back to the sin itself, he thought, and not forward to transformation, thus torturing the conscience into despair or pretense. Scripture, Calvin believed, authorizes voluntary private confession to any member of the church but ordinarily to the pastor.[137] Calvin encouraged people to seek pastoral help in times of difficulty, especially when "troubled and afflicted with a sense of sins that without the aid of others [they are] unable to find freedom from them."[138]

Calvin faithfully attended the sick and dying. When the plague came to Geneva in 1542, even though the council forbade him to visit its victims, Calvin insisted that he, too, be available for this work. He explained to Viret that "so long as we are in this ministry, I do not see that any excuse will avail us if, through fear of infection, we are found wanting in the discharge of our duty where we are most needed."[139]

---

133. Mary Beaty and Benjamin W. Farley, trans., *Calvin's Ecclesiastical Advice* (Louisville: Westminster John Knox, 1991), 13.

134. John T. McNeill, *The History and Character of Calvinism* (New York: Oxford University Press, 1954), 231.

135. Olson, "Calvin as Person," 394.

136. Quoted by Wallace, *Calvin, Geneva and the Reformation*, 180–81.

137. *Institutes*, 3.4.1; 4.4.2–3.

138. *Institutes*, 3.4.12.

139. Calvin to Pierre Viret, October 1542, in *Letters*, 1:358.

Both Calvin's *Form of Prayers* and *Ecclesiastical Ordinances* provided instruction about how pastors should minister to the sick. Calvin stated that

> it is the duty of a minister to visit the sick and comfort them with the word of the Lord, exhorting them that all which they suffer and endure comes from the hand of God and His good providence, that God who never sends anything to His faithful people except for their good and salvation. The minister will offer the appropriate testimonies from the scriptures.[140]

Calvin added that "if the minister has anything by which he can aid or console the poor afflicted ones physically, let him not spare these means but show to all a good example of love."[141]

Calvin's ministry of counsel, correction, and encouragement reached beyond Geneva through his extensive correspondence (eleven volumes of his collected writings) with a wide range of people—with royalty, men and women imprisoned for their faith, people troubled by personal and theological issues, and church leaders of many countries. Ronald Wallace notes "the extraordinary variety of [Calvin's] expressions and counsel in his letters which never became stereotyped." For Calvin "each soul is new, each situation is new, and God's way must always be found out afresh."[142] J. I. Packer has written, "As his pastoral letters show, [Calvin] was a superb physician of the soul, unerring in diagnosis and supremely skilful in applying the remedies of the gospel."[143]

Jean-Daniel Benoit writes that "Calvin was a pastor and counselor for martyrs! This is one light in which he is too little known. However, perhaps this facet of his career reveals the genuine depth of his life and is the clearest illustration of his piety."[144] Receiving the sad news of the massacre of some Waldensians in Provence, Calvin's heart went out to them. He closed his letter to Farel on May 4, 1545, with the words, "I

---

140. Quoted in McKee, *Writings on Pastoral Piety*, 292.
141. Quoted in McKee, *Writings on Pastoral Piety*, 293.
142. Wallace, *Calvin, Geneva and the Reformation*, 179.
143. J. I. Packer, "Calvin: A Servant of the Word," in *Able Ministers of the New Testament: Papers Read at the Puritan and Reformed Studies Conference, December 1964* ([London]: Puritan and Reformed Studies Conference, 1964), 41. In a long article, Ian M. Tait has collected many examples of Calvin's pastoral counsel from his letters. See Tait, "Calvin's Ministry of Encouragement," *Presb* 11 (1985): 43–99.
144. Benoit, *Calvin, directeur d'âmes*, 61.

write, worn out with sadness, and not without tears, which so burst forth that every now and then they interrupt my words."[145]

Through continuing conflict with a host of enemies, acute and enduring physical suffering, the premature birth and death of his son, and the death of his wife, Calvin knew how to suffer with those who suffered. When Idelette and John's baby died soon after birth, Calvin wrote to Viret, "The Lord has certainly inflicted a severe and bitter wound in the death of our infant son. But he is himself a Father, and knows best what is good for His children."[146] In another instance, Calvin wrote to a friend, "When I first received the intelligence of the death . . . of your son Louis, I was so utterly overpowered that for many days I was fit for nothing but to grieve." He was one "whom I loved as a son."[147] When Idelette died, Calvin wrote to Farel that he was doing what he could to keep himself "from being overwhelmed with grief."[148] So when Calvin exhorted and comforted the sick with assurance that everything comes to believers from the hands of their loving Father, they knew that he believed what he said and had experienced God's comforting presence in his own times of trouble. After the death of a French woman in Geneva, Calvin wrote a long letter to a friend of hers reporting the sad news and asking her to inform the woman's father. "Our consolation is that He has gathered her unto Himself," he wrote, "for He has guided her even to the last sigh, as if visibly He had held out a hand to her."[149]

"As the Saving Doctrine of Christ Is the Soul of the Church, So Does Discipline Serve As Its Sinews, through Which the Members of the Body Hold Together"[150]

For Calvin, "discipline was a pastoral measure, a part of the proclamation of the Word of God," states Parker.[151] In the *Institutes*, Calvin described the threefold function of discipline: it is "like a bridle to restrain and tame those who rage against the doctrine of Christ; or like a spur to arouse those of little inclination; and also sometimes"—and one senses

---

145. Calvin to Guillaume Farel, May 4, 1545, in *Letters*, 1:459.
146. Calvin to Pierre Viret, August 19, 1542, in *Letters*, 1:344.
147. Calvin to Monsieur De Richebourg, April 1541, in *Letters*, 1:246.
148. Calvin to Guillaume Farel, April 11, 1549, in *Letters*, 2:217.
149. Quoted in McKee, *Writings on Pastoral Piety*, 301.
150. *Institutes*, 4.12.1.
151. Parker, *Portrait of Calvin*, 90.

that this is where Calvin's heart was—"like a father's rod to chastise mildly and with the gentleness of Christ's Spirit those who have more seriously lapsed."[152] Calvin stipulated that the elders "show mildness in correcting the faults of brethren," remembering "to begin with ourselves and then, conscious of our own weakness," to be gentle with others.[153]

Sins requiring church discipline included forbidden sexual activity, unfair economic practices, and personal conflicts involving quarrels and slander. Calvin wrote voluminously on many of these topics, including sex, marriage, and family. He was "interested in good order on these subjects, but he could also be very humane" and "flexible," write John Witte Jr. and Robert M. Kingdom; Calvin's work "stands today as one of the enduring models of marriage and family life in the Protestant world and well beyond."[154]

The goal of church discipline was repentance and reconciliation. The usual penalty was temporary suspension from the Lord's Supper. "The 'reason' for the Calvinist discipline is not, as is often supposed, to be discovered in premises of ethical or scriptural legalism," explains McNeill, "but in the sense of 'the Holy' and in reverence for the sacrament as the meeting of Christ and his people, and of the people as one body in Christ."[155]

"A Pastor Needs Two Voices, One for Gathering the Sheep and the Other for Driving Away Wolves and Thieves"[156]

Pastors are called to lead people to Christ and also to "repel the machinations of those who strive to impede the work of God."[157] Calvin wrote to the pastors of Bern in May 1555 that he wished that "the duty of [his] office and [his] conscience" would permit him to keep silent. He continued, "But when I see the heavenly doctrine of Christ, of which he has been pleased to make me a minister," attacked, "how disgraceful it would be for me to hold my peace as if I were tongue-tied!"[158]

---

152. *Institutes*, 4.12.1.
153. *CNTC*, 11:108–9.
154. John Witte Jr. and Robert M. Kingdon, *Sex, Marriage, and Family in John Calvin's Geneva*, vol. 1, *Courtship, Engagement, and Marriage* (Grand Rapids, MI: Eerdmans, 2005), xix, xxiii, 2.
155. McNeill, *History and Character of Calvinism*, 138.
156. *CNTC*, 10:361.
157. Calvin, *Reformation Debate*, 53.
158. Calvin to the pastors of Bern, May 1555, in *Letters*, 3:173.

Enemies to God's truth are to be found within as well as outside the church. "There is no plague more destructive to the Church than when wolves go about under the mask of shepherds," Calvin wrote. Christ warns that there are times when "those who rule in the Church in the place of shepherds are hostile and opposed to the Gospel."[159]

Calvin was usually moderate in his criticism of fellow Protestants, except for the Anabaptists—although at times Lutheran intolerance for the Reformed tried his patience. Calvin made fairly frequent and often sharp and sarcastic comments about Catholics, whom Calvin called "papists," "apostates," and even "the devil's children."[160] In his reforming city and dangerous times, "Calvin had to win people over to become Bible Christians," Parker comments, "and the negative side of that was to convince them that sometimes (certainly not always) the Catholic position or practice was contradicted by the Bible itself."[161] Protestant Christians, including his closest associates and the people of his own congregation, did not escape Calvin's correction. In a sermon on Titus 1:10–12, he asserted that it is necessary not only to fight against the teaching of Muslims and Catholics but also to be "careful and diligent to withstand" those he called "home enemies." Ministers, "when they see any wickedness among them which are committed to their charge," must not fail to plainly point out and correct the errors of the faithful.[162]

"He Will Never Steadfastly Persevere in This Office Unless the Love of Christ So Reigns in His Heart That Forgetting Himself and Devoting Himself Entirely to Him, He Surmounts Every Obstacle"[163]

Calvin's pastoral life was not an easy one. He said to friends as he and Farel were being harried out of Geneva in 1538, "Certainly, had I been the servant of men I had obtained a poor reward, but it is well that I have served him who never fails to perform to his servants whatever

---

159. *CNTC*, 4:258–59.
160. Calvin, *Sermons on the Beatitudes*, 60. In his extreme language Calvin was not unusual. Robert White notes that "the demonizing of opponents, a procedure not unknown in our day, was common currency in sixteenth-century debate." In Calvin, *Sermons on the Beatitudes*, 106n14.
161. Parker asserts that Calvin's anti-Catholic polemic, as harsh as it often was, "lacked the fierce anger bestowed on lawlessness and licentiousness in the city [of Geneva]." Parker, *Calvin's Preaching*, 127.
162. Calvin, *Sermons on Timothy and Titus*, 1105, 1107.
163. *CNTC*, 5:219.

he has promised."[164] In the preface to his *Commentary on the Book of Psalms*, Calvin described his deep affinity with David in his struggles to lead God's people. As David suffered many bitter trials in his service to God and the people in Israel, so did Calvin in Geneva. He was an exile for his faith, living as a resident alien in often uncongenial circumstances. As late as 1556, he could write, "I am a stranger in this city."[165]

Calvin noted the "innumerable hindrances" that could discourage "the most prudent" pastor—ungrateful people, long hours and laborious work, and Satan's hatred and opposition—and reminded him of the "only remedy"—"to turn his eyes to the coming of Christ."[166] "We are harassed in many different ways on every side," Calvin wrote; "the only remedy for all these difficulties is to look forward to Christ's appearing and always to put our trust in it."[167] In a letter to Farel written just after their expulsion from Geneva, he complained that their successors had defamed them:

> But if we know that they cannot calumniate us, excepting in so far as God permits, we know also the end God has in view in granting such permission. Let us humble ourselves, therefore, unless we wish to strive with God when He would humble us. Meanwhile, let us wait upon God.[168]

Commenting on John 21:15, Calvin stated,

> None can faithfully serve the Church and sustain the task of feeding the flock unless he looks higher than men. In the first place, the office of feeding is in itself laborious and troublesome, for nothing is more difficult than to keep men under the yoke of God, many of whom are weak, others light and unsteady, others dull and sluggish and yet others hard and unteachable. Satan now attacks with all the stumbling-blocks he can, to break or weaken the courage of a good pastor. Add to this the ingratitude of many and other causes of weariness.[169]

---

164. Theodore Beza, *Life of John Calvin*, trans. Henry Beveridge, in *Tracts and Treatises*, 1:lxxi.
165. Calvin to Nicholas Zerkinden, February 21, 1556, in *Letters*, 3:250.
166. *CNTC*, 12:317.
167. *CNTC*, 10:279.
168. Calvin to Guillaume Farel, August 4, 1538, in *Letters*, 1:75.
169. *CNTC*, 5:219.

In his commentary on 1 Peter 5:1–4, Calvin noted the three vices that especially tempt pastors—sloth, desire for gain, and lust for power—and urged, as Peter does, hard work, a generous spirit, and humble hearts.[170] Sloth was not one of Calvin's sins. In fact, he could probably be faulted for working too much. Calvin himself warned that men "wear themselves out and torment themselves in vain, when they are more busy than their calling permits or compels."[171] He may have been thinking of himself when he remarked in a sermon that "a great many people are their own executioners through working constantly and without measure."[172] When he was dying, he refused to cease his laborious work on his Ezekiel commentary. Urged by friends to rest, he replied, "Would you have the Lord find me idle?"[173] He finally stopped dictating about eight hours before he died, when his voice gave out. Calvin certainly lived out what he wrote in his commentary on Luke 17:7:

> Let each of us remember that he has been created by God for the purpose of laboring, and of being vigorously employed in his work, and that not only for a limited time, but till death itself, and what is more, that he should not only live, but die, to God.[174]

Neither did a desire for gain tempt Calvin. Calvin informed Sadoleto that the Reformers had "counseled that as much should be distributed to ministers as might suffice for a frugal life befitting their order without luxurious superabundance" and that beyond that the money of the church be used, according to the practice of the ancient church, to help the poor.[175] At one time, Calvin asked that his salary be reduced to bring it into line with that of the other ministers (despite the fact that his expenses were greater), but the council would not agree. When Calvin died in 1564, Pope Pius IV is said to have commented that his strength lay in the fact that he could never be corrupted by money.[176]

---

170. *CNTC*, 12:314.
171. *CNTC*, 1:220.
172. Cited by William J. Bouwsma, *John Calvin: A Sixteenth-Century Portrait* (New York: Oxford University Press, 1988), 199.
173. Beza, *Life*, 1:cxxii.
174. *CNTC*, 2:213.
175. Calvin, *Reformation Debate*, 56.
176. Philip Schaff, *A History of the Christian Church* (New York: Charles Scribner's Sons, 1910), 7:839.

Calvin never sought personal power (although he is falsely ma-
ligned as the "dictator" of Geneva), but he struggled with an impatience that sometimes gave way to harshness and anger. When charged
with anti-Trinitarian heresy by Pierre Caroli, Calvin acknowledged in
a letter to Farel that "I have sinned grievously in not having been able
to keep within bounds. . . . I poured out bitterness on all sides."[177] He
gently (and humorously) rebuked Francis Hotman (1524–1590) for
his excessive anger in conflict with a colleague but reminded him that
"these counsels are given you by a man, who, though he is conscious
of possessing a more vehement temper than he could wish," was learning to bear more patiently similar aggravations.[178]

Calvin summoned the ministers of Geneva to his home for a farewell message on April 28, 1564.[179] Calvin told them, "I have had
many infirmities which you have been obliged to bear with." "My
vices have always displeased me," he added, asking them to forgive
the "evil" that he had done, "and if there was any good," to profit by
it.[180] Ganoczy writes, "One can say that Calvin was so radically fixed
on the grace of God that his own mistakes never gave him occasion to
despair."[181] This was true of him to the end.

"My Conscience Told Me How Strong the Zeal Was with Which I Burned for the Unity of [the] Church, Provided ... Truth Were Made the Bond of Concord"[182]

Calvin became an influential leader for the whole Protestant community, especially in France, the Netherlands, England, and Scotland.
He maintained that, in an important sense, there is already "one
flock" of Christians in that "believers who are scattered throughout
the world are enclosed within common bounds, in that the same
Word is preached to all and the same Sacraments are used."[183] The

---

177. Calvin to Guillaume Farel, October 8, 1539, in *Letters*, 1:154.
178. Calvin to Francis Hotman, May 27, 1559, in *Letters*, 4:41.
179. It was, Steinmetz comments, "a curious combination of piety and truculence." Steinmetz, *Calvin in Context*, 19.
180. Calvin, "Farewell to the Ministers of Geneva," April 28, 1564, in *Letters*, 4:375. Another source records that Calvin asked "his brethren to forgive him for having been so violent, choleric, and hasty." *Letters*, 4:375n2.
181. Ganoczy, "Calvin's Life," 24.
182. Calvin, *Reformation Debate*, 86. See John T. McNeill, "Calvin as an Ecumenical Church-man," *CH* 32, no. 4 (1963): 379–91.
183. *CNTC*, 4:267–68.

"only bond of holy unity," according to Calvin, was Christ; "he who departs from him disturbs and violates unity, while out of him there is nothing but sacrilegious conspiracy."[184] Calvin ended his letter to Sadoleto with a prayer:

> The Lord grant, Sadoleto, that you and all your party may at length perceive, that the only true bond of ecclesiastical unity would exist if Christ the Lord, who has reconciled us to God the Father, were to gather us out of our present dispersion into the fellowship of His Body, that so, through His one Word and Spirit, we might join together with one heart and one soul.[185]

But as important as unity is, truth, for Calvin, is to be prized even more. Calvin quoted with great delight Augustine's "beautiful and shrewd dictum": "Christ does not give Himself the name Custom but Truth."[186]

Although Calvin's hope for a reunion of Catholics and Protestants faded with the political realities of the time and the dogmatism of the Catholic Counter-Reformation, he continued to long for greater visible unity among the various branches of Protestantism. In 1552 he wrote to Thomas Cranmer (1489–1556), Archbishop of Canterbury, that "among the chief evils of our time" is the fact "that the Churches are so divided. . . . Thus it is that the members of the Church being severed, the body lies bleeding. So much does this concern me, that, could I be of any service, I would not grudge to cross even ten seas, if need were, on account of it."[187]

"The Lord Orders the Ministers of the Gospel to Go Far Out to Scatter the Teaching of Salvation throughout All the Regions of the Earth"[188]

In his writings and sermons (from both the Old Testament and the New), Calvin stressed the biblical theme of the worldwide extension of Christ's reign and challenged Christian people to spread zealously

---

184. Cited by Bouwsma, *John Calvin*, 215.
185. Calvin, *Reformation Debate*, 94.
186. Calvin, *Concerning Scandals*, 233.
187. Calvin to Thomas Cranmer, April 1552, in *Letters*, 2:347–48.
188. CNTC, 3:251.

the gospel message. In treating Isaiah 2:4, Calvin wrote that Christ was "not sent to the Jews only, that he may reign over them, but that he may hold his sway over the whole world."[189] Commenting on Isaiah 12:4, Calvin wrote that the Jews, the special recipients of God's blessing in the Old Testament, "ought to have been heralds to sound aloud the name of God through every country in the world." That goal should now be the desire "among all the godly"—that is, "that the goodness of God may be made known to all, that all may join in the same worship of God."[190] Calvin wrote to Somerset that Christian people must work wisely "to gain over the whole world to God, if that were possible."[191] In his exposition of the words "Thy kingdom come" in the Lord's Prayer, Calvin shifted his emphasis from individual obedience in the first edition of the *Institutes* (1536) to the planting of churches in the last edition (1559), when he wrote that "we must daily desire that God gather churches unto himself from all parts of the earth." Calvin noted that this prayer instructs us "in bearing the cross. For it is in this way that God wills to spread his Kingdom."[192] Calvin's closing prayer following his sermons on Deuteronomy included these world-embracing words: "May it please [God] to grant this grace, not only to us, but also to all peoples and nations of the earth."[193]

With Calvin's leadership, Geneva became, according to Philip E. Hughes, "a dynamic center or nucleus from which the vital missionary energy it generated radiated out into the world beyond."[194]

"It Is Enough That I Live and Die for Christ, Who Is to All His Followers a Gain Both in Life and Death"[195]

The above words Calvin wrote to his friend Guillaume Farel several weeks before Calvin himself died on May 2, 1564. In the minutes of the Consistory of Geneva, there is a simple cross beside his name and

---

189. John Calvin, *Commentary on the Book of the Prophet Isaiah* (Grand Rapids, MI: Eerdmans, 1958), 1:99.
190. Calvin, *Commentary on Isaiah*, 1:402–3.
191. Calvin to the Protector Somerset, October 22, 1548, in *Letters*, 2:195–96.
192. *Institutes*, 3.20.42.
193. Calvin, *Sermons on Deuteronomy*, 12.
194. Philip E. Hughes, "John Calvin: Director of Missions," in *The Heritage of John Calvin*, ed. John H. Bratt, Heritage Hall 2 (Grand Rapids, MI: Eerdmans, 1973), 45. See also David B. Calhoun, "John Calvin: Missionary Hero or Missionary Failure?," in *Presb* 5 (1979): 16–33.
195. Calvin to Guillaume Farel, May 2, 1564, in *Letters*, 4:364.

the words: "Gone to God, May 27th of the present year, between 8 and 9 o'clock, p.m."[196] A few days later, Farel wrote a friend,

> Oh why was I not taken away in his stead, and he preserved to the church which he has so well served, and in combats harder than death? He has done more and with greater promptitude than any one, surpassing not only the others but himself. Oh, how happily he has run a noble race! May the Lord grant that we run like him, and according to the measure of grace that has been dealt out to us.[197]

---

196. *Letters*, 4:377n3.
197. Farel to [Christopher] Fabri, June 6, 1564, in *Letters*, 4:364n1.

4

Calvin and the Consistory

Douglas F. Kelly

Every man should endeavor to admonish his brother. But let
pastors and presbyters be especially watchful to do this.
—John Calvin, *Institutes of the Christian Religion*

Thursday Nights in Geneva[1]

John Calvin's chief legacy to the Christian church was undoubtedly his preaching and theological writing. Much has been written
on this subject, of very high quality.[2] But far less material is available on his significant work as a pastor. For that reason, it is well
to introduce readers to a rich resource of the pastoral theology
and practice of John Calvin: *Registres du Consistoire de Genève*
(*Registers of the Consistory of Geneva*). These "session minutes"
(in Presbyterian terminology) comprise twenty-one volumes, running from the year of Calvin's return to Geneva in 1541 after his

---

1. This chapter is an English translation of the French original, "Cauvin Pasteur, presentè par
les proces-verbux du consistoire de Geneve," given at Colloque Biblique Francophone in Belly,
France, in March 2008.
2. For example, see T. H. L. Parker, *Calvin's Preaching* (Edinburgh: T&T Clark, 1992).

banishment in Strasbourg to the time of his death in 1564. The voluminous manuscripts of these handwritten minutes of the Consistory had been safely kept in the archives of Geneva for centuries, but they were very little used. The handwriting is hard to read, and they were thus never published.[3]

In the 1980s, Robert Kingdon began arranging for the transcription and publication of these valuable, largely unknown Consistory minutes. Jeffrey and Isabella Watt, with their knowledge of French paleography, began the painstaking task of transcribing these minutes for eventual publication. Thomas Lambert also did a great deal of work on this project. All twenty-one volumes were transcribed by 1992, and the first volume, covering the years 1542–1544, was published in Geneva in 1996. To date, eleven volumes have been published, which include the minutes for the years 1542–1557.

Although we learn much from Calvin's *Institutes*, commentaries, sermons, tracts, treatises, and many letters, we can never really know what kind of pastor he was until we study these Consistory minutes. For they show him at work once a week (on Thursday nights) dealing with pastoral problems, often for hours at a time, in what was a very busy life, and one often characterized by poor health. There can be no doubt that the pastoral problems he faced caused him to rethink and refine many areas of theology and pastoral and liturgical practice as the years went by. His dealings with the people deepened his theology and frequently drove him back to renewed study of relevant passages of Holy Scripture.[4] John Witte and Robert Kingdon, for instance, demonstrate how years of work on the Consistory bench in Geneva caused Calvin to deepen, broaden, and more fully apply the theology of the covenant to marriage.[5]

Another reason for rejoicing at the publication of these *Registres* is that delving into them gives us a much more balanced view of the Calvinist Reformation in Geneva than we previously had from the

3. See *Registres*, viii. Unless otherwise noted, all translations from the *Registres* in this chapter are by the author.

4. See the splendid book by John Witte Jr. and Robert M. Kingdon, *Sex, Marriage, and Family in John Calvin's Geneva*, Vol. 1, *Courtship, Engagement, and Marriage* (Grand Rapids, MI: Eerdmans, 2005).

5. See especially chap. 14, "Concluding Reflections: The Emerging Covenantal Model of Engagement and Marriage," in Witte and Kingdon, *Sex, Marriage, and Family*, 1:481–90.

nineteenth- and twentieth-century biographies and studies of Calvin's tenure there. Kingdon, in his introduction to volume 1 of these *Registres*, notes that only 5 percent of this hard-to-read material has ever been drawn upon by Calvin's biographers. And interestingly, it is the very same 5 percent! These extracts were made by Frederic-Auguste Cramer in 1853, and according to recent experts, they not infrequently included misreading of handwriting and other mistakes.[6] The great Emile Doumergue drew only from these transcriptions of Cramer, and all other biographers for the next 150 years drew from exactly the same source.

The problem with this narrowness of original source material is that we are not given a balanced survey of the truly broad and deep scope of the work of the Consistory from 1541 to 1564. Most of what Cramer drew out of the larger mass tended to be more dramatic or extreme. If we read only these episodes, we may think of Calvin and the Consistory members as harsh Puritans, but this would be to neglect the vast amount of material in the minutes that reflects generally normal pastoral counseling, ecclesiastical discipline, and personal nurture. A case in point is the famous biography of Calvin by Williston Walker (1906). The Consistory cases he mentions are generally of a somewhat extreme nature, which would have been the most offensive to twentieth-century sensibilities.[7]

Yes, of course, these things did happen, such as discipline of a man for singing a song defamatory of Calvin, or of a widow for praying *requiescat in pace* over her husband's grave. Or one that Walker does not mention would be the short-lived attempt to force taverns to have the drinkers sing hymns and songs rather than bawdy ditties. But when you take together the mass of the material, many of the scenes that seem to us silly or inappropriate for discipline, are only a very small part of a much more serious and pastorally responsible body of work, even from our perspective some 450 years later.

Calvin personally attended most of the Consistory meetings each Thursday night, and these at times lasted for several hours. Calvin

---

6. *Registres*, 1:viii.
7. Williston Walker, *John Calvin: The Organiser of Reformed Protestantism, 1509–1564* (1906; repr., New York: Schocken Books, 1969), 281–84.

was not the moderator; one of the "syndics" appointed by the city council moderated the meetings. And Calvin does not appear to have dominated the meeting. At times he is listed as having cross-examined someone or as having given the admonition, and sometimes he was sent to the town council on Mondays to explain why the Consistory had taken a particular action or, indeed, to protest the council's failure to act. But always, his presence was felt, even though he was only one among many.

What Kind of Body Was the Consistory?

But before we examine more closely what the Consistory minutes teach us about Calvin's pastoral ministry, we must mention very briefly just what this body was and what was its relationship to the civil magistrate in Geneva. In terms of the history of medieval Christian Europe, the Genevan Consistory was a replacement of the traditional Bishop's Courts, which had handled moral and minor civil questions for over a thousand years throughout the Christian countries of the West. An interesting review of the typical work of these courts is found in Peter Brown's biography *Augustine of Hippo*.[8]

In 1536 the bishop had been expelled from Geneva when the town voted for the Reformation. That left them with a vacuum in handling moral and minor civil cases. François Bonivard stated in his famous work *Police* (written in the late 1550s) that with the rejection of pope and bishops, the work of the Bishop's Court was handed over to the ministers in conjunction with the various town councils. He explained that this body was the Consistory, and to it were committed the censuring of morals, marriages, and lighter civil cases. Punishments and more serious cases were to be brought before the town councils.[9]

This indicates a strong distinction (though not a strict separation) between church and civil authorities. For the sake of space, we need not enter into the details of the various town councils of Geneva at that period. For our purposes, it suffices to note that the Consistory was most directly related to the Small Council (i.e., the executive com-

---

8. Peter Brown, *Augustine of Hippo: A Biography* (Berkeley: University of California Press, 1969), 195–97.
9. Cf. *Registres*, 1:391.

mittee), which was under the Council of Sixty, which in turn was under the Council of Two Hundred. After Calvin's return from exile, he quickly proposed the *Ordonnances ecclésiastiques* (or *Ecclesiastical Ordinances*), in 1541, which for the most part was accepted by the civil magistrate and immediately put into practice. The *Ecclesiastical Ordinances* specified that twelve lay elders be chosen by the Small Council, subject to consultation with the ministers (depending on the year, there could be between nine and thirty-two pastors)[10] and under the final approval by the Council of Two Hundred.

The following substantial section from the 1541 *Ecclesiastical Ordinances* illuminates the duties of the Consistory:

> If there be anyone who dogmatizes against the received doctrine, conference is to be held with him. If he listen to reason, he is to be dismissed without scandal or dishonour. If he be opinionative, he is to be admonished several times, until it is seen that measures of greater severity are needed. . . .
>
> If anyone is negligent in coming to church, so that a noticeable contempt of the communion of the faithful is evident, or if any show himself contemptuous of the ecclesiastical order, he is to be admonished, and if he prove obedient dismissed in friendliness. . . .
>
> As for each man's conduct, for the correction of faults, proceedings should be in accordance with the order which our Lord commands.
>
> Secret vices are to be secretly admonished; no one is to bring his neighbour before the Church to accuse him of faults that are not in the least notorious or scandalous, unless having found him contumacious. . . .
>
> As for vices notorious and public which the Church cannot dissimulate, if they are faults that merit admonition only, the duty of the elders will be to summon those who are implicated to make friendly remonstrance to them in order that they make correction, and if amendment is evident, to do them no harm. If they persevere in doing wrong, they are to be admonished as despisers of God, they must abstain from the Supper until a change of life is seen in them.

---

10. *Registres*, 1:viii.

As for crimes which merit not merely remonstrance in words but correction by chastisement, should any fall into them, according to the needs of the case, he must be warned that he abstain for some time from the Supper, to humble himself before God and to acknowledge his fault the better. . . .

Yet all this should be done with such moderation, that there be no rigour by which anyone may be injured; for even the corrections are only medicines for bringing back sinners to our Lord.[11]

The Small Council, before accepting Calvin's original draft, added this article to make clear that the ministers would not intrude on civil authority in serious cases:

All this is to take place in such a way that the ministers have no civil jurisdiction, nor use anything but the spiritual sword of the Word of God, as Paul commands them; nor is the Consistory to derogate from the authority of the Seigneury or ordinary justice. The civil power is to remain unimpaired. Even where there will be need to impose punishments or to constrain parties, the ministers with the Consistory having heard the parties and used such remonstrances and admonitions as are good, are to report the whole matter to the Council, which in their turn will advise sentence and judgment according to the needs of the case.[12]

An oath administered to the Consistory in February 1544 instructed the members (some of them newly elected) of their duties:

The Syndic (a lay representative from the Small Council, who was moderator of the Consistory) commanded them to carry out their office with regard to the Word of God [considering] idolatry, those who lead dishonest lives, the Lord's Supper, and drunkards, whoremongers, violent persons, blasphemers, people who live badly and in superstition. All of them responded that they would do their duty.[13]

The ministers sat on one bench, and the elders sat on another as together they did their work of hearing cases week by week on Thurs-

---

11. *Draft Ecclesiastical Ordinances*, in *Theological Treatises*, 70, 71.
12. *Draft Ecclesiastical Ordinances*, 71n84.
13. *Registres*, 1:312.

day evenings. It must have been heavy work, for Calvin indicated great sorrow when his close ministerial colleague, Pierre Viret, was sent from Geneva (where he assisted Calvin most ably) to Lausanne. Viret had made Calvin's load much lighter. In January 1542, Calvin wrote that "since my arrival here I can only remember having been granted two hours in which no-one has come and disturbed me."[14]

Why Calvin Wanted the Consistory

What did Calvin think that the Consistory, to whose work he devoted so many hours, was doing? In his *Institutes*, he argued that sessional discipline is an extension of the pastoral care that must always accompany the preaching of the gospel. He believed that preaching is insufficient unless people are dealt with personally and pastorally by the officers of the church. He wrote,

> The first foundation of discipline is to provide a place for private admonition; that is, if anyone does not perform his duty willingly, or behaves insolently, or does not live honorably, or has committed any act deserving blame—he should allow himself to be admonished; and when the situation demands it, every man should endeavor to admonish his brother. But let pastors and presbyters be especially watchful to do this, for their duty is not only to preach to the people, but to warn and exhort in every house, wherever they are not effective enough in general instruction. Paul teaches this when he relates that he taught privately and from house to house [Acts 20:20], and declares himself "innocent from the blood of all" [v. 26], because he "ceased not to admonish everyone night and day with tears" [v. 31]. For doctrine obtains force and authority where the minister not only explains to all together what they owe to Christ, but also has the right and means to require that it be kept by those whom he has observed are either disrespectful or languid toward his teaching.[15]

In other words, Calvin believed that pastoral work (of which Consistory discipline was a constituent part) was one of the three marks

---

14. Quoted in Jean Cadier, *The Man God Mastered: A Brief Biography of John Calvin*, trans. O. R. Johnston (London: Inter-Varsity Fellowship, 1964), 119.
15. *Institutes*, 4.12.2.

of the true church. At one time, it was thought that Calvin believed, along with Martin Luther, that there were only two marks to identify a true church: true preaching of the word and pure administration of the sacrament. Those are in fact the only ones he mentions in his *Institutes*,[16] following the words of the Lutheran Augsburg Confession (1530). But Robert Kingdon has effectively pointed out that Calvin held to a third mark of the true church: discipline. This is brought out in his *Reply to Sadoleto* (1539), where he lists all three marks.[17] Thus, discipline as the third mark of the church was not an innovation with Calvin's Scottish disciple John Knox (ca. 1514–1572).

Calvin was convinced that the Holy Spirit used not merely frequent preaching of the word of God to shape men and women into the renewed image of Christ but frequent preaching backed by sincerity and relative purity of life in church members, a sincerity and relative purity that could only be achieved by careful pastoral care, visitation, and at times official discipline. Christlikeness—that was the major overall goal of all churchly activity. Calvin expanded on the theme of Christlikeness in his *Commentary on Ephesians*, in which he argued that the gifts of the ascended Christ to his church are generally concentrated on various church officers, who are gifted precisely so they may assist in the shaping of people into the image of Christ.[18] The apostle Paul explains it in Ephesians 4:11–13:

> And he gave the apostles, the prophets, the evangelists, the shepherds and teachers, to equip the saints for the work of ministry, for building up the body of Christ, until we all attain to the unity of the faith and of the knowledge of the Son of God, to mature manhood, to the measure of the stature of the fullness of Christ.

Ronald Wallace clearly grasped Calvin's vision of what he wanted to happen in Geneva through a well-disciplined church. He states,

> Calvin believed that what happens when humanity is redeemed in Christ gives us a true picture of what was meant to happen originally in society in its natural form. For grace always tends to

---

16. *Institutes*, 4.1.9.
17. See Robert Kingdon, preface to *Registres*, 1:vii.
18. See *Comm.*, 21:277–86.

reveal and restore the original form of nature. Therefore he found the ideal human order described for him in Paul's account of the Church in the New Testament—an organism, or a body, in which each member derives its life and health and nourishment from the whole body, and has a quite unique and irreplaceable function. In Geneva he wanted even civil society to reflect as far as it could the pattern of mutual dependence, cooperation, close intercommunion between the whole body and its members which he expected to find first especially in the Church. Earthly citizenship was to be patterned on heavenly citizenship. The whole social body in the city itself, therefore, was meant to be an organism with a great variety of members, each member finding significance in his part in, and service to, the whole body, and the health and wealth of the whole depending on the faithful functioning of each. . . .

He believed, moreover, that the whole realm of human and secular affairs in Geneva, in spite of its frailty and its persistent tendency to alienation from God, could become penetrated and invaded powerfully by the Word of God, and thus, by the influence of the grace and Kingdom of God. The proximity of the realm of grace could thus powerfully affect the realm of nature, and the life of the "world" could in Geneva become dominated and moulded by the same regenerating divine influences as were at work within the Church. Calvin therefore expected to see great changes taking place in how Geneva as a secular city worked and lived.[19]

Yet Calvin's great expectations for thorough reformation and renewal in the Genevan church and then society were carefully bounded by the teachings of Scripture on the tension between the "already" and the "not yet." Hughes Oliphant Old strikes the right note here as he comments on Calvin's fifteenth sermon on the prophecy of Micah:

Yet it should be noted, Calvin cautions, that those blessings of Christ's reign will never be completely realized in this world. As much as the reign of Christ has indeed begun and advances and grows in us, and as much as the blessings of the kingdom may

---

19. Ronald S. Wallace, *Calvin, Geneva and the Reformation: A Study of Calvin as Social Reformer, Churchman, Pastor, and Theologian* (Edinburgh: Scottish Academic Press, 1988), 117, 120.

already be experienced in this world, they are never completely fulfilled on earth. It should also be noted that the reign of Christ is above all spiritual and is not the same thing as the peace and prosperity of a merely secular society. God does not want us to be misled into thinking that our paradise is here below, or that our happiness is to be found in worldly vanities. Nevertheless, it is also true, as Saint Paul teaches us, that when we serve God with a pure conscience, the blessings of God will belong to us not only in the world to come but in this world as well (I Tim. 4:8). In this world also, to be sure, God supplies all the needs of the faithful. God is even now helping us, establishing us in all his blessings and encouraging us with his generosity and grace.[20]

The Reformation: A Pastoral-Care Movement

Reformation of the church and considerable renewal of society through word, sacrament, and discipline (or effective pastoral care): this was the grand vision that motivated this overworked man to spend yet more grueling hours at the Consistory, in addition to his regular pastoral visitation and extensive letter writing, in which he conveyed much detailed personal counsel, in addition to his preaching, his theological writing, and his church, city, and Pan-European statesmanship. While we most frequently think of the sixteenth-century Reformation as a renewal of the preaching of the word of God (which is true), it was more than that. As Eduard Thurneysen has pointed out, "The Reformation itself was a pastoral-care movement growing directly out of care for the salvation of the soul."[21]

Calvin would not have thought that a pastoral-care movement was a totally new thing in church history, for he argued at large in book 4 of the *Institutes* that pastoral care and Consistory church discipline among the Reformed constituted a return to central concerns of the early church. I suspect there is much to commend in this view, for I have noticed in recent years while visiting the catacombs of Rome that the earliest Christian "logo" (in addition to the fish) was not the cross but rather a shepherd carrying a lamb on his shoulders. This is par-

---

20. Hughes Oliphant Old, *The Reading and Preaching of the Scriptures in the Worship of the Christian Church*, vol. 4, *The Age of the Reformation* (Grand Rapids, MI: Eerdmans, 2002), 120.
21. Quoted in Wallace, *Calvin, Geneva and the Reformation*, 169.

ticularly the case with the second-century paintings in the Catacombs of Saint Priscilla on the Via Salaris in Rome. And of course, there are multiplied references to intensive pastoral care and discipline in the early church fathers of both East and West (but that subject goes beyond the scope of this chapter).

I will grant that one has a different feeling when going from a catacomb fresco of the good shepherd gently carrying a lamb on his shoulders to a regular Thursday-night Consistory meeting at the Cathedral of Saint Pierre, when people are being interrogated by the elders as to various moral offenses! But maybe they are not so different after all. It is not unlike raising children; to do so has its unspeakably tender moments, but it also entails close attention, self-sacrifice, demanding duty, and at times, very unpleasant conflicts with them. The work of mutual sanctification within the body of Christ is not essentially different. It is sweet and tender; it is tough and nasty. One finds some of both—"agony and ecstasy," melting love and chilling severity—in the Genevan Consistory meetings. This is where Calvin's pastoring skills developed more than anywhere else, so we do well to survey some of its work.

Heavy Caseload of the Consistory

First, let us note the heavy caseload of the Consistory and what a large percentage of the Genevan population they dealt with between 1541 and 1564. It is estimated that in the 1540s, Geneva had about 12,000 inhabitants in and around the small commercial city. Year by year between 6 and 7 percent of the adults in that population came before the session (whether as defendants, plaintiffs, or witnesses). Kingdon says that during its first twenty-four months of activity, it called before it some 850 persons.[22] Since it met only one night per week, and since it interviewed very carefully each person in close detail, this would have taken many, many hours.

The giving up of so many hours each week in a highly pressured life in and of itself shows the pastoral heart of Calvin. I suspect that no one can be an effective pastor (whether in a small church or in a

---

22. Kingdon, preface to *Registres*, 1:xiii.

congregation of thousands) without self-sacrifice. Self-sacrifice probably hurts us most (assuming that we are conscientious servants of
Christ) when it requires us to give up what little precious time we might
otherwise have had. Calvin was never one to say, "My preaching and
theological work are so important that I cannot possibly be expected
to expend my valuable time visiting people and dealing with their sins
and foibles." He could have argued, "I am writing for the ages; the temporal problems of these foolish church members are merely ephemeral
and unworthy of my time." Not a bit of it! He felt that he was doing
the shepherd work of Christ sitting in those long meetings with sinners
as much as when he was proclaiming the word of God from the pulpit
or writing the *Institutes* or letters to important figures in Europe. That
is, the preached word and the theological tract had not been communicated until their truths permeated the thinking and behavior of the
people through close and at times uncomfortable interpersonal dealings
with them—a process that took time, energy, and patience.

Various Types of Cases

Second, we must consider what sorts of cases regularly came before
the Consistory in Geneva. This is where it simply will not do to restrict
our gaze to the 5 percent of mostly dramatic cases reported in nearly
all the Calvin biographies. That unbalanced sampling makes the serious work of the Consistory seem to verge on the foolish or fanatical.
But if we take the whole caseload over the twenty-three years of diligent, weekly work, we get a very different picture, one that shows a
sincere and serious Christian attempt of church elders to encourage
holiness by reproving vice and pointing out a better way in the most
practical detail.

In other words, here were men determined to hold those who pro-
fessed to follow Christ accountable to his word. Of course, the Genevan elders had behind them the police power of the state in a way that
our churches have not had since the late seventeenth century. Still, the
issues that the Consistory had to deal with, the points on which they
had to hold their people pastorally accountable, were much the same as
today (or as in the days of Moses, David, and the Corinthians). By the
way, even a cursory reading of these minutes of the Consistory will con-

firm the biblical teachings of original sin, of the essentially unchanging nature of fallen humanity, and of the ceaseless struggle between flesh and spirit in the lives of those who are being redeemed. The different types of cases Calvin and his colleagues dealt with show that sixteenth-century Geneva was no better, no worse, nor even very different from our congregations in twenty-first-century America or Europe.

Thomas Lambert and Isabella Watt outline the various types of cases regularly brought before the Consistory.[23] More than any other issues were problems related to marriage, family, and sexuality. Witte and Kingdon devote a large volume to these questions, which took up approximately 60 percent of the time of the Consistory.[24] They state,

> First, in each year, roughly 60 percent of the Consistory's entire case load was devoted to issues of sex, marriage, and family. But the volume of cases on these issues nearly doubled in a decade— from 182 cases in 1546 to 323 in 1557. This reflected, in part, the growing population of Geneva. But it also reflected the growing aggressiveness of the Consistory in governing Genevan life.[25]

Lambert and Watt note that "the Consistory watched over drunk-ards, blasphemers, usurers, dissipated persons, beggars, dancers, sing-ers of 'dishonest songs,' healers, diviners (i.e., occult practitioners), players and other 'bad-livers.'"[26] In addition to these types of cases, the elders of Reformed Geneva were charged with extirpating residual Roman Catholic practices. Again, Lambert and Watt write,

> The Consistory was charged with suppressing the practices and beliefs of the ancient faith, and with introducing those of the Ref-ormation. To reach this goal, the Consistory interrogated peo-ple suspected of attachment to the Church of Rome as well as those who neglected their duties: chiefly those whose poor atten-dance at the sermons did not demonstrate an ardent zeal for the Reformation. . . . [The minutes] state that they continued to pray to the saints and to the Virgin Mary, that they prayed for the dead,

---

23. Thomas Lambert and Isabella Watt, introduction to *Registres*, 1:xiv–xvii.
24. See Witte and Kingdon, *Sex, Marriage, and Family*.
25. Witte and Kingdon, *Sex, Marriage, and Family*, 74.
26. Lambert and Watt, introduction to *Registres*, 1:xiv, xv.

that they fasted on Fridays and during Lent, that they disdained taking the Reformed Lord's Supper, that they read Books of Hours, and sometimes took advantage of living near Catholic countries so that they left the city in order to attend Mass. Sometimes the persistence of Catholic beliefs is explained by their will and by an informed refusal to accept the Reformation. Sometimes it is explained merely by ignorance.[27]

Lambert and Watt state that by 1545, most of the Consistory inquisitions of the Genevans for praying to saints and to the Virgin Mary had ceased.[28] The preaching of Calvin (and his colleagues) and the work of the Consistory had prevailed to shape the popular piety of Geneva from lingering Catholicism into a Reformed mode.

We may take as a representative example of most years of Consistory work the year 1546. Witte and Kingdon give a table of cases pertaining to sex, marriage, and family (which, as we have seen, took up 60 percent of their time). Let me cite the types of cases and their number from that year:[29]

> Fornication/Adultery: 94 cases
> Other Sexual Immorality: 23
> Rape / Sexual Assault: 1
> Disputed Engagements: 20
> Spouse/Family Quarrels: 66
> Abortion: 1
> Baptism Disputes: 3
> Child Mistreatment: 5
> Schooling Disputes: 1
> Disobeying Parents: 1
> Wife Beating: 1
> Divorce: 6

An Overview of Some Representative Cases

Third, let us now take a look at some representative cases and how the Consistory dealt with them. I will restrict myself here to volume 1 of

---

27. Lambert and Watt, introduction to *Registres*, 1:xv.
28. Lambert and Watt, introduction to *Registres*, 1:xvi.
29. Witte and Kingdon, *Sex, Marriage, and Family*, 75.

the *Registres*, covering the years 1542–1544. The nature of the problems and the way they were resolved gives us insight into early Reformed pastoral practice, specifically that of Calvin and his colleagues.

One could summarize the various types of cases in several different ways, but for our purposes, I look at them under the following main headings: sexual morality, marriage and family, sermon attendance, prayer, personal Christian knowledge, sincerity of life, a community of reconciliation, and godly examples for a godly society.

Sexual Morality

Sexual morality along with marriage took up some 60 percent of the time of the Consistory. I suspect that this would be more or less in line with the counseling load in most churches today, although I am not certain. God has created us with the good gift of sexuality, and it is a major aspect of our human existence, for good or for ill. Certainly the Christians in Calvin's time were not like the "nice people" of Victorian times who did not discuss sex. The Reformed of Geneva were much more frank about this crucial area of our lives, and in this respect were more like the English Puritans, as Leland Ryken has shown.[30]

By far the largest percentage of cases involving sexual misconduct that came before the Consistory dealt with premarital (and at times extramarital) fornication, particularly pregnancy out of wedlock. Sometimes we wonder how far Western society has declined morally with the great number of people living together and having children (or more likely abortions) outside marriage. Yet a close look at these minutes shows that we may not be that different in our generally accepted immoral practices from sixteenth-century Christian Europe.

Those with expertise in the social history of that period tell us that in the early period of Calvin's ministry in Geneva, premarital intercourse of those who were engaged was rather widely accepted, and a pregnancy before marriage (assuming that the partners were actually engaged) was not considered particularly shameful (though it could have its problems). In general, if a couple decided that they wanted to marry, and they drank wine together, and one or both gave some

---

30. Leland Ryken, *Worldly Saints: The Puritans as They Really Were* (Grand Rapids, MI: Zondervan, 1986).

kind of gift, particularly in front of witnesses, then it was not unusual for them to engage in premarital sex. Hence, in the first volume of the *Registres* (particularly in the early months of it), girls who were pregnant before wedlock were for the most part not rebuked by the Consistory for having done so, assuming that they were indeed voluntarily engaged. The Consistory response was that they must marry without delay.[31] On occasion they asked the Small Council to imprison a man for fornication but then required him to marry after he had served his short sentence (usually three days on bread and water).[32] Sometimes an engaged man committed fornication with someone other than his betrothed, and generally he was punished by a brief imprisonment,[33] though sometimes by more serious measures.

It is important to remember here that the Consistory did not have civil or police powers, so they could not directly have anyone beaten or put into prison. The most they could do would be to send them to the Small Council with such a recommendation on Monday (after the Consistory meeting on Thursday). And of course, the Consistory could suspend transgressors from the Lord's Supper. No doubt, the Consistory had the power of excommunication, but it took considerable conflict with the Small Council to make this ecclesiastical authority clear. In fact, it was not until 1557, very late in Calvin's ministry, that the Consistory clearly gained the legal right of excommunication.[34] Even so, as Witte and Kingdon show, the Consistory used admonition (or the temporary ban from the Supper) forty times for every one person they excommunicated.[35]

As for premarital relations, views changed after the legal acceptation of Calvin's 1545–1546 "Ordinance on Marriage," which forbade premarital intercourse.[36] And even before that time, the Consistory became far less tolerant of this practice, especially as the population was being more deeply affected by the preaching of the word, and by their accountability to the elders. It is interesting to realize that even at

---

31. E.g., see *Registres*, 1:11, 76, 177–78, 211–12, 366.
32. E.g., see *Registres*, 1:333, 334.
33. E.g., see *Registres*, 1:298, 299.
34. Witte and Kingdon, *Sex, Marriage, and Family*, 73.
35. Witte and Kingdon, *Sex, Marriage, and Family*, 68.
36. For the text of the "Marriage Ordinance," see Witte and Kingdon, *Sex, Marriage, and Family*, 51–56.

the height of the Reformation, Christian leaders were realistic enough to know that it would take time and patience to bring about purity of sexual morals.

However, even before the "Ordinance on Marriage," from the very beginning of Consistory meetings, the elders and ministers did not tolerate mere fornication without a view to marriage. Not infrequently, when a girl was pregnant, the boyfriend would deny that they had ever been engaged, and in such cases, it seems to me that the Consistory did the best they could to follow due process of law to ascertain the truth, if possible.[37]

Sheer adultery was dealt with much more strictly. More than once men were put into prison for having impregnated their servant[38] or for other kinds of adultery.[39] Sometimes the minutes specify exactly where the adultery took place: one time in the kitchen[40] and another time in the barn.[41] One widow was put in prison for having had a child long after her husband was dead.[42] Yet even so, she was told to be more faithful in attending sermons in the future. One man denied that he had ever put his hands up a girl's dress in public, and the Consistory, having no firm proof of it, let him go, admonishing him to learn the Lord's Prayer and the Apostle's Creed and to live honestly.[43] Capital punishment for repeated adultery was possible (under the Justinian Code to which Geneva and nearly all Europe still largely adhered), but it was highly unusual. Robert Kingdon shows that Geneva did not have an explicit provision for adultery until 1566, two years after Calvin's death.[44] Even so, before that time, capital punishment for adultery did on occasion occur. Kingdon discusses one such case, in which both Anne Le Moine and Antoine Cossonex were executed in 1560.[45]

But more usually, repeated adultery or repeated illegitimacy could get one fined, beaten, or banished from the city (by the Small Council,

---

37. E.g., see *Registres*, 1:13, 177, 178.
38. E.g., see *Registres*, 1:220–21.
39. E.g., see *Registres*, 1:199n160.
40. *Registres*, 1:220.
41. *Registres*, 1:358.
42. *Registres*, 1:103.
43. *Registres*, 1:98, 99.
44. Robert M. Kingdon, *Adultery and Divorce in Calvin's Geneva* (Cambridge, MA: Harvard University Press, 1995), 116.
45. Kingdon, *Adultery and Divorce*, 116–41.

if and when they followed the Consistory's recommendation). Pierre Rapid was condemned to be publicly whipped, to go through the streets wearing a dunce cap, and to be banished from the city for having become engaged to two women and having consummated marriage with both of them.[46] But far more often than beating or prison, the normal response of the Consistory to the fornicator or adulterer was to repent, to abstain from the Lord's Supper for a time, to learn better the Lord's Prayer and the Apostle's Creed, and to begin living chastely and charitably with others. In due time, they could come back before the elders, and if they showed sincere repentance and increased Christian knowledge, they would be readmitted to the Supper.[47] Indeed, one woman was given merciful treatment and "a second chance" after she had gotten pregnant by a married man.[48] Even when someone was banned temporarily from the Supper, he or she was still told to frequent the sermons.[49]

This response of the Consistory to an impoverished woman who had never been married and yet had two children is not atypical: "The opinion of the Consistory: given that we have seen her repentance, and that she has made confession, we should have pity upon her, and speak to her words of admonition and remonstrance."[50]

The Consistory consistently showed humane consideration for the lives of women who were pregnant out of wedlock, as well as for their illegitimate children. Not infrequently, they sought to make sure that sufficient funds were available for them to survive without a father. Even when they recommended punishment (usually three days in prison), they still in a sense considered such transgressors to be under their care and kept the door open for reconciliation with the church. There were also times when a fallen woman (especially after two illegitimate children) would be banished from the city (for a year and a day), although even in that case, the woman was given some money to help care for the child.[51]

Jeffrey Watt (one of the transcribers of the handwritten Consistory minutes into print) has shown the forward-looking nature of the Consistory's dealing with women:

---

46. *Registres*, 1:15.
47. *Registres*, 1:70, 201.
48. *Registres*, 1:203.
49. *Registres*, 1:70.
50. *Registres*, 1:365.
51. *Registres*, 1:9.

But unlike other contemporary institutions, the Genevan Consistory convoked as many men as women for fornication, and made a decided effort to establish paternity for the benefit of unwed mothers. Indeed, the Consistory went so far as to require a married man to take custody of the illegitimate child he had fathered (see *Registres du Consistoire de Genève*, I.86v).[52]

Issues of abortion,[53] infanticide,[54] pimpery,[55] and other sexual deviations seem to have been fairly rare but certainly not unknown. In this area, if in no other, the general morals of sixteenth-century Geneva appear (at least from the records we have) to put the modern West to shame. It is important for the modern church to consider what a clear stand the Christian church in Calvin's time took on sexual morality. Although we in no sense have the police power of the state behind us in the way that most of European Christianity had in the sixteenth century, at the very least it is incumbent on us to hold the people of the church accountable to a high sexual morality. Not to do so is an uncharitable failure to give moral light to the general society so desperately in need of it. While we may despair of ever having much influence on an immoral society at large, we would probably be surprised at the widespread godly suasion the church could exercise by keeping her own house in order. Unbelievers have every right to expect this of us.

Marriage and Family

Here we consider a representative fraction of typical pastoral problems that Calvin and his Consistory had to deal with as they sought to have families of the congregations live in accordance with the word of God. Again, we find that their family problems were not very different from the ones Christian pastors face in our own day.[56]

---

52. Jeffrey R. Watt, "Women and the Consistory in Calvin's Geneva," *SCJ* 24, no. 2 (1993): 438.
53. *Registres*, 1:269.
54. *Registres*, 1:130.
55. *Registres*, 1:354, 374.
56. While it lies outside the purview of this essay, I commend the significant work of Witte and Kingdon on how Calvin's understanding of biblical covenant was deepened as he dealt with marital issues over the years and how it enabled him to draw together the diverse aspects of marriage and family into a more coherent whole. Witte and Kingdon, *Sex, Marriage, and Family*, 481–90.

Calvin was concerned to see to it that all marriages were consensual by both parties. If the couple were under age (twenty for men and eighteen for women), the parents' permission was necessary. But otherwise, they were free to marry (unless there were impediments to it such as consanguinity or disease[57]). Calvin's 1546 "Marriage Ordinances" required that the wedding be held in the church, before sermon time. (Medieval weddings had usually been held outside the church, at the front door). At first, dancing was allowed at wedding receptions, but later this permission was revoked.

The vast majority of Consistory cases dealing with the family were concluded by a call to forgiveness and full reconciliation, after the conflicts were discussed. This was a sort of forced marriage counseling service, and before we are critical of it, it would be wise to consider whether our churches are nearly so effective in resolving family conflicts and preventing divorce.

Spousal conflict is nothing new. Here are some examples. Benoyte Ameaux (or Amyaulx) complained that her husband was always angry with her and beat her and that he was never satisfied with anything she did. "It was the opinion of the Consistory that one remonstrate with them and that she live in peace and union with her husband, and frequent the sermons."[58] Benoyte's problems, however, did not go away, and the Consistory had to keep dealing with her. Kingdon has devoted an entire chapter to the divorce case between her and her husband, Pierre.[59] It would appear that Benoyte was mentally ill, as we would say today, and appropriate action had to be taken to protect both her and the public. Kingdon explains what happened after the council decided that she was guilty of both adultery and blasphemy:

> Given the record laid before it, the council really had no other choice. But it then decided on a sentence that, in the circumstances, proved to be surprisingly lenient. It ordered that Benoite be condemned to be imprisoned "perpetually, unless by the grace of God

---

57. See chaps. 6, 7, and 8 in Witte and Kingdon, *Sex, Marriage, and Family*, 202–309.

58. *Registres*, 1:102, 103.

59. Kingdon, "The Pierre Ameaux Case: Divorce for Adultery and Blasphemy," in *Adultery and Divorce*, 31–70.

she repents her misdeeds." The reason given for this leniency is that Benoite was clearly "in a frenzy and weak of spirit" (*Registres du Conseil*, vol. 39, fol. 109, 22 January 1545). The real conclusion of the trial of Benoite Ameaux, therefore, was that she was mentally ill and that this explained much of her talk and behavior. The punishment inflicted on Benoite Ameaux is, indeed, the treatment usually ordered by courts of the period for people regarded to be suffering from severe cases of mental illness. It was recognized that some people were so ill mentally that they had to be restrained, for both their own safety and the safety of others. And yet there were no institutions equipped to handle them. So it was usually considered that they be confined, by force if necessary, often in the homes of relatives, as long as symptoms of their mental illness remained evident, for life if necessary.[60]

Actually, poor Benoyte (or Benoite) was released from prison after only a few months. The Small Council recommended to the Council of Two Hundred that petitions—both from her and from her relatives—be accepted for her being set free. It was promised that Benoyte would continually remain in her bedroom, "so as not to give scandal to others."[61] By this time, her husband, Pierre, was remarried and was a member of the Small Council.

Another couple fought over money, and the Consistory advised the husband to come to a fair understanding on finances with his wife.[62] There were other arguments over money.[63] In another case, a wife was told to be submissive to her husband and to stop doing things to make him angry.[64] Sometimes the reasons for the quarrels were not specified, but the couple were exhorted "to live together in good peace."[65] In another case, a man beat his wife because she was always getting into conflicts with other people.[66] In one case, a husband was angry because his wife would not keep the house clean.[67]

---

60. Kingdon, *Adultery and Divorce*, 60 with 193n43.
61. Kingdon, *Adultery and Divorce*, 62, 63.
62. *Registres*, 1:110.
63. *Registres*, 1:308.
64. *Registres*, 1:168.
65. *Registres*, 1:180.
66. *Registres*, 1:104.
67. *Registres*, 1:93.

At times, parents fought over children.[68] On occasion, the Consistory called in the parents for not disciplining their children and failing to train them in good morals.[69] One widow was called in and told to control her children.[70] But the elders wished to help by having her bring her disobedient son to them after the sermon for consultation and reconciliation with his mother.

Jeffrey Watt has written an intriguing article in which he states that "Luther, Calvin, and other reformers definitely encouraged religious education in the home, promoting private family devotions and exhorting parents to lead the religious education of their children."[71] He notes moreover that "on 21 May 1536, at the same time that Geneva opted for the Reformation, the General Council ordered mandatory elementary education, a goal that would not be met for centuries."[72] And the founding of the Academy of Geneva late in Calvin's career showed his commitment to godly education at all levels, including that of the university.

But possibly the most important contribution of Calvin to the life of the youth in Geneva was his many sermons. As Barbara Pitkin has pointed out: "It is in the pulpit that Calvin often addresses such practical concerns as child rearing."[73] That was one good reason among others why the Consistory insisted that troubled families more faithfully attend the regular sermon.

I might add that his pulpit advice on handling children is a species of the general principle of Reformational Christianity that much (though by no means all) pastoral counseling is done through the sermon. Great twentieth-century preachers and pastors in the Calvinist tradition such as D. Martyn Lloyd-Jones (1899–1981) of Westminster Chapel in London and William Still (1911–1997) of Gilcomston South Church of Scotland in Aberdeen taught and fruitfully exemplified this same principle. In his fascinating *Preaching and Preachers*, Lloyd-

---

68. *Registres*, 1:254.

69. *Registres*, 1:154, 281.

70. *Registres*, 1:264.

71. Jeffrey R. Watt, "Calvinism, Childhood, and Education: The Evidence from the Genevan Consistory," *SCJ* 33, no. 2 (2002): 445.

72. Watt, "Calvinism, Childhood, and Education," 449.

73. Barbara Pitkin, "Children and the Church in Calvin's Geneva," in *Calvin and the Church: Papers Presented at the 13th Colloquium of the Calvin Studies Society, May 24–26, 2001*, ed. David Foxgrover (Grand Rapids, MI: Calvin Studies Society, 2002), 146.

Jones frequently discusses how most of his counseling work was handled in the pulpit (although his two-volume biography by Iain Murray shows how very much time he gave to counseling needy individuals).[74] The same principle is true of William Still, as he explains in his lectures to theological students, *The Work of the Pastor*.[75] He, too, I can personally testify, gave immense amounts of time to people who wished his advice on their problems. Similarly, we will not grasp the immense influence of Calvin as pastor, unless we understand how much of his preaching actually handled pastoral issues (though his biographies also demonstrate the willingness of this hard-worked man to talk to his people one-on-one).

This direct relation of preaching to the solution of people's sins, difficulties, and challenges is a prime reason why until recent years, so many churches in the Calvinist tradition insisted on holding two preaching services (morning and evening) each Sunday and another one (for both prayer and preaching) on Wednesday night. One service per week was felt to be insufficient to help people know which truths of the sixty-six books of Holy Scripture to apply to the daily demands of their lives in a complex world. In this frequency of preaching, thousands of congregations were true heirs of Calvin, whose sermons continually dealt with nearly every kind of pastoral issue, as one can find from reading them.

One of the most intriguing subjects is what we now call "anger management." I counted at least nine or ten cases dealing with that problem, which we may think exists only in our highly pressured times. One couple got angry whenever one of them lost something. The Consistory called for them to live in peace and to attend the sermons.[76] One man said that he did not get angry with his mother but was frequently angry with his wife.[77] The elders told him to be reconciled with his wife

---

74. D. Martyn Lloyd-Jones, *Preaching and Preachers* (Grand Rapids, MI: Zondervan, 1970); Iain H. Murray, *D. Martyn Lloyd-Jones: The First Forty Years, 1899–1939* (Edinburgh: Banner of Truth, 1982); Murray, *D. Martyn Lloyd-Jones: The Fight of Faith, 1939–1981* (Edinburgh: Banner of Truth, 1990).

75. William Still, *The Work of the Pastor* (1976; repr., Fearn, Ross-shire, Scotland: Christian Focus, 1996); see also the discussion in Nigel M. de S. Cameron and Sinclair B. Ferguson, eds., *Pulpit and People: Essays in Honour of William Still on His 75th Birthday* (Edinburgh: Rutherford House, 1986).

76. *Registres*, 1:170.

77. *Registres*, 1:195.

and to attend the sermons. A widowed mother and her daughters were said to have a disordered house owing to their frequent anger.[78] One man admitted that he got very angry with his wife but denied ever having beaten her.[79] One woman was furious with her husband because he owed her some money that he had not paid back.[80] A widow was infuriated with her children for wasting time.[81] A man was angry with his wife for spending so much time with her mother.[82] Always the Consistory advised them to make things right, to forgive and live in peace, and to attend the sermons. Serious punitive actions were not very often taken against them, but rather they were held to a high moral standard of forgiveness, kindness, and personal restraint in a God-centered context.

Sometimes marital anger descended into violent action. Many cases of wife abuse came before the Consistory (or even the Small Council). The council punished a man for abusing his wife.[83] A minister was actually deposed for mistreating his wife.[84] One violent husband was sent to the council for having put out his wife's eye.[85] One mistreated wife was asked to return to her husband (from her father's house) to give him another chance. The elders admonished him henceforward to treat her well and to live in good peace with her.[86] One man slapped his wife for having cursed him. The elders told them to be reconciled and to live together in peace.[87] Another man admitted that he had been angry with his wife but denied that he had actually thrown her out the window.[88] In another case, a man slapped his wife, and she hit him in the stomach with her fist.[89] A different couple had fights because, according to the husband, the wife wanted to rule the roost. He was instructed to stop beating his wife, and she to submit to him.[90] Another violent man hit his wife with a rock.[91]

78. *Registres*, 1:201.
79. *Registres*, 1:211.
80. *Registres*, 1:214.
81. *Registres*, 1:224.
82. *Registres*, 1:368.
83. *Registres*, 1:78.
84. *Registres*, 1:88.
85. *Registres*, 1:104.
86. *Registres*, 1:174.
87. *Registres*, 1:228, 229.
88. *Registres*, 1:253, 354.
89. *Registres*, 1:301.
90. *Registres*, 1:303.
91. *Registres*, 1:316.

As would be expected, most spousal abuse was from the husband to the wife. But there are some interesting exceptions, showing that Geneva had at least a few who would fit the category of "battered husband" syndrome. One high-spirited woman threatened to cut her husband's nose off.[92] Another case was even worse. An angry or frustrated wife violently attacked her husband's anatomy.[93] If I described it, even the most sophisticated of people would be shocked!

The Consistory also had to deal with problems between parents and grown children. Someone's mother complained to the Consistory that her son (who was morally obligated to help support his mother) was sending his mother bad, cheap wine. The elders ordered him to start sending good wine![94] A grown son was rebuked for having been insolent to his father.[95] Other sons were told to give financial support to their elderly parents.[96] A woman was called in for having gotten into a fight with both her mother and grandmother![97] Bad relationships between grown siblings were dealt with by the elders.[98]

The elders without fail addressed the problems and called for true reconciliation within the family. In these cases (except for violence), they usually applied moral suasion, rather than sending them for legal action to the council, although in a number of cases they certainly did so. But always they told them to frequent the sermons.

Sermon Attendance

Some of the able scholars who have worked on these sources in Genevan and Calvinist history have expressed surprise at how the Consistory nearly always, no matter what the issue or problem before them, after addressing particular actions that must be carried out by the offender, told the offender to frequent the sermons faithfully.[99] Why?

Here we are taken to the very heart of the Reformation: revival of the church and transformation of life and of every relationship by the

92. *Registres*, 1:280.
93. *Registres*, 1:246.
94. *Registres*, 1:266, 267.
95. *Registres*, 1:72.
96. *Registres*, 1:98, 142, 143, 179, 218.
97. *Registres*, 1:235.
98. *Registres*, 1:53, 80, 205.
99. E.g., *Registres*, 1:15, 18, 30, 88, 89.

"ordinary means of grace." Calvin and most of the Reformers believed that many developments in medieval Catholicism had obscured the gospel of Christ, which comes to us primarily through the preaching of the word, the administration of the sacrament, congregational accountability (i.e., discipline), and also prayer. Calvin often said that the risen Christ rules his church through his written word and his Holy Spirit. Those conjoined realities make the Lord personally present to carry on his supernatural ministry of salvation and transformation until the end of time.

From that point of view, every problem can in principle begin to be worked out, if those who bear those burdens and sins submit themselves to the word of God in the Spirit of God. The Spirit-empowered explanation and application of the word is a way of strengthening our union with Christ so that we "walk in the light, as he is in the light" (1 John 1:7). It may certainly take a good while, but at length, grasping even something of the truth of God with a tender heart profoundly changes attitudes and liberates the soul from all sorts of oppression (including the worst possible oppression—that of the egocentric, unmortified self-life), and it equips one for fruitful Christian service in the most practical ways. The preaching of the word, in sum, is like the hands of God reshaping us from the inside out to love God above all and our neighbor as ourselves. That and that alone enables us to find the chief end of human life, which is "to glorify God and to enjoy him forever."[100]

Some people excused nonattendance at sermons on poor hearing, sick children, inability to remember what would be said, and so forth.[101] On occasion, women said that they did not have nice enough clothes to wear to church; that was the reason for their absence![102] One lady who was asked by the Consistory what she remembered of the sermon said that she had forgotten the content but that it was preached by "a pretty man with a beard" (*un joly homme barbu*)—namely, Calvin.[103]

What is clear is that thousands of people several times a week were hearing biblical preaching in the three churches of Geneva, and an

---

100. WSC 1.
101. *Registres*, 1:104, 114, 124, 136, 146.
102. *Registres*, 1:97, 223.
103. *Registres*, 1:278.

entire society was beginning to be gradually transformed. This shows that the Consistory's intrusive questioning of people over the years on what they remembered of the sermon at last had its good effect.[104]

Prayer

Another means of grace is prayer. It may come as a surprise that the traditional Protestant Wednesday night prayer meeting started in Geneva under Calvin's ministry.[105] I had always assumed that it came from seventeenth-century Puritan England or Presbyterian Scotland or perhaps from the eighteenth-century revivals in the Anglo-Saxon realm. But it is actually older and goes back to the very fount of the Reformation.

I cannot think that it is a mere coincidence that the powerful preaching and worldwide reforming influence of Geneva took place at a period when there was so much regular, fervent congregational prayer. They knew who God was and how he has promised to bless. That is why they prayed as they did, for they realized that God expects his people to plead his promises as the forerunner of his execution of those promises.

In addition to attendance at the public prayer meeting, the elders expected the people to be able to pray individually and in families. That is one reason why they required that at the very least, people would be able to recite the Lord's Prayer. A typical example is that of May 1544, when three persons were given one month to memorize this model prayer of all prayers.[106] And as we have already noted, daily family worship in every home was encouraged.[107]

Personal Christian Knowledge

The Consistory regularly quizzed people whether they knew the Lord's Prayer and the Apostles' Creed and whether they remembered anything from the sermons. The Consistory minutes indicate the specific detail that La Maurisaz Talluchete only knew one-fourth of the creed: she could get to "born of the Virgin Mary" and no further.[108] Anthoyne

---

104. E.g., *Registres*, 1:100, 101, 137, 195, 276.
105. *Registres*, 1:16, 91, 112.
106. *Registres*, 1:372.
107. Cf. Watt, "Calvinism, Childhood, and Education," 445.
108. *Registres*, 1:196.

Servoz was typical of many: he could recite the Lord's Prayer but not the creed.[109] Some claimed to have remembered parts of the sermon,[110] while others said they had forgotten.[111] One elderly woman blamed her inability to remember sermon content on her advanced age,[112] while another claimed to be only "a thick-head."[113]

It is significant to note that the Consistory did not require arcane "denominational" theology but rather the mainstream of the once-undivided Christian tradition. This indicates that Calvin saw himself not as an innovator but as a reformer of the Catholic tradition, and it was that tradition that he wished his people to know. That is why he wrote two catechisms and ran weekly catechism classes not only for children but also for adults whose knowledge of God's truth was thin or defective. This was especially the case with those suspected of "papist" sentiments. The Consistory required many people who were still stuck in Roman Catholic practices to attend catechism as well as sermons.[114] And constantly they admonished these people to buy Bibles and to read them.[115]

If space permitted, we could go into the kinds of Roman ideas and practices that the Consistory worked to root out.[116] By 1545 they had been largely successful through teaching and preaching, even more than through physical constraint (though that was not totally absent, for some people who refused to accept the Reformation were banished or otherwise disadvantaged). Yet most of the changed attitude of the vast majority of the Genevan population really does seem to have been in the main voluntary.

Sincerity of Life

In addition to the centralities of family and sexuality, the Consistory sought to bring people into line with God's holy law in terms of hon-

---

109. *Registres*, 1:15.
110. *Registres*, 1:137, 195, 276.
111. *Registres*, 1:101, 134.
112. *Registres*, 1:114.
113. *Registres*, 1:104.
114. E.g., *Registres*, 1:106, 140.
115. *Registres*, 1:32, 110, 127.
116. E.g., for prayers in Latin, see *Registres*, 1:106, 123, 140, 232, 322; for prayers to the Virgin, see *Registres*, 1:26, 36, 62, 63, 107, 112, 125, 182, 330; for controversies over (Catholic-type) baptismal names, see *Registres*, 1:252, 279; and for belief in salvation through both works and grace, see *Registres*, 1:214.

est business practice,[117] payment of debts,[118] faithful work, and personal diligence. In this last regard, they frequently rebuked wasting of time[119] and wasting of money.[120] Sometimes the Consistory appointed a *tuteur* to discipline the husband in properly managing the family's finances.[121] They also consistently insisted on the necessity of Christian people's exercising charity to the poor.[122] They sought to suppress tavern haunting and other ways of wasting the family's money.[123] But they also stood against avarice among their constituency.[124]

In other areas, they saw holiness as requiring the suppression of things that most of us fail to see as biblically mandated, such as plays,[125] dancing,[126] and card playing.[127] Some tavern keepers were instructed to buy a Bible for their guests to read rather than playing cards and dice.[128] It is also hard to know what to make of their denial of the legitimacy of usury (a position also generally held by medieval Catholicism).[129] Our modern world economy is based on a certain type of usury.[130] But we can heartily agree with them in seeking to suppress cursing and swearing and ugly talk.[131] Increasing crudeness in language is one of the plagues of our own time, even among church people. The Genevan Consistory never forbade drinking but did take action against serious drunkenness.[132]

Less familiar to us (though it is going to become far more familiar in this society, whether we like it or not) is their determination to stamp out magic and the occult. This requires more knowledge and thought than I am able to give it. All I will say is this: we should not automatically laugh it off as nothing but mere medieval superstition

---

117. *Registres*, 1:102, 343.
118. *Registres*, 1:280, 309.
119. *Registres*, 1:132, 270.
120. *Registres*, 1:274.
121. See Witte and Kingdon, *Sex, Marriage, and Family*, 385.
122. E.g., *Registres*, 1:35, 204.
123. *Registres*, 1:169, 353.
124. *Registres*, 1:222.
125. *Registres*, 1:xv.
126. *Registres*, 1:192, 261.
127. *Registres*, 1:10, 203.
128. *Registres*, 1:10.
129. *Registres*, 1:182, 183, 229, 238.
130. For a brief discussion of usury by Calvin, see *Calvin's Ecclesiastical Advice*, trans. Mary Beaty and Benjamin W. Farley (Edinburgh: T&T Clark, 1991), 139–43.
131. E.g., *Registres*, 1:117, 120, 127, 159, 164, 352.
132. *Registres*, 1:279, 280.

and hysteria (though no doubt, elements of that were not lacking among both Protestants and Catholics). But there is more to the malign side of spiritual powers than can be explained away by a facile assumption of materialism. One can go to the local bookstore and see whether they have more Christian books or new age and occult books.

A Community of Reconciliation

A close reading of the Consistory minutes will indicate that the widely held idea of Calvin and his followers as primarily harsh and unloving in their dealing with sinners is untenable. Certainly, the *Registres* do contain their share of hard questions and harsh sentences, but for the most part, the proceedings of the Genevan elders indicate a loving desire to see people sincerely reconciled with one another, whether warring spouses, parents and children, business associates, or neighbors. Often those who have been deeply offended are asked for the sake of Christ to forgo revenge.[133] They are told that they must forgive those who have done them wrong.[134] Guillaume Blant was told that "he must hold nothing against anyone, must forgive everyone."[135]

Especially was this the case as the city neared the administration of the Lord's Supper. Before the Lord's Supper in September 1542, the *dizeniers* (or those who watched over morals in the different neighborhoods) were told to bring together those who were at odds with each other, so they might be reconciled before receiving the Lord's Supper.[136] At another time, two women who had fallen out with each other were told to be reconciled so that they could receive Communion.[137] In August 1543, two well-known men who had cursed each other were exhorted "to forgive one another in order to receive the holy Supper of our Lord in a holy fashion, and to live in peace and good charity with one another."[138] In December of the same year, Pierre Joly and his wife were told that if they wished to receive Communion, they had to forgive everyone against whom they had anything whatsoever.[139]

---

133. *Registres*, 1:216, 217.
134. *Registres*, 1:29, 69.
135. *Registres*, 1:108.
136. *Registres*, 1:108.
137. *Registres*, 1:144.
138. *Registres*, 1:255.
139. *Registres*, 1:289.

This practice of serious reconciliation before the quarterly Communions became the mainstay of the Scottish Presbyterian tradition (although in the Highlands, Communion was often held only twice a year, or less). People in the Scottish congregations were to appear before the elders to receive a Communion token, admitting them to the Table. If the elders knew of any controversies in their lives, in family or community, the disagreeing parties were required to be reconciled before receiving a token. It would be hard to exaggerate the good effects this kind of accountability and call to reconciliation would have in a churchgoing community over the generations.[140]

Calvin and the elders of Geneva, in order to better achieve true reconciliation between enemies, asked that after the warring parties had spoken words of forgiveness, they touch one another. Here they showed keen psychological insight into the way we instinctively draw away from those who have hurt us (or whom we have hurt). A touch is a way of showing a new start; a willingness to come back together in renewed hope and trust. In May 1542, two disgruntled neighbors are said by the Consistory "to have pardoned one another and then to have touched one another."[141] A year later, two brothers who had fallen out accepted the call of the elders to forgive and forgo all vengeance. The minutes state rather movingly, "Having heard the holy doctrine, they pardoned one another, made peace together, and touched each other as a sign of peace."[142] In May 1544, two women who had sharp differences over a business deal, listened to the elders and "forgave one another and took each others' hand in a sign of peace."[143] Sometimes former enemies embraced one another before the elders.[144]

Thus, while Geneva, like all the rest of Western Europe at that time, did not lack certain elements of a police state, from reading the *Registres* one concludes that it was more than anything else a place of forgiveness, reconciliation, and new beginnings in imperfect human relationships. That may well be one of the reasons why so many thousands of emigrants willingly went into it during Calvin's

---

140. For an excellent study on these (and other) aspects of the Lord's Supper in historic Scottish practice, see Malcolm MacLean, *The Lord's Supper* (Fearn, Ross-shire, Scotland: Mentor, 2009).
141. *Registres*, 1:64.
142. *Registres*, 1:206.
143. *Registres*, 1:370.
144. Cf. Lambert and Watt, introduction to *Registres*, 1:xvii.

later ministry.[145] Because of the vital Christianity they saw being lived out there, they were inspired to expand it elsewhere, so that Geneva became (in the words of Heiko Oberman) "a bridgehead for the expansion of the kingdom of Christ."[146] Jean-Marc Berthoud devotes an entire volume to the moral influence of Calvin and Geneva in the explosive spread of Reformed Christianity in France in the 1560s.[147] And others have spoken of how the godly atmosphere of Geneva was taken by those who experienced it to the British Isles and later to the American colonies.[148] For all Geneva's stringency, there had to have been something powerfully attractive in the way Calvinism was lived out in the sixteenth century, for otherwise, it could not have won the hearts of millions and expanded across the nations the way it did.

Godly Examples for a Godly Society

In the expansion of true religion in the earth, nothing is more important than people seeing flesh-and-blood examples of sincere godliness. I think that Ronald Wallace is right in emphasizing how Calvin expected the church to be the transforming agent for godly change in Geneva and then for Geneva to become "a city set on a hill" for the rest of Europe.[149]

Holy Scripture is full of the power of good example as a powerful agent of societal change. Israel as the Lord's wife was an example of the blessing of belonging to him, and in her apostasy was a warning of the disaster of religious whoredom. Think of how this is worked out in Hosea, Isaiah, Jeremiah, and Malachi, among others. In the New Testament, the church as the bride of Christ is the prime example of the beauty of a holy love relationship to the Lord (as we are shown, for instance, in Eph. 5). And the seven churches of Asia in the

---

145. See the discussion of reasons for this huge emigration to Calvin's Geneva in Ernst Pfisterer, *Calvin's Wirken in Genf: Neu geprüft und in Einzelbildern dargestellt*, ZZ 5 (Neukirchen: Buchhandlung des Erziehungsvereins, 1940), 18.

146. Heiko A. Oberman, *The Reformation: Roots and Ramifications* (Grand Rapids, MI: Eerdmans, 1994), 216.

147. Jean-Marc Berthoud, *Calvin et la France: Genève et le Déploiement de la Réforme au XVIe Siècle* (Lausanne: L'Age d'Homme, 1999).

148. See Douglas F. Kelly, *The Emergence of Liberty in the Modern World: The Influence of Calvin on Five Governments from the 16th through 18th Centuries; Calvin's Geneva, Huguenot France, Knox's Scotland, Puritan England, Colonial America* (Phillipsburg, NJ: P&R, 1992).

149. See his discussion on Calvin's achievements in Geneva. Wallace, *Calvin, Geneva and the Reformation*, 110–28.

early chapters of Revelation show how the responses to Christ's love of these churches—both good and bad—provide vivid examples for all future history of what it means to keep or break covenant with the Lord.

The New Testament clearly makes ministers and elders prime examples of true Christianity to the society around them; that is one of their major functions in facilitating the expansion of the gospel. First Timothy 3:7 requires that a bishop "have a good report of them which are without" (KJV). Paul charges Timothy, "Let no one despise you for your youth, but set the believers an example in speech, in conduct, in love, in faith, in purity" (1 Tim. 4:12).

With this biblical background in mind, the elders had to take an appropriate oath. This oath was put to the Consistory on October 12, 1542, and all of them agreed to it. It shows how the elders, in company with the ministers, were called above all else to be godly examples in order to form a godly society:

Called into the Consistory in order to equip the church to watch over those who live badly in their villages, and to conserve the holy church, in order to demonstrate a good example to others, who would otherwise go astray in the church, if they do not carefully hear the Word of God. It is understood that the elders must be honest and peaceful as a good example to others, that they must warn them along with the minister of the Word of God, and that thus they do their duty as well as the others. And no one must be spared from being instructed after dinner; neither their families, wives, children, or servants. And that they bring the erring to the Consistory, including those who still follow some papal superstitions from older times. And they must seriously remonstrate with keepers of taverns, blasphemers, and others who live badly; also with those who hold bitterness or hatred against others, as well as people who rebel against the Word of God and the honour of justice as far as possible. The Consistory is of the view that since they are here, one should present them to the magistrate to be administered the oath which they are to keep as has been explained.[150]

---

150. *Registres*, 1:126–27.

It is clear that Calvin knew these men well, as a faithful pastor and colleague would, for on his deathbed he said to many of them, "I know the disposition and character of each of you."[151] And he had learned his flock, in sickness and in health, in season and out of season. He had worn himself out at age fifty-five by constantly giving of himself to them in preaching, visiting, and pastoral service.

Calvin carried out as a pastor what he had written in his 1538 catechism:

> For however others may appraise it, we certainly do not think our function confined within such narrow limits that, having assembled for preaching and as it were having discharged one's duty, one is allowed to be idle. Those whose blood is required of us if it should fail through our idleness ought to be cared for much more closely and with more vigilant effort.[152]

Likewise, his old mentor in Strasbourg, Martin Bucer, had written him in 1547, "I must greatly praise you for visiting the brethren, for you know with what pain I have observed that the duty of piety and love, on the part of the clergy—to visit, warn, and comfort the people—is greatly neglected."[153]

A colleague who knew Calvin well, Nicholas Des Gallars, described his pastoral sensitivity in dealing with so many people:

> No words of mine can declare the fidelity and prudence with which he gave counsel. The kindness with which he received all who came to him, the clearness and promptitude with which he replied to those who asked his opinion on the most important questions, and the ability with which he disentangled the difficulties and problems which were laid before him. Nor can I express the gentleness with which he could comfort the afflicted and raise the fallen and distressed.[154]

---

151. Quoted in Theodore Beza, *Life of John Calvin*, trans. Henry Beveridge, in *Tracts and Treatises*, 1:cxxx.

152. John Calvin, *Calvin's Catechism of 1538*, trans. Ford Lewis Battles, in I. John Hesselink, *Calvin's First Catechism: A Commentary*, CSRT (Louisville: Westminster John Knox, 1997), 3; cf. CO, 5:319. See also the citation in Wallace, *Calvin, Geneva and the Reformation*, 173.

153. Quoted in Wallace, *Calvin, Geneva and the Reformation*, 173n21.

154. Nicholas Des Gallars to Crespin, preface to *Commentary on Isaiah*, in CO, 36:n.p.

In the interests of realism, let me add here that Calvin well knew that he was far from perfect. On his deathbed, he apologized to his colleagues of church and state for his irascibility. Probably he had made some progress over the years in controlling his temper but never entirely achieved it. At times, even for the sixteenth century, he could be very harsh to opponents.

Yet the epochal fruitfulness of his life shows that God does use cracked, flawed vessels of clay to show, as Paul says in 2 Corinthians 4:7, that the transcendent power comes from God and not from the human vessel. Calvin's preaching and pastoral ministry was a rare combination of sharp irritability and sweet, humble consecration. It should encourage us to think that one does not have to possess sinless perfection to be widely used as a good Christian pastor.

I believe that the fruitfulness of Calvin's pastoral ministry demonstrates that the resurrection power of Christ in our lives is far greater than the fallenness and deadness in us, so that time and again, Christian character wins out over the indwelling sin and self-centered behavior that accompany us in what Saint Paul terms "the body of this death" (Rom. 7:24 KJV). Moral victories over self are continually won in the pastoral ministry as we seek—day and night—to keep our hearts and minds on the crucified, risen Christ, to whom we are united by the Holy Spirit. Our personal imperfections will not keep him from shining through, if only we will sincerely say with Calvin, *Cor meum tibi offero, Domine, prompte et sincere in opera domini* ("Lord, I offer my heart to thee, promptly and sincerely in thy work").

Of course, Calvin's unique genius and his unparalleled self-discipline entered into the historic effectiveness of his preaching and pastorate. All the greatest theologians—Athanasius, Augustine, Anselm, Aquinas, and Calvin—were gifted with intellectual genius, and their lives were marked by tremendous self-discipline. But it is clear that Calvin, simply by virtue of superior intellectual gifts and massively hard work, could still never have achieved such heights for the Lord had he not stayed in close fellowship with that good shepherd, who "giveth his life for the sheep" (John 10:11 KJV). One of the reasons why Calvin eschewed all pomp, show, and pretense was in the interests of keeping his life "hidden with Christ in God" (Col. 3:3), for that secret reality is far better than any sort of externally impressive religiosity (and indeed, is inconsistent with it). The controlling reality of his self-sacrifice in union with the risen Christ influenced elders, magistrates, and the general population at a deeper level than could be resisted, resulting in deep and wide societal transformation.

That is no doubt why Calvin's younger colleague John Knox, the mighty Reformer of Scotland, spoke of Geneva as "the most perfect school of Christ since the days of the apostles."[155] God is willing and able to build other such schools across the earth, for his saving work goes on half a millennium after Calvin's birth in 1509.

Still the Lord is looking for imperfectly sanctified people who are determined "to know nothing . . . except Jesus Christ and him crucified" (1 Cor. 2:2). Still the words of 2 Chronicles 16:9 are true: "For the eyes of the LORD run to and fro throughout the whole earth, to shew himself strong in the behalf of them whose heart is perfect toward him" (KJV)—an imputed perfection, of course! God "raiseth up the poor out of the dust, and lifteth the needy out of the dunghill; that he may set him with princes, even with the princes of his people" (Ps. 113:7–8 KJV). And still it is true that for those little folk who will open their ears and attune their hearts, God will do something very great. Psalm 68:11–13 explains, "The Lord gave the word; great was the company of those that published it. . . . Though ye have lien among the pots, yet shall ye be as the wings of a dove covered with silver, and her feathers with yellow gold" (KJV). The divine grace that worked in Calvin is still available, for God's strength is always made perfect in our weakness.

---

155. Quoted in George D. Henderson, *Presbyterianism* (Aberdeen: Aberdeen University Press, 1954), 59.

5

Calvin and Friends

W. Robert Godfrey

We have good reason to glory before God and have the clearest evidence to show to men that our alliance and friendship have been entirely consecrated to Christ's name, have hitherto been profitable to His Church, and have no other aim than that all men should be at one with us in Him.

—John Calvin, dedication to Guillaume Farel and Pierre Viret, *Commentary on Titus*

The Humanity of Calvin?

John Calvin was one of the greatest theologians and scholars of the Reformation era. His *Institutes of the Christian Religion* and his biblical commentaries have been studied and treasured for centuries. His thought has been so revered that sometimes Calvin has been treated simply as a great mind—almost a disembodied mind. Of what other theologian would anyone have thought to write a book titled *The Humanity of Calvin*,[1] as if his humanity were somehow in doubt?

---

1. Richard Stauffer, *L'humanité de Calvin* (Neuchâtel: Delachaux et Niestlé, 1964).

The humanity of Calvin appears clearly in the network of friends that he had throughout his life, with whom he sought to advance the cause of reforming the church. For all the profundity of Calvin's thought, he was first and foremost a reformer and pastor. The work of reforming and pastoring the church was not the work of one man or one city. It was the work of many people in many cities and countries. In that work, Calvin had many friends.

Friendship is fascinating and elusive, almost universally experienced but very difficult to define. Friendship between two people rests on several factors, not all of equal importance in every friendship. First, friendship can truly form only when two people have some time together. Although Calvin and Philipp Melanchthon (1497–1560) met only a few times and relatively briefly, they could not have been the friends they were without those meetings. Second, friendship must rest on a measure of admiration for one another and on pleasure in one another's company. Third, friendship requires some common interests and goals. Fourth, it must be able to express itself honestly, including the freedom to criticize the friend. Finally, friendship must offer a measure of encouragement and the bearing of burdens for one another. Every true friendship must have these qualities to some extent.

The ancient Roman Cicero, carefully studied by young Renaissance scholars like John Calvin for his natural wisdom and eloquence, wrote a treatise on friendship, *De Amicitia*. One of his reflections summarized the qualities of friendship brilliantly:

> For friendship is nothing else than an accord in all things, human and divine, conjoined with mutual goodwill and affection. . . . What is sweeter than to have someone with whom you may dare discuss anything as if you were communing with yourself? . . . For friendship adds a brighter radiance to prosperity and lessens the burden of adversity by dividing and sharing it.[2]

Calvin had such friends.

While it is easy to reconstruct from the historical record the names and general relationship of many of Calvin's friends, it is not easy to

---

2. Cicero, *De Amicitia*, LCL 154 (Cambridge, MA: Harvard University Press, 1923), 131–32.

examine in detail the character and course of these friendships. For someone who lived five hundred years ago, what record of friendship can we expect to find? The fullest record is preserved for us in letters, but letters are necessarily very limited. Letters tell us little about the friends who lived geographically near Calvin. For example, in a letter to Theodore Beza, written August 27, 1561, Calvin expressed his grief on the occasion of the death of his close friend and neighbor in Geneva for eleven years Guillaume de Trie, Seigneur de Varennes. Calvin wrote,

> I am obliged to dictate this letter to you from bed, and in the deepest affliction from the loss of my dear friend De Varennes, who has hitherto been my principal stay and comfort in all my troubles. One thing affords me no slight consolation in my sorrow, which is that nothing could have been more calm than the manner of his death, which he seemed to invite with outstretched arms as cheerfully as if it had been some delicious enjoyment. . . . All his thoughts and conversation turned only on eternal happiness. . . . He then is happy—I wretched.[3]

Although de Varennes was a close friend and neighbor of Calvin in Geneva from 1549 to 1561, the historical record leaves us largely ignorant of the details of their friendship.

Even where we have letters, they are not as revealing as we might wish. Letter writers in the sixteenth century knew that letters were sometimes intercepted by unintended readers and so did not always state everything on their minds. For example, Calvin wrote to Guillaume Farel in 1547 relating some of his troubles in Geneva. Then he added that when Farel came to Geneva, he "would hear everything that cannot be committed to writing."[4] Although Calvin may have been particularly cautious as a letter writer, his friend Pierre Viret complained that Calvin was very careless with letters written to him. In 1556 Viret wrote to Calvin,

> For you, when we write to you, do not be so negligent and do not leave our letters lying around as you often do. Because, when I came to you to stay with you, I have often taken my letters away with me when I found them scattered all over the house. You know

3. Calvin to Theodore Beza, August 27, 1561, in *Letters*, 4:215–16.
4. Calvin to Guillaume Farel, August 21, 1547, in *Letters*, 2:138.

the kind of men with whom we have had trouble. Destroy these papers, or at least take good care of them.[5]

Another complication with sixteenth-century letters is a certain epistolary convention in which friendship and devotion are expressed sometimes more strongly than they are felt. We must sometimes look below the surface politeness to evaluate the real closeness of the friendship.

Despite the limits of letters as a record of friendship, they reveal many aspects of Calvin's feelings, frustrations, and joys in cooperating with his friends in the work of reformation. The humanity of Calvin in its strengths and weaknesses shines in these letters, and the importance of friends to him personally and in his work becomes clear. While his letters do not allow us to overhear Calvin's most intimate conversations with his friends, they do permit us to experience something of his relationships with his friends.

While Calvin certainly had a number of friends throughout his life,[6] those friendships were still marked by diverse characteristics. Some friendships, while having a personal dimension, were pursued for strategic reasons to advance the Reformation—such as those with the Reformers Philipp Melanchthon and Heinrich Bullinger. Other friendships were strong for a time but for a variety of reasons did not continue. Here we can think of Louis du Tillet, a friend from university days, and Jacques de Bourgogne, Seigneur de Falais, a very distinguished religious refugee. Still other friendships were of a more personal and intimate kind, such as those with Guillaume Farel, Pierre Viret, and Theodore Beza. Calvin had many more friends than these, of course, but these represent key relationships in his life. In what follows, we let Calvin speak at length in his own words to hear the variety of ways in which he expressed himself to his friends.

---

5. Cited in Robert D. Linder, "Brothers in Christ: Pierre Viret and John Calvin as Soul-Mates and Co-Laborers in the Work of the Reformation," *Calvin and Spirituality: Papers Presented at the 10th Colloquium of the Calvin Studies Society, May 18–20, 1995, Calvin Theological Seminary; Calvin and His Contemporaries: Colleagues, Friends and Conflicts: Papers Presented at the 11th Colloquium of the Calvin Studies Society, April 24–26, 1997, Louisville Theological Seminary,* ed. David Foxgrover, CSSP 1995, 1997 (Grand Rapids, MI: Calvin Studies Society, 1998), 151.

6. See, for example, Carter Lindberg, ed., *The Reformation Theologians: An Introduction to Theology in the Early Modern Period,* Great Theologians (Oxford: Blackwell, 2002); David C. Steinmetz, *Reformers in the Wings: From Geiler von Kaysersberg to Theodore Beza,* 2nd ed. (Oxford: Oxford University Press, 2001); M. A. van den Berg, *Vrienden van Calvijn: Een amicale biografie* (Utrecht: De Banier, 2006).

Strategic Friends

Philipp Melanchthon

Calvin first met Philipp Melanchthon in 1539 in Frankfurt at a conference to discuss the resolution of the religious divisions in the Holy Roman Empire. Calvin was at that time exiled from Geneva and ministering in Strasbourg. While Calvin was young and relatively unknown, Melanchthon was famous—as Martin Luther's close friend and ally, as the author of the Reformation's first true systematic theology, his *Loci Communes*, and as a remarkable commentator, scholar, and educator. They seem to have developed a genuine appreciation of one another, reinforced by other meetings during the time Calvin remained in Strasbourg and sustained throughout the rest of Melanchthon's life by occasional correspondence.[7]

In addition to Calvin's personal affection for Melanchthon, he believed that Melanchthon was a crucial figure in the desired reconciliation of the Lutherans and the Reformed, especially in the understanding of the Lord's Supper. Calvin hoped that Melanchthon's stature as a theologian and a friend of Luther would enable him to lead other sensible Lutherans into eucharistic unity with the Reformed. Calvin was frustrated by Melanchthon's timidity and ultimate failure in this matter, but he never really understood how precarious Melanchthon's influence was with the strict Lutherans. The correspondence of Calvin to Melanchthon was not extensive—about twelve letters—but it was significant.

Calvin expressed, no doubt in somewhat exaggerated terms, his real appreciation for Melanchthon and desire to learn from him:

> Would, indeed, as you observe, that we could oftener converse together, were it only by letter. To you, indeed, that would be no advantage; to me, however, nothing in this world could be more desirable than to take solace in the mild and gentle spirit of your correspondence . . . because I am so far removed from yourself and a few others, and therefore am deprived of that sort of comfort and consolation which would prove a special help to me. . . .

---

7. See Timothy Wengert, "'We Will Feast Together in Heaven Forever': The Epistolary Friendship of John Calvin and Philip Melanchthon," in *Melanchthon in Europe: His Work and Influence beyond Wittenberg*, ed. Karin Maag, TSRPRT (Grand Rapids, MI: Baker Academic, 1999), 19–44.

> This comfort we have at least, of which no far distant separation
> can deprive us,—I mean, that resting content with this fellowship
> which Christ hath consecrated with his own blood, and hath also
> confirmed and sealed by his blessed Spirit in our hearts, while we
> live on the earth, we may cheer each other with that blessed hope
> to which your letter calls us, that in heaven above we shall dwell
> for ever, where we shall rejoice in love and in continuance of our
> friendship.[8]

He even made a little joke in this letter about Melanchthon's unpublished commentary on Daniel: "I wonder what can be the reason why
you keep your *Daniel* a sealed book at home."[9] While Calvin was not
famous for his humor, he did allow it to show occasionally in letters
to his friends.

Calvin could also be sharply critical with Melanchthon, as in this
letter reacting to Melanchthon's acceptance of the Augsburg Interim,
imposed on Protestants by Emperor Charles V:

> In the mean while, let it be well understood, that in openly ad-
> monishing you, I am discharging the duty of a true friend; and if
> I employ a little more severity than usual, do not think that it is
> owing to any diminution of my old affection and esteem for you.
> . . . This is the sum of your defence: that provided purity of doc-
> trine be retained, externals should not be pertinaciously contended
> for. . . . In our day, indeed, the enemy has not troubled us about
> circumcision, but that they may not leave us anything pure, they
> are tainting both doctrine and every exercise of worship with their
> putrid leaven. . . . Lest you may perhaps have forgotten what I
> once said to you, I now remind you of it, namely, that we consider
> our ink too precious if we hesitate to bear testimony in writing to
> those things which so many of the flock are daily sealing with their
> blood. . . . Your position is different from that of many, as yourself
> [*sic*] are aware. For the trepidation of a general or leader is more
> dishonourable than the flight of a whole herd of private soldiers.
> Accordingly, while the timidity of others may be overlooked, unless
> you give invariable evidence of unflinching steadfastness, all will

---

8. Calvin to Philipp Melanchthon, February 16, 1543, in *Letters*, 1:373–74.
9. Calvin to Philipp Melanchthon, February 16, 1543, in *Letters*, 1:376.

say that vacillation in such a man must not be tolerated. . . . You know why I am so vehement. I had rather die with you a hundred times, than see you survive the doctrines surrendered by you. . . . Pardon me for loading your breast with these miserable, though ineffectual groans.[10]

Calvin began his rebuke with genuine protestations of friendship but ended it with an indirect yet severe reminder: "Multitudes, to avoid idolatry in France, are making choice of a voluntary exile among us."[11] Calvin clearly thought that Melanchthon should do the same.

Despite their differences, Calvin wrote as a friend in 1558 to comfort Melanchthon in the face of criticism from his former students, saying that he was "a man who had discharged with the highest fidelity and diligence the functions of a teacher, and also deserved the highest honours from the whole church." Even in this comforting letter, though, he expressed his disappointment that Melanchthon had not worked more publicly to promote unity on the Lord's Supper:

I shall not for all that cease to press towards the mark at which I had begun to aim; in the controversy respecting the Lord's Supper, not only your enemies traduce what they calumniously style your weakness, but your best friends also, and those who cherish you with the pious feelings which you deserve, would wish that the flame of your zeal burned more brightly, of which we behold but some feeble sparks, and thus it is that these pigmies strut like giants. Whatever happen [sic], let us cultivate with sincerity a fraternal affection towards each other, of which no wiles of Satan shall ever burst asunder the ties.[12]

Another area where Calvin differed from Melanchthon was on the important doctrine of predestination. The relative mildness of Calvin's critique of Melanchthon on this doctrine reflected Calvin's patience and abiding friendship with Melanchthon as well as his belief that Melanchthon might play a key ecumenical role in the Protestant cause. Still, his rather gentle criticism of Melanchthon on predestination[13] is

---

10. Calvin to Philipp Melanchthon, June 18, 1550, in *Letters*, 2:271–74.
11. Calvin to Philipp Melanchthon, June 18, 1550, in *Letters*, 2:275.
12. Calvin to Philipp Melanchthon, November 19, 1558, in *Letters*, 3:484.
13. See, for example, Calvin to Philipp Melanchthon, November 28, 1552, in *Letters*, 2:379–81.

surprising in light of the severe reactions of Calvin to Jerome Bolsec (ca. 1524–1584) and Albert Pighius (ca. 1490–1542) on predestination. Randall Zachman, drawing on the work of Gary Remer, has suggested that Calvin was following a rhetorical tradition well known since the days of Cicero.[14]

Cicero divided spoken communication into two categories:

The classification of discourse [*orationis*] is a two-fold one— conversation [*sermo*], on the one side; oratory [*contentio*], on the other—there can be no doubt that of the two this debating power (for that is what we mean by eloquence) counts for more toward the attainment of glory; and yet, it is not easy to say how far an affable and courteous manner in conversation may go toward winning the affections.[15]

Cicero expanded on this distinction more fully:

The power of speech [*orationis*] in the attainment of propriety is great, and its function is twofold: the first is oratory [*contentionis*]; the second, conversation [*sermonis*]. Oratory is the kind of discourse to be employed in pleadings in court and speeches in popular assemblies and in the senate; conversation should find its natural place in social gatherings, in informal discussions, and in intercourse with friends; it should also seek admission at dinners. There are rules for oratory laid down by rhetoricians; there are none for conversation; and yet I know not why there should not be. . . .

Conversation, then, in which the Socratics are the best models, should have these qualities. It should be easy and not in the least dogmatic; it should have the spice of wit. And the one who engages in conversation should not debar others from participating in it, as if he were entering upon a private monopoly; but, as in other things, so in a general conversation he should think it not unfair for each to have his turn. He should observe, first and foremost,

---

14. See Randall C. Zachman, "The Conciliating Theology of John Calvin: Dialogue among Friends," in *Conciliation and Confession: The Struggle for Unity in the Age of Reform, 1415– 1648*, ed. Howard P. Louthan and Randall C. Zachman (Notre Dame, IN: University of Notre Dame Press, 2004), 91, drawing on Gary Remer, *Humanism and the Rhetoric of Toleration* (University Park, PA: Penn State University Press, 1996).

15. Cicero, *De Officiis*, 2.48, LCL 30 (Cambridge, MA: Harvard University Press, 1913), 217.

what the subject of conversation is. If it is grave, he should treat it with seriousness; if humorous, with wit. And above all, he should be on the watch that his conversation shall not betray some defect in his character. . . .

But as we have a most excellent rule for every phase of life, to avoid exhibitions of passion, that is, mental excitement that is excessive and uncontrolled by reason; so our conversation ought to be free from such emotions: let there be no exhibition of anger or inordinate desire, of indolence or indifference, or anything of the kind. We must also take the greatest care to show courtesy and consideration toward those with whom we converse.[16]

At the risk of oversimplification, we might say that Cicero saw oratory as a way to demolish enemies and conversation as a way to win friends.

Calvin did indeed seem to use this distinction. Those whom he considered wicked and dangerous enemies of the truth, like Bolsec and Pighius, he attacked with all the vehemence of his considerable eloquence and learning. Those whom he considered good and faithful, even if seriously flawed, like Melanchthon, he treated with respect and careful discussion. Melanchthon remained a friend with whom Calvin carried on Christian conversation.

Heinrich Bullinger

Calvin cultivated another strategic friendship with Heinrich Bullinger.[17] Calvin had met Bullinger while living in Basel in 1535 and writing the first edition of his *Institutes*. This was a year in which Calvin met several future close friends, including Viret and Farel.

In 1535 Bullinger had already replaced Huldrych Zwingli as the principal minister in Zurich and would become a key figure in Calvin's developing efforts to unify the Reformation cause. Bullinger was a strong defender of Zwingli's heritage, including his approach to the Lord's Supper. He was an influential preacher and theologian who often frustrated Calvin by failing to support him strongly on predestination and on the freedom of the church to discipline sinners.

16. Cicero, *De Officiis*, 1.132, 134, 135, LCL 30, 135–39.
17. See Aurelio A. Garcia, "Bullinger's Friendship with Calvin: Loving One Another and Edifying the Churches," in Foxgrover, *Calvin and Spirituality; Calvin and His Contemporaries*, 119–33.

Calvin seemed to regard Melanchthon personally more highly than Bullinger, just as he admired Luther more than Zwingli. But he was able to cooperate more successfully with Bullinger in unifying and advancing the cause of the Reformation.

Calvin wrote Bullinger early in his career, expressing his eager desire for a sincere alliance between them:

> What ought we rather, dear Bullinger, to correspond about at this time than the preserving and confirming, by every possible means in our power, brotherly kindness among ourselves? We see indeed of how much importance that is, not only on our own account, but for the sake of the whole body of professing Christians everywhere, that all those on whom the Lord has laid any personal charge in the ordering of his Church, should agree together in a sincere and cordial understanding. Indeed, Satan himself perceives that very clearly, who while he plots, by every method he can devise, the ruin of Christ's kingdom, plies none more earnestly with all his might, than to sow division and discord among us, or somehow at least to estrange the one from the other. . . . Our friendship, I trust, in virtue of the happy auspices which presided at its commencement, and resting as it does on so solid a foundation, will continue firm and entire to the last. For myself, assuredly, so far as depends upon me, I undertake to persevere in maintaining it firm and unimpaired, because, indeed, I have always very much deferred to you. I have also, as was meet and reasonable, embraced you with singular delight, nor will I ever cease to entertain that affection. Between this church and yours, although I do not see that there really exists any disagreement or secret grudge, yet I might wish there was a closer connection or rather relationship.[18]

In writing this way from his exile in Strasbourg, Calvin was seeking to promote closer Protestant unity, an issue close to the heart of Strasbourg's lead pastor and Calvin's mentor, Martin Bucer.

Some years later, when Bullinger was unhappy with the criticisms Calvin had sent him on his treatise on the sacraments, Calvin replied that he wanted harmony and agreement. He also, however, added,

---

18. Calvin to Heinrich Bullinger, March 12, 1539, in *Letters*, 1:113–14.

I made a note of those points in your book that did not satisfy myself, or that might prove unsatisfactory to others, or such as I thought might not meet the approbation of the pious and learned. I did that at your request. I discharged the duty of a friend; if you think differently, you are at liberty to do so, as far as I am concerned.[19]

Calvin reminded him that true friends must from time to time criticize one another.

Calvin also complained rather sharply to Bullinger for failing to support Calvin fully and clearly in his contest with Bolsec. After explaining the problems with the character and teaching of Bolsec, Calvin wrote,

Now that your answer has been ambiguous, the sorry wretch is making his boast that you countenance his error. . . . Now, if I have laid bare my inmost feelings in making these complaints to you, let that have no weight as far as our reply is concerned. Although you disappointed my expectations, I nevertheless gladly offer you our friendship.[20]

Calvin did not readily accept criticism from others when it came to important doctrinal truths.

Most of Calvin's letters to Bullinger largely contained news about the reform in Geneva and France or discussed the issue of the Lord's Supper, seeking to keep Bullinger informed and to support Calvin's views on the best way of advancing the Reformation. Still, at times he expressed more personal frustrations:

The unfortunate issue of the conference at Worms does not so much distress me, as the inconstancy of Philip [Melanchthon] moves both my anger and detestation. For though I had not forgotten how pliant and weak he has always been, and knew that on the present occasion also he is too timid and indolent, nevertheless he has exceeded himself far beyond what I could ever have suspected.[21]

Even here, however, Calvin was being strategic. He was implicitly reminding Bullinger that he and Bullinger were publicly united on the

---

19. Calvin to Heinrich Bullinger, March 1, 1548, in *Letters*, 2:160.
20. Calvin to Heinrich Bullinger, January 1552, in *Letters*, 2:334.
21. Calvin to Heinrich Bullinger, February 23, 1558, in *Letters*, 3:410–11.

Lord's Supper by writing the Consensus Tigurinus in 1549 together, while Melanchthon refused to support them publicly.

Friendships That Did Not Last

Cicero recognized that friendships do not always last: "Nothing was harder than for a friendship to continue to the very end of life."[22] Friendships fail where friends fail in duty to one another: "It is in the case of friendships, however, that men's conceptions of duty are most confused; for it is a breach of duty either to fail to do for a friend what one rightly can do, or to do for him what is not right."[23] We see such friendships in Calvin's life.

Louis du Tillet

Louis du Tillet was a friend of Calvin from their university days together. He joined Calvin in the cause of the Reformation for several years and then returned to France and to the Roman Catholic Church. Their friendship did not survive in the long run, but we do have three letters from Calvin in 1538 that show us his attitude toward his departed friend.

Calvin's first letter after du Tillet's departure reflected his affection and his disappointment:

> It is indeed true, that I derived such advantage from your society and conversation, that your absence could not be joyous to me. . . . This so sudden change has appeared very strange to me, seeing the constancy and firmness which you manifested. . . . Moreover, I think that I perceive such a fear of God to be in you that I must see great arguments to move me from the persuasion which I have entertained. Be assured, then, that the first slight reports will not have such power over me as to overturn the experience I have had of you for many long years. . . . I can by no means approve your conduct; and would choose rather that I should be taken out of the world by a bitter death, than approve your deed, which I know to be damnable in itself. . . . I pray the Lord to keep you in his holy protection, and so to direct you that you may not go astray in that

---

22. Cicero, *De Amicitia*, 10.33, LCL, 145.
23. Cicero, *De Officiis*, 3.43, LCL, 311.

slippery path whereon you are, until himself shall have manifested to you his complete deliverance.[24]

Calvin made clear the spiritual dangers of du Tillet's course but still addressed him as a friend in conversation.

Du Tillet later wrote to Calvin, challenging his calling and ordination to the ministry outside the Roman church. Calvin defended himself and his calling: "When first I entered upon it I could discern the calling of God which held me fast bound, with which I consoled myself."[25]

Calvin again defended his calling in the third letter. He acknowledged many faults in himself but vigorously defended his own ministry and the legitimacy of the Reformation:

Whatsoever are my peculiar faults as an individual, while I can discern very many, yet I hold, nevertheless, that I do not perceive the greatest of them, even the grosser faults. Wherefore, I pray the Lord that he would make them more clearly manifest to me from day to day. Those which you point out are not to be laid to my charge. If there was any ground to dispute my call, I believe that you have got no such reasons to impugn my ministry, but the Lord has furnished me with more firm and stable ones for confirmation. If you entertain some doubt about that, it is enough for me that it is quite clear to my own satisfaction, and not only so, but that I can approve it to those who are willing to submit their censures to the test of truth. . . . I shall not enter upon a disputation, for neither is that your intention; but I would like to know what equity there is in a person who passes judgment in his closet, condemning all those who maintain their doctrine daily openly before all the world, and who thinks notwithstanding, that it is presumption in those others to dare to condemn the manifest enemies of God and of his majesty. . . . One of my companions [Augustin Courault] is now before God to render account of the cause which has been common to him and me. When we come thither, it will be known on which side the rashness and desertion has been. It is thither that I appeal from the judgments of all the worldly-wise sages, who

---

24. Calvin to Louis du Tillet, January 31, 1538, in *Letters*, 1:61–65.
25. Calvin to Louis du Tillet, July 10, 1538, in *Letters*, 1:72.

think their simple word has weight enough for our condemnation. There, the angels of God will bear witness who are the schismatics. . . . I shall entreat our Lord that he would uphold and keep you in his holy protection, so directing you, that you decline not from his way.[26]

Again we see Calvin treating du Tillet as a friend, unwilling to attack him as if in a disputation. But their correspondence—and apparently their friendship—did not continue.

Monsieur de Falais

Between 1543 and 1552, Calvin wrote over forty letters to Jacques de Bourgogne, Seigneur de Falais, and his wife.[27] Monsieur de Falais was the natural great-grandson of Philip the Fair, Duke of Burgundy, and was raised as a very distinguished nobleman at the court of Emperor Charles V. In embracing the Reformed faith, he lost much of his wealth and needed to seek exile. Calvin wrote to encourage him in his faith and to urge him to settle in Geneva, where he finally arrived in 1548.

Calvin's letters reflected his great respect for this noble personage, and in a letter to Madame de Falais, he expressed his genuine affection: "The love and reverence which I may well bear toward him in our Lord are so strong, that I am very sorry that I cannot devote myself more to his and your service, to shew what is in my heart."[28] Monsieur de Falais was often ill, and Calvin wrote several times to comfort him:

We shall not give over praying to God that it would please him to confirm you entirely, with thanksgiving that he has brought you back from the brink of the grave. Besides, I hope, from present appearances, that he is minded yet to make use of you in health, since he has employed you in sickness. For although laid powerless upon a bed, we are by no means useless to him, if we testify our obedience by resigning ourselves to his good pleasure,—if we give proof of our faith by resisting temptation,—if we take advantage of the

---

26. Calvin to Louis du Tillet, October 20, 1538, in *Letters*, 1:95–99.
27. See Mirjam G. K. van Veen, "'In excelso honoris gradu': Johannes Calvin und Jacques de Falais," *Zwing* 32 (2002): 5–22.
28. Calvin to Madame de Falais, November 20, 1546, in *Letters*, 2:86.

consolation which he gives us in order to overcome the troubles of the flesh. It is in sickness, especially when prolonged, that patience is most needful; but most of all in death.[29]

Calvin's last letter to his friend was written after Monsieur De Falais had sided with Bolsec, who had helped him medically but had sharply attacked Calvin on predestination. Calvin summarized Bolsec's attack to Monsieur de Falais in this way: "The God of Calvin is hypocritical, mendacious, perfidious, unjust, the provoker and patron of crimes, and worse than the Devil himself."[30] Calvin exhorted him to uphold the truth and honor of God against Bolsec:

> If from the humanity and mildness of your disposition, you are content not only to remain ignorant of the character of the man who makes war on God, but also, by lending no credit to our testimony, furnish a handle for rendering us odious, suffer me, to entreat you, to have some zeal in maintaining the honour of my Master.[31]

Calvin concluded the letter, and as far as we know his relationship with Monsieur de Falais, by commending him to God: "I will supplicate him [God], Monseigneur, that in having pity on me, and receiving me to his mercy, he may preserve and guide you by his Spirit, and increase you in all prosperity."[32] Monsieur de Falais left Geneva for Basel after the rupture with Calvin and passed into historical obscurity.

Intimate Friends

Calvin had many friends.[33] Among his closest friends throughout his life were Farel, Viret, and Beza. Calvin reflected on his strong personal relationship with Farel and Viret in the dedication of his *Commentary on Paul's Epistle to Titus* (1549). He dedicated the commentary to Guillaume Farel and Pierre Viret, calling them "two eminent servants of Christ and his own dearly beloved colleagues and brethren." He stated why he dedicated the commentary to these two friends:

---

29. Calvin to Monsieur de Falais, November 16, 1546, in *Letters*, 2:82.
30. Calvin to Monsieur de Falais, 1552, in *Letters*, 2:382.
31. Calvin to Monsieur de Falais, 1552, in *Letters*, 2:382.
32. Calvin to Monsieur de Falais, 1552, in *Letters*, 2:383.
33. See, for example, Jeannine E. Olson, "The Friends of John Calvin: The Budé Family," in Foxgrover, *Calvin and Spirituality; Calvin and His Contemporaries*, 159–68.

It was the subject of the Epistle with which it deals that led me to dedicate it to you. . . . For when with great labour and much risk you had set your hands to raise up this church in Geneva, I arrived later first of all as your assistant, and then afterwards I was left behind as your successor, to strive to the best of my ability to carry on the work that you had begun so successfully and so well. . . . It will at least be a testimony to this present age and perhaps also to posterity of the holy bond of friendship that unites us. I think there has never been in ordinary life a circle of friends so heartily bound to each other as we have been in our ministry. With both of you I discharged here the office of pastor, and so far from there being any appearance of rivalry, I always seemed to be of one mind with you. . . . This also I count among the benefits of our union, that unclean dogs whose bites cannot succeed in tearing and rending the Church only stir it up to no effect by their barking. We cannot hold their influence in too great scorn, since we have good reason to glory before God and have the clearest evidence to show to men that our alliance and friendship have been entirely consecrated to Christ's name, have hitherto been profitable to His Church, and have no other aim than that all men should be one with us in Him. . . . We have good reason to glory before God and have the clearest evidence to show to men that our alliance and friendship have been entirely consecrated to Christ's name, have hitherto been profitable to His Church, and have no other aim than that all men should be at one with us in Him.[34]

Here indeed is the spirit of warm friendship in the service of the gospel.

Theodore Beza in his sympathetic biography of Calvin, *Life of Calvin* (1575), wrote about the work of these three friends together:

He availed himself much of the aid of old Farel and Viret, while, at the same time, he was also of great service to them. This friendship and intimacy was not less hateful to the wicked than delightful to all the pious, and, in truth, it was a pleasing spectacle to see and hear those three distinguished men, carrying on the work of God

---

34. *CNTC*, 10:347–48.

so harmoniously, and yet differing so much from each other in the nature of their gifts. Farel excelled in a certain sublimity of mind, so that nobody could either hear his thunders without trembling, or listen to his most fervent prayers without feeling almost as it were carried up into heaven. Viret possessed such winning eloquence, that his entranced audience hung upon his lips. Calvin never spoke without filling the mind of the hearer with the most weighty sentiments. I have often thought that a preacher compounded of the three would have been absolutely perfect.[35]

Beza was younger than these three and became a close friend of Calvin later, but he had ample opportunity to observe the genuine friendship of these three pastors.

Guillaume Farel

Guillaume Farel was the preacher who introduced the Reformation to Geneva and convinced Calvin in 1536 to remain there to help with the consolidation of the reform of the church. Farel and Calvin made a strong team, united as they were in their understanding of theology and their vision for the life of the church.[36] They were both exiled from Geneva in 1538 for their insistence that the church needed freedom from the city council in matters of ecclesiastical discipline. After this exile, Calvin in time settled in Strasbourg, ministering to a small congregation of French refugees, until his return to Geneva in 1541. Farel settled in the Swiss town of Neuchâtel (about 75 miles northeast of Geneva), where he remained as minister until his death.

In an early letter to Farel after his exile from Geneva, Calvin expressed his feelings about the work they had done there together:

We may indeed acknowledge before God and his people, that it is in some measure owing to our unskilfulness, indolence, negligence, and error, that the Church committed to our care has fallen into such a sad state of collapse; but it is also our duty to assert

---

35. Theodore Beza, *Life of John Calvin*, trans. Henry Beveridge, in *Tracts and Treatises*, 1:lxxvii.

36. See David N. Wiley, "Calvin's Friendship with Guillaume Farel," in Foxgrover, *Calvin and Spirituality; Calvin and His Contemporaries*, 187–204; Heiko A. Oberman, "Calvin and Farel: The Dynamics of Legitimation in Early Calvinism," *RRR* 1 (1999): 7–40.

our innocence and our purity against those who, by their fraud, malignity, knavery, and wickedness, have assuredly brought about this ruin.[37]

Calvin often wrote his candid feelings to Farel. For example, he complained of the quarrelsomeness of the Zurich theologians:

> The good men flame up into a rage if any one dares to prefer Luther to Zuingli, just as if the Gospel were to perish if any thing is yielded by Zuingli. Nor, indeed, is there any injury thereby done to Zuingli; for if the two men are compared with each other, you yourself know how much Luther has the preference. . . . But these things are intended for your ear alone.[38]

He went on to urge Farel to come to Strasbourg for his wedding so that they could talk more fully:

> Would that only a single opportunity were allowed me, in a familiar and confidential way, to confide to you all my hopes and fears, and in turn to hear your mind and have your help, whereby we might be the better prepared. An excellent opportunity will occur for your repairing hither, if, as we hope, the marriage shall come to pass. . . . First of all, then, I request of you, as an act of friendship, that you should come. For it is altogether indispensable that some one from thence be here to solemnize and ask a blessing upon the marriage. I would rather have you than any one else.[39]

Farel would long remain Calvin's chief confidant in his letters.

Calvin wrote to encourage Farel when he was discouraged: "If our calling is indeed of the Lord, as we firmly believe that it is, the Lord himself will bestow his blessing, although the whole universe may be opposed to us. . . . When I perceive you to be so much cast down, at times I desire to be with you, that I might suggest some comfort."[40]

Calvin shared with Farel both his disappointment and his fundamental agreement with Melanchthon on Lutheran ceremonies in worship:

---

37. Calvin to Guillaume Farel, September 1538, in *Letters*, 1:81.
38. Calvin to Guillaume Farel, February 28, 1539, in *Letters*, 1:109.
39. Calvin to Guillaume Farel, February 28, 1539, in *Letters*, 1:110.
40. Calvin to Guillaume Farel, March 1539, in *Letters*, 1:131.

Of late, I have plainly told Philip to his face how much I disliked that over-abounding of ceremonies; indeed, that it seemed to me the form which they observe was not far removed from Judaism. When I pressed him with argument, he was unwilling to dispute with me about the matter, but admitted that there was an over-doing in these either trifling or superfluous rites and ceremonies. . . . But he made a small reservation, to the effect that the ceremonies which they had been compelled to retain were not more approved of by Luther than was our sparing use of them. . . . Besides, as to Bucer's defense of Luther's ceremonies, he does not do so because he eagerly seeks them, or would endeavour to introduce them. By no means can he be brought to approve of chanting in Latin. Images he abhors. Some other things he despises, while others he cares nothing at all about. There is no occasion to fear that he would be for restoring those things which have been once abolished; only he cannot endure that, on account of these trifling observances, we should be separated from Luther. Neither, certainly, do I consider them to be just causes of dissent.[41]

In his letters to Farel and others, Calvin often praised the virtue of moderation in ministers. His understanding of moderation was no doubt that of Cicero: moderation [*modestia*] is "the science of doing the right thing at the right time."[42] Calvin was concerned from time to time to call Farel back to moderation:

We do not exhort you to keep a good and pure conscience, as to which, we entertain no doubt whatever; we only desire earnestly that, in so far as your duty will admit, you will accommodate yourself more to the people. There are, as you know, two kinds of popularity: the one, when we hunt after favour from motives of ambition and the desire of pleasing; the other, when, by fairness and moderation, we gain upon their esteem, so as to make them willing to be taught by us. . . . Even were there nothing else to complain of, you sin to this extent, because you do not satisfy those to whom the Lord has made you a debtor. You are aware how much we love and revere you. This very affection, yea truly,

---

41. Calvin to Guillaume Farel, April 1539, in *Letters*, 1:136–37.
42. Cicero, *De Officiis*, 1.142, LCL, 145–46.

this respect impels us to a more exact and strict censoriousness, because we desire earnestly that in those remarkable endowments which the Lord has conferred upon you, no spot or blemish may be found for the malevolent to find fault with.[43]

Here Calvin in effect urged Farel to communicate with his people more in terms of *sermo* than *contentio*.

Calvin's experience of advising Farel to be moderate may have influenced his writing in his *Commentary on Paul's Epistle to Titus*:

One of the most important parts of the tact and wisdom needed by a bishop is the ability to adapt the manner of his teaching to the character and habits of his people. He will not deal with the stubborn and insubordinate in the same way as with the meek and teachable. To the latter we should show a mildness suited to their teachableness, but the stubbornness of the former must be corrected with severity.[44]

Only with reticence and difficulty did Calvin criticize Farel's writing:

I have written nothing regarding your book, as I laid the whole burden on Viret. I said from the first, what is true, that I mistrusted my own judgment regarding your writings, seeing that our mode of writing is so different. You know with what respect I regard Augustine. Not, however, because I disguise from myself how much his prolixity dissatisfies me. Perhaps my style, in the mean time, is over-concise. . . . I am only afraid that the involved style and tedious discussion will obscure the light which is really in it. I know, and that not without pleasure too, that nothing but what is excellent is expected from you. I speak without flattery.[45]

Prolixity was indeed a recurring flaw in Farel's writing.

Calvin felt free to write Farel about his frustrations with Zurich and Bullinger: "Should you be displeased with the general letter of the men of Zurich, let me tell you, that Bullinger's private letter to me was not a whit better. . . . It is not fair that I should be troubled with his

---

43. Calvin to Guillaume Farel, September 16, 1541, in *Letters*, 1:285.
44. Calvin, comm. on Titus 1:13, *CNTC*, 10:364.
45. Calvin to Guillaume Farel, September 1, 1549, in *Letters*, 2:247.

trifles, while he is, at the same time, looking down on our wants with supreme contempt."[46] Calvin also expressed briefly the depths of his pain on his struggles with the Libertines in Geneva:

> For I think it better silently to repress the very sad cares which torture me, rather than seek consolation by inconveniencing you. Even if I did throw part of the burden on your shoulders, I should rather increase than diminish the evil. The very act of writing, moreover, by awakening the memory, irritates the wound.[47]

Calvin offered very pointed advice to Farel on his troubles with a fellow minister, Christopher Fabri. The advice showed Calvin's friendship and his willingness to criticize his friend:

> I wish, my dear Farel, I could find a better remedy for your evils than that which I here think of offering you. But as you yourself are well aware that there are many things which we must endure, because it is not in our power to correct them, I shall not spend many words in exhorting you to show yourself gentle and moderate, in a contest which is evidently not embittered by personal hostility. . . . One thing we know that the man is pious and zealous in the discharge of his duty. Add to that—he loves you, is anxious to have your approbation, and both considers and respects you as a parent. Now if he sometimes carries himself rather more forwardly than he ought, the chief cause of such conduct appears to me to be this: he fancies that you are too rigid and morose, and so he aims at a certain popularity which may smooth down offences. Thus the good man, while he is consulting your tranquillity, and guarding against ill will, which he believes neither of you can stand against, forgets the firmness and dignity which should belong to a minister of Christ. . . . I see how vexatious and provoking a proceeding this is, nor am I ignorant how much blame his fault deserves. But your own prudence and love of fair dealing will suggest to you that you ought on the other hand to number up the good qualities which counterbalance his defects. . . . With how much greater reason, then, should you

---

46. Calvin to Guillaume Farel, December 8, 1551, in *Letters*, 2:329.
47. Calvin to Guillaume Farel, October 26, 1552, in *Letters*, 2:370.

strive to foster peace with a man who both desires faithfully to serve the Lord along with you, and abhors all rancorous dissensions! But you are found not only to maintain peace with him, but to cultivate friendship also.

For if you bear in mind how few tolerable good ministers we have in the present day, you will be on your guard how you slight a man who is both honest and diligent, endowed, moreover with other most estimable gifts. . . . Let him only feel that you love him, and I answer for it, you will find him tolerably docile.[48]

Calvin often wrote letters to promote peace between good ministers.

In the midst of his troubles with Michael Servetus in Geneva, Calvin expressed his appreciation for Farel's comforting words to him:

It is as you say, my dear Farel. Although we may be severely buffeted hither and thither by many tempests, yet, seeing that a pilot steers the ship in which we sail, who will never allow us to perish even in the midst of shipwrecks, there is no reason why our minds should be overwhelmed with fear and overcome with weariness.[49]

Here we see Calvin and Farel's mutual encouragement in their pastoral labors.

The greatest test of their friendship came when Farel, who had never married, announced his intention at age sixty-nine to marry a young woman (possible only sixteen or seventeen).[50] Calvin expressed his deep distress in a letter to the ministers of Neuchâtel:

It is certain that poor Master William has been for once so ill-advised that we cannot but blush for his weakness. . . . Since there is no law which forbids such a marriage, to break it off when it is contracted is, I am afraid, beyond our power. . . . Since the only objection that can be raised is the inequality of their years, I consider this fact as an evil that cannot be cured. It is for this reason that, after having made him sufficiently sharp reproaches, I forbore to say any thing more to him on the subject, for fear of reducing him to despair altogether. And, in fact, I have always feared and

---

48. Calvin to Guillaume Farel, July 19, 1553, in *Letters*, 4:419–21.
49. Calvin to Guillaume Farel, August 20, 1553, in *Letters*, 2:416–17.
50. Wiley, "Calvin's Friendship with Guillaume Farel," 202.

conjectured that the consequences which I had anticipated from this affair would occasion his death.[51]

Calvin was appalled at such a marriage but had to recognize that it was not illegal.

Calvin also wrote to Farel, refusing to come to the wedding: "But, should no obstacle stand in my way, yet as my coming would afford an admirable handle for the ungodly and the badly disposed to vent their malice in evil speaking, you neither seem to do prudently in inviting me, nor should I act with due consideration if I complied with your wishes."[52] Calvin was amazed that Farel could not see how such a marriage might damage the reputation of the Reformation.

Calvin wrote only four letters to Farel between 1559 and his death in 1564.[53] One might conclude that Farel's marriage had permanently poisoned their relationship. But the tone of the letters belies that conclusion. They are as warm as they ever were. In the two letters written in 1561, Calvin addressed Farel as "excellent man and most blameless brother" and "that most pre-eminent servant of Christ . . . brother and most blameless church colleague."[54] Even allowing for epistolary flattery, the greeting is very warm. In his last letter, Calvin wrote,

> Farewell, my most excellent and upright brother; and since it is the will of God that you should survive me in the world, live mindful of our intimacy, which, as it was useful to the church of God, so the fruits of it await us in heaven. . . . It is enough that I live and die for Christ, who is to all his followers a gain both in life and death.[55]

Calvin urged Farel in light of his age not to make a last visit to him, but Farel did, and they had a most friendly parting.

---

51. Calvin to the ministers of Neuchâtel, September 26, 1558, in *Letters*, 3:473–74.
52. Calvin to Guillaume Farel, September 1558, in *Letters*, 3:476.
53. Only two of those letters, one dated February 26, 1559, telling Farel of Viret's being deposed in Lausanne, and the other, dated May 1564, from Calvin's deathbed, are contained in the standard English translation of Calvin's letters. Oberman states that perhaps as many as one-half of Calvin's letters have not been preserved, which might in part account for the number of letters from this period. Oberman's fascinating study of the strategic elements in the roles and relationships of Calvin, Farel, Viret, and Beza does not affect the argument of this study of their friendship. See Oberman, "Calvin and Farel," 9.
54. These letters are printed as letters 3591 and 3670 in *CO*, 19:84, 209.
55. Calvin to Guillaume Farel, May 2, 1564, in *Letters*, 4:364.

The reasons for the paucity of letters to Farel—and Viret—in the last years of Calvin's life are most likely to be found elsewhere than in some alleged permanent alienation after Farel's marriage. Calvin had finally achieved a strong and stable position in Geneva and had Beza as his right-hand man. He probably had less to complain of and was in less need of the encouragement that Farel and Viret gave him. These were also years in which Calvin was writing a great deal and declining in his health and strength. He sensed that his time was short, and he used his energy for other activities. His friendships with Farel and Viret remained strong.

Pierre Viret

Pierre Viret was born near Lausanne in Switzerland and received a humanist education in Paris, where he was converted to the Reformation. In 1531 he was persuaded by Farel to enter the Reformed ministry and joined Farel in the reform of the church in Geneva from 1534 to 1536. He was in Geneva when Farel convinced Calvin to stay there. From 1536 to 1559, he served as leading minister in Lausanne, returning to Geneva from 1559 to 1561 to preach and teach. For reasons of health, he left Geneva for the south of France, serving the Queen of Navarre there from 1561 until his death in 1571.[56]

Calvin's close friendship with Viret was expressed in these words of comfort and desire for conversation: "Again adieu; may the Lord be with you. Would that you could make a run as far as this, I would willingly have half a day's free conversation with you."[57]

Calvin was open with Viret even about his frustrations with their mutual friend Farel:

> I may therefore say of Farel what Cicero said of Cato, "That he acts indeed with good judgment, but in counsel does not always shew the best." The cause of this is chiefly, that being carried away

56. In addition to Linder, "Brothers in Christ" (cited above), see Jean-Marc Berthoud, "Pierre Viret: The Apologetics and Ethics of the Reformation," in *Adorning the Doctrine: Papers Read at the 1995 Westminster Conference* (London: Westminster Conference, 1996), 28–57; Willem Balke, "Jean Calvin und Pierre Viret," in *Calvin in Kontext der Schweizer Reformation: Historische und Theologische Beiträge zur Calvinforschung*, ed. Peter Opitz (Zurich: TVZ Theologischer Verlag, 2003).
57. Calvin to Pierre Viret, August 19, 1542, in *Letters*, 1:344.

by the vehemence of his zeal, he does not always discern what is expedient, and either does not foresee dangers, or despises them; and there is to be added the evil, that he cannot bear with patience those who do not comply with his wishes.[58]

Calvin also felt free to complain to Viret about the strong opposition he faced in Geneva in 1547: "Their wickedness has, however, reached such a pitch, that I hardly hope to be able any longer to retain any kind of position for the Church, especially under my ministry. My influence is gone, believe me, unless God stretch forth his hand."[59] Calvin was clearly willing to open his heart and share his burden with Viret.

After his wife died, Calvin wrote Viret how much his friends had helped him:

Although the death of my wife has been exceedingly painful to me, yet I subdue my grief as well as I can. Friends, also, are earnest in their duty to me. It might be wished, indeed, that they could profit me and themselves more; yet one can scarcely say how much I am supported by their attentions. But you know well enough how tender, or rather soft, my mind is. Had not a powerful self-control, therefore, been vouchsafed to me, I could not have borne up so long.[60]

Calvin worried about the struggles of Viret in Lausanne and urged him to come to Geneva, but he was also willing in the same letter to criticize some of Viret's actions, concluding, "I both think and speak of you as a man guided by zeal for piety, but deceived by a too great propensity to hope for the best. You think otherwise; I forgive and endure your sentiment, provided only you accord me the same liberty."[61] Clearly this criticism did not cause any permanent estrangement. Viret did come to Geneva, where he and Calvin worked together well for two years.

Viret was certainly a close friend of Calvin. Robert Linder has argued that he was Calvin's closest friend over the longest period of time: "In fact, Viret seems to have been Calvin's most enduring friend—the

---

58. Calvin to Pierre Viret, October 24, 1545, in *Letters*, 2:25.
59. Calvin to Pierre Viret, December 14, 1547, in *Letters*, 2:149.
60. Calvin to Pierre Viret, April 7, 1549, in *Letters*, 2:216.
61. Calvin to Pierre Viret, August 28, 1558, in *Letters*, 3:458.

only individual who enjoyed an intimate relationship with Calvin from his early days in Geneva in 1536 to the end of his life in 1564."[62] Linder develops this thought in these terms:

> The Viret-Calvin connection was more intimate and more endur-
> ing than that of Farel-Calvin. . . . In the late 1530s and during the
> first two years of the next decade, Farel and Calvin exchanged
> more written communications than did Viret and Calvin. However,
> after 1542, the balance shifted and the reverse was true for the
> remainder of their lives.[63]

Linder's judgment is not entirely convincing. Calvin's letters to Viret generally seem less personal and intimate than his letters to Farel. Calvin certainly spent more time with Viret than Farel, since Lausanne was much closer to Geneva than Neuchâtel for visits and since Viret spent the years 1559–1561 in Geneva. After 1561 Calvin did not correspond with Viret any more than he did with Farel. He wrote only two letters to Viret from 1558 to 1564. Certainly, from the evidence of the letters, Calvin's friendship with Farel was closer until at least 1558.

Theodore Beza

Theodore Beza was born in Vézelay, France, to a minor noble family. His education followed the same path as that of Calvin, including the study of law. He formally renounced the Roman Catholic Church and became Reformed in 1548. In 1549 he began to teach Greek in Lausanne, and in 1558 he moved to Geneva, where he was professor and minister. Beza was a great scholar and theologian as well as a noted poet. He became the leading minister in Geneva after Calvin's death, a position he held for more than forty years.

Calvin had learned to value Beza as a friend and ally even before they had spent much time together. For example, Calvin wrote in 1551 to someone in France on hearing of the serious illness of Beza:

> I was therefore not only troubled about the danger he was in, but
> from my very great affection for him I felt almost overpowered, as

---

62. Linder, "Brothers in Christ," 158.
63. Linder, "Brothers in Christ," 139.

if I was already lamenting his death; although, indeed, this grief did not rise so much from private regard, as from my public anxiety for the prosperity of the Church. Indeed, I were destitute of human feeling, did I not return the affection of one who loves me with more than a brother's love, and reveres me like a very father. But the Church's loss afflicted me more deeply, when I pictured a man, of whom I had so very high expectations, suddenly snatched away from us by death, at the very outset of his career—a man whose gentle disposition, polished manners, and native candour, had endeared him to all good men.[64]

Writing to Madame de Cany in 1552, Calvin highly recommended Beza: "I shall not even touch upon many virtues, which would have won your affections, had you seen them as I have done. I will only tell you, that he has received excellent graces from God, and has so improved them for the general benefit of the Church, that he is truly a pearl."[65]

Shortly before Beza moved permanently to Geneva, Calvin wrote him words of encouragement during the troubles in the school and church of Lausanne: "Meanwhile, the reward of your labours is more certain with God, in proportion as you shall see these labours detested by the Devil; and do not murmur that these perverse animals discharge their violence on you, provided the angels who are in heaven applaud your conduct."[66]

After Beza had worked for about three years in Geneva, Calvin even joked with him in one of his letters,

If you desire to give pleasure to a great many persons, profit in that school in which your name is at present so celebrated, and learn to lie a little more audaciously; for when others recount marvels, you alone scarcely let us have one glimpse of hope. But joking apart, remember that you are writing to me who care for nothing more than to be made acquainted with the present state of affairs by a plain narrative.[67]

---

64. Calvin to a French gentleman, June 30, 1551, in *Letters*, 2:314.
65. Calvin to Madame de Cany, January 1552, in *Letters*, 2:340.
66. Calvin to Theodore Beza, December 5, 1557, in *Letters*, 3:379.
67. Calvin to Theodore Beza, September 10, 1561, in *Letters*, 4:218–19.

Calvin complimented Beza for his reports on the Colloquy of Poissy in France, and especially his speech there: "Your speech is now before us, in which God in a marvelous manner directed your mind and tongue." He closed this letter with another little joke: "As often as you shall keep silence longer than ten days, which has now happened to you the second time, I shall proclaim you a sluggard."[68]

Calvin's genuine concern and affection for Beza was expressed in this advice: "Consult your health, I entreat you, and do not suffer yourself to be overwhelmed by harassing labours, for it is not without sorrow that I learn that you are worn to a shadow."[69] Calvin, who never limited his own work for the sake of his health, showed real fatherly care for Beza and his health.

Conclusion

The record of friendships found in Calvin's letters shows us something of the workings of the network of Reformers in sixteenth-century Europe. They also give us a window into the life and personality of Calvin, displaying his humanity as expressed in his love, concern, frustrations, criticisms, and commitment. Calvin was dedicated to the reform of the church according to the word of God. His friends were indispensable to advancing that great cause and to upholding Calvin for his role in it. Calvin would have agreed with Cicero: "But of all the bonds of fellowship, there is none more noble, none more powerful than when good men of congenial character are joined in intimate friendship."[70]

---

68. Calvin to Theodore Beza, September 24, 1561, in *Letters*, 4:229–30.
69. Calvin to Theodore Beza, November 19, 1561, in *Letters*, 4:239.
70. Cicero, *De Officiis*, 1.55, LCL, 59.

6

The Expository Pulpit
of John Calvin

Steven J. Lawson

> The Scripture is the fountain of all wisdom, from which
> pastors must draw all that they place before their flock.
>
> —John Calvin, *Commentary on 1 Timothy*

A Tribute to the Reformation

Hidden below street level in the Old Town of Geneva, nestled behind
the University of Geneva, there stands an imposing monument that
pays lasting tribute to the Reformation, which occurred in that city
nearly five hundred years ago.[1] Known as the Reformation Wall, this
memorial rises 30 feet high and stretches 325 feet long, commemorat-
ing the history-altering movement that galvanized this ancient city in
the sixteenth century. In the middle of the wall are positioned the four

---

1. Portions of this chapter are adapted from Steven J. Lawson, "The Preacher of God's
Word," in *John Calvin: A Heart for Devotion, Doctrine, and Doxology*, ed. Burk Parsons (Or-
lando, FL: Reformation Trust, 2008), 71–82; Lawson, *The Expository Genius of John Calvin*
(Orlando, FL: Reformation Trust, 2007). Used by permission of Reformation Trust.

leading figures of the Genevan Reformation. These four individuals stand together as one man, representing their unified commitment to the lofty ideals that once swept through Europe.

On the left is Guillaume Farel, the man who first came to Geneva and helped turn the city to the cause of the Reformation. On the right are Theodore Beza and John Knox, two men who carried Protestant beliefs into the next generation. But standing resolutely between Farel and Beza is its chief influencer—the great theologian, the master expositor, whose preaching and teaching shaped much of the Reformation—John Calvin. Poised slightly taller than the others, Calvin is the central figure in this epic monument. Dressed in his Genevan robe, he is postured erect, leaning forward, both hands confidently gripping an opened Bible. Appropriately, his left hand is in the Scripture, ready to turn to the appointed text and unleash its life-giving power.

No Weapon but the Bible

This graphic depiction of John Calvin represents the true genius of his prolific ministry. For some twenty-five years, this magisterial Reformer stood in the pulpit of Saint Pierre's Cathedral in Geneva, armed only with an open Bible, preaching the inspired word. Of this famed man, James Montgomery Boice writes,

> Calvin had no weapon but the Bible. From the very first, his emphasis had been on Bible teaching. Calvin preached from the Bible every day, and under the power of that preaching the city began to be transformed. As the people of Geneva acquired knowledge of God's Word and were changed by it, the city became, as John Knox called it later, a New Jerusalem.[2]

To be sure, every great season of reformation in the history of the church and every great hour of spiritual awakening is always ushered in by a recovery of biblical preaching. J. H. Merle d'Aubigné, the noted historian of the Reformation in Geneva and Europe, has written, "The only true reformation is that which emanates from the Word of God."[3]

---

2. James Montgomery Boice, *Whatever Happened to the Gospel of Grace? Rediscovering the Doctrines That Shook the World* (Wheaton, IL: Crossway, 2001), 83–84.
3. J. H. Merle d'Aubigné, *History of the Reformation of the Sixteenth Century*, trans. Henry White (Grand Rapids, MI: Baker, 1976), 728.

That being so, the Reformation of the sixteenth century was certainly no exception. And positioned at the headwaters of this mighty movement stood John Calvin, the great Genevan Reformer, the man supremely used by God to embolden the Protestant cause and bring about the recovery of biblical preaching.

Primarily a Pastor and Preacher

John Calvin was many things—a revered exegete, a world-class theologian, a prolific author, a renowned teacher, an ecclesiastical statesman, an influential Reformer, and more. But first and foremost, Calvin was a pastor, the faithful shepherd of a local flock, and as a pastor, he was, above all, "preeminently a preacher."[4] Amid his many responsibilities, Calvin regarded "the pulpit as the heart of his ministry."[5] For this leading Reformer, "the centre of his pastoral work, around which all else revolved, was the preaching of the gospel."[6] Every pastor has many demands on his time, and Calvin, because of his elevated status in Geneva, had more responsibilities than most. But amid these many pastoral duties, Calvin nevertheless saw "his most important work to be preaching."[7]

During Calvin's first pastoral stint in Geneva (1536–1538), it is uncertain which books of Scripture he expounded and how often he preached, though preaching was his main ministry. After his banishment from Geneva, Calvin retired to Strasbourg (1538–1541), where he preached twice on Sundays, expounding Romans, the Gospel of John, and 1 Corinthians. At the request of the city fathers, this "expositor in exile" returned to Geneva (1541–1564), where he labored until his death. Initially, he preached twice on Sunday, from the New Testament in the morning and mostly from the Psalms in the afternoon. In addition, he preached from the Old Testament, three times during the week, on Monday, Wednesday, and Friday mornings. Then, beginning in 1549, Calvin rearranged his schedule to preach six mornings a week, Monday through Saturday, every other week. Thus, in the course of two weeks, he filled the pulpit ten

---

4. James Montgomery Boice, foreword to *Sermons on Psalm 119*, by John Calvin (1580; repr., Audubon, NJ: Old Paths, 1996), viii.
5. Douglas Kelly, introduction to *Sermons on 2 Samuel*, vol. 1, *Chapters 1–13*, by John Calvin, trans. Douglas Kelly (Edinburgh: Banner of Truth, 1992), ix.
6. T. H. L. Parker, *Portrait of Calvin* (London: SCM, 1954), 81.
7. Boice, foreword to Calvin, *Sermons on Psalm 119*, viii.

times. This indefatigable preacher expounded "some 4000 sermons after his return to Geneva,"[8] approximately two hundred sermons per year. The sheer volume of this preaching demonstrates its primary importance to Calvin, regarded by some as a "master preacher."[9]

To be sure, Calvin restored the ministry of biblical preaching to its principal place in the Reformed church. He viewed the pulpit as "the primary means by which God's presence becomes actual to us and by which God's work is accomplished."[10] Consequently, this illustrious Reformer gave himself to the exposition of the word as perhaps no one else in the history of the church. If preaching was this central to Calvin's ministry, and it most surely *was*, then certain questions need to be addressed: What was Calvin's view of preaching? How did he prepare to preach? What were some of the distinctives of his expository pulpit? Answering these questions is the focus of this chapter. As we survey the expository preaching of Calvin, it is with the prayer that God will raise up a new generation of expositors in this hour, cast in the mold of the Genevan master.

Calvin's View of Expository Preaching

In his approach to preaching, John Calvin was an expositor. That is, he was one who relentlessly expounded the word, explaining the original meaning of the text and applying its life-changing relevance to the needs of his congregation. In simplest terms, expository preaching involves "an explanation and application of a passage of Scripture."[11] The preacher, Calvin believed, stood between two worlds—the ancient world of the biblical author and the present-day world of his listeners. In biblical exposition, the preacher brings these two worlds together. This was Calvin. He took the inspired text of Scripture, explaining the authorial intent of the passage, and then brought it forward to the present hour, applying it to the challenges of his day, showing its practicality for contemporary living. Calvin then called for a favorable hearing from his congregation, "challenging the listener to greater

---

8. William J. Bouwsma, *John Calvin: A Sixteenth-Century Portrait* (New York: Oxford University Press, 1988), 29.

9. Timothy George, introduction to *John Calvin and the Church: A Prism of Reform*, ed. Timothy George (Louisville: Westminster John Knox, 1990), 24.

10. John H. Leith, "Calvin's Doctrine of the Proclamation of the Word and Its Significance for Today," in George, *John Calvin and the Church*, 206.

11. T. H. L. Parker, *Calvin's Preaching* (Louisville: Westminster John Knox, 1992), 79.

faith, obedience, and piety."[12] This is the essence of expository preaching, and this is the expository genius of Calvin's pulpit.

Though Calvin never wrote a formal definition of expository preaching, the great Genevan did leave behind a vast body of works from which his views can be constructed. In its most basic terms, Calvin stated, "Preaching is the public exposition of Scripture by the man sent from God, in which God Himself is present in judgment and in grace."[13] By this simple statement, the Genevan leader maintained that all preaching must be a "public exposition of Scripture." He was "not willing to select among the traditions of men, and to preserve the least anti-scriptural; he put them all aside, to set up in their place the Word of God only."[14] For Calvin, those preachers who "mingle their own inventions with the Word of God, or who advance anything that does not belong to it, must be rejected, how honourable soever may be their rank."[15] Succinctly put, expository preaching for Calvin was the pure preaching of the word. Five key components marked his approach to the pulpit, as follows.

Biblical in Content

First, Calvin believed that preaching must be biblical in its content. His entire approach to the pulpit was dictated "by his extraordinarily high regard for the authority and power of God's written Word."[16] This fundamental commitment to preaching the infallible word was based on the "formal principle" of the Reformation—*sola Scriptura*, or Scripture alone. The sole authority of the Bible, he insisted, gives "form" to all the beliefs and ministries of the church. Thus, the unwavering allegiance of Calvin in the pulpit was to preach the Bible only. He stated, "Their [i.e., ministers'] whole task is limited to the ministry of God's Word; their whole wisdom to the knowledge of His Word; their whole eloquence, to its proclamation."[17] For Calvin, "the words of scripture are the source and content of preaching," John

---

12. William B. Evans, "John Calvin's Sermons on Acts 1–7," *BTM* 533, 2008, 18.
13. Quoted in John Blanchard, comp., *Gathered Gold* (Darlington, UK: Evangelical Press, 1984), 238.
14. J. H. Merle D'Aubigné, *Let Christ Be Magnified: Calvin's Teaching for Today* (1864; repr., Edinburgh: Banner of Truth, 2007), 11.
15. John Calvin, *Commentary on a Harmony of the Evangelists, Matthew, Mark, and Luke*, trans. William Pringle (repr., Grand Rapids, MI: Baker, 1979), 2:284.
16. Evans, "Sermons on Acts 1–7," 16.
17. *Institutes* (1536), 195.

Leith explains.[18] To this end, Calvin started with a specific text of Scripture and stayed with it throughout the entirety of his message.

Calvin had such a high view of preaching that he believed that when the word is expounded, "the word goeth out of the mouth of God."[19] The Bible, he asserted, is "the unchangeable oracles of our heavenly Father."[20] Thus, when the Scripture is proclaimed, it is as if we "heard the very words pronounced by God Himself."[21] Calvin insisted, "Wherever the gospel is preached, it is as if God Himself came into the midst of us."[22] He believed that expository preaching makes the voice of God heard in the life of the church. However, the Reformer claimed, "As soon as men depart, even in the smallest degree from God's Word, they cannot preach anything but false-hoods, vanities, impostures, errors, and deceits."[23] It is a dangerous step for the preacher to depart even in the slightest from the pure teaching of the word. D'Aubigné notes, "In Calvin's view, every thing that had not for its foundation the Word of God was futile and ephemeral boast; and the man who did not lean on Scripture ought to be deprived of his title of honor."[24] Consequently, he saw his God-assigned role and the duty of every preacher as being merely the mouthpiece for the divine word.

Sequential in Pattern

Second, Calvin held that preaching should be sequential in its pattern. That is, biblical exposition is best fulfilled when moving consecutively, verse by verse, through entire books of the Bible. T. H. L. Parker notes, "Almost all Calvin's sermons are connected series on books in the Bible."[25] He would begin in chapter 1, verse 1, of a particular book and then preach steadily verse by verse through the entire book until he concluded with the last

---

18. Leith, "Calvin's Doctrine," 212.

19. *Comm.*, 8:172.

20. John Calvin, "Epistle Dedicatory to His Most Mighty and Most Serene Prince, Sigismund Augustus, King of Poland," in *Comm.*, xxi.

21. John Calvin, *Institutes of the Christian Religion*, trans. John Allen (Philadelphia: Philip H. Nicklin and Hezekiah Howe, 1816), 1.7.1.

22. Calvin, *Commentary on a Harmony*, 1:227.

23. John Calvin, *Commentaries on the Book of the Prophet Jeremiah and the Lamentations*, trans. John Owen (repr., Grand Rapids, MI: Baker, 1979), 2:226–27.

24. J. H. Merle D'Aubigné, *History of the Reformation in Europe in the Time of Calvin* (1880; repr., Harrisonburg, VA: Sprinkle, 2000), 7:85.

25. Parker, *Calvin's Preaching*, 80.

verse of the last chapter. Each verse and each phrase received his careful attention. By this manner, the full counsel of God was ensured to be heard. Controversial subjects were unavoidable. Hard sayings could not be skipped. Difficult doctrines could not be overlooked. This verse-by-verse style—*lectio continua*, the "continuous expositions"[26]—guaranteed that Calvin preached *tota Scriptura*, "all Scripture." Upon completing one book, he immediately began the next book.

Table 17.1   Old Testament books Calvin preached through

Biblical book	Number of sermons	Dates preached
Genesis	123 sermons	1559–1561
Deuteronomy	201 sermons	1555–1556
Judges	short series	1561
1 Samuel	107 sermons	1561–1562
2 Samuel	87 sermons	1562–1563
1 Kings	various sermons	1563–1564
Job	159 sermons	1554–1555
Individual psalms	72 sermons	at various times
Psalm 119	22 sermons	1553
Isaiah	343 sermons	1556–1559
Jeremiah	91 sermons	1549
Lamentations	25 sermons	1550
Ezekiel	175 sermons	1552–1554
Daniel	47 sermons	1550–1552
Hosea	65 sermons	1551
Joel	17 sermons	1551
Amos	43 sermons	1551–1552
Obadiah	5 sermons	1552
Jonah	6 sermons	1552
Micah	28 sermons	1550–1551
Nahum	unknown	unknown
Zephaniah	17 sermons	1551

---

26. Boice, foreword to Calvin, *Sermons on Psalm 119*, viii.

Table 17.2   New Testament books Calvin preached through

Biblical book	Number of sermons	Dates preached
Harmony of the Gospels	65 sermons	1559–1560
Gospel of John	unknown	while exiled in Strasbourg
Acts	189 sermons	1549–1554
Romans	unknown	while exiled in Strasbourg
1 Corinthians	110 sermons	1555–1556
2 Corinthians	66 sermons	1557
Galatians	43 sermons	1557–1558
Ephesians	48 sermons	1558–1559
1–2 Thessalonians	46 sermons	1554
1 Timothy	55 sermons	1554–1555
2 Timothy	31 sermons	1555
Titus	17 sermons	1555

In this consecutive fashion, Calvin preached through over half the books of the Old Testament. These expositions were protracted series, often lasting more than a year. During his Genevan pastorate, Calvin preached through the Old Testament books listed in table 17.1. For the most part, he preached these Old Testament books at 6:00 in the morning (7:00 a.m. during the winter months) each weekday, Monday through Saturday, at Saint Pierre's Cathedral.

In addition, Calvin preached through much of the New Testament, treating during his ministry in Geneva and Strasbourg the books listed in table 17.2.[27] This kind of "connected exposition" gave "a great breadth to his preaching."[28] No single doctrine was unduly pursued to the exclusion of others. By preaching systematically through every verse in a book of the Bible, Calvin maintained a healthy balance in his preaching. Thus, all truths of Scripture were emphasized, both law

---

27. For a compilation of these sermons, see the following sources, Parker, "Catalogues of the Sermons" and "Bibliographies: Sermons in Manuscripts," in *Calvin's Preaching*, 153–98; Bernard Cottret, *Calvin: A Biography*, trans. M. Wallace McDonald (Grand Rapids, MI: Eerdmans, 2000), 354–55; Robert L. Reymond, *John Calvin: His Life and Influence* (Fearn, Ross-shire, Scotland: Christian Focus, 2004), 83–84; "Publishers Introduction," in John Calvin, *Sermons on the Epistle to the Ephesians* (Edinburgh: Banner of Truth, 1998), ix; Wulfert de Greef, *The Writings of John Calvin: An Introductory Guide*, trans. Lyle D. Bierma, expanded ed. (Louisville: Westminster John Knox, 2008), 93–100.

28. Parker, *Portrait of Calvin*, 83.

and grace, doctrine and duty, divine sovereignty and human responsibility, correction and consolation, evangelism and edification, time and eternity, and heaven and hell.

So committed to sequential exposition was Calvin that after his three-and-a-half-year exile to Strasbourg, having last preached in Geneva on Easter Day 1538, he resumed his pulpit ministry in Geneva on September 13, 1541, at the very next verse. This was "the better to show the nature of his ministry as a mere servant of the Word of God written."[29] On another occasion, in October 1558, Calvin became seriously ill and did not return to the pulpit for eight months. But when he did return in June 1559, he commenced at the very next verse in his exposition of Isaiah. These two incidents represent how disciplined and determined Calvin was in preaching consecutively through entire books in the Bible.

Authoritative in Delivery

Third, Calvin maintained that preaching must be authoritative in its delivery. This was the unshakable foundation of Calvin's preaching—the divine authority of Scripture itself. As a result, Calvin believed that the word preached demands the deepest respect and wholehearted response of both the preacher and the people: "We owe to Scripture the same reverence which we owe to God because it has proceeded from Him alone."[30] In other words, when the Bible speaks, God speaks. Consequently, John Murray notes that to understand Calvin's preaching, we must always be mindful of "the reverence with which Calvin approaches and deals with the Scripture. He is never forgetful that it is the Word of God."[31] Philip Schaff, the highly regarded Protestant historian, writes that Calvin had "the profoundest reverence for the Scriptures, as containing the Word of the living God and as the only infallible and sufficient rule of faith and duty"[32]—which is to say, Calvin was blood earnest as he exposited the Scripture.

---

29. Kelly, introduction to *Sermons on 2 Samuel*, 1:ix.
30. *Comm.*, on 2 Tim. 3:16; quoted in J. I. Packer, "Calvin the Theologian," in *John Calvin: A Collection of Distinguished Essays*, ed. G. E. Duffield, CourtSRT 1 (Grand Rapids, MI: Eerdmans, 1966), 166.
31. John Murray, *Collected Writings of John Murray*, vol. 1, *The Claims of Truth* (Edinburgh: Banner of Truth, 2001), 310.
32. Philip Schaff, *History of the Christian Church*, vol. 8, *Modern Christianity; the Swiss Reformation* (1910; repr., Grand Rapids, MI: Eerdmans, 1984), 535.

Hughes Oliphant Old explains, "Calvin's sermons . . . [reveal] a high sense of the authority of Scripture. The preacher himself believed he was preaching the Word of God. He saw himself to be the servant of the Word."[33] When the word is expounded, he asserted, the divine will is made binding on both the preacher and all who sit under the sermon. Expository preaching comes with the authority of God himself; it is the word of God that is being heard, not the mere babblings of men. T. H. L. Parker notes, "For Calvin the message of Scripture is sovereign, sovereign over the congregation and sovereign over the preacher. His humility is shown by his submitting to this authority."[34] In other words, Calvin saw himself under the supreme authority of the word, while speaking with its sovereign command.

Explanatory in Nature

Fourth, Calvin insisted that preaching must be explanatory in its nature. The sermon, he maintained, must be rooted and grounded in the explication of the biblical text. That is, it must give the God-intended meaning of a specific passage. Calvin's primary duty was to "explain the meaning" of the biblical author,[35] "unfolding the writer's 'mind.'"[36] This necessitated that Calvin give himself to "establishing historical contexts and background, searching for the precise meaning of terms in the original Hebrew or Greek, worrying over geography and chronology, and so on."[37] Only by so doing was he able to "make his case for what the biblical authors intended."[38] Thus, Calvin devoted himself to explaining "the meaning of sentences and paragraphs by appealing to what the apostle intended."[39] Throughout the sermon, the Reformer would "explain the meaning of a word more carefully," giving "deceptively simple explanations of his author's meaning."[40]

33. Hughes Oliphant Old, *The Reading and Preaching of the Scriptures in the Worship of the Christian Church*, vol. 4, *The Age of the Reformation* (Grand Rapids, MI: Eerdmans, 2002), 131.
34. Parker, *Calvin's Preaching*, 39.
35. Parker, *Calvin's Preaching*, 86.
36. John L. Thompson, "Calvin as a Biblical Interpreter," in *The Cambridge Companion to John Calvin*, ed. Donald K. McKim (Cambridge: Cambridge University Press, 2004), 60.
37. Thompson, "Calvin as a Biblical Interpreter," 61.
38. Thompson, "Calvin as a Biblical Interpreter," 61.
39. Thompson, "Calvin as a Biblical Interpreter," 61.
40. Parker, *Calvin's Preaching*, 86.

For Calvin, the proper interpretation of the biblical text *is* the very unshakable foundation of the sermon.

In the dedication of his *Commentary on the Epistle to the Romans,* Calvin revealed that the right interpretation of the biblical text was his fundamental priority. He stated,

> Since it is almost his [the interpreter's] only task to unfold the mind of the writer whom he has undertaken to expound, he misses his mark, or at least strays outside his limits, by the extent to which he leads his readers away from the meaning of his author. . . .
>
> It is . . . presumptuous and almost blasphemous to turn the meaning of Scripture around without due care, as though it were some game that we were playing. And yet many scholars have done this at one time.[41]

Throughout his ministry, this primary concern marked Calvin's expository pulpit. Hearers felt the saving and sanctifying power of God as Calvin unveiled what God was saying through his word.

Practical in Application

Fifth, Calvin asserted that expository preaching must also be practical in its application. The Scripture must be directly connected to the individual lives of people. In Calvin's view, expository preaching must never stop with the mere transference of biblical information. Instead, he believed, the exposition must also be "applicatory" and "intensely practical."[42] From the very outset of the sermon, Calvin was "applying the teaching of the passage to the experience and life of the congregation."[43] Authentic exposition must be heart sifting, sin exposing, soul elevating, duty imposing, and will summoning. The Reformer said, "We have not come to the preaching merely to hear what we do not know, but to be incited to do our duty."[44] To be sure, Calvin, after explaining the biblical passage, was "driven by a passion for

---

41. *CNTC,* 8:1, 4.
42. David J. Engelsma, foreword to John Calvin, *Sermons on Election and Reprobation* (1579; repr., Willow Street, PA: Old Paths, 1996), viii.
43. Engelsma, foreword to Calvin, *Sermons on Election and Reprobation,* viii.
44. *CR,* 79:783, cited in John H. Gerstner, "Calvin's Two-Voice Theory of Preaching," in *Reformed Review* 13, no. 2 (1959): 20.

application."[45] He believed that it was his duty to show the practical relevance of his text, relating it to the lives of those under his ministry.

Such heart-searching challenge was interwoven throughout the entire sermon. "Just as Calvin explicated Scripture word by word," Leith observes, "so he applied the Scripture sentence by sentence to the life and experience of his congregation."[46] Consequently, his sermons had "a strong note of reality" as they "move[d] directly from Scripture to the concrete, actual situation in Geneva."[47] Calvin's expositions were continually "moving toward practical spiritual applications."[48] The Reformer said, "Doctrine is not an affair of the tongue, but of the life."[49] By this, he meant that the issue is not what his listeners merely say they believe but how they live. Accordingly, Calvin contended, "Doctrine is not apprehended by the intellect and memory merely, like other branches of learning; but is received only when it possesses the whole soul, and finds its seat and habitation in the inmost recesses of the heart."[50] Thus, a right understanding of the truth is foundational, but it is not final. After the truth is learned, it must be lived. Calvin wrote that doctrine must be "given the first place" in the sermon, "but it must be transformed into the breast, and pass into the conduct, and so transform us."[51] For Calvin, the bottom line in preaching is the application of truth that leads to the transformation of life.

The Expository Commitment of Calvin

In summary, these five distinctives marked the unwavering commitment of Calvin in his expository preaching. He believed that the public proclamation of Scripture must be biblical, sequential, authoritative, explanatory, and applicational. In other words, Calvin insisted that expository preaching (1) be rooted in the biblical text, (2) move consecutively through books in the Bible, (3) come with the recognized authority of God, (4) properly explain a passage of Scripture, and (5) show

---

45. Thompson, "Calvin as a Biblical Interpreter," 71.
46. Leith, "Calvin's Doctrine," 215.
47. Leith, "Calvin's Doctrine," 215.
48. Leith, "Calvin's Doctrine," 215.
49. John Calvin, *Institutes of the Christian Religion*, trans. Henry Beveridge, 2nd ed. (Edinburgh: T&T Clark, 1895), 3.6.4.
50. Calvin, *Institutes*, trans. Beveridge, 3.6.4.
51. Calvin, *Institutes*, trans. Beveridge, 3.6.4.

its practical relevance in the life of the congregation. This is the heart and soul of expository preaching as Calvin perceived it, and *this* is how he practiced it. Such a high standard for the pulpit requires considerable preparation, and Calvin modeled extensive preparation for preaching.

Calvin's Preparation for Expository Preaching

When Calvin stepped into the pulpit, he drew from a deep well of the knowledge of God and Scripture. To rightly preach, Calvin had to be rightly prepared before God. This necessitated that he be disciplined in both his spiritual life and his scriptural learning. For Calvin, the essential prerequisites for being an effective expositor were personal piety and thorough study. The basic components in Calvin's preparation for the pulpit are as follows.

The Knowledge of God

For Calvin, the first step in sermon preparation was growing in the personal knowledge of God. This is precisely where Calvin began his *Institutes of the Christian Religion*. The Christian life, he believed, begins with the true knowledge of God. So does preaching. To know God is not simply to have intellectual knowledge about him. Rather, it is to enter into a personal relationship with him and to grow experientially closer to him. This true knowledge of God begins with genuine conversion. Calvin had experienced such a personal encounter with the living God while studying in France. Calvin described his new birth as "a sudden conversion" in which, he said, God "subdued and brought my mind to a teachable frame."[52] Immediately, he "received some taste and knowledge of true godliness" and was "inflamed" with an intense desire to make progress in holiness.[53] All preaching is the overflow of this heart communion with God.

Throughout his Christian life, Calvin steadfastly grew in the personal knowledge of God. It was out of this intimate communion with the living God that this magisterial Reformer preached. Benjamin B. Warfield, renowned professor at Princeton, wrote, "Here we have the

---

52. Calvin, preface to *Commentary on the Book of Psalms*, trans. James Anderson (repr., Grand Rapids, MI: Baker, 2003), xl–xli.
53. Calvin, preface to *Commentary on the Psalms*, xl–xli.

secret of Calvin's greatness and the source of his strength unveiled to us. No man ever had a profounder sense of God than he; no man ever more unreservedly surrendered himself to the Divine direction."[54] Calvin preached out of the overflow of beholding the supreme glory of God in the pages of Scripture. As John Piper states, "Nothing mattered more to Calvin than the supremacy of God over all things."[55] Thus, his preaching could be described as "exaltational" preaching, that which magnifies the greatness of God.

The Knowledge of Scripture

In the second place, Calvin possessed an extensive knowledge of the Scriptures. His commitment to apprehend the God-intended meaning of the biblical text drove him to diligent study. For the Genevan Reformer, his knowledge of the Bible was the result of a lifetime of learning. Calvin wrote that the preacher "ought to be prepared by long study for giving to the people, as out of a storehouse, a variety of instruction concerning the Word of God."[56] To be an expositor, he made the disciplined inquiry into Scripture a way of life. The Genevan wrote,

> We must all be pupils of the Holy Scriptures, even to the end; even those, I mean, who are appointed to proclaim the Word. If we enter the pulpit, it is on this condition, that we learn while teaching others. I am not speaking here merely that others may hear me; but I too, for my part, must be a pupil of God. The most accomplished in the Scripture . . . [must] acknowledge that they have need of God for their schoolmaster all the days of their life.[57]

For Calvin, this comprehensive study was buttressed through his continuous lecturing, writing, and commentary work. His massive commentary on the Bible is one of the largest Bible commentaries ever written by a single individual, spanning forty-five large volumes, each

54. Benjamin B. Warfield, *Calvin and Calvinism* (1932; repr., Grand Rapids, MI: Baker, 2000), 24.

55. John Piper, *The Legacy of Sovereign Joy: God's Triumphant Grace in the Lives of Augustine, Luther, and Calvin* (Wheaton, IL: Crossway, 2000), 115.

56. *Comm.*, 16:134.

57. John Calvin, quoted in D'Aubigné, *History of the Reformation in Europe*, 7:84–85.

more than four hundred pages. This work occupied "the largest share of his life after his return to Geneva."[58] In his commentaries, Calvin "analyzed in great detail one book of Scripture at a time, beginning with the New Testament and eventually moving to the Old."[59] This massive project covers almost every book in the Old Testament, with the exception of fifteen books, three of which he preached through (Job and 1 and 2 Samuel). Further, he wrote a commentary on every book in the New Testament except three books, 2 John, 3 John, and Revelation. This extensive grasp of Scripture was further evidenced by his *Institutes*, which contains 1,755 quotations from the Old Testament and 3,098 from the New Testament.[60] In addition, Calvin wrote dozens of theological treatises that were careful presentations and defenses of important biblical doctrines. It was out of this deep and detailed knowledge of Scripture that Calvin stepped into the pulpit to preach.

Calvin's thorough study of God's word gave him an immediate recall and command of its truths. The Reformer "knew much of it virtually by memory, and most of it was available to him by quick and effective reference."[61] Calvin said,

> If I should enter the pulpit without deigning to look at a book and should frivolously think to myself, "Oh, well, when I preach, God will give me enough to say," and come here without troubling to read or think what I ought to declare, and do not carefully consider how I must apply Holy Scripture to the edification of the people, then I should be an arrogant upstart.[62]

To the contrary, Calvin gave himself to the rigorous study of the Bible as few in church history have.

The Knowledge of Literary Analysis

During his days at the Universities of Paris, Orléans, and Bourges (1523–1532), Calvin became "a scholar trained in the humanist

---

58. Bouwsma, *John Calvin*, 28.
59. Bouwsma, *John Calvin*, 28.
60. John H. Leith, *John Calvin's Doctrine of the Christian Life* (Louisville: Westminster John Knox, 1989), 62n195.
61. Leith, "Calvin's Doctrine," 223.
62. Calvin, "Sermon on Deuteronomy 6:13–15," quoted in Leith, "Calvin's Doctrine," 35.

tradition of the Renaissance."[63] In this academic discipline, he was taught the skills of textual analysis, including a working knowledge of authorial intent, literary genre, figures of speech, and stylistic differences between writers. This emphasis emerged out of the Renaissance, and Calvin was well trained in this endeavor. During his university days, Calvin's first love was the study of classical literature. His first published book was a secular commentary on *De Clementia* (*On Mercy*), written by the Roman philosopher Seneca the Younger. This early work revealed Calvin's ability to break down language and grasp the intentions of an author. In subsequent years, this was precisely what Calvin did with the Scriptures. He searched out the God-intended meaning of a biblical text by grappling with the literature of the scriptural writers.

Further, Calvin graduated from the University of Bourges with a doctor of laws degree. This exposure gave him incredible skills in public rhetoric and persuasive argument, skills he would use in the pulpit. So efficient did Calvin become in presenting a convincing argument that he was nicknamed "the accusative case." These same powers of inductive and deductive reasoning, fortified by convincing logic, valid conclusions, and a proper defense of propositions, would become an integral part of Calvin's faculties to stand in the pulpit and present the truthfulness of Scripture and refute those who contradicted it. Through these previously acquired skills, the Genevan expositor was well prepared to interpret the biblical text and convincingly argue his point.

The Knowledge of Biblical Languages

The advent of the Reformation was preceded by the scholastic pursuit of the Renaissance, which began in the fourteenth century in Italy and extended into the seventeenth century. The Renaissance witnessed a revival of interest in classical writings, including an interest in Hebrew and Greek. John Reuchlin wrote several books on Hebrew grammar, including *A Grammatical Interpretation of the Seven Penitential Psalms*. Desiderius Erasmus, the leading humanist of

---

63. Evans, "Sermons on Acts 1–7," 16.

the Renaissance, edited and published in 1516 the first edition of the Greek New Testament. For Calvin, this renewed interest enabled him to become proficient in the original languages. Calvin was first introduced to Hebrew while a student at the University of Paris (1531) under the venerable François Vatable, "the greatest Hebraist of his day" and "the restorer of Hebrew scholarship in France."[64] Calvin also learned Greek, while pursuing a law degree at Orléans and Bourges (1531–1532) under the teaching of Melchior Wolmar. This renowned Greek scholar gave Calvin "a good grounding in the rudiments of the language."[65] Calvin later resided in Basel (1535–1536), where he deepened his conviction that "the Bible was to be read and understood according to the original texts."[66] There he met Simon Grynaeus, a Greek professor at the University of Basel, who "significantly contributed to Calvin's study of and ability in the Greek language."[67] Calvin further studied Hebrew under Sebastian Münster during his exile from Geneva while in Strasbourg (1538–1541). The point is, it was this proficiency in Hebrew and Greek that deepened Calvin's ability to exegete the biblical text.

John Currid notes, "The biblical languages were foundational to Calvin's exegetical prowess."[68] It was this linguistic skill in the original languages that undergirded his study of the Scripture. John Murray says, "Calvin was the exegete of the Reformation and in the first rank of biblical exegetes of all time."[69] This ability to probe the biblical text included grappling with individual words, grammatical syntax, literary genre, historical contexts, and geography. This study required Calvin to examine the meaning of words in the Hebrew and Greek languages and how they are associated in sentences. Calvin brought this linguistic knowledge and exegetical skill into his study for the pulpit, enabling him to plumb the depths of the Scripture.

---

64. John Currid, *Calvin and the Biblical Languages* (Fearn, Ross-shire, Scotland: Mentor, 2006), 14, 15.
65. CNTC, 10:1.
66. Currid, *Calvin and the Biblical Languages*, 19.
67. Currid, *Calvin and the Biblical Languages*, 20.
68. Currid, *Calvin and the Biblical Languages*, 13.
69. Murray, "Calvin as Theologian and Expositor," in *Collected Writings of John Murray*, 1:308.

The Knowledge of Historical Theology

In addition, Calvin's understanding of Scripture was further aided by his extensive reading of historical theology. He was conversant with the writings of the church fathers, church councils, medieval theologians, and other Reformers of his day. Certainly, *sola Scriptura* was the battle cry of the Reformation, but this does not mean that Calvin was unacquainted with the contributions of these other gifted individuals. In fact, he was sharpened by their writings. John Currid states, "Calvin did not shy away from using extrabiblical texts in order to explain a meaning of a Scriptural passage."[70] For example, in the *Institutes*, Calvin quoted heavily the church fathers and medieval theologians, referencing such notable men as Irenaeus, Tertullian, Origen, Cyprian, Eusebius, Hilary of Poitiers, Gregory Nazianzus, Basil of Caesarea, Ambrose, Jerome, John Chrysostom, Augustine, Cyril of Alexandria, Theodoret, Gregory the Great, Anselm, Bernard of Clairvaux, Peter Lombard, Thomas Aquinas, Clement V, and more.[71] This reveals how well read Calvin was—and, no doubt, how influenced he was by the Patristics, ecclesiastical councils, and medieval teachers.

So great was the influence of Augustine on Calvin's thinking that the Reformer wrote, "Augustine is so much at one with me that, if I wished to write a confession of my faith, it would abundantly satisfy me to quote wholesale from his writings."[72] In his *Institutes*, Calvin makes nearly seven hundred references to the works of Augustine, a staggering number. There is an inseparable connection between Calvin and the great church father Augustine, considered the greatest theologian of the first 1500 years of church history. In addition, the noted medieval theologian Bernard of Clairvaux "deeply influenced the early Calvin."[73] The other major works of Calvin, such as his *Bondage and Liberation of the Will* (1543), cite the theological insights of the church fathers in order to refute his opponents. As he stepped into the

---

70. Currid, *Calvin and the Biblical Languages*, 24.
71. Anthony N. S. Lane, *John Calvin: Student of the Church Fathers* (Grand Rapids, MI: Baker, 1999), 55–61.
72. John Calvin, *Concerning the Eternal Predestination of God*, trans. J. K. S. Reid (Cambridge: James Clark, 1961), 63.
73. Lane, *John Calvin*, 8.

pulpit to preach, Calvin's understanding of Scripture had been molded by these earlier leaders and their writings.

Calvin's Launching of the Sermon

Whenever Calvin mounted the lofty pulpit in Geneva, he stood before an open Bible, ready to expound the divinely inspired word. In launching the sermon, the introduction played a key role. His goal was to draw the listeners into the text as quickly as possible, orienting them to the mind of the biblical author. The following are some of the peculiar traits of how Calvin chose to begin his sermons.

Scripture Reading

As the sermon commenced, Calvin would first "read his text of Scripture."[74] He did not begin with a compelling quote, captivating illustration, personal anecdote, or cultural reference. Instead, the Reformer launched the message with the public reading of the Scriptures in the pulpit. In commenting on 1 Timothy 4:13, Calvin agreed with what Paul required, that there must be "reading before doctrine and exhortation."[75] The reason for the Scripture reading, Calvin asserted, is that "the Scripture is the fountain of all wisdom, from which pastors must draw all that they place before their flock."[76] Therefore, the reading of the Scripture set the direction and tone for the entire sermon. This entire sermon would be an exposition of this passage.

For Calvin, the Scripture reading was from his Bible in the original language. That is, as he read the word, he translated from either the Hebrew or Greek Bible, depending on which testament he was preaching from. Calvin was a Frenchman by birth, background, and education. Thus, French was his native tongue, the language in which he preached in Geneva to French-speaking people. But the Reformer did not preach from a French Bible. Rather, when expounding the Old Testament, Calvin sight-read the Hebrew text without any linguistic aids, translating into French as he read. When expounding a New Testament book, Calvin carried his Greek Bible into the

---

74. Currid, *Calvin and the Biblical Languages*, 24.
75. *Comm.*, 11:115.
76. *Comm.*, 11:115.

pulpit,[77] translating into French. To be sure, Calvin was well versed and equally at home in the original languages of the Scripture. As a result, this brilliant man used them exclusively in the pulpit as he ministered the word.

Direct Beginning

Having read his text, Calvin then proceeded to give "a brief introduction."[78] The intent was to immediately acclimate his listeners to the biblical text and establish the larger context. Most often, Calvin began by "reminding the congregation of where he had left off in the last sermon."[79] Generally, he briefly restated "what he had usually been treating in the previous sermon."[80] In other words, he typically began by reviewing the central thrust of the previous sermon. Calvin was reestablishing the historical and biblical context of his passage, as well as reintroducing the developing argument of the biblical author.

Calvin next directed the congregation to the unique emphasis of this particular text. In so doing, Calvin put the listener into the central thought of the biblical author. And he attempted to build a connection between the biblical author and his congregation. In the introduction, Calvin would often say something like, "And now St. Paul brings us to the origin and source, or rather to the principal cause that moved God to take us into His favor."[81] Or he would say, "But now it remains to be seen how God receives us into His favor by means of our Lord Jesus Christ."[82] Or he stated, "But let us notice here how Saint Paul uses two words to express how we are reconciled to God."[83] These statements are representative of how Calvin narrowed his focus and drew in the listener to the passage. Further, he would also attempt to show something of the practical relevance of the passage. For Calvin, the introduction was direct, succinct, and straightforward.

---

77. See especially Parker, *Calvin's Preaching*, 172–78.
78. Boice, foreword to Calvin, *Sermons on Psalm 119*, ix.
79. Dawn DeVries, "Calvin's Preaching," in McKim, *Cambridge Companion to John Calvin*, 112.
80. Boice, foreword to Calvin, *Sermons on Psalm 119*, ix.
81. Calvin, *Sermons on Ephesians*, 22.
82. Calvin, *Sermons on Ephesians*, 50.
83. Calvin, *Sermons on Ephesians*, 51.

Spontaneous Delivery

As Calvin delivered his sermon, he used no written manuscript, no sermon notes, and no visual aids.[84] This is not to suggest that he was unprepared. To the contrary, such a style demanded extensive study. Calvin spoke extemporaneously, relying on the Holy Spirit to draw from his study. Calvin was mindful that he must speak to common people in the pew, not professional theologians in a classroom. He wanted his heart to be engaged, his delivery to be natural, and his vocabulary to be understandable. Thus, he stood with only an open Bible before him, spontaneously giving a clear, concise explanation of the text. An easy, deliberate flow resulted, offered with a personal pastoral tone.

Hughes Oliphant Old observes that it was Calvin's powers of concentration and recall that "enabled him to preach without notes or manuscript."[85] In this impromptu manner of delivery, "the sermon content emerged spontaneously out of Calvin's deep and detailed knowledge of Scripture."[86] Old remarks, "The sermon itself was put together before the congregation."[87] This impulsive style stood in stark contrast to the lifeless preaching of his day, in which the preacher merely read his sermon notes in stoic fashion. Such a stale delivery was usually carried out in a dry, cold manner—something Calvin sought to avoid. The Reformer said, "It appears to me that there is very little preaching of a lively kind in the Kingdom; but that the greater part deliver it by way of reading from a written discourse."[88] To counter this deadening trend, Calvin preached as he did, without reading or referencing any notes. This, he believed, would enhance the dynamic of his sermon delivery.

Singular Theme

As Calvin concluded the introduction, he usually stated the central theme of the passage. The primary thrust of the text was announced and became the main idea of his message. Parker explains, "The theme [of his sermon] is the theme of Holy Scripture."[89] For example, Parker

---

84. T. H. L. Parker, *John Calvin: A Biography* (Philadelphia: Westminster, 1975), 92.
85. Old, *Reading and Preaching*, 4:129.
86. Evans, "Sermons on Acts 1–7," 17.
87. Old, *Reading and Preaching*, 4:129.
88. John Calvin, *Letters of John Calvin: Selected from the Bonnet Edition with an Introductory Biographical Sketch* (Edinburgh: Banner of Truth, 1980), 95.
89. Parker, *John Calvin*, 94.

states, "If his text is a passage from Job he will expound and apply that passage. If from Ephesians, then he will expound and apply that passage. He will never commit the contempt of Scripture that prevails today of reading a verse from the Bible and preaching about something quite different."[90] That is, Calvin was not imposing his "pet doctrines" on each sermon. Eisegesis was not his goal; exegesis was. Whatever truths were in this particular passage became his main preaching idea.

Despite the misconceptions of many, Calvin's messages were "not severely logical lectures on the sovereignty of God, predestination, providence and Church discipline."[91] Regardless of the stereotype, Calvin's messages were not a constant threat of excluding people from the Lord's Table. Not every exposition was an "attack" on "the papacy for ecclesiastical abuses, or on theological opponents for their stupidity."[92] Granted, these truths were addressed in his sermons but only when his passage addressed them. Parker concludes, "The consistent focus of Calvin's preaching was the passage that was before him. His sermons have as many themes as Scripture."[93] In other words, the biblical text will not say one thing but the Reformer preach something else. To the contrary, Calvin let each individual passage speak its own message.

Calvin's Explaining of the Text

After the introduction, Calvin immediately proceeded into the exposition of the Scripture passage itself. The humanist cry of the day was *ad fontes*—"to the sources." The Reformers applied this maxim to their preaching, and Calvin was no exception. Calvin's earlier humanist education "taught him to return to the sources and trained him in the skills of interpretation."[94] He applied this learning to the Bible, which enabled him to obtain a proper handling of the biblical passage. Thus, the vast majority of his sermon was spent plunging into the sacred text to excavate the depth of its riches and discover its true meaning. This, Calvin believed, was an absolute prerequisite for God-honoring exposition.

---

90. Parker, *John Calvin*, 94.
91. Parker, *John Calvin*, 94.
92. Parker, *John Calvin*, 94.
93. Parker, *John Calvin*, 94.
94. Leith, "Calvin's Doctrine," 209.

Specific Passage

As Calvin began the exposition, he always had a specific text before him. The length of the Scripture passage varied according to the genre of the literature and the specific emphasis Calvin desired to make. If preaching from an epistle, Calvin typically expounded one or two verses, sometimes even two or three messages from one verse. When preaching from one of the Old Testament prophets, he unfolded four or five verses. And if preaching a narrative, Calvin preached from as many as ten to twelve verses.[95]

For Calvin, the entirety of the sermon was an exposition of one passage of Scripture. He began with a specific text and stayed with it throughout the message. The entire sermon was an explanation and application of the passage. The introduction directly led into the text, and all that followed flowed out of the passage. The entire message lay within the parameters of this unit of Scripture.

Sound Exegesis

In expounding any passage, Calvin gave himself to the solid exegesis of the text. This required analyzing literary style, word meanings, grammatical structure, historical background, book context, and authorial intent. Owing to his classical education and further studies, Calvin was well trained for this discipline. Schaff notes, "Calvin is the founder of the modern grammatico-historical exegesis."[96] And David Puckett writes, "Calvin can neither uproot a text from its immediate literary context nor neglect the environment in which the document was originally produced. The exegete may not neglect the audience to whom the writer was originally addressed."[97] In this exegetical endeavor, Calvin was among the best.

As Calvin stood in the pulpit, preaching from a Hebrew or Greek Bible, he gave strict attention to the linguistic nuances of the biblical text. His eye was attuned to the emphatic position of words, verb tenses, subordinate clauses, supportive phrases, connecting conjunctions, and the like. His exegetical skill allowed Calvin to

---

95. Cf. Parker, *Calvin's Preaching*, 84.
96. Schaff, *History of the Christian Church*, 8:532.
97. David L. Puckett, *John Calvin's Exegesis of the Old Testament*, CSRT (Louisville: Westminster John Knox, 1995), 67.

step, as close as humanly possible, into the mind of the biblical author. As he advanced verse by verse, Calvin kept the larger context before him. The Reformer, Puckett observes, "almost always favors the interpretation that he believes best suits the context."[98] That is, any possible interpretation that could not be justified contextually was disregarded.

Literal Interpretation

Regarded as "one of the greatest interpreters of the Bible,"[99] Calvin insisted on the *sensus literalis*—the literal sense of the biblical text. He put it this way: "The true meaning of Scripture is the natural and obvious meaning."[100] Like the other Reformers, he rejected allegorical interpretations, calling them "frivolous games" that torture the Scripture, stripping the text of its true meaning. He refused the medieval *quadriga*, the ancient interpretation scheme that allowed for a fourfold meaning of a text: literal, moral, allegorical, and anagogical. Instead, Calvin insisted that the words within each specific passage were to be understood literally within its historical context and grammatical structure. In so doing, he sought to unfold the plain, or natural, meaning of Scripture. Schaff notes, "[Calvin] affirmed . . . the sound and fundamental hermeneutical principle that the biblical authors, like all sensible writers, wished to convey to their readers one definite thought in words which they could understand."[101]

The literalism of Calvin's interpretation was influenced by the Renaissance scholars' desire to get at "the original and genuine meaning of a text"[102] in classical literature. For Calvin, discovering the literal meaning of the text was his primary hermeneutical goal. He declared, "I have observed . . . a simple style of teaching. . . . I have felt nothing to be of more importance than a literal interpretation of the biblical text."[103] As John Leith puts it, "Calvin's purpose in preaching was to

---

98. Puckett, *John Calvin's Exegesis*, 64.

99. James D. Wood, *The Interpretation of the Bible: A Historical Introduction* (London: Gerald Duckworth, 1958), 91.

100. John Calvin, *Sermons on Galatians*, trans. Kathy Childress (1563; repr., Edinburgh: Banner of Truth, 1997), 136.

101. Schaff, *History of the Christian Church*, 8:532.

102. Joseph Haroutunian, "General Introduction," in *Calvin: Commentaries*, trans. and ed. Joseph Haroutunian with Louise Pettibone Smith, LCC 23 (Philadelphia: Westminster, 1958), 28.

103. *Calvin: Commentaries*, 359.

render transparent the text of Scripture itself."[104] This commitment was the cornerstone of Calvin's preaching. The true meaning of the text is the text. The Reformer stated, "The important thing is that the Scripture should be understood and explained; how it is explained is secondary."[105] Thus, Calvin valued substance over style—the proper interpretation over a captivating presentation.

Cross-References

In establishing the literal meaning, Calvin often cited other passages of Scripture. In this way, Calvin held to the analogy of faith. This is the fundamental belief that the Bible speaks with one voice, nowhere contradicting itself. The Reformers held that the entire Bible, from Genesis to Revelation, teaches one body of truth, one system of theology, one view of history, and one ethic for morality. Because Scripture is the word of God, it is seamlessly consistent. Calvin declared, *Sacra Scriptura sui interpres*—Scripture interprets Scripture. Therefore, when seeking to determine the right meaning of a text, Calvin was ready to appeal to other passages to find additional light and support. The clearer passages should interpret the less clear ones.

In so doing, Calvin used cross-references strategically and, at times, sparingly. He desired not to wander away from the primary passage that lay before him. His cross-references were carefully chosen, intending not to deviate from the central thrust of the sermon. He chose to remain within the focus of a clear exposition of the main passage. In cross-referencing, Calvin often cited a biblical passage and paraphrased it. On other occasions, he directly quoted a verse, reciting it from memory. In these instances, he would say something like "as Saint Paul says" without giving the specific reference. At other times, he would give the actual textual citation, such as which psalm he was quoting.

Calvin's Style in the Delivery

Expository preaching is both a science and an art. The science of biblical exposition is governed by certain laws of exegesis, hermeneutics, and

---

104. Leith, "Calvin's Doctrine," 214.
105. John Calvin, quoted in T. H. L. Parker, *Calvin's New Testament Commentaries* (Grand Rapids, MI: Eerdmans, 1971), 50.

communication. These principles cannot be broken, and they demand the strict adherence of all preachers. There should be only one and the same interpretation of any passage of Scripture. But there is also the art of expository preaching. Here the issue is not in what the text says but in how the preacher relays it. Here each preacher is as unique as each person is different. Calvin was well prepared in both the science and art of exposition. The Reformer saw that his primary aim was to rightly interpret Scripture, but it must be communicated in a way that is clear, concise, and compelling. In his delivery, Calvin was never seeking to impress his congregation with his own brilliance. Rather, he sought to imbue them with the awe-inspiring majesty of God. The following can be said for the cogent style with which he preached the word.

Familiar Language

In the pulpit, Calvin communicated in simple and familiar language. Alister McGrath notes, "One of the most significant moments in the history of the Reformation is Martin Luther's decision in 1520 to switch from being an academic reformer (arguing in Latin to an academic public) to a popular one (arguing in German to a broader one)."[106] Calvin followed suit, choosing to preach on a popular level to reach a broad audience. As a result, Calvin chose to employ simple words and understandable language: "His words are straightforward, the sentences simple."[107] The Reformer intended to make the meaning of Scripture "as clear as possible to his listeners."[108] Thus, his sermons were easily comprehensible by his congregation. Parker explains that Calvin's vocabulary was "nearly always familiar and easy. . . . He is so intent on making himself understood that now and then he will think it necessary to explain a simple word which is nevertheless ambiguous from similarity of sound with a quite different word."[109] Parker explains that this familiarity of speech is "made possible and also heightened by his preaching extemporarily."[110] His spontaneity allowed him to express himself with common clichés, colloquial expressions, verbal

---

106. Alister E. McGrath, *A Life of John Calvin: A Study in the Shaping of Western Culture* (Oxford: Blackwell, 2001), 134.
107. Boice, foreword to Calvin, *Sermons on Psalm 119*, x.
108. Boice, foreword to Calvin, *Sermons on Psalm 119*, x.
109. Parker, *Calvin's Preaching*, 141–42.
110. Parker, *Calvin's Preaching*, 140.

repetition, and simple vocabulary. The profoundness of the truth that Calvin expounded was "never at the expense of comprehensibility."[111]

Even Calvin's sentences were marked by simplicity. The longer sentences in the English translations of his sermons were probably shorter in the original language. He said, "Preachers must be like fathers dividing bread into small pieces to feed their children."[112] Joel Beeke observes that Calvin's towering intellect lies "nearly always concealed, behind [his] deceptively simple explanations of his author's meaning."[113] He spoke in "simple and general terms"[114] so as not to speak over the heads of his sheep but to connect with them. Parker writes,

> His language was clear and easy. He spoke in a way that the Genevese could understand, even, it would seem, to the point of using some of their idiosyncrasies of French. . . . To clarity of sense and diction he paid great attention, carefully explaining unusual or technical words in the biblical text.[115]

"There is little rhetorical flourish,"[116] Boice writes. Calvin "delighted in the simple and straightforward rhetoric of the Bible" and "attempted to imitate it in his preaching style," Currid adds.[117] The Reformer recognized "the clear brevity of the Word of God," which in turn required "the simple eloquence of preaching from the pulpit."[118]

Vivid Expressions

Calvin used striking expressions as he preached. Educated in the finest liberal arts universities of the day, he possessed and used an arsenal of literary devices in his preaching. Included were such weapons as metaphors, similes, comparisons, hyperbole, colloquial expressions, provocative questions, rhetorical questions, dramatic repetition, and simple restatements. All these figures of speech and manners of

---

111. Richard C. Gamble, foreword to John Calvin, *The Deity of Christ and Other Sermons*, trans. Leroy Nixon (1581; repr., Audubon, NJ: Old Paths, 1997), 8.

112. John Calvin, quoted in Joel Beeke, "John Calvin: Teacher and Practitioner of Evangelism," *R&R* 10, no. 4 (2001): 69.

113. Beeke, "John Calvin," 87.

114. Parker, *Calvin's Preaching*, 86.

115. Parker, *John Calvin*, 93.

116. Boice, foreword to Calvin, *Sermons on Psalm 119*, x.

117. Currid, *Calvin and the Biblical Languages*, 28.

118. Currid, *Calvin and the Biblical Languages*, 28.

expression made Calvin's preaching colorful, compelling, memorable, and easy to understand. Further, Calvin had learned from his days in law school powers of persuasive rhetoric. He employed airtight logic and inductive and deductive reasoning—establishing a premise, supporting an argument, rebutting an opponent, refuting an error, and convincing a listener. Like a lawyer before the jury presenting his final argument, Calvin knew the high value of calling for a verdict in the heart of the listener. Calvin used all these rhetorical tools in his pulpit ministry, making his preaching powerful.

Timothy George notes, "A proper understanding of Calvin must take seriously his masterful use of figurative language."[119] David Engelsma observes that his communication style was "vivid, forceful, and thus popular."[120] Leith adds, "His sermons are replete with metaphors, comparisons, and proverbial images and wisdom that appeal to the imagination."[121] He used "colloquial expressions"[122] that were striking to the ear of his congregation. For example, Calvin called his opponents "barking dogs," "vile goats," and "ravenous wolves."[123] The good works in which men trust, Calvin said, are "like smoke in our hands."[124] Calvin spoke of unlearned men in the Scripture as "tavern theologians."[125] Such men are "swollen with pride, to the point of bursting."[126] False teachers are "rogues" and "deadly plagues."[127] Those who refuse to acknowledge their sin, he declared, "play make-believe and hide their depravity."[128] Men who resist God's word are "like wild beasts throwing off their yokes,"[129] "ready to kick us in the teeth."[130] People who refuse to confess their iniquity "shut their eyes, or blindfold themselves."[131] Humor was scarce in Calvin's pulpit—he was "no

---

119. George, introduction to *John Calvin and the Church*, 24.
120. Engelsma, foreword to Calvin, *Sermons on Election and Reprobation*, ix.
121. Leith, "Calvin's Doctrine," 221.
122. Gamble, foreword to Calvin, *Deity of Christ*, 8.
123. John Calvin, sermon on 2 Tim. 2:16–18, in *A Selection of the Most Celebrated Sermons of John Calvin* (New York: S. & D. A. Forbes, 1830), 65.
124. Calvin, *Sermons on Galatians*, 215.
125. John Calvin, *Sermons on the Book of Micah*, trans. and ed. Benjamin Wirt Farley (Phillipsburg, NJ: P&R, 2003), 378.
126. Calvin, *Sermons on Galatians*, 215.
127. Calvin, *Sermons on Galatians*, 112.
128. Calvin, *Sermons on Galatians*, 220.
129. Calvin, *Sermons on Galatians*, 223.
130. Calvin, *Sermons on Galatians*, 409.
131. Calvin, *Sermons on Galatians*, 410.

smiling, positive preacher."[132] Nevertheless, he used dry wit and biting sarcasm that presumably drew a smile or shocked his listeners.

Simple Restatements

Moreover, Calvin used simple restatements in explaining a biblical text. By restating a verse in alternative words, he could convey its meaning in simpler terms. Accordingly, Calvin was wont to adopt a different sentence structure and use synonyms to be more easily understood. According to Ford Lewis Battles, Calvin was a superb explicator of Scripture because he was "a master of the paraphrase."[133] He could reword Scripture with precision and clarity, "translating it into the language of the common human discourse of his own time."[134] This elucidating skill was developed through his training in liberal arts and classical literature, applied with theological and spiritual insight to his preaching.

For example, in Calvin's sermons on Micah and Galatians, he used certain signature phrases to introduce a restatement, such as these: "It is as if he were saying . . ."; "In effect, he is saying . . ."; or "In other words . . ."[135] This ability to restate a biblical text with substitute language, while speaking without prepared notes, was an important component of Calvin's skill in explaining the meaning of the text in an understandable fashion.

Unspoken Outline

As Calvin preached, he had a clear structure of thought for the sermon in his orderly, brilliant mind, though he announced no sermon outline from the pulpit. As Leith puts it, Calvin "did not fashion his sermons according to logical outline."[136] For the most part, he omitted homiletical headings. Calvin did articulate his major thrusts, which were arranged in tight paragraphs of well-developed thought. But the arrangement of the message did not follow a stated outline with

---

132. Engelsma, foreword to Calvin, *Sermons on Election and Reprobation*, xiii.

133. Ford Lewis Battles and André Malan Hugo, eds. and trans., *Calvin's Commentary on Seneca's "De Clementia": With Introduction, Translation, and Notes*, RTS 3 (Leiden: Brill, 1969), 79.

134. Leith, "Calvin's Doctrine," 212.

135. Calvin, *Sermons on Micah*, 55; Calvin, *Sermons on Galatians*, 321, 314.

136. Leith, "Calvin's Doctrine," 217.

recognizable divisions. For Calvin, there were no polished, alliterated headings, such as "The *Purpose* of Prayer," "The *Particulars* of Prayer," and the like. Calvin instead moved through the biblical text "sentence by sentence, sometimes even word by word, explaining what each part means,"[137] which resulted in a natural flow to the message and an unhindered, conversational feel to the delivery.

The sermon was certainly not without form and structure. The text itself provided the shape that the message would take. Parker notes,

> The form of his sermons is determined by the exposition. In theory it follows the pattern of explanation of a clause or sentence and its application to the people, sometimes in the context of an immediate situation. In practice, the form is flexible, even loose. It is saved from being rambling by his capacity for keeping to the point and breaking the material up into short sections.[138]

Parker continues, "His manner of delivery was lively, passionate, intimate, direct, and clear."[139] Calvin's goal was to "speak from the heart."[140] As he expounded the passage, the Reformer established subordinate truths under the major thoughts, though he did not necessarily state these supporting thrusts as such.

Smooth Transitions

In addition, Calvin used smooth transitions as he advanced from one thought to the next. Such transitions served as bridges in communication, ushering the listener to the next heading of truth. Because he was concerned with the flow of thought in his messages, Calvin made sure his sermons were connected at the seams. He did not want to leave behind any of his listeners with abrupt, disconnected changes in direction. Because of this, it cannot be said that Calvin was a sterile exegete, devoid of linguistic skills. Rather, he was smooth, graceful, and purposeful as he conveyed biblical truth. In this, Calvin was easy to follow.

---

137. Boice, foreword to Calvin, *Sermons on Psalm 119*, ix.
138. Parker, *John Calvin*, 92.
139. Parker, *John Calvin*, 93.
140. Parker, *John Calvin*, 93.

A sampling of the transitional phrases from his first sermon on Micah reveal this practice. Calvin pulled his listeners along as he introduced new paragraphs of thought with the following segues:

At the same time . . .
Furthermore . . .
But let us consider . . .
It is time, now, to summarize . . .
In addition, we might wonder why . . .
Now it is quite true that . . .
On the contrary . . .
From this example it can be seen that . . .
Accordingly, we should infer from the foregoing that . . .
Now from this text we glean . . .
But, on the contrary, one finds . . .
We now come to what the prophet adds . . .
In the meanwhile, let us note . . .
That, I say, is how proud and presumptuous . . .
Now the prophet specifically says to them . . .
That is the similarity that the prophet alludes to here . . .
In truth . . .
Having said that, however, we should note . . . [141]

Transitional phrases, such as these, applied a structural polish to Calvin's messages.

Focused Intensity

What is more, as Calvin spoke, he did so with a focused intensity that held captive the attention of his congregation. Singularly absorbed in the biblical text, Calvin preached with riveting powers of concentration, convictions, and sacred passion. "Doctrine without zeal," he declared, "is either like a sword in the hand of a madman, or else it lieth still as cold and without use, or else it serveth for vain and wicked boasting."[142] Calvin's deep beliefs drew people to the truth as he preached. Old writes, "Let us ask why Calvin was

---

141. Calvin, *Sermons on Micah*, 4–16.
142. *Comm.*, 19:201.

regarded so highly as a preacher. Why did people listen to him?" He then answers,

> Although Calvin is never thought of as a great orator, he did have some important gifts of public speaking. He seems to have had an intensity which he focused on the text of Scripture which was so powerful that he drew his hearers into the sacred text along with him. This intensity comes from his tremendous power of concentration.[143]

Philip Schaff notes that it was the building intensity in Calvin's delivery that made him so compelling. The Reformer, Schaff notes, "lacked the genial element of humor and pleasantry; he was a Christian stoic: stern, severe, unbending."[144] Yet in spite of this absolute seriousness, there were "fires of passion and affection glowing beneath the marble surface."[145] In Schaff's view, this zeal—this burning, internal energy—was a key component of Calvin's success as a preacher. He writes, "History furnished no more striking example of a man of so little personal popularity, and yet such great influence upon the people; of such natural timidity and bashfulness combined with such strength of intellect and character, and such control over his and future generations."[146] In Calvin's words, the preacher must speak "in a way that shows he is not pretending."[147] This the Genevan Reformer did.

Calvin's Application of the Truth

As Calvin explained the word, he sought to apply it in an edifying manner to his congregation. From his pulpit, he addressed real people with real needs. He spoke to them right where they lived. In his Genevan congregation were countless persecuted believers, who had fled from beleaguered France, Scotland, and other parts of Europe to this Reformed city. Many of them were troubled, separated from their families, bereft of funds. Calvin aimed not to tear them down but to build them up. Other Genevans were barely new to the Christian

---

143. Old, *Reading and Preaching*, 4:128–29.
144. Schaff, *History of the Christian Church*, 8:258.
145. Schaff, *History of the Christian Church*, 8:258.
146. Schaff, *History of the Christian Church*, 8:259.
147. Quoted in Parker, *Calvin's Preaching*, 115.

faith and needed encouragement. Still others were living in sin and needed his loving rebuke. As a result, he preached with the intent of prompting, encouraging, and, at times, challenging his congregation to follow the word. Richard Gamble notes, "No ivory tower preaching here!"[148]

Pastoral Exhortation

As a shepherd before his flock, Calvin was full of loving exhortation, warm persuasion, and fervent appeal. He preached with the intent of encouraging the congregation to live the truth of the biblical passage. In so doing, the Reformer "stood in solidarity with his congregation,"[149] using, for the most part, the inclusive language of the first-person plural pronouns—"us," "we," "our"—as opposed to the second-person "you." By doing so, he avoided speaking down to his listeners. He in no way wanted to bury them under any overbearing intimidation or false guilt. Instead, Calvin stood together with the people, under the authority of God's word, including himself in the need to act on biblical truth.

Further, loving rebuke was a part of Calvin's application of the biblical text. Sin must always be confronted in the lives of people from the pulpit—and Calvin knew this. As he was aware that members of his flock were being tempted by the world, or were already living in sin, Calvin issued loving admonitions from the word. He openly confronted vice, calling his listeners to pursue paths of holiness. He explicitly attacked the sexual immorality and spiritual license with which some in Geneva presumed on God's grace. Fearlessly, he called for their repentance as he addressed their promiscuous lifestyles.

Self-Examination

In the midst of his exhortations, Calvin frequently called his listeners to self-examination. He urged the members of the congregation to search their hearts and see how they measured up to the passage at hand: "We must all, therefore, examine our lives not against one of God's precepts but against the whole law. Can any of us truly say that

---

148. Gamble, foreword to Calvin, *Deity of Christ*, 8.
149. Evans, "Sermons on Acts 1–7," 19.

we are blameless? Surely we are all put to shame when we judge ourselves by the standards of the law."[150] On another occasion, he said,

> The way to apply this text of Paul's to our instruction is as follows: inasmuch as we are unaware of the sins that lurk within us, it is necessary for God to come and examine our lives. . . . Yet if each of us were more careful to examine ourselves in this way, we would all surely have occasion to tremble and sigh; all haughtiness and pride would be cast down and we would be ashamed of every aspect of our lives.[151]

It was Calvin's clear desire that the people not look into the mirror of the word and then turn away and forget what they had seen. Instead, he called them to search their lives, carefully, in light of the truth he had proclaimed.

Polemic Defense

For Calvin, part of applying the truth was applying it to the times in which one lives. This included refuting the error that pervades the surrounding world scene. Thus, sermon application also required defending the faith, while refuting those who contradict it. Calvin saw it as his duty to confront those who opposed sound doctrine. Such false teaching is always a danger to the health of the church. Four groups in particular elicited Calvin's rebuke:

> (1) Geneva's civic leaders, its merchants, and judicial system; (2) the Roman Catholic Church, its forms of worship and doctrines, as they were then being reinterpreted and restated by the Council of Trent; (3) the Anabaptists, primarily because of their hermeneutical and political positions; and finally, (4) the Libertines, or Spiritualists, whose mystical views struck Calvin as bizarre, if not foolish and tragic.[152]

Further, he attacked "the Muslims," though "his greatest polemic" was "directed toward the Roman Catholic Church."[153] Calvin "rarely missed an opportunity to skewer the pope of Rome and his minions"

---

150. Calvin, *Sermons on Galatians*, 264.
151. Calvin, *Sermons on Galatians*, 543.
152. Benjamin Wirt Farley, introduction to Calvin, *Sermons on Micah*, vii–viii.
153. Leith, "Calvin's Doctrine," 222.

for their "idolatry."[154] In the face of such opposition, his sermons were "vigorously polemical" as he "defended the truth of God."[155]

Calvin believed that he had received, as one called to preach, a divine mandate to guard the truth. Calvin wrote, "To assert the truth is only one half of the office of teaching . . . except all the fallacies of the devil be also dissipated."[156] In a sermon on Titus 1:10–12, Calvin exclaimed, "If these vain talkers and deceivers be let alone, if we take no notice of them, what will become of the church? Will not the devil win all?"[157] He concluded that "it [is] the duty of those who are called to preach the Word of God to use plainness, and point out the errors to the faithful."[158] Thus, systematic exposition, Calvin believed, necessitates confronting the devil's lies. They must be exposed in the pulpit for what they are—damnable errors. Nevertheless, on the whole, "his overriding concern was clearly constructive."[159] For the most part, he was far more interested in "edifying the faithful than in conquering the naysayers."[160]

Calvin's Conclusion of the Sermon

Once he had carefully explained and applied the Scripture, Calvin knew he must bring his sermon to a strong conclusion. The message must not taper off at the end but must increase in intensity and build in momentum. Thus, the Reformer sought to end with a dramatic culmination. As the closing approached, he sought to conclude his exposition with direct impact and lasting impression. The preacher must be a persuader, he believed. Thus, he must call his listeners to respond to God with submission and allegiance. Such a climactic conclusion involved the following elements.

Succinct Summary

As Calvin concluded his exposition, he often summarized the central thrust of what had been stated. This final restatement served to

---

154. Evans, "Sermons on Acts 1–7," 20.
155. Engelsma, foreword to Calvin, *Sermons on Election and Reprobation*, xiii.
156. John Calvin, quoted in J. Graham Miller, *Calvin's Wisdom: An Anthology Arranged Alphabetically by a Grateful Reader* (Edinburgh: Banner of Truth, 1992), 252.
157. John Calvin, *Sermons on the Epistles to Timothy and Titus* (Edinburgh: Banner of Truth, 1983), 1105; archaic spelling updated.
158. Calvin, *Sermons on Timothy and Titus*, 1105.
159. George, introduction to *John Calvin and the Church*, 21.
160. George, introduction to *John Calvin and the Church*, 21.

underscore—and even drive home and reinforce—the main theme of the message. Last words are lasting words, and nowhere was this more true than in Calvin's pulpit. As a symphony escalates toward a final crescendo, Calvin's expositions rose in their intensity and soared to the end. He desired, one last time, to seal the primary truths in the hearts of his listeners.

Often, in the final summary, Calvin would issue one final word of practical application. On one occasion, he concluded, "Now, since we cannot expound the whole at this time, let us seek to profit from this doctrine."[161] Having said this, he would reiterate for his people the relevance of the passage in their lives. In another final summation, Calvin stated,

> Moreover, we must gather from this passage that the doctrine of predestination does not serve to carry us away into extravagant speculations, but to beat down all pride in us and the foolish opinion we always conceive of our own worthiness and deserts, and to show that God has such free power, privilege, and sovereign dominion over us that He may reprobate whom He pleases and elect whom He pleases.[162]

With such a summarizing statement, Calvin would restate the central thrust of the entire message and fix it in the minds of the listeners. In one sermon, Calvin concluded, "Here, then, is a summary of what we must always keep in mind."[163] On another occasion, he ended by saying, "That, in summation, is what lies behind Micah's intention."[164] These are representative ways in which Calvin brought his sermon to climactic conclusion.

Persuasive Appeal

As the sermon climaxed, Calvin made pressing appeals to his listeners. He passionately called for their unqualified submission to the Lord. He summoned their wills to unwavering faith in Christ. They must choose obedience from the heart. As he concluded, Calvin almost al-

---

161. Calvin, *Sermons on Ephesians*, 34.
162. Calvin, *Sermons on Ephesians*, 48.
163. Calvin, *Sermons on Galatians*, 15.
164. Calvin, *Sermons on Micah*, 30.

ways exhorted his congregation with these words: "Let us fall before the majesty of our great God."[165] Or Calvin concluded,

> In light of this holy teaching, let us prostrate ourselves before the face of our gracious God, acknowledge our faults, praying that, if it pleases God, He might touch our hearts better than we have ever been touched before, and that by acknowledging our poverty, we ask only to be drawn in everything to Him.[166]

With this passionate appeal, he called for deep humility and personal surrender to the Lord. Whatever the individual text, fervent words like these underscored that all who sat under his preaching must submit unconditionally to God. Calvin simply could not step down from his pulpit without urging his listeners to act on the truth he had just proclaimed.

Included in this appeal, Calvin often issued an evangelistic plea. The Reformer was fervent in his call to the unconverted listeners to come to faith in the Lord Jesus Christ. With passion, he pleaded with his congregation to renounce their sin and fully trust in Christ for salvation. The great expositor did not hesitate to invite all under his voice to faith in Jesus Christ. The following is one such appeal:

> We must realize that we would be sent to the pit a hundred thousand times if God did not pity us and raise us up in His infinite mercy. Then we will know that we cannot be justified by the law, for we are all under condemnation every time we compare ourselves with God. We need to have such fear, that we cannot find rest until the Lord Jesus Christ has saved us.[167]

Closing Prayer

Finally, after calling the people to turn to God, he appealed to God to help the people. His intent was to leave them *coram deo*—"in the presence of God." These concluding prayers by Calvin were vertical in their thrust, ushering his listeners before God. His closing intercessions appealed to God to bless the people. They unveiled the glorious

---

165. Calvin, *Sermons on Galatians*, 340.
166. Calvin, *Sermons on Micah*, 123.
167. Calvin, *Sermons on Galatians*, 186.

majesty of God as he made a final plea for the spiritual good of his congregation. The focus of the prayer was adapted to the subject of the message preached. In this manner, Calvin reinforced the truth preached to each heart.

One such passionate prayer, offered by Calvin, heard him express,

> Almighty God, our heavenly Father, since you have willed for us to be governed by the preaching of your Holy Word, grant that those who are charged with fulfilling this office may be increasingly endued with your heavenly power, that they might not attempt anything of their own, but with all their power truly employ themselves in service to you and to us, that as we become edified by them, you might ever dwell among us, and that we might truly become the temple of your majesty, all the days of our life, that we might finally one day come into your heavenly sanctuary, to which you daily invite us, since you have opened that door, once and for all, through the blood of your only-begotten Son, our Lord Jesus Christ. Amen.[168]

With this final intercession, the sermon concluded at the throne of grace.

The Call for a New Reformation

Across the top of the Reformation Wall, the motto of the Genevan reformation is etched in stone for all to read: *post tenebras lux*—"after darkness, light." This was the hope of John Calvin and all those in Geneva who gathered under his expository preaching. Amid the spiritual darkness of the sixteenth century, there came shining in the Reformation the glorious light of the truth of God's word. The Scripture, which had been opened in Wittenberg and Zurich and Strasbourg and Basel, was opened, at last, in Geneva.

There, nestled amid the Swiss Alps in Geneva, the expository preaching of John Calvin burst aflame like a blazing torch. The light of divine truth pierced the darkness. Like a city set on a hill, the glory of God shone forth from this Geneva pulpit, beaming throughout continental Europe. So bright was its flame that its illuminating rays reached Scotland and England and then, crossing the Atlantic Ocean,

---

168. Calvin, *Sermons on Micah*, 183.

the American Colonies. Eventually, this pure light extended to the faraway corners of the earth.

The radiance of truth that emanated from Calvin's pulpit still shines brightly in this day. The expository messages of the great Reformer were not a mere reflection of his own brilliance. Instead, his expository preaching sends forth gospel light that reveals the supreme glory of our triune God. May God raise up in this day a new generation of expositors in the mold of the gifted Genevan Reformer. May we live to see *post tenebras lux* yet again in this hour. After the darkness of this generation, may there be light. May there once more be the sending forth of the pure, penetrating light of Scripture through the expository preaching of the word. *Soli Deo gloria.*

7

The Development of the
Institutes from 1536 to 1559

Derek W. H. Thomas

In the first edition of this work of ours I did not in the least expect that success which, out of his infinite goodness, the Lord has given. . . . Although I did not regret the labor spent, I was never satisfied until the work had been arranged in the order now set forth. Now I trust that I have provided something that all of you will approve.
—"John Calvin to the Reader," *Institutes of the Christian Religion*, 1559 edition

A Basic Manual of Christianity

When Calvin completed the first edition of the *Institutes* in 1535 and saw it through to publication the following year in Basel, he could not have known that 450 years later, his first Christian book,[1] both

---

1. Calvin had written what was more or less a secular commentary on Seneca's well-known work *On Clemency* a few years earlier, in 1532, as part of what today would be regarded as the equivalent of a doctoral dissertation; cf. John Calvin, *Calvin's Commentary on Seneca's "De Clementia": With Introduction, Translation, and Notes*, ed. and trans. Ford Lewis Battles and André Malan Hugo, RTS 3 (Leiden: Brill, 1969).

its form and content, would continue to be the subject matter of enormous amounts of scholarly research and debate and remain a standard text in the preparation of students for ministry in conservative seminaries around the globe. Apart from the Bible itself, John Calvin's *Institutes* and John Bunyan's *Pilgrim's Progress*, for several centuries following their initial publication, have been the books Christians have turned to the most for instruction on Christian faith and practice.[2] In a recent volume celebrating the publication of the fifth edition of the *Institutes* (first published in 1559), J. I. Packer refers to it as "one of the wonders of the literary world."[3] Similarly, B. B. Warfield wrote in 1899, "From the point of view of mere literary standing, the *Institutes* of John Calvin holds a position so supreme in its class that every one who would profess to know the world's best literature must perforce make himself acquainted with it."[4]

Though it reveals its historical setting all too obviously (a feature that many of its readers sometimes forget), the *Institutes* has an uncanny way of anticipating theological discussions that belong both to the sixteenth century and our own day. For all its serious and ultimately fatal flaws, the movement known as neoorthodoxy—largely associated with the monumental figure of Karl Barth (1886–1968)—was, and remains to a great extent, a supposed return to Calvin and the theology of the *Institutes*, however distorted the attempt has been.[5] For half a millennium, in ways that are both legitimate and illegitimate, the *Institutes* has shaped Reformed theology as well as provided grist for those whose theological formulations have been largely a reaction to it. Calvin's *Institutes* is also cited as the source for Reformed

---

2. The first part of *Pilgrim's Progress* was published in 1678 and the second part, six years later, in 1684.

3. J. I. Packer, foreword to *A Theological Guide to Calvin's "Institutes": Essays and Analysis*, ed. David W. Hall and Peter A. Lillback, Calvin 500 Series (Phillipsburg, NJ: P&R, 2008), ix. Ronald S. Wallace says of the *Institutes* that "it began to be recognized even in his lifetime as one of the greatest text books on theology ever to be written." *Calvin, Geneva and the Reformation: A Study of Calvin as Social Reformer, Churchman, Pastor, and Theologian* (Grand Rapids, MI: Baker, 1988), 42.

4. B. B. Warfield, "The Literary History of Calvin's *Institutes*," *PRR* 38 (1899): 193–219; also found in Richard C. Gamble, ed., *Influences upon Calvin and Discussion of the 1559 Institutes*, vol. 4 of *Articles on Calvin and Calvinism: A Fourteen-Volume Anthology of Scholarly Articles* (New York: Garland, 1992), 181–207.

5. On Barth's use of Calvin and the Reformed tradition, see Carl Trueman, "Calvin, Barth, and Reformed Theology: Historical Prolegomena," in *Calvin, Barth, and Reformed Theology*, ed. Neil B. MacDonald and Carl Trueman (Milton Keynes, UK: Paternoster, 2008), 3–26.

interpretations on issues as diverse as mercy ministry, church government, the use of the law in the Christian life, the decentralization of
politics, and even capitalism.[6]

The success of the *Institutes* can be measured in part by the reaction to its publication in French. This bulky translation made its way
into France in 1542 only to be met by an official but unsuccessful cam-
paign to burn it two years later by French authorities. Translating the
Institutes into French was clear strategy on Calvin's part. The growing number of French exiles in Europe, particularly French-speaking
Strasbourg and Geneva, encouraged Calvin to make Geneva the base
of operations for a printing industry with a particular eye for the
French market. Exiled French printers, now living in Geneva, caught
the vision to import easily hidden books, including the *Institutes*, into
their native country.[7]

It is important to remember that when the first edition of the *Institutes* was published in 1536, the process of printing with the aid
of moveable type was relatively new. The process was cheaper by far
than parchment and, more to the point, was capable of producing
multiple copies. It has been estimated that in Geneva in the 1540s, a
skilled craftsman could produce in one day 1,300 copies of a single
sheet (for the average-sized book, a single sheet translated to eight
pages of the finished product). Seven hundred copies of a small book
(such as the first edition of the *Institutes*) could be produced in half a
day. The larger volumes (more intensive to re-create once the typeface
had been dismantled) were generally produced in batches of three to
four thousand at a time.[8] This alone signals the importance of writing and publication in the early Reformation period and explains the
speed with which Reformation truths spread across Europe in a relatively brief time. And Calvin, as much as other Reformers before and
after him, especially Martin Luther, used this providential blessing

---

6. See David W. Hall, *The Legacy of John Calvin: His Influence on the Modern World*, Calvin
500 Series (Phillipsburg, NJ: P&R, 2008).

7. Diarmaid MacCulloch, *The Reformation: A History* (London: Viking, 2003), 190–92; see
also Bruce Gordon, *John Calvin's "Institutes of the Christian Religion": A Biography*, Lives of
Great Religious Books (Princeton, NJ: Princeton University Press, 2016).

8. Andrew Pettegree, "Printing and the Reformation: The English Exception," in *The Beginnings of English Protestantism*, ed. Peter Marshall and Alec Ryrie (Cambridge: Cambridge
University Press, 2002), 158–59.

for all it was worth. As it was true of the Renaissance generally, so also was it true for the leaders of the Reformation: the printing of books, small and large, was viewed as vital in the dissemination of truth and ideas.

Before we examine the *Institutes* as we know it today in its fifth and final edition (1559), it is worth asking ourselves why Calvin began this project in the first place. Though the first edition can be found more or less intact in the final edition, its expansion and substantial reordering makes the final edition appear almost as a brand-new work.[9]

The name "the *Institutes*" is, of course, a common colloquial expression for the more cumbersome title *Institutes of the Christian Religion*. Not that the abbreviated title helps us in understanding the nature of the book itself; *institute* for most of us is a synonym for a place of learning, a school or training college, perhaps. But that is only a part of what the word meant in the original Latin. *Institutio* means "instruction" or "manual of instruction," and we should note that the Latin term is in the singular, not, as in the English, in the plural. It is, literally, the *Institute of the Christian Religion*, a title which is sure to confuse us even further! In common parlance, the title could be rendered *Basic Manual in Christian Doctrine* or *Basic Manual of Christianity*.

It is perhaps testimony to how highly people regard this book that we do not bother to ask what the title means. The term *institutio* was in many respects unexpected even in Calvin's time. The medieval term for such a volume would undoubtedly have been *summa*. Thus, for example, the most well-known text of theology prior to Calvin was Thomas Aquinas's (1225–1274) unfinished *Summa Theologiae*. *Summa* here means "whole" or even "summation" and has connotations of a compendium of theology or even a "systematic" theology. The original title given to the first edition of the *Institutes* (1536) was *Basic Instruction* [institutio] *in the Christian Religion, Embracing Just about* [fere] *the Whole Sum of Godliness* [pietatis summam], *and All That Needs to Be Known in the Doctrine of Salvation; a Work Very Well Worth Reading*

---

9. On the organization of Calvin's *Institutes*, see Richard A. Muller, "Establishing the *Ordo Docendi*: The Organization of Calvin's Institutes, 1536–1559," in *The Unaccommodated Calvin: Studies in the Foundation of a Theological Tradition*, OSHT (New York: Oxford University Press, 2000), 118–39.

by Everyone Zealous for Godliness.[10] Too much can be made of the difference between Aquinas's *Summa Theologiae* and Calvin's *Pietatis Summam*, as though one represents an arid discourse on abstruse points of theology, while the other has a more practical objective. Calvin was certainly concerned with the cultivation of piety— *biblical* piety, as the first edition of the *Institutes* was explicitly designed to help the growing French Christian community cultivate genuine piety. But we cannot pit this concern against his concern for doctrine—*systematized* doctrine! To separate doctrine (*doctrina*) and piety (*pietatis*) was the very issue Calvin was most eager to avoid.[11] But it is important to note that whatever Calvin envisioned for the *Institutes* as initially written, the book took on a life of its own as it went through its various editions and translations (in Latin and French). What culminated in 1559 bore only a faint reflection of what he had originally envisioned; in the words of Wulfert de Greef, "The material has increased to such an extent that it can almost be spoken of as a new work."[12] It grew from a theological-catechetical exercise based largely on the Apostles' Creed to a greatly expanded series of doctrinal points, or *loci communes* ("common places") and *disputationes*, purporting to cover the summation of Christian theology and practice. Philipp Melanchthon had written a summary of doctrine a decade before Calvin, the *Loci Communes* (1521, and several editions until its final one in 1555),[13] and Huldrych Zwingli had written a similar volume in 1525, *On True and False Religion*. Similarly, Calvin's friend Guillaume Farel had also published a book in 1525, the *Sommaire*, purporting to be a summary of doctrine.[14]

---

10. In Latin, *Christianae religionis institutio totam fere pietatis summam et quidquid est in doctrina salutis cognitu necessarium complectens omnibus pietatis studiosis lectu dignissimum opus ac recens editum. CO*, 1:1.

11. Calvin could write, for example, of the "doctrine of godliness" (*pietatis doctrina*) in *Institutes*, 3.2.13; *CO*, 2:408. For discussion on the significance of these and similar terms, see Muller, *Unaccommodated Calvin*, 107; cf. Joel R. Beeke, "Calvin on Piety," in *The Cambridge Companion to John Calvin*, ed. Donald K. McKim (Cambridge: Cambridge University Press, 2004), 125–52.

12. Wulfert de Greef, "Calvin's Writings," in McKim, *Cambridge Companion to John Calvin*, 43.

13. Luther once quipped that he loved Melanchthon's *Loci Communes* so much that he thought it should be included in the canon (*canone ecclesiastico*)! See Luther, *De servo arbitrio* (1525), in *D. Martin Luthers Werke, Kritische Gesamtausgabe*, ed. Rudolph Hermann et al. (Weimar: Hermann Böhlaus Nachfolger, 1883–2009), 18:601; cf. Luther, *The Bondage of the Will*, trans. J. I. Packer and O. R. Johnston (Grand Rapids, MI: Revell, 1990), 63. Melanchthon's work, however, is nowhere near as well organized as the 1536 *Institutes*.

14. The book bore a French title: *Sommaire et briefve déclaration d'auscuns lieux fort nécessaires à ung chascun chrestien pour mettre sa confiance en Dieu et ayder son prochain.*

It is a matter of almost incredulity, were it not easily proved, that Calvin was only twenty-seven years old, having been converted less than four years earlier, when the first edition of the *Institutes* appeared. He had up to that point never pastored a church or given a theological lecture! There are hints of early preaching in France but nothing to account for the maturity of the work that emerged in 1535. It was in the brief period of leisure in Basel, before Guillaume Farel's famous charge to his friend that he remain in Geneva, that the *Institutes* took shape. Did he bring with him to Basel notes already written in France? We have no way of knowing. The book appeared in six chapters. Some have suggested that the first four chapters were written earlier, especially in the library of his friend Louis du Tillet at Claix in Angoulême, but Alexandre Ganoczy doubts it, suggesting that it was written in its entirety in the first seven months of Calvin's sojourn in Basel.[15]

Whatever the precise timetable of his production of the *Institutes*, Calvin clearly spelled out his intention in the introductory letter to Francis I, in which he declared his "purpose . . . to transmit certain rudiments by which those who are touched with any zeal for religion might be shaped to true godliness." Calvin explains that among his fellow countrymen in France who were "hungering and thirsting for Christ . . . very few . . . had been imbued even a slight knowledge of him."[16] If this was indeed the case, why did Calvin choose to write the book in Latin? And having done so, why did he not immediately provide a French translation? A French edition of the *Institutes*, not of this first edition but of the expanded second (Latin) edition of 1539, did not appear until 1541–1542.[17] The answer to these questions is a matter of conjecture, of course, but the sequence of events that occurred in these years—as Calvin found himself a pastor in Geneva, then summarily evicted less than three years later, only to return again

---

15. See Alexandre Ganoczy, *The Young Calvin*, trans. David Foxgrover and Wade Provo (Philadelphia: Westminster, 1987), 91–102; cf. Ford Lewis Battles, *Interpreting John Calvin*, ed. Robert Benedetto (Grand Rapids, MI: Baker, 1996), 92; Karl Barth, *The Theology of John Calvin*, trans. Geoffrey W. Bromiley (1922; repr., Grand Rapids, MI: Eerdmans, 1995), 160–61.

16. "Epistle Dedicatory to Francis, King of the French," in *Institutes* (1536), 1; CO, 1:9.

17. See the recent translation into English of the 1541 French edition by Robert White, *Institutes of the Christian Religion: Calvin's Own "Essentials" Edition* (Edinburgh: Banner of Truth, 2014).

in 1542—is itself sufficient to explain why a French translation was not in fact produced. What we do know is that Calvin adapted the first Latin edition to form the French catechism in the first year of his ministry in Geneva, but even this proved too difficult for the French exiles, and shortly afterward Calvin produced the so-called Geneva and Strasbourg Catechisms in the familiar question-and-answer format.[18]

A catechism in the early sixteenth century often summarized the contents of the law, the Apostles' Creed, the Lord's Prayer, and the sacraments. Luther, for example, had written his Small Catechism in 1522 and Large Catechism in 1529, and these catechisms had basically done just that. Calvin's first edition of the *Institutes*, which seems to have been modeled after Luther's Large Catechism,[19] did the same, adding a refutation of the papal Mass to the close of chapter 4 and a lengthier refutation of the other five so-called sacraments of medieval Catholicism. The concluding chapter contained three related essays on Christian freedom, ecclesiastical power, and political power.

Some of Calvin's distinctives were already apparent: the emphasis on sin as idolatry in his exposition of the law, the stress on justification by faith apart from the works of the law (where Luther's influence is obvious), assertions of Trinitarianism's crucial importance to Christianity, a nonliteral interpretation of the "descent into hell" (*descendit in inferno*) passage of the Apostles' Creed, the importance of prayer (this section, greatly enlarged, constitutes for many the most eloquent section of the final edition of the *Institutes*), and a distancing of his view of the Lord's Supper from "those who weaken the force of the sacraments" (showing his familiarity with Zwingli's memorialist view of the Supper) and from those who attach to the sacraments some sort of secret power (Roman Catholics).[20]

The final chapter of the 1536 edition of the *Institutes* contained three sections that were designed to address the work's dedicatee, the

---

18. See I. John Hesselink, *Calvin's First Catechism: A Commentary*, with the 1538 catechism trans. Ford Lewis Battles, CSRT (Louisville: Westminster John Knox, 1997).

19. Williston Walker, *John Calvin: Revolutionary, Theologian, Pastor* (1906; repr., Fearn, Ross-shire, Scotland: Christian Focus, 2005), 112.

20. Calvin's extensive reading on the sacraments, particularly in the church fathers, was already obvious. In October 1536, Calvin gave two speeches at the Colloquy of Lausanne, a discussion organized by the Bernese authorities between Roman Catholics and the Reformed on the Lord's Supper, in which, from memory, he cited extensively from the church fathers. See *Deux discours de Calvin au colloque de Lausanne*, in CO, 9:877–86.

king of France, Francis I. In advocating the rule of law against anti-
nomian license, Calvin was walking a delicate tightrope in this section.
Calvinism has always appeared austere and oppressively legalistic to
its detractors, whether ecclesiastical or civil, despite the fact that only
Calvinism can maintain true liberty of conscience.[21] On one level,
he wanted the king to know that the Reformed were not a threat to
civil power. He was not advocating civil unrest. He was pleading for
civil tolerance of his position as well as informing the king that the
(Roman) church had usurped civil authority. It was not the Reformed
that the king needed to be concerned about but the Catholic Church's
insistence on controlling features of society beyond its legitimate jurisdiction. Consequently, Calvin argued for a separation of powers that
included the role of the civil authority to legislate the rule of civil law
in such a way as to enable true religion to prosper.

What emerged, then, in 1536 was a not-so-small, though often
referred to as "pocket-sized," volume of over 520 pages designed to
catechize Calvin's fellow French countrymen in the rudiments of the
Christian faith. It is a testimony to his belief in the power of literature as much as to the need for the systematic, unified, and coherent
integration of core truths for the fledgling church of Europe to grow
and flourish.

Assessing the first edition of the *Institutes* could engage us in more
space than this chapter warrants, but a few summary statements
should be made. To begin with, the 1536 edition is a deliberate piece
of catholic theology. The oft-repeated argument made by Calvin's
Catholic contemporaries that evangelicals had abandoned the church
fathers, jettisoning the historic lineage of the catholic (universal)
faith of the church, was wholly without foundation. Calvin knew his
Patristic theology and knew it well. Far from jettisoning the fathers,
evangelicals (in the sixteenth century) were standing in their tradition.
It was Roman Catholicism that had introduced such things as Lenten

---

21. It is in this tradition that a century later the Westminster Confession could assert one of
its distinctive and pivotal statements on the nature of Christian liberty of conscience: "God alone
is Lord of the conscience, and hath left it free from the doctrines and commandments of men,
which are in anything contrary to His Word; or beside it, if matters of faith or worship. So that,
to believe such doctrines, or to obey such commands, out of conscience, is to betray true liberty
of conscience: and the requiring of an implicit faith, and an absolute and blind obedience is to
destroy liberty of conscience, and reason also" (WCF 20.2).

observance, images of Christ and the saints, prayers for the dead, transubstantiation, clerical celibacy, and so on—none of which the fathers avowed. The persecution of evangelicals that had manifested itself in France was misguided.[22]

Calvin had, after all, faced the anger of Francis I on All Saints' Day (November 1) in 1533, forcing both Calvin and Nicolas Cop to leave the city a few weeks later, never to return to it again. According to his friend and colleague Theodore Beza, Calvin's hand was evident in the address given by Cop upon his assumption of the rectorship of the University of Paris.[23] Cop's address, a sermon on the lectionary reading for the day, Matthew 5:1–12, had included the following words: "The world and the wicked are wont to label as heretics, imposters, seducers and evil speakers those who strive purely and sincerely to penetrate the minds of believers with the Gospel."[24] Francis had responded with threats of "grievous punishment" as a "correction to the accursed heretics and an example to others."[25] French Reformed Christians now found themselves at the mercy of an unstable monarch whose opinions, so it is said, often reflected those of the last person with whom he spoke. The threat of death in the years 1534–1535 was real enough that many had fled to Switzerland and the cities of Bern, Neuchâtel, Basel, Zurich, Strasbourg, and eventually Geneva. French exiles, emboldened by their new freedoms in Switzerland, were keen to teach the "poor ignorant" ones left behind, and they smuggled back into France a series of placards or posters containing detailed instructions on why the Mass was an abomination, one of which, on the night of October 17, 1534, was fixed to the king's bedchamber in Blois! The reaction was swift and bloody, and the cause of the Reformation was rapidly being viewed by the king as one of insurrection and political intrigue.

It is in this light that we must consider the intent of Calvin's preface to Francis I that appeared in the first edition of the *Institutes*. As the title to the preface suggests, it was a less-than-subtle attempt to achieve

---

22. Battles, *Interpreting John Calvin*, 100–104.
23. Theodore Beza, *The Life of John Calvin*, trans. Henry Beveridge (Darlington, UK: Evangelical Press, 1997), 22, 24.
24. The full text of this sermon can be found in "Appendix III: The Academic Discourse," in *Institutes* (1536), 363–72; quotation on 371.
25. Cited by Ford Lewis Battles, introduction to *Institutes* (1536), xviii; cf. CO, 1:25–26.

the support of the "most mighty and most illustrious monarch Francis, most Christian King of the French, [Calvin's] esteemed Prince and Lord," for the evangelical cause. It didn't work. As Alister McGrath notes, "On 1 July 1542, the Parisian *parlement* directed that all works containing heterodox doctrines, especially Calvin's *Institutes*, were to be surrendered to the authorities within three days."[26]

1539 Edition

Over the next three years, Calvin's life would undergo a significant *volte-face*: his ambitions of a reclusive life of study were summarily cut short by the imprecatory words of Farel that he should stay in Geneva and pastor the emerging church of French exiles. Somewhere amid the demands of Calvin's painstaking approach to ministry, he found time to work on the *Institutes*, producing in 1539 an edition of considerably greater length, bearing the title *Basic Instruction in the Christian Religion, Now at Last Truly Answering to Its Description* [*nunc vere demum suo titulo respondens*], and eventually growing, in the fifth and final edition in 1559, to five times its original length. Work on the *Institutes* in one form or another occupied the entire span of Calvin's ministry, and had he lived longer (he died five years after the final edition), we might have seen a sixth edition. It is a sign of his attempt to justify a reprint of a book already widely read and available that the final edition bore the words (what we might today call a subtitle) *So Greatly Enlarged That It Can Almost Be Regarded as a New Work.*

New this second edition certainly was, in terms of size (now having seventeen chapters) and structure. New sections included a seminal chapter on the relationship of the Old and New Testaments and another on infant baptism. Yet while this edition grew in volume and expanded the themes treated, even rearranging order (the placement of a discussion of election, for example),[27] there is little evidence of any substantive change in Calvin's thought. It would be difficult to advance a "young Calvin versus old Calvin" antithesis as could be done with, for example, Luther or Zwingli.

---

26. See Alister E. McGrath, *Reformation Thought: An Introduction*, 3rd ed. (Oxford: Blackwell, 1999), 14.
27. Discussed later in this chapter.

Having settled in Basel in 1538, following his banishment from Geneva, Calvin began revising his *Institutes*, once again in Latin. Three times as large, this edition already showed evidence of a larger intended audience.[28] In the words of Richard Muller,

> The 1539 edition of Calvin's *Institutes* marks a crucial solidification of purpose and yet a significant alteration of direction. It was at this point that the *Institutes* ceased to be a brief, catechetical work and took on a new appearance—arguably the appearance of what one might call a sixteenth century "system" of theology.[29]

The first sign of this shift was the change of title. Dropped was the reference to the *Institutes* as a *pietatis summam*; instead, maintaining the word *institutio* (showing continuity in intent as a volume of instruction in doctrine), Calvin declared its purpose as embracing "the sum of religion [*religionis summam*] in all its parts," primarily for the aim of instructing "candidates in sacred theology [*sacrae theologiae candidatos*] for the reading of the divine Word."[30]

Whatever Calvin's desire for a book to help the French Christian laity in discerning those truths "necessary to know for salvation," a French edition of the *Institutes* was still three years away from publication, and the tone of the book now focused on "candidates in sacred theology." Moreover, since Calvin wrote the prefaces to the 1539 edition of the *Institutes* in the same period as his *Commentary on the Epistle to the Romans* (1540), Muller has argued that they should be considered a reflection of Calvin's methodology at this point. Significantly, in the *Romans* preface, Calvin found it necessary to explain why his exposition took the form of a running commentary on the text with recourse to identifying theological *loci* or *topoi*, in distinction to the somewhat differing practices of Martin Bucer, Philipp Melanchthon,

---

28. See B. B. Warfield, "On the Literary History of Calvin's *Institutes*," *PRR* 10 (1899): 193–219; Jean-Daniel Benoit, "The History and Development of the *Institutio*: How Calvin Worked," in *John Calvin: A Collection of Distinguished Essays*, CourtSRT 1, ed. Ford Lewis Battles and Gervase E. Duffield (Grand Rapids, MI: Eerdmans, 1966), 102–17; Battles, "Calculus Fidei," in *Interpreting John Calvin*, 139–78; Wulfert de Greef, *The Writings of John Calvin: An Introductory Guide*, trans. Lyle D. Bierma (Grand Rapids, MI: Baker, 1993), 195–202.
29. Muller, *Unaccommodated Calvin*, 102.
30. "John Calvin to the Reader," *Institutes*, 1:4. These words, as Battles observes in his editorial notation, appeared in the second edition of the *Institutes*, published in August 1539. See *CO*, 1:255.

and Heinrich Bullinger. In short, Calvin saw a symbiotic relationship between the *Institutes* and the commentaries.[31] What emerges, then, is a clear theological method: the running exposition of a biblical text in the commentaries (employing Calvin's description of the model employed: *brevitas et facilitas*)[32] and sermons, in which reference is given to theological doctrines culled from the text. These *loci*, or doctrines, are then gathered and ordered systematically and addressed against the various theological disputes of the time in the form of a basic instruction manual in theology, or *institutio*.

1543, 1550, and 1559 Editions

The development of the *Institutes* in its editions of 1543 (reprinted in 1545) and 1550 and in its final edition in 1559 is an interesting story but need not detain us unduly here. The 1543 edition expanded the number of chapters from seventeen to twenty-one, including a chapter on monasticism, expanded material on the Apostles' Creed to four chapters, and an extensive section on office in the church. The fourth Latin edition in 1550 (reprinted in 1553 and 1554) added an exposition of the conscience and showed greater division of the material into paragraphs.

The final (1559) edition was markedly different from its predecessors. The work was now divided into four "books" (reflecting the highly successful work by the twelfth-century theologian Peter Lombard, *Sententiarum libri quatuor*, or *Four Books of the Sentences*)[33] and into a total of eighty chapters. The first book covers the knowledge of God the Creator, and the second, the knowledge of God the Redeemer in Christ, first disclosed to the fathers under the law and then also to us in the gospel. The third book deals with the way the grace of Christ is received and with the benefits and effects that follow, and the final book, which occupies as much space as the first three

---

31. Calvin scholarship in the past has not always emphasized this relationship sufficiently and has therefore failed to see the precise role of the *Institutes* in the overall scheme of Calvin's work. See Muller, *Unaccommodated Calvin*, 28–29.

32. I.e., "brief and simple." See Richard C. Gamble, "*Brevitas et facilitas*: Toward an Understanding of Calvin's Hermeneutic," *WTJ* 47 (1985): 1–17; Gamble, "Exposition and Method in Calvin," *WTJ* 49 (1987): 153–65. For a slightly different point of view as to the significance of these terms in Calvin's methodology, see Muller, *Unaccommodated Calvin*, 236n94.

33. Speculation continues as to whether Calvin's division of four books was a deliberate reflection of Lombard's *Sentences*. See McGrath, *Reformation Thought*, 246.

put together, covers the nature and organization of the church, the sacraments, and the civil government, arranged under the rubric of the external aids that God uses to bring us to Jesus Christ.

The *Institutes* was an immediate success for the burgeoning publishing industry. In 1541 the anonymously written *Benefits of Christ*, which contained numerous references to the first edition of the *Institutes*, attained the status of a religious best seller before being suppressed by the Inquisition with its list of banned books in June 1542 and July 1545.[34] After the final edition was published, numerous "summary" or "compendium" abridgments were published in Western Europe, resulting in considerable commercial success. In 1562 Augustin Marlorat published a set of indexes facilitating the location of various subjects and biblical references. In 1576 Nicolas Colladon, who wrote a biography of Calvin, produced an edition of the *Institutes* that included brief marginal summaries. Thomas Vautrollier, a Huguenot refugee and one of London's most important publishers, printed two study guides to the *Institutes*: Edmund Bunny's *Compendium* (1576) "attempted to deal with Calvin's difficult style and subtleties of argumentation for the benefit of perplexed students,"[35] and Guillaume Delaune (a Huguenot refugee who Anglicized his name to William Lawne) also produced a summary of the *Institutes* in 370 pages that included flowcharts and diagrams.[36] The Elizabethan Thomas Norton translated Calvin's Latin into English,[37] the work going through eleven editions by 1632.[38] It would be impossible to exaggerate Calvin's theological influence, not just on the seventeenth century and the shaping of the various confessions of faith but on the shape of theological reflection ever since. Indeed, interest in Calvin's theology, particularly the *Institutes*, shows no sign of abating.[39]

---

34. The 1545 list included a total of 121 titles in French, half of which were printed in Geneva. French booksellers protested that because of the book banning, they faced bankruptcy, since the evangelicals were their best customers.

35. McGrath, *Reformation Thought*, 248.

36. Other "study guides" were produced by Caspar Olevianus (1586), Johannes Piscator (1589), and Daniel de Coulogne (or Colonius, 1628).

37. J. I. Packer suggests that no English translation fully matches Calvin's original but that Norton gets closest. Foreword to Hall and Lillback, *Theological Guide to Calvin's "Institutes,"* x.

38. Calvin's catechism went through eighteen editions by 1628.

39. See, for example, Collin Hansen, *Young, Restless, Reformed: A Journalist's Journey with the New Calvinists* (Wheaton, IL: Crossway, 2008).

Sacred Theology

Since Calvin's claim in the preface to the 1539 and subsequent editions of the *Institutes* was to provide a systematized volume for "candidates in sacred theology," it is helpful for us to investigate in broad detail what this actually meant for the Reformer. What truths in particular did Calvin believe belonged in such a volume as this? Obviously, this question could detain us to a degree that outweighs the nature of this chapter, and therefore, we endeavor to select some highlights in response to this issue.

A few things in general should now be pointed out to those relatively unfamiliar with the *Institutes*. The first feature is its historical or occasional setting, which gives the work a distinctive style. Those reading the book for the first or second time might, for example, draw the conclusion that the doctrine of creation *ex nihilo* ("out of nothing") was relatively unimportant to Calvin since he devotes almost no attention to it at all. But this merely reflects that Calvin, in returning to the book for most of his adult life, took up certain issues and elaborated on them when he found them to be in the center of theological disputation. This gives to the *Institutes* a certain uneven feel: some things are given greater attention than others—the Lord's Supper, predestination, or the incarnation of Jesus Christ, for example, all three of which were undergoing severe distortions during Calvin's lifetime. It would therefore be a great mistake to draw hard-and-fast conclusions as to the relative weightiness or importance of any given topic from the brevity of the material in the *Institutes*.

The *Institutes* is, then, a *disputatio* in the sense that it takes aim at various opponents in a manner that may appear offensive by contemporary literary standards.[40] The "papists," "Sorbonnists," or "schoolmen," whether euphemistic for Thomists, Augustinians, Occamists, Jesuists, or obscurantist Parisian seminary faculty, were often in the crosshairs of Calvin's scope. The language of dispute in the sixteenth century, even (*especially!*) in theology, sounds decidedly acerbic in our ears, but it would be an error of cultural chronology to judge it by contemporary standards.

---

40. That said, Calvin's sermonic rhetoric is understandably coarser in places than the more reflective nature of the *Institutes*.

A second feature of the *Institutes* is its unabashed advocacy of a system of truth and that this truth is essential to salvation and growth in grace. What occasioned such impassioned language as we referred to above? A belief that more was at stake than the reputations of theologians and philosophers. Salvation itself was at stake, and for Calvin this meant more than a concern for a defense, say, of Luther's understanding of justification by faith *alone*; *all revealed doctrine* was important and worthy of defense. It is a mark of Calvin's theology that he saw clearly the coherence of truth: that revelation was capable of a unified, logical presentation. Indeed, Karl Barth's dialectic, based as it was in part on a return to Calvin, would have made no sense to the Reformer at all![41]

The *Institutes* does not read like the systematic theology texts of Charles Hodge or Herman Bavinck or Louis Berkhof. But it is as committed to a principle of unity of truth as any one of these examples. Few would argue that Calvin was insensitive to the nuances of biblical exegesis or for that matter to the need for contextualizing a text relative to the history of redemption. So careful is Calvin, for example, to do just that in his Old Testament preaching and commentaries that Lutherans, one in particular, accused him of being no better than an enlightened rabbi.[42] Calvin did not think of himself as a dogmatician in the modern sense of the term; rather, as most of his contemporaries did, he saw himself primarily as a preacher and exegete of Scripture. In sheer volume, the *Institutes* is roughly the same size as his 159 sermons on Job preached in 1554–1555 and dwarfed by the volume of 200 sermons on Deuteronomy preached in 1555–1556, as well as by his commentaries on Psalms, Isaiah, Jeremiah, and the Pentateuch.

Here we should mention the modern tendency to speak of "Calvin's doctrine of . . . ," an expression that would have horrified Calvin himself, not least because he saw himself as expounding, however naively to our ears, the historical church's understanding of a particular doctrine rather than his own viewpoint. Armed with renewed

---

41. Barth's dialectical theological method attempts to find epistemic certainty in paradox and tension between the infinite and finite. Barth's stress on the unknowability of God apart from divine self-disclosure set him apart from the mainstream Protestant liberalism of his day.

42. The Lutheran in question, Aegidius Hunnius, wrote three decades after Calvin's death a work titled *Calvin the Judaizer*. See David L. Puckett, *John Calvin's Exegesis of the Old Testament*, CSRT (Louisville: Westminster John Knox, 1995).

enthusiasm for Renaissance emphases on language and grammar, Calvin did indeed pave new ground by way of exegetical insights, but these were in the main corroborative of central catholic dogma rather than expressions of Calvin's own stamp on theological endeavor.

Third, we should also mention the tendency to suggest a "central" or "organizing theme" in the *Institutes*. A variety of suggestions have been given, more or less dogmatically, including the sovereignty of God (Paul Tillich and to a certain extent J. I. Packer[43]), the knowledge of God (Edward Dowey and to some extent T. H. L. Parker), union with Christ (T. F. Torrance and Charles Partee), Christology generally (E. David Willis), or even the Holy Spirit (B. B. Warfield).[44] None is entirely convincing, even if some do show dominating influence in certain sections of the book. The truth seems to be that Calvin himself gave no hint that one single theme dominates his theological system. Rather, a symbiotic relationship exists between several important themes. An examination of the whole rather than the individual parts of the *Institutes* favors the view that what we have is a systematic theology, where the integration of the various strands provides a unified canvas. Uneven as the final work is for the reasons that we have already mentioned—specifically because Calvin enlarged certain sections to meet the exigencies of the 1540s and 1550s—the 1559 *Institutes* nevertheless does manifest what Calvin himself describes as an *ordo*, or organization. In a much debated statement, Calvin held that he "was never satisfied until the work had been arranged in the order [*ordo*] now set forth."[45] Whatever else he may have meant by this phrase, Calvin was affirming that the evolution of the *Institutes* was in part a desire to find the right structure.

Specific Theological Emphases

Having noted these general points, we next inquire as to some of the more central themes in the *Institutes* as a whole, those aspects that distinguish it from similar treatments of the doctrinal corpus and make

---

43. See J. I. Packer, "Calvin the Theologian," in Battles and Duffield, *John Calvin*, 155.

44. See I. John Hesselink, "Calvin's Theology," in McKim, *Cambridge Companion to John Calvin*, 78–84.

45. "John Calvin to the Reader," *Institutes*, 1:3; "Ioannes Calvinus Lectori," CO, 2:1. For an extended discussion, see Muller, *Unaccommodated Calvin*, 137–39.

us say immediately, "This is Calvin!" Other chapters in this volume treat these themes in greater length, and our purpose here is merely to draw attention to a few of them to familiarize ourselves with the topographical-theological landscape of the *Institutes*.

One of the first things we find in the *Institutes* is the importance given to the doctrine of the knowledge of God, or more precisely, the twofold knowledge of God (*duplex cognitio Dei*)—the knowledge of God the Creator and the knowledge of God the Redeemer. Attempts to make this the central key in the *Institutes* are understandable since it does play a key role in establishing the direction of the rest of the book. But it would be better to view it as foundational rather than central.

The issue of the knowledge of God dominates the first two books in the *Institutes*—the knowledge of God the Creator in book 1 and of God the Redeemer in Christ in book 2.[46] One of Calvin's memorable sections is to be found at the start of the *Institutes*, where the Reformer is meditating on the nature of our knowledge of God. The oft-cited opening sentence is itself a remarkable summary of the aim of the *Institutes* as a whole. In the 1536 edition, it reads, "Nearly the whole of sacred doctrine consists in these two parts: the knowledge of God and ourselves." In the final edition this statement is amplified: "Nearly all the wisdom we possess, that is to say, true and sound wisdom, consists of two parts: the knowledge of God and of ourselves. But, while joined by many bonds, which one precedes and brings forth the other is not easy to discern."[47] This knowledge is more than a set of beliefs, though Calvin does not in any way mean to discount the cognitive element of our knowledge. But it is more than a set of propositions. Certain truth, Calvin suggests, "merely flits about the brain,"[48] but the knowledge of

---

46. T. H. L. Parker criticizes the *duplex cognitio Dei* as an ordering principle of the *Institutes*, insisting instead that the work is governed by the ordering of the Apostles' Creed. See Parker, *Calvin's Doctrine of the Knowledge of God*, rev. ed. (Grand Rapids, MI: Eerdmans, 1959). But this observation seems entirely beside the point, not least because Calvin is explicit in saying, "First, as much in the fashioning of the universe as in the general teaching of Scripture the Lord shows himself to be simply the Creator. Then in the face of Christ [cf. 2 Cor. 4:6] he shows himself the Redeemer. Of the resulting twofold knowledge of God [*duplex cognitio*] we shall now discuss the first aspect; the second will be dealt with in its proper place." *Institutes*, 1.2.1; CO, 2:34. For further discussion, see Hesselink, "Calvin's Theology," 78.

47. For the 1536 quotation, see *Institutes* (1536), 15; CO, 1:27. For the 1559 citation, see *Institutes*, 1.35; CO 2:31.

48. *Institutes*, 1.5.9; CO, 2:47.

God that he is keen to write about is much more than that. To know God truly, we must listen to him in the Scriptures and acknowledge him precisely as Scripture reveals him. Whatever knowledge of God exists in creation, we still need the "spectacles" of Scripture to bring that information into sharp focus:

> Just as old or bleary-eyed men and those with weak vision, if you thrust before them a most beautiful volume, even if they recognize it to be some sort of writing, yet can scarcely construe two words, but with the aid of spectacles will begin to read distinctly; so Scripture, gathering up the otherwise confused knowledge of God in our minds, having dispersed our dullness, clearly shows us the true God.[49]

Several features of Calvin's understanding of the knowledge of God are worth noting, including the following:

1. We can only know ourselves when we know that we are wretched by nature, and we cannot know our wretchedness unless we first of all have some knowledge of God as he has revealed himself in his law. It is difficult to be precise as to how much Calvin was influenced by individual church fathers like Augustine or Bernard of Clairvaux or even the later medieval philosopher John Major. But it cannot really be disputed that Calvin knew and cited Augustine's *Confessions* to a point that can only imply some considerable influence.[50] As with Augustine, Calvin saw that the holiness of God affects our current knowledge of him. In other words, there exist moral preconditions for knowing God, and our present willful rebellion militates against our ability to know him. Saving knowledge of God comes as a result of the work of the Holy Spirit in us, bringing us into union with Christ and reckoning us as members of the kingdom of God: "Christ, when he illumines us into faith by the power of his Spirit, at the same time so engrafts us into his body that we become partakers of every good."[51]

No one reading the *Institutes* could fail to note Calvin's stress on the wretchedness of human nature. We are fallen, defiled, full of rot-

---

49. *Institutes*, 1.6.1; CO, 2:53.
50. On this point, see A. N. S. Lane, *John Calvin: Student of the Church Fathers* (Grand Rapids, MI: Baker, 1999).
51. *Institutes*, 3.2.35; CO, 2:427.

tenness, utterly debased, and unable to do any spiritual good. This is not, as some have conjectured, a sign of psychological trauma or a man suspended in "an age of anxiety," saying more of Calvin himself than of the general human condition, but an honest assessment of the biblical record on human depravity and the condition of unregenerate human will in union with Adam.[52] Calvin's aim, as J. I. Packer points out, was

> to convey a sense which Scripture had given him of the tragic quality of the human predicament. Here was the noblest of this world's occupants, a creature made for fellowship with God and given great intellectual and moral potentialities, now spiritually ruined; he had lost his *rectitude* (uprightness), the image of God in which he was made, and had been banished from God's favour; and yet in this condition he was so perverse as to be proud, and vain glorious, and self-satisfied! Calvin wished to bring out the tragic folly of the human attitude.[53]

2. There is a fundamental difference between God as he is in himself (*in se*) and God as he is revealed to us (*quoad nos*). This is a basic distinction in Calvin, applied to the entirety of his thought and writings about God, and is a distinction made also by Aquinas, among others; it shows once again a trajectory of thought in Calvin that was not in the least embarrassed by its medieval roots.[54] The aim in view by this distinction was not to posit a Kantian divide rendering the knowledge of God epistemologically impossible. Rather, Calvin's aim was to avoid speculation about God, something he found distasteful. The secret things belong to God and to God alone (cf. Deut. 29:29), and it is none of our business to probe where no revelation has been given. For Calvin, all our knowledge of him has been accommodated to compensate for our creaturely status. He states,

---

52. Since its appearance in 1988, William J. Bouwsma's *John Calvin: A Sixteenth-Century Portrait* (New York: Oxford University Press), in which just such a description is given, has received much attention. Note, however, T. H. L. Parker's uncharacteristically terse response, suggesting that Bouwsma understood Calvin better than Calvin understood himself and that this "seems to me to end all meaningful commerce with the past." *Calvin: An Introduction to His Thought* (Louisville: Westminster John Knox, 1995), 11.

53. Packer, "Calvin the Theologian," 159.

54. See Paul Helm, *John Calvin's Ideas* (Oxford: Oxford University Press, 2004), 11; cf. Arvin Vos, *Aquinas, Calvin, and Contemporary Protestant Thought: A Critique of Protestant Views on the Thought of Thomas Aquinas* (Grand Rapids, MI: Eerdmans, 1985).

For who even of slight intelligence does not understand that, as nurses commonly do with infants, God is wont in a measure to "lisp" in speaking to us? Thus such forms of speaking do not so much express clearly what God is like as accommodate the knowledge of him to our slight capacity. To do this he must descend far beneath his loftiness.[55]

It can hardly be missed as we begin to read the *Institutes* for the first time that Calvin is eager to expound the greatness of God. To know God, both in creation[56] and redemption, is to know a God who is great: "The teaching of Scripture is from heaven. And . . . all the books of Sacred Scripture far surpass all other writings. Yes, if we turn pure eyes and upright senses toward it, the majesty of God will immediately come to view, subdue our bold rejection, and compel us to obey."[57]

How this knowledge comes to fruition in the heart and soul of an individual depends entirely on the operations of the Holy Spirit. B. B. Warfield's suggestion, over a century ago, that Calvin was "the theologian of the Holy Spirit" has received much attention, and a case could be (and has been) made that the central dogma in the *Institutes* is the doctrine of the Holy Spirit.[58] But it would be more accurate to suggest that Calvin was a Trinitarian-centered theologian rather than a Spirit-centered or even Christ-centered theologian. God the Father

55. *Institutes*, 1.13.1; CO, 2:90.
56. Calvin has a pronounced view of the revelation of God in the created order, being "completely overwhelmed by the boundless force of its brightness" (*Institutes*, 1.5.1; CO, 2:42), likening it to a "dazzling theater" of God's glory (*Institutes*, 1.5.8; 1.6.2; CO, 2:47, 54). Much agitated controversy exists, however, in discussing Calvin's relationship to natural theology. Does Calvin, for example, derive any theological conclusions from nontheological starting points (whether by use of reason or by observation of events in creation)? This, in part, divided the two neoorthodox giants of the twentieth century, Karl Barth and Emil Brunner. Calvin did, for example, lay enormous emphasis on Scripture, insisting on the self-authenticating (Gk. *autopistos*) nature of Scripture's own testimony to itself: "Let this point therefore stand: that those whom the Holy Spirit has inwardly taught truly rest upon Scripture, and that Scripture indeed is self-authenticated; hence, it is not right to subject it to proof and reasoning." *Institutes*, 1.7.5; CO 2:60. See Sinclair B. Ferguson, "How Does the Bible Look at Itself?," in *Inerrancy and Hermeneutic: A Tradition, a Challenge, a Debate*, ed. Harvie M. Conn (Grand Rapids, MI: Baker, 1988), 47–66. But this is not all that Calvin says, and his use of "common" or "external proofs" for the authenticity of Scripture, for example, albeit secondary to Scripture's self-authenticating character and the testimony of the Holy Spirit, shows that Warfield's contention that Calvin did have a place for natural theology is correct. See B. B. Warfield, "Calvin's Doctrine of the Knowledge of God," in *Calvin and Calvinism* (Grand Rapids, MI: Baker, 2003), 29–130; cf. Paul Helm, "Natural Theology and the *Sensus Divinitatis*," in *John Calvin's Ideas*, 209–45.
57. *Institutes*, 1.7.4; CO, 2:59.
58. B. B. Warfield, "Calvin as a Theologian," in *Calvin and Augustine*, ed. Samuel G. Craig (Philadelphia: Presbyterian and Reformed, 1956), 484–85.

makes himself known in union with Jesus Christ and by the testimony of the Holy Spirit. In a passage that owes a great deal to the early church theologian Hilary of Poitiers, Calvin says, "For as God alone is a fit witness of himself in his Word, so also the Word will not find acceptance in men's hearts before it is sealed by the inward testimony of the Spirit [*interiore Spiritus testimonio*]."[59] Throughout the *Institutes*, Calvin elaborates extensively on the role of the Holy Spirit in relationship to the doctrine of God as Trinity, the inspiration and interpretation of Scripture, and the application of redemption (particularly in book 3) and on the Spirit's role in the life and ministry of the church.

Interestingly, given recent speculations and the implications of a view that emphasizes both the divine and human role in the production of Scripture, Calvin seems peculiarly modern. Giving full credence to the fact that Scripture is both a human and divine production, he nevertheless affirms that Scripture comes from God's mouth and is to be received as "oracles of God": "Yet this, as I have said, is the difference between the apostles and their successors: the former were sure and genuine scribes of the Holy Spirit, and their writings are therefore to be considered oracles of God."[60]

When Calvin here refers to the apostles as "scribes" (suggesting dictation), he is not affirming a theory of the psychology of inspiration as though the individual writers were themselves passive in the process. Calvin did not affirm any such theory. His point is that at the point of inspiration, what results on the page corresponds exactly (precisely) to the intent of the divine author. Men wrote but only (in the end) as God intended them to write.[61]

3. Calvin's doctrine of God includes the key themes of election and reprobation, a topic he initially placed where it logically belongs— in discussing the rule of God in providence in book 1. At least this is where it was found in the early editions of the *Institutes*, but in the final

---

59. *Institutes*, 1.7.4; CO, 2:59. Cf. Hilary of Poitiers, *On the Trinity*, 1.18: "For He whom we can know only through his own utterances is a fitting witness concerning himself." *Nicene and Post-Nicene Fathers of the Christian Church*, 2nd ser., ed. Philip Schaff and Henry Wace (1890–1900; repr., Grand Rapids, MI: Eerdmans, 1987), 9:45. The original Latin reads, "Idoneus enim sibi testis est, qui nisi per se cognitus non est." *Patrologiae Cursus Completus, Series Latina*, ed. Jacques-Paul Migne (Paris, 1844–1864), 10:38.

60. *Institutes*, 4.8.9; CO, 2:851–52.

61. See Warfield, *Calvin and Augustine*, 62–64.

edition, he moved it to book 3, at the point where he considered the application of redemption in the life of the believer.[62] Part of the explanation for this was the fact that Calvin had met some stiff resistance to the doctrine, particularly the so-called doctrine of double predestination, or the *decretum horribile*, as he would later refer to it.[63] For pastoral reasons, therefore, it was easier to maintain the doctrine of election within a consideration of grace than in the more abstract (sovereign) considerations of God's decree. Election, in that respect, is a "family secret."[64] But Calvin had also become convinced, partly through the influence of Philipp Melanchthon's 1536–1537 *Loci Communes*, that this was where the doctrine was located in Paul's epistle to the Romans.[65]

Mention should also be made in this context of the related doctrine of providence (*Institutes*, 1.16–18), one of the finest sections in the entire work: "Let them inquire and learn from Scripture what is pleasing to God so that they may strive toward this under the Spirit's guidance. At the same time, being ready to follow God wherever he calls, they will show in very truth that nothing is more profitable than the knowledge of this doctrine."[66]

Space does not allow for elaboration on such issues as union with Christ (surely a key theme in Calvin generally and particularly in the *Institutes*),[67] the threefold office of Christ (the *munus triplex*)

---

62. Calvin, for example, moved the vexed issue of the doctrine of election from its logical location as a precursor to the doctrine of providence at the beginning of the *Institutes* to its final location *after* the discussion of the role of the Holy Spirit in the application of redemption (soteriology) and Calvin's beautifully written section on prayer. Calvin is giving practical expression to the view that election is a "family secret" best understood *after* conversion rather than before, as well as attempting a pastoral response to many critics of predestination and election that surfaced in the 1540s and 1550s. It is true that much that has been written on the motivation behind this change has been speculative, often reflecting a negative bias toward the issue in question, and the reason for the change owes as much to its location in Romans as to any other consideration. Richard Muller has written that "Calvin did not, as has often been stated, remove the doctrine of predestination from the doctrine of God and place it in an a posteriori position in order to avoid the theological problems of the '*Deus nudus absconditus*,' speculative determinism, and central *dogmas*." See Muller, *Unaccommodated Calvin*, 129. For an assessment of Calvin's doctrine of election, see R. Scott Clark, "Election and Predestination: The Sovereign Expressions of God (3.21–24)," in Hall and Lillback, *Theological Guide to Calvin's "Institutes*," 90–122.

63. *Institutes*, 3.23.7; CO, 2:704.

64. See, e.g., *Institutes*, 3.21.1–2; cf. CO, 2:678–81.

65. In that sense, we might argue that the 1536 edition, which locates the doctrine of predestination in book 1, reflects the location given to it by Paul in Ephesians, whereas the 1559 edition reflects the location of the doctrine in Romans. See Muller, *Unaccommodated Calvin*, 128–29.

66. *Institutes*, 1.17.3; CO, 2:156.

67. Those who are united to him are both justified and sanctified: God declares the believing sinner righteous in Christ apart from works. But those who are united to Christ are also sanctified and called to do good works, thus avoiding both legalism and antinomianism.

as prophet, priest, and king,[68] Calvin's high (Cyprianic) view of the church "as our mother,"[69] or his discussions of the sacraments, particularly the Lord's Supper. Other contributors to this volume do so at some length.

First-Time Readers of the *Institutes*

What advice should be given to those picking up a copy of the *Institutes* for the very first time, unfamiliar with the theological nuances of the sixteenth century, expecting perhaps to find something similar to J. I. Packer's *Knowing God* or a tract on the five points of Calvinism? At first glance, the *Institutes* is intimidating.[70] Parts of the *Institutes* have in the course of time been published separately and have therefore had a life of their own. Sections, for example, of book 3, particularly the section dealing with the Christian life and prayer, have been published numerous times and testify to the immediate appeal of this material.[71] But there is a sense in which these sections are also part of a whole, an elaboration of a theme that suggests that a sovereign God (book 1) saves sinners through faith in Jesus Christ (book 2) to a life of holiness and obedience by the sovereign help of the Holy Spirit (book 3) through the instrumentality and encouragement of the visible church (book 4). Oversimplified as that is, it nevertheless demonstrates the need to view not just a part of Calvin's theological output but to see it as part of a whole.

---

68. See Derek W. H. Thomas, "The Mediator of the Covenant (2.12–15)," in Hall and Lillback, *Theological Guide to Calvin's "Institutes,"* 205–25.

69. Calvin's statement that we cannot have God as our Father without also having the church as our mother, citing Cyprian, is startling in an age when the institutional church receives little or no emphasis among Christians. Calvin's statements can sometimes appear, therefore, shockingly Catholic in modern ears, even if they were viewed as entirely at odds with Rome in the sixteenth century. For example, Calvin stated,

> For there is no other way to enter into life unless this mother conceive us in her womb, give us birth, nourish us at her breast, and lastly, unless she keep us under her care and guidance until, putting off mortal flesh, we become like the angels [Matt. 22:30]. Our weakness does not allow us to be dismissed from her school until we have been pupils all our lives. Furthermore, away from her bosom one cannot hope for any forgiveness of sins or any salvation, as Isaiah [Isa. 37:32] and Joel [Joel 2:32] testify. Ezekiel agrees with them when he declares that those whom God rejects from heavenly life will not be enrolled among God's people [Ezek. 13:9]. (*Institutes*, 4.1.4; CO 2:748–49)

70. Ford Lewis Battles, for example, refers to "the cumbrous bulk" of the *Institutes* in his introduction to the 1559 edition. *Institutes*, xlviii.

71. See, for example, one of the latest publications on these sections in Book 3 of the *Institutes*, John Calvin, *A Little Book on the Christian Life*, trans. and ed. Aaron Clay Denlinger and Burk Parsons (Orlando, FL: Reformation Trust, 2017).

Abridgments, too, have appeared from time to time,[72] which largely omit the more polemical aspects of the work. Nothing, however, beats the sense of accomplishment that reading the entirety of the *Institutes* brings. Writing over forty years ago, J. I. Packer summarized it this way:

> The *Institutio*, which sets out and safeguards this knowledge, should accordingly be read as a vast expository sermon with the whole Bible as its text, a systematic confession of divine mysteries learned from God's own mouth. Its analytical structure, its sustained theocentrism, and its leading themes—the unacknowledged majesty of the Creator; God's judgment-seat; the shame of sin; the quenching of God's wrath by the blood of Christ; the knowledge of God in Christ as a reconciled Father; the life of faith as the work in us of the Holy Spirit; the believer's hardships and hopes; predestination as guaranteeing glory; the church as the ministering fellowship of elect believers; the state as a servant of God; the unity of both Testaments in their witness to Christ—are sufficiently accounted for by reference to Calvin's key to Scripture, the epistle to the Romans. The Calvin-critic's first task is to grasp Calvin's theological method, and to learn to see his tenets as its products. Failing this, our praise and blame of Calvin will inform men, not about him, but merely about ourselves.[73]

Those who wish to understand the Bible better should need no encouragement to read a book that has influenced the course of theology for the past four and a half centuries. Calvin's *Institutes* belongs in a list of Christian classics, no matter what our theological sympathies may be, and becoming acquainted with it will prove to be a life-changing experience.

---

72. E.g., *Calvin's Institutes: Abridged Edition*, ed. Donald K. McKim (Louisville: Westminster John Knox, 2001). Others include *A Compend of the Institutes of the Christian Religion*, ed. Hugh T. Kerr (1939; repr., Philadelphia: Westminster, 1964), and a modernized version based on the Beveridge translation, *The Institutes of the Christian Religion*, ed. Tony Lane and Hilary Osborne (Grand Rapids, MI: Baker, 1986). Several abridgments were also published in the sixteenth century, including Latin editions by Edmund Bunny (1576), from which Edward May developed an English translation (1580), and Guillaume Delaune (1583), from which Christopher Featherstone developed an English translation (1585).

73. Packer, "Calvin the Theologian," 172.

PART 2

The TEACHING *of* JOHN CALVIN

8

The Divinity and Authority of Scripture

K. Scott Oliphint

> But because the church recognizes Scripture to be the truth of its own God, as a pious duty it unhesitatingly venerates Scripture.
> —John Calvin, *Institutes of the Christian Religion*

The Alone Foundation

During the Reformation, there were two "principles" that served to define the importance of the movement itself. While these two principles were only part of the overall project as it progressed historically, they highlighted the central matters of conflict between the established church and those calling for its reform. The two principles were delineated as *formal* and *material*.

The formal principle of the Reformation provided the ground of authority, the structure and context for the material principle. The material principle was the doctrine of justification by faith alone. This was the central matter that needed to be clarified against the backdrop of the predominant theology of the church in the sixteenth century. The formal principle was summed up in the Latin phrase *sola Scriptura*—Scripture alone—and was designed to call the church back to its sole ground of authority. It was meant to emphasize again the necessity of Scripture as the only foundation on which all matters of theology were to be based.

It would be difficult to overestimate the importance of John Calvin's theology in this movement. His prolific output—in his commentaries, the *Institutes*, and his miscellaneous letters and treatises—forms the centerpiece of what became the central tenets of Reformed theology. Specifically, for our purposes, Calvin's insight into the nature and function of Scripture provided the catalyst for all things Reformed coming after him. Our focus in this chapter is to highlight some of the most salient points that Calvin develops as he calls the church back to a proper (i.e., biblical) view of Scripture.

To think about the importance of Scripture in Calvin's *Institutes*, we must first attend to some preliminary matters. We should look initially at the context of his discussion of the doctrine of Scripture. That is, the reason why Calvin organized his topics in the way that he did says something about our particular topic. So we must say something briefly about Calvin's design as he wrote the *Institutes*.

After noting Calvin's organizational rationale, we can then set out the particular context of his view of Holy Scripture. As we proceed, however, it might be helpful to offer two significant "bookends" to this topic that give it its proper context. The first bookend has to do with Calvin's understanding of God's general revelation to man. Given that Calvin is interested in explaining just how it is that we come to a true and proper knowledge of God, any exposition of Calvin on Scripture should at least summarize his view of the knowledge of God available through God's revelation in creation. The second bookend, featured at the end of our discussion, comes in the century after Calvin in the Westminster Confession of Faith (1646). Because this confession gives us, in summary fashion, the gist of Calvin's concerns with respect to Scripture, it is useful for us to conclude with it after we see Calvin's own emphases with respect to a Reformed doctrine of Scripture.

Organization: Method and Structure[1]

One of the primary purposes of Calvin's *Institutes* is to develop and explicate a series of theological topics that would help and guide students of theology in their approach to Scripture.[2] Like us all, Calvin was a man of his time. His influences, goals, and content are, therefore, to a greater or lesser degree, reflective of that time. It should help us, then, to note some significant contours of Calvin's thinking. In this regard, we focus, albeit briefly, on two important aspects of Calvin's thought in order to better understand the content and development of his view of Holy Scripture.[3]

Despite Alister McGrath's contention that some editions of the *Institutes* were "poorly organized,"[4] there seems to be little question that Calvin was consciously developing and deepening the *Institutes* from the beginning.[5] From the publication of the second edition in 1539 on, according to Richard Muller, Calvin organized the *Institutes* according to the then-popular idea of "common places" (*loci communes*)[6] and

---

1. Both method and structure are important for understanding the rationale behind the *Institutes* and so need to be set forth and kept in mind in this chapter; for more on the distinction between method and structure, see n11 below. The following section is slightly edited from K. Scott Oliphint, "A Primal and Simple Knowledge (1.1–5)," in *A Theological Guide to Calvin's "Institutes": Essays and Analysis*, ed. David W. Hall and Peter A. Lillback (Phillipsburg, NJ: P&R, 2008), 17–21. Used by permission of P&R Publishing.

2. Cf. "John Calvin to the Reader, 1559," in *Institutes*, 1:4. Richard Muller notes,

> One might fairly argue that Calvin never set out to produce a theological system in the modern sense of the term. At the same time, it must be emphasized (against several modern accommodations of his work) that he certainly did intend to produce a theological system or body of doctrine in and for his own time. Specifically, he determined in his *Institutes* to develop a fairly cohesive set of theological topics and disputations that would guide *theological students* in their approach to Scripture—and he expanded the text in the light of insights gained in his work of preaching and exegesis and in the course of his polemical defense of the Reformation.

The Unaccommodated Calvin: Studies in the Foundation of a Theological Tradition (New York: Oxford University Press, 2000), 5, italics added; see also *PRRD*, 1:56–59.

3. We focus not on all or most of the influences on Calvin's thinking but instead pick two of those most centrally related to our topic. For a fuller understanding of Calvin's context and influences, see, for example, Muller, *Unaccommodated Calvin*; *PRRD*, 1:273–76; 3:173–74; Muller, "*Duplex Cognitio Dei* in the Theology of Early Reformed Orthodoxy," *SCJ* 10, no. 2 (1979): 51–61; Peter J. Leithart, "The Eminent Pagan: Calvin's Use of Cicero in *Institutes* I:1–5," *WTJ* 52 (1990): 1–12; Egil Grislis, "Calvin's Use of Cicero in the *Institutes* I:1–5: A Case Study in Theological Method," *ARG* 62, no. 1 (1971): 3–37.

4. Alister E. McGrath, *Reformation Thought: An Introduction*, 2nd ed. (Oxford: Blackwell, 1993), 246.

5. According to Muller, what we find in successive editions of the *Institutes* (after the 1536 edition, which was patterned after Luther's Small Catechism) is that Calvin was developing a more formal, doctrinal theology. See *PRRD*, 1:56–57.

6. Cf. "John Calvin to the Reader, 1559," in *Institutes*, 1:5. *Loci communes* was an organizational term in which Christian doctrine was explained according to different *loci* in Scripture. In this sense, the *Institutes* depends, at least in part, on Melanchthon's methodology in his *Loci*

disputations (*disputationes*).[7] The *Institutes*, in other words, contains the doctrinal elaborations that flow from the exegetical work that Calvin undertook in his commentaries.

Important and central for our purposes, given this general organizational method, is the fact that Calvin developed the *Institutes*, more specifically, according to the *loci* of the epistle to the Romans. Book 1 of the *Institutes* should be seen, therefore, as an explication of Paul's own order as he wrote the book of Romans. Specifically, what we find in the beginning of book 1 is "the relationship of God to humanity, the character of the human predicament, and the fact that humanity is left 'without excuse' in the presence of the revelation of God in nature."[8]

So the first point to be made with respect to our particular topic is that while Calvin no doubt refers to a number of humanist and Renaissance sources in the beginning sections of the *Institutes*, and while there are similarities at points between, for example, the arguments of Cicero and those of Calvin,[9] the driving force behind the content and arguments set forth by Calvin resides in the order of argumentation set forth by the apostle Paul in Romans. This is an important interpretive point that must be kept in mind and one that is central to understanding what Calvin is saying and why he is saying it.

Edward Dowey, for example, notes that Calvin's notion of the *sensus divinitatis* ("sense of divinity") shows "much dependence" on Cicero in the latter's *Nature of the Gods*.[10] There can be no question that Calvin refers to Cicero and others in his elaboration of the *sensus*. However, to think that Calvin's concept of that notion derives,

---

Communes: "The order of *loci* identified by Melanchthon in Paul's Epistle to the Romans thus established a standard for the organization of Protestant theology." Muller, *Unaccommodated Calvin*, 129.

7. Cf. "John Calvin to the Reader, 1559," in *Institutes*, 1:5. Muller states,

That Calvin, from 1539 on, did understand his *Institutes* as a gathering of *loci communes* and *disputationes* appears also from the even more explicit statements presented in his introductory "Argument" to the French translation of 1541. . . . In this "argument," Calvin once again indicates the purpose of the *Institutes* and, this time, omits all reference to piety, identifying his purpose, first, as providing a "sum of Christian doctrine" and, second, as offering a point of entry into the study of the Old and New Testaments.

Unaccommodated Calvin, 105.

8. Muller, *Unaccommodated Calvin*, 137.

9. Leithart, "Eminent Pagan," 1–12; Grislis, "Calvin's Use of Cicero," 3–37.

10. Edward A. Dowey Jr., *The Knowledge of God in Calvin's Theology*, 3rd ed. (Grand Rapids, MI: Eerdmans, 1994), 51.

in the main, from sources other than Scripture is to miss the point of Calvin's argument.

The second contextual point, which goes hand in hand with the first point above, has to do with Calvin's organizing structure in these initial chapters.[11] Calvin states,

> First, as much in the fashioning of the universe as in the general teaching of Scripture the Lord shows himself to be simply the Creator. Then in the face of Christ he shows himself the Redeemer. Of the resulting twofold knowledge of God [*hinc duplex emergit eius cognitio*] we shall now discuss the first aspect; the second will be dealt with in its proper place.[12]

This *duplex cognitio* is oftentimes hailed as the organizing principle of Calvin's *Institutes*.[13] Here Calvin states plainly that he will be discussing this *duplex* throughout the *Institutes*. Certainly, given the four books as a whole, his emphasis on the twofold knowledge of God is easily seen. This organizing structure is not original with Calvin but has its precedent both in Luther and in the Christian tradition generally.[14]

What must be kept in mind, however, is that while the *duplex* is important for Calvin, it is not the organizing structure of the beginning sections of the *Institutes*. That structure is articulated clearly in the first sentence of the *Institutes*:

> Nearly all the wisdom we possess, that is to say, true and sound wisdom, consists of two parts: the knowledge of God and of ourselves.[15]

---

11. We are making a (somewhat artificial) distinction in this section between Calvin's organizing method and his organizing structure. The point to be made is that, as we have noted, the way that Calvin chose the topics presented and the order of those topics are dependent on Paul's order in Romans. The general headings under which he chose to structure those topics, as we will see, have their source in the theological tradition on which Calvin depended. See Muller, *Unaccommodated Calvin*, 127–30, 134, 138.

12. *Institutes*, 1.2.1; cf. CO, 2:34.

13. "The really significant ordering principle of the *Institutes* in the 1559 edition is the *duplex cognitio Domini*, not the Apostles' Creed." Dowey, *Knowledge of God*, 42.

14. Muller explains, "Luther's theology, specifically his exegesis of Galatians, may also be the proximate source of the theme of twofold knowledge of God that became so prominent a feature of Calvin's *Institutes* in 1559." *PRRD*, 1:99. Elsewhere, Muller says, "The *duplex cognitio* in Calvin is not original with him, but probably also reflects the medieval Augustinian identification of the *obiectum theologiae* as God the Creator and Redeemer (Giles of Rome) or God the Creator, Redeemer, and Glorifier (Gregory of Rimini)." *Unaccommodated Calvin*, 73.

15. *Institutes*, 1.1.1.

Therefore, before proceeding to the overall *duplex cognitio Dei*, Calvin needs first to flesh out the relationship of our knowledge of God to our knowledge of ourselves. Hence, Muller states,

> [T. H. L.] Parker is certainly correct in arguing against Dowey that the initial and most basic twofold knowledge in the *Institutes* is not the "twofold knowledge of God" but the "knowledge of God and ourselves" the knowledge of God and self that was identified as basic to Calvin's thought in the first sentence of the 1536 text and that became the two foundational introductory chapters in 1539: this introductory structure remains in 1559.[16]

We now have before us two organizing principles that provide the backdrop for our understanding of Calvin's doctrine of Scripture. We take for granted that behind all that Calvin is saying in the opening chapters of the *Institutes* is the apostle Paul's discussion in Romans, and that at the heart of Calvin's concern in these initial chapters is the relationship of our knowledge of God to our self-knowledge.

How then does Calvin initiate the training of theological students in these beginning chapters? What matters are central and important for Calvin if his readers are to think biblically about the relationship of our knowledge of God and man? These seem to be the central questions to ask as we look at Calvin's argumentation.

"Nearly All the Wisdom We Possess"

We should not pass over too quickly the radical and penetrating way in which Calvin begins the *Institutes* with his discussion on "the knowledge of God and of ourselves."[17] Here Calvin is not concerned,

---

16. Muller, *Unaccommodated Calvin*, 134.
17. *Institutes*, 1.1.1. According to Muller, in the 1539 edition of the *Institutes*,

Calvin . . . added two introductory chapters in which he juxtaposed the knowledge of God with the knowledge of man and thereby recast the whole system in the light of the problem of human knowing in its finitude and sinfulness after the fall. . . . The final edition of Calvin's *Institutes*, published in 1559, not only expands the number of chapters and distributes the text, roughly, in terms of the outline of the Apostles' Creed, it also adds the theme of a twofold knowledge of God, the *duplex cognitio Dei*—knowledge of God as Creator and as Redeemer—that provides not only a further presuppositional focusing of Calvin's theology but also a structuring device identifying Scripture as the ground of all true knowledge of God and then setting forth the order of the first two books of the *Institutes*: "Knowledge of God the Creator" and "Knowledge of God the Redeemer."

PRRD, 1:104.

first of all, with elaborating a biblical doctrine of God. Neither is he intent, in the first place, on defending a biblical doctrine of Christ or of salvation. Instead, Calvin begins with covenantal relationship.[18] His primary and initial concern is to establish the fact that all people are related to the God who created them, and then to underscore that this relationship has everything to do with the way that we all think and act. Given the impetus of Calvin's thinking (i.e., Paul's order of topics in Romans), what we have in the initial chapters of the *Institutes* is the foundation for a Reformed Christian apologetic.

According to B. B. Warfield (speaking of Calvin),

> But we can attribute to nothing but his theological genius the feat by which he set a compressed apologetical treatise in the forefront of his little book—for the "Institutes" were still in 1539 a little book, although already expanded to more than double the size of their original form (edition of 1536). Thus he not only for the first time supplied the constructive basis for the Reformation movement, but even for the first time in the history of Christian theology drew in outline the plan of a complete structure of Christian Apologetics. For this is the significance in the history of thought of Calvin's exposition of the sources and guarantee of the knowledge of God, which forms the opening topic of his "Institutes."[19]

In other words, the *Institutes* is for Calvin an apologetic. It is more than that, but it is clearly no less than that. It is meant to provide for the church the structure in which one can defend the true, biblical faith against errors. In that way, Calvin's concerns were aimed at the destruction of strongholds that were raised up in his time against the knowledge of God (cf. 2 Cor. 10:5). His chosen organizational method provided the Protestant church a rich and deep foundation from which a Reformed apologetic could be developed.

To highlight the apologetic aspect of these initial discussions in the *Institutes*, we provide a brief overview of Calvin's view of God's revelation in nature and then set our sights on three crucial topics that he

---

18. This is not to say that Calvin uses the word "covenant" here; it is only to note that Calvin begins with man's relationship to God, his Creator, first of all.

19. Benjamin B. Warfield, "Calvin's Doctrine of the Knowledge of God," in *Calvin and Calvinism* (New York: Oxford University Press, 1931), 30.

emphasized with respect to a Reformed doctrine of Scripture. These three topics were not the only ones that Calvin dealt with. They were, however, central to his defense of a theology that had its foundations in Scripture. Because of his concern to address the errors of the church, Calvin was forced to confront the issue of ultimate authority, a matter of fundamental importance in the Christian culture of his time.

But that question is no less important in our own time. Even though Calvin's context and time were quite different from ours today, the issues he addressed and the answers he provided transcend that context and time (because they are biblical answers), and thus they remain crucially relevant to us today. As a matter of fact, with respect to apologetics, the argument could plausibly be made that the issue of ultimate authority is the issue that must be addressed by us all, Christian and non-Christian. Moreover, just how we begin to address this matter goes a long way toward demonstrating where our ultimate allegiance lies. This was Calvin's concern; it is our present concern as well.

"Pure and Clear Knowledge of God"

It may be useful at this point to offer a brief summary of the inaugural five chapters of Calvin's *Institutes*, which set up his discussion of Holy Scripture. One way to summarize these chapters is by using a selection of Calvin's own words from each chapter:

> It is certain that man never achieves a clear knowledge of himself unless he has first looked upon God's face, and then descends from contemplating him to scrutinize himself.[20]

> Our knowledge should serve first to teach us fear and reverence; secondly, with it as our guide and teacher, we should learn to seek every good from him.[21]

> Since, therefore, men one and all perceive that there is a God and that he is their Maker, they are condemned by their own testimony because they have failed to honor him and to consecrate their lives to his will.[22]

---

20. *Institutes*, 1.1.2.
21. *Institutes*, 1.2.2.
22. *Institutes*, 1.3.1.

Miserable men do not rise above themselves as they should, but measure him by the yardstick of their own carnal stupidity, and neglect sound investigation; thus out of curiosity they fly off into empty speculations.[23]

Yet hence it appears that if men were taught only by nature, they would hold to nothing certain or solid or clear-cut, but would be so tied to confused principles as to worship an unknown god.[24]

Calvin's concern in the first five chapters of the *Institutes* is two-fold: First, he wants to make clear that because we are made in the image of God, it is certainly the case that all men know God; they have within them a "sense of divinity" (*sensus divinitatis*) or a "seed of religion" (*semen religiones*). Second, this knowledge of God is sufficient only to condemn us; it is never, while we remain in Adam, taken and used for its proper purposes.

Once we take hold of the truth about God that he gives to each of us, we, in Adam, fashion a god of our own image. In so doing, we proceed to build a religion around the false god(s) that we have created. This response is, for those who remain in Adam, the inevitable reaction to the knowledge of God implanted in us and given all around us in creation and providence.

It is important for us to see that Calvin, like Paul in Romans, sees no reaction to natural revelation that would provide a foundation for a true, biblical (natural) theology. Our problem, however, is not a lack of knowledge of God but our suppression and distortion of it. Commenting on Romans 1:22, Calvin notes,

It is commonly inferred from this passage, that Paul alludes here to those philosophers, who assumed to themselves in a peculiar manner the reputation of wisdom. . . . But they seem to me to have been guided by too slender a reason; for it was not peculiar to the philosophers to suppose themselves wise in the knowledge of God, but it was equally common to all nations, and to all ranks of men. There were indeed none who sought not to form some ideas of the majesty of God, and to make him such a God as they

---

23. *Institutes*, 1.4.1.
24. *Institutes*, 1.5.12.

could conceive him to be according to their own reason. This presumption I hold is not learned in the schools, but is innate, and comes with us, so to speak, from the womb. . . . The arrogance then which is condemned here is this—that men sought to be of themselves wise, and to draw God down to a level with their own low condition, when they ought humbly to have given him his own glory. For Paul holds this principle, that none, except through their own fault, are unacquainted with the worship due God.[25]

In our rebelliousness, therefore, according to Calvin, sinners culpably commit idolatry. Not only so, but instead of fearing the God they know, "they do not desist from polluting themselves with every sort of vice, and from joining wickedness to wickedness, until in every respect they violate the holy law of the Lord and dissipate all his righteousness."[26]

There is no thought in Calvin's initial discussion of God's revelation in creation that mortal man, in Adam, could take that revelation and conclude for the true God. In our sins, we immediately pervert, suppress, and distort that which God clearly and constantly reveals concerning himself. Calvin is clear enough about our lack of ability to conclude for truth on the basis of God's revelation in creation. He states,

And where Paul teaches that what is to be known of God is made plain from the creation of the universe (Rom. 1:19), he does not signify such a manifestation as men's discernment can comprehend; but, rather, shows it not to go farther than to render them inexcusable. . . . But although we lack the natural ability to mount up unto the pure and clear knowledge of God, all excuse is cut off because the fault of dullness is within us.[27]

Likewise, in his comment on Paul's Areopagus address, Calvin notes, "After their boldness they fashion [God] so as they may comprehend him. By such inventions is the sincere and plain knowledge of God corrupt; yea, his truth, as saith Paul, is turned into a lie (Rom. i.25)."[28]

---

25. *Comm.*, on Rom. 1:22.
26. *Institutes*, 1.4.4.
27. *Institutes*, 1.5.14–15.
28. *Comm.*, on Acts 17:24.

In sum, Calvin argues that sinful man cannot take God's revelation in nature and, by a process of inference, conclude for the true God.

"Another and Better Help"

Given our sinful natures, it becomes all the more urgent, therefore, in Calvin's mind, that we move from the knowledge of God given in creation—a knowledge that, because given by God, is clear and universal but that, because taken by sinful man, is inevitably corrupted—to the knowledge of God given in Holy Scripture.[29] As Calvin puts it,

> That brightness which is borne in upon the eyes of all men both in heaven and on earth is more than enough to withdraw all support from men's ingratitude—just as God, to involve the human race in the same guilt, sets forth to all without exception his presence portrayed in his creatures. Despite this, it is needful that another and better help be added to direct us aright to the very Creator of the universe. It was not in vain, then, that he added the light of his Word by which to become known unto salvation.[30]

Having established the need for "another and better help," we can now turn our attention to three essential aspects of Calvin's teaching on Holy Scripture: the divinity of Scripture, the authority and self-authentication of Scripture, and the use of internal and external evidences with respect to Scripture.

"From the Very Mouth of God"

All-important for Calvin was the fact that the Bible is the very word of God. Because the phrase *word of God* can be understood in various

---

29. The relationship of general and special revelation in Calvin is summarized well by Warfield:

[Calvin] means only that in the absence of Scripture, that is of special revelation, the general revelation of God is ineffective to preserve any sound knowledge of Him in the world: but in the presence of Scripture, general revelation is not set aside, but rather brought back to its proper validity. The real relation between general and special revelation, as the matter lay in Calvin's mind, thus proves to be, not that the one supersedes the other, but that special revelation supplements general revelation indeed, but in the first instance rather repeats and by repeating vivifies and vitalizes general revelation, and flows confluently in with it to the one end of both, the knowledge of God (I.vi.2).

"Calvin's Doctrine of the Knowledge of God," 69.
30. *Institutes*, 1.6.1.

ways,[31] Calvin was anxious to set forth just what should be meant when one confesses that Scripture is God's word.

It would be difficult to imagine a more central and all-determining focus for the church of Jesus Christ today. If one goes wrong with respect to Scripture, even in perhaps subtle and unassuming ways, one is set to go wrong with the entirety of Christianity. Even that most basic of all doctrines—the doctrine of God—is itself properly gleaned from Scripture and can be construed only once Scripture is understood in its proper light.[32]

For Calvin, Scripture is a divine book. It is not, in the first place, a divine and human book. It is a divine book and therefore partakes of those characteristics of divinity that transcend and supersede whatever human marks are present. Calvin, of course, was certainly aware that Scripture was written by human agents. But it was just that awareness that motivated him to make clear that the human agency used by God to record his word was secondary, concerning the character of that word.[33] So, says Calvin (just to use a couple of the many examples),

> Hence the Scriptures obtain full authority among believers only when men regard them as having sprung from heaven, as if there the living words of God were heard.[34]

> We affirm with utter certainty (just as if we were gazing upon the majesty of God himself) that [Scripture] has flowed to us from the very mouth of God by the ministry of men.[35]

---

31. This was true in Calvin's day and is even more so in ours. One need only think of Karl Barth's view of the Bible as the *word of God*, as well as various permutations of that view (e.g., in postconservatives), to realize the importance of explaining just what is meant by the phrase *word of God*.

32. This is not to say that every Christian must have a full-orbed, biblical doctrine of Scripture to affirm what it teaches. It is rather to say that for those who set out to delineate a doctrine of Scripture, it is imperative that such a doctrine be firmly grounded in what Scripture is, first of all.

33. Calvin here is echoing the medieval tradition and anticipating the Protestant scholastics. Muller observes that

> the Protestant scholastics looked both to the medieval scholastic tradition and to the works of the Reformers. From the medieval teachers they received the definition of God as the *auctor principalis sive primarius Scripturae* [the principal or primary author of Scripture] and of human beings, the prophets and apostles, as secondary authors or instruments. From the Reformers they received no new language, but they did find confirmation of the point in the repeated identification of Scripture as God's Word, as given by God.

PRRD, 2:226.

34. *Institutes*, 1.7.1.

35. *Institutes*, 1.7.5.

This notion that God himself is Scripture's author and that his authoring Scripture took place "by the ministry of men" cannot be overemphasized, especially in our day.[36] For example, in a recent book on the character of theology, the author, ignoring the divine character of Scripture in Calvin's teaching, misconstrues Calvin's doctrine of Scripture altogether. Speaking of God's accommodation to us, the author says,

> For John Calvin, this means that in the process of revelation God "adjusts" and "descends" to the capacities of human beings in order to reveal the infinite mysteries of divine reality, which by their very nature are beyond the capabilities of human creatures to grasp.[37]

It is, of course, true that God condescends to us, and that teaching is a marvelous feature of Calvin's theology. Like any theological emphasis, however, once wrested from its proper context and used for a task it was never meant to perform, such a teaching is so misdirected as to become unrecognizable. The author continues to draw out what he sees as proper implications of Calvin's view of accommodation:

> The use that God makes of the creaturely medium of human language in the inspiration and witness of Scripture does not entail its divinization. Language, like the human nature of Jesus, remains subject to the historical, social, and cultural limitations and contingencies inherent in its creaturely character. Yet this does not in any way negate the reality of biblical inspiration as a gracious act of the Holy Spirit or detract from the authority of Scripture.[38]

---

36. Calvin's clear and emphatic insistence that Scripture is *God's* word, not man's, led to the Reformed affirmation that God, not man, was the efficient cause of Scripture. The human authors were instrumental causes, and thus secondary with respect to Scripture's identity. So, says Muller, "'considered essentially,' Scripture proceeds from God, while considered 'accidentally,' it was written by human beings." Muller adds, "When the human author of the text is an instrumental cause and God is identified as the *auctor primarius* [primary author], *the historical situation of the human author cannot ultimately limit the doctrinal reference of the text.*" *PRRD*, 2:242, 254, italics for non-Latin material added.

37. John R. Franke, *The Character of Theology: An Introduction to Its Nature, Task, and Purpose* (Grand Rapids, MI: Baker Academic, 2005), 75.

38. Franke, *Character of Theology*, 77.

For this author, because he ignores Calvin's view of Scripture, God's accommodation negates divinization. And we should note that the reason given for this negation is the analogy of the incarnation, such that he appeals to the "human nature of Jesus."[39]

But it should be obvious that such a construal is well wide of the mark—not only because Jesus Christ was, in fact, *divine*, and that essentially so,[40] but also because Calvin clearly articulates that Holy Scripture is in its character *divine*, given that it comes from the very mouth of God. Here Calvin is following the apostle Paul, who clearly states that "all Scripture is breathed out [Gk. *theopneustos*] by God" (2 Tim. 3:16). Paul, of course, knew that human beings had used human language to write the Scriptures. He could have deferred to an incarnational analogy and said, "All Scripture is breathed out by both God and man." But he did not do that, and for one reason: because the human authors of Scripture and the accommodation that is presupposed in the writing of Scripture do not in any way negate Scripture's divinity. Divinity accommodated is not humanity. Divinity accommodated is still divinity. Calvin understood this. Modern-day postconservatives do not.

So strong is Calvin's affirmation of Scripture's divinity that he can say, "This is the first clause, that we owe to the Scripture the same reverence which we owe to God; because it has proceeded from him alone, and has nothing belonging to man mixed with it."[41] Of course, Calvin is well aware of the fact that human language, authors, and so forth play their role in the constitution of Holy Scripture. His point, and a point that must be maintained by anyone who wants to hold to a Reformed view of Scripture, is that an admixture of human or accommodated elements in Scripture does not make Scripture a human

---

39. For another example of an incarnational analogy that goes wrong with respect to a biblical doctrine of Scripture, see Peter Enns, *Inspiration and Incarnation: Evangelicals and the Problem of the Old Testament* (Grand Rapids, MI: Baker Academic, 2005). For an example of a proper use of the incarnational analogy with respect to Scripture, see Richard B. Gaffin Jr., *God's Word in Servant-Form: Abraham Kuyper and Herman Bavinck on the Doctrine of Scripture* (Jackson, MS: Reformed Academic Press, 2008).

40. To say that Christ is *essentially* divine is simply to say, with historic Christianity, that the one who took on a human nature is the same one who is, eternally, the Son of God. So the human nature of Christ does not determine who he is essentially; he is, and will forever be, divine. He became human for us and for our salvation. That humanity, however, in no way eliminates his being divine, whereas his divinity determines his humanity.

41. *Comm.*, on 2 Tim. 3:16.

document or even a divine-human document with respect to its initial identity. Here Warfield's analysis of Calvin's view is on the mark:

> The diversity of the human authors thus disappears for Calvin before the unity of the Spirit, the sole responsible author of Scripture, which is to him therefore not the *verba Dei* [words of God], but emphatically the *verbum Dei* [word of God]. It is *a Deo* ("Institutes," I.vii.5); it has "come down to us from the very mouth of God" (I.vii.5); it has "come down from heaven as if the living words of God themselves were heard in it" (I.vii.1); and "we owe it therefore the same reverence which we owe to God Himself, since it has proceeded from Him alone, and there is nothing human mixed with it" (Com. on II Tim. iii.16). According to this declaration the Scriptures are altogether divine, and in them, as he puts it energetically in another place, "it is God who speaks with us and not mortal men" (Com. on II Pet. i.20). Accordingly, he cites Scripture everywhere not as the word of man but as the pure word of God.[42]

Scripture is the word of God; it did not simply come from God, nor does it simply contain what God wants. It *is*, in its very nature, the word of God. It is God breathed. It is *not* God and man breathed. It is *not* the word of God and the word of men.

It should be clear, then, that God's *use* of human authors and contexts in no way makes God *subject to* those means. They are mere means used by God to set forth his own transcendent truth.[43] That truth, even as it comes to us over time, in history, and by way of contexts and communities remains the truth of the one true God. *He* is the author of Scripture. Any other "authoring" with respect to Scripture is, in every sense of the word, *secondary* and should be treated as such in all our study and affirmations of Scripture. Embedded in his *accommodation*, in other words, is his *divine communication*.[44]

---

42. Warfield, "Calvin's Doctrine of the Knowledge of God," 61–62.

43. In commenting on the Reformed-orthodox view of Scripture's divinity, Muller notes, "The intention of Scripture is *not to draw attention to itself or its human authors*, but to lead human beings to worship and reverence God alone, to resign themselves to his will, and to direct all that they have and do to the glory of God." *PRRD*, 2:274, italics added.

44. This does not mean that Calvin was in any way unaware or ignorant of some of the harmonization and other issues that might arise with respect to Scripture. For an analysis of Calvin's handling of some such questions, see John Murray, "Calvin's Doctrine of Scripture," in *Collected Writings of John Murray* (Edinburgh: Banner of Truth, 1977), 4:158–75.

"Manifest Signs of God Speaking"

Holy Scripture is holy because it comes from the mouth of Holy God. It is holy because it is his word. It is *not* holy because God providentially accommodated himself to us and used otherwise common and human elements to produce it.[45] That can be said of a multitude of things. But it is holy because it is God breathed (Gk. *theopneustos*, cf. 2 Tim. 3:16).[46] It is *not* holy simply because it comes from God; it is holy because it is his very word.

For Calvin, and the other Reformers, the divinity of Scripture was closely connected to the question of authority. As can be seen in Richard Muller's analysis, the definitions of biblical authority offered by the Reformed orthodox in the seventeenth century were initiated, at least in part, by Calvin:

> The definitions of biblical authority offered by the orthodox lead directly to a series of related concepts that further characterize the authority of the text: the specific kind of "authenticity" it bears, yielding its principial status in theology, further defined and qualified by its self-authentication as "worthy of faith" or belief (*autopistos*) in itself. The written Word has authority if it is authentically divine—if it is authentically divine and, therefore, authoritative, it can stand as the *fundamentum* [foundation], the sustaining power of Christian faith and life through which the Spirit works, having the authority to adjudicate all theological controversies and all disputes over morals: it is the "authentic norm" (*authentian norma*) which stands above and directs faith and life.[47]

---

45. Any view that sees God's accommodation as the divine becoming human *simpliciter* would be anathema to a Reformed understanding of Scripture's divinity. Against the traditional Reformed view of accommodation, this view of accommodation became predominant in the eighteenth century and continues to the present. See *PRRD*, 2:305. For a contemporary example of what Muller describes as a rationalist understanding of accommodation, see Peter Enns, *Inspiration and Incarnation*. To use just one, of many, examples from that work, Enns argues, "This is surely what it means for God to reveal himself to people—he accommodates, condescends, meets them where they are. The phrase *word of God* does not imply disconnectedness to its environment. In fact, if we can learn a lesson from the incarnation of God in Christ, it demands the exact opposite. . . . We must resist the notion that for God to enculturate himself is somehow beneath him." Enns, *Inspiration and Incarnation*, 56.

46. There has been much discussion on just exactly *how* Calvin understood Scripture to be "God breathed," that is, inspired. For a brief discussion of this topic, see *PRRD*, 2:234–39. Note, for example, that, according to Muller, "Calvin was not interested in defining precisely how the biblical writers were to be considered as amanuenses or secretaries receiving dictation." *PRRD*, 2:237.

47. *PRRD*, 2:264.

It is because Scripture is the very word of God, from his mouth, that Calvin defends the character of Scripture in terms of its "self-authentication," or "self-attestation" (Gk. *autopistos*). What Calvin means by this needs some explanation. According to Calvin,

> It is utterly vain then to pretend that the power of judging Scripture so lies with the church that its certainty depends upon churchly assent. Thus, while the church receives and gives its seal of approval to the Scriptures, it does not thereby render authentic what is otherwise doubtful or controversial. But because the church recognizes Scripture to be the truth of its own God, as a pious duty it unhesitatingly venerates Scripture. As to their question—How can we be assured that this has sprung from God unless we have recourse to the decree of the church?—it is as if someone asked: Whence will we learn to distinguish light from darkness, white from black, sweet from bitter? Indeed, Scripture exhibits fully as clear evidence of its own truth as white and black things do of their color, or sweet and bitter things do of their taste.[48]

The point that Calvin is making here might be seen more clearly against the historical, ecclesiastical debates in which he was engaged.

One of the questions that loomed large during the time of the Reformation was the question of ultimate authority with respect to faith. The question was not whether God was the ultimate authority; that issue was noncontroversial. But the question that came most naturally after that was the question of what "vehicle" or "instrument" God uses, ultimately, to communicate himself and his truth to his people. At the time of the Reformation, the case had been made, and was generally accepted, that God had determined that the church would be the instrument through which his truth was given to his people. This, of course, is true as far as it goes. It is the church of Jesus Christ that is commissioned to spread the gospel and to proclaim the whole counsel of God to the world.

But the issue ran deeper than that. It had to do with just how one could know what God's truth was and what he was saying to the church. To oversimplify, the Roman church developed the idea of what was called "implicit faith," in which those in the church were

---

48. *Institutes*, 1.7.2.

to trust the tradition and officers of the church in matters of faith and life. It was the church that was commissioned by God to determine, propagate, and preserve the truth of God as it is found in Scripture. In other words, we are to believe that Scripture is God's word because the church has determined it to be so.

Calvin understood, and set forth clearly, that to think in this way was to put our trust ultimately in the church, rather than in the word of God itself.[49] It is, as Calvin notes above, the church's "pious duty" to acknowledge Scripture for what it is. This entails, unquestionably, that the church itself is to be subject to Scripture, as the very truth of God, and is not commissioned to determine that Scripture is true. The natural question comes, of course, and Calvin anticipates it: If it is the church's responsibility and duty to venerate Scripture (since it is the very word of God), how then are we to know that Scripture is God's own word?

Calvin's initial answer to this question is with another question: "Whence will we learn to distinguish light from darkness, white from black, sweet from bitter?" The answer to this latter question is simple, on the one hand, but contains within it a profound Reformed truth concerning the character of Scripture itself. Simply put, we learn to distinguish light from darkness, white from black, sweet from bitter by the experiencing of those things. All that is needed, therefore, for the attributes of those elements to be known and affirmed is the proper means of experience. Is Calvin saying, then, that the truth of God is itself dependent on something internal to us, something that we have and must use?

To answer that question, we must make another distinction, a distinction that was less precise in Calvin's mind but that became more precise, and important, as Reformed theology developed after Calvin. The distinction has to do with the work of the Holy Spirit and the relationship of his work to the word written.

Confusion has sometimes reigned regarding Calvin's understanding of the relationship of the Holy Spirit to the authority of Scripture. For example, Edward Dowey notes,

---

49. Recall above that Calvin so identifies God's word with God himself (in terms of our allegiance) that he can say, "We owe to the Scripture the same reverence which we owe to God." *Comm.*, on 2 Tim. 3:16.

True enough, the Bible has intrinsic validity. But this does not constitute its authority or even one source of its authority. The authority derives solely from the inner witness of God himself through which the intrinsic validity or inherent truth of the sacred oracles is recognized or confirmed.[50]

What Dowey seems to intimate here, and what could, given a certain reading, be mistakenly attributed to Calvin, is that Scripture's authority obtains only in such cases where the internal testimony of the Holy Spirit also obtains. If there is no internal testimony of the Spirit, there is no authoritative Scripture.

This reading, however, can have disastrous implications for the nature of Scripture itself.[51] Calvin understood this, albeit it in nascent form. He knew that the Spirit's work included not only the inner testimony, which itself is applied to all who come to Christ, but also the very "speaking" of Scripture as the word of God. Note, for example, how strongly Calvin can state this relationship: "As for the word 'Spirit,' it appears from what [Paul] calls his 'ministerial preaching of the Spirit' (II Cor. 3:8) that Spirit and Scripture are one and the same."[52] This identity of the Spirit with Scripture is not an identity in us, such that it requires the internal testimony of the Spirit. Rather, Calvin goes on to say,

> For after admonishing the Thessalonians not to "quench the Spirit," he adds that they should "not despise the prophets" (I Thess. 5:19f.). *By this he means that we choke out the light of God's Spirit if we cut ourselves off from His Word.*[53]

---

50. Dowey, *Knowledge of God*, 108.

51. One such implication would be tantamount to a Barthian view of Scripture, in which it is not the words themselves that carry the authority of God but rather the "Event" wherein the words "become" the word of God to me. This locates the authority of God's word in the individual subject, rather than in what God has objectively *said*. Another implication of this bifurcation of word and Spirit can be seen in the following:

> The Bible is the instrumentality of the Spirit in that the Spirit appropriates the biblical text for the purpose of speaking to believers today. . . . We must not conclude that exegesis alone can exhaust what the Spirit can say through the text. While the Spirit appropriates the text in its internal meaning, the goal of this appropriation is to guide the church in the variegated circumstances of particular contemporary settings.

Franke, *Character of Theology*, 133. Franke does try, to his credit, to maintain that word and Spirit are not to be separated, but his elaboration and methodology end up doing just that.

52. John Calvin, *Treatises against the Anabaptists and against the Libertines*, trans. Benjamin Wirt Farley (Grand Rapids, MI: Baker, 1982), 224.

53. Calvin, *Treatises against the Anabaptists and against the Libertines*, 224–25, italics added.

It is, therefore, the Holy Spirit who himself is speaking in and through the text of Scripture. "Thus, the highest proof of Scripture derives in general from the fact that God in person speaks in it."[54] The "speaking" to which Calvin refers is never independent of the words of Scripture themselves. As and when Scripture speaks, God himself, in the person of the Holy Spirit, speaks. The Spirit does not speak "through" the word; he does not speak as one who "appropriates" the word; the word is not, for him, an "instrumentality." Rather, the word just *is* the Spirit speaking.

It is this speaking of God in Scripture that provides for Calvin the apologetic "punch" that can silence the objector. Scripture needs no other proof to establish it as the word of God. So Calvin notes the following:

> True, if we wished to proceed by arguments, we might advance many things that would easily prove—if there is any god in heaven—that the law, the prophets, and the gospel come from him. Indeed, ever so learned men, endowed with the highest judgment, rise up in opposition and bring to bear and display all their mental powers in this debate. Yet, unless they become hardened to the point of hopeless impudence, this confession will be wrested from them: that they see manifest signs of God speaking in Scripture. From this it is clear that the teaching of Scripture is from heaven.[55]

The notion of self-authentication, therefore, is an affirmation that when Scripture speaks, God himself speaks. The authority of Scripture is not (contra Dowey above) something that only obtains if and when it is affirmed by us. It is an intrinsic attribute of Scripture itself, or better, an objective attribute of Scripture, whether or not we affirm it. When Scripture goes out—whether in preaching, in reading, in evangelizing—it goes out with all the authority of God himself. It is no "dead letter"; it is the very word of God himself, and it never goes out without carrying the authoritative demands of God with it.

It should be noted here that Calvin is not saying that Scripture is the word of God because it says it is. That, of course, is true enough.

---

54. *Institutes*, 1.7.4.
55. *Institutes*, 1.7.4.

But Calvin is making a more substantive point. His point is that Scripture is the word of God because God is its author. We only know that, of course, because Scripture tells us so. But we should not lose sight of the fact that it is God's speaking in Scripture that gives it its power and defines its identity.[56]

This is an important, perhaps *the* important, point to make regarding Scripture: it attests to its own authority. Two related matters need to be mentioned in this context, one related to Calvin's view of the Spirit's work in us and the other related to the apologetic nature of self-authentication.

The Holy Spirit is the one who speaks in Scripture.[57] The words of Scripture are his words. Because these words are God's, they carry his authority. But Calvin was just as adamant that, even though the word of God goes out with the full authority and power of God, no one can be convinced that Scripture is the word of God apart from the inner testimony of the Holy Spirit:

> Let this point therefore stand: that those whom the Holy Spirit has inwardly taught truly rest upon Scripture, and that Scripture indeed is self-authenticated; hence, it is not right to subject it to proof and reasoning. *And the certainty it deserves with us, it attains by the testimony of the Spirit.* For even if it wins reverence for itself by its own majesty, it seriously affects us only when it is sealed upon our hearts through the Spirit.[58]

What is needed, therefore, for the full assurance and individual certainty that Scripture is the very word of God himself is a necessary

---

56. The inevitable circularity of this affirmation did not escape the Reformed. Without engaging the entire debate, two matters can be mentioned here. First, this understanding of Scripture was consistent with the notion, going all the way back to Aristotle, of a ground, or foundation (*principium*), of knowledge (which, it should be noted, is *not* foundationalism). See *PRRD*, 2:162. Second, and after Calvin, John Owen provided a substantial and penetrating argument for the necessity of this biblical view, over against the circularity of the Roman view. Owen assigns to the church of Rome, not one efficient of belief and one motive of belief; rather, he says, Rome is caught between two different motives of faith, neither of which can prove the other without at the same time contradicting itself as the motive of faith. See John Owen, "The Testimony of the Church Is Not the Only Nor the Chief Reason of Our Believing the Scripture to Be the Word of God," in *The Works of John Owen*, ed. William H. Goold (Edinburgh: Banner of Truth, 1977), 8:527. For more on the issue of circularity, see K. Scott Oliphint, "Gauch's 'Gotchas': *Principia* and the Problem of Public Presuppositions," *Philosophia Christi* 17, no. 2, (2015): 441–54, esp. 450–53.

57. As the Westminster Confession of Faith (written after Calvin but surely influenced by him) affirms, the Holy Spirit is the one who himself is speaking in Scripture; cf. WCF 1.10.

58. *Institutes*, 1.7.5, italics added.

"connection" between the Spirit who speaks in Scripture and that same Spirit who testifies to us and in us, by that very word, that it is the word of God.

Second, we should keep in mind that Scripture's self-authentication, while being of great encouragement to us, is not of itself an apologetic *argument* that is meant to be lodged against unbelief. It is certainly the case that any document can proclaim itself to be God's word or in some way ultimately authoritative (and some writings actually do just that). But Scripture as self-authenticated by virtue of the Spirit speaking is an apologetic tool in that we can be assured and confident of Scripture's power and effectiveness whenever its truth is set forth. Our goal, therefore, in apologetics is to set forth the truth of Scripture clearly and accurately, because therein is the voice of the true God, confronting and challenging unbelief through the power of his word.[59]

"Very Useful Aids"

It remains for us now to explain briefly how Calvin views the use of "evidences" with respect to Holy Scripture. It might be thought that if Scripture is self-authenticating, and if it attests to its own authority, there would be nothing else to say about it. If we remember what we have just said above, however, we can begin to see that this is certainly not the case. If we remember that the fact of Scripture's self-authentication is not a part of the apologetic argument, it remains for us to see if there is, as a matter of fact, an apologetic argument to be made. In other words, it should not be the case (at least not normally the case) that we confront those who do not believe in Scripture's divinity and authority with the statement, "It is self-attesting." Since self-attestation accrues to Scripture objectively, and since it cannot be affirmed without the inner testimony of the Holy Spirit, we can expect that its self-attestation will not be recognized by those who do not have the Spirit. What, then, can we say in such circumstances?

---

59. Note John Murray:

The sum of this is clear. God speaks in Scripture. In it he opens his sacred mouth. In Scripture the majesty of God confronts us. This divinity inheres in the Scripture and it therefore exhibits the plainest evidence that it is God's Word. When we bring sound minds it compels our submission and obedience. And our conclusion must be that this is but another way of saying that Scripture is by its nature divinely authoritative.

"Calvin and the Authority of Scripture," in *Collected Writings of John Murray*, 4:188.

Calvin addresses this question, and while we do not need to delve into the complexities of detail regarding the internal and external evidences of Scripture, we should note the primary emphases that Calvin presses. He states,

> Unless this certainty, higher and stronger than any human judgment, be present, it will be vain to fortify the authority of Scripture by arguments, to establish it by common agreement of the church, or to confirm it with other helps. For unless this foundation is laid, its authority will always remain in doubt. Conversely once we have embraced it devoutly as its dignity deserves, and have recognized it to be above the common sort of things, those arguments—not strong enough before to engraft and fix the certainty of Scripture in our minds—become very useful aids.[60]

In this opening statement of chapter 8 of the *Institutes*, Calvin is moving our consideration from the "connection" of the Spirit's work—in his objective speaking (in Scripture) and his subjective inner testimony (in an individual)—to a consideration both of Scripture's characteristics and of those external and outward attestations to Scripture's own power.

Why does Calvin move in this direction? If Scripture is self-authenticating and can be known as such only by way of the inner testimony of the Spirit, why mention evidences of Scripture's power and divinity? What is his concern here? One interpretation has it that Calvin is arguing the necessity of external evidences for the inner testimony of the Holy Spirit to have its proper content.[61] This, however, does not seem to be Calvin's concern.

To the extent to which he discusses evidences of Scripture's divinity, Calvin is making an apologetic point.[62] Once we understand the absolute ground and foundation of Scripture's divinity—that is, that it authenticates itself objectively and that the Spirit's work is necessary,

---

60. *Institutes*, 1.8.1.

61. This argument is given by B. B. Warfield. Note, for example, how Warfield understands Calvin's notion of the evidences (*indicia*) of Scripture: "It is . . . in [Calvin's] general teaching as to the formation of sound faith in the divinity of Scripture that we find the surest indication that he thought of the *indicia* as co-working with the testimony of the Spirit to this result." "Calvin's Doctrine of the Knowledge of God," 89.

62. An "apologetic point" is not only made to rank unbelief but is also beneficial to any who have elements of unbelief residing in their hearts.

subjectively, for any affirmation of that divinity—Calvin recognizes that there is a certain and substantial usefulness in pointing out those characteristics and attributes related to Scripture's divinity to any who might doubt it. Though Calvin will affirm that "they who strive to build up firm faith in Scripture through disputation are doing things backwards,"[63] he spends a considerable amount of time and energy in this section of the *Institutes* demonstrating that there is an abundance of evidence to show that "the Sacred Scriptures, which so far surpass all gifts and graces of human endeavor, breathe something divine."[64]

To put it into common apologetic vernacular, Calvin is arguing that once the authority (including the self-attestation) of Scripture is presupposed, evidences that point to its divinity, though not able to establish its authority, provide fodder for demonstrating what Scripture actually is.

Richard Muller, in speaking of the relationship of the "subjective condition" of the Spirit's internal testimony relative to the objective evidence of Scripture's divinity, argues that the objective evidence "must be present if the subjective conviction is to be grounded in reality."[65] Muller continues,

> Thus, Calvin begins his discussion of the objective divinity of Scripture with the disclaimer that "unless this foundation is laid," namely, the foundation provided by the work of the Spirit, "its authority will always remain in doubt." Once this work of the Spirit is accomplished, however, Calvin *knows of no bounds to the usefulness and the power of the evidences of divinity present in Scripture.*[66]

Apologetically speaking, to add to Muller's point, Calvin sees these evidences not only as useful "once this work of the Spirit is accomplished" but also as useful to those who "try to gnaw at" Scripture's divinity.[67]

Without spelling out the details, we ought to note that the list of evidences for Scripture's authority and divinity in the *Institutes*

---

63. *Institutes,* 1.7.4.
64. *Institutes,* 1.8.1.
65. *PRRD,* 2:259.
66. *PRRD,* 2:259, italics added.
67. *Institutes,* 1.8.2.

can be categorized as internal evidences—that is, those evidences that are found in Scripture itself—and external evidences—that is, those evidences that are outside of Scripture per se but that testify to its character. It is the internal evidences that receive priority, because in them is the guarantee (given what we have already seen with respect to Scripture's divinity) that the Spirit is speaking with power and authority. The external evidences are supportive and useful but carry no such guarantee. Among the internal evidences of which Calvin speaks are majesty, eloquence, truthfulness, miracles, fulfilled prophecies, and heavenly character.[68] Among the external evidences are such things as Scripture's antiquity, its providential preservation, the consent of the church, and the faithfulness of the martyrs.[69] These are all, with varying effect, worthy of discussion when Scripture's divinity and authority are in question.

Conclusion

Much more could be said regarding Calvin and his monumental and penetrating elaboration of a Reformed understanding of Holy Scripture.[70] One way to summarize the influence that Calvin's view of Scripture had on theological discourse after him is by referring to the second "bookend" mentioned at the beginning of this chapter—the Westminster Confession of Faith. The first chapter of the confession sets forth a doctrine of Scripture. Sections 4 and 5 state concisely what Calvin was at pains to argue a century earlier. Section 4 lays out the self-authentication of Scripture, in contrast to a Romanist view:

> The authority of the Holy Scripture, for which it ought to be believed and obeyed, dependeth not upon the testimony of any man, or Church; but wholly upon God (who is truth itself) *the author* thereof: and therefore it is to be received *because it is the Word of God*.[71]

Section 5 takes up the topic of the internal evidences of Scripture, as well as the internal testimony of the Holy Spirit:

---

68. See *Institutes*, 1.8.1; 1.8.2; 1.8.4; 1.8.5–6; 1.8.7–8; 1.8.11, respectively.
69. See *Institutes*, 1.8.3; 1.8.9–10; 1.8.12; 1.8.13, respectively.
70. Anyone interested in delving into this topic should consult Muller, *Unaccommodated Calvin*, and the first two volumes of *PRRD*.
71. WCF 1.4, italics added.

We may be moved and induced by the testimony of the Church to an high and reverent esteem of the Holy Scripture. And the heavenliness of the matter, the efficacy of the doctrine, the majesty of the style, the consent of all the parts, the scope of the whole (which is, to give all glory to God), the full discovery it makes of the only way of man's salvation, the many other incomparable excellencies, and the entire perfection thereof, are arguments whereby it does abundantly evidence itself to be the Word of God: yet notwithstanding, our full persuasion and assurance of the infallible truth and divine authority thereof, is from the inward work of the Holy Spirit bearing witness by and with the Word in our hearts.[72]

The point to be made here is that Calvin's views on Sacred Scripture did not remain in Geneva. His able arguments, as well as his firm grasp on the all-important formal principle of the Reformation, gained such ground in the Reformed world from his time forth that the points he labored to argue became the very points on which Reformed theology stood.[73] To understand what a Reformed doctrine of Scripture is, one must spend time with Calvin.

---

72. WCF 1.5.

73. When this truth of the self-authentication of Scripture is ignored, disastrous consequences can follow. Note, for example, former evangelicals at Southern Evangelical Seminary recounting their "conversions" to Roman Catholicism in Douglas M. Beaumont, *Evangelical Exodus: Evangelical Seminarians and Their Paths to Rome* (San Francisco, CA: Ignatius, 2016), and see my review of that book in *Themelios* 41, no. 2, August 2016, http://themelios.thegospelcoalition .org/review/evangelical-exodus-evangelical-seminarians-and-their-paths-to-rome. Much of their confusion is owing to a deficient view of Scripture and its authority.

9

Creation and Humanity

J. V. Fesko

The Celestial Creator himself, however corrupted man may be, still keeps in view the end of his original creation.

—John Calvin, *Commentary on Genesis*

A Neglected Doctrine

Ever since the sixteenth-century Reformation, John Calvin has received a great deal of attention, as he was one of the key second-generation Reformers that moved the fledging Protestant church forward. Though a number of other theologians contributed to the work of reformation, it is Calvin who has often been front and center. This is likely due to the popularity of his chief theological work, *Institutes of the Christian Religion*.

Over the years historical theologians have intensely studied Calvin's theology, especially his *Institutes*—though some doctrines have received more attention than others. The doctrine of predestination, of course, has been a hot commodity in Calvin research, although other doctrines, such as his teaching on union with Christ, providence, or the sacraments, have also featured prominently.[1] One doctrine that has received less attention, however, has been Calvin's doctrine of creation and humanity.[2] In one sense, this is easily explainable for two reasons. First, during the Reformation a number of doctrines were under debate, such as the nature of human freedom and human will, justification, predestination, and the sacraments. A quick perusal of Calvin's writings shows that he gave these doctrines greater attention.[3] Second, Calvin's doctrine of creation and humanity, at least in its broad contours, was no different from his Patristic forefathers or his contemporaries, Roman Catholic or Protestant.[4]

Hence, it seems only natural that this doctrine would receive less attention than its more debated counterparts. At the same time, although Calvin's teaching on this subject is very similar to his predecessors and contemporaries, this does not mean that it has no unique aspects. To see the unique aspects of Calvin's doctrine of creation and humanity, in this essay we first survey the general contours of his view. We then focus on the specific aspects of his teaching, and we conclude by exploring the practical implications of his doctrine. By the end of our study, we will see why Calvin believed that even in a fallen world, the whole created order, including fallen man, is still the theater of God's glory.

---

1. For a cross section of recent works on these subjects, see, for example, Richard A. Muller, *Christ and the Decree: Christology and Predestination in Reformed Theology from Calvin to Perkins,* SHT 2 (1986; repr., Grand Rapids, MI: Baker, 1988), 17–38; Muller, *Calvin and the Reformed Tradition: On the Work of Christ and the Order of Salvation* (Grand Rapids, MI: Baker, 2012); Horton Davies, *The Vigilant God: Providence in the Thought of Augustine, Aquinas, Calvin and Barth* (New York: Peter Lang, 1992), 95–126; Dennis E. Tamburello, *Union with Christ: John Calvin and the Mysticism of St. Bernard,* CSRT (Louisville: Westminster John Knox, 1994), 84–101; Ronald S. Wallace, *Calvin's Doctrine of the Word and Sacrament* (Edinburgh: Scottish Academic Press, 1995); B. A. Gerrish, *Grace and Gratitude: The Eucharistic Theology of John Calvin* (Edinburgh: T&T Clark, 1993).

2. A notable exception is Susan E. Schreiner, *The Theater of His Glory: Nature and the Natural Order in the Thought of John Calvin* (Grand Rapids, MI: Baker, 1991). There is also, of course, the well-known essay by Benjamin B. Warfield, "Calvin's Doctrine of the Creation," in *The Works of Benjamin B. Warfield,* ed. E. D. Warfield et al. (1931; repr., Grand Rapids, MI: Baker, 1981), 5:287–352.

3. See, for example, the following sample of Calvin's writings: *Institutes,* 3.11–18; 3.21–25; 4.14–17; *The Bondage and Liberation of the Will: A Defence of the Orthodox Doctrine of Human Choice against Pighius,* ed. A. N. S. Lane, trans. G. I. Davies, TSRPRT 2 (Grand Rapids, MI: Baker, 1996); *Concerning the Eternal Predestination of God,* trans. J. K. S. Reid (1961; repr., Cambridge: James Clarke, 1982); *Calvin's Calvinism: Treatises on the Eternal Predestination of God and the Secret Providence of God,* trans. Henry Cole (1856; repr., Grand Rapids, MI: Reformed Free Publishing Association, [1987?]); *Canons and Decrees of the Council of Trent, with the Antidote (1547),* in *Selected Works of John Calvin,* ed. Henry Beveridge and Jules Bonnet (Grand Rapids, MI: Baker, 1983), 3:17–188; *True Partaking of the Flesh and Blood of Christ,* in Beveridge and Bonnet, *Selected Works of John Calvin,* 2:495–572.

4. Schreiner, *Theater of His Glory,* 2.

Broad Contours of Calvin's Doctrine

Creation out of Nothing

Like generations of theologians before him, Calvin holds that God created the universe *ex nihilo*, "out of nothing." Scholars trace the origins of this teaching to Theophilus of Antioch (d. ca. 183–185), who wanted to show the superiority of the Christian doctrine of creation to the teachings of Greek philosophy concerning the supposed eternality of the world. Creation *ex nihilo* became standard fare in the theology of early church fathers such as Origen (ca. 185–ca. 254), Diodore of Tarsus (ca. 330–ca. 392), Lactantius (ca. 240–ca. 320), and Basil of Caesarea (ca. 329–379).[5] It is the work of Basil and of Ambrose of Milan (ca. 338–397), whom Calvin calls "saintly men," that he cites favorably on the doctrine of creation. Calvin explains that the opening chapters of the Bible briefly set forth the doctrine of creation, namely, that "God by the power of his Word and Spirit created heaven and earth out of nothing." By his word, God spoke the creation into existence and brought forth living things, animate and inanimate, endowed each with its own nature, assigned functions, and appointed each thing in the creation its place and station. Moreover, God also provided for the preservation of each species until the conclusion of all history.[6]

Providential Ordering of the Creation

From these points we can see that Calvin clearly distinguishes God from the creation. God alone is eternal and self-existent. Not only did God create what we can see, the visible creation, but he also created what we cannot see, the invisible creation. Although the opening Genesis narrative does not speak of the invisible creation, Calvin nevertheless acknowledges that the rest of Scripture does speak of it.[7] In this regard, Calvin has in mind the creation of the heavens and particularly angels. God alone is the sovereign Creator, and there is no sort of cosmic dualism, where God and the devil are competing forces in the universe.[8] If God, therefore, created the visible and invisible creation,

---

5. Schreiner, *Theater of His Glory*, 8.
6. *Institutes*, 1.14.20.
7. *Institutes*, 1.14.3.
8. Wilhelm Niesel, *The Theology of Calvin*, trans. Harold Knight, LEH (1956; repr., Cambridge: James Clarke, 2002), 63.

then it flows naturally from this point that God also preserves the created order through his providence.

Calvin's time was one when the traditional foundations of the world had been shaken by political and theological unrest, particularly the conflict between the Roman Catholic Church and the Protestant Reformation. One scholar writes, "Calvin had sensed that the foundations of the late 'medieval' world had crumbled."[9] Yet the concomitant doctrine of Calvin's doctrine of creation, God's providence, was reason for hope and peace despite the apparent tumult. In contrast to the philosophical view of fate or its antithetical twin, chance (or fortune), Calvin believed that God not only created the cosmos but also upholds it by his providential care. God does not idly observe his creation from heaven but governs all events. In Calvin's view, each individual event in the cosmos takes place because of God's set plan, and nothing takes place by chance.[10] Calvin goes as far as to say, "Not one drop of rain falls without God's sure command."[11]

In a sermon on Job 38, Calvin encourages his hearers to recognize God's providence at all times:

> He sends many adversities and miseries: One man loses his goods, another is smitten with sickness, another falls into reproach and slander, and another is wronged and beaten. It might be thought that God is far overseen in handling men so roughly. No, not so. In all these things it behooves us to learn to confess, that God is always righteous, and that he knows cause why to handle us so, and that the same cause is good and rightful though it be unknown to us.[12]

Calvin believed that God created and sustained the entire creation both to uphold the created order, a necessary corollary of the doctrine of creation, and to "reveal his concern for the whole human race, but especially his vigilance in ruling the church, which he deigns to watch more closely."[13] For Calvin, humanity is the

---

9. Schreiner, *Theater of His Glory*, 3.
10. *Institutes*, 1.16.4–5.
11. *Institutes*, 1.16.5.
12. John Calvin, "Sermon 143," in *Sermons on Job* (1574; repr., Edinburgh: Banner of Truth, 1993), 697. I have updated all Early Modern English quotations with contemporary spelling.
13. *Institutes*, 1.17.1.

pinnacle of the creation and therefore the supreme object of God's providential care.

Humanity as the Pinnacle of the Creation

Calvin firmly teaches that humanity is the pinnacle of God's good creation. Man, made in the image of God, is the noblest and most remarkable example of God's justice, wisdom, and goodness.[14] For Calvin, man is the "most illustrious ornament and glory of the earth." Furthermore, he says that if mankind were to vanish, "the earth would exhibit a scene of desolation and solitude, not less hideous than if God should despoil it of all its other riches."[15] In addition to this, because man is the pinnacle of the creation, the entire created order was made for humanity's benefit. In the creation, Calvin argues that one can see God's fatherly care toward mankind. He explains that God did not create man until he had lavished on the universe all manner of good things. God disposed the movements of the sun and stars, filled the earth, waters, and air with living things, and brought forth an abundance of fruits to serve as food, all of which manifested God's kindness toward humanity.[16]

The reason that man is the pinnacle of God's creation is because he is made in the image of his Creator, which sets him apart from all the other creatures. In a sermon on Job 10:7–15, Calvin explains,

> When John declares that all things are quickened by the word of God, and that the said eternal wisdom which is in God is the wellspring of life and power: he shows that men have not only life, so as they can eat and drink: but (says he) there is also a light shining in them. By this word *light*, he means that the image of God is imprinted in us because we have understanding and reason, because we discern between good and evil, and because men are borne to have some order and common society among themselves, so as every man has a conscience of his own to tell him what is evil and what is good.[17]

What one can see from this statement is the Reformer's belief that though God's glory shines in the outer man, in his body, the primary

---

14. *Institutes*, 1.15.1.
15. *Comm.*, on Ps. 24:1.
16. *Institutes*, 1.14.2.
17. Calvin, "Sermon 39," in *Sermons on Job*, 183.

seat of the image of God is in his inner man, in his soul. This is evident in the emphasis Calvin places on understanding, reason, and discerning between good and evil.[18]

Calvin, of course, is quick to acknowledge that man has fallen because of the disobedience of the first Adam in the garden. It is through the second Adam, Jesus, that God will restore man to his unspoiled integrity.[19] In this regard, it is important to note Calvin's methodology in explaining the nature of the image of God in man. Calvin does not primarily use the Genesis creation narratives as the source material for his understanding of the image of God. Rather, he uses New Testament texts that relate primarily to Christ and man's redemption to explain the nature of man's prefall characteristics. Commenting on Colossians 3:10, Calvin writes,

> We are renewed after the image of God. Now, the image of God resides in the whole of the soul, since it is not only the reason that is upright, but also the will. Hence, too, we learn both what is the end of our regeneration (that is, that we may be made like God and that His glory may shine forth in us) and also what is the image of God which Moses speaks of; that is, the rectitude and integrity of the whole soul, so that man represents as in a mirror the wisdom, righteousness and goodness of God.[20]

In man's redemption, Calvin argues, it is Jesus, the second Adam, who bears the unblemished image of God, and it is to this unblemished image that man will be restored. Though this aspect of Calvin's understanding might arguably be a part of his soteriology, we should note, nevertheless, that his Christology and eschatology inform his understanding of the creation, or more specifically, the nature of the image of God in man in the initial creation: "Now we see how Christ is the most perfect image of God; if we are conformed to it, we are so restored that with true piety, righteousness, purity, and intelligence we bear God's image."[21]

---

18. *Institutes*, 1.15.3. Cf. François Wendel, *Calvin: Origins and Development of His Religious Thought*, trans. Philip Mairet (1950; repr., Grand Rapids, MI: Baker, 1997), 173.

19. *Institutes*, 1.15.4.

20. *CNTC*, 11:349–50.

21. *Institutes*, 1.15.4; cf. Niesel, *Theology of Calvin*, 69; Peter Wyatt, *Jesus Christ and Creation in the Theology of John Calvin*, PrTMS 42 (Allison Park, PA: Pickwick, 1996), 73.

Summary

The broad contours of Calvin's doctrine of creation and humanity can be summarized by saying that God created everything, visible and invisible, out of nothing. God not only created the cosmos, but he also continues to sustain the creation by his providence, both for the creation in general and even down to the minutest detail, including the actions of man. God exercises his providential care over creation and man not only because he is sovereign but also because he is showing his care for humanity, the pinnacle of his creation. Since man is the "most illustrious ornament and glory of the earth," as he shines forth the wisdom, righteousness, and goodness of God, the whole creation was ordered for man's benefit and enjoyment. Calvin uses primarily the New Testament to explain not only the nature of man's redemption but also the nature of man at his creation before the fall. More specifically, Calvin emphasizes that man is made in the image of God but that God's unblemished image is revealed in Jesus. Given these broad contours, we can now turn to explore some of the specific aspects of Calvin's doctrine of creation and humanity.

Specific Aspects of Calvin's Doctrine
Creation as the Theater of God's Glory

When we turn to consider some of the specific aspects of Calvin's doctrine of creation and humanity, we can begin by noting an important observation in his understanding of the creation of man. Calvin writes, "Certain philosophers, accordingly, long ago not ineptly called man a microcosm because he is a rare example of God's power, goodness, and wisdom, and contains within himself enough miracles to occupy our minds, if only we are not irked at paying attention to them."[22] Calvin is reflecting positively on the teaching of Aristotle (384–322 BC). Aristotle taught that man is a miniature version of the greater universe as a whole. Man, the microcosm, is analogous to the macrocosmic universe.[23] Calvin observes that in man's physical construction, one can see the wisdom and creativity of God:

---

22. *Institutes*, 1.5.3.
23. See John T. McNeill's editorial comment in *Institutes*, 1:54n9.

> In regard to the structure of the human body one must have the greatest keenness in order to weigh, with Galen's skill, its articulation, symmetry, beauty, and use. But yet, as all acknowledge, the human body shows itself to be a composition so ingenious that its Artificer is rightly judged to be a wonder-worker.[24]

Here we see Calvin marvel at the physical construction of humans, even positively speaking of Galen (ca. 131–ca. 200), a Greek philosopher, physician, and anatomist who was renowned for his medical knowledge.[25]

Continuing in this line of thought—namely, that of man as the microcosm of God's wisdom, power, and beauty—Edward Dowey explains that in Calvin's theology, "man, the image of God, is the summit of general revelation, and Christ the God-man is the brightest mirror of both God's self-revelation and man's essential nature."[26] If man, then, is the image of God and as a mirror reflects God's wisdom, power, and beauty, and if he is also a microcosmic creation, then the same may be said of God's attributes reflected in the macrocosmic creation. Commenting on Hebrews 11:3, "By faith we understand that the worlds have been framed by the word of God, so that what is seen hath not been made out of things which do appear" (ASV), Calvin writes,

> These words contain the very important teaching that in this world we have a clear image of God, and in this passage our apostle is saying the same thing as Paul in Rom. 1.20 where he says that the invisible things of God are made known to us by the creation of the world, since they are seen in His works. In the whole architecture of His world God has given us clear evidence of His eternal wisdom, goodness and power and though He is invisible in Himself He shows Himself to us in some measure in His work. The world is therefore rightly called the mirror of divinity not because there is enough clarity for men to know God by looking at the world but because He makes Himself clear to unbelievers in such a way that they are without excuse for their ignorance. On the other hand,

---

24. *Institutes*, 1.5.2.

25. See John T. McNeill's editorial comment in *Institutes*, 1:54n8.

26. Edward A. Dowey Jr., *The Knowledge of God in Calvin's Theology* (1952; repr., Grand Rapids, MI: Eerdmans, 1994), 19; cf. *Institutes*, 1.15.1; 1.15.3–4; 2.12.6.

believers to whom He has given eyes to see discern the sparks of His glory as it were shining out in every individual creature. The world was founded for this purpose, that it should be the sphere of divine glory.[27]

Here we see that Calvin is willing to say that man bears the microcosmic image of God and that the creation bears the macrocosmic image of God. Of course, as always, Calvin stipulates that because of the fall, the data that fallen man can see serves for his condemnation and renders him without excuse for his disbelief and rebellion before the tribunal of God.[28] Nevertheless, redeemed man has been given the eyes to see the glory of God in the creation.

Calvin has famously explained that when one places a beautiful volume before a "bleary-eyed man," he can recognize that there is some writing before him, but he can scarcely make out two words. Yet when he wears spectacles, the bleary-eyed man can begin to read the beautiful book. So it is with sinful man, who knows that God exists and that he should worship him, but it takes the Holy Spirit to open his eyes and also requires the Scriptures to help him see clearly. Scripture, Calvin writes, gathers up the otherwise confused knowledge of God in the mind of man and enables him to see God clearly.[29] In this way, then, Scripture enables redeemed man to read the "book" of creation aright and to discern and see God's glory in the creation that was otherwise obscured by his sin. With the spectacles of Scripture, the Christian is enabled to behold the powers and attributes of God as they are displayed in the creation, which Calvin likens to a painting.[30] Or another metaphor Calvin employs is that the creation is a mirror: "The Lord represents both himself and his everlasting Kingdom in the mirror of his works with very great clarity."[31] Switching metaphors, Calvin also compares the creation to a "dazzling" or "glorious theater" in which God displays his glory.[32]

---

27. *CNTC*, 12:159–60.
28. On the importance and necessity of faith in Christ for salvation in Calvin's theology, see Barbara Pitkin, *What Pure Eyes Could See: Calvin's Doctrine of Faith in Its Exegetical Context*, OSHT (Oxford: Oxford University Press, 1999), 25–26, 79–80, 100–113.
29. *Institutes*, 1.6.1.
30. *Institutes*, 1.5.10.
31. *Institutes*, 1.5.11.
32. *Institutes*, 1.5.8; 1.6.2; 2.6.1.

In Calvin's *Commentary on Genesis*, he explains that God has described the visible form of the world in the opening chapter of the Bible, specifically Genesis 1:6. He writes,

> Here the Spirit of God would teach all men without exception; and therefore what Gregory declares falsely and in vain respecting statues and pictures is truly applicable to the history of creation, namely, that it is the book of the unlearned. The things, therefore, which he relates, serve as the garniture of that theater which he places before our eyes.[33]

Here Calvin reacts negatively to the idea promoted by Pope Gregory I (ca. 540–604), namely, that icons and religious art are the "book of the unlearned," pictures for those who are unable to read the Bible. Calvin rejects this idea but applies it instead to the creation, saying that it is the theater of God's glory and that in this theater the unlearned can "read" about the glory of God. In this regard, Calvin encourages theological students and lay Christians to explore the creation and with the spectacles of Scripture to read this wonderful and beautiful book, to behold God's glory in the dazzling and wondrous theater.

In Calvin's sermon on Job 9:7–15, he explains, "Let us mark well that Job's intent here is to teach us to be astronomers, so far as our capacity will bear, that we may refer all to the glorifying of God, so goodly order in the heaven as we see." Calvin is not merely telling his congregation that they should use the Bible for science. In this same sermon, he explains that Moses wrote of two great lights in the sky, the sun and the moon, though it appears at times that the moon is bigger than the sun. Certainly, some stars and planets are bigger than the moon, Calvin observes, but we cannot recognize this because they are at a great distance from us. But Calvin also adds, "God speaks unto us of these things, according to our perceiving of them, and not according as they be."[34] In other words, the Bible describes the creation as

---

33. *Comm.*, on Gen. 1:6.
34. Calvin, "Sermon 34," in *Sermons on Job*, 157. Over the years some have claimed that Calvin was hostile to the latest scientific developments in his day, specifically the heliocentric theories of Nicolaus Copernicus (1473–1543). Calvin, citing the opening verse of Ps. 93, is reported to have written in his Genesis commentary, "The earth is established, that it cannot be moved," in rebuttal to Copernicus's theory. Based on Ps. 93:1, Calvin supposedly writes, "Who will venture

things appear; the Bible does not give us a scientific description of the universe. This means that Calvin is encouraging his congregation to explore the book of nature, and with the spectacles of Scripture, one can do so profitably and see the glory of God in astronomy. Calvin's appreciation for the study of creation, however, is not limited to astronomy.

Calvin lamented that in his day learning and the liberal arts were despised and that noblemen did not want to be known as men of education and of letters.[35] Calvin believed that Christians should have an appreciation of the liberal arts and sciences. He thus teaches that innumerable evidences in heaven and earth declare the wonderful wisdom of God, and for this reason Christians should explore astronomy, medicine, and all the natural sciences. Calvin writes, "Men who have either quaffed or even tasted the liberal arts penetrate with their aid far more deeply into the secrets of divine wisdom." At the same time, Calvin nevertheless affirms that even without study of the liberal arts and sciences, a person can still behold enough of God's workmanship in the creation to lead him to break forth in admiration of his Lord.[36]

Calvin encourages Christians to study these things because their ultimate source is not man but God:

---

to place the authority of Copernicus above that of the Holy Spirit?" Thomas S. Kuhn, *The Copernican Revolution: Planetary Astronomy in the Development of Western Thought* (Cambridge, MA: Harvard University Press, 1985), 192. The problem with Kuhn's quotation is that he obtains it from a secondary source. Calvin never wrote the statement. Kuhn relies on Andrew D. White, *A History of Warfare of Science with Theology in Christendom* (New York: Appleton, 1896), 127. However, Edward Rosen has shown that White relied on the earlier work of F. W. Farrar, *History of Interpretation* (1886; repr., Grand Rapids, MI: Baker, 1960), xvii; cf. Edward Rosen, "Calvin's Attitude toward Copernicus," *JHI* 21, no. 3 (1960): 431–41. It is without question that Calvin held to geocentricity, which can be confirmed from *Comm.*, on Ps. 93:1. However, given Calvin's commitment to the phenomenological description of the creation in Scripture, it seems that he would not be opposed to heliocentricity, as he was aware of the teaching, and his comments on Ps. 136:7 leave the possibility open:

The Holy Spirit had no intention to teach astronomy; and, in proposing instruction meant to be common to the simplest and most uneducated persons, he made use by Moses and the other prophets of popular language, that one might shelter himself under the pretext of obscurity. . . . Accordingly, as Saturn though bigger than the moon is not so to the eye owing to his greater distance the Holy Spirit would rather speak childishly than unintelligibly to the humble and unlearned.

Comm., on Ps. 136:7; cf. Robert White, "Calvin and Copernicus: The Problem Reconsidered," *CTJ* 15, no. 2 (1980): 233–43; David F. Wright, "Calvin's Accommodating God," in *Calvinus Sincerioris Religionis Vindex: Calvin as Protector of the Purer Religion*, ed. Wilhelm H. Neuser and Brian G. Armstrong, SCES 36 (Kirksville, MO: Sixteenth Century Journal Publishers, 1997), 3–20.

35. See *Comm.*, on Dan. 1:4.
36. *Institutes*, 1.5.2.

If we ought to form such an opinion about agriculture and me-
chanical arts, what shall we think of the learned and exalted
sciences, such as Medicine, Jurisprudence, Astronomy, Geometry,
Logic, and such like? Shall we not much more consider them to
have proceeded from God? Shall we not in them also behold and
acknowledge his goodness, that his praise and glory may be celebrated both in the smallest and in the greatest affairs?[37]

Calvin holds that man's learning and knowledge, even in a fallen
world, still declared the glory of God. While Calvin teaches that these
gifts come ultimately from God, he is willing to admit that God has
given them to the heathen nations and that the liberal arts and sciences have descended to Christians from them.[38] Nevertheless, Calvin
proclaims that God's glory is written across the heavens—not in small
obscure letters but richly engraved in large and bright characters—and
can be read with the greatest of ease. Indeed, the splendor and magnifi-
cence of the heavenly bodies preach "the glory of God like a teacher
in a seminary of learning."[39]

Calvin's appreciation for the arts and sciences even expands to the
musical talents of unbelievers. Like the liberal arts and sciences, music
is also a gift from God that reflects his glory and therefore is in no
way to be despised. In fact, these gifts are to be commended. Calvin
explains in his comments on Genesis 4:21 that Jubal was the father
of those who played the pipe and the lyre and that "the sons of Cain,
though deprived of the Spirit of regeneration, were yet endued with
gifts of no despicable kind." Indeed, Moses wrote of these things to
show that the family of Cain "was not so accursed by the Lord but
that he would still scatter some excellent gifts among his posterity."
Calvin teaches that the harp and similar musical instruments have
been created for our pleasure rather than for our necessity. Nevertheless, music is therefore not altogether superfluous, nor should it be
condemned. Rather, Calvin holds that pleasure as a self-referential
end, pleasure for the sake of pleasure, should be condemned. But
pleasure combined with the fear of God, and with the common benefit

---

37. *Comm.*, on Isa. 28:29.
38. *Comm.*, on Gen. 4:20–21.
39. *Comm.*, on Ps. 19:4; cf. Randall C. Zachman, "The Universe as the Living Image of God:
Calvin's Doctrine of Creation Reconsidered," *CTQ* 61, no. 4 (1997): 308–9.

of society in view, is appropriate.[40] In other words, in the same way that the Christian can with the spectacles of Scripture appreciate the liberal arts and sciences, he or she can also appreciate and enjoy music, even if it is generated from unbelievers. The believer can appreciate the beauty and order even in music. Calvin writes, "The use of God's gifts is not wrongly directed when it is referred to that end to which the Author himself created and destined for us, since he created them for our good, not for our ruin."[41]

God's Order Even in a Fallen World

When we turn to other areas in Calvin's thought, we find the same principles at work, namely, that God reveals himself in the creation and in humanity, and though man is sinful and fallen, one can still see God's fingerprints in the creation. One such area where we see the fingerprints of God is in the societal order that exists throughout the world. Calvin acknowledges that in addition to liberal arts, science, philosophy, medicine, and astronomy, all descending from the heathen nations, one can also add the order of civil government.[42] Calvin is, of course, famous for his insistence on the depravity of man and his explanation of the noetic effects of sin—that is, the effects of sin on the human mind. Calvin argues that in matters of salvation, man is completely blind and that his ability to reason is useless. At the same time, however, Calvin does not hold that human reason is utterly and totally shut down as a consequence of the fall.[43] This, therefore, means that even fallen man is capable of exercising and employing justice to maintain societal order. Once again, we must remember that for Calvin, this is ultimately the image of God in humanity, albeit fallen.

Calvin teaches that all people have the contents of the Ten Commandments engraved on their hearts.[44] In terms of humanity's redemption, this natural knowledge of God's law renders man inexcusable; he cannot claim ignorance to what God requires of his

---

40. *Comm.*, on Gen. 4:20–21; cf. Paul Helm, *John Calvin's Ideas* (Oxford: Oxford University Press, 2004), 386–87.
41. *Institutes*, 3.10.2.
42. *Comm.*, on Gen. 4:20–21.
43. Schreiner, *Theater of His Glory*, 71.
44. *Institutes*, 2.8.1.

creatures. Nevertheless, Calvin acknowledges that we cannot say that unbelievers are "utterly blind as to the conduct of life."[45] In Calvin's commentary on Romans 2:14–15, he qualifies his position by stating that man does not have a full knowledge of the law but that nonetheless seeds of justice still remain in fallen man. To support his exegesis, Calvin writes,

> This is evidenced by such facts as these, that all the Gentiles alike institute religious rites, make laws to punish adultery, theft, and murder, and commend good faith in commercial transactions and contracts. In this way they prove their knowledge that God is to be worshipped, that adultery, theft, and murder, are evils, and that honesty is to be esteemed.[46]

While Calvin recognizes and teaches a robust doctrine of original sin, he nevertheless gives a place to the natural knowledge of the law of God, or natural law, in his theology.[47] Aside from the general order that natural law gives human society, Calvin also recognizes that natural law is the standard for civil government. Calvin writes,

> It is a fact that the law of God which we call the moral law is nothing else than a testimony of natural law and of that conscience which God has engraved upon the minds of men. Consequently, the entire scheme of this equity of which we are now speaking has been prescribed in it. Hence, this equity alone must be the goal and rule and limit of all laws. . . . For the Lord through the hand of Moses did not give that law to be proclaimed among all nations and to be in force everywhere; but when he had taken the Jewish nation into his safekeeping, defense, and protection, he also willed to be a lawgiver especially to it; and as became a wise lawgiver— he had special concern for it in making its laws.[48]

It is important that we see what Calvin argues in terms of the standard for earthly government, namely, that the Mosaic law was never intended to be the standard for earthly governments but was peculiar

---

45. *Institutes*, 2.2.22.
46. *CNTC*, 8:48.
47. R. S. Clark, "Calvin on the *Lex Naturalis*," *STJ* 6, nos. 1–2 (1998): 3.
48. *Institutes*, 4.20.16.

to Israel. In fact, Calvin outright rejects the idea of the use of Mosaic law as a blueprint for government:

> For there are some who deny that a commonwealth is duly framed which neglects the political system of Moses, and is ruled by the common laws of nations. Let other men consider how perilous and seditious this notion is; it will be enough for me to have proved it false and foolish.[49]

While there are certainly many details to be fleshed out, Calvin affirms that the Mosaic law finds its purpose and telos not in the earthly governments of this world but in the person and work of Christ.[50] How, then, does Calvin correlate the function of natural law, or equity, as the standard for the governments of the nations to the Christian and the person and work of Christ?[51] Calvin teaches that man is under a "twofold government." The one government pertains to eternal life and resides in the soul, or inner man; the other government pertains only to the establishment of civil justice and outward morality. In formal theological terminology, the two governments of which Calvin writes are the kingdoms of grace and of power. The kingdom of grace is the realm of God's saving grace, and the kingdom of power is the realm of God's common grace. The former has special revelation as its moral standard, and the latter has natural law, or general revelation, as its standard. Calvin explains,

> Whoever knows how to distinguish between body and soul, between this present fleeting life and that future eternal life, will without difficulty know that Christ's spiritual Kingdom and the civil jurisdiction are things completely distinct. Since, then, it is a Jewish vanity to seek and enclose Christ's Kingdom within the elements of this world, let us rather ponder that what Scripture clearly teaches is a spiritual fruit, which we gather from Christ's

---

49. *Institutes*, 4.20.14.

50. See, e.g., *CNTC*, 3:235–36. On Calvin's understanding of typology, see David L. Puckett, *John Calvin's Exegesis of the Old Testament*, CSRT (Louisville: Westminster John Knox, 1995), 106–24.

51. On *equity*, see Helm, *Calvin's Ideas*, 363–67; cf. A. Craig Troxel and Peter J. Wallace, "Men in Combat over the Civil Law: 'General Equity' in WCF 19.4," *WTJ* 64, no. 2 (2002): 307–18. For a treatment of Calvin's views on natural law and his relationship to the broader sixteenth- and seventeenth-century Reformed tradition, see Stephen J. Grabill, *Rediscovering the Natural Law in Reformed Theological Ethics* (Grand Rapids, MI: Eerdmans, 2006), esp. 70–97.

grace; and let us remember to keep within its own limits all that freedom which is promised and offered to us in him.[52]

Calvin teaches that the two kingdoms, while always under God's providential rule, nevertheless have different and distinct ends. In the kingdom of grace, the heavenly eternal kingdom is already among us in the church because of the work of Christ, and it comes through the ministry of word and sacrament. The kingdom of power, on the other hand, has a temporary role to play, one that will endure only until the return of Christ. The kingdom of power is supposed to cherish and protect the outward worship of God, to defend sound doctrine and piety in the church, to adjust our life to the society of men, to conform our social behavior to civil righteousness, to bring temporal peace between men, and to promote general societal order and tranquility.[53] The civil magistrate is to bring these goals about through use of the sword, not the word of God. The responsibility of the civil magistrate, for example, is to promote the "public good."[54]

What one must realize is that though the two kingdoms arose because of the fall of humanity, an outcome certainly within the purview of God's sovereignty and providential rule over creation, the general stability of earthly government is a result of the original creation. In other words, the image of God in fallen man was not totally obliterated, but some remnant of it remained, and that remaining wisdom, power, and goodness of God is reflected in the law of God written on the heart of humanity, or natural law.

Calvin writes, "The Celestial Creator himself, however corrupted man may be, still keeps in view the end of his original creation."[55] And for this reason, Calvin wants Christians to understand that the inaugurated kingdom of heaven in the church is not a rejection of the past or of the creation but rather is to coexist alongside the church until the consummation.[56]

---

52. *Institutes*, 4.20.1.
53. *Institutes*, 4.20.2.
54. CNTC, 8:282–83.
55. *Comm.*, on Gen. 9:6; cf. Schreiner, *Theater of His Glory*, 80.
56. In his sermons on Deuteronomy, for example, Calvin proclaims,

True it is that men are sore blinded by reason of Adam's sin: but yet has our Lord left still a certain discretion engraved in their hearts, and that is but only to make them inexcusable, as says S. Paul in the first chapter of Romans. Howbeit, there was this further regard also,

This means that Christians are not supposed to separate themselves from the earthly sphere but instead to participate in it, at the same time being careful to distinguish between the spiritual and civil realms and between the respective tools and ends of each kingdom.[57] So this means for Calvin that the Christian can become a civil magistrate, but he is supposed to recognize that as a magistrate, his implements are natural law and the sword, not word and sacrament. The Christian civil magistrate can go about his duty confident in the tools of his trade not because he is informed by man's fallen reason but because, aided by the spectacles of Scripture, he can appeal to the wisdom and goodness still inscribed on the heart of man. God, not man, is the author of natural law.[58] Recall Calvin's comments on Genesis 4:20–21, that God had bestowed gifts on the family of Cain to show that he was "not so accursed by the Lord." And among the gifts that he gave to Cain's unbelieving descendants was "the order of civil government."[59]

Calvin, of course, was not naive. He was well aware that because man was sinful and fallen, he could and would abuse his civil authority and even ignore and rebel against his knowledge of natural law. Nevertheless, this did not cause Calvin to abandon his commitment to natural law. He writes,

> If anyone objects and says that we ought not to obey princes who, as far as they can, pervert the holy ordinance of God, and thus become savage wild beasts, while magistrates ought to bear the image of God, I reply that the order established by God ought to be so highly valued by us as to honor even tyrants when in power. There

that mankind might be maintained, and that there might be some difference between men and beasts. That is the thing which we have to learn by the agreeableness that is found to be between the law of Moses and all the states of government that have been among all the heathen in the world.

John Calvin, "Sermon 114" (on Deut. 19:14–15), in *Sermons on Deuteronomy*, trans. Arthur Golding (1583; repr., Edinburgh: Banner of Truth, 1987), 699; cf. Wyatt, *Jesus Christ and Creation*, 126.

57. Cf. Schreiner, *Theater of His Glory*, 85.

58. For a fuller treatment of Calvin's views and the relationship between natural law and the two kingdoms, see David VanDrunen, "The Context of Natural Law: John Calvin's Doctrine of the Two Kingdoms," *JChSt* 46, no. 3 (2004): 503–25; VanDrunen, "Medieval Natural Law and the Reformation: A Comparison of Aquinas and Calvin," *ACPQ* 80, no. 1 (2006): 77–98; VanDrunen, *Natural Law and the Two Kingdoms: A Study in the Development of Reformed Social Thought* (Grand Rapids, MI: Eerdmans, 2010), 67–118.

59. *Comm.*, on Gen. 4:20–21.

is yet another reply still more evident, that there has never been a tyranny, nor can one be imagined, however cruel and unbridled, in which some portion of equity has not appeared. God never allows His just order to be destroyed by the sin of men without some of its outlines remaining obscured. And finally, some kind of government, however deformed and corrupt it may be, is still better and more beneficial than anarchy.[60]

Calvin, therefore, completely aware of the abuse of civil authority, nonetheless urges Christians to submit even to tyrants. This is not to say that Calvin does not conceive of times when disobedience to civil authorities is warranted.[61] Nevertheless, he affirms that even in tyrannical governments, there is still an echo of equity, or natural law, and that God's creation order is still present.

Doxology as the Goal of Creation

When we stop to contemplate Calvin's understanding of creation and humanity, namely, that the creation is the theater of God's glory, we are irresistibly led to the conclusion that for Calvin, doxology is the goal of creation, even in a fallen world. Calvin writes in his commentary on Psalm 104:1 that Christians can never know God according to his essence, but through the creation we can see his glory. Calvin likens the creation to a "garment in which He, who is hidden in himself, appears in a manner visible to us." Moreover, when the psalmist says that the heavens are a curtain, "It is not meant that under them God hides himself, but that by them his majesty and glory are displayed; being, as it were, his royal pavilion."[62] Calvin teaches that when we as Christians see God's glory and majesty, we will be led "to love and serve him with all our heart."[63]

In other words, while certainly many blessings come to man from God through the creation and while God dispenses many gifts to humans, both unbeliever and believer alike, the telos of God's revelation of his goodness, power, and wisdom is doxology, the praise of God.

---

60. CNTC, 12:271.
61. See *Institutes*, 4.20.31–32; also *Comm.*, on Dan. 6:21–22.
62. *Comm.*, on Ps. 104:1.
63. *Institutes*, 1.14.22.

In a sermon from Job, Calvin captures this doxological goal and summarizes it for his congregation. Calvin writes,

> Yet notwithstanding it behooves us to come back to this point, namely why God sets the earth before us as a looking glass. It is to the end that we might behold his infinite glory, wisdom, power, and might, to guide us and lead us, as it were by the hand, to the considering, thereby to be ravished into wonderment of purpose to humble ourselves under his incomprehensible greatness, and to honor him.[64]

If a theater is a place where people come to watch a play and then applaud the performance, then it seems more than warranted to conclude that for Calvin, the theater of God's glory is filled with Christians who wear the spectacles of Scripture and are enabled to see the wisdom, power, and glory of their Creator and are thus led not merely to applause but to doxology.

Pastoral Observations

Given that Calvin was himself both a theologian and a pastor, it seems only natural that some pastoral observations are in order, observations that show the practical implications of Calvin's doctrine of creation and humanity. We may begin by reflecting on Calvin's teaching concerning the "living image" of God in the broader creation. In recent years it seems that when one hears the term *Christian art*, one invariably finds pictures or paintings of Jesus, crosses, or perhaps churches. Those who have been gifted with artistic abilities are thus given a very narrow view of the spectrum in which they can express their artistic abilities. Yet for Calvin, such expressions of art are problematic because, in his view, they are violations of the second commandment. Calvin rejects as unbiblical the iconography of the Roman Catholic Church, believing that "whatever visible forms of God man devises are diametrically opposed to His nature; therefore, as soon as idols appear, true religion is corrupted and adulterated."[65] It should be no

---

64. Calvin, "Sermon 148," in *Sermons on Job*, 695. Cf. Susan E. Schreiner, *Where Shall Wisdom Be Found? Calvin's Exegesis of Job from Medieval and Modern Perspectives* (Chicago: University of Chicago Press, 1994), 137–38; Derek Thomas, *Calvin's Teaching on Job: Proclaiming the Incomprehensible God* (Fearn, Ross-shire, Scotland: Mentor, 2004).

65. *Institutes*, 2.8.17.

surprise, then, that as a result of the Reformation, artists influenced by Reformed teaching moved away from painting religious art, such as pictures of crosses and Jesus, and began painting landscapes.

Pieter Bruegel (1525–1569) was a famous artist of the sixteenth century who largely painted portraits of landscapes or sixteenth-century peasant life. Another famous painter who was influenced by the teachings of the Reformation was Rembrandt (1606–1669). Though Rembrandt did paint what one might call "religious art," such as his well-known *Raising of the Cross*, he also painted portraits of everyday life. Still yet, Pieter Claesz (ca. 1597–1661) was a Dutch painter for whom "everyday reality was seen as God's creation."[66] Claesz was famous for his still-life paintings, such as *Still Life with Roemer and Oysters* or *Vanitas Still Life*. Both portraits appear ordinary, in that the former looks like a place setting with food and the latter, the upper portion of a skull resting atop a small stack of books. Christians in our own day might scratch their heads in confusion and wonder how such paintings could be considered in any way "religious" or "Christian." Yet for one such as Calvin, such paintings are indeed "religious" and "Christian." Once again, through the spectacles of Scripture one can behold the living image of God in the creation. In what may appear to be ordinary and mundane, such as a landscape, through the spectacles of Scripture, one sees the robe of God's glory, where he manifests his power, wisdom, and goodness. The same may be said, of course, for literature, music, and science.

Often it seems that Christians in our day have little interest in literature, music, or science. If there is an interest in science, it seems to be driven by a desire to disprove the scientific theories of Charles Darwin (1809–1882); or, if there is an interest in the writings of non-Christians, it is merely an effort to answer their claims apologetically or point out what is deficient. In other words, there seems to be little genuine interest in literature or science produced by unbelievers, as it is viewed as tainted and therefore taboo. This is especially true of "non-Christian" music. In its place, one finds "Christian" literature, music, and science. Calvin would have rejected such practices.

66. Francis A. Schaeffer, *How Should We Then Live? The Rise and Decline of Western Thought and Culture* (Wheaton, IL: Crossway, 1976), 98–104.

Instead, he firmly teaches that because the Spirit of God is the sole fountain of truth, Christians should neither reject the truth nor despise it regardless of the source. To do so is to dishonor the Spirit of God. Calvin writes,

> Shall we deny that the truth shone upon the ancient jurists who established civic order and discipline with such great equity? Shall we say that the philosophers were blind in their fine observation and artful description of nature? Shall we say that those men were devoid of understanding who conceived the art of disputation and taught us to speak reasonably? Shall we say that they are insane who developed medicine, devoting their labor to our benefit? What shall we say of all the mathematical sciences? Shall we consider them the ravings of madmen? No, we cannot read the writings of the ancients on these subjects without great admiration.

Calvin can appreciate truth and beauty wherever he finds it because he recognizes that God is the source, and in this way man, even fallen man, is a mirror of God's wisdom, power, and goodness. Calvin argues that those who ignore or marginalize pagan learning should "be ashamed of such ingratitude." He holds that those whom Paul calls "natural men" are "indeed, sharp and penetrating in their investigation of inferior things." He teaches that we should "learn by their example how many gifts the Lord left to human nature even after it was despoiled of its true good."[67]

This means that as Christians, yes, we have been redeemed and have had our spiritual blinders removed, enabling us to worship the one true God as he has revealed himself in Christ. At the same time, however, though we have been regenerated, that does not necessarily make us more intelligent or talented. Yes, we can account for the telos and goal of all learning, but that does not mean that we cannot learn truth from unbelievers in literature, science, or medicine or appreciate the order and beauty in their musical expression. Of course, Christians should always read, listen, and learn critically, never forgetting the differing presuppositions that exist between the believer and unbeliever.

---

67. *Institutes*, 2.2.15. Cf. Charles Partee, *Calvin and Classical Philosophy* (1977; repr., Louisville: Westminster John Knox, 2005).

And to this end, Christians should always approach the knowledge of unbelievers with the spectacles of Scripture. However, with those spectacles affixed to one's face, one can study and appreciate the literature, science, medicine, and music produced by "natural men" and learn from them. Indeed, to do so is merely to recognize that glimmers of God's wisdom, power, and goodness still flicker in the fallen world.

Another area in which Christians can benefit from Calvin's understanding of the doctrine of creation and humanity is the manner in which Christians engage in culture and politics. Christian reaction to culture and politics runs the gamut from total withdrawal to complete involvement. On the one hand, there are those who believe that unbelievers run culture and politics, and therefore Christians should not intertwine themselves with the world. On the other hand, there are those who believe that Christians must involve themselves in culture and politics so that eventually Christianity can be the dominant force. Those who seek cultural and political influence also usually believe that the Bible is the only book that gives the Christian a blueprint for the takeover of the cultural and political realms.

Once again, it behooves us to account for Calvin's understanding of creation and humanity. Calvin holds that though man is fallen, there are still glimmers of God's creation order left in him, such as the law of God inscribed on his heart. If God is the author of creation and nature, then to appeal to natural law in the political realm is in no way appealing to autonomous human reason. Rather, with the spectacles of Scripture, the Christian can employ and appeal to natural law, or equity, which is written on man's heart. This is not to say that such appeals will always be successful, as even Calvin recognizes that there are tyrannical forms of government. Nevertheless, by recognizing that God is the author of creation and that there are still echoes of the initial creation order in both culture and politics, Christians can engage in these activities as individuals not in an effort to control them or to join fallen mankind in building the city of man to sinful ends. Rather, as Susan Schreiner notes regarding the societal implications of Calvin's doctrine of creation and humanity, "Christians are to be active in the ordering of society, the upbuilding of the church, the combating of demons, and the study of nature, not because this world can offer salvation or fulfillment but because these activities express the glory of God within the created order."[68]

The way the Christian as an individual can participate in cultural and political endeavors to the glory of God in Calvin's thought is ultimately founded on the proper understanding of the differing ends and goals of the two kingdoms to which the Christian belongs. Calvin comments regarding the two kingdoms,

> All of this I admit to be superfluous, if God's Kingdom, such as it is not among us, wipes out the present life. But if it is God's will that we go as pilgrims upon the earth while we aspire to the true fatherland, and if the pilgrimage requires such helps, those who take these from man deprive him of his very humanity.[69]

Calvin recognizes the transitory nature of the existing creation and that the kingdom of God will eventually supersede it. Even in our pilgrimage to the new Jerusalem, Calvin nevertheless teaches that the existing structures of the creation, whether cultural or political, are essential to man's humanity—echoes of God's wisdom, goodness, and power, even in a fallen world. With this knowledge, Christians can be better equipped to interact with the cultural and political realms, and we need not withdraw from the world, nor need we think that we must control it. Rather, we can manifest God's glory in it by ordering society as we pilgrim to our fatherland.

Conclusion

Calvin's doctrine of creation and humanity is certainly marked by both sadness and joy. Yes, God's creation before the fall was an unsullied mirror of his wisdom, power, and goodness—indeed, the robe of his glory. This is especially true of the pinnacle of the creation, humanity, those made in his image. This is reason for sadness—man's rebellion against his Creator. At the same time, even in a fallen world, the creation is still the theater of God's glory, which is reason for great joy. Hopefully this means that with the fresh breeze of the centuries blowing through our minds, especially those currents originating from

---

68. Schreiner, *Theater of His Glory*, 122.
69. *Institutes*, 4.20.2.

sixteenth-century Geneva, we can regain a renewed appreciation for the book of nature. And with the spectacles of Scripture, we can once again read the book of nature to great profit until the creation culminates in the new heavens and new earth, when God's people will be restored to their original glory, to the perfect image of the second Adam.

10

The Providence of God

Burk Parsons

There is nothing more calculated to increase our faith,
than the knowledge of the providence of God.

—John Calvin, *Commentary on the Psalms*

Surrender to God

The providence of God is one of the most overwhelming and liberating doctrines that humanity has had the privilege and burden of
beholding, though by a mere glimpse.[1] Thus, for anyone to under-
take the task of discerning the supreme weightiness of the doctrine
of divine providence would be to demonstrate one's own indiscre-
tion. Nevertheless, in his wisdom the Lord has set the matter of
his providence before our eyes, and insofar as he has removed the
blindfolds from our sight, the Lord has summoned us to himself that

---

1. Calvin writes concerning the liberating quality of our knowledge of divine providence, "In
a word, as the Providence of God, rightly considered, does not bind our hands, but frees them for
work, so it not only does not hinder prayer, but strengthens and confirms its earnestness." John
Calvin, *Defence of the Secret Providence of God*, in *Calvin's Calvinism: Treatises on the Eternal
Predestination of God and the Secret Providence of God*, trans. Henry Cole (1856; repr., Grand
Rapids, MI: Reformed Free Publishing Association, [1987]), 236.

we might "trust, invoke, praise, and love him" as he has revealed himself to us.[2]

For anyone to commence a study of the providence of God in an appropriate frame of mind, he must empty himself of all presumptuous gleanings and rid himself of all speculative endeavors.[3] Indeed, writing about the providence of God is a daunting task. What is more, preaching about the providence of God is a significant undertaking; however, living with the knowledge of the providence of God is impossible—impossible without having a heart and mind that have been conquered and regenerated by the life-giving Holy Spirit.[4] Such was the reality of the heart and mind of one man whom God mastered, namely, John Calvin.[5] He was a man who not only wrote and preached about the providence of God but lived in light of the providence of God throughout his life.[6]

Calvin was not an ivory-tower academician who lived in isolation and experienced no suffering or grief. One example of this reality in his life was the death of his only son, Jacques. On July 28, 1542, Jacques was born prematurely and died shortly thereafter. In writing to his dear friend Pierre Viret, Calvin provides a glimpse into the grief that he and his wife, Idelette, experienced and into his unwavering acknowledgment of the wisdom and providence of God: "Certainly the Lord has afflicted us with a deep and painful wound in the death of our beloved son. But he is our Father: he knows what is best for his children."[7]

In his life and in his writings, we do not observe a man who presumed to know the mind of God; rather, we observe a man who surrendered himself to God without qualification and who manifested his trust in God's providential character every day of his life and on every page of his writings.[8] In his _Commentary on the Psalms_, Calvin writes,

---

2. _Institutes_, 1.14.22.
3. See _Institutes_, 1.5.9; 1.6.3.
4. See _Institutes_, 1.5.1; 1.13.21.
5. Jean Cadier, _Calvin: The Man God Mastered_, trans. O. R. Johnston (Grand Rapids, MI: Eerdmans, 1960).
6. See Richard Stauffer, _The Humanness of John Calvin_, trans. George H. Shriver (Nashville: Abingdon, 1971).
7. Calvin to Pierre Viret, August 19, 1542, in _CO_, 11:430. Quoted by Stauffer, _Humanness of John Calvin_, 42.
8. Perhaps the most succinct and stimulating biography on Calvin is from the pen of Thomas Smyth: _The Life and Character of Calvin, the Reformer, Reviewed and Defended_ (Philadelphia: Presbyterian Board of Publication, 1844).

In assigning the cause of their afflictions he corrects the false impressions of those persons who imagine that these happen by chance. Were they to reflect on the judgments of God, they would at once perceive that there was nothing like chance or fortune in the government of the world. Moreover, until men are persuaded that all their troubles come upon them by the appointment of God, it will never come into their minds to supplicate him for deliverance.[9]

According to Calvin, nothing was, nothing is, and nothing ever will exist by chance, fortune, or happenstance.[10] Just as we live, move, and have our being in God, so all things live, move, and have their being in God (cf. Acts 17:28).[11] Affliction brings us to the end of ourselves and to our knees in surrender to God.[12] Spirit-wrought surrender to God compels us to seek him and "supplicate him for deliverance." This is the supreme advantage of Calvin's doctrine of the providence of God, namely, that people would come to the end of themselves, repent of their self-sufficiency, and surrender themselves to God unconditionally.[13]

The *Institutes* and the Word of God

In our lifelong pursuit to know and worship God, we must immerse ourselves in his word. Similarly, in order to understand more fully Calvin's teaching on the providence of God, we need to immerse ourselves in all his writings and (what is perhaps more indicative of his doctrine) examine how this doctrine affected his life and ministry.[14] Nevertheless, we may let Calvin's *Institutes of the Christian Religion* suffice as the primary source for our present study, for in it we observe his summary of Christian doctrine, which was written in order to assist those studying for ecclesiastical ministry so that they might study the word of God and have "easy access to it and to advance in it without stumbling."[15] This supreme trait of the

---

9. *Comm.*, on Ps. 107:11.
10. See *Institutes*, 1.16.2.
11. See *Institutes*, 1.16.1.
12. See *Institutes*, 3.22.7.
13. See *Institutes*, 3.14.6.
14. See Stauffer, *Humanness of John Calvin*.
15. "John Calvin to the Reader," in *Institutes*, 1:4.

Institutes we would do well to remember; for if we study the *Institutes* rightly, we will, by God's humbling grace, advance in the word of God rightly.[16] Moreover, according to Calvin, we are to be "daily taught in the school of Jesus Christ."[17] Thus, we must be students of Scripture if we are to possess right and sound doctrine: "Now in order that true religion may shine upon us, we ought to hold that it must take its beginning from heavenly doctrine and that no one can even get the slightest taste of right and sound doctrine unless he be a pupil of Scripture."[18] Elsewhere, Calvin writes, "Let us not take it into our heads either to seek out God anywhere else than in his Sacred Word, or to think anything of him that is not prompted by his Word, or to speak anything that is not taken from that Word."[19] This, writes T. H. L. Parker, is "Calvin's theological programme—to build on the Scripture alone."[20]

The Providence of God and the *Institutes*

Calvin expounds God's providence on virtually every page of his *Institutes*. Though his development of the doctrine is not explicit on every page, one can hardly read a single paragraph of the *Institutes* without feeling the liberating weight of God's providence contained therein. While many have pointed out that Calvin's ordering and formulation of the doctrine of providence within the *Institutes* differs somewhat from the first edition in 1536 to the final edition in 1559, it is not the intention of this short study to examine all the possible reasons for such differentiation.[21] Nevertheless, to appreciate Calvin's classification of the doctrine of providence more fully, it is perhaps helpful to examine a few of the reasons for his organization of the doctrines of providence and predestination in his last edition of the *Institutes*.

---

16. See "John Calvin to the Reader," in *Institutes*, 1:4–5; cf. "Subject Matter of the Present Work: From the French Edition of 1560," in *Institutes*, 1:6–8.

17. John Calvin to the Duchess of Ferrara, July 20, 1558, in *Letters of John Calvin*, ed. Jules Bonnet, 4 vols. (repr., Eugene, OR: Wipf and Stock, 2007).

18. *Institutes*, 1.6.2.

19. *Institutes*, 1.13.21.

20. T. H. L. Parker, *Portrait of Calvin* (Philadelphia: Westminster, 1954), 52.

21. For example, Charles B. Partee, "Calvin on Universal and Particular Providence," in *Readings in Calvin's Theology*, ed. Donald K. McKim (Grand Rapids, MI: Baker, 1984), 79. See also Etienne de Peyer, "Calvin's Doctrine of Divine Providence," *EvQ* 10 (1938): 30–44.

The Development of Providence and Predestination in the Institutes

In the 1559 edition of the *Institutes*, Calvin's treatment of the doctrine of providence follows his explanation of God's work of creation at the end of book 1, "The Knowledge of God the Creator."[22] This is a characteristic unique to the 1559 edition.[23] Whereas in previous editions of the *Institutes* Calvin had formulated his doctrines of predestination and providence in the same chapter, in his final edition he sets forth the doctrine of predestination in book 3 while he establishes the doctrine of providence at the outset of the *Institutes*.[24] Although Calvin in no way intends to separate the doctrines of predestination and providence from the perspective of God's salvation of his people, Calvin does distinguish them on account of the fact that God's providence is the all-encompassing foundation of the character of God, whereas God's predestination is an expression of his providential character.[25] In an article titled "Calvin on Providence: The Development of an Insight," P. H. Reardon makes this basic point as he conveys the aim of his study:

> It would readily be thought, then, that Calvin's doctrine of Providence is scarcely separable from his theory of predestination. The present study, by pursuing the evolution of his ideas on Providence, intends to demonstrate that such is not the case. To be sure, the two doctrines are closely related in the Reformer's mind, as indeed they were in the thinking of earlier theologians. None the less it will be seen that his view of Providence underwent a separate development meriting a separate treatment.[26]

---

22. For a helpful analysis of Calvin's doctrine of creation, see John Murray, "Calvin's Doctrine of Creation," *WTJ* 17, no. 1 (1954): 21–43.

23. For a full discussion on the various editions of the *Institutes*, see François Wendel, *Calvin: Origins and Development of His Religious Thought*, trans. Philip Mairet (1950; repr., Grand Rapids, MI: Baker, 1997), 111–49, 177–84.

24. John T. McNeill states, "In editions 1539–1554, Calvin treated the topics of providence and predestination in the same chapter. In the final edition they are widely separated, providence being here set in the context of the knowledge of God the Creator, while predestination is postponed to III.xxi–xxiv, where it comes within the general treatment of the redemptive work of the Holy Spirit." *Institutes*, 1:197n1.

25. Charles Partee's examination of Calvin's doctrine of providence is helpful on this point:

> God's care for believers is the basis of both the doctrines of providence and predestination. However it is not easy to specify the relation between the doctrine of providence and of predestination in Calvin's theology. The problem is whether predestination is an aspect of the doctrine of providence or whether providence is a part of the doctrine of predestination or are they two similar but separate doctrines? This topic has long been the subject of debate.

"Calvin on Universal and Particular Providence," 77.

26. P. H. Reardon, "Calvin on Providence: The Development of an Insight," *SJT* 28 (1975): 517.

It is important to observe Calvin's distinction between God's providential character and God's work of predestination, as well as to observe Calvin's classification of the doctrine of predestination under the rubric of God's work of salvation.[27] By so doing, we are better able to assess matters pertaining to God's predestining work of election, God's work of creation, the fall of humanity, the salvation of humanity, and the persons and work of the Godhead.[28] Werner Krusche observes the relationship between providence and predestination in Calvin's last edition of the *Institutes*:

> The Holy Spirit is the author of providence and, since very special providence equals predestination, the author of the doctrine of predestination. He is the first as the Spirit of the Eternal Son, the second as the Spirit of the Mediator Jesus Christ. The position of the doctrine of providence and predestination in the last edition of the *Institutes* shows this most clearly. Since it is the Spirit of the Eternal Word that brings the action of divine providence to fruition, the doctrine of providence can be developed in connection with the doctrine of the Trinity. Since it is the Spirit of the Mediator Jesus Christ, who makes the action of God's election efficacious, the doctrine of predestination must form the conclusion of Christology and Pneumatology.[29]

The Holy Spirit makes the providential work of predestination effectual in the work of God's salvation of his people. This is the essential point of correspondence between providence and predestination and the fundamental reason the two doctrines are appropriately distinguished in Calvin's last edition of the *Institutes*. Charles Partee writes, "Calvin's understanding of God's government of the world and his care of his own are closely related to each other and crucial to his theology."[30]

The question may still remain, however, "What, precisely, have these reflections on predestination got to do with providence?"[31] Paul Helm answers this question sufficiently for the purposes of our study:

---

27. See Susan E. Schreiner, *The Theater of His Glory: Nature and the Natural Order in the Thought of John Calvin* (Grand Rapids, MI: Baker, 1991), 33–34.
28. These are subjects covered elsewhere in the *Institutes*.
29. Werner Krusche, *Das Wirken des Heiligen Geistes nach Calvin*, FKDG 7 (Göttingen: Vandenhoeck & Ruprecht, 1957), 14. Quoted by Partee, "Calvin on Universal and Particular Providence," 78.
30. Partee, "Calvin on Universal and Particular Providence," 78.
31. Paul Helm, *Calvin's Ideas* (Oxford: Oxford University Press, 2004), 96.

First, for Calvin predestination is one aspect of providence, that aspect of God's governance of things that concerns the destiny of the elect and of the reprobate. Secondly, the locus on providence *is* placed appropriately early in the final edition of the *Institutes* and it is also noticeably predestinarian in character. There Calvin claims that all events are governed by God's secret plan and that nothing takes place without his deliberation. God so intends the regulation of individual events, and they all so proceed from his set plan, that nothing takes place by chance.[32]

All things were created by God, and all things are governed by him. We can thus conclude that salvation, in its fullness, is created and governed by God—from beginning to end.[33] Simply put, if we understand the doctrine of the providence of God, we must, by necessity, acknowledge and accept the doctrine of predestination, keeping in mind the words of the apostle Paul:

> Blessed be the God and Father of our Lord Jesus Christ, who has blessed us in Christ with every spiritual blessing in the heavenly places, even as he chose us in him before the foundation of the world, that we should be holy and blameless before him. In love he predestined us for adoption to himself as sons through Jesus Christ, according to the purpose of his will, to the praise of his glorious grace, with which he has blessed us in the Beloved. (Eph. 1:3–6)

There are many within our churches who claim to believe in the providence of God but who, in the same breath, deny God's providential work of predestination. Moreover, as the doctrine of God's providence is under attack in our day, so it was in Calvin's day, as Susan Schreiner explains:

> When Calvin discussed the continuing *administration* or providence of God, he confronted contemporary opponents. Crucial to understanding Calvin's view of providence is the fact that he perceived providence to be under attack in the sixteenth century.[34]

32. Helm, *Calvin's Ideas*, 96.
33. See *Institutes*, 3.14.5.
34. Schreiner, *Theater of His Glory*, 16.

While some in our churches may not think the doctrine of providence is under attack, supposing merely that the doctrine of predestination is under attack, they would do well to consider the matter again. It is on account of such attacks that we must rightly formulate and defend the biblical doctrine of God's providence, so that we might rightly explain and defend the biblical doctrine of God's salvation, which, of course, includes God's providential work of predestination. This is likely a factor in Calvin's rationale for classifying the doctrines of providence and predestination in the locations he did.[35] It is as if, in combating the enemies of God's word—enemies such as the Libertines, the Stoics, the determinists, the pantheists, and the deists of his day—Calvin could explain and defend the doctrines of providence and predestination from the generally accepted belief in the biblical doctrine of creation.[36]

When it comes right down to it, in order to explain the reasons one should acknowledge the biblical doctrine of predestination, we could simply inquire of a fellow church member as to his belief in the biblical doctrine of creation, asking simply, first, if he believes that God created all things; second, if he believes that God in his providence governs all his creation; and third, if he would grant that God is Creator and that God providentially governs all things. If so, he should concede that God providentially governs all the affairs of men and the salvation of his people. While it is certainly never that easy to convince another of the biblical doctrine of predestination (nor perhaps should it be), Calvin makes his case in a similar manner in his 1536 edition of the *Institutes*:

> By this we confess that we have all our trust fixed in God the Father, whom we acknowledge to be Creator of ourselves and of absolutely all things that have been created, which have been established by the Word, his eternal Wisdom (who is the Son), and by his Power (who is the Holy Spirit). And, as he once established, so now he sustains, nourishes, activates, preserves, by his goodness and power, apart from which all things would immediately collapse and fall into nothingness.

---

35. See Heinrich Heppe, *Reformed Dogmatics*, trans. G. T. Thomson (London: George Allen and Unwin, 1950), 251–80.
36. See Schreiner, *Theater of His Glory*, 7–38.

But when we call him almighty and creator of all things, we must ponder such omnipotence of his whereby he works all things in all, and such providence whereby he regulates all things. . . .

We should so reverence such a Father with grateful piety and burning love, as to devote ourselves wholly to his service, and honor him in all things. We should also receive all adverse things with calm and peaceful hearts, as if from his hand, thinking that his providence so also looks after us and our salvation while it is afflicting and oppressing to us. Therefore whatever may finally happen, we are never to doubt or lose faith that we have in him a propitious and benevolent Father, and no less are to await salvation from him.[37]

Grasping God as Creator and Sustainer

While Calvin thus ordered his primary treatment of the doctrine of divine providence in chapters 16, 17, and, to some degree, 18 of book 1, his discussion of God's providence runs throughout the opening chapters of the *Institutes*.[38] In fact, Calvin's continual reference to providence is so frequent that it seems that the Genevan pastor can barely wait to explain the matter to his readers more fully. When one reads through book 1, it is easy to get the impression that Calvin could very well have expounded at length the subject of providence at the end of every paragraph.[39] His references to providence come to a head at the beginning of chapter 10, concerning the doctrine of God the Creator, wherein he must restate his intentions and "warn [his] readers" what he intends to accomplish as to the ordering of his treatment of God the Creator and his treatment of the secondary, yet fundamental, matter of the providence of God as Creator. He writes,

But even if it shall be worth-while a little later to cite certain passages from the New Testament, in which the power of God the Creator and of his providence in the preservation of the primal nature are proved, yet I wish to warn my readers what I now intend to do, lest they overlap the limits set for them. Finally, at present

---

37. *Institutes* (1536), 66–67.
38. Calvin also addresses many of the implications pertaining to the doctrine of providence in *Institutes*, 2.1–5.
39. See, for example, *Institutes*, 1.2.1; 1.4.2; 1.5.2; 1.5.7; 1.5.10–11; 1.6.2; 1.8.1.

let it be enough to grasp how God, the Maker of heaven and earth, governs the universe founded by him.[40]

Throughout book 1, Calvin is laying the groundwork for his treatment of providence, yet it is a matter of direct import that the subject of divine providence is contained within his discussion of our knowledge of God as Creator. God is not only the Creator of all, he is the Sustainer of all as well. For Calvin, the fundamental truths that God is both Creator and Sustainer cannot be separated; rather, the truth of God's providential work of sustaining his creation necessarily emerges from the truth of God's work of creation.[41] Paul Helm observes, "Calvin's views on providence cannot be separated from his views of creation, for God is not a 'momentary Creator' and so we do not understand what it is to say that God is the Creator unless we consider his providence."[42] According to Calvin, not only did God create the world, but, as Donald McKim points out, God also preserves and provides for the world he created:

> Our comfort is that our world and our lives are held secure in God's hand. God preserves creation and our human existence. God provides for the world, orders the world, and cares for the world. Our lives are entrusted to the God who created us and loves us utterly, as we see in Jesus Christ. This God guides our lives and provides for our needs. As Calvin said in speaking of our knowledge of God's providence, "Gratitude of mind for the favorable outcome of things, patience in adversity, and also incredible freedom from worry about the future all necessarily follow upon this knowledge."[43]

From the outset of chapter 16, it is clear what Calvin intends to accomplish in his discussion on the doctrine of providence. In fact, his title to the chapter provides us with a concise summary of what is con-

---

40. *Institutes*, 1.10.1.

41. Herman J. Selderhuis writes, "According to Calvin, one will only believe that God cares for this world if one acknowledges him as the Creator. Furthermore, it is evident that the providence of God is a consequence of his role in creation." Selderhuis, *Calvin's Theology of the Psalms*, TSRPRT (Grand Rapids, MI: Baker Academic, 2007), 89.

42. Helm, *Calvin's Ideas*, 99.

43. Donald K. McKim, *Introducing the Reformed Faith: Biblical Revelation, Christian Tradition, Contemporary Significance* (Louisville: Westminster John Knox, 2001), 54.

tained therein: "God by his power nourishes and maintains the world created by him, and rules its several parts by his providence."[44] This title is a necessary transition for readers to understand the relationship between Calvin's treatment of God the Creator and his treatment of God the providential Sustainer. He writes,

> Moreover, to make God a momentary Creator, who once for all finished his work, would be cold and barren, and we must differ from profane men especially in that we see the presence of divine power shining as much in the continuing state of the universe as in its inception. For even though the minds of the impious too are compelled by merely looking upon earth and heaven to rise up to the Creator, yet faith has its own way of assigning the whole credit for creation to God. To this pertains that saying of the apostle's to which we have referred before, that only "by faith we understand that the universe was created by God" [Heb. 11:3]. For unless we pass on to his providence—however we may seem both to comprehend with the mind and to confess with the tongue—we do not yet properly grasp what it means to say: "God is Creator." . . .
>
> But faith ought to penetrate more deeply, namely, having found him Creator of all, forthwith to conclude he is also everlasting Governor and Preserver—not only in that he derives the celestial frame as well as its several parts by a universal motion, but also in that he sustains, nourishes, and cares for, everything he has made, even to the least sparrow [cf. Matt. 10:29].[45]

From the very beginning of his treatment of providence, Calvin argues that it is a doctrine comprehended only through the word of God by faith. Against the claims of the philosophers, he makes the charge that providence is not an obvious matter that all men can apprehend but that it is only recognized by faith.[46] Reardon explains,

> In 1552 he had already asserted that it was known by a certain experience of faith (". . . *agnoscitur fidei sensu* . . ."). This perspective, of course, rendered it unnecessary and superfluous to attempt to

---

44. See *Institutes*, 1.16.
45. *Institutes*, 1.16.1.
46. For a full treatment on this, see Derek W. H. Thomas, *Calvin's Teaching on Job: Proclaiming the Incomprehensible God* (Fearn, Ross-shire, Scotland: Mentor, 2004), 151–303.

prove the doctrine of Providence. One had only to consult the Bible in faith. One does not simply believe that there is a Providence, according to Calvin: one gives himself over to it in the full commitment of personal faith. As he was later to assert in the definitive edition of the *Institutes*, faith "is a firm and sure knowledge of the divine favor toward us, founded on the truth of a free promise in Christ, and revealed to our minds, and sealed on our hearts by the Holy Spirit."[47]

Thus, in the *Institutes*, as well as in Calvin's *Defence of the Secret Providence of God*, we observe Calvin's efforts to set forth the biblical-theological rationale for the doctrine of divine providence without necessarily attempting to offer an extrabiblical defense of it.[48] According to Calvin, providence is not an "empirical doctrine."[49] Rather, it is a doctrine ascertained by faith.[50] Schreiner points out,

> The dark and threatening aspect of creation surfaces repeatedly in those texts where Calvin defended divine providence against empirical evidence. Like Chrysostom, Calvin was acutely aware that nature and history did not equally reflect the providence of God. Calvin believed that although history *can* reflect the providence of God, he also knew that the disorders in history often cast a "cloud" between human perception and God's providential rule. Believers can now only "see through a mirror dimly" and "only in part," because they cannot perceive God's providence at work or comprehend the rational governance of the world. It is not always evident that God is at work restraining the wicked and the forces of societal chaos. No wonder, Calvin said, there exists an almost universal belief that all things are governed by chance and that the world is aimlessly tossed about by the blind impulse of fortune.[51]

In his natural condition, man is blind to the secret providence of God. Nevertheless, as Schreiner rightly observes, even though believers have

47. Reardon, "Calvin on Providence," 524. See also *Institutes*, 3.2.7.
48. Helm, *Calvin's Ideas*, 103–4.
49. Schreiner, *Theater of His Glory*, 33.
50. Calvin, *Defence of the Secret Providence of God*, 190.
51. Schreiner, *Theater of His Glory*, 32. See also *Institutes*, 1.16.2; *Comm.*, on Pss. 73:1; 94:15; 116:11.

the eyes to behold the providence of God, we now only have the advantage of seeing through a mirror dimly (1 Cor. 13:12).[52] G. C. Berkouwer writes,

> But now we still see through a glass, in riddles, and our knowledge is made up in fragments. Now we are menaced by unbelief, doubt, and disloyalty. Temptation levels itself on the reality of our time, in which, however, the living God is at work. We cannot fathom it. We can only listen to the voice of the Word—listen, as it speaks warning and comfort.[53]

As believers, though we see only dimly, we do still see, having been given eyes to behold God's providential manifestations and ears to listen to the voice of God as he communicates his word to us. Calvin proffers, "As nurses commonly do with infants, God is wont in a measure to 'lisp' in speaking to us?"[54] It is in our perception of the word of God by the Spirit of God through faith that we give ourselves wholeheartedly to the reality of divine providence. Indeed, the Lord God Almighty is the foundation and focus of our faith as he has revealed himself to us. Our faith, therefore, is not based on our arrogantly perceived ability to comprehend all his ways.[55] In Derek W. H. Thomas's treatment on this subject in *Calvin's Teaching on Job*, he examines the pastoral implications of Calvin's doctrine of providence from his teaching on the book of Job. Thomas writes,

> In fact, Calvin finds multiple applications for his understanding of the doctrine of providence. He ranges over the entire scope of the Christian life as he unravels the story of Job's trial. One lesson, however, receives consistent emphasis: providence is essentially incomprehensible, and that, because God himself is incomprehensible to us. Just as we know God only in part, so we understand God's ways in part.[56]

---

52. Susan E. Schreiner, "Through a Mirror Dimly: Calvin's Sermons on Job," *CTJ* 21 (1986): 175–93.

53. G. C. Berkouwer, *The Providence of God*, SDog (1952; repr., Grand Rapids, MI: Eerdmans, 1983), 160.

54. *Institutes*, 1.13.1.

55. See *Institutes*, 1.14.1.

56. Thomas, *Calvin's Teaching on Job*, 226.

It is for this reason—namely, the incomprehensibility of God—that Calvin establishes the doctrine of providence on the word of God and our perception of providence by the instrument of Spirit-wrought faith.[57] For if Calvin were to have argued from man's supposed natural ability to comprehend the incomprehensible, he would have lost the argument on both sides. He not only would have lost the battle in his attempt to make the case for the providence of God but also would have lost the entire war in his attempt to make the case that God is Creator and Sustainer, infinite in his being, glory, blessedness, and perfection—all-sufficient, eternal, unchangeable, everywhere present, almighty, knowing all things, most wise, most holy, most just, most merciful and gracious, long suffering, abundant in goodness and truth, and essentially, though not completely, incomprehensible.[58] Calvin writes,

> Therefore no one will weigh God's providence properly and profitably but him who considers that his business is with his Maker and the Framer of the universe, and with becoming humility submits himself to fear and reverence. Hence it happens that today so many dogs assail this doctrine with their venomous bitings, or at least with barking: for they wish nothing to be lawful for God beyond what their own reason prescribes for themselves. . . .
>
> But if they do not admit that whatever happens in the universe is governed by God's incomprehensible plans, let them answer to what end Scripture says that his judgments are a deep abyss [Ps. 36:6]. . . . And it is, indeed, true that in the law and the gospel are comprehended mysteries which tower far above the reach of our senses. But since God illumines the minds of his own with the spirit of discernment [Job 20:3 or Isa. 11:2] for the understanding of these mysteries which he has designed to reveal by his Word,

---

57. See *Institutes*, 3.2.11.
58. See WLC 7. Louis Berkhof writes,

To Calvin, God in the depths of His being is past finding out. "His essence," he says, "is incomprehensible; so that His divinity wholly escapes all human senses." The Reformers do not deny that man can learn something of the nature of God from His creation, but maintain that he can acquire true knowledge of him only from special revelation, under the illuminating influence of the Holy Spirit. . . . Reformed theology holds that God can be known, but that it is impossible for man to have a knowledge of Him that is exhaustive and perfect in every way. To have such a knowledge of God would be equivalent to comprehending Him.

Systematic Theology (Grand Rapids, MI: Eerdmans, 1996), 29–30.

now no abyss is here; rather a way in which we ought to walk in safety, and a lamp to guide our feet [Ps. 118:105, Vg.; 119:105, EV], the light of life [cf. John 1:4; 8:12], and the school of sure and clear truth.[59]

Essentially, the providence of God is a reality perceived not by our natural senses but by the supernatural gift of faith.[60] Such faith is not the fruit of an arrogant mind that presumes to comprehend God and his providential ways of governing that which he created; rather, it is a faith that is conceived in humble surrender to God and birthed in "deepest reverence"[61] of God, whose incomprehensibility should "shut our mouths"[62] as we "worship him both with perfect innocence and with unfeigned obedience, then to depend wholly upon his goodness."[63]

The Nature of the Providence of God[64]

Up to this point we have considered how Calvin's doctrine of divine providence relates to the doctrine of predestination. We have also examined briefly the manner in which we as regenerate yet finite creatures are able to grasp the "mystery of providence," to employ the language of Puritan John Flavel (ca. 1630–1691).[65] However, it is only now that we come to that inevitable point in our short study wherein we must examine, with much trepidation and humility, the nature of divine providence. For it is not as if there is a united Christian voice on the doctrine of providence, nor, to this author's dismay, is there a united Reformed voice on the matter. And while it would do our faith well to examine with precision all the intricacies of disparity on the matter of divine providence within the Reformed tradition, let alone the whole realm of Christian thought, it is the attempt of this

---

59. *Institutes*, 1.17.2.

60. For discussion on these matters, see Paul Helm, *Faith and Understanding*, Reason and Religion (Edinburgh: Edinburgh University Press, 1997).

61. Thomas, *Calvin's Teaching on Job*, 239.

62. John Calvin, "Sermon 37" (on Job 9:29–35), in *Sermons on Job*, trans. Arthur Golding (1574; repr., Edinburgh: Banner of Truth, 1993), 173; quoted in Thomas, *Calvin's Teaching on Job*, 239.

63. *Institutes*, 1.10.2.

64. Portions of this section are adapted from Burk Parsons, "What's the Problem?," *Tabletalk* 30, no. 6 (June 2006): 2. Used by permission of *Tabletalk*.

65. John Flavel, *The Mystery of Providence* (1678; repr., Edinburgh: Banner of Truth, 2002).

study to focus chiefly on the nature of providence as formulated in Calvin's *Institutes*. Nevertheless, we do not yet escape the conundrum of disparity even when we turn solely to Calvin's *Institutes*, for there remains a great deal of ongoing discussion on Calvin's formulation of providence in his magnum opus.

Definition and Aim

At the beginning of his treatment of the nature of divine providence, Calvin, in his usual manner, helps define the doctrine and establishes the matter from Scripture:

> At the outset, then, let my readers grasp that providence means not that by which God idly observes from heaven what takes place on earth, but that by which, as keeper of the keys, he governs all events. Thus it pertains no less to his hands than to his eyes. And indeed, when Abraham said to his son, "God will provide" [Gen. 22:8], he meant not only to assert God's foreknowledge of a future event, but to cast the care of a matter unknown to him upon the will of him who is wont to give a way out of things perplexed and confused. Whence it follows that providence is lodged in the act; for many babble too ignorantly of bare foreknowledge. Not so crass is the error of those who attribute a governance to God, but of a confused and mixed sort, as I have said, namely, one that by a general motion revolves and drives the system of the universe, with its several parts, but which does not specifically direct the action of individual creatures.[66]

In this section wherein Calvin argues that divine providence is more than a "bare foreknowledge" of things to come, he begins with the teaching of Scripture. According to Calvin, the question of divine providence is not a question instigated by the vain speculations of men but a matter set forth by the very word of God. Although the subject of providence is in many ways mysterious to us, it is nevertheless revealed to us by God in his word that we might worship him in an acceptable manner.[67]

---

66. *Institutes*, 1.16.4.
67. See *Institutes*, 1.16.2.

Let our study of providence therefore not merely result in a greater vocabulary but in a greater mind and heart for God. The doctrine of divine providence is given to us by God with the divine intention not merely that we learn about him but that we "fear and worship God in very truth."[68] In this vein, the phrase often attributed to Thomas Aquinas expresses the point well: *Theologia a Deo docetur, Deum docet, et ad Deum ducit* ("Theology is taught by God, teaches God, and leads unto God").[69] If our theological investigation is truly of God, we will, by necessity, be instructed by God and about God, and we will be led to God in true devotion, doctrine, and doxology. Accordingly, if we maintain our study of Calvin's doctrine of providence with this disposition, we will surely proceed and conclude with humble hearts that are not only directed but also consumed by Scripture. Still, for those who "insolently scoff" at this whole matter of providence, let them heed Calvin's concluding admonition in book 1, wherein he brings his primary treatment of the doctrine of providence to a close:

> Let those for whom this seems harsh consider for a little while how bearable their squeamishness is in refusing a thing attested by clear Scriptural proofs because it exceeds their mental capacity, and find fault that things are put forth publicly, which if God had not judged useful for men to know, he would never have bidden his prophets and apostles to teach. For our wisdom ought to be nothing else than to embrace with humble teachableness, and at least without finding fault, whatever is taught in sacred Scripture. Those who too insolently scoff, even though it is clear enough that they are prating against God, are not worthy of a longer refutation.[70]

Although Calvin's admonition may seem brash to some, we must understand that such fervency is a result of his great care for the people whom he served. Therefore, in addressing the nature of providence according to Calvin, we must look at the entire matter from the perspective of a compassionate pastor who not only loved God

---

68. "Prefatory Address to King Francis," in *Institutes*, 1:30.
69. Quoted in Berkhof, *Systematic Theology*, 39.
70. *Institutes*, 1.18.4.

and his congregation but also thought that this doctrine was "one of the most important principles in divine philosophy."[71] Herman Selderhuis observes,

> Here, perhaps even more than in the case of other themes, one can appreciate that Calvin interpreted the Bible within the context of his own time and with an eye towards his and his readers' circumstances. Calvin knows from personal experience how many dangers threaten one's life. The account of these in his *Institutes* is quite memorable in a paragraph that forms a subdivision of the chapter dealing with providence. These very same convictions resonate in his commentary on the Psalms. Calvin knows how vulnerable life is: "One's life is exposed to a thousand deaths. It hangs by a thin thread of silk and presents nothing more than a breath that passes away suddenly." . . . Calvin repeatedly refers in autobiographical terms to "our fears." At the same time he realizes that he is preaching, teaching and writing to those who have experienced by and large the same things.[72]

General and Special Providence

It is for this reason that Calvin cannot bring himself to accept a providence that is merely *general* in nature. For Calvin, the matters of life and death, faith and hope, and past and future events demand that he uphold a *special* providence as well.[73] And although he is concerned with the general providence of God in the *Institutes*, he gives most of his attention to the formulation and defense of the special providence of God, which can be summarized in Calvin's explanation that God "sustains, nourishes, and cares for, everything he has made, even to the least sparrow."[74] Moreover, Partee observes, "Unlike the philosophers, Calvin's point of view is more concerned with the particularity of God's care rather than its universality."[75]

We should therefore not be satisfied, as some theologians seem to be, with a general adherence to general providence. For example,

---

71. *Comm.*, on Ps. 49:1–2.
72. Selderhuis, *Calvin's Theology of Psalms*, 89–90.
73. Schreiner, *Theater of His Glory*, 32.
74. *Institutes*, 1.16.1. Also see chap. 14 of Calvin's 1545 treatise *Against the Libertines*.
75. Partee, "Calvin on Universal and Particular Providence," 69.

in his book *The God Who Risks*, open-theism proponent John Sanders asserts,

> The overarching structures of creation are purposed by God, but not every single detail that occurs within them. Within general providence it makes sense to say that God intends an overall purpose for the creation and that God does not specifically intend each and every action within the creation.[76]

Sanders goes on later to conclude regarding "meticulous providence," or particular providence, in contradistinction to his open-theistic view of general providence, "Although meticulous providence provides *God* with a great deal of security, it does not necessarily lead to *our* having less anxiety or uncertainty about what we are to do."[77]

However, that is precisely the reason for acknowledging and trusting in God's special, or "meticulous," providence. Calvin writes,

> Yet, when that light of divine providence has once shone upon a godly man, he is then relieved and set free not only from the extreme anxiety and fear that were pressing him before, but from every care. For as he justly dreads fortune, so he fearlessly dares commit himself to God. His solace, I say, is to know that his Heavenly Father so holds all things in his power, so rules by his authority and will, so governs by his wisdom, that nothing can befall except he determine it. . . .
>
> From this, also, arises in the saints the assurance that they may glory. . . . Whence, I pray you, do they have this never-failing assurance but from knowing that, when the world appears to be aimlessly tumbled about, the Lord is everywhere at work, and from trusting that his work will be for their welfare?[78]

It is precisely for the sake of our freedom from anxiety and our security in "never-failing assurance" that we must cling to the special providence of God.[79] Calvin continues his charge: "But they wrongly

---

76. John Sanders, *The God Who Risks: A Theology of Divine Providence*, 2nd ed. (Downers Grove, IL: IVP Academic, 2007), 272.
77. Sanders, *The God Who Risks*, 287.
78. *Institutes*, 1.17.11.
79. See Selderhuis, *Calvin's Theology of the Psalms*, 99–100. See also *Comm.*, on Ps. 112:7.

conceal and obscure by this excuse that special providence which is so declared by sure and clear testimonies of Scripture that it is a wonder anyone can have doubts about it."[80]

Louis Berkhof explains the relationship between general and special providence in this way: "These are not two kinds of providence, but the same providence exercised in two different relations."[81] Thus, it seems appropriate that when speaking of the different aspects of divine providence, it is better to speak in terms of divine providence as it is generally manifested and providence as it is specially manifested. For it is not as though there are two providences, and what is more, it is not as if we can subscribe to "general providence" without simultaneously subscribing to "special providence."[82]

Concurrence

In the *Institutes*, Calvin is careful to explain that God's special providence governs all things. And although he is certainly concerned with the various aspects of divine providence, namely, preservation (*sustenatio*), governance (*gubernatio*), and concurrence (*concursus*), Calvin's language demonstrates that his primary emphases concern the manner in which God *preserves* his creation and *governs* all things within his creation.[83] Nevertheless, simply because we primarily observe such language of preservation and governance in Calvin does not necessarily indicate that he was not concerned about the doctrine of concurrence, for it is a matter he deals with throughout all his writings, though his treatment of it is ever so brief in the *Institutes*.[84] Berkhof reasons,

> Calvin, the Heidelberg Catechism, and some of the more recent dogmaticians (Dabney, the Hodges, Dick, Shedd, McPherson) speak of only two elements, namely preservation and government. This does not mean however, that they want to exclude the element

---

80. *Institutes*, 1.16.4.
81. Berkhof, *Systematic Theology*, 168.
82. Concerning the language of the word *providence*, see Selderhuis, *Calvin's Theology of the Psalms*, 90.
83. For a full treatment of the aspects of providence, see Berkhof, *Systematic Theology*, 166–78.
84. For example, see *Institutes*, 1.18.4; 2.3.11.

of concurrence but only that they regard it as included in the other two as indicating the manner in which God preserves and governs the world.[85]

Berkouwer agrees, yet he sheds more light on the matter of concurrence and even calls attention to the way in which the word *concurrence* might be misconstrued. In his explanation as to why the term is not generally employed by the Reformed confessions and our forefathers, he defends their case by explaining, "Our fathers were, with their insight into Providence as they expressed it in their confessions, well armed against deism and pantheism without having the doctrine of concurrence." He goes on to add,

> It is hardly avoidable that the idea of cooperation—be it unintended—carries with it the suggestion that God *co*-operates with His creatures. The term does not sufficiently avoid the appearance that we begin with human activity and then see God as co-operator or co-runner (*con*currence) with already active man. . . . There is no poverty of insight in the confessions. The ramparts over which the Church must stand watch, against pantheism and deism, are quite evident in them. That we have found it necessary to posit a third locus, concurrence, alongside sustenance and government certainly is no indication of progress.[86]

So although the word is not generally employed by Calvin and our confessions, and although it may run the risk of being misconstrued outside the appropriate context and without appropriate assignment under the rubric of divine governance, the word *concurrence,* together with its theological import, is helpful as long as we possess a right understanding of the two all-encompassing notions of governance and preservation. For Calvin, the entire matter of divine providence, particularly as we observe it displayed and acknowledged by historical characters in the biblical narrative, is a matter for personal application, piety, and solace. In his comments on those particular biblical narratives in which we often broach the notion of concurrence in our day (e.g., Gen. 45:5; 50:20; Job 1:21;

---

85. Berkhof, *Systematic Theology*, 166.
86. Berkouwer, *Providence of God*, 129–30.

2 Sam. 16:11), under the editors' heading "Certainty about God's providence helps us in all adversities," Calvin writes,

> If there is no more effective remedy for anger and impatience, he has surely benefited greatly who has so learned to meditate upon God's providence that he can always recall his mind to this point: the Lord has willed it; therefore it must be borne, not only because one may not contend against it, but also because he wills nothing but what is just and expedient. To sum this up: when we are unjustly wounded by men, let us overlook their wickedness (which would but worsen our pain and sharpen our minds to revenge), remember to mount up to God, and learn to believe for certain that whatever our enemy has wickedly committed against us was permitted and sent by God's just dispensation.[87]

Primary and Secondary Causality

Thus, insofar as Calvin's formulation of concurrence in the *Institutes* is concerned, we are able to understand how he figured it into the equation of divine governance by exploring his treatment of primary and secondary causality, which is indeed the rub of the whole matter of divine providence. For we understand that God is active and that man is active; as such, we recognize that man makes his own decisions on how to live his life—what to do, what to say, and so on. We understand, as the Westminster divines explained, that

> when God converts a sinner, and translates him into the state of grace, He freeth him from his natural bondage under sin; and, by His grace alone, enables him freely to will and to do that which is spiritually good; yet so, as that by reason of his remaining corruption, he doth not perfectly, nor only, will that which is good, but doth also will that which is evil.[88]

And we also "admit," with the divines, that God governs and sustains all his creation.[89]

---

87. *Institutes*, 1.17.8.
88. WCF 9.4.
89. See WCF 5.1; WLC 18; WSC 11.

We certainly understand that bad things happen to seemingly "good" people and that seemingly good things happen to bad people. But, of course, the nagging question remains—how? How is it that God in his providence works in us, both to will and to do for his good pleasure (Phil. 2:13)? How is it that God works all things together for good for those whom he loves and who are called according to his purpose (Rom. 8:28)? How is it that Joseph could say to his brothers, "As for you, you meant evil against me, but God meant it for good" (Gen. 50:20)? How is it true that "the Lord has made everything for its purpose, even the wicked for the day of trouble" (Prov. 16:4)? And how can the apostle Paul make the same such argument in Romans (Rom. 9:6–24)? Interestingly, Calvin employs a similar method of biblical interrogation:

> But because we know that the universe was established especially for the sake of mankind, we ought to look for this purpose in his governance also. The prophet Jeremiah exclaims, "I know, O Lord, that the way of man is not his own, nor is it given to man to direct his own steps" [Jer. 10:23, cf. Vg.]. Moreover, Solomon says, "Man's steps are from the Lord [Prov. 20:24 p.] and how may man dispose his way?" [Prov. 16:9 p., cf. Vg.]. Let them now say that man is moved by God according to the inclinations of his nature, but that he himself turns that motion whither he pleases. Nay, if that were truly said, the free choice of his ways would be in man's control. Perhaps they will deny this because he can do nothing without God's power. . . . It is an absurd folly that miserable men take it upon themselves to act without God, when they cannot even speak except as he wills![90]

We can do nothing without God's power, Calvin argues. We cannot "even speak" apart from his will. It is on this foundation that Calvin is able to build his formulation of the biblical doctrine of secondary causality.[91] With a simple explanation as to the identity and nature of the first cause, Calvin says plainly, "The sum of the doctrine . . . is, that God, in wondrous ways and in ways unknown to us, directs all

---

90. *Institutes*, 1.16.6.
91. See Selderhuis, *Calvin's Theology of the Psalms*, 103–14.

things to the end that he wills, that His eternal will might be the first cause of all things."[92] The will of God is not some sort of temporary or arbitrary divine whim directed by chance or fortune, Calvin frequently explains.[93] Rather, the will of God is eternal and unchangeable. Regardless of whether all men cast all events to the devilish realm of chance, it is, in reality, a notion foreign to Scripture. Calvin states,

> We must know that God's providence, as it is taught in Scripture, is opposed to fortune and fortuitous happenings. Now it has been commonly accepted in all ages, and almost all mortals hold the same opinion today, that all things come about through chance. What we ought to believe concerning providence is by this depraved opinion most certainly not only beclouded, but almost buried.[94]

In the same section, Calvin further clarifies the nature of providence as it relates to inanimate objects:

> But anyone who has been taught by Christ's lips that all the hairs of his head are numbered [Matt. 10:30] will look farther afield for a cause, and will consider that all events are governed by God's secret plan. And concerning inanimate objects we ought to hold that, although each one by nature has been endowed with its own property, yet it does not exercise its own power except in so far as it is directed by God's ever-present hand. These are, thus, nothing but instruments to which God continually imparts as much effectiveness as he wills, and according to his own purpose bends and turns them to either one action or another.[95]

Whether we are speaking of rational creatures with immortal souls or inanimate objects, God's "ever-present" hand directs them all. With this in mind, whether we call it God's general providence or God's special providence, we must recognize not only that all things were created by God but that all things are sustained by God and that he directs all things according to his eternal will. For it is not merely a doctrinal matter to state that God governs not only the ends but also

---

92. Calvin, *Defence of the Secret Providence of God*, 190.
93. For example, see *Institutes*, 1.16.2; 1.16.3; 1.16.8.
94. *Institutes*, 1.16.2.
95. *Institutes*, 1.16.2.

the means to those ends; it is a severely practical matter.[96] Indeed, it is not just any means or ends that God governs but his eternally established means and his eternally established ends.[97] As the Westminster divines plainly state that "God, in his ordinary providence, maketh use of means, yet is free to work without, above, and against them, at His pleasure,"[98] so Calvin concurs:

> Three things, indeed, are to be noted. First, God's providence must be considered with regard to the future as well as the past. Secondly, it is the determinative principle of all things in such a way that sometimes it works through an intermediary, sometimes without an intermediary, sometimes contrary to every intermediary. Finally, it strives to the end that God may reveal his concern for the whole human race, but especially his vigilance in ruling the church, which he deigns to watch more closely.[99]

The Problem of Evil

Where God's providential hand bestows prosperity and beneficence, there is no argument in acknowledging that he has ordained whatsoever comes to pass. Yet it is when our eyes behold sin, Satan, and spiritual death that we question the providence of God, and additionally, it is then that we question the goodness and love of God. It is precisely when we observe the seeming chaotic nature of this world, the corrupt nature of all mankind, and the confused nature of our own hearts and minds that we question the nature of God. It is along these lines of spiritual awareness, leading to our attempts in formulating a definitive theodicy that we would do well to stop for a moment and consider the more appropriate question regarding the supposed problem of evil.[100]

In this fallen world, we are bombarded with evil from every direction—not only the evil of this world but also the evil within our own hearts. In Calvin's words, we are "laden and stuffed with all kinds of

---

96. See Flavel, *Mystery of Providence*, chap. 9, "How to Meditate on the Providence of God," 117–42.
97. See *Institutes*, 1.14.5; 1.17.4.
98. WCF 5.3.
99. *Institutes*, 1.17.1.
100. *Theodicy* may be defined as follows: "The justification of a deity's justice and goodness in light of suffering and evil." Donald K. McKim, *Westminster Dictionary of Theological Terms* (Louisville: Westminster John Knox, 1996), s.v.

evils."[101] And that is where the real problem exists. As fallen creatures who live in this fallen world of sin and misery, we do not reflect the light of God's glory as we should.[102] We are but a dim and distorted shadow of the glorious light of Almighty God, who created both light and darkness and who makes "well being" and "creates calamity."[103] Calvin writes,

> But if the destruction and misery that press upon us happen without human agency, let us recall the teaching of the law: "Whatever is prosperous flows from the fountain of God's blessing, and all adversities are his curses" [Deut. 28:2 ff., 15 ff. p.]. . . . It is for this same reason that Jeremiah and Amos bitterly expostulated the Jews, for [the Jews] thought both good and evil happened without God's command [Lam. 3:38; Amos 3:6]. In the same vein is Isaiah's declaration: "I, God, creating light and forming darkness, making peace and creating evil: I, God, do all these things" [Isa. 45:7 cf. Vg.].[104]

Considering this teaching, the Westminster divines rightly and succinctly state,

> The almighty power, unsearchable wisdom, and infinite goodness of God, so far manifest themselves in His providence, that it extendeth itself even to the first fall, and all other sins of angels and men; and that not by a bare permission, but such as hath joined with it a most wise and powerful bounding, and otherwise ordering and governing of them, in a manifold dispensation, to His own holy ends; yet so, as the sinfulness thereof proceedeth only from the

---

101. *Institutes*, 3.17.4.
102. See *Institutes*, 2.1.11.
103. Selderhuis writes,

Calvin explains this paradox employing the terms "light" and "darkness." The light of God's grace is intended for those who are surrounded with darkness and know that God uses the darkness, but the ungodly on the other hand are blind in the midst of the light. By a variation on the famous motto of the city of Geneva (*post tenebras lux*), this view of God's providence suggests both *inter tenebras lux* as well as *per tenebras lux*. There is not only light amidst darkness; there is also light by means of the darkness when they stand in contrast to one another.

Calvin's Theology of the Psalms, 97.
104. *Institutes*, 1.17.8.

creature, and not from God, who, being most holy and righteous, neither is, nor can be the author or approver of sin.[105]

While some may suggest that this statement is merely the by-product of post-Reformation scholasticism, we should not presume that it is far beyond the scope of Calvin's formulation of divine providence.[106] For Calvin plainly asserts, "The figment of bare permission vanishes: because it would be ridiculous for the Judge only to permit what he wills to be done, and not also to decree it and to demand its execution by his ministers."[107] Moreover, as to the inquiry of the ages concerning the origination of sin, Calvin wholeheartedly concurs with the Westminster divines that Almighty God is neither the author nor approver of sin. He writes,

> Now away with those persons who dare write God's name upon their faults, because we declare that men are vicious by nature! They perversely search out God's handiwork in their own pollution, when they ought rather to have sought it in that unimpaired and uncorrupted nature of Adam. Our destruction, therefore, comes from the guilt of our flesh, not from God, inasmuch as we have perished solely because we have degenerated from our original condition. Let no one grumble here that God could have provided better for our salvation if he had forestalled Adam's fall. Pious minds ought to loathe this objection, because it manifests inordinate curiosity. Furthermore, the matter has to do with the secret of predestination, which will be discussed later in its proper place. Let us accordingly remember to impute our ruin to depravity of nature, in order that we may not accuse God himself, the Author of nature. True, this deadly wound clings to nature, but it is a very important question whether the wound has been inflicted from outside or has been present from the beginning. Yet it is evident that the wound was inflicted through sin. We have, therefore no reason to complain except against ourselves. Scripture has diligently noted this fact. For Ecclesiastes says: "This I know, that

---

105. WCF 5.4.
106. See Carl R. Trueman, "Calvin and Calvinism," in *The Cambridge Companion to John Calvin*, ed. Donald K. McKim (Cambridge: Cambridge University Press, 2004), 225–44.
107. *Institutes*, 1.18.1.

God made man upright, but they have sought out many devices."
[Ch. 7:29] Obviously, man's ruin is to be ascribed to man alone;
for he, having acquired righteousness by God's kindness, has by
his own folly sunk into vanity.[108]

In our rebellion, which God providentially authorized by his eternal will,[109] we not only authored sin but approved it as well and
thereby "sunk" ourselves into "vanity." Thus, in accordance with
the eternal will of God, the problem of evil is our problem, one that
we authored and one we have to live with until the Lord returns and
establishes the new heavens and new earth, which is the ultimate
fulfillment of Jeremiah's great prophecy of the new covenant (Jer.
31:31–40).[110]

When we understand the genesis of the problem of evil, we will
cease asking the Lord why so much evil exists. Having been confronted by our own guilt and shame before our holy and righteous
Lord, we should realize the foolishness of the commonly uttered assertion, "If God is a good God, he would not allow so much evil to
exist." Instead, we would begin to ask the more appropriate questions:
If God is a just God, why doesn't more evil exist? Why is there not
more sin, death, and destruction on this earth? Why do we not struggle
more than we do? Do we not justly deserve to experience more pain
and misery in this world of sin? We will cease asking the nagging question that Rabbi Kushner had the audacity to put before us, namely,
Why do bad things happen to good people? And we will begin asking
the more appropriate question: Why do good things happen to bad
people? Calvin answers both questions in the following way, using the
Old Testament character Job as an example:

> How may we attribute this same work to God, to Satan, and to
> man as author, without either excusing Satan as associated with
> God, or making God the author of evil? Easily, if we consider first
> the end, and then the manner, of acting. The Lord's purpose is to
> exercise the patience of His servant by calamity; Satan endeavors

---

108. *Institutes*, 2.1.10.
109. Or, in Calvin's language, "he has permitted, indeed commanded." *Institutes*, 1.17.11.
110. See Thomas, *Calvin's Teaching on Job*, 176–77.

to drive him to desperation; the Chaldeans strive to acquire gain from another's property contrary to law and right. So great is the diversity of purpose that already strongly marks the deed. There is no less difference in the matter. The Lord permits Satan to afflict His servant; He hands the Chaldeans over to be impelled by Satan, having chosen them as His ministers for this task.[111]

And in what is perhaps one of Calvin's more succinct explanations of all matters pertaining to general and special providence, secondary causality, the righteousness of God, and the wickedness of Satan, he reasons,

I pass over here the universal activity of God whereby all creatures, as they are sustained, thus derive the energy to do anything at all. I am speaking only of that special action which appears in every particular deed. Therefore we see no inconsistency in assigning the same deed to God, Satan, and man; but the distinction in purpose and manner causes God's righteousness to shine forth blameless there, while the wickedness of Satan and of man betrays itself by its own disgrace.[112]

We must make no mistake about it: as Calvin contends for the distinction between purpose and matter, God's righteousness shines forth blamelessly. His righteous and holy character shines forth not only in spite of his providence but in, through, and on account of his providence. It is the invisible yet ever-present hand of our providential God through which we behold his nature. Praise be to the Lord God Almighty that his nature is to care for his creation, sustain it, govern it, and redeem it! But why, the inquisitive one maintains, why did God permit the fall of Satan and the fall of man? Why did God in his providence covenant to save only some men out of the mass of fallen humanity? Although the answers to such questions are shrouded in the glorious and humbling mystery of providence, the mysterious veil of which may be partially lifted in the world to come, we would do much better to ask the far more mysterious questions, such as, Why did God create anything at all? Why did he choose to sustain that which he

---

111. *Institutes*, 2.4.2.
112. *Institutes*, 2.4.2.

created? Why did he covenant to save anyone? These are the questions that are at the very heart of the doctrine of providence. And it is only from such an attitude of humble inquiry that we can begin to learn the many practical lessons of divine providence.[113]

Free from Every Care

Although we have not even begun to scratch the hard surface of the weighty matter of divine providence, it is certainly a doctrine with which every believer is familiar, for it is our caring Father who has provided us with eyes to behold his providence, even though it be a mere glimpse. In so doing, he has shown us not only that he is Creator and Sustainer of the world but also that he is Creator and Sustainer of our faith (cf. Heb. 1:1–2; 12:1–2). As Thomas observes, "Providence is proof of God's interest in us."[114] It is the liberating foundation of providence set forth by God that commands our immediate attentions, provoking us to offer our hearts and minds to God ever so promptly, sincerely, and humbly. Such was Calvin's daily attitude, and it is precisely that attitude that he would desire to exist within us as well. For it is in such true Christian piety and obedience that our understanding of the true doctrine of providence is most clearly manifested, directing us to revere God rightly, fear him rightly, and worship him rightly.[115]

In knowing God rightly, we shall know ourselves rightly,[116] and, in turn, we shall be instructed by the providence of God in the following ways: Providence makes us humble.[117] Providence brings us to utter dependence on God in complete surrender to God.[118] Providence makes us eternally grateful and rids us of all vain self-centeredness.[119] Providence forces us to lift our hands to the heavens and admit that it is not what our hands have done. Providence makes us patient in adversity, in God's fatherly discipline, and in the chaos of world events.[120] Providence liberates us from anxiety about tomorrow, about our lives,

---

113. See Thomas, *Calvin's Teaching on Job*, chap. 4, "Interpreting the Hand of God: Calvin's Pastoral Understanding of Job."
114. Thomas, *Calvin's Teaching on Job*, 229.
115. Thomas, *Calvin's Teaching on Job*, 303.
116. This is one of Calvin's premises in *Institutes*, 1:1–4.
117. *Institutes*, 1.17.2; 2.1.3.
118. *Institutes*, 2.1.2.
119. *Institutes*, 1.17.7.
120. See Thomas, *Calvin's Teaching on Job*, 231–32.

and about our deaths.[121] Providence quickens us to serve the Lord, his church, and the world, enabling us to live by principle and not pragmatically—to be concerned primarily with faithfulness, not successfulness.[122] Providence gives us comfort and assurance, and it thereby guards us against apathy and cynicism. "When that light of divine providence has once shone upon a godly man," Calvin writes, "he is then relieved and set free not only from the extreme anxiety and fear that were pressing him before, but from every care."[123] Regarding the great benefit of comfort, Calvin continues, the Christian's "solace, I say, is to know that his Heavenly Father so holds all things in his power, so rules by his authority and will, so governs by his wisdom, that nothing can befall except he determine it."[124]

The glory of the doctrine of divine providence is not in the notion that we have discerned the ways of Almighty God, but it is in this, namely, that we have been provided with wisdom from above, which reveals that God has not left us to our own carnal whims, selfish desires, and natural devices.[125] "Nothing," Calvin writes, is "more calculated to increase our faith, than the knowledge of the providence of God."[126] This is the great comfort and assurance of providence that motivates us to worship, which is not only a means but an end as well, for it is God's "active delight," according to Herman Bavinck,[127] in that God "supports and maintains his people in this world with this view, that they may employ their whole life in praising him."[128] If we understand this truth only, I believe Calvin would be pleased, but what is even more essential, I believe our Lord would be pleased, for this is his command with the promise of his providential care: "Humble yourselves, therefore, under the mighty hand of God so that at the proper time he may exalt you, casting all your anxieties on him, because he cares for you" (1 Pet. 5:6–7).

---

121. *Institutes*, 1.16.9.
122. See Thomas, *Calvin's Teaching on Job*, 236–37.
123. *Institutes*, 1.17.11.
124. *Institutes*, 1.17.11.
125. *Institutes*, 3.3.10.
126. *Comm.*, on Ps. 107:42.
127. Herman Bavinck, *Reformed Dogmatics*, vol. 2, *God and Creation*, ed. John Bolt, trans. John Vriend (Grand Rapids, MI: Baker Academic, 2004), 345.
128. *Comm.*, on Ps. 146:1.

11

The Law of God

Guy Prentiss Waters

There is nothing more common than for a man to be sufficiently instructed in a right standard of conduct by natural law.

—John Calvin, *Institutes of the Christian Religion*

Calvin and the Law

Law, in many respects, defined the life of John Calvin. As a young man, Calvin received a thorough legal education. His legal training and concern for political and ecclesiastical law are evident as early as 1532, when his *Commentary on Seneca's "De Clementia"* was published.[1] As a pastor, Calvin shared responsibility for applying biblical law to the lives and circumstances of God's people. As a theologian,

---

1. Irena Backus, "Calvin's Concept of Natural and Roman Law," *CTJ* 38 (2003): 15–25. See especially Ford Lewis Battles, "Calvin and Law," in Ford Lewis Battles and André Malan Hugo, eds. and trans., *Calvin's Commentary on Seneca's "De Clementia": With Introduction, Translation, and Notes*, RTS 3 (Leiden: Brill, 1969), 134*–140*. Battles comments,

> That Calvin had freshly come from his legal studies is evidenced not only by the copious references to the ancient jurisconsults, but by numerous fleeting allusions to legal matters and terms for which sometimes no precise citation is given. The *Leitmotif* of the *De Clementia* itself—the proper relation of ruler to subject—is fraught not only with philosophical but with juristic questions; in fact, it would be difficult if not impossible to draw a line between the two disciplines as they bear upon the *Commentary*. (137*)

Calvin came to define his understanding of biblical law in relation to the positions advocated by Rome, the Lutherans, the Anabaptists, and the Libertines. As a minister of the word of God, Calvin tirelessly preached the Scriptures of the Old and the New Testaments. In the course of his preaching, Calvin faced countless questions concerning biblical law. What is "law" according to the Bible? How does biblical law function in the different epochs of redemptive history? Does biblical law play a role in the justification of the believer? Are all the laws revealed in the Bible binding on believers today?

These are precisely the questions that ministers, elders, and students of the Bible routinely encounter in the study and application of the Scripture. As such, Calvin's reflections on biblical law in his *Institutes*, commentaries, and sermons are both enduring and contemporary. Although these works were authored half a millennium ago, their biblical fidelity ensures that they have much to teach the church today.

In this chapter, we explore Calvin's understanding of law along three lines. First, we consider law in relation to the creation, giving attention to Calvin's doctrine of natural law and to the place of the law in Adam's state of innocency. Second, we consider law in relation to the entrance of sin into the world. Specifically, what now is the relationship between fallen human beings and the eternal law of God? Third, we consider law in relation to the history of redemption. In so doing, we explore how Calvin's sensitivity to the successive epochs of redemptive history affects his understanding of biblical law and its application to the contemporary church.[2]

The Law and Creation

Calvin's Doctrine of Natural Law

In continuity with medieval theology and in company with other sixteenth-century Reformers, John Calvin maintained a doctrine of

---

2. Since this chapter was drafted, two works have appeared that have bearing on the aspects of Calvin's thought addressed in this chapter. On Calvin and natural law, see now David VanDrunen, *Natural Law and the Two Kingdoms: A Study in the Development of Reformed Social Thought* (Grand Rapids, MI: Eerdmans, 2010), 67–118, esp. 93–115. For a trenchant critique of the view that there is "a doctrine of Adamic representation in Calvin's thought" (227), see Aaron Denlinger, "Calvin's Understanding of Adam's Relationship to His Posterity: Recent Assertions of the Reformer's 'Federalism' Evaluated," *CTJ* 44 (2009): 226–50. For a brief statement of the case for Adamic representation as true to Calvin's thought, see n23 later in this chapter.

natural law.[3] In the mid-twentieth century, Karl Barth, T. H. L. Parker, T. F. Torrance, and other influential students of Calvin vigorously resisted a positive place for natural law in the thought of the Reformer.[4] More recently, scholars have increasingly recognized the Genevan's favorable stance toward natural law.[5]

What is natural law according to Calvin? Citing Romans 2:14–15, Calvin observes that "there is nothing more common than for a man to be sufficiently instructed in a right standard of conduct by natural law."[6] Natural law, then, is "a right standard of conduct." People have "a discrimination and judgment by which they distinguish between what is just and unjust, between what is honest and dishonest."[7] At root, natural law concerns the discernment of a set of ethical principles.

Calvin claims that natural law is grounded in the character of God. Because this law is a reflection of God's own character, if one were to observe its precepts, he would "express the image of God, as it were, in his own life."[8] The ethical standards of natural law, then, are a reflection of the divine righteousness.

How do people come to know natural law? Negatively, Calvin stresses that natural law is not "a written law."[9] Calvin speaks rather

---

3. On the medieval discussions concerning natural law, see Stephen J. Grabill, *Rediscovering the Natural Law in Reformed Theological Ethics* (Grand Rapids, MI: Eerdmans, 2006), 54–69. On natural law in the writings of sixteenth- and seventeenth-century Protestant theologians, see Grabill, *Rediscovering the Natural Law*, 175–91.

4. Representative are Karl Barth, *The Knowledge of God and the Service of God according to the Teaching of the Reformation: Recalling the Scottish Confession of 1560*, trans. J. L. M. Haire and Ian Henderson (London: Hodder and Stoughton, 1938); T. H. L. Parker, *Calvin's Doctrine of the Knowledge of God*, rev. ed. (Grand Rapids, MI: Eerdmans, 1959). Invaluable for this period is the discussion in Grabill, *Rediscovering the Natural Law*, 21–53; and the bibliography in I. John Hesselink, *Calvin's Concept of the Law*, PrTMS 30 (Allison Park, PA: Pickwick, 1992), 57–58.

5. In addition to Grabill and Backus, see Paul Helm, "Calvin and Natural Law," *SBET* 2 (1984): 5–22; Helm, *John Calvin's Ideas* (Oxford: Oxford University Press, 2004), 209–45, 347–88; Susan E. Schreiner, *The Theater of His Glory: Nature and the Natural Order in the Thought of John Calvin*, SHT 3 (Durham, NC: Labyrinth, 1991); Schreiner, "Calvin's Use of Natural Law," in *A Preserving Grace: Protestants, Catholics, and Natural Law*, ed. Michael Cromartie (Washington, DC: Ethics and Public Policy Center; Grand Rapids, MI: Eerdmans, 1997), 51–76; Hesselink, *Calvin's Concept of the Law*, 51–85; David VanDrunen, "Natural Law, Custom, and Common Law in the Theology of Aquinas and Calvin," *UBCLR* 33, no. 3 (2000): 699–717.

6. *Institutes*, 2.2.22.

7. *Comm.*, on Rom. 2:15. See also *Comm.*, on Rom 1:32; "The Use of the Law," in *Comm.*, 3:196–201.

8. *Institutes*, 2.8.51. In context, Calvin is speaking about the moral law as promulgated in the Decalogue. Because for Calvin natural law at the very least substantially overlaps with the moral law (discussed later), these comments apply *mutatis mutandis* to the natural law.

9. *Comm.*, on Rom. 2:14.

of the "natural light of righteousness."[10] The medium of natural law is the created order. More specifically, natural law is "inward," that is, "written, even engraved, upon the hearts of all."[11] It is written or engraved by none other than God himself. That God thus ensures the communication of natural law does not mean that the faculties of the individual person are inactive in accessing it. Each human being's God-given "reason," rather, is quite active in discerning good and evil.[12]

Is there any other way to access the content of natural law? Calvin answers this question in the affirmative. Natural law "in a sense asserts the very same things that are to be learned from the two Tables [of the Decalogue]."[13] Elsewhere, Calvin states, "It is a fact that the law of God which we call the moral law is nothing else than a testimony of natural law and of that conscience which God has engraved upon the minds of men."[14] Calvin defines what he means here by "the moral law":

> The moral law . . . is contained under two heads, one of which simply commands us to worship God with pure faith and piety; the other, to embrace men with sincere affection. Accordingly, it is the true and eternal rule of righteousness, prescribed for men of all nations and times, who wish to conform their lives to God's will. For it is his eternal and unchangeable will that he himself indeed be worshipped by us all, and that we love one another.[15]

The moral law and natural law, then, are both expressions of "the true and eternal rule of righteousness" and bind "men of all nations and times."[16] Neither standard is relative to a particular individual,

---

10. *Comm.*, on Rom. 2:14.
11. *Institutes*, 2.8.1.
12. Sermon on Job 27:19–28:9, in *Sermons on Job*, trans. Arthur Golding (1574; repr., Edinburgh: Banner of Truth, 1993), 477a.
13. *Institutes*, 2.8.1.
14. *Institutes*, 4.20.16. Compare Calvin's similar language in his sermon on Deut. 19:14–15: "Our Lorde left stil a certaine discretion ingraven in their hearts. . . . That is the thing which we have to learn by the agreeablenes that is found to be betweene the law of Moses & al the states of government that have bin among all the Heathen in the world." *Sermons on Deuteronomy*, trans. Arthur Golding (1583; repr., Edinburgh: Banner of Truth, 1987), 699a.
15. *Institutes*, 4.20.15.
16. Scholars debate whether Calvin understood the Decalogue to be strictly identical with natural law, or whether the two significantly overlap one another. See the discussions at Grabill, *Rediscovering the Natural Law*, 89–90; Helm, *John Calvin's Ideas*, 379–80.

culture, or moment in history because both are grounded in God's unchangeable character.

These observations are important for a biblical understanding of human nature. Natural law is inextricably and indelibly part of what it means to be a human being made after the image of God.[17] Every human being without exception has some inward testimony to natural law, is aware of God's standards of right and wrong, and is therefore accountable to those standards.

What contemporary significance does this truth have? Calvin reminds us that no human being is a moral blank slate. Nor do individuals or societies legislate morality in the sense that they authoritatively dictate what is morally right and wrong. On the contrary, humanity's sense of right and wrong is received, not legislated. The mind, heart, and conscience of every human being join in bearing witness to unchangeable divine standards engraved on the individual. This does not mean that people by nature approve and obey the dictates of natural law. (We consider below Calvin's reflections on the way sin affects how humans receive natural law.) It does mean, however, that they are inescapably aware of them.

When Christians engage in apologetics with unbelievers, they have a powerful ally within every unbeliever—an indelible sense of right and wrong implanted by the Creator and Judge of humanity. This truth is a crucial starting point for a compelling case for the existence of God—God can be demonstrated to exist from the presence of the natural law that he has written on the hearts of every human being. It is this moral argument for the existence of God that Calvin raises early in the *Institutes*[18] and that subsequent Christian thinkers have developed as well.

Before the Fall: Adam and the Law

Another aspect of the law in relation to the creation in Calvin's writings is the place of the law in the life of Adam before Adam's first sin. Adam from the moment of his creation had within him testimony to

---

17. On the question whether for Calvin knowledge of natural law is innate or acquired, see Helm, "Calvin and Natural Law," 7. For the relation of natural law to the image of God, see *Comm.*, on Gen. 1:26–27.

18. See *Institutes*, 1.3.1.

natural law. Adam was not only aware of natural law but was also conformed to natural law:

> Adam was endued with a right judgment, had affections in harmony with reason, had all his senses sound and well-regulated, and truly excelled in everything good. . . . In the mind perfect intelligence flourished and reigned, uprightness attended as its companion, and all the senses were prepared and moulded for due obedience to reason; and in the body there was a suitable correspondence with this internal order.[19]

Righteous God gave righteous Adam one additional commandment— the prohibition of eating from the tree of the knowledge of good and evil (Gen. 2:16–17). Unlike the natural law, which inherently reflects the upright character of God, this prohibition was "imposed upon him in token of his subjection; for it would have made no difference to God, if he had eaten indiscriminately of any fruit he pleased." This prohibition was "a test of obedience."[20]

The biblical narrative records both Adam's disobedience to this prohibition and the consequences of that disobedience for Adam and his posterity, excepting Jesus. Calvin speculates what consequences would have followed upon Adam's continued obedience to the commandments of God:

> Truly the first man would have passed to a better life, had he remained upright; but there would have been no separation of the soul from the body, no corruption, no kind of destruction, and, in short, no violent change.[21]

> We must, I say, remember from what kind of life man fell. He was, in every respect, happy; his life, therefore, had alike respect to his body and his soul, since in his soul a right judgment and a proper government of the affections prevailed, there also life reigned; in his body there was no defect, wherefore he was

---

19. *Comm.*, on Gen. 1:26.
20. *Comm.*, on Gen. 2:16.
21. *Comm.*, on Gen. 3:9. Both this and the preceding quotation are drawn from Peter A. Lillback, "Ursinus' Development of the Covenant of Creation: A Debt to Melanchthon or Calvin?," *WTJ* 43 (1981): 281, 282.

wholly free from death. His earthly life truly would have been temporal; yet he would have passed into heaven without death, and without injury.[22]

Calvin underscores here an important point that will surface later in our discussion. Had Adam continued in obedience to the law of God, two things would have resulted. Negatively, Adam would have been spared the experience of death, sin's wage. Positively, Adam would have continued in life until "passing into heaven without death, and without injury." Confirmed life would have been the consequence of obedience.

Adam, however, disobeyed the command of God. The consequence was death for himself and for his ordinary posterity. Adam's posterity died, Calvin taught, because the first sin of their representative, Adam, was imputed or accounted to them.[23]

What we have outlined from Calvin's writings is what came to be known in the later sixteenth and seventeenth centuries as the "covenant of works." Much attention has been given to the progress and development of this doctrine in British and Continental theology after Calvin.[24] What we have observed is that the origins of the doctrine of the covenant of works expressed in later Reformed theology lie in the writings of John Calvin. This is not to say that Calvin formally articulated a doctrine of the covenant of works. Nor is it to say that

---

22. *Comm.*, on Gen. 2:16.

23. See the compelling case made here by Lillback, "Ursinus' Development," 278–80. We may summarize Lillback's case as follows. Calvin understood Adam to be not only the "root" from which the corruption of Adam's ordinary posterity sprang but also his posterity's "representative 'head.'" By divine appointment, the first sin of this representative was counted to those whom he represented. The relationship between Adam and his posterity is one that is parallel with the relationship between Christ and the elect. As the elect's representative head, Christ has done what Adam failed to do (by obeying God perfectly) and has remedied what Adam did (by paying the penalty for sin). *Institutes*, 2.12.3. Since Christ's obedience and satisfaction come into the possession of the elect by imputation in justification, Adam's sin must also have come into the possession of his posterity by imputation. One further consequence of this imputation was the corruption of those whom Adam represented. *Comm.*, on John 3:6.

24. For an overview of this period, see Robert Letham, "The *Foedus Operum*: Some Factors Accounting for Its Development," *SCJ* 14, no. 4 (1983): 457–67; David A. Weir, *The Origins of the Federal Theology in Sixteenth-Century Reformation Thought* (New York: Oxford University Press, 1990). For Britain, see especially Michael McGiffert, "From Moses to Adam: The Making of the Covenant of Works," *SCJ* 19, no. 2 (1988): 131–55. For the Continent, see Lillback, "Ursinus' Development"; Lillback, *The Binding of God: Calvin's Role in the Development of Covenant Theology*, TSRPRT (Grand Rapids, MI: Baker, 2001), 276–304; Lyle D. Bierma, *German Calvinism in the Confessional Age: The Covenant Theology of Caspar Olevianus* (Grand Rapids, MI: Baker, 1996); Willem J. van Asselt, *The Federal Theology of Johannes Cocceius (1603–1669)*, trans. Raymond A. Blacketer, SHCT 100 (Leiden: Brill, 2001).

bicovenantal theology explicitly structured Calvin's writings.[25] It is to say, however, that the doctrine of the covenant of works formulated in the later sixteenth and seventeenth centuries is the legitimate off-spring of John Calvin. Without claiming in this matter a strict identity between Calvin and his heirs, we may surely claim an unbroken line of continuity between them.

What do Calvin's writings on this point have to say to the church today? First, they are a sober explanation of the somber human condition. As a faithful biblical theologian, Calvin holds no illusions about fallen human nature. Unregenerate human beings universally are des-titute of all that is spiritually good, are morally corrupt, are spiritu-ally blind, are singly devoted to the service of idols, and are unable to please God.[26]

Calvin rejects the doctrine that fallen people are only "half dead." He acknowledges that the unregenerate have "some kind of life" in them, "for unbelief does not altogether destroy the spiritual senses, or the will, or the other faculties of the soul." This life, however, has nothing to do with the "kingdom of God" or "a happy life." This is because "out of Christ we are altogether dead, because sin, the cause of death, reigns in us."[27]

This state of affairs is traceable to a single cause—the one sin of our father Adam: "For the corruption of all mankind in the person of Adam alone did not proceed from generation, but from the ap-pointment of God, who in one man had adorned us all, and who has in him also deprived us of his gifts."[28] The universal depravity of mankind does not exist because individuals born with morally virtuous or morally neutral natures universally make poor choices. The universal depravity of mankind exists because the imputation

---

25. Scholars have observed that the covenant concept dominates Calvin's understanding of the progress and details of redemptive history while recognizing, for instance, that Calvin refrains in the *Institutes* and in the catechisms and confessions that he authored from appealing to the cove-nant concept as the organizing principle of those writings. See here M. Eugene Osterhaven, "Cal-vin on the Covenant," in *Readings in Calvin's Theology*, ed. Donald K. McKim (Grand Rapids, MI: Baker, 1984), 89–106, esp. 89–91; Peter A. Lillback, "Calvin's Interpretation of the History of Salvation: The Continuity and Discontinuity of the Covenant (2.10–11)," in *A Theological Guide to Calvin's "Institutes": Essays and Analysis*, ed. David W. Hall and Peter A. Lillback, Calvin 500 Series (Phillipsburg, NJ: P&R, 2008), 168–204, esp. 178–80.

26. For Calvin's analysis of the biblical assessment of the human condition, see especially *Institutes*, 2.1–3.

27. *Comm.*, on Eph. 2:1.

28. *Comm.*, on John 3:6. Cf. *Comm.*, on Ps. 51:5.

of Adam's sin to his posterity has resulted in the universal depravity of that posterity.

This truth means that biblically faithful preaching and evangelism must uncompromisingly proclaim the inability of the sinner to please God or to turn to God in faith and repentance. Sinners must be told that all that they are capable of doing as sinners is sinning. They must never be led to think that anything they do can commend them to the favor of God. They must never be led to think that any hope for salvation rests within themselves.

This leads to a second point. The only hope for salvation comes from without. Calvin summarizes Jesus's words to Nicodemus in John 3:

> [Jesus] intended to exhort Nicodemus to newness of life, because he was not capable of receiving the Gospel, until he began to be a new man. It is, therefore, a simple statement, that we must be born again, in order that we may be the children of God, and that the Holy Spirit is the Author of this second birth.[29]

Until the Spirit renews a person in this way, until he is joined to Jesus Christ in his death and resurrection,[30] he is incapable even of "receiving the Gospel." Once that individual is born again, however, he is alive to God. The new birth, Calvin stresses, is authored by the Holy Spirit. It is not produced or induced by the sinner, the minister, or the evangelist. It is a sovereign gift of God. Biblically faithful preaching and evangelism must direct sinners to the feet of the divine Savior, who alone is able to bring the dead to life.

The Law and Sin

Calvin teaches that because of sin, the ordinary descendants of Adam relate to God in a fundamentally different way than Adam related to God in his state of innocence. This fact raises questions about the relationship of fallen people to the law of God. We first observe Calvin arguing that the fall has resulted in no change to the law itself. We then observe Calvin holding that what changed is the relationship of sinful people to that law.

---

29. *Comm.*, on John 3:5.
30. *Comm.*, on Eph. 2:4.

After the Fall: The Law of God

We have observed Calvin claim that all human beings are aware of and accountable to the natural law that God has engraved on each person's heart. Calvin insists that the fact of sin has not destroyed, much less weakened, the sinner's accountability to that standard. He gives no quarter to the position that the law is "so accommodated to our capacities that we are of necessity able to fulfill all their demonstrable requirements."[31] God has not relaxed the requirements of the law to suit our sinful failure to keep its demands and our sinful propensity to violate its precepts. When we study the moral law, rather, "we are rendered more inexcusable"[32] because we are unable as sinners to fulfill its demands.[33]

Calvin's biblical observation is a timely one. People in our own day persist in believing that God's requirements for entering into eternal life are commensurate with their ability. If sin has restricted the degree to which they can be righteous, they reason, then God must accommodate his standards to meet them where they are. As a result, they deceive themselves into thinking that they actually meet the divine standard of righteousness. Calvin reminds us that God's standard of righteousness is as unalterable and inflexible as God's own character is unchangeable. The law, as we shall see Calvin argue, has only bad news for the sinner trusting in his own performance for acceptance with God.

After the Fall: The Law of God and the Sinner

The fall of humanity has not changed the standards and demands of the law of God. The fall, however, most certainly has altered the relationship of man to the law of God. We may reflect on two ways in which Calvin addresses how this relationship has changed.

The Law Obscured

One effect of sin is to obscure natural law. Natural law is in itself clear. Its obscurity to people is a consequence of sin: "Man is so shrouded in the darkness of errors that he hardly begins to grasp through this

---

31. *Institutes*, 2.5.6. "And we cannot pretend the excuse that we lack ability and, like impoverished debtors, are unable to pay. It is not fitting for us to measure God's glory according to our ability; for whatever we may be, he remains always like himself: the friend of righteousness, the foe of iniquity." *Institutes*, 2.8.2.

32. *Institutes*, 2.7.3.

33. *Institutes*, 2.7.5.

natural law what worship is acceptable to God. Surely he is very far removed from a true estimate of it."[34] Calvin understands Romans 2:15 to teach not "that there is in men a *full* knowledge of the law, but that there are only some seeds of what is right implanted in their nature."[35]

If sin both obscures this standard of conduct and prevents people from obeying its dictates, does natural law serve any purpose at all? Calvin, following Paul, argues in the affirmative: "The purpose of natural law, therefore, is to render man inexcusable."[36] This purpose lays bare the claim that people "sin only out of ignorance."[37] Since natural law is known to all people alike, no individual has any excuse to sin.

What does it mean to be rendered inexcusable? It means, in part, that the sinner continually realizes that he is subject to divine judgment for sin. There is a genuine sense in which the judgment of the last day breaks into the present life of the sinner when conscience continually "reproves us for our vices."[38]

Calvin identifies another purpose of the natural law in a fallen context. Although the natural law is obscured to sinners, it nevertheless explains the presence of the remnants of morality among the Gentiles.[39] This is true not only at the individual level but also at the level of civic or public life, where "all nations, of themselves and without a monitor, are disposed to make laws for themselves [and] have some notions of justice and rectitude."[40] Calvin is careful to say that this individual and public recognition of virtue and vice does not constitute the approbation of virtue. It is more appropriate to say that "they were so mastered by the power of truth, that they could not disapprove of it."[41] Even so, natural law plays a vital and continuing role in the restraint of vice and of the preservation of virtue in the lives of both individuals and societies.[42]

---

34. *Institutes*, 2.8.1.
35. *Comm.*, on Rom. 2:15, italics original.
36. *Institutes*, 2.2.22.
37. *Institutes*, 2.2.22.
38. *Comm.*, on Rom. 2:15. See also *Institutes*, 4.10.3.
39. *Comm.*, on Rom. 2:14.
40. *Comm.*, on Rom. 2:14.
41. *Comm.*, on Rom. 2:15.
42. For the way in which Calvin counsels nations to frame their laws, see *Institutes*, 4.20.14–16. Calvin vehemently denies that nations must adopt the "political system of Moses," that is, the judicial legislation of the Mosaic legal code. *Institutes*, 4.20.14. Rather, "every nation is left free to make such laws as it foresees to be profitable for itself. Yet these must be in conformity to that

The entrance of sin had one further implication for the relation of fallen humanity to the natural law. Because of the culpable obscurity of natural law to sinners, God has formally promulgated the natural law in written form: "Accordingly (because it is necessary both for our dullness and for our arrogance), the Lord has provided us with a written law to give us a clearer witness of what was too obscure in the natural law, shake off our listlessness, and strike more vigorously our mind and memory."[43] This promulgation is found in the moral law, the two tables of the Decalogue given by God to Israel through Moses.[44] The purpose of this promulgation was to clarify what sin had obscured. The promulgation of the law itself conveys no power to any sinner to keep the demands of the moral law.[45]

Justification by Works?

Had Adam continued in perfect obedience to the law, he could have received the reward of eternal life.[46] In that light, Calvin explicitly addresses the question whether the law may play any role in the basis or ground of the sinner's justification. In other words, may the sinful son of Adam enter into life on the basis of his own performance? This question Calvin categorically answers in the negative.

Calvin responds to unbiblical attempts to qualify the Scripture's prohibition on justification by works. Some claim that the prohibition on works in justification extends only to such ceremonial works of the Mosaic law as circumcision. Calvin argues that the apostle Paul's statements in Galatians 3:10 and 3:12 prohibit works of the moral law for justification.[47] Others claim that Paul excludes only the works of the unregenerate from the works by which a person is

---

perpetual rule of love, so that they indeed vary in form but have the same purpose." *Institutes*, 4.20.15. Specifically, Calvin points the civil magistrate to the moral law as sufficient to guide the state in framing its laws: "The entire scheme of this equity of which we are now speaking has been prescribed in [the moral law]. Hence, this equity alone must be the goal and rule and limit of all laws." *Institutes*, 4.20.16. He recognizes, however, that the "judicial law" of Moses "imparted certain formulas of equity and justice" for Israel. *Institutes*, 4.20.15. Presumably, these "formulas of equity and justice" are instructive as examples of the equity required by the moral law. As a code of civil law, however, the Mosaic legislation was never intended to bind any nation other than biblical Israel.

43. *Institutes*, 2.8.1. See also *Comm.*, on Ex. 19:1, in *Comm.*, 2:313–16.
44. *Institutes*, 4.20.14–15; 2.8.1.
45. See *Comm.*, on 2 Cor. 3:6.
46. *Institutes*, 3.11.19. See also *Comm.*, on Gen. 2:16.
47. *Comm.*, on Gal. 2:15.

not justified. A regenerate person may therefore be justified by his works done in obedience to the moral law.[48] To this position Calvin responds that Paul's prohibition of works for the ground of justification is a categorical one: "All works are excluded, whatever title may grace them."[49]

Why is it that a sinner's efforts to keep the moral law cannot justify him? The law and the gospel offer two mutually exclusive paths to justification.[50] "The gospel promises are free and dependent solely upon God's mercy, while the promises of the law depend upon the condition of works."[51] Since "no one, not only of the common folk, but of the most perfect persons . . . can fulfill [the law],"[52] and since "unceasing obedience to the law is necessary" for justification,[53] the avenue of justification by works of the law is therefore closed to sinners. Even if one were to have "some wholly pure and perfect works . . . one sin is enough to wipe out and extinguish every memory of that previous righteousness."[54] In short, "no other righteousness than the complete observance of the law is allowed in heaven"—"partial righteousness" is a "fiction."[55]

The sinner's problem, then, is twofold. The sinner is unable to produce the kind of righteousness that the law requires. Further, even if he were able to produce such a righteousness,[56] he would undo it entirely by a single sin.[57] What, then, does the law pronounce to one who has failed to keep perfectly its demands? It pronounces "curse"[58] and "death and judgment."[59] However much "life" was extended to Adam by obedience, justification by the avenue of the law is entirely closed to the sinner because of his sin.

---

48. *Institutes*, 3.11.14.
49. *Institutes*, 3.11.14.
50. On law and gospel in Calvin's writings, see Hesselink, *Calvin's Concept of the Law*, 155–215.
51. *Institutes*, 3.11.17.
52. *Institutes*, 3.11.17. Calvin argues at length the impossibility of a sinner being able to keep the law in *Institutes*, 2.7.5.
53. *Institutes*, 3.14.10.
54. *Institutes*, 3.14.10.
55. *Institutes*, 3.14.13.
56. On the impossibility of this hypothetical scenario, see *Comm.*, on Rom. 2:13; *Institutes*, 3.17.13.
57. "God's most holy servants . . . are far from fulfilling the law, hemmed in as they are by many transgressions," *Institutes*, 3.17.3.
58. *Institutes*, 3.14.13. See also *Comm.*, on Gal. 3:10.
59. *Institutes*, 3.14.10.

This is why only the imputation of Christ's righteousness will avail for justification.[60] Our dilemma—namely, that "the Lord promises nothing except to perfect keepers of his law, and no one of the kind is to be found"[61]—is answered by Christ and his imputed righteousness alone. God answers our dilemma "not by leaving us a part of righteousness in our works, and by supplying part out of his loving-kindness, but by appointing Christ alone as the fulfillment of righteousness."[62] It is therefore through the "promises of the gospel," and these promises only, that the believer has "the free forgiveness of sins," "acceptance with God," and the assurance that God is pleased to accept and to bless our good works.[63]

Calvin's words have continued application in the church today. The Reformation was a glorious recovery of the gospel of grace. It thundered the justification of the sinner solely on the basis of the righteousness of Christ, imputed to the sinner, and received by faith alone. The tendency of the sinful heart is to seek some credit or glory in justification by interjecting its own performance in place of or even alongside Christ's righteousness. Calvin reminds us that there can be no mixture of our righteousness and Christ's righteousness for justification: "A man who wishes to obtain Christ's righteousness must abandon his own righteousness."[64] Calvin's refutations of these errors in the sixteenth century help us faithfully present the gospel of grace to men and women in the twenty-first century. We must point sinners not to a Christ who can help them justify themselves but to the Christ of the Scripture, who clothes his people with his own divine righteousness for justification—the only righteousness a sinner could ever need.

The Law in the History of Redemption

In the final part of our study of Calvin's writings on law, we consider how Calvin understands law to function in the different epochs of

---

60. *Institutes*, 3.11.2.
61. *Institutes*, 3.17.1.
62. *Institutes*, 3.17.2.
63. *Institutes*, 3.17.3. Calvin stresses in this section that these good works in no way merit the divine blessing. God "attributes some value to them . . . of his fatherly generosity and loving-kindness, and without considering their worth." They must, further, "be cleansed of spots" and in no way rival or share in the imputed righteousness of Christ that alone grounds the sinner's justification.
64. *Institutes*, 3.11.13.

redemptive history. It is at this point in our discussion that we witness the explicit intersection of *law* and *covenant* in Calvin's writings. First, we briefly observe that Calvin understands God to have made a single redemptive covenant with his people. Second, we consider the place of the law within that covenant by giving attention to two distinct administrations of that one covenant, the Mosaic covenant and the new covenant. Such attention allows us to explore Calvin's understanding of the continuity and discontinuity of these administrations with respect to the law.

A Single Redemptive Covenant

Calvin stresses the impossibility of fallen man attaining to anything other than death and judgment on the basis of his own record. If "life" is to come to the sinner, it must come through Christ, by the gospel. This principle is true not only for new covenant saints but also for Old Testament saints.[65] There is and always has been, therefore, a single way of redemption for the fallen sons of Adam:

> Now we can clearly see from what has already been said that all men adopted by God into the company of his people *since the beginning of the world* were covenanted to him by the same law and by the bond of the same doctrine as obtains among us. . . . The patriarchs participated in the same inheritance and hoped for a common salvation with us by the grace of the same Mediator.[66]

One is not surprised, then, to discover that this common salvation is administered through a single redemptive covenant: "The covenant made with all the patriarchs is so much like ours in substance and reality that the two are actually one and the same."[67]

This redemptive covenant is one, but it is not monolithic. Calvin understands this single covenant to have been administered in historically successive dispensations or administrations. Immediately after

---

65. *Institutes*, 2.10.2; 2.10.4.
66. *Institutes*, 2.10.1, italics added.
67. *Institutes*, 2.10.2. For helpful surveys of this redemptive covenant in Calvin's writings, see Hesselink, *Calvin's Concept of the Law*, 87–101, 160–61; Lillback, "Calvin's Interpretation of the History of Salvation"; Osterhaven, "Calvin on the Covenant."

stating that the covenant that God made with the patriarchs is "one and the same" with "ours," Calvin adds, "Yet they differ in the mode of dispensation."[68]

The accent in Calvin's discussion of the covenant of grace in the *Institutes* is nevertheless on that covenant's unity or continuity. The various dispensations are not essentially different or discontinuous. They are administrations of a single redemptive covenant. Within that covenant's unity or continuity, Calvin notes, there exists a legitimate measure of discontinuity among the various administrations of that covenant.[69] For Calvin, then, we must speak of discontinuous continuity rather than essential discontinuity.

Calvin is sensitive to the charge that the historical succession of the administrations of this gracious covenant strikes at the self-consistency of God. In Calvin's words, should God "be considered changeable merely because he accommodated diverse forms to different ages"?[70] Calvin answers in the negative. He compares the successive stages of redemptive history to the successive stages of a person's life. Just as a human being proceeds from youth to adulthood, the people of God mature in like fashion:

> Paul likens the Jews to children, Christians to young men [Gal. 4:1ff.]. What was irregular about the fact that God confined them to rudimentary teaching commensurate with their age, but has trained us through a firmer and, so to speak, more manly discipline? Thus, God's constancy shines forth in the fact that he taught the same doctrine to all ages, and has continued to require the same worship of his name that he enjoined from the beginning. In the fact that he has changed the outward form and manner, he does not show himself subject to change. Rather, he has accommodated himself to men's capacity, which is varied and changeable.[71]

---

68. *Institutes*, 2.10.2.

69. See *Institutes*, 2.11.1–12. This chapter follows a chapter (2.11.10) devoted to establishing the essential unity of God's gracious covenant. The sequence of the discussion (continuity proceeding to discontinuity) further suggests that Calvin emphasizes continuity in his discussion of the administrations of this covenant. See the helpful discussion in Lillback, "Calvin's Interpretation of the History of Salvation," 185–201.

70. *Institutes*, 2.11.13.

71. *Institutes*, 2.11.13; see also *Institutes*, 2.11.5. Compare the Westminster divines' description of Israel as "a church under age." WCF 19.3.

Calvin here draws two important observations about changes in covenantal administration. First, they reflect no change or inconstancy in God. They are, rather, accommodations to the "capacity" of people. Second, the changes are changes in "outward form and manner." The doctrine and worship of God remains unchanged from administration to administration. In this respect, these administrations are administrations of the same covenant. This covenantal dynamic of unity-in-essence and diversity-in-form helps us understand the way in which Calvin addresses the role and form of "law" in the various administrations of the covenant of grace. We turn now to consider the place of the law in two of those administrations—the Mosaic covenant and the new covenant.

The Law and the Mosaic Covenant

Calvin gives particular attention to the place of the law within the Mosaic administration of this covenant.[72] In addition to calling the commandments of God "law," the Scripture frequently denominates this administration "law." To appreciate Calvin's conception of the law's place within the Mosaic covenant, a rehearsal of the various ways in which Calvin, following Scripture, uses the term "law" is in order.

First, as we have observed, Calvin does not understand the Mosaic covenant to have introduced the law afresh. The natural law "in a sense asserts the very same things that are to be learned from the two Tables."[73] There is, then, a materially close relationship between the content of the natural law and the content of the Decalogue. The promulgation of the Decalogue at Sinai is therefore a confirmation of the divine standards of which humans have been aware since the creation of Adam.

Second, Calvin recognizes that part of the Sinaitic legislation was new. Calvin affirms the classical threefold categorization of the moral, civil, and ceremonial laws.[74] For the Genevan Reformer, these were

---

72. Interestingly and importantly, Calvin defends, in response to "certain rascals [who] display the keenness of their wit in assailing God's truth," not only the historicity of Moses but also the authenticity of the Mosaic legislation. *Institutes*, 1.8.9; 1.8.10. Calvin appears to be responding to individuals who claimed that the Pentateuch was a "spurious" text. *Institutes*, 1.8.10.

73. *Institutes*, 2.8.1.

74. *Institutes*, 4.20.15.

distinct but not entirely separate categories of law. The ceremonial laws "properly belonged to the doctrine of piety," although they "could be distinguished from piety itself." Similarly, the judicial legislation sought "best to preserve that very love which is enjoined by God's eternal law" but "had something distinct from that precept of love." The ceremonial and judicial laws therefore adhered to the moral law but could be and were abrogated without any injustice to the "perpetual duties and precepts of love."[75]

Third, Calvin teaches that the Scripture denominated the Mosaic covenant in terms of "law." Referencing Galatians 3:17 ("This is what I mean: the law, which came 430 years afterward, does not annul a covenant previously ratified by God, so as to make the promise void"), Calvin says, "I understand by the word 'law' not only the Ten Commandments, which set forth a godly and righteous rule of living, but the form of religion handed down by God through Moses."[76] Calvin recognizes with the apostle Paul that God did not intend the Mosaic covenant to rival or supplant the Abrahamic covenant in the economy of salvation. God intended the Mosaic covenant to reinforce and advance the Abrahamic covenant: "We see [Moses] repeatedly reminding the Jews of that freely given covenant made with their fathers of which they were the heirs. It was as if he were sent to renew it."[77]

The Mosaic covenant has an equally complementary relationship with the new covenant. This is evident from the ceremonial laws of the Mosaic covenant. The ceremonies were intended to "guide [Israel] to Christ," particularly by setting forth his sacrificial and reconciling death for sinners.[78] Calvin, following Paul, understands Christ to be the substance of the promise of the Abrahamic covenant. By pointing Israel to Christ, the ceremonial laws of the Mosaic covenant not only confirm the Abrahamic promise but also demonstrate to us the essential continuity between the Mosaic and the new covenants.

We may also underscore Calvin's contention that the ceremonial laws were suited for an immature people: "For, since [the Jews] had not yet

---

75. *Institutes*, 4.20.15.
76. *Institutes*, 2.7.1.
77. *Institutes*, 2.7.1.
78. *Institutes*, 2.7.2. Calvin emphasizes in this section that these ceremonies had no redemptive virtue or efficacy in themselves. The ceremonies' goal was to "lift [the Israelites'] minds higher," that is, to Christ. *Institutes*, 2.7.1.

come to know Christ intimately, they were like children whose weakness could not yet bear the full knowledge of heavenly things."[79] These laws have, in other words, a built-in obsolescence. When Christ the substance appears, when the people of God attain to their maturity, the ceremonial laws (along with the covenantal administration that promulgated them) will have fulfilled their divinely appointed purpose.[80]

Fourth, there is a sense in which Calvin uses the term *law* in close connection with the term *gospel*. This law-gospel relationship itself admits of further distinction. Calvin sometimes articulates this relationship in complementary fashion. At other times, he articulates this relationship in antithetical fashion. This twofold relationship exists because Calvin intentionally uses the words *law* and *gospel* in both a broad and a narrow sense.

In its broad denomination, *gospel* "includes those testimonies of [God's] mercy and fatherly favor which God gave to the patriarchs of old." In its narrow denomination, *gospel* "refers . . . to the proclamation of the grace manifested in Christ."[81] This distinction allows Calvin to apply the term *gospel* to the Abrahamic and Mosaic covenants as administrations of divine promise. In this respect, *law* (defined broadly as the Mosaic covenant) overlaps with *gospel* (defined in this broad sense).[82] This *law* may be said to be in complementary relationship with *gospel* defined in its narrower sense ("the proclamation of the grace manifested in Christ") because each of these administrations is an administration of promise.

There is, according to Calvin, a legitimate antithetical relationship between *law* and *gospel*, provided that these terms are properly defined. Calvin contrasts *law* (defined as the Old Testament) and *gospel* (defined narrowly as the New Testament) in three ways.[83] First, the Old Testament "in the absence of the reality . . . showed but an image and shadow in place of the substance; the New Testament reveals the very substance of truth as present."[84] "The gospel points out with

---

79. *Institutes*, 2.7.2.
80. See *Institutes*, 2.11.4–6.
81. *Institutes*, 2.9.2.
82. Calvin expresses concern that this complementary relationship not be overlooked through attention to the legitimate antithetical relationship between *law* and *gospel. Institutes*, 2.9.4.
83. *Institutes*, 2.11.10.
84. *Institutes*, 2.11.4.

the finger what the law foreshadowed under types,"[85] and the gospel "confirmed and satisfied whatever the law had promised, and gave substance to the shadows."[86]

A second point of contrast consists in what Calvin terms the literality of the law and the spirituality of the gospel. Calvin elaborates this contrast with reference to Paul's statements in 2 Corinthians 3: "The former he speaks of as carved on tablets of stone, the latter as written upon men's hearts; the former is the preaching of death, the latter of life; the former of condemnation, the latter of righteousness; the former to be made void, the latter to abide."[87]

A third and related point of contrast is that "the Scripture calls the Old Testament one of 'bondage' because it produces fear in men's minds; but the New Testament, one of 'freedom' because it lifts them to trust and assurance."[88]

What precisely does Calvin mean when he ties "condemnation" to the law? Calvin states, "Paul often means by the term 'law' the rule of righteous living by which God requires of us what is his own, giving us no hope of life unless we completely obey him, and adding on the other hand a curse if we deviate even in the slightest degree." It is in this sense that the apostle "justly makes contraries of the righteousness of the law and of that of the gospel"[89] and that sinners invariably fall under the law's condemnation.

These latter two points of contrast in particular appear to pose difficulty for Calvin's understanding of the law. Calvin argues that the Mosaic covenant is an evangelical administration of God's gracious covenant. Its divinely intended goal was to point the Israelites to Christ through its types and shadows. One must not understand the Mosaic and the new covenants to be advocating "different way[s] of salvation."[90]

And yet, Calvin acknowledges that the New Testament appeals to the Old Testament commandments to articulate the principle that eternal life is suspended upon one's flawless obedience to the precepts

---

85. *Institutes*, 2.9.3.
86. *Institutes*, 2.9.4.
87. *Institutes*, 2.11.7.
88. *Institutes*, 2.11.9.
89. *Institutes*, 2.9.4.
90. *Institutes*, 2.9.4.

of the law. He understands the New Testament to teach that the Old Testament commandments leave sinners condemned. Does this mean that the Old Testament is advocating a way of salvation antithetical to that proposed by the New Testament? Does this mean that the Old Testament, on the Genevan Reformer's reading, is advocating two mutually exclusive ways of salvation: one of grace and the other of works?

Calvin addresses and resolves this very question with a crucial distinction:

> Jeremiah and Paul, because they are contrasting the Old and New Testaments, consider nothing in the law except what properly belongs to it. For example: the law contains here and there promises of mercy, but because they have been borrowed from elsewhere, they are not counted part of the law, when only the nature of the law is under discussion. They ascribe it only to this function: to enjoin what is right, to forbid what is wicked; to promise a reward to the keepers of righteousness, and threaten transgressors with punishment; but at the same time not to change or correct the depravity of heart that by nature inheres in all men.[91]

The antithesis between condemnatory "law" and life-bringing "gospel," then, exists between "gospel" (whether defined narrowly or broadly) and "the bare law," understood in what Calvin terms "a narrow sense." The antithesis does not lie between "gospel" and the law understood as "the covenant of free adoption."[92] The law understood as an evangelical covenant advocates salvation through Christ alone. But the law understood strictly in terms of bare commandment testifies that it offers eternal life only to those who perfectly keep its demands.[93]

Calvin elaborates on this distinction in his comments on Romans 10:5 ("For Moses writes about the righteousness that is based on the law, that the person who does the commandments shall live by them"):

> But we ought to understand the reason why Paul harmonizes the law with faith, and yet sets the righteousness of one in opposition

---

91. *Institutes*, 2.11.7.
92. *Institutes*, 2.7.2.
93. *Comm.*, on Lev. 18:5, in *Comm.*, 3:204–5.

to that of the other:—The law has a twofold meaning; it sometimes includes the whole of what has been taught by Moses, and sometimes that part only which was peculiar to his ministration, which consisted of precepts, rewards, and punishments.[94]

Moses, Calvin argues, has a twofold office. His "own and peculiar office" is to set forth "the real righteousness of works."[95] It is to this office that Paul makes reference in Romans 10:5. This specific office, however, is not "the whole office of Moses," for his "common office [was] to teach the people the true rule of religion." In this capacity, he was "a preacher of the gospel; which office he faithfully performed, as it appears from many passages."[96]

Interestingly, Calvin does not restrict the exercise of Moses's "peculiar office" to the Israelites. There is a sense in which all human beings, Jew and Gentile, stand under this aspect of Moses's ministry. Calvin explicitly states that the law, so defined, condemns all people. Commenting on Galatians 3:10 (cf. Deut. 27:26), Calvin observes that "the law holds *all living men* under its curse; and from the law, therefore, it is in vain to expect a blessing." He adds, "The sentence of the law is, that all who have transgressed any part of the law are cursed. Let us now see if there be *any living man* who fulfils the law."[97] Because all stand accursed by the law, we can be delivered only by the laying of "our curse" on Christ.[98]

How can the Mosaic legislation, given to Israel at Sinai, condemn all men? In a sermon on Galatians 3:11–14, Calvin claims that the law of which Moses is minister and that condemns all men is the moral law:

It is told us here [Gal. 3:11–14], that the righteousness of the law is the fulfilling of God's commandments. And hereby it might seem to us that the doctrine of the law were sufficient to save us, forasmuch as God having rehearsed the ten commandments that are contained in the law, hath finally told us that that is the thing

---

94. *Comm.*, on Rom. 10:5. For the same distinction, see *Comm.*, on Ex. 19:1.
95. *Comm.*, on Rom. 10:5.
96. *Comm.*, on Rom. 10:5.
97. *Comm.*, on Gal. 3:10, italics added.
98. *Comm.*, on Gal. 3:13.

whereby we should live, the thing whereby we should direct our life, the infallible rule, and that we must not seek any other perfection of righteousness than that.[99]

That Calvin understands the "law" that condemns all people universally to be the moral law explains how it is that he can elsewhere say, "The Old [Testament] brings death, for it can but envelop the whole human race in a curse."[100] It is as the moral law, or the natural law promulgated, condemns humanity that Calvin can say that Moses and the Mosaic law bring death and condemnation to all people.

It is here that we see in Calvin's thought a conscious intersection of the covenant of works and the Mosaic covenant.[101] Calvin affirms that the Mosaic covenant is an administration of the single, postlapsarian covenant of grace. It is essentially an evangelical covenant. The Mosaic covenant, stripped down to "bare law," gives voice to the covenant of works. It does so by articulating the suspension of eternal life upon perfect obedience to the commandments of the moral law. In so doing, it pronounces condemnation on every fallen son of Adam. To those who look to Moses for salvation by the Mosaic precepts, only condemnation awaits. Those, however, who heed "the whole of what was taught by Moses" will be directed to Christ and to his righteousness for salvation.

The Law and the New Covenant

The hallmark of the new covenant is that in it, Christ, the substance of Old Testament shadows, is now revealed.[102] New covenant

---

99. John Calvin, *Sermons on Galatians* (1574; repr., Audubon, NJ: Old Paths, 1995), 378.

100. *Institutes*, 2.11.8.

101. This observation is broached but not fully articulated in Lillback, "Ursinus' Development," 282–83. For later Reformed articulations of the relationship between the covenant of works and the Mosaic covenant, see Heinrich Heppe, *Reformed Dogmatics Set Out and Illustrated from the Sources*, rev. and ed. Ernst Bizer, trans. G. T. Thomson (1950; repr., Grand Rapids, MI: Baker, 1978), 288–89; Anthony Burgess, *Vindiciae Legis: Or, A Vindication of the Morall Law and the Covenants, from the Errours of Papists, Arminians, Socinians, and more especially, Antinomians. In XXX. Lectures, preached at Laurence-Jury, London*, 2nd ed. (London, 1647); Francis Turretin, *Institutes of Elenctic Theology*, trans. George Musgrave Giger, ed. James T. Dennison Jr. (Phillipsburg, NJ: P&R, 1992–1997), 2:267 (12.12.18); Mark W. Karlberg, "Reformed Interpretation of the Mosaic Covenant," *WTJ* 43, no. 1 (1980): 1–57. For an exegetical treatment of this relationship, see Guy Prentiss Waters, "Romans 10:5 and the Covenant of Works?," in *The Law Is Not of Faith*, ed. Bryan D. Estelle, J. V. Fesko, and David VanDrunen (Phillipsburg, NJ: P&R, 2009), 210–39.

102. *Institutes*, 2.11.4.

revelation possesses a clarity absent in old covenant revelation.[103] It is therefore not surprising, Calvin reasons, to witness changes to the Mosaic legislation prompted by this momentous redemptive-historical transition.

Two changes merit discussion. Calvin, we have seen, understands the Mosaic law to admit of a threefold distinction: moral, civil, and ceremonial. The new covenant entails the abrogation of the ceremonial laws. These "shadows whose substance exists for us in Christ" have now passed because Christ "has already plainly revealed himself."[104] Christ's abrogation of the ceremonial laws does not mean, however, that he has "deprived them of anything of their sanctity; rather, he has approved and honored" them.[105] These laws, in other words, have fulfilled their divine purpose and have been honorably discharged from service to the people of God.

The new covenant also entails the passing of the Mosaic judicial code. Calvin not only states this doctrine as fact[106] but also supplies a rationale for the judicial law's abrogation. Under the old covenant, the covenant of grace was primarily confined within the nation of Israel. Referencing Ephesians 2:14–17; Galatians 3:28; 6:15; and other passages, Calvin argues that the new covenant extends to the ends of the earth.[107] The Mosaic judicial laws, however, were peculiar to Israel. God intentionally tailored the Mosaic legislation for Israel's "safekeeping, defense, and protection." They were "never enacted for us." Judicial laws that better suit the "condition of times [and] place" of particular nations should be adopted.[108]

One change that the transition from the old covenant to the new covenant does not entail is the abrogation of the moral law as a rule of life. This is evident from Calvin's statements on the nature of the moral law. Since the moral law is "the true and eternal rule of righteousness, prescribed for men of all nations and times,"[109] it could no sooner be abrogated than men and women could cease to be.

---

103. *Institutes*, 2.9.1.
104. *Institutes*, 2.7.16.
105. *Institutes*, 2.7.16.
106. See n42 above.
107. *Institutes*, 2.11.11.
108. *Institutes*, 4.20.16.
109. *Institutes*, 4.20.15.

While the moral law can never be abrogated, the curse that is attached to breaking it has been abrogated in Christ. Each believer in every age, justified because of the perfect righteousness of Christ, is freed from the curse of the law.[110] This is what Paul is saying in Romans 7:6 ("But now we are released from the law, having died to that which held us captive, so that we serve in the new way of the Spirit and not in the old way of the written code"). Calvin reminds those who have been delivered from the law's curse that we must "always . . . receive [the law] with the same veneration and obedience," since "no part of the authority of the law is withdrawn."[111]

The new covenant has no superadded obligation to the moral law. The moral law is "the perfect teaching of righteousness" and therefore has "a perpetual validity."[112] Christ, far from being "another Moses, suppl[ying] what was lacking in the Mosaic law," or "add[ing] to the law," simply "restored [the law] to its integrity."[113] The church, moreover, has no legislative authority and may not therefore "lawfully bind consciences by its laws."[114]

The new covenant believer, in company with believers in all ages, continues to relate to the moral law in one of three ways. These are the celebrated "three uses" of the law, the first two of which apply to all human beings alike.[115] Calvin likens the "first use" of the law to a "mirror."[116] It shows people "God's righteousness, that is, the righteousness alone acceptable to God. [It] warns, informs, convicts, and lastly condemns, every man of his own unrighteousness."[117] Since sin remains in every believer, this use of the law applies to believers as well as to the reprobate.[118] Citing Augustine, Calvin stresses that the aim of this use for the believer is to "convict [him] of his infirmity and move him to call upon the remedy of grace which is in Christ."[119]

---

110. *Institutes*, 2.7.14.
111. *Institutes*, 2.7.15.
112. *Institutes*, 2.8.5.
113. *Institutes*, 2.8.7.
114. *Institutes*, 4.10.1.
115. *Institutes*, 2.7.6–13. The first use is discussed in *Institutes*, 2.7.6–9; the second use in *Institutes*, 2.7.10–11; the third use in *Institutes*, 2.7.12–13.
116. *Institutes*, 2.7.7.
117. *Institutes*, 2.7.6.
118. *Institutes*, 2.7.8.
119. *Institutes*, 2.7.9, citing a letter from Augustine to Asellicus; cf. Letter 196.2.6, in *Saint Augustine Letters*, trans. Wilfrid Parsons, FC 30 (New York: Fathers of the Church, 1955), 336. Compare Calvin's comments in "The Use of the Law."

The aim of this use for the reprobate is to leave him inexcusable in the sense of his sin.[120]

The second use of the law applies particularly to the unregenerate. The law "by fear of punishment restrains certain men who are untouched by any care for what is just and right unless compelled by hearing the dire threats in the law."[121] This restraint is simply that—restraint from doing what one would otherwise do. The unregenerate person does not refrain from vice because of a love of virtue but because of a fear of punishment. This use is valuable for civil order. God has also used this restraining work of the law in the preregenerate experience of his people. The result is that "when they are called, they are not utterly untutored and uninitiated in discipline as if it were something unknown."[122]

The third and "principal" use of the law is unique to believers. Enabled by the Spirit to desire to obey God, the law shows them "the nature of the Lord's will to which they aspire."[123] Furthermore, the law itself stirs up the believer to renewed and continued obedience. It is the master's "whip" to an intransigent beast of burden. Even so, the "accompanying promise of grace" ensures that the otherwise "bitter" law is "sweet" to the believer.[124] The law remains the standard of the believer's conduct "throughout [his] life."[125] The law sets forth nothing less than the perfection for which the believer daily strives but never, in this life, attains. Believers have the assurance, however, that when the "course" of our life has been "run," "the Lord will grant us to attain that goal to which our efforts now press forward from afar."[126] The believer's desire for moral perfection, never realized in this life, will be granted in heaven.

Conclusions

Let us conclude our discussion of Calvin's treatment of the law by considering three ways in which Calvin's understanding of the place of the law in redemptive history speaks to the church today. First, Calvin

---

120. *Institutes*, 2.7.9.
121. *Institutes*, 2.7.10.
122. *Institutes*, 2.7.10. See also *Institutes*, 2.7.11.
123. *Institutes*, 2.7.12.
124. *Institutes*, 2.7.12.
125. *Institutes*, 2.7.13.
126. *Institutes*, 2.7.13.

helps us read the Old Testament with spiritual profit. The ceremonial laws of the Old Testament pointed Israel to the Christ who was to come. They "have been abrogated not in effect but only in use."[127] Although the church no longer observes these laws, our reading of them continues to point us to the Christ who has come in the fullness of time. The Abrahamic and the Mosaic covenants, moreover, are covenants of promise. They proclaim the same redemptive mercies contained in the new covenant. The church must therefore read, properly interpret, meditate on, and apply the books of the Old Testament. It is inexcusable for any Christian to be deprived of the spiritual treasures that God has given his people in the Old Testament.

Second, Calvin has helped us respond thoughtfully to the antinomianism prevalent within the church today. Antinomianism claims that the Christian is not obligated to observe the law of God as a rule of life. Calvin reminds us that every human being, by virtue of being a human being, is obligated to keep the rule of righteousness that his Creator has engraved on his heart and has formally promulgated in the Decalogue. Sin in no way alters this obligation to keep the moral law. Redemption, far from weakening the ties of a person's existing obligation to God, rather strengthens them. Calvin is clear that one's obedience to the law in no way contributes to the ground of a person's justification. The work of Christ alone grounds one's justification. Calvin insists, however, that the justified person necessarily obeys the commandments of God.

Third, Calvin points us to the incomparable privileges and advantages that belong to the new covenant believer. God has revealed himself fully and most clearly in the new covenant. The bondage of the old covenant era has yielded to the freedom of the new covenant. The mercies of God now extend beyond the boundaries of old covenant Israel to the very ends of the earth. Furthermore, "today the grace of which [the prophets] bore witness is put before our eyes. They had but a slight taste of it; we can more richly enjoy it."[128] One cannot help but recall our Lord's admonition—to whom much is given, much is expected (Luke 12:48). What then is expected of us? Calvin points us

---

127. *Institutes*, 2.7.16.
128. *Institutes*, 2.9.1.

to the law of God—that we might be humbled in the sense of our sin and emptiness; that we might behold the majesty and perfection of the God who has made us, sustains us, and has redeemed us; and that we might gratefully and joyfully respond in the worship and service that God has prescribed in his holy commandments.[129]

---

129. *Institutes*, 2.8.1.

12

The Person and Work of Christ

Paul Wells

Whatever has been consecrated through the Mediator is pleasing to God.

Apart from the Mediator, God never showed favor toward the ancient people, nor ever gave hope of grace to them. . . . God cannot without the Mediator be propitious toward the human race.

—John Calvin, *Institutes of the Christian Religion*

Calvin's Christology[1]

Perhaps there is no better way to get a taste of John Calvin on the work of Christ than to compare the structure of Thomas Aquinas's *Summa Theologiae* and Calvin's *Institutes of the Christian Religion*. You have to dig deep into Aquinas to turn up Christology, but in

---

1. Portions of this chapter are adapted from Paul Wells, "John Calvin's *Munus Triplex*: A Hermeneutic of Salvation History: Alternative to 'Wandering in Uncertain and Stormy Paths,'" in *Reading and Listening: Meeting One God in Many Texts: Festschrift for Eric Peels on the Occasion of His 25th Jubilee as Professor of Old Testament Studies*, ed. Jaap Dekker and Gert Kwakkel, Amsterdamse Cahiers voor Exegese van de Bijbel en zijn Tradities, Supplement Series 16 (Bergambacht, the Netherlands: 2VM, 2018), 275–83. Used by permission of the editors.

Calvin there is no need for a machete to find it—it stands out in a pivotal place in the second book of Calvin's catechetical exposition.[2]

In spite of this prominence, Calvin's doctrine of the work of Christ has not always been given the place of honor it merits in the context of his theology or with regard to its originality and influence.[3] In popular expositions its importance tends to be eclipsed by interest in predestination, a fact noted by Wilhelm Niesel decades ago.[4] Just as strictness and Puritanism are synonymous in the popular imagination, so also are predestination and Calvin, with negative connotations attached in both cases.

The present chapter seeks to illustrate the centrality of the work of Christ in Calvin's thought and also the inventive contributions he made to Christology. The Genevan Reformer presents, both in the *Institutes* and in his commentaries, a theological perspective that hinges on mediation and Christ as mediator, not only in the incarnation but also with a much broader perspective.[5]

Mediation implies a dialectic fundamental to all that can be said about the relation between God and creation, including human beings. The position and act of mediation assumed by Christ is focused in his work as it relates to God and to man and creation, and also as it involves the person of Christ himself. It is set in a historical perspective—eternal, past, present, and future—that is appropriate to the biblical witness: "There is one mediator between God and men, the man Christ Jesus" (1 Tim. 2:5), and "Jesus Christ is the same yesterday and today and forever" (Heb. 13:8). Mediation finds expression in the incarnation, the progression from suffering to exaltation, and the fulfillment of the divine promises, which because of the success of the work of the mediator is as broad as the cosmos itself. The three

2. Thomas Aquinas, *Summa Theologica*, vol. 2 (New York: Benziger Brothers, 1947), 3a.1–59. This is not to deny possible influences of Aquinas on Calvin. See Arvin Vos, *Aquinas, Calvin and Contemporary Protestant Thought: A Critique of Protestant Views on the Thought of Thomas Aquinas* (Grand Rapids, MI: Eerdmans, 1985); Richard A. Muller, *The Unaccommodated Calvin: Studies in the Foundation of a Theological Tradition*, OSHT (Oxford: Oxford University Press, 2000), chap. 3.

3. In some recent presentations of Calvin's life and work, the references to his Christology are hardly satisfying. See, for example, William J. Bouwsma, *John Calvin: A Sixteenth-Century Portrait* (New York: Oxford University Press, 1988); Bernard Cottret, *Calvin: Biographie* (Paris: J. C. Lattès, 1995).

4. Wilhelm Niesel, *The Theology of Calvin*, trans. Harold Knight, LEH (1956; repr., Grand Rapids, MI: Eerdmans, 1980), 159.

5. Hendrik Schroten, *Christus, de Middelaar, bij Calvijn* (Utrecht: P. den Boer, 1948).

offices of Christ as prophet, priest, and king provide a hermeneutical key to the interpretation of redemption. Mediation has a triple finality: reconciliation, Christ for us; union with Christ, Christ in us; and the promise of new creation, Christ with us eternally. As such, mediation is an aspect of the representative covenant headship of Christ.[6]

God and Man

The Reformation bears witness to a recentering of Christian theology on Christ and the incarnation in the sixteenth century, which in turn implies a revision of the concept of mediation. This affected not only the Protestant churches and their view of *solus Christus* but also Roman Catholicism and the subsequent development of the role of the church and its sacraments as a bodily continuation of the mediation of Christ.[7] Calvin's placing of Christ as mediator implies no such linear extension but is grounded in a vertical contrast between God and the cosmos. His doctrine of the work of Christ is best understood against a theocentric backdrop. As François Wendel states,

> Calvin places all his theology under the sign of what was one of the essential principles of the Reform: the absolute transcendence of God and his total "otherness" in relation to man. No theology is Christian and in conformity with the Scriptures but in the degree to which it respects the infinite distance separating God from his creature and gives up all confusion, all "mixing" that might tend to efface the radical distinction between the Divine and the human. Above all, God and man must again be seen in their rightful places. That is the idea that dominates the whole of Calvin's theological exposition, and underlies the majority of his controversies.[8]

Quite apart from humanity's fallen nature, an irreducible space between God and man limits any human access to the divine and presents

---

6. Robert Letham, *Union with Christ: In Scripture, History, and Theology* (Phillipsburg, NJ: P&R, 2011), 57–84; Paul Wells, "Calvin and Union with Christ: The Heart of Christian Doctrine," in *Calvin: Theologian and Reformer*, ed. Joel R. Beeke and Garry J. Williams (Grand Rapids, MI: Reformed Heritage Books, 2010), 65–88.

7. Philippe Denis, *Le Christ étendard: L'Homme-Dieu au temps des réformes (1500–1565)* (Paris: Editions du Cerf, 1987).

8. François Wendel, *Calvin: Origins and Development of His Religious Thought*, trans. Philip Mairet (London: Collins, 1965), 151.

an insurmountable barrier to any imagined contiguity between them. Man is radically subordinate to God, and theology can never forget the reality of this situation.[9] Creation, the covenant, redemption, and eschatology, together with their specific orders, express the difference between God and all else and institutionalize the primacy of God. It is into the distance between the "otherness" of the transcendent God and his creatures that mediation is introduced as a *sine qua non* for contact between them.

Mediation is therefore a key concept in Calvin's theology, placing all reality under the sign of accommodation and divine grace.[10] God "must descend far beneath his loftiness" as "the situation would surely have been hopeless had the very majesty of God not descended to us, since it was not in our power to ascend to him."[11] In addition, continues Calvin, "Even if man had remained free from all stain, his condition would have been too lowly for him to reach God without a Mediator."[12]

The distance between God and man not only implies the necessity of a mediator but also has profound implications for orthodox Christology. The beautiful chapter 12 of book 2 of the *Institutes* says that we need not be troubled about where to find the mediator, for Christ became man to exercise this function, and so he was near to us, "indeed touches us, since he is our flesh."[13] Since we could never behold God in the splendor of his majesty, God takes on humanity, makes himself small, so we can have access to him: "This self-mortification of the divine means a concealment of His revelation."[14] Yet the mediator was not only true man but also true God: "It was his task to swallow up death. Who but the Life could do this? It was his task to conquer sin. Who but very Righteousness could do this? . . . Our most merciful God, when he willed that we be redeemed made himself our Redeemer in the person of his only-begotten Son."[15]

9. Alexandre Ganoczy, *Calvin, théologien de l'Eglise et du ministère* (Paris: Editions du Cerf, 1964), 75.

10. Pierre Gisel, *Le Christ de Calvin*, CJJC 44 (Paris: Desclée, 1990), 29–37, 142, 151.

11. *Institutes*, 1.13.1.

12. *Institutes*, 2.12.1. On accommodation, see Paul Helm, *John Calvin's Ideas* (Oxford: Oxford University Press, 2004), chap. 7.

13. *Institutes*, 2.12.1.

14. Niesel, *Theology of Calvin*, 113.

15. *Institutes*, 2.12.2.

In affirming that both God and man "reside" in the person of Christ, Calvin's reasons are primarily exegetical; however, he is also motivated by theological considerations, namely, the Chalcedonian tradition. In the person of Christ there is no "mixing" of the divine and human natures. Both natures exist in the one person and yet without any fusion of the divine and human.[16] For this reason it is not possible to speak of the "nature" of Jesus Christ in the singular, which would imply confusion of the divine and human, even though there are two distinct natures in one person.[17] "Mixing" the natures would be confusing heaven and earth, and the result would be an idol or a monster.

Each nature is present, however, in unmodified form in the unity of the person. For this reason, in his debate with Francesco Stancaro about whether Christ as mediator acted in his complete person as the God-man and not only in his human nature, Calvin argued that both natures were involved in the act of mediation.[18] Calvin adopts in full the doctrine of the two natures of the mediator to illustrate how Christ satisfies the double condition of salvation by being at one and the same time the spotless Lamb of God and by being made sin for us.[19]

Calvin's interest in the two natures is not a formal one born out of a desire for harmony or symmetry in the person of the mediator. The natures are of complementary importance in light of the function Christ assumed. It is not the fact of humanity that interests Calvin as such but what it implies, because the true humanity of the mediator is humanity shared with us and involves the brotherhood of Christ. Only on the basis of shared humanity can we approach God. The humanity of the Son is therefore a requisite for fulfilling the office of mediator, not a mere appendix to divinity, even though the value of

---

16. Egbert Emmen, *De Christologie van Calvijn* (Amsterdam: H. J. Paris, 1935), remains one of the most complete treatments of Calvin's doctrine of the person of Christ, but it touches only briefly on Christ's work.

17. Gisel, *Le Christ*, 37–38. Thus Calvin's critique of Eutychianism. On Luther and Calvin and the "communication of idioms," see Wendel, *Calvin*, 221–22.

18. Joseph Tylenda, "Christ the Mediator: Calvin versus Stancaro," *CTJ* 7 (1972): 5–16; Tylenda, "The Controversy on Christ the Mediator: Calvin's Second Reply to Stancaro," *CTJ* 8 (1972): 131–57. See also Stephen Edmondson, *Calvin's Christology* (Cambridge: Cambridge University Press, 2004), chap. 1.

19. Wendel, *Calvin*, 215, 218.

Christ's human nature accrues from its unity with the divine: "The humanity of Christ is only of value as a result of the union with divine nature; it draws its worth from the fact that it is the humanity not of a man, but of the Mediator, in a word it is the humanity of God."[20] As such, Christ's humanity draws God closer to us, revealing love and compassion and providing us with a concrete pledge of salvation. As Calvin says,

> Relying on this pledge, we trust that we are sons of God, for God's natural Son fashioned for himself a body from our body, flesh from our flesh, bones from our bones that he might be one with us. He took our nature upon himself to impart to us what was his, and to become both Son of God and Son of man in common with us.[21]

Similarly, the famous doctrine known as the *extra calvinisticum*, or better, *catholicum*, does not betray the wandering of a speculative spirit, nor is it an invention of Calvin's.[22] It owes its importance to the context of mediation and thus underlines not only the unchangeability of God but also divine sovereignty in salvation. In his incarnation Jesus Christ is fully divine. None of his deity was laid aside when the Logos became flesh and was incarnate in Jesus and at the same time wholly outside him (*extra*). In the person of the mediator, the divine undergoes no mutation, and thus transcendence is included under the rubric of Christology, giving the history and acts of redemption divine weight. Divinity is not limited by, or dependent on, humanity in the least degree but dwells in it. Two passages of the *Institutes* are particularly well known in this respect:

> The Son of God descended from heaven in such a way that, without leaving heaven, he willed to be borne in the virgin's womb, to go about the earth, and to hang upon the cross; yet he continuously filled the world as he had done from the beginning![23]

---

20. Max Dominicé, *L'humanité de Jésus d'après Calvin* (Paris: Editions Je Sers, 1933), 48, trans. mine.

21. *Institutes*, 2.12.2.

22. On this subject, see in particular E. David Willis, *Calvin's Catholic Christology: The Function of the So-Called Extra Calvinisticum in Calvin's Theology*, SMRT 2 (Leiden: E. J. Brill, 1966), chap. 2; Heiko A. Oberman, "The 'Extra' Dimension in the Theology of Calvin," *JEH* 21, no. 1 (1970): 43–64. See also Helm, *Calvin's Ideas*, chap. 3; Edmondson, *Christology*, 210–15.

23. *Institutes*, 2.13.4. This passage appears only in the 1559 edition of the *Institutes*.

The very same Christ, who according to the flesh, dwelt as Son of man on earth, was God in heaven. In this manner, he is said to have descended to that place according to his divinity, not because divinity left heaven to hide itself in the prison house of the body, but because even though it filled all things, still in Christ's very humanity it dwelt bodily (Col. 2:9), that is, by nature, and in a certain ineffable way.[24]

Niesel has correctly pointed to the fact that the *extra calvinisticum* is not the most essential feature of Calvin's Christology, that it is referred to in few passages, and that its context is often polemical.[25] Its functional value, however, is significant in the context of mediation, as it underpins Calvin's teaching that God has revealed himself only in Christ and that God cannot be savingly known apart from the mediator. In the person of Jesus, we encounter the eternal God:

> The *extra-calvinisticum* emphasizes that the God at work in Jesus Christ is one and the same with the God who sustains and orders the universe. . . . Calvin is asserting that Christ is able to be God for us because he does not cease to be God over us in the incarnation and because the humanity of Christ never ceases to be our humanity in the movement of God towards us.[26]

To sum up, fundamental to all Calvin's thought is the sovereign difference of God, who stands over against all else. A mediator is necessary to bridge this gulf, and the true mediator is the one who incarnates the realities of divinity and humanity in unmodified fashion. Hence, the two natures of Christ are united in one person without change and without "mixing." The outcome of this unique mediation is salvation, which is at once a divine work and also appropriate to human responsibilities and needs.

The Mediator

The centrality of Christ and redemption in the context of the divine-human dialectic leads us to expect that this perspective is important

---

24. *Institutes*, 4.17.30. This passage, taken from the context of discussion on the Lord's Supper, is present in germ in the 1536 edition of the *Institutes*. See also *Institutes*, 2.14.2; *Comm.*, on John 3:13; Acts 20:28.
25. Niesel, *Theology of Calvin*, 119.
26. Willis, *Calvin's Catholic Christology*, 6–7.

for Calvin's theology as a whole. The distance between God and humanity, further aggravated by the enmity resulting from sin, is the situation into which the mediator steps, and his work is all-important. Richard Muller goes as far as to suggest that "the function of mediation becomes determinative, and the person of Christ must be considered in and through his office."[27] Three points in particular can be considered here: the person of the mediator, the primacy of his work, and the relation to God the Father.

It is in the incarnation that the mediator is known, and in his person the freely given love of God and his grace are expressed. The ground of salvation is the immense love of God toward sinners expressed in the work of Christ as a whole. God "did not spare his own Son" (Rom. 8:32). Commenting on Matthew 3:17, "This is my beloved Son, with whom I am well pleased," Calvin says,

> Christ was presented to us by the Father with this proclamation, in His coming forth to fulfill His task of Mediator, that we might rely on this pledge of our adoption and without fear call God Himself our Father. The title of Son truly and by nature belongs to Christ alone, yet He was revealed as Son of God in our flesh, that He who alone claimed Him as Father by right, could win Him for us also. So God, in introducing our Mediator with words that praise him as the Son, declares Himself to be a Father to us all. This is exactly the aim of the word *beloved*, for as in ourselves we are hateful to God, His fatherly love must flow to us in Christ.[28]

Christ "comes forth" from the Father; he does so as the one who alone bears the name of the Son. He is revealed as the Son of God in his humanity, and through him, as the mediator, the love of God flows out to us. This formulation is striking because of its exclusiveness, a reason why it would be offensive to many people, particularly in our day. If God is the only Father, then Christ is the only Son in whose manifestation the unique love of God is to be found. In him alone, as

27. Richard A. Muller, *Christ and the Decree: Christology and Predestination in Reformed Theology from Calvin to Perkins*, SHT 2 (Durham, NC: Labyrinth, 1984), 28.

28. *Comm.*, on Matt. 3:17; quoted in Robert A. Peterson, *Calvin and the Atonement* (Fearn, Ross-shire, Scotland: Mentor, 1999), 17.

mediator, the love of God is expressed, and through him it "flows to us." This amounts to saying, as in Peter's apostolic proclamation, that "there is salvation in no one else, for there is no other name under heaven given among men by which we must be saved" (Acts 4:12).

God has come in the flesh in the person of Christ. Not only does this reveal the eternal divinity of the Son, but also, for Calvin, "by saying that Christ came we must note the cause of his coming; for the Father did not send Him for nothing. Christ's office and power depend on this."[29] It is by assuming a human nature in the incarnation that Christ carries out the office of mediator, and through it we are led into a relation with his divinity and thereby with the Father.[30] So "whoever does not know the office of Jesus Christ, can never trust in God, nor make prayers and supplications: he will be always in anxiety and doubt and dissimulation. Unless faith comes and shows us the way, it is certain (I say) that we shall never have access to God."[31]

For Calvin, Christ as mediator is more than an intermediary or a go-between, a third person standing between God and man, like a conciliator called in to negotiate a settlement between two parties. He is mediator in a special sense in that he has a part in God and a part in man in the incarnation because of the divine plan of salvation. The God-man is what Christ is in himself as a person. For this reason, he is what he does, and he does what he is. As Robert Peterson observes, "Calvin's favorite way of saying 'the person and work of Christ' is simply to speak of the 'Mediator.'"[32]

A good deal has been made recently of the primacy of the work of the mediator in Calvin, as over against the person, and this sometimes goes together with an appreciation of the rhetorical, narratival, or dramatic nature of Calvin's presentation.[33] This is said to be one of the innovative aspects of Calvin's Christology, and there is a large

---

29. *Comm.*, on 1 John 4:2. Cf. Edmondson, *Christology*, chap. 6, esp. 186–93, on "persona."

30. On Christ as mediator in general, see Emil Brunner, *The Mediator: A Study of the Central Doctrine of the Christian Faith*, trans. Olive Wyon (London: Lutterworth, 1934); T. F. Torrance, *The Mediation of Christ*, rev. ed. (Edinburgh: T&T Clark, 1992); Peter Lewis, *The Glory of Christ* (Carlisle: Paternoster, 1992), chap. 15; Paul Wells, *Cross Words: The Biblical Doctrine of the Atonement* (Fearn, Ross-shire, Scotland: Christian Focus, 2006), chap. 13.

31. Calvin, "Sermon on Luke 2:9–14," in T. H. L. Parker, *The Oracles of God: An Introduction to the Preaching of John Calvin*, LEH (London: Lutterworth, 1947), 150.

32. Peterson, *Atonement*, 42.

33. Edmondson, *Christology*, 1–14; Gisel, *Le Christ*, 27–28. Cf. Serene Jones, *Calvin and the Rhetoric of Piety* (Louisville: Westminster John Knox, 1995), chap 1; Olivier Millet, *Calvin et la*

element of truth to it. It can hardly be gainsaid that Calvin's thought is a form of personalism rather than the metaphysical approach exemplified by some of his scholastic predecessors. It is also obvious from what we have already said, however, that person and work are complementary. In the *Institutes*, discussion of Christ's person (2.12–14) directly precedes the work (2.15–17), yet even where Calvin presents the person, the work is never far away.[34] Christ in person is the mediator, and mediation is an act or operation that embodies an economy of accommodation or divine condescension. Recent commentators, such as Stephen Edmondson, for example, consider that such an approach is justified by the character of Scripture itself, which presents the economy of divine salvation in the form of a dynamic narrative, far removed from concerns about God's essence.[35]

Person and office are therefore two sides of the same coin. The *persona* of Christ describes the role or function he assumes in the divine economy. Calvin says that Christ speaks "in the *persona* of Mediator or minister when he says he teaches only what he has received from the Father."[36] The person of Christ is actively defined, and the action of Christ is personally defined. This implies that in the economy of redemption (though *not* in the eternal ontology of the Trinity), Christ is subordinate to the Father. Calvin writes,

> As long as Christ sustains the role of mediator, he does not hesitate to submit Himself to the Father. He does this not because his divinity had lost its rank when he was clothed in the flesh but because he could not in any other way interpose himself as intermediary between us and the Father without the Father's glory, in the present dispensation, becoming clearly visible in the person of the mediator.[37]

Why is Christ economically (though not eternally) subordinate as mediator, and why must the glory be hidden? Without doubt, it is because

---

dynamique de la parole: Étude de rhétoriqe réformée, BLR, ser. 3, no. 28 (Paris: Librairie Honoré Champion, 1992).

34. Muller maintains the priority of the work of Christ. Calvin speaks about Christ's work in the *Institutes* before the person, in connection with the revelation of the Old Testament. *Christ and the Decree*, 27–35.

35. Edmondson, *Christology*, 33–37.

36. *Comm.*, on John 17:8.

37. Quoted in Tylenda, "Christ the Mediator," 15.

we could not behold his glory face-to-face and survive. Christ's economic submission to the Father is in line with the function of his person and office as the means of bringing us back to God. Commenting on "the man Christ Jesus" as mediator in 1 Timothy 2:5, Calvin says that if we are overawed by the idea of God, we ought to remember that Christ "invites us as a man and with such goodness, takes us by the hand as it were, in order to render the Father favorable to us. . . . This is the only key that opens the door to the heavenly kingdom, by which we can appear before the divine majesty with full assurance."[38]

Finally, the fear and anxiety we experience with regard to God as sinners requires the intervention of the mediator and the manifestation of the love of the Father that we need because of our infirmity and our guilt. Calvin begins his exposition of the office of Christ in the *Institutes* with the statement that "since our iniquities, like a cloud cast between us and him had completely estranged us from the Kingdom of Heaven," "our most merciful Father decreed what was best for us."[39] Sin, for Calvin, has a double consequence. Man is an object of horror for God, but also man holds God in horror, hates him, and consequently tries to flee from him. The divine answer to this situation is not a reaction but an action rooted in the divine decree. God's presence mediated in the lowliness of the incarnation takes on a form that we need not fear. By descending to our level, Christ short-circuits our desire to escape from the presence of God and reveals his grace and love toward us as human beings and sinners:

> God, who is the highest righteousness, cannot love the unrighteousness that he sees in us all. All of us have in ourselves something deserving of God's hatred. . . . However much we have brought death upon ourselves, yet he has created us unto life. Thus he is moved by pure and freely given love of us to receive us into grace. . . . Therefore by his love God the Father goes before and anticipates our reconciliation in Christ. Indeed, "because he first loved us" (1 John 4:19) he afterward reconciles us to himself. But until

---

38. John Calvin, *Commentaires de Jean Calvin sur le Nouveau Testament*, vol. 7, *Épîtres aux Thessaloniciens, à Timothée, Tite et Philémon* (Aix-en-Provence: Éditions Kerygma, 1991), 120, trans. mine.
39. *Institutes*, 2.12.1.

Christ succors us by his death, the unrighteousness that deserves God's indignation remains in us and is accursed and condemned before him. Hence we can be fully and firmly joined with God only when Christ joins us with him.[40]

This is then the reason why divinity clothes itself in humanity. Behind the incarnation stands the free electing love of God, and before Christ incarnate stands the reconciliation that is the final end of election, resulting from the work of the mediator.[41] This work unfolds itself in a historical economy, in a personal way through the acts of the incarnate one, and is expressed by the triple ministry of Christ as prophet, priest, and king.

The Economy of Mediation

In Calvin's view of the economy of mediation, even if the moment of the incarnation is decisive, it does not fall on the earth like a bolt from the blue. Mediation itself cannot be limited to the work of Christ on earth; Christ is mediator both before and after this time. Calvin's view of mediation is much broader and, one might even say, all-embracing. If it has a climactic point, it also has creational and historical precedents. Christ is mediator as the covenant head of creation, and this broader perspective is legitimate, in Calvin's view, in light of the biblical witness. This question is theologically complex; Calvin is discreet and here, as elsewhere, resists the temptation to say more than Scripture. We shall limit ourselves to two aspects of the economy of mediation: the creation and the covenant history with its fulfillment in the coming of Christ.

Could any of Adam's children be the mediator? No, because like their father, they are terrified by the sight of God. Could an angel then? No, replies Calvin, for "they also had need of a head, through whose bond they might cling firmly and undividedly to their God."[42] As head of the angels, which are created beings, Christ is seen to be the head and

---

40. *Institutes*, 2.16.3.
41. See Peterson, *Atonement*, chap. 1.
42. *Institutes*, 2.12.1. In his chapter on God the Creator in the *Institutes*, Calvin includes a long section on angels. Their function is to lead us "by the hand" to Christ and "keep us in the one Mediator, that we may wholly depend on him." *Institutes*, 1.14.12. See also *Comm.*, on Col. 1.17, where Calvin extends what is said of the angels to the whole creation.

mediator of all creation. In the Son we behold the "bond" tying the creation to God. All God's relations with created reality—past, present, and future—are grounded in Christ, the eternal Word and wisdom of God. God has no dealings with creation that do not pass through the Christ connection. This perspective is consistent with the Pauline presentation of the headship of Christ in Ephesians 1:22–23 and Colossians 1:15–18.

As a moment in God's plan, the incarnation points back to the fact that all created reality is tributary of a covenant economy in which Christ is the head. Creation is instituted as a divinely sanctioned reality under the auspices of the mediator. Ever antispeculative, Calvin says little about this. As the eternal Word, Christ, from "the beginning of creation . . . already truly was Mediator, for he always was Head of the Church, has primacy over the angels and was the firstborn of every creature."[43] What Herman Bavinck later affirmed would stand true for Calvin as well: "While the creation is a work of the whole Trinity, it cannot be denied that in Scripture it also stands in a peculiar relation to the Son. . . . Christ is not only the mediator of re-creation but also of creation."[44] Commenting on John 1:3, "All things were made by Him," Calvin says, "After having stated that the Word is God and of eternal essence, John displays His divinity by his works. . . . From the creation of the world, the Word was disclosed by an external act. And as previously the Word was incomprehensible in essence, His power was now made manifest by its effects."[45] As firstborn of creation, Christ is the "'mode of communication from which otherwise hidden source, the grace of God flowed to men'; he is a mid-point (*medium*) between the Father and creation; and as Head of the angels he maintains them under his command and unites them to God."[46] As the active presence in creation, the Word and wisdom of God sets the scene for subsequent

43. Calvin, quoted in Tylenda, "Christ the Mediator," 12. Cf. *Comm.*, on John 1:1, 25; *Comm.*, on Gen. 1:3.

44. Herman Bavinck, *Reformed Dogmatics*, vol. 2, *God and Creation*, ed. John Bolt, trans. John Vriend (Grand Rapids, MI: Baker Academic, 2004), 423.

45. John Calvin, *Commentaires de Jean Calvin sur le Nouveau Testament*, vol. 2, *Evangeli selon Saint Jean* (Aix-en-Provence: Éditions Kerygma, 1978), 15, trans. mine.

46. Tylenda, "Calvin's Second Reply," 147; Tylenda, "Christ the Mediator," 13, quoted by Edmondson, *Christology*, 30.

action as the Word revealed in the unfolding of divine revelation in covenantal history.[47]

The covenant history is played out against the backdrop of the Adamic drama, interpreted in an Augustinian perspective of original integrity, its loss and restoration through the mediator.[48] Where Adam failed in his task, a second Adam is called for to repair the fault. Calvin draws on the comparison made by the apostle Paul in Romans 5:12–19 to affirm that the righteousness and life lost in Adam are recovered only in Christ: "Here then is the relationship between the two: Adam implicating us in his ruin, destroyed us with himself; but Christ restores us to salvation by his grace."[49] Christ was promised "from the beginning to restore the fallen world and succor lost men."[50]

In view of this perspective, which is developed in a less systematic fashion than in subsequent Reformed theology,[51] the entire Old Testament history finds its unity in the promise of the covenant. The differences between the testaments are subordinate to a unity of substance that has a Christological focus via the promise of the Savior to come and its soteriological consequences. This is highlighted by the structure of the second book of the *Institutes* in the 1559 edition, "The Knowledge of God the Redeemer, First Disclosed to the Fathers under the Law, and Then to Us in the Gospel." Chapters 1–6 concern the obscuring of the image of God and the loss of knowledge through Adam's fall. Calvin's originality, over against Luther's dialectic of law and gospel, is seen in the introduction of the law in chapters 7–9, followed by the relationship between the two testaments in chapters 10–11. This indicates the preparatory nature of the Old Testament revelation, accomplished in Christ, who is presented as the mediator

---

47. In *Calvin's Doctrine of the Work of Christ* (London: James Clark, 1956), John F. Jansen argues at length in favor of the two offices of Christ, priest and king, as constituting the essence of Calvin's teaching on the ministry of the mediator. He argues that the prophetic office, added in the final version of the *Institutes* to the two others, is a dogmatic imposition that Calvin's exegesis cannot justify. Rather, it is a retrogression on Calvin's part, motivated perhaps by his desire to bolster the teaching office in the Reformed churches. Although the point would have to be argued at length, it appears to this writer that the function of the eternal Logos in creation, which is the substantial foundation for all God's subsequent speaking, could provide adequate theological justification for Calvin's move, even if exegetically this would be hard to demonstrate.

48. Gisel, *Le Christ*, chap. 1.

49. *Institutes*, 2.1.6.

50. *Institutes*, 2.12.4.

51. Muller, *Unaccommodated Calvin*, 152–57.

in chapter 12. Chapters 13–14 concern the incarnation and the two natures of Christ in one person. Chapter 15 provides a presentation of the fulfilled promise through the three offices of Christ as prophet, priest, and king and is followed by the nature of the redemption accomplished through the death, resurrection, and ascension of Christ in chapter 16. The conclusion in chapter 17 is that Christ has fully merited God's grace and salvation for us.

What is Calvin saying through this precise structuring of book 2? The structure of the whole presents one persuasive argument. On the one hand, looking forward, under the sign of promise, the covenant history tends toward eschatological fulfillment in the person of the mediator. From the perspective of the person of the mediator, looking backward, redemption is the reconciliation of creation and fallen humanity, and the mediation of Christ is written into the covenantal perspective that characterizes the relation of God and man in creation: "There is an intimate relationship between the economy and who Christ is: we can even say that Christ is the substance of the economy."[52] The history of the covenant flows through Abraham, Moses, and David to Christ to revive the fallen church and establish God's people; it is mediated by and in him through the giving of prophets, priests, and kings. An illustration: Calvin holds that Matthew 2:15 correctly interprets Hosea 11:1, "Out of Egypt I called my son," not as a prediction but because "Christ cannot be separated from his Church, as the body will be mutilated and imperfect without a head. Whatever then happened formerly in the Church, ought at length to be fulfilled in the head."[53] This case in point is the application of a general principle. The principle is that Christ is the mediator of the entire history of his people, as its head. The concept of mediation provides the fundamental perspective for a Christological interpretation of Scripture.[54]

To summarize, we can say that God has made one covenant with his people; that covenant is historically mediated by Christ in both testaments. As John Jansen states,

---

52. Edmondson, *Christology*, 40; cf. chap. 2, "Christ and the Covenant History."
53. *Comm.*, on Hos. 11:1.
54. See Jansen, *Calvin's Doctrine*, chap. 3, which provides an excellent development of this point.

This covenant may vary in its administration, but is substantially one in its gracious content. Both Old and New Testaments have the same three promises: eternal life, a covenant based on unmerited grace, and a knowledge and possession of Christ as the Mediator. Although the promises are the same, however, their administration is quite different, for the New Testament leaves the shadow and figures of the Old for the direct contemplation of God's grace through the gospel.[55]

Covenant Fulfillment in the Mediator

The covenant history finds its fulfillment and its substance in a person, Jesus Christ the mediator. In the incarnation the covenant presence of God reaches its full expression. Christ is revealed as the true image of God, the head over humanity, and the captain of salvation, themes that are recurrent in Calvin's presentation. In a debate with Andreas Osiander, Calvin says,

> I admit that Adam bore God's image, in so far as he was joined to God (which is the true and highest perfection of dignity). . . . Whatever excellence was engraved upon Adam derived from the fact that he approached the glory of the Creator through the only-begotten Son. . . . Adam was advanced to this degree of honor, thanks to the only-begotten Son. But I add: the Son was the common Head over angels and men.[56]

As the "residence" of God with man, the incarnation recapitulates the covenant institution and in the person of Christ reveals, as never before, the truth of the relationship between God and man through the work that he undertakes. The Word made flesh (John 1:14) "chose for himself the virgin's womb as a temple in which to dwell [and] he who was the Son of God became the Son of man."[57]

How are we to understand the fulfillment of the covenant in light of the divine plan? François Wendel raises the classic question whether Calvin's simultaneous affirmation of predestination and redemption by incarnation does not contain a contradiction. If God

---

55. Jansen, *Calvin's Doctrine*, 67–68. See also Wendel, *Calvin*, 109–10.
56. *Institutes*, 2.12.6.
57. *Institutes*, 2.14.1.

has decreed the salvation of some and the perdition of others, why should the incarnation be necessary to achieve a differentiation that already exists? Wendel refers to the German theologian Paul Jacobs' judgment: "The work of salvation is as unthinkable, apart from its relations with election as would be an election eternal in itself; the history of salvation unfolds itself in relation with election and completes the latter."[58] Calvin regards the problem from the standpoint of two orders, the divine and the human, orders that for us remain complementary but impossible to combine in a univocal statement. He says rather tersely, "As for God, his love was first in time and in order, but with regard to us, the beginning of the love of God toward us is at the sacrifice of Christ."[59]

It has been proposed that some headway can be made with this perennial question by considering the role of Christ as mediator, since in this function Christ is both the second person of the Trinity and the incarnate one. In the person of the mediator, both eternal election and historical accomplishment are expressed as complementary axes. Following Paul Jacobs and Wendel, Muller points out that Calvin in the *Institutes* begins his discussion of the office of mediator with specific reference to the divine decree.[60] That Christ is true God and true man stems "from a heavenly decree, on which men's salvation depended. Our most merciful Father decreed what was best for us."[61] This means, according to Muller, that Calvin sets forth Christ not as a simple enactor of the decree but as its author together with God the Father:

> The mediator reveals the truth of God because he himself is God. Christ witnesses faithfully to the election of all believers eternally in God since he himself is one with the Father who had chosen the elect in eternity. Yet as mediator he is designated to the work. As mediator Christ is subordinate to the decree while as Son of God he is one with the Father and in no way subordinate. The Son as

---

58. Wendel, *Calvin*, 229; quoting Paul Jacobs, *Prädestination und Verantwortlichkeit bei Calvin* (Neukirchen: Kreis Moers, 1937), 78–79.

59. *Comm.*, on 2 Cor. 5:19; quoted in Wendel, *Calvin*, 230.

60. Muller, *Christ and the Decree*, 28; cf. *Institutes*, 2.12.1. See especially chap. 2 for the whole of Muller's argument, which is highly attractive in spite of Edmondson's reservations. Edmondson, *Christology*, 147–51.

61. Muller, *Christ and the Decree*, 35.

God stands behind the decree while the Son as mediator is the executor of the decree.[62]

Calvin insists, then, on a primordial mediation of the Son, one that lies beyond the bounds of time and space and that expresses the eternal grace of God in election. The transcendent office is the register that precedes the incarnation and that the coming of the mediator brings to light. The incarnate Son in history is the personal concretization of an eternal act, in which salvation is made known through the historical process of suffering and exaltation, through the historical stages of the work of Christ from the birth to the ascension. In this context Calvin can speak of the merit of Christ in the fulfillment of the eternal plan of God. In reply to Laelius Socinus, and drawing on Augustine, Calvin asserts that "in discussing Christ's merit, we do not consider the beginning of merit to be in him, but we go back to God's ordinance, the first cause. For God solely of his own good pleasure appointed him Mediator to obtain salvation for us."[63]

In chapter 16, preceding this conclusion to book 2 of the *Institutes*, Calvin presents the Redeemer in his work of delivering us from the wrath of God. He narrates the sequence of condemnation under Pilate, crucifixion, death, and burial, and he comments at length on the descent into hell (following the Apostles' Creed) before speaking of Christ's resurrection, ascension, session at God's right hand, and coming in judgment. The historical mediation of Christ is therefore played out under the sign of obedience and fulfillment.

The movement of suffering to glory is traditional. Calvin portrays the work of the Son in two distinct moments or states.[64] The depth of suffering Christ knew, which lasted all his life but particularly marked its end,[65] stands in stark contrast not only to the eternal glory of the mediator but also to the subsequent enthronement. The resurrected

---

62. Muller, *Christ and the Decree*, 37–38. References are given to *Comm.*, on John 6:38; 17:6–8. Muller considers this interpretation to tally with the *extra calvinisticum*.

63. *Institutes*, 2.17.1.

64. That said, Muller seems right in affirming that the states of humiliation and exaltation are not "a specific doctrinal determination in the argument of the *Institutes*." *Christ and the Decree*, 32.

65. Heidelberg Catechism, q. 37.

and ascended glory is not simply sequential but is the consequence of the suffering and the success of the work recognized by the Father. The two states of suffering and glory in the fulfillment of the covenant underline not only the representative function of the work of Christ but also its eschatological orientation.

However, if the two states provide a fundamental structure for covenant fulfillment, the way they are construed by the Reformer shows some originality. Although he follows a historical sequence, it is not as though suffering and glory are two watertight compartments cut off from each other, precisely because of the intricate nature of the work and the complexity of the person of Christ. Calvin cannot forget that there are two natures residing in the person of the mediator. A careful reading of his commentary on Christ's self-humiliation in Philippians 2:7–9 shows that for Calvin, it is not simply a case of two successive states. The tension of the humiliation is all the more palpable because it coexists with the exalting of human nature through its union with the divine in the one person. Thus,

> Christ could not have renounced his divinity, but he held it hidden for some time so that it did not appear in the weakness of flesh. Thus he laid aside his glory before men, not by lessening it, but by concealing it. . . . The humiliation of the flesh was as a veil, hiding the divine majesty. . . . Christ revealed himself as a man before men. However, he was something other than a mere man, even though he was truly man.[66]

It would appear that, for all intents and purposes, there is already in the union of the natures in the one person of the mediator an elevation of the humanity of Christ in the context of his humbling, something that heightens the mystery of the incarnation and renders the doctrine of the two states more complex.[67]

---

66. John Calvin, *Commentaires de Jean Calvin sur le Nouveau Testament*, vol. 6, *Epîtres aux Galates, Ephésiens, Philippiens et Colossiens* (Aix-en-Provence: Éditions Kerygma, 1978), 270–71, trans. mine. For an ample documentation on this subject, see Gisel, *Le Christ*, 72–81. The motivations and content of Calvin's presentation are not to be equated with Karl Barth's dialectic, in which the Lord is servant and the servant is Lord. *Church Dogmatics*, vol. 4, *The Doctrine of Reconciliation*, pt. 1 (Edinburgh: T&T Clark, 1956), §59.

67. See Marvin P. Hoogland, *Calvin's Perspective on the Exaltation of Christ in Comparison with the Post-Reformation Doctrine of the Two States* (Kampen: J. H. Kok, 1966).

The preceding considerations are not without their import for the finality of the work of the mediator, redemption from sin through the death and resurrection of Christ. The obedience of Christ, "even unto death, yea, the death of the cross" (Phil. 2:8 ASV), is understood in terms of a logic of representation and substitution. Calvin says, "It was already a great humbling for the Lord to be made a servant. But he went even further: for even though he was immortal and Lord of life and death, he was all the same obedient to the Father to the point of enduring death."[68] The death of the cross is then the climax of a life of obedience, the obedience of the second Adam, who paid the penalty we deserved.

There is no one unified theology of the saving work of Christ in Calvin, who develops the meaning of the death of Christ in complementary and varied ways. Peterson proposes that Calvin presents six different biblical themes that contribute to his theology of atonement. Christ is the obedient second Adam, the victor, the legal substitute, our sacrifice, our merit, and our example.[69] Even though this may be the case, all the colors of atonement in the kaleidoscope of themes are not equally dominant. Against the background of the Anselmian tradition of satisfaction rendered to God, the notion of substitution, Christ in our place, is capital in Calvin's exposition.[70] Calvin, however, unlike Anselm, does not speak of penalty and satisfaction as alternatives, with Christ supposedly satisfying the divine honor. Satisfaction in Calvin refers to the paying of the debt owed to divine justice as a vicarious punishment, a fate Christ assumed on the cross.[71] A multitude of texts could be quoted. Calvin's summation in the *Institutes* (2.16.2) is classic, since it joins the sin of man, the obedience of Christ in assuming the consequences, and the resulting deliverance. To illustrate this approach, I have broken up the text into its constituent parts:

---

68. Calvin, *Commentaires*, 6:271, trans. mine.

69. An excellent introduction to the subject is found in Peterson, *Atonement*, chaps. 4–9.

70. Brunner indicates Calvin's adherence to Anselm's substitutionary doctrine in *Mediator*, 248–49, 458, 507. See also Paul van Buren, *Christ in Our Place: The Substitutionary Character of Calvin's Doctrine of Reconciliation* (Edinburgh: Oliver and Boyd, 1957).

71. Henri Blocher, "The Atonement in John Calvin's Theology," in *The Glory of the Atonement: Biblical, Historical and Practical Perspectives; Essays in Honor of Roger Nicole*, ed. Charles E. Hill and Frank A. James III (Downers Grove, IL: IVP Academic, 2004), 279–303. On 281–82, Blocher refers to Timothy George's enumeration of five original features of Calvin's view compared to Anselm. George, *The Theology of the Reformers* (Nashville: Broadman, 1988), 221–23.

[Someone] learns, as Scripture teaches,

that he was estranged from God through sin, is an heir of wrath, subject to the curse of eternal death, excluded from all hope of salvation, beyond every blessing of God, the slave to Satan, captive under the yoke of sin, destined finally for a dreadful destruction and already involved in it;

and that at this point Christ interceded as his advocate,

took upon himself and suffered the punishment that, from God's righteous judgment, threatened all sinners; that he purged with his blood those evils which had rendered sinners hateful to God; that by this expiation he made satisfaction and sacrificed duly to God the Father; that as intercessor, he has appeased God's wrath; that on this foundation rests the peace of God with men; that by this bond his benevolence is maintained toward them.

Will the man not then be even more moved by all these things that so vividly portray the greatness of the calamity from which he has been rescued?[72]

This fine expression of eloquence shows how Calvin teaches vicarious penal substitution through the cross of Christ.

In his section on the crucifixion, Calvin indicates the way the cross fulfills the sacrificial types of the Mosaic covenant. The blood of Christ, shed as sacrificial victim for our sins, is the pledge of the reality of our redemption:

We could not believe with assurance that Christ is our redemption, ransom and propitiation unless he had been a sacrificial victim. Blood is accordingly mentioned wherever Scripture discusses the mode of redemption. Yet Christ's shed blood served not only as a satisfaction, but also as a laver (Eph. 5:26; Titus 3:5; Rev. 1:5) to wash away our corruption.[73]

It could be said that the incarnation itself, Christ taking our flesh, is a primary form of substitution. The finality of substitution, however, lies

---

72. *Institutes*, 2.16.2, italics added.
73. *Institutes*, 2.16.6.

in the fact that Christ sheds blood to undergo punishment in the stead of sinners. "Our Lord," says Calvin, "came forth as true man and took the person and the name of Adam in order to take Adam's place in obeying the Father to present our flesh as the price of satisfaction to God's righteous judgment and, in the same flesh, to pay the penalty that we had deserved."[74] The incarnation and the death of Christ are complementary aspects of obedience rendered to God and issue in resurrection and new life, which are the result of the victory of Christ. Whenever we mention the death of Christ, Calvin says, we are to understand at the same time what belongs to the resurrection, "because the victory of our faith over death lies in his resurrection alone."[75]

Finally, the old question whether the atonement for Calvin is general or particular is of such complexity and has generated so much debate that it cannot be reasonably treated here.[76] A proposition regarding limited atonement in Calvin that bears consideration is Muller's brief comment in his book *Christ and the Decree*.[77] Much of the dispute can be laid to rest, claims Muller, by examining Calvin's language and recognizing that *atonement* is not Calvin's word. The Reformer uses the words *expiation* and *satisfaction* in an unlimited sense to portray the sufficiency of Christ's work but uses *reconciliation* and *redemption* (and *intercession*) in a limited sense for the efficacy of the benefits Christ bestows in the restoration and purchase of individuals. The latter sense is restricted to the elect. Muller comments that this "fits what is loosely called 'limited atonement' not only in Calvin's thought but also in later Reformed theology."[78]

The Hermeneutical Function of the Three Offices (the *Munus Triplex*)

"In Calvin's thought," Muller states, "the doctrine of the *munus triplex* becomes for the first time in the history of dogma a strict doctrinal category and a formula determinative of the shape of Christology."[79]

---

74. *Institutes*, 2.12.3.
75. *Institutes*, 2.16.13; cf. 3.25.3.
76. See especially Paul Helm, *Calvin and the Calvinists* (Edinburgh: Banner of Truth, 1982), which, although it is a reply to R. T. Kendall, *Calvinism and English Calvinism to 1649* (Oxford: Oxford University Press, 1979), nonetheless gives a good view of the contours of the terrain.
77. Muller, *Christ and the Decree*, 33–35.
78. Muller, *Christ and the Decree*, 34.
79. Muller, *Christ and the Decree*, 31.

In this light, it can be said to represent an innovative aspect in Calvin's Christology, particularly as it functions to bind together the person and the work of the mediator.

The threefold office of Christ is used by Calvin to explain the meaning of the saving activity of Christ.[80] As mediator between God and man, Christ embodies the messianic functions of prophet, priest, and king.[81] The offices of Christ, which give substance to understanding his person and work, have a long history in the Christian tradition.[82] In the *Institutes* of 1536, Calvin refers to the two traditional offices, those of priest and king, but later in the Geneva Catechism (1541) and the *Institutes* of 1545, the prophetic office appears, and in the final edition in 1559, it takes definitive form in Calvin's exposition of the messianic titles. The three-office Christology sets the scene for subsequent developments in Reformed theology as well as problems that arose through accentuating one of the offices over against the others.[83]

Calvin gives as title to book 2, chapter 15, of the *Institutes* "To Know the Purpose for Which Christ Was Sent by the Father, and What He Conferred upon Us, We Must Look above All at Three Things in Him: The Prophetic Office, Kingship, and Priesthood." The offices have a hermeneutic function as an aid in understanding why and wherefore Christ was sent and the dimensions of the salvation he accomplished through his work. They are a substantiation and an illustration of the unique work of the mediator. "Office" implies a representative capacity, understood here as a ministry, a charge, or a function into which Christ is officially inducted as mediator, with a dual reference to the Father and to humanity.[84] As such, the offices interpret the name of *Christ*, who, as mediator, is anointed in a messianic

---

80. See the useful monograph by Klauspeter Blaser, *Calvins Lehre von den drei Ämtern Christi* (Zürich: EVZ-Verlag, 1970); also Willis, *Calvin's Catholic Christology*, 78–79.

81. See n47 above. Space forbids that we enter into the debate concerning two versus three offices of Christ and its history. We refer the reader to the works of Jansen, Edmondson, and Peterson (esp. chap. 3 of his *Atonement*) cited earlier in the chapter; see also Heinrich Heppe, *Reformed Dogmatics Set Out and Illustrated from the Sources*, rev. and ed. Ernst Bizer, trans. G. T. Thompson (1950; repr., Grand Rapids, MI: Baker, 1978), chap. 18. My comments in this chapter concern mainly the *Institutes*.

82. Wendel traces it back to Eusebius (*Hist. eccl.* 1.3.9) and says that Calvin may have derived the idea from Martin Bucer's *Enarrationes in Evangelia* (1536). *Calvin*, 225.

83. Jansen, *Calvin's Doctrine*, 16–23. See also Bavinck, *Dogmatics*, 2:475–82; G. C. Berkouwer, *The Work of Christ*, trans. Cornelius Lambregtse (Grand Rapids, MI: Eerdmans, 1965), chap. 4.

84. Jansen, *Calvin's Doctrine*, 71–72.

capacity for his work: to proclaim divine truth as prophet, to intervene as priest, and to rule as king.

Calvin's definition of the offices has no frills, either in the Geneva Catechism or in the *Institutes*, and here, as elsewhere, brevity and clarity are the rule:

Prophet

He was the sovereign messenger and ambassador of God His Father, to give a full exposition of God's will toward the world and so put an end to all prophecies and revelations.[85]

The prophetic dignity in Christ leads us to know that in the sum of doctrine as he has given it to us all parts of perfect wisdom are contained.[86]

Priest

It is the office and prerogative of presenting Himself before God to obtain grace and favor, and appease his wrath in offering a sacrifice which is acceptable to him.[87]

As a pure and stainless Mediator he is by his holiness to reconcile us to God. . . . As priest Christ obtains God's favor for us and appeases his wrath. To perform this office Christ had to come forward with a sacrifice.[88]

King

[Kingship] is spiritual, and consists in the Word and Spirit of God and includes righteousness and life.[89]

It would be pointless to speak of this without first warning my readers that it is spiritual in nature. From this we infer its efficacy and benefit for us, as well as its whole force and eternity.[90]

When one studies the passages from which these excerpts are taken, the triple reference of the three offices emerges in greater detail. The

---

85. *Calvin's Geneva Catechism, 1541*, in *The School of Faith: The Catechisms of the Reformed Church*, trans. and ed. Thomas F. Torrance (London: James Clarke, 1959), 11 (answer 39).
86. *Institutes*, 2.15.2.
87. *Calvin's Geneva Catechism*, 11 (answer 38).
88. *Institutes*, 2.15.6.
89. *Calvin's Geneva Catechism*, 10 (answer 37).
90. *Institutes*, 2.15.3.

offices all concern the function of mediation; they refer primarily to God the Father; and they bring the benefits of salvation down to earth in terms of divine doctrine, redemption, and rule for "the gentle."

The root of the three-office doctrine is no doubt the eternal Sonship of the Word with the Father. The kingship of Christ has priority over the other offices.[91] As king, Christ implements his rule through the priestly office exercised at the cross, the empty tomb, and in the eternal intercession as great high priest. As prophet, the Son is not the bearer of the message of salvation but the Word made flesh in person, the truth-act of God as light coming into the world and as such communicating sovereignty and deliverance.

The three offices bind together the saving activity of God in the covenant by anticipation in the divine promise, by enactment in the person of the Son incarnate, and by eschatological announcement of the eternal reign of Christ. We will briefly consider these three dimensions of the *munus triplex*.

The eternal Word is the fullness and culmination of all revelation, and as such, there is nothing "before" the truth that he makes known in creation and grace: "We know that, inasmuch as He is the eternal Wisdom of God, He is the only fount of all doctrine and that all the prophets who have been from the beginning spoke by His Spirit."[92] The Son is behind the revelation of the Old Testament messengers, who anticipate the coming of the perfect teacher. The prophetic office in terms of anticipation is what confers on Scripture the structure of promise and fulfillment, the giving of the law in its preparatory function "until Christ," and the prophetic predictions concerning the future.[93] It operates in the establishment of the covenant as an implementation of divine kingship:

> God, by providing his people with an unbroken line of prophets, never left them without useful doctrine sufficient for salvation, yet the minds of the pious had always been imbued with the conviction that they were to hope for the full light of understanding only at the coming of the Messiah.[94]

---

91. Willem Adolph Visser 't Hooft, *The Kingship of Christ: An Introduction of Recent European Theology* (London: SCM, 1948).
92. *Comm.*, on John 14:24.
93. Blaser, *Calvins Lehre*, 27–34.
94. *Institutes*, 2.15.1.

Because the content of the prophetic expectation concerns salvation, revelation has ever been linked to sacrifice. The priestly office belongs to Christ alone, and for that reason any sacrifice before Christ could only be in anticipation of the one sacrifice; in and of themselves, these offerings could not propitiate God. Nor can there be any other sacrifice or priest after Christ.[95] The Old Testament priests are copies and shadows that are to come to an end, and Christ alone in his priestly office is the author of salvation. Calvin very often joins the priestly to the kingly office in his commentaries. Commenting on Psalm 2:6, "Yet have I set my king upon my holy hill of Zion" (ASV), Calvin says,

> Although David in these words had a regard to the promise of God, and recalled the attention of himself and others to it, yet, at the same time, he meant to signify that his own reign is holy and inseparably connected with the temple of God. But this applies more appropriately to the Kingdom of Christ, which we know to be both spiritual and joined to the priesthood, and this is the principal part of the worship of God.[96]

The temple and the kingdom go together in the Old Testament. Therefore, with theocratic anticipation and sacrifices correctly offered, salvation and blessing of the people went hand in hand: "By these two things [i.e., kingdom and priesthood] God testified that He was allied to the children of Abraham."[97]

All this was temporary and preparatory yet at the same time illuminated by the promised Messiah. The unity of salvation and the unity of revelation are in play here; the person of the mediator is tied to a temporal economy that is incomplete without incarnation. As Muller puts it, "The prophet, the king, and the priest are united in Christ, are perfected, and are thereby fulfilled and brought to a conclusion in the one who is both king and priest forever after the order of Melchizedek."[98]

The incarnation of the mediator finally enacts and makes concrete the three offices in the person of the Son, who receives the messianic anointing. The work of mediation focuses on the human fulfillment

---

95. *Institutes*, 2.15.6.
96. *Comm.*, on Ps. 2:6.
97. *Comm.*, on Hos. 8:4.
98. Muller, *Christ and the Decree*, 32.

of the offices. The historical incarnate Son is anointed as man in the office of Messiah (how could divinity be anointed?), but what belongs to the human nature is communicated to the person, who represents "a degree midway" between God and us. Calvin states his rule: "Let this, then, be our key to right understanding; those things which apply to the office of the Mediator are not spoken simply either of the divine nature or of the human."[99]

As prophet, Christ bears "the perfection of the gospel doctrine." Quoting Isaiah 61:1–2 and Luke 4:18, Calvin says that Christ "was anointed by the Spirit to be herald and witness of the Father's grace." He then indulges in hyperbole: "Outside Christ there is nothing worth knowing, and all who by faith perceive what he is like have grasped the whole immensity of heavenly benefits."[100] Christ's teaching is enacted and effective because it is truly redemptive. Commenting on the same passage in his *Commentary on Luke*, Calvin says that Christ "was endowed with the fullness of the Spirit, to be a witness and ambassador for our reconciliation with God," and, "alone by the power of His Spirit, effects and provides the benefits promised here."[101]

As prophet, Christ brings the covenant to fruition since his message concerns his priestly ministry.[102] The title "Lamb of God who takes away the sins of the world" encapsulates the "principal office of Christ briefly and clearly":[103]

> He takes away the sins of the world by the sacrifice of his death and reconciles men to God. There are other favors indeed, which Christ bestows upon us, but this is the chief favor, and the rest depend on it; that, by appeasing the wrath of God, he makes us to be reckoned holy and righteous. From this source flow all the streams of blessing, that, by not imputing our sins, God receives us into favor.[104]

Not only is Christ the priest, he is also the offering and the altar. All three have redemptive connotations. The priest is close to the people

99. *Institutes*, 2.14.3.
100. *Institutes*, 2.15.2.
101. *Comm.*, on Luke 4:17.
102. For a detailed treatment of "expiating crime," see Blocher, "Atonement," 283–88.
103. *Comm.*, on John 1:29.
104. *Comm.*, on John 1:63.

in experiencing their miseries, and Christ "by his own experience learned what it is to succor the weak."[105] "The Son of God had no need of experience, that he might know the emotions of mercy," Calvin explains, "but we could not be persuaded that He is merciful and ready to help us, had he not become acquainted by experience with our miseries."[106] As priest, to perform his office, Christ had to enter the sanctuary with a sacrifice, and this he did with his own blood. This was "a new and different order" from the animal sacrifices commanded by the law: "The same one was to be both priest and sacrifice. This was because no other satisfaction adequate for our sins, and no other man worthy to offer to God his only-begotten Son, could be found."[107] As priest, Christ is also "the altar of God, and on Him we must offer, if we wish that God should accept our sacrifices."[108]

Finally, how does the incarnate Son reveal his kingship in the "days of his suffering"? We have noticed that Calvin insists heavily on the spiritual nature of this office. Christ rules for God by his truth and the power of the Spirit; when Christ came into the world, it was by these weapons that he established his kingdom, overcoming the devil and his works.[109] As Christ accomplished this messianic office, he was gifted with the kingdom. There is no change in the divine kingship of the Father when Christ is appointed to rule "as vice-regent governing the world," "since God is the Son and works in Him."[110] For this reason, although "Christ was anointed as king by the Holy Spirit," Calvin assigns no moment in the life of Christ when he began to reign.[111] The kingdom is always present with him, and Calvin is reticent to reduce a spiritual reality to a temporal moment. The kingdom, however, is invested in due form at the moment of the ascension when, "having laid aside the mean and lowly state of mortal life and the shame of the cross, Christ by rising again began to show forth his glory and power

---

105. *Comm.*, on Rom. 8.3.
106. *Comm.*, on Heb. 2:17.
107. *Institutes*, 2.15.6.
108. *Comm.*, on Isa. 60:7. This is a strange expression, but Calvin refers to Matt. 23:19 and the idea that the altar sanctifies offerings that would elsewhere be unacceptable. He means, I think, that we are acceptable to God only through faith in the sacrifice of Christ.
109. *Comm.*, on John 18:6.
110. *Comm.*, on John 5:22; 20:26.
111. *Institutes*, 2.15.5.

more fully. Yet he truly inaugurated his kingdom only at his ascension into heaven."[112]

On earth Christ's kingdom work extends through his teaching and miracles, considered as expressing the anointing of his human nature with power from on high, in order to overcome the sin and corruption in the world. These manifestations of Christ's power culminate in the victory of the cross, often portrayed by Calvin as the triumphal chariot of the conqueror.[113] Christ entered Jerusalem as a conqueror for his encounter with evil and subdued Satan in a violent struggle: "By means of his crucifixion salvation was obtained for the world, and Christ himself obtained a splendid triumph over death and Satan."[114]

While Calvin repeatedly emphasizes that Christ is victor, nowhere does he diminish the terror and anguish experienced by the mediator in the encounter with Satan, death, and hell. On the contrary, he speaks about Christ's serious struggle, the weakness of the flesh, wrestling in anguish, pain, the dread of death, and the curse of God and his judgment. Because he knew this, Christ "emerged from the pains of death as Conqueror, was upheld by the saving hand of the Father, and after a brief encounter gained a glorious victory over Satan, sin and the powers of hell."[115]

The messianic work of Christ as mediator is a unity that expresses how the one Christ was before all things and before us in the promise, how he acted for humanity in the incarnation, and how he is now with his people through his eschatological presence, both now and forever. For Calvin, Christ continues his mediatorial office in glory as Lord, head of the church, brother, captain, and leader.[116] Christ incorporates us into his body. The whole alphabet of redemption is written by and in Christ, the Alpha and

---

112. *Institutes*, 2.17.14.
113. Jansen refers to the commentaries on Acts 16:22, Col. 2:15, and the sermon on Isa. 53. *Calvin's Doctrine*, 89.
114. *Comm.*, on John 6:15. On Christ's victory over death and Satan, see Peterson, *Atonement*, chap. 5; Edmondson, *Christology*, 133–36. On the victory theme, see Henri Blocher, "*Agnus Victor*: The Atonement as Victory and Vicarious Punishment," in *What Does It Mean to Be Saved? Broadening Evangelical Horizons of Salvation*, ed. John G. Stackhouse Jr. (Grand Rapids, MI: Baker Academic, 2002); Wells, *Cross Words*, chap. 9.
115. *Comm.*, on Heb. 5:7.
116. Blaser, *Calvins Lehre*, 44.

Omega. In considering this continuing aspect of Calvin's thought, we touch briefly on the link between Christology and its soteriological implications.

As the steward of the Spirit, Christ continues his prophetic activity in drawing his people to himself and thus fulfilling the Abrahamic promise. In heaven Christ continues the prophetic office he exercised while on earth, because as head he diffuses his anointing to his members. He received it "not only for himself that he might carry out the office of teaching, but for his whole body that the power of the Spirit might be present in the continuing preaching of the gospel." It is certainly a marvelous privilege to preach the gospel, as Christ ministers prophetically through his witnesses! Not only so, but the prophetic proclamation leads to deliverance because of the work of the Spirit, who extends the external teaching to make it internally effective. As the heavenly master, Christ "not only addresses [us] with the words of his mouth, but also teaches inwardly and effectively by His Spirit."[117] He is the great high prophet who not only continues to dispense the "doctrine of life" outwardly but who also shapes the hearts of believers in obedience to the gospel through saving faith. The prophetic proclamation of pardon and healing makes believers citizens of Christ's kingdom.

Beyond the one sacrifice for sin, the office of priest has an eschatological extension in heaven through the intercession of Christ, the great advocate at the right hand of God, who pleads the cause of his own before the Father. Reconciliation with God, based on the finality of the work of Christ, is the first part of his priestly office. It is currently expressed though the heavenly mediation of Christ, who by his intercession continually applies the fruits of his death in our favor to salvation. So "the intercession of Christ, according to Calvin, is not an additional act which Christ performs in heaven, different from His death and resurrection. His intercession is the presence of this death and resurrection themselves before the Father."[118] To put it another way, intercession and the remission of sin are two sides of the same priestly activity. Calvin says it better:

---

117. *Comm.*, on Rom. 8:15.
118. Hoogland, *Calvin's Perspective*, 198–99.

Having entered a sanctuary not made with hands, he appears before the Father's face as our constant advocate and intercessor [Heb. 7:25; 9:11–12; Rom. 8:34]. Thus he turns the Father's eyes to his own righteousness to avert his gaze from our sins. He so reconciles the Father's heart to us that by his intercession he prepares a way and access for us to the Father's throne. He fills with grace and kindness the throne that for miserable sinners would otherwise have been filled with dread.[119]

This is the foundation on which we are able to approach the throne of grace with "trust in prayer, but [it is] also peace for godly consciences, while they safely lean upon God's fatherly mercy and are surely persuaded that whatever has been consecrated through the Mediator is pleasing to God." Not only so, but equally remarkable is the fact that as great high priest, Christ receives us at his side "as his companions in this great office," and we "freely enter the heavenly sanctuary that the sacrifices and prayers and praise that we bring may be acceptable and sweet-smelling before God."[120] This, says Calvin, is the meaning of John 17:19, "For their sakes I sanctify myself" (ASV).

Election is in Christ before the foundation of the world, and its end owes its efficacy to the royal work of the mediator, as Christ is anointed king for his people's sake. All power is in the hands of the shepherd-king to "govern, nourish and sustain us, keep us in his care, and help us. . . . Christ stands in our midst, to lead us little by little to a firm union with God."[121] In his kingly office, Christ is "armed with eternal power," and "the perpetuity of the church is secure in this protection. Hence, amid the violent agitation with which it is continually troubled, amid the grievous and frightful storms that threaten it with unnumbered calamities, it still remains safe."[122] Christ is ruler over all but also protector and defender of his own. Believers who know him in this capacity can wait in confidence for his triumph in the last judgment. Then he will complete the separation of the wheat and the tares that has already begun through the preaching of the gospel.[123]

---

119. *Institutes*, 2.16.16.
120. *Institutes*, 2.15.6.
121. *Institutes*, 2.15.5.
122. *Institutes*, 2.15.3.
123. *Comm.*, on Ps. 15:1.

In conclusion, it must be said that the three offices distinguished by Calvin are ultimately not three but one, the one saving office incarnated in the person of the mediator. The *munus triplex* distinguishes the three because Scripture does so in order to accommodate the intricacy of the messianic work to our need of saving understanding and faith. "The office-bearing is not something rigid but has a wondrous and saving effect," observes G. C. Berkouwer. "In fulfilling this office Christ accomplishes the one work of salvation. That is why Christ's office does not conflict with his personal spontaneity; in Christ there never existed such a conflict."[124] If the one work of salvation has a historical rooting without which there would be no redemption, no change from wrath to grace in history, it is also transhistorical and suprahistorical. In presenting this profound truth, Calvin

> keeps in the foreground the assertion that the incarnation was not the eternal Son's abdication of his universal empire but the reassertion of that empire over rebellious creation. This continuity of gracious order over creaturely attempts at discontinuity depends on the identity of the redeeming Mediator in the flesh with the Mediator who is the eternal Son of God by whom, and with whose Spirit, all things were created according to the Father's will.[125]

Conclusion

We mentioned at the beginning of this essay that Calvin's Christology has not always been valued as much as it deserves to be. No doubt one of the reasons for this is because its central motifs are theocentric and not humanistic. It became an increasingly countercurrent doctrine over against the dominant trends of man-centered modernism in later centuries; its transcendent aspects became more and more strange for those working in the cadre of historical immanentism. This is not only the case with philosophical or cultural developments. It applies also to theological developments within Christianity, deeply affected by horizontalism. Calvin's doctrine of the work of Christ as a mediation theology fits nicely neither with the accents of Christology "from below"

---

124. Berkouwer, *Work of Christ*, 62.
125. Willis, *Calvin's Catholic Christology*, 99–100.

or "from above." Although Calvin would no doubt have approved more of the latter, it may be doubted that he would have found any accentuation other than a mediatorial one to be totally satisfactory. In light of this, and in the context of our current situation, Calvin's Christology still demands attention and presents a challenge in two particular respects.

It can hardly be doubted that a doctrine of Christ as the mediator is what Christianity lacks at present, as a robust Christ- and gospel-honoring alternative to the woolly waffling of pluralistic religion, where a hidden Jesus is found in every religious aspiration. In the multi-religious and multiethnic winds like those in the air we breathe, the church and believers are swamped by a relativism that reduces Jesus of Nazareth to being another illustration of a general principle. The problem is the finality of Christ.[126] Whatever one thinks of Emil Brunner's theological presuppositions, Brunner no doubt got it right when he insisted in his book *The Mediator* on the fact that there are only two types of theology—that which is erected on the basis of the one mediator, implying exclusivity and finality in revelation, and all other religions or theologies, which are fundamentally naturalistic and cannot reveal God. Mediation is the only way humans *could* know God or have any hope of salvation. We have not taken seriously enough Calvin's dictum "Outside Christ there is nothing worth knowing."[127] Calvin is not saying, of course, that nothing is worth knowing at all but that all the riches of human knowledge pale in significance when one knows the glories of Christ.

Second, this kind of truth brings a real and personal knowledge of Christ into lost lives. It is experiential and involves us in a living relationship with the one who not only is human like us but who also holds the cards of history, death and hell, time and eternity, in his hand. This is the surest safety net anyone could have in this vale of tears, where disaster can strike at any moment, even though we all live as though we were permanent fixtures. The notes of Calvin's theology of mediation are sweet music to anyone searching for personal

---

126. D. A. Carson speaks eloquently about this in *The Gagging of God: Christianity Confronts Pluralism* (Leicester, UK: Apollos, 1996), chap. 7.

127. *Institutes*, 2.15.3, quoting 1 Cor. 2:2.

meaning in life. Because he is mediator, Christ is for, in, and with us.[128] Christ is Lord and brother, head of a family, and the one who gives his Spirit to unite us to him in mystic union. As Redeemer, he is ever the man Christ Jesus for us:

> Indeed, if this were deeply impressed on the hearts of all, that the Son of God holds out to us the hand of a brother, and that we are united to Him by the fellowship of our nature, in order that, out of our low condition, He may raise us to heaven; who would not choose to keep by this straight road, instead of wandering in uncertain and stormy paths?[129]

---

128. For a development of these concepts in the context of eschatology, see Adrio König, *The Eclipse of Christ in Eschatology: Toward a Christ-Centered Approach* (Grand Rapids, MI: Eerdmans, 1989).

129. *Comm.*, on 1 Tim. 2:5.

13

The Holy Spirit

Joel R. Beeke

We have not received the Holy Spirit for a single day, or for any short period, but as a perennial fountain, which will never fail us.

—John Calvin, *Commentary on the Gospel according to St. John*

Theologian of the Holy Spirit

The sixteenth-century Reformers examined afresh the doctrine of the Holy Spirit.[1] The Reformers most commonly associated with the theology of the Spirit are Huldrych Zwingli, Martin Bucer, and John Calvin.[2] But as Benjamin B. Warfield famously said, "Calvin was "*the* theologian of the Holy Spirit." He then added, "The doctrine of the Holy Spirit is a gift from Calvin to the church."[3]

---

1. Portions of this chapter are adapted from Joel R. Beeke, "Calvin on Piety," in *The Cambridge Companion to John Calvin*, ed. Donald K. McKim, Cambridge Companions to Religion (Cambridge: Cambridge University Press, 2004), 125–52; Beeke, "Appropriating Salvation: The Spirit, Faith and Assurance, and Repentance (3.1–3, 6–10)," in *A Theological Guide to Calvin's "Institutes": Essays and Analysis*, ed. David W. Hall and Peter A. Lillback, Calvin 500 Series (Phillipsburg, NJ: P&R, 2008), 270–300. Used by permission of Cambridge University Press through PLSclear and by permission of P&R Publishing, respectively.

2. Willem van 't Spijker, "The Doctrine of the Holy Spirit in Bucer and Calvin" (paper delivered at the International Congress on Calvin Research, 1986), 1.

3. Benjamin B. Warfield, "Calvin as a Theologian," in *Calvin and Augustine*, ed. Samuel G. Craig (Philadelphia: Presbyterian and Reformed, 1956), 484–85.

Warfield's statements about Calvin are perhaps better known than Calvin's actual teaching on the Holy Spirit. Thankfully, recent scholarship has drawn more attention to Calvin's work on the Holy Spirit, despite earlier negligence. Though many explanations of Calvin on the Holy Spirit have been published in chapters or scholarly journals,[4] some in non-English books,[5] and in unpublished English theses and dissertations,[6] only a few thorough, contemporary English works on

4. Some of the best representatives include J. K. Parratt, "The Witness of the Holy Spirit: Calvin, the Puritans and St. Paul," *EvQ* 41, no. 3 (1969): 161–68; M. Eugene Osterhaven, "John Calvin: Order and the Holy Spirit," *RefR* 32, no. 1 (1978): 23–44; Anthony N. S. Lane, "John Calvin: The Witness of the Holy Spirit," in *Faith and Ferment* (London: Westminster Conference Papers, 1982), 1–17; I. John Hesselink, "Calvin, Theologian of the Holy Spirit," in *Calvin's First Catechism: A Commentary*, with the 1538 catechism trans. Ford Lewis Battles, CSRT (Louisville: Westminster John Knox Press, 1997), 177–87, 230–33; Hesselink, "Calvin, the Theologian of the Holy Spirit: The Holy Spirit and the Christian Life," in *Calvin in Asian Churches*, ed. Sou-Young Lee (Seoul: Korean Calvin Society, 2002), 113–28; Stanley M. Burgess, "John Calvin (1509–1564)," in *The Holy Spirit: Medieval Roman Catholic and Reformation Traditions* (Peabody, MA: Hendrickson, 1997), 161–71; Howard Griffith, "The First Title of the Spirit: Adoption in Calvin's Soteriology," *EvQ* 73, no. 2 (2001): 135–53; Adrian A. Helleman, "John Calvin on the Procession of the Holy Spirit," *OiC* 37, no. 4 (2002): 21–36; Paul Chung, "Calvin and the Holy Spirit: A Reconsideration in Light of Spirituality and Social Ethics," *Pneuma* 24, no. 1 (2002): 40–55; Yang-en Cheng, "Calvin on the Work of the Holy Spirit and Spiritual Gifts," *TaiJT* 27 (2005): 173–206; Willem van 't Spijker, "The Sealing with the Holy Spirit in Bucer and Calvin," in *John Calvin and the Interpretation of Scripture: Calvin Studies X and XI, Papers Presented at the 10th and 11th Colloquiums of the Calvin Studies Society at Columbia Theological Seminary*, ed. Charles Raynal (Grand Rapids, MI: Calvin Studies Society by CRC Product Services, 2006), 246–88; I. John Hesselink, "Pneumatology: The Cosmic Dimension," in *The Calvin Handbook*, ed. Herman J. Selderhuis (Grand Rapids, MI: Eerdmans, 2009), 299–312; Shu-Ying Shih, "The Doctrine of Holy Spirit in the Theology of John Calvin," *TaiJT* 31 (2009): 77–96; Elias Dantas, "Calvin, the Theologian of the Holy Spirit," in *John Calvin and Evangelical Theology: Legacy and Prospect*, ed. Sung Wook Chung (Louisville: Westminster John Knox, 2009), 128–41; David A. Höhne, "The Secret Agent of Natural Causes: Providence, Contingency, and the Perfecting Work of the Spirit," in *Engaging with Calvin: Aspects of the Reformer's Legacy for Today*, ed. Mark D. Thompson (Nottingham, UK: Apollos, 2009), 158–78; Sinclair B. Ferguson, "Christology and Pneumatology: John Calvin, the Theologian of the Holy Spirit," in *Always Reformed: Essays in Honor of W. Robert Godfrey*, ed. R. Scott Clark and Joel E. Kim (Escondido, CA: Westminster Seminary California, 2010), 15–36; Ferguson, "Calvin and Christian Experience: The Holy Spirit in the Life of the Christian," in *Calvin: Theologian and Reformer*, ed. Joel R. Beeke and Garry J. Williams (Grand Rapids, MI: Reformation Heritage Books, 2010), 89–106; Gerard Booy, "The Holy Spirit in the Thoughts of John Calvin," in *Calvin@500: Theology, History, and Practice*, ed. Richard R. Topping and John A. Vissers (Eugene, OR: Pickwick, 2011), 38–51; Stafford Carson, "Calvin and the Holy Spirit," in *Living in Union with Christ in Today's World: The Witness of John Calvin and Ignatius Loyola*, ed. Brendan McConvery (Dublin: Veritas, 2011), 105–26; David Wenkel, "The Logic and Exegesis behind Calvin's Doctrine of the Internal Witness of the Holy Spirit to the Authority of Scripture," *PRJ* 3, no. 2 (2011): 98–108; Keith D. Stanglin, "*Spiritus Propheticus*: Spirit and Prophecy in Calvin's Old Testament Exegesis," *CTJ* 50, no. 1 (2015): 23–42.

5. The two most important non-English works are in Dutch and German, respectively: Simon van der Linde, *De Leer van den Heiligen Geest bij Calvijn: Bijdrage tot de Kennis der Reformatorischen Theologie* (Wageningen: H. Veenman & Zonen, 1943); Werner Krusche, *Das Wirken des Heiligen Geistes nach Calvin*, FKDG 7 (Göttingen: Vandenhoeck & Ruprecht, 1957). Both volumes are strongly polemical—van der Linde in opposing Barthianism and Krusche in challenging Emil Brunner and his followers.

6. Jack La-Vere Zerwas, "The Holy Spirit in Calvin" (STM thesis, Union Theological Seminary, 1947); Jean Abel, "The Ethical Implications of the Doctrine of the Holy Spirit in John Calvin" (ThM thesis, Union Theological Seminary, Richmond, VA, 1948); Margaret Virginia Cubine,

this subject have been published.[7] One reason for this relative neglect may be the vastness of the subject; Calvin weaves the work of the Spirit into nearly every chapter of his *Institutes* as well as throughout his commentaries, sermons, and letters. Another reason may be that Calvin does not provide a detailed treatment of the doctrine of the Holy Spirit in his *Institutes* or anywhere else.[8] This is understandable, however, since Calvin stresses that the Holy Spirit's goal is to focus on Christ rather than on himself. Furthermore, by Calvin's continual reference to the Holy Spirit in lieu of devoting a particular chapter to him, Calvin communicates a profound truth about the Spirit. Sinclair Ferguson writes, "By holding a high view of the Spirit's person and work, yet refraining from a specific locus exposition, Calvin thus demonstrates that the Spirit's personal influence must pervade all theology, and touch it at every point precisely because he is the Executive Member of the Godhead."[9]

After addressing the question of who the Holy Spirit is in Calvin's theology, I summarize Calvin's thinking on the Spirit in relation to the Scriptures and to Christ; the Spirit and the order of salvation (*ordo salutis*), focusing both on union and communion with Christ and on faith, justification, and sanctification; the Spirit and the assurance and application of redemption; and the Spirit's relationship to spiritual gifts.

"John Calvin's Doctrine of the Work of the Holy Spirit Examined in the Light of Some Contemporary Theories of Interpersonal Psychotherapy" (PhD diss., Northwestern University, 1955); Henry O'Brien, "The Holy Spirit in the Catechetical Writings of John Calvin: A Comparative Study with Other Constructive Presentations of Christian Doctrine between 1529 and 1566" (PhD diss., Pontificia Universitas Gregoriana, Facultas Theologiae, Rome, 1991); Christopher J. Ganski, "Spirit and Flesh: On the Significance of the Reformed Doctrine of the Lord's Supper for Pneumatology" (PhD diss., Marquette University, 2012); David M. Sarafolean, "Tracing the Person and Work of the Holy Spirit in the Early Protestant Reformation" (ThM thesis, Puritan Reformed Theological Seminary, 2016).

7. A helpful step in this direction is Peter De Klerk, ed., *Calvin and the Holy Spirit: Papers and Responses Presented at the Sixth Colloquium on Calvin and Calvin Studies* (Grand Rapids, MI: Calvin Studies Society, 1989). Essays include Jelle Faber, "The Saving Work of the Holy Spirit in Calvin"; John Bolt, "Spiritus Creator: The Use and Abuse of Calvin's Cosmic Pneumatology"; Willem van 't Spijker, "*Extra nos* and *in nobis* by Calvin in a Pneumatological Light"; Richard C. Gamble, "Word and Spirit in Calvin"; Brian G. Armstrong, "The Role of the Holy Spirit in Calvin's Teaching on the Ministry"; Leonard Sweetman Jr., "What Is the Meaning of These Gifts?" Two additional volumes have furthered this area of Calvin studies: Gwyn Walters, *The Sovereign Spirit: The Doctrine of the Holy Spirit in the Writings of John Calvin*, ed. Eifion Evans and Lynn Quigley, RSHT (Edinburgh: Rutherford, 2009); Daniel Y. K. Lee, *The Holy Spirit as Bond in Calvin's Thought: Its Functions in Connection with the* Extra Calvinisticum (Oxford: Peter Lang, 2011).

8. The *Institutes* offers only one brief chapter directly on the Holy Spirit: 3.1.

9. Ferguson, "Christology and Pneumatology," 17.

Who Is the Holy Spirit?

Calvin's views on who the Spirit is are largely traditional, following the fathers of the ancient church, who held to the full equality of the three persons of the Trinity. In affirming the full deity of the Spirit, Calvin emphasizes the Spirit's divine works. Many of the divine works ascribed to the Son are also attributed to the Spirit; hence, the Spirit, like the Son, must be fully God. For example, the Spirit works regeneration and immortality by his own divine power.[10]

The Holy Spirit is thus to be confessed as the third person of the Trinity, equal in deity with the Father and the Son. Calvin defines "person" in relation to Hebrews 1:3 as "a subsistence in God's essence, which, while related to the others, is distinguished by an incommunicable quality."[11] He acknowledges that such theological terms, though needed to refute heresies, have their limitations. Based on texts such as Matthew 28:19 and Ephesians 4:5, Calvin says that it is important to maintain that "in God's essence reside three persons in whom one God is known." Since there is only one God, "Word and Spirit are nothing else than the very essence of God."[12]

The one God, however, has a "threeness" about him. Calvin quotes Gregory of Nazianzus, who says, "I cannot think on the one without quickly being encircled by the splendor of the three; nor can I discern the three without being straightway carried back to the one."[13] To avoid tritheism, Calvin hastens to add that this "splendor of the three" manifests only a distinction in the Trinity, not a division.[14] He writes, "To the Father is attributed the beginning of activity, and the fountain and well-spring of all things; to the Son, wisdom, counsel, and the ordered disposition of all things; but to the Spirit is assigned the power and efficacy of that activity."[15] A natural economic order of equality, then, flows from the Trinity. This order coincides with revelatory and redeeming activity, enabling us to contemplate the Father

---

10. See *Institutes*, 1.13.14.
11. *Institutes*, 1.13.6.
12. *Institutes*, 1.13.16.
13. *Institutes*, 1.13.17.
14. *Institutes*, 1.13.17.
15. *Institutes*, 1.13.18.

as the first person, the Son as the second person, and the Spirit as the third person. Calvin says, "For the mind of each human being is naturally inclined to contemplate God first, then the wisdom coming forth from him, and lastly the power whereby he executes the decrees of his plan."[16]

Little more need be said about the ontological Trinity, Calvin concludes. Theologians may multiply words on the subject, but that is unnecessary: "In the one essence of God there is a trinity of persons; you will say in one word what Scripture states, and cut short empty talkativeness."[17]

Calvin is more interested in the practical work of the relational Trinity than the theological abstractions of the ontological Trinity. His major goal is to promote practical, experiential Christian living. In his 1538 catechism, Calvin writes, "When we name Father, Son, and Holy Spirit, we are not fashioning three Gods, but in the simplest unity of God, Scripture and the very experience of godliness disclose to us the Father, his Son, and the Spirit."[18] I. John Hesselink points out that Calvin speaks similarly of the Spirit's divinity in the *Institutes*: "What Scripture attributes to him [the Holy Spirit] we ourselves learn by the sure experience of godliness."[19] Hesselink goes on to say that "Calvin frequently appeals to experience as a secondary sort of confirmation of Scripture, and in this case particularly godliness (or piety)."[20] Likewise, B. B. Warfield says of Calvin, "The doctrine of the Trinity did not stand out of relation to his religious consciousness but was a postulate of his profoundest religious emotions; was given, indeed, in his experience of salvation itself."[21]

This experiential effect of the Spirit permeates Calvin's theology, giving life to it. For Calvin, experiencing the work of the Spirit is more important than attempting to describe the essence of the Spirit, since the latter remains a mystery that we can never fully grasp. Willem van 't Spijker summarizes this point well:

---

16. *Institutes*, 1.13.18.
17. *Institutes*, 1.13.5.
18. John Calvin, *Calvin's Catechism of 1538*, trans. Ford Lewis Battles, in Hesselink, *Calvin's First Catechism: A Commentary*, sec. 20.
19. *Institutes*, 1.13.14.
20. Hesselink, "Calvin, Theologian of the Holy Spirit," 179.
21. Warfield, *Calvin and Augustine*, 195.

The Institutes possesses a unity, but not that of a closed system. It is a unity which always remains open to God, man, and the world. However, this unity is not anthropologically determined. It is rooted in the Spirit, who brings about the encounter between God and man through the real presence of Christ. It can also be said that the presence of the Spirit in almost all *loci* has preserved Calvin's doctrine from petrification. . . . It is the Spirit who blows through his garden and who makes it alive and blooming. . . . [His] sound is heard everywhere.[22]

The Spirit and the Scriptures

Holy Scripture is the classroom of the Holy Spirit, Calvin asserts. As its author, the Holy Spirit draws people into his service through the Bible and works in perfect harmony with it.[23] A summary of what Calvin teaches on these important matters highlights two key themes: the Spirit's internal testimony and the Spirit's harmony with Scripture.

The Internal Testimony of the Spirit and Scripture's Self-Authenticating Character

To those who teach that rational proof is required to affirm the divine authority of the biblical writers, Calvin responds by appealing to the internal testimony of the Holy Spirit (*testimonium internum Spiritus Sancti*):

The testimony of the Spirit is more excellent than all reason. For as God alone is a fit witness of himself in his Word, so also the Word will not find acceptance in men's hearts before it is sealed by the inward testimony of the Spirit. The same Spirit, therefore, who spoke through the mouth of the prophets, must penetrate our hearts to persuade us that they faithfully proclaimed what had been divinely commanded.[24]

---

22. Van 't Spijker, "Holy Spirit in Bucer and Calvin," 3–4; cf. *Institutes*, 1.13.14.

23. Contrary to what John T. McNeill says, I believe that Calvin frequently used the terms "God's word," "the Bible," and "Scripture" as convertible terms; hence, I use them as such in this section of the chapter without entering into this complex debate here. Suffice it to say that at times, of course, Calvin speaks of Jesus Christ and of preaching as "the word of God," but these usages will not be used in this chapter. For a sampling of various views on this issue, see Gamble, "Word and Spirit in Calvin," 75–77. For Calvin on the inspiration of Scripture, see Walters, *Sovereign Spirit*, 24–34. For Calvin on inerrancy, see Frederick S. Leahy, "Calvin and the Inerrancy of Scripture," *RTJ* 17 (2001): 44–56.

24. *Institutes*, 1.7.4.

The Spirit's internal witness, or testimony, confirms the authority of Scripture for the believer, Calvin says. It does not establish that authority, for the Scriptures are self-authenticating (Gk. *autopiston*). There are self-evidencing "proofs" from Scripture (*indicia*, i.e., statements about Scripture) that argue for the credibility of Scripture, Calvin asserts, but ultimately such proofs are secondary to the Spirit's illumination of our minds and our consciences that the Bible contains the very words of God. Though secondary, however, these proofs—such as the antiquity of Scripture, miracles, fulfilled prophecies, and the preservation of the law—ought not to be lightly dismissed; they provide confirmation but only for those who are already believers.[25] No human argument will convince an unbeliever that the Bible is the word of God. Thus, the Spirit's witness does not relate to evidentiary proofs but to the authority of the word itself, which is confirmed by the Spirit's witness. Later, Warfield would mistakenly reverse that position, as Robert Reymond says, because of Warfield's "empirical apologetic based on Thomas Reid's Scottish common sense realism that ruled at Princeton."[26]

Reymond summarizes Calvin well when he says that if the Bible needed "anyone or anything other than itself to authenticate and validate its divine character—based on the principle that the validating source is always the higher and final authority (see Heb. 6:13)—it would not be the Word of God because the validating sources would be the higher authority."[27] Calvin regards the principle of Scripture's self-authentication as critical to avoid the Roman Catholic error of making Scripture's credibility dependent on the judgment of the church. The believer's ultimate authority in matters of faith and practice is the Bible, not the church.[28] As T. H. L. Parker notes, "All the Church can do is to accept this authority [of the Scriptures] over herself obediently. . . . She cannot do otherwise than obey it—i.e., regard it as her Lord, because as the Word of her Lord it is the presence of her Lord with her."[29] Ronald Wallace similarly states, "For Calvin the

---

25. *Institutes*, 1.8.
26. Robert L. Reymond, "Calvin's Doctrine of Holy Scripture (1.6–10)," in Hall and Lillback, *Theological Guide to Calvin's "Institutes,"* 52–53.
27. Reymond, "Calvin's Doctrine of Holy Scripture," 51.
28. See *Institutes*, 1.7.1–2.
29. T. H. L. Parker, *Calvin's Doctrine of the Knowledge of God*, rev. ed. (Grand Rapids, MI: Eerdmans, 1959), 43–44.

Bible is not only the sole source of Church proclamation but also the sole authority that must rule the life of the Church."[30]

God communicates through the work of the Holy Spirit. Consequently, the Scripture's authority for belief and behavior rests on its ultimate author, the Holy Spirit, who is truth itself. The Spirit-based, authoritative nature of Scripture is unique to Christians.[31] The Spirit imprints Scripture's divine authority on their hearts with an indubitable certainty "that piety requires."[32]

For Calvin, the Spirit graciously removes the blindness of sin and the soul and gives the believer new eyes to see Scripture for what it is: the divinely inspired word of God. Through the spectacles of Scripture, we see God for who he is and ourselves, with our sinful nature, for who we are. The Holy Spirit gives us a new desire for God and his word within the realm of faith. The Spirit's witness is the means of faith, not the final ground of faith, which is Scripture itself. Calvin would thus agree with Louis Berkhof, who writes, "The ground of faith is identical with [Scripture's] contents, and cannot be separated from it. But the testimony of the Spirit is the moving cause of faith. We believe Scripture, not because of, but through the testimony of the Holy Spirit."[33]

The testimony of the Holy Spirit is at the center of Calvin's theological system. Without this testimony, the word cannot be understood, knowledge cannot be gained, and faith cannot be genuine. Apart from the Spirit's testimony, the word is of no avail, knowledge is reduced to opinion, and faith is falsified. But when the believer receives the testimony of the Holy Spirit, he experiences that Scripture is the living word of God that opens his heart before God, soothes it with assurances of God's grace in Christ, and motivates him to live to the glory of God. The believer then knows that the Scriptures are from God with an assurance that neither the church nor reason can provide.[34]

---

30. Ronald S. Wallace, *Calvin's Doctrine of the Word and Sacrament* (Edinburgh: Oliver and Boyd, 1953), 99. Cf. Rupert E. Davies, *The Problem of Authority in the Continental Reformers: A Study in Luther, Zwingli, and Calvin* (London: Epworth, 1946).

31. H. Jackson Forstman, *Word and Spirit: Calvin's Doctrine of Biblical Authority* (Stanford, CA: Stanford University Press, 1962), 15.

32. *Institutes*, 1.7.4.

33. Louis Berkhof, *Systematic Theology* (Grand Rapids, MI: Eerdmans, 1996), 1:185.

34. Cf. Douglas Schuurman, "Calvin's Doctrine of the *Testimonium Spiritus Sancti*" (paper for Calvin's *Institutes* seminar conducted by Ford Lewis Battles, Calvin Theological Seminary, fall 1978), 9–10.

Martin Luther and Huldrych Zwingli allude to the doctrine of the Spirit's internal witness,[35] but Calvin was the first to develop it and show that it involves "a recognition of the evidential value of religious experience."[36] Though much has been written to support that development, some have challenged it on the grounds that it is subjective and circular. In response to these objections, I. John Hesselink writes,

> In a sense [Calvin's] argument is circular. For how do we know the Bible is the Word of God? Answer: The Spirit tells us so. How do we know it is truly the Spirit who gives us this assurance? Answer: The Bible itself convinces us of this. Yet it should be noted that this kind of argumentation is no invention of the theologians! There are several passages in the New Testament which suggest this approach: John 8:13ff.; 1 Corinthians 2:11; Romans 8:16; and 2 Corinthians 3:1–3, for example.[37]

Hesselink reports Karl Barth calling Calvin's argument a "logical circle," in which the objective word and the subjective Spirit coalesce. The Bible, which appears to be "objective," is, as Otto Weber notes, "by its very essence also 'subjective'" in the persuasion of its divine origin. When the Spirit internally persuades us of its authority, the "polarity of object and subject is overcome."[38]

John Murray is convinced that Calvin could have been clearer in distinguishing between the objective, intrinsic authority that resides in the Scriptures and the believer's subjective recognition of that authority. Calvin requires both intrinsic authority and its recognition, but Murray asserts that distinguishing between them would help us reconcile statements of Calvin that emphasize the objective (e.g., "The Scripture exhibits as clear evidence of its truth as white and black things do of their color, or sweet and bitter things of their taste"[39]) and the subjective (e.g., "[The Scriptures] obtain complete authority

35. Hartmann Grisar, *Luther*, trans. E. M. Lamond, ed. Luigi Cappadelta (London: Kegan Paul, Trench, Trubner, 1915), 4:391–92; S. M. Jackson, *Huldreich Zwingli: The Reformer of German Switzerland* (New York: G. P. Putnam's Sons, 1901), 42.

36. Walters, *Sovereign Spirit*, 41.

37. Hesselink, "Calvin, Theologian of the Holy Spirit," 181–82; cf. Otto Weber, *The Foundations of Dogmatics*, trans. Darrell L. Guder (Grand Rapids, MI: Eerdmans, 1981), 1:244.

38. Hesselink, "Calvin, Theologian of the Holy Spirit," 182.

39. *Institutes*, 1.7.2.

with believers only when they are persuaded that they proceed from heaven"[40]).[41] For Calvin, however, these two emphases are seamless since the Spirit's testimony persuades us of Scripture's authority.[42]

In summary, several points can be made about Calvin's witness of the Spirit to the word. First, full conviction of scriptural authority comes only through the witness of the Spirit. Though we should not despise rational argument or the church's testimony, we must not rely too heavily on these sources, for in themselves they can only produce probable conclusions. To build hope on reason or the church only fosters instability.

Second, the witness of the Spirit to Scripture is what believers alone experience.[43] Certainty evolves from paying heed to that witness, while uncertainty results from ignoring that witness. We must not look to reason or to inner light or to the church for certainty but to the Spirit's witness in our conscience.

Third, the inner witness of the Spirit does not deny the church's role in recognizing the sacred canon. Not every believer feels the Spirit's witness for each of the sixty-six books of Scripture in equal measure, since one believer's feelings about a particular book in the canon may differ somewhat from another's. Rather, the self-authenticating canon has imposed itself on the church in such a manner that the Spirit has "opened the eyes of the worldwide church over the ages to discern the limits of the canon."[44]

The Harmony of Word and Spirit

Calvin says there is a reciprocal relationship between the word and the Spirit; the word without the Spirit is ineffective, and the Spirit without the word is a delusion.[45] The Holy Spirit converts and di-

---

40. *Institutes*, 1.7.1.

41. John Murray, "Calvin and the Authority of Scripture," in *Collected Writings of John Murray* (Edinburgh: Banner of Truth, 1982), 4:183–84. Cf. Derek Naves, "The Internal Witness of the Spirit in the Theology of John Calvin" (MDiv paper for Prolegomena, Puritan Reformed Theological Seminary, fall 2007), 7–9.

42. Wallace, *Calvin's Doctrine*, 101–2; Jack Rogers and Donald K. McKim, *The Authority and Interpretation of the Bible: An Historical Approach* (San Francisco: Harper & Row, 1979), 104.

43. See *Institutes*, 1.7.5.

44. This paragraph is a summary of the thoughts of Lane, "Witness of the Holy Spirit," 4–5.

45. See *Institutes*, 1.9. For Calvin's polemics against the Spirit-without-word theology of some Anabaptists, particularly the Spiritualists among them, see William Klassen, "Anabaptist Hermeneutics: The Letter and the Spirit," *MQR* 40 (1966): 91; George Hunston Williams, *The Radical*

rects believers by the word. Unlike Luther, who stresses the objective, external word in his debates with spiritual radicals, resulting in "the danger of uniting Word and Spirit so completely as to run the risk of identifying them,"[46] Calvin maintains that, though word and Spirit are intimately related, they remain distinct from each other. They work together to establish God's kingdom. In explaining the petition "Thy kingdom come," Calvin writes that the kingdom comes partly by the preaching of the word and partly by the secret power of the Spirit: "He would govern us by his Word, but as the voice alone, without the inward influence of the Spirit, does not reach down into the heart, the two must be brought together for the establishment of God's kingdom."[47] Though Calvin does not say that the believer is continually being led by some special inner light, he does acknowledge that the Spirit occasionally works independently from the word in governing and guiding the believer.[48] Those independent workings, however, do not conflict with Holy Scripture but always harmonize with it.[49]

In the ultimate sense, then, the word and Spirit are bonded together. So Calvin writes,

> By a kind of mutual bond the Lord has joined together the certainty of his Word and of his Spirit so that the perfect religion of the Word may abide in our minds when the Spirit, who causes us to contemplate God's face, shines; and that we in turn may embrace the Spirit with no fear of being deceived when we recognize him in his own image, namely, in the Word.[50]

Bringing the word and Spirit into the closest proximity helped Calvin maintain his theological method of striving for a genuine *via media*, that is, a middle way between false extremes, says Richard Gamble.

Reformation (Philadelphia: Westminster, 1962), 821–28; Willem Balke, *Calvin and the Anabaptist Radicals*, trans. William Heynan (Grand Rapids, MI: Eerdmans, 1981).

46. I. John Hesselink, "Calvin's Theology," in McKim, *Cambridge Companion to John Calvin*, 80.

47. Hesselink, "Calvin's Theology," 81; cf. *Comm.*, on Matt. 6:10.

48. For illustrations of this point, see I. John Hesselink, "Governed and Guided by the Spirit: A Key Issue in Calvin's Doctrine of the Holy Spirit," in *Das Reformierte Erbe: Festschrift für Gottfried W. Locher zu seinem 80. Geburtstag*, ed. H. A. Oberman, Ernst Saxer, et al. (Zurich: Theologischer Verlag, 1992), 161–71.

49. Lane, "Witness of the Holy Spirit," 5.

50. *Institutes*, 1.9.3.

Those extremes were the Roman Catholics, who deemphasized the word to exaggerate the Spirit's work in the church;[51] the Anabaptists, who deemphasized the word to exaggerate the Spirit's work in the individual;[52] and "rationalistic"-leaning apologists, who emphasized the rational evidences of the word at the expense of the Spirit.[53] Calvin's close proximity of word and Spirit has far-reaching consequences for public worship and preaching as well as for the experiential and practical dimensions of Christian living. When word and Spirit are properly coalesced, worship, preaching, and personal experience are enriched and empowered in a way that glorifies the triune God.[54]

The Spirit and the Order of Salvation

The Spirit and Union and Communion with Christ

Calvin supports the tradition of the councils and the Fathers of the church in affirming the *filioque* (literally, "and the Son")—an addition in the Western form of the Niceno-Constantinopolitan Creed that states that the Spirit proceeds not only from the Father but also from the Son.[55] Thus the Spirit is sometimes called "Spirit of the Father" and sometimes "Spirit of the Son."[56] This doctrine of the double procession of the Spirit (from the Father and the Son) has been the dominant teaching of Western Trinitarianism since Augustine.[57]

Here, too, Calvin is less interested in the ontological relationship between the Son and the Spirit than in their practical working relationship. The Son and the Spirit are both "inner teachers," Calvin says, but their roles are different. The Holy Spirit stays in the background, focusing all attention on the crucified and risen Lord. The Spirit does not initiate new work but honors the finished work of Christ, reveal-

---

51. See *Institutes*, 4.8.13.

52. Gamble, "Word and Spirit in Calvin," 81–85.

53. Bernard Ramm, *The Witness of the Spirit* (Grand Rapids, MI: Eerdmans, 1960), 12. See Schuurman, "Calvin's Doctrine," 2–7.

54. Cf. Cheng, "Holy Spirit and Spiritual Gifts," 175–76; Forstman, *Word and Spirit*, 66–85.

55. This is clear from article 6 of the French Confession of Faith (1559), written by Calvin and his student Antoine de la Roche Chandieu; see *The Creeds of Christendom*, ed. Philip Schaff (Grand Rapids, MI: Baker, 1993), 3:356–82.

56. *Institutes*, 3.1.2.

57. For a study on Calvin's sparse references to the Spirit's double procession, see Helleman, "Procession of the Holy Spirit," 21–36.

ing it to believers for their salvation and comfort. The Spirit works for Christ, and Christ works through the Spirit. In this reciprocal dependence, believers are made doubly secure and are kept from errors such as false mysticism or from imagining that the Spirit can be obtained without obtaining Christ. Calvin elaborates,

> We are partakers of the Holy Spirit in proportion to the intercourse which we make with Christ; for the Spirit will be found nowhere but in Christ, on whom he is said, on that account, to have rested. . . . But neither can Christ be separated from his Spirit; for then he would be said to be dead, and to have lost all his power.[58]

The Holy Spirit, Calvin explains, is the bond by which Christ unites us to himself.[59] No doctrine is more important than union with Christ. As David Willis-Watkins writes, "Calvin's doctrine of union with Christ is one of the most consistently influential features of his theology and ethics, if not the single most important teaching that animates the whole of his thought and his personal life."[60] Daniel Lee states, "Through the office of the Holy Spirit, the Mediator is 'personalized' to us so that He can be said to dwell and work in us."[61]

Calvin did not intend to present theology through a single doctrine. Nonetheless, his sermons, commentaries, and theological works are so permeated with the doctrine of union with Christ that it becomes his focus for Christian faith and practice.[62] He writes, "That joining together of Head and members, that indwelling of Christ in our hearts—in short, that mystical union—are accorded by us the highest degree of importance, so that Christ, having been made ours, makes us sharers with him in the gifts with which he has been endowed."[63]

---

58. *Comm.*, on Eph. 3:17.
59. *Institutes*, 3.1.1.
60. David Willis-Watkins, "The *Unio Mystica* and the Assurance of Faith according to Calvin," in *Calvin: Erbe und Auftrag; Festschrift für Wilhelm Heinrich Neuser zum 65. Geburtstag*, ed. Willem van 't Spijker (Kampen: Kok, 1991), 78.
61. Lee, *Holy Spirit as Bond*, 189.
62. E.g., Charles Partee, "Calvin's Central Dogma Again," *SCJ* 18, no. 2 (1987): 194. Cf. Otto Gründler, "John Calvin: Ingrafting into Christ," in *The Spirituality of Western Christendom*, ed. E. Rozanne Elder (Kalamazoo, MI: Cistercian, 1976), 172–87; Brian G. Armstrong, "The Nature and Structure of Calvin's Thought according to the *Institutes*: Another Look," in *John Calvin's "Institutes": His Magnum Opus* (Potchefstroom, South Africa: Institute for Reformational Studies, 1986), 55–82; Guenther H. Haas, *The Concept of Equity in Calvin's Ethics* (Waterloo, ON: Wilfred Laurier University Press, 1997).
63. *Institutes*, 3.11.10.

Since salvation is rooted in the believer's union with Christ, this union must be our starting point in understanding salvation.[64] None of the subsequent elements of the order of salvation (*ordo salutis*), such as justification, sanctification, and perseverance, are possible without the union with Christ that the Spirit effects through faith.[65] Calvin says, "We must understand that as long as Christ remains outside of us, and we are separated from him, all that he has suffered and done for the salvation of the human race remains useless and of no value for us."[66] Such union is possible only because Christ took on our human nature, filling it with his virtue. Union with Christ in his humanity is historical, ethical, and personal, but there is no crass mixture (*crassa mixtura*) of human substance between Christ and us. We are not absorbed into Christ or united to him in such a way that our human personalities are annulled even in the slightest degree. Nonetheless, as Calvin states, "Not only does he cleave to us by an indivisible bond of fellowship, but with a wonderful communion, day by day, he grows more and more into one body with us, until he becomes completely one with us."[67]

Union with Christ by the Spirit is a great mystery.[68] If Christ had died and risen but had not applied his salvation by his Spirit to believers for their regeneration and sanctification, his work would have been ineffectual. The fruits of true godliness reveal that the Spirit of Christ is working in us what has already been accomplished in Christ.

Only the Spirit can unite Christ in heaven with the believer on earth. The Spirit not only initiates this union but also works the communion (*communio*) with Christ that flows from it. This involves participation (*participatio*) in his benefits, which are inseparable from union with Christ.[69] Just as the Spirit united heaven and earth in the incarnation, so

---

64. Howard G. Hageman, "Reformed Spirituality," in *Protestant Spiritual Traditions*, ed. Frank C. Senn (New York: Paulist, 1986), 61.

65. François Wendel, *Calvin: Origins and Development of His Religious Thought*, trans. Philip Mairet (Grand Rapids, MI: Baker, 1997), 238.

66. *Institutes*, 3.1.1.

67. *Institutes*, 3.2.24.

68. Dennis Tamburello points out that "at least seven instances occur in the *Institutes* where Calvin uses the word *arcanus* or *incomprehensibilis* to describe union with Christ" (2.12.7; 3.11.5; 4.17.1, 9, 31, 33; 4.19.35). *Union with Christ: John Calvin and the Mysticism of St. Bernard*, CSRT (Louisville: Westminster John Knox, 1994), 89, 144. Cf. William Borden Evans, "Imputation and Impartation: The Problem of Union with Christ in Nineteenth-Century American Reformed Theology" (PhD diss., Vanderbilt University, 1996), 6–68.

69. Van 't Spijker, "Pneumatological Light," 39–62; Merwyn S. Johnson, "Calvin's Ethical Legacy," in *The Legacy of John Calvin: Papers Presented at the 12th Colloquium of the Calvin*

in regeneration the Spirit raises the elect from earth to commune with Christ in heaven and brings Christ into the hearts and lives of the elect on earth.[70] Communion with Christ is always the result of the Spirit's work, which is astonishing and experiential rather than comprehensible.[71] The Holy Spirit is thus the link that binds the believer to Christ and the channel through which Christ is communicated to the believer.[72] By the Spirit, Christ outside us (*extra nos*) becomes Christ within us (*in nobis*).[73] As Calvin writes to Peter Martyr Vermigli,

> We grow up together with Christ into one body, and he shares his Spirit with us, through whose hidden operation he has become ours. Believers receive this communion with Christ at the same time as their calling. But they grow from day to day more and more in this communion, in proportion to the life of Christ growing within them.[74]

Believers experience union and communion with Christ not because they participate in the essence of Christ's nature[75] but because the Spirit of Christ unites believers so intimately to Christ that they become as flesh of his flesh and bone of his bone (Eph. 5:30). Indeed, the spiritual union with Christ that the Holy Spirit forges in us is even closer than physical union. Calvin writes,

> Let us know the unity that we have with our Lord Jesus Christ; to wit, that he wills to have a common life with us, and that what he has should be ours: nay, that he even wishes to dwell in us, not in imagination, but in effect; not in earthly fashion but spiritually; and that whatever may befall us, he so labors by the virtue of his Holy Spirit that we are united with him more closely than are the limbs with the body.[76]

Studies Society, April 22–24, 1999, Union Theological Seminary and Presbyterian School of Christian Education, Richmond, Virginia, ed. David Foxgrover (Grand Rapids, MI: Calvin Studies Society, 2000), 63–83.

70. See *Institutes*, 4.17.6; *Comm.*, on Acts 15:9.
71. See *Comm.*, on Eph. 5:32.
72. See *Institutes*, 3.1.1; 4.17.12.
73. Van 't Spijker, "Pneumatological Light," 44–53.
74. "Calvinus Vermilio," August 8, 1555, in CO 15:723–24 (no. 2266).
75. Calvin roundly defeats Osiander's doctrine of "essential righteousness" with Christ in *Institutes*, 3.11.5–12.
76. Cited in Wendel, *Calvin*, 235.

The culmination of this union with Christ in both body and soul will be fully realized when we rise from the dead on judgment day.[77]

Calvin moves beyond Luther in this emphasis on communion with Christ. He stresses that, by his Spirit, Christ empowers those who are united with him by faith. Being "engrafted into the death of Christ, we derive from it a secret energy, as the twig does from the root," Calvin writes. The believer "is animated by the secret power of Christ; so that Christ may be said to live and grow in him; for as the soul enlivens the body, so Christ imparts life to his members."[78]

Christ and the Spirit work together for our salvation. Though distinct, they are inseparable. Calvin moves fluidly from saying "The Spirit dwelling in us" to "Christ dwelling in us."[79] Jesus Christ bears and bestows the Spirit. Every action of the Spirit is, in essence, the action of Christ. The Spirit bestows a saving nature on us through Christ, and Christ bestows on us a saving nature only through the Spirit.[80] Calvin hints of this in the title of his opening chapter in book 3 of the *Institutes*: "The Things Spoken concerning Christ Profit Us by the Secret Working of the Spirit." Christ works salvation through the Spirit, and the Holy Spirit works salvation for Christ in sinners' hearts.[81]

Calvin further explains this collaboration between Christ and the Spirit. He says that the Spirit in his "whole fullness" is given by the Father to Christ in a special way, so that we, through the "Spirit of sanctification," might each be given the Spirit "according to the measure of Christ's gift" (Eph. 4:7).[82] The Spirit's work in us helps us separate from the world and brings us by faith and hope into our eternal inheritance.[83] This work is reflected in the titles Scripture gives to the Holy Spirit, such as the "spirit of adoption," "the guarantee and seal" of our inheritance, "water," "oil," and "anointing."[84]

---

77. See *Comm.*, on 1 Cor. 6:15.

78. *Comm.*, on Gal. 2:20; CO 50:199. Cf. Barbara Pitkin, *What Pure Eyes Could See: Calvin's Doctrine of Faith in Its Exegetical Context*, OSHT (New York: Oxford University Press, 1999).

79. *Institutes*, 3.2.39.

80. Faber, "Saving Work," 3.

81. *Institutes*, 3.1.1.

82. *Institutes*, 3.1.2.

83. *Institutes*, 3.1.2.

84. *Institutes*, 3.1.3.

The Spirit and Faith, Justification, and Sanctification

From God's perspective, the Spirit is the bond between Christ and believers, Calvin says, whereas from our perspective, faith is the bond. Those perspectives do not clash with each other, since one of the Spirit's primary tasks is to work faith in a sinner. As Calvin explains, "Faith itself has no other source than the Spirit."[85] In his formal definition of faith, Calvin gives a prominent role to the Holy Spirit:

> Now we shall possess a right definition of faith if we call it a firm and certain knowledge of God's benevolence toward us, founded upon the truth of the freely given promise in Christ, both revealed to our minds and sealed upon our hearts through the Holy Spirit.[86]

Human initiative cannot contribute to this work; rather, faith is an entirely supernatural gift given by the Spirit. It would be easier to mix fire and water than to mix faith-righteousness and works-righteousness.[87] Without the Spirit's work in us through faith in Christ, all our knowledge would be worthless; only by his work can we truly come to know the Redeemer. Thus, "the virtue and the hidden working of the Holy Spirit are the cause of our enjoyment of Christ and of all his benefits."[88]

Calvin's definition of faith also emphasizes that the Spirit's saving work involves knowledge—not mere abstract, speculative, or external knowledge but soteriological, heartfelt knowledge. Such knowledge includes an understanding rooted in the inmost depth of man's existence. Like Luther, Calvin believes such knowledge is fundamental to faith, for it embraces the word of God as well as the proclamation of the gospel.[89] Since the written word is exemplified in the living Word, Jesus Christ, faith cannot be separated from Christ, in whom all God's promises are fulfilled.[90] The work of the Spirit does not supplement or supersede the revelation of Scripture but authenticates it. As Calvin says, "Take away the Word, and no faith will remain."[91]

---

85. *Institutes*, 3.1.4.
86. *Institutes*, 3.2.7.
87. *Institutes*, 3.11.13.
88. Calvin, quoted in Wendel, *Calvin*, 239.
89. See *Institutes*, 2.9.2; *Comm.*, on 1 Pet. 1:25. Cf. David Foxgrover, "John Calvin's Understanding of Conscience" (PhD diss., Claremont Graduate School, 1978), 407–9.
90. See *Comm.*, on Gen. 15:6 and Luke 2:21.
91. *Institutes*, 3.2.6.

Spirit-worked faith unites the believer to Christ by means of the word, enabling him to receive Christ as presented in the gospel and graciously offered by the Father.[92] God also dwells in the believer through faith. Consequently, Calvin says, "We ought not to separate Christ from ourselves or ourselves from him" but ought to participate in Christ by faith, for this "revives us from death to make us a new creature."[93]

Calvin exalts this faith, saying that it rises "from the flesh of Christ to his divinity" to penetrate "above all the heaven, even to those mysteries which the angels behold and adore."[94] The Holy Spirit uses faith to bring the heavenly graces of Christ down into the human soul and to raise our souls up to heaven in return. Communion with Christ through faith is so real and profound that even though Christ remains in heaven, he is so firmly grasped by faith and so fully possessed by us that he actually dwells in our hearts.[95] By faith we "come to possess the Heavenly Kingdom."[96]

Faith derives all its value from Jesus Christ. Without Christ, faith is of "no dignity or value," for it is "only instrumental."[97] But when focused on Christ, faith is of inestimable value because by it we receive Christ and all his benefits, including the double grace of justification and sanctification, which together provide a twofold cleansing.[98] Justification offers imputed purity; sanctification, actual purity.[99]

Calvin views justification as "the acceptance with which God receives us into his favor as righteous men."[100] He explains, "Since God justifies us by the intercession of Christ, he absolves us not by the confirmation of our own innocence but by the imputation of righteousness, so that we who are not righteous in ourselves may be reckoned as such in Christ."[101] Justification includes the remission of sins and the right to eternal life, of which the Spirit delights to assure the believer.

---

92. See *Institutes*, 3.2.30–32.
93. *Institutes*, 3.2.24; *Comm.*, on 1 John 2:12.
94. *Comm.*, on John 12:45; 8:19.
95. See *Comm.*, on Acts 15:9.
96. *Institutes*, 3.2.1.
97. *Institutes*, 3.11.7.
98. *Institutes*, 3.11.1.
99. See John Calvin, *Sermons on Galatians*, trans. Kathy Childress (1563; repr., Edinburgh: Banner of Truth, 1997), on Gal. 2:17–20.
100. *Institutes*, 3.11.2.
101. *Institutes*, 3.11.3.

Justification by works is not possible for a sinner, because of his sin. The believer, "excluded from the righteousness of works, grasps the righteousness of Christ through faith, and clothed in it, appears in God's sight not as a sinner but as a righteous man."[102] For Christ's sake, the believer is declared acquitted, "as if his innocence were confirmed."[103] Such truths lead Calvin to define justification as follows: "The sinner, received into communion with Christ, is reconciled to God by his grace, while, cleansed by Christ's blood, he obtains forgiveness of sins, and clothed with Christ's righteousness as if it were his own, he stands confident before the heavenly judgment seat."[104]

Calvin regards justification as the central doctrine of the Christian faith. He calls it "the main hinge on which religion turns"; it is the soil out of which the Christian life develops and is the substance of piety.[105] Justification not only serves God's honor by satisfying the conditions for salvation, it also offers the believer's conscience "peaceful rest and serene tranquility."[106] As Romans 5:1 says, "Therefore being justified by faith, we have peace with God through our Lord Jesus Christ" (KJV). The Spirit teaches believers that they need not worry about their status with God because they are justified by faith.

Justification, however, does not stand alone. As Richard Gaffin writes, it is "a component, with regeneration, of the principal 'twofold grace' that flows from the believer's underlying union with Christ. The 'hinge' of justification, if I may put it this way, is not a 'skyhook.' It is anchored firmly, without in any way diminishing its pivotal importance, in that union" with Christ.[107]

Sanctification is the process through which the believer, by the Spirit's gracious work, increasingly becomes conformed to Christ in heart, conduct, and devotion to God. It is the continual remaking of the believer by the Holy Spirit as well as the increasing consecration of

---

102. *Institutes*, 3.11.2.
103. *Institutes*, 3.11.3.
104. *Institutes*, 3.17.8.
105. *Institutes*, 3.11.1; 3.15.7.
106. *Institutes*, 3.13.1.
107. Richard B. Gaffin Jr., "Justification and Union with Christ (3.11–18)," in Hall and Lillback, *Theological Guide to Calvin's "Institutes,"* 257.

body and soul to God so that "we grow into one body with Christ."[108] Calvin explains:

> By contemplating the face of Jesus Christ in the mirror of the gospel, we may conform ourselves to him from glory to glory. Whereby the apostle means that in proportion as we draw nearer to Jesus Christ and know him more intimately, the grace and virtue of his Spirit will at the same time grow and be multiplied in us.[109]

In sanctification, the believer offers himself to God as a sacrifice. This does not come without great struggle, for it requires cleansing from the pollution of the flesh and the world.[110] It requires repentance, mortification, daily conversion, and separation from pollution.[111] But by the Spirit's grace, the believer perseveres in sanctification. The Spirit grants the resources the believer needs to abide in the vine (John 15:1–16). As Calvin says, the Holy Spirit did not begin the work of our salvation to leave it imperfect but rather makes himself continually available to draw from: "We have not received the Holy Spirit for a single day, or for any short period, but as a perennial fountain, which will never fail us."[112] The Spirit is no "spasmodic visitor but a resident purifier of the inmost recesses of the soul."[113]

The Spirit labors to complete salvation, moving the believer to work at sanctification as well. Though all spiritual fruit in sanctification must be attributed to the Spirit, the Spirit uses the believer. In the paradox of grace, sanctification is both God's work and man's work. The Holy Spirit works in the believer even as the believer is empowered by the Holy Spirit. Gwyn Walters concludes, "Calvin thus avoids the extremes of a spiritual absolutism on the one hand, and those of an equally invidious moralistic humanism on the other."[114]

---

108. *Institutes*, 3.1.1–2; cf. 1.7.5.
109. Quoted in Walters, *Sovereign Spirit*, 105.
110. See *Comm.*, on John 17:17–19.
111. See *Comm.*, on 1 Cor. 1:2.
112. *Comm.*, on John 4:13.
113. Walters, *Sovereign Spirit*, 109.
114. Walters, *Sovereign Spirit*, 111.

Justification and sanctification are inseparable, Calvin says. To separate one from the other is to tear Christ in pieces.[115] It is like trying to separate the sun's light from the heat that light generates.[116] Gaffin summarizes Calvin's metaphor this way:

> Christ, our righteousness, is the sun; justification, its light; sanctification, its heat. The sun is at once the sole source of both such that its light and heat are inseparable. At the same time, only light illumines and only heat warms, not the reverse. Both are always present, without the one becoming the other.[117]

By the Spirit's influence, justification is never a cul-de-sac; believers are justified by faith for the purpose of worshiping God in holiness of life.[118]

The Spirit and the Assurance and Application of Redemption

Calvin teaches that the Holy Spirit has a vital role in the application of redemption. God speaks to us in his word and by his Spirit.[119] He sounds in our ears the preaching of his servants, and he sounds in our hearts the promptings of his Spirit.[120] The inner work of the Spirit, which opens our eyes to the truth in our minds and consciences, is absolutely essential. That truth consists in the gospel, Christ, God's promises, and salvation itself.[121] Calvin says that without the Spirit, "Christ is in a manner unemployed, because we view him coldly without us, and so at a distance from us."[122]

The Holy Spirit witnesses to and assures the believer of his adoption. Calvin writes, "The Spirit of God gives us such a testimony, that when he is our guide and teacher our spirit is made sure of the adoption of God; for our mind of its own self, without the preceding testimony of the Spirit, could not convey to us this assurance."[123]

---

115. *Institutes*, 3.11.6.
116. Calvin, *Sermons on Galatians*, on Gal. 2:17–20.
117. Gaffin, "Justification and Union with Christ," 268.
118. See *Comm.*, on Rom. 6:2.
119. See *Institutes*, 3.24.2.
120. See *Comm.*, on John 14:26; 17:26.
121. See *Institutes*, 3.1.1; 3.2.36; 3.2.41.
122. *Institutes of the Christian Religion*, ed. Henry Beveridge (Edinburgh: Calvin Translation Society, 1845–1846), 3.1.3.
123. *Comm.*, on Rom. 8:16. Cf. *Institutes*, 3:2.11; 3.2.34; 3.2.41; *Comm.*, on John 7:37–39; Acts 2:4; 3:8; 5:32; 13:48; 16:14; 23:11; Rom. 8:15–17; 1 Cor. 2:10–13; Gal. 3:2; 4:6; Eph. 1:13–14; 4:30; *Tracts and Treatises*, 3:253–54; Parratt, "Witness of the Holy Spirit," 161–68.

Calvin's repeated references to adoption embrace "the whole ethos of the Christian life," despite his lack of apportioning adoption a specific section in the *Institutes*.[124] For Calvin, adoption is the apex of salvation as well as "a half-way point between justification and sanctification, inasmuch as in adoption there are both forensic and dynamic aspects."[125] In dynamic, experiential aspects, the Spirit persuades the believer to call out unashamedly, "Abba, Father."[126]

The Holy Spirit assures us of the forgiveness of sins, of the love and goodwill of our Father, and of election and eternal life,[127] all without detracting from the role of Christ. As the Spirit *of Christ*, he assures the believer by leading him to Christ and his benefits, and by bringing those benefits to fruition in the believer.[128]

The unity of Christ and the Spirit has great implications for the doctrine of assurance. Recent scholars often minimize Calvin's emphasis on the necessity of the Spirit's work in assuring a believer of God's promises. They say that Calvin teaches that the *ground* of assurance is God's promises in Christ and in the word of God, whereas the *cause* of assurance is the Spirit, who works it in the heart. Cornelis Graafland argues, however, that this distinction is simplistic, since the Spirit always works as the Spirit of Christ. Hence the objective and subjective elements in assurance cannot be so readily separated; objective salvation in Christ is bound to subjective sealing by the Spirit. Graafland concludes that "Christ in and through his Spirit is the ground of our faith."[129]

Moreover, Calvin teaches that a believer's objective reliance on God's promises as the primary ground for assurance must be sub-

---

124. Joel R. Beeke, *Heirs with Christ: The Puritans on Adoption* (Grand Rapids, MI: Reformation Heritage Books, 2008), 5–6. For a thorough study of Calvin on adoption, see Tim J. R. Trumper, "An Historical Study of the Doctrine of Adoption in the Calvinistic Tradition" (PhD diss., University of Edinburgh, 2001), 38–214. See also Griffith, "'First Title of the Spirit,'" 135–53.

125. Walters, *Sovereign Spirit*, 93.

126. Walters, *Sovereign Spirit*, 95.

127. See *Comm.*, on Rom. 5:5; *Institutes*, 3.2.11; *Comm.*, on 1 Cor. 2:12; Rom. 8:33; *Institutes*, 3.1.3.

128. *Institutes*, 3.2.34.

129. Cornelis Graafland, "'Waarheid in het Binnenste': Geloofszekerheid bij Calvijn en de Nadere Reformatie," in *Een Vaste Burcht voor de Kerk der Eeuwen: Opstellen, Opgedragen aan Drs. K. Exalto ter Gelegenheid van Zijn Zeventigste Verjaardag*, ed. K. Exalto (Kampen: Kok, 1989), 58–60. For more on the sealing of the Spirit, see Johannes De Boer, *De Verzegeling met de Heilige Geest volgens de Opvatting van de Nadere Reformatie* (Rotterdam: Brunder, 1968).

jectively sealed by the Holy Spirit. The reprobate may claim God's promises without experiencing the feeling (*sensus*) or consciousness of those promises. The Spirit often works in the reprobate but in an inferior manner. Calvin says that the minds of the reprobates may be momentarily illumined such that they may seem to have a beginning of faith; nevertheless, they "never receive anything but a confused awareness of grace."[130]

By contrast, the elect are regenerated with incorruptible seed.[131] They receive subjective benefits that the reprobate will never taste: they receive the promises of God as truth in the inward parts; they alone receive the testimony that can be called "the enlightening of the Spirit"; they alone receive experiential, intuitive knowledge of God as he offers himself to them in Christ.[132] Calvin says that the elect alone come to "be ravished and wholly kindled to love God; [they] are borne up to heaven itself [and] admitted to the most hidden treasures of God."[133] "The Spirit, strictly speaking, seals forgiveness of sins in the elect alone, so that they apply it by special faith to their own use."[134] The elect alone come to know a special faith and a special inward testimony.

When distinguishing the elect from the reprobate, Calvin speaks more about what the Spirit does *in us* than what Christ does *for us*, for here the line of demarcation is clearer. He speaks much of inward experience, feeling, enlightenment, perception, even "violent emotion."[135] Though aware of the dangers of excessive introspection, Calvin also recognizes that the promises of God are efficient only when they are brought by the Spirit within the scope, experience, and obedience of faith.[136]

By insisting that the Spirit's *primary method* of working assurance is to direct the believer to embrace the promises of God in

---

130. *Institutes*, 3.2.11.
131. *Institutes*, 3.2.11–12.
132. *Institutes*, 1.4.1; 2.6.4; 2.6.19.
133. *Institutes*, 3.2.41.
134. *Institutes*, 3.2.11.
135. M. Charles Bell states, "Too few scholars have been willing to recognize the intensely experiential nature of Calvin's doctrine of faith." *Calvin and Scottish Theology: The Doctrine of Assurance* (Edinburgh: Handsel, 1985), 20.
136. *Institutes*, 3.1.1. Cf. Randall C. Zachman, *The Assurance of Faith: Conscience in the Theology of Martin Luther and John Calvin* (Minneapolis: Fortress, 1993), 198–203.

Christ, Calvin rejects any confidence in the believer himself. Nevertheless, Calvin does not deny that a *subordinate means* to strengthen assurance is provided by the Spirit through his work within the believer, which bears fruit in good works and marks of grace. Specifically, the Holy Spirit may assure the believer that he is not a temporary believer by revealing to him that he possesses "signs which are sure attestations" of faith,[137] such as "divine calling, illumination by Christ's spirit, communion with Christ, receiving Christ by faith, the embracing of Christ, perseverance of the faith, the avoidance of self-confidence, and [filial] fear."[138]

To summarize Calvin's position, all the members of the Trinity are involved in the believer's assurance of faith. The Father's election, the Son's work, and the Spirit's application of redemption are complementary. When Calvin writes that "Christ is a thousand testimonies to me," he is saying that Christ is a primary source of assurance for him precisely because of the Spirit's application of Christ and his benefits to him as one elected by the Father. No one can be assured of Christ without the Spirit.[139] The Holy Spirit reveals to the believer through his word that God is a well-disposed Father and also enables the believer to embrace Christ's promises by faith and with assurance.

The Spirit and Spiritual Gifts

Governing Calvin's understanding of the gifts of the Spirit is that the Spirit intends them to be used for the common good of the church.[140] When any gift deviates from this purpose, it loses its proper function.

Calvin views the specific gifts mentioned in passages such as 1 Corinthians 12 as part of a larger body of gifts. In the *Institutes*, he mentions science, art, and sculpture as gifts of God.[141] In this light, Calvin's understanding of gifts becomes clearer. For instance, Calvin understands the gift of knowledge as "acquaintance with sacred

---

137. *Institutes*, 3.24.4.
138. Paul Helm, *Calvin and the Calvinists* (Edinburgh: Banner of Truth, 1982), 28.
139. *Institutes*, 3.2.35.
140. Burgess, *The Holy Spirit*, 166. For studies of Calvin and spiritual gifts not otherwise cited here, see Cheng, "Holy Spirit and Spiritual Gifts," 195–204; Peter F. Jensen, "Calvin, Charismatics and Miracles," *EvQ* 51, no. 3 (1979): 131–44; Paul Elbert, "Calvin and the Spiritual Gifts," *JETS* 22, no. 3 (1979): 235–56. Thanks to Derek Naves for assistance in this section.
141. See *Institutes*, 1.11.8–16; 2.2.15.

things" or "ordinary information."[142] Wisdom, on the other hand, represents "revelations that are of a more secret and sublime order."[143]

The gift of faith mentioned in 1 Corinthians 12 represents not saving faith but faith in the miracles performed in Christ's name. Such was the faith possessed by Judas.[144] Calvin does not comment on the gift of healing, since "everyone knows what is meant"[145] by that. He explains that miracles in conjunction with healing, however, "manifest the goodness of God" and the destruction of Satan.[146] The gift of prophecy refers to Spirit-anointed preaching, not a supernatural understanding of the future.[147] The ability to discern between spirits does not refer to natural wisdom, Calvin says; it was a special gift of God to the early church whereby believers could distinguish between true and false ministers.[148]

Calvin understands the tongues mentioned in Acts and 1 Corinthians as the spoken languages of various nations surrounding Israel. The ability to speak in those languages was not acquired through study but by supernatural endowment. The interpretation of these tongues was also a gift that allowed the entire church to benefit from the tongue being spoken.[149] These gifts helped the church quickly disseminate the knowledge of Christ throughout the entire Roman world.[150]

Calvin's position on the cessation of gifts is clearly stated in his *Commentary on Acts*: "The gift of the tongues, and other such like things, are ceased long ago in the Church."[151] In keeping with his conviction that the gifts were to be used for the good of the corporate church rather than for personal gain, Calvin says that sinful ambition eventually deprived the church of these gifts. Though the gift of tongues was present in the early church, God "took away that shortly after which he had given, and did not suffer the same to be corrupted with longer abuse."[152] The administration of those gifts has not been

---

142. *Comm.*, on 1 Cor. 12:8.
143. *Comm.*, on 1 Cor. 12:8.
144. *Comm.*, on 1 Cor. 12:9.
145. *Comm.*, on 1 Cor. 12:9.
146. *Comm.*, on 1 Cor. 12:10.
147. *Comm.*, on 1 Cor. 12:10.
148. *Comm.*, on 1 Cor. 12:10.
149. *Comm.*, on 1 Cor. 12:10.
150. Sweetman, "Meaning of These Gifts?," 120.
151. *Comm.*, on Acts 10:44.
152. *Comm.*, on Acts 10:46.

committed to the church today.[153] As Walters observes, Calvin coupled his conviction of the "finality" of the Bible with his belief that the special revelation of "the New Testament dispensation was extraordinary" and does not continue today.[154]

Stepping back from the debates surrounding the gifts of the Spirit, Calvin emphasizes the true function of the works of the Spirit. In his *Commentary on Acts*, Calvin summarizes his thought:

> For although we do not receive [the Spirit], that we may speak in tongues, that we may be prophets, that we may cure the sick, that we may work miracles; yet it is given us for a better use, that we may believe with the heart unto righteousness, that our tongues may be framed unto true confession, (Rom. 10:10,) that we may pass from death to life, (John 5:24,) that we, which are poor and empty, may be made rich, that we may withstand Satan and the world stoutly.[155]

Such gifts, says Calvin, we should recognize as the Spirit's work, acknowledging "that God has bestowed superlative gifts upon us for the purpose of perfecting what He has begun." Instead of filling us with pride, this should greatly humble us.[156]

The Spirit's Comprehensive Role

Calvin's word-based understanding of the Holy Spirit is a binding principle of his theology. As Walters writes of Calvin, "There are no major, and hardly any minor, aspects of theology which he can discuss without explicit reference to, and dependence upon, the Spirit of God. His doctrine of the Holy Spirit integrates his entire theology. . . . The Spirit is never relegated to the incidentals or periphery of faith."[157] That emphasis confirms Calvin's reputation of being "the theologian of the Holy Spirit."

More aspects of Calvin's pneumatology are addressed elsewhere in this book. These include the Spirit's role in relation to creation

---

153. *Institutes*, 4.19.18.
154. Walters, *Sovereign Spirit*, 191. See 192–202 for Calvin's negation of claims to special revelation today, while allowing for the Spirit's continuing illumination and assistance of believers.
155. *Comm.*, on Acts 2:38.
156. *Comm.*, on 1 Thess. 1:2.
157. Walters, *Sovereign Spirit*, 233.

and providence (chaps. 9, 10),[158] the Christian life (chaps. 14, 15),[159] the church and the sacraments (chaps. 17, 18),[160] and preaching (chap. 6).[161]

More than any other theologian, Calvin teaches us how radically dependent we must be on the Holy Spirit for every temporal, spiritual, and eternal blessing. Without the Spirit, we could not live; our religion would be a sham, and we would be relegated to the abyss of condemnation. Without the Spirit, there would be no real ministry of

---

158. I. John Hesselink, "The Spirit of God the Creator in Calvin's Theology," in *Sola Gratia: Bron voor de Reformatie en uitdaging voor nu*, ed. A. van de Beek and W. M. van Laar (Zoetermeer, the Netherlands: Boekencentrum, 2004), 53–69; Bolt, "Spiritus Creator," 17–34; Joseph A. Pipa Jr., "Creation and Providence (1.14, 16–18)," in Hall and Lillback, *Theological Guide to Calvin's "Institutes*," 123–50; Hesselink, "Pneumatology," 302–4; Höhne, "Secret Agent of Natural Causes," 169–178; Walters, *Sovereign Spirit*, 12–21; Yuzo Adhinarta, *The Doctrine of the Holy Spirit in the Major Reformed Confessions and Catechisms of the Sixteenth and Seventeenth Centuries* (Carlisle, UK: Langham Monographs, 2012), 105–33; cf. John Calvin, *Sermons on Genesis: Chapters 1:1–11:4*, trans. Rob Roy McGregor (Edinburgh: Banner of Truth, 2009), 15–17, 92.

159. John H. Leith, *John Calvin's Doctrine of the Christian Life* (Louisville: Westminster John Knox, 1989); I. John Hesselink, "Calvin, the Theologian of the Holy Spirit: The Holy Spirit and the Christian Life," in Lee, *Calvin in Asian Churches*, 113–27; Chung, "Calvin and the Holy Spirit," 40–55; Guenther H. Haas, "Calvin's Ethics," in McKim, *Cambridge Companion to John Calvin*, 93–105; David Clyde Jones, "The Law and the Spirit of Christ (2.6–9)," in Hall and Lillback, *Theological Guide to Calvin's "Institutes*," 301–19; William Edgar, "Ethics: The Christian Life and Good Works according to Calvin (3.6–10, 17–19)," in Hall and Lillback, *Theological Guide to Calvin's "Institutes*," 320–46.

For Calvin on the Spirit's work in prayer, see D. B. Garlington, "Calvin's Doctrine of Prayer: An Examination of Book 3, Chapter 20 of the *Institutes of the Christian Religion*," BRT 1, no. 1 (1991): 21–36; Robert Douglas Loggie, "Chief Exercise of Faith: An Exposition of Calvin's Doctrine of Prayer," HQ 5, no. 2 (1965): 65–81; Jae Sung Kim, "Prayer in Calvin's Soteriology," in *Calvinus Praeceptor Ecclesiae: Papers of the International Congress on Calvin Research, Princeton, August 20–24, 2002*, ed. Herman J. Selderhuis, THR 388 (Geneva: Librairie Droz, 2004), 265–74; Stephen Matteucci, "A Strong Tower for Weary People: Calvin's Teaching on Prayer," FJ 69 (2007): 19–24; David B. Calhoun, "Prayer: 'The Chief Exercise of Faith' (3.20)," in Hall and Lillback, *Theological Guide to Calvin's "Institutes*," 347–67; Joel R. Beeke, "Communion of Men with God," in *John Calvin: A Heart for Devotion, Doctrine, and Doxology*, ed. Burk Parsons (Lake Mary, FL: Reformation Trust, 2008).

160. Hughes Oliphant Old, "Calvin's Theology of Worship," in *Give Praise to God: A Vision for Reforming Worship; Celebrating the Legacy of James Montgomery Boice*, ed. Philip Graham Ryken, Derek W. H. Thomas, and J. Ligon Duncan III (Phillipsburg, NJ: P&R, 2003), 412–35; Peter Ward, "Coming to Sermon: The Practice of Doctrine in the Preaching of John Calvin," SJT 58, no. 3 (2005): 319–32; I. John Hesselink, "The Role of the Holy Spirit in Calvin's Doctrine of the Sacraments," in *Essentialia et Hodierna: Oblata P. C. Potgieter*, ed. D. François Tolmie, AcTS 3 (Bloemfontein: University of the Free State, 2002), 66–88; Jill Raitt, "Three Inter-Related Principles in Calvin's Unique Doctrine of Infant Baptism," SCJ 11, no. 1 (1980): 51–62; John W. Riggs, *Baptism in the Reformed Tradition: A Historical and Practical Theology*, CSRT (Louisville: Westminster John Knox, 2002); Wallace, *Calvin's Doctrine*; Kilian McDonnell, *John Calvin, the Church, and the Eucharist* (Princeton, NJ: Princeton University Press, 1967); Brian A. Gerrish, *Grace and Gratitude: The Eucharistic Theology of John Calvin* (Minneapolis: Fortress, 1993); Thomas J. Davis, *The Clearest Promises of God: The Development of Calvin's Eucharistic Teaching* (New York: AMS, 1995); Keith A. Mathison, *Given for You: Reclaiming Calvin's Doctrine of the Lord's Supper* (Phillipsburg, NJ: P&R, 2002); W. Robert Godfrey, "Calvin, Worship, and the Sacraments (4.13–19)," in Hall and Lillback, *Theological Guide to Calvin's "Institutes*," 368–89; Walters, *Sovereign Spirit*, 146–75; Osterhaven, "Order and the Holy Spirit," 23–44.

161. Dawn DeVries, "Calvin's Preaching," in McKim, *Cambridge Companion to John Calvin*, 106–24; Armstrong, "Role of the Holy Spirit," 99–116.

the word, no real church, and no real commemoration of the sacraments. How much we must thank God for the person and ministry of
his precious, indispensable Spirit! And how much we should pray to
exercise the faith that the Spirit produces in us as we wait for greater
measures of his sovereign outpouring in our lives and in the life of
our churches.

14

The Christian Life

Edward Donnelly

We are not our own. . . . We are God's.
—John Calvin, *Institutes of the Christian Religion*

The *Golden Booklet*

As Alister McGrath describes, "Calvin is widely regarded as a cool and dispassionate systematizer, a mind rather than a personality, a withdrawn and socially isolated figure who felt more at home in the world of ideas than in the real world of flesh, blood and human relationships."[1] In other words, a remote, cerebral genius. Genius he certainly was, a man of towering intellect, but never cold and never remote from the pastoral needs of ordinary men and women. Benjamin B. Warfield observes,

> The prime characteristic of Calvin as a theologian is precisely the practical interest which governs his entire thought and the religious profundity which suffuses it all. It was not the head but the heart

---

1. Alister E. McGrath, *A Life of John Calvin: A Study in the Shaping of Western Culture* (Oxford: Blackwell, 1990), 147.

which made him a theologian, and it is not the head but the heart which he primarily addresses in his theology.[2]

His "practical interest" meant that he was in effect dealing with the Christian life in everything he preached and wrote. In his sermons and commentaries, lectures, letters, and occasional writings, he is constantly seeking to show how truth promotes piety. This is especially true of the *Institutes*, originally designed as a simple catechism for teaching young believers the elements of the Christian faith. As he explained in his prefatory address to King Francis of France, "My purpose was solely to transmit certain rudiments by which those who are touched with any zeal for religion might be shaped to true godliness."[3] Even when he revised and lengthened it to provide training for theological students, this pastoral emphasis remained uppermost.

At the heart of Calvin's theology is a profound sense of God in his majestic glory, with the accompanying realization of human littleness and sin. Like the prophet, he could say, "Woe is me! For I am lost; for I am a man of unclean lips, and I dwell in the midst of a people of unclean lips; for my eyes have seen the King, the LORD of hosts!" (Isa. 6:5). Yet this God, so intimidating in his holiness, is also sovereignly gracious, reaching down to sinners whom he has moved to seek his mercy in Christ and proclaiming, "Your guilt is taken away, and your sin atoned for" (Isa. 6:7). To those who have been thus forgiven then comes the call to service, to which the only appropriate response is "Here am I! Send me" (Isa. 6:8), or, in the words of Calvin's life motto, "My heart I offer to you, Lord Jesus, eagerly and sincerely."

This combining of divine glory and grace with human guilt and gratitude, which is nothing other than biblical Christianity in its purest form, has produced people of a distinctive character. Calvinists at their best are serious and joyful, energetic and serene, orderly and creative. They are exultingly certain that the Lord whom they fear and revere loves them everlastingly. Holding a low opinion of themselves, they are at the same time convinced that they are men and women of high destiny. Over the centuries they have proved themselves extra-

---

2. Benjamin B. Warfield, *Calvin and Calvinism*, in *The Works of Benjamin B. Warfield*, ed. E. D. Warfield et al. (1931; repr., Grand Rapids, MI: Baker, 1981), 5:23.

3. *Institutes*, 1:9.

ordinarily useful on earth precisely because of their heavenly minded-
ness. Their daily lives bear the stamp of the doctrine to which they
have entrusted themselves. To stay in the homes of such believers, as
has been my privilege—talking around their tables, kneeling with them
in family worship, accompanying them to their daily work—is to be
struck by a pronounced similarity of ethos. American or Welsh, Scots
or Dutch, Canadian or English, there is an unmistakable family resem-
blance—very like the Ulster Reformed Presbyterians among whom I
was raised. It is the imprint of John Calvin's system of theology.

But while all the doctrines he expounds make their contribution to
his treatment of the Christian life, a section of the *Institutes*, located
since the 1559 edition in book 3, chapters 6–10, deals with the subject
in a concentrated form. "The Life of the Christian Man" is Calvin at
his most accessible. He writes simply and passionately, rising at times
to what are for him unusual heights of eloquence. This section had
the distinction of being the first part of the *Institutes* to be published
separately,[4] and it has proved influential ever since, sometimes appearing under the title *Golden Booklet of the True Christian Life*. In
these pages Calvin opens his heart and sets out his deepest convictions about how the believer is to live from day to day. It would be
an ideal starting point for anyone embarking on the *Institutes* for the
first time. "If you would know the man," advises Warfield, "how he
lived with and for God and the world, read first of all in the *Institutes* the section *On the Life of the Christian Man*. It is the portrait
of himself."[5]

These chapters were not part of the original edition but were
added at the end of the more comprehensive *Institutes* of 1539, and
we may wonder why such an important section was not included
from the beginning. The answer may lie in Calvin's circumstances
over the preceding months, for he had been following a steep learning curve. It had been for him a period of exhilaration, turmoil, and
eventual disillusionment, in that the early Reformation in Geneva
appeared to have failed. All had gone well at first, and on May 21,

---

4. It was published in 1549, in Thomas Broke's English translation, with French and Latin
editions published in Geneva in the following year.
5. Warfield, *Calvin and Calvinism*, in *Works*, 5:26.

1536, the General Council had voted unanimously to abolish the Mass and other Roman abuses and had covenanted to live in obedience to God's word. Encouraged by this commitment, Guillaume Farel and Calvin had embarked on a vigorous program aimed at enforcing acceptance of the confession and catechisms and overseeing morals throughout the city. Their attempt was premature, opposition boiled up and gained the ascendancy, and on April 23, 1538, the Reformers were banished. The young enthusiast had bruised himself against the obduracy of fallen human nature. He was being compelled to realize that to explain doctrine, no matter how clearly, would not be enough to bring men to love and follow the truth. "A deeper reflection on the christological foundations of the Christian life, particularly as they had been set forth by the apostle Paul, was called for," Ford Lewis Battles observes. "This short treatise supplied the lack."[6]

Imitation of Christ

In an introductory chapter, Calvin explains that as children of God, we are to be like our Father. It is characteristic of God's glory that he have no fellowship with uncleanness, for "it is highly unfitting that the sanctuary in which he dwells should be like a stable crammed with filth."[7] Since he is holy, we, too, must be holy, for he is redeeming us in order to restore within us his image, defaced by the fall: "When we hear mention of our union with God, let us remember that holiness must be its bond. . . . This is the goal of our calling to which we must ever look."[8] Our pursuit of holiness will therefore promote his glory and prove that we really are his children.[9]

Renewal in God's image takes place when we are united by faith to Jesus Christ, for the Christian life is literally life "in him." We are called to reflect him in the world, "for we have been adopted as sons by the Lord with this one condition: that our life express Christ, the

---

6. Ford Lewis Battles, *Interpreting John Calvin*, ed. Robert Benedetto (Grand Rapids, MI: Baker, 1996), 297.
7. *Institutes*, 3.6.2.
8. *Institutes*, 3.6.2.
9. Joel R. Beeke, "Appropriating Salvation: The Spirit, Faith and Assurance, and Repentance (3.1–3, 6–10)," in *A Theological Guide to Calvin's "Institutes": Essays and Analysis*, ed. David W. Hall and Peter A. Lillback, Calvin 500 Series (Phillipsburg, NJ: P&R, 2008), 272.

bond of our adoption."[10] In other words, to live as a believer means to be a disciple of Jesus. Calvin takes us back into the Gospels and places us in the position of the first disciples. To us, as to them, comes Christ's definitive summons: "If anyone would come after me, let him deny himself and take up his cross and follow me" (Matt. 16:24). His exposition of the Christian life is an expansion and application of this verse. We are pilgrims on the road from earth to heaven, walking in the steps of our Master. He not only went before us but now, as risen and reigning Lord, accompanies us on the journey, motivating us for every challenge, empowering us along the way and awaiting us at the end. Being a Christian involves participation in his death and resurrection, dying to sin and rising to a new life of righteousness. To imitate Christ means to deny ourselves and take up the cross as he did. As we travel, we look forward to our future life in heaven, being careful at the same time to serve God faithfully in the present world through which we are passing. Such is the outline that he is about to develop. The conception is brilliantly simple and profound, demanding and inviting. The Christian life is following the Lord Jesus.

As Calvin knew from recent painful experience in Geneva, however, not all who call themselves Christians are true disciples,

> whatever they meanwhile learnedly and volubly prate about the gospel. For it is a doctrine not of the tongue but of life. It is not apprehended by the understanding and memory alone, as other disciplines are, but it is received only when it possesses the whole soul and finds a seat and resting-place in the inmost affection of the heart.[11]

From there it must pass "into our daily living, and so transform us into itself that it may not be unfruitful for us."[12]

This is a dauntingly high requirement, and the believer should not expect instant perfection or be unduly downcast when spiritual progress is "at a feeble rate." Nor, on the other hand, should the ultimate target be abandoned as unrealistic.

---

10. *Institutes*, 3.6.3; cf. Beeke, "Appropriating Salvation," 272–74; Michael Horton, *Calvin on the Christian Life: Glorifying and Enjoying God Forever*, Theologians on the Christian Life (Wheaton, IL: Crossway, 2014), 104.

11. *Institutes*, 3.6.4.

12. *Institutes*, 3.6.4.

Let each one of us, then, proceed according to the measure of his puny capacity and set out upon the journey we have begun. No one shall set out so inauspiciously as not daily to make some headway, though it be slight. Therefore, let us not cease so to act that we may make some unceasing progress in the way of the Lord. And let us not despair at the slightness of our success; for even though attainment may not correspond to desire, when today outstrips yesterday the effort is not lost. Only let us look toward our mark with sincere simplicity and aspire to our goal: not fondly flattering ourselves, nor excusing our own evil deeds, but with continuous effort striving toward this end: that we may surpass ourselves in goodness until we gain to goodness itself.[13]

After this preface, an admirable blend of challenge and encouragement, Calvin is ready to deal with the four central features of the Christian life.

Self-Denial

Denial of the self was a staple in the ascetic theology of the Middle Ages, the means by which the spiritual elite could ascend to perfection. By mortifying the flesh—that is, practicing celibacy and poverty and inner contemplation—the candidate could hope to pass through the stages of purgation and illumination to final union with God. Calvin was familiar with this teaching, but his perspective was radically different. For him, self-denial is not a special requirement for the few but a norm for all believers, and we deny self because we *have* been united with God, not because we want to achieve such a union. The discipline, though costly at times, is overwhelmingly positive and joyful, as we can see from two exhilarating emphases.

Self-Denial Is Gospel Based

We are saved in the first place by turning away from ourselves and trusting God. We confess and forsake our sins, repudiate our imagined righteousness, and abandon all attempts to earn God's favor, literally "denying ourselves." In return, we receive Christ in all the fullness

---

13. *Institutes*, 3.6.5.

of his salvation. This is not a sacrifice or something to regret but is cause for the most profound gladness. To lose a self that is worse than useless in order to gain Christ, the pearl of great price, is the best of exchanges, for as he himself said, "Whoever loses his life for my sake will find it" (Matt. 16:25).

Self-denial in the ongoing Christian life is simply a continuation of this enriching pattern, to be engaged in life not with grim resignation but with joyful eagerness. For "we are God's," cries Calvin, in one of his most memorable passages:

> We are not our own: in so far as we can, let us therefore forget ourselves and all that is ours. Conversely, we are God's: let us therefore live for him and die for him. . . . We are God's: let all the parts of our life accordingly strive toward him as our only lawful goal. . . . For, as consulting our self-interest is the pestilence that most effectively leads to our destruction, so the sole haven of salvation is to be wise in nothing and to will nothing through ourselves but to follow the leading of the Lord alone. Let this therefore be the first step, that a man depart from himself in order that he may apply the whole force of his ability in the service of the Lord.[14]

The privilege of believers, and it is a privilege, is "to present [our] bodies as a living sacrifice, holy and acceptable to God" in order to "be transformed by the renewal of [our] mind" (Rom. 12:1–2).

Self, in other words, is our great enemy, the root of all sin. It is, in its very nature, hostile to God, resisting his word and will, unwilling to yield to his authority. Ronald Wallace explains,

> The self constitutes the first and most continuous and most baffling problem that every Christian has to face. . . . Our own hearts are the battlefield where by far the fiercest conflicts with evil are to be waged, and if we can succeed in overcoming Satan in this sphere we will find no difficulty in overcoming him in any other sphere of life where we may encounter him.[15]

---

14. *Institutes*, 3.7.1.
15. Ronald S. Wallace, *Calvin's Doctrine of the Christian Life* (repr., Eugene, OR: Wipf and Stock, 1997), 58.

To deny self is to erase from our minds "the yearning to possess, the desire for power, and the favor of men, . . . ambition and all craving for human glory and other more secret plagues."[16] It is "to renounce ungodliness and worldly passions, and to live self-controlled, upright, and godly lives in the present age" (Titus 2:12).

As Christina Rossetti artfully puts it,

God, harden me against myself . . . :

Myself, arch-traitor to myself;
My hollowest friend, my deadliest foe,
My clog whatever road I go.[17]

Self-denial is liberation from this lethal bondage, and to put it to death is to come closer to Christ and to experience true life. To borrow Calvin's epigram, "Man becomes happy through self-denial."[18] This is a far cry from medieval asceticism.

Self-Denial Is Outward Looking

Far from being a process of endless introspection, a Sisyphean pursuit of complete self-emptying, self-denial finds its focus in love of our fellow man, as required in the apostolic injunction to "do nothing from selfish ambition or conceit, but in humility count others more significant than yourselves" (Phil. 2:3). Self-denial is not, in other words, an end in itself, but one engages in it to make room for other people. We are naturally proud, overvaluing our good qualities and minimizing our defects while exaggerating the failures and depreciating the gifts of others. This makes us mean spirited and competitive, and it destroys community. Self-denial, however, leads us, "unremittingly examining our faults," to "call ourselves back to humility," while "on the other hand we are bidden so to esteem and regard whatever gifts of God we see in other men that we may honor those men in whom they reside."[19]

---

16. *Institutes*, 3.7.2.

17. Christina Rossetti, "Who Shall Deliver Me?," in *The Poetical Works of Christina Georgina Rossetti* (London: Macmillan, 1904), 238.

18. *CR*, 55:48; cited in Wilhelm Niesel, *The Theology of Calvin*, trans. Harold Knight, LEH (1956; repr., Cambridge: James Clarke, 2002), 144. See also Horton, *Calvin on the Christian Life*, 251.

19. *Institutes*, 3.7.4.

This is a difficult duty, and it requires us to "do no little violence to nature, which so inclines us to love of ourselves alone that it does not easily allow us to neglect ourselves and our possessions in order to look after another's good." But we are to "let this be our rule for generosity and beneficence: We are the stewards of everything God has conferred on us by which we are able to help our neighbor, and are required to render account of our stewardship."[20]

People may not deserve help, but that does not alter our obligation, grounded as it is on the twin realities of creation in the image of God and a common humanity. Calvin writes,

> Assuredly there is but one way to achieve what is not merely difficult but utterly against human nature. . . . It is that we remember not to consider men's evil intention but to look upon the image of God in them, which cancels and effaces their transgressions, and with its beauty and dignity allures us to love and embrace them.[21]

We are to love our neighbor as ourselves, and "for anyone to be a neighbour, it is enough that he be a man; it is not in our power to deny the common ties of nature."[22] To refuse to help the needy is to dehumanize ourselves and to place ourselves outside the human race. No matter how challenging and costly such love of others may be, we remember, in Rossetti's words,

> One there is can curb myself,
> Can roll the strangling load from me,
> Break off the yoke and set me free.[23]

Self-denial also enables us to submit tranquilly to God's ordering of our lives, being delivered from "an immoderate desire to grow rich or ambitiously pant after honors"[24] and seeking the Lord's blessing as our chief good in every circumstance. This makes us contented and

---

20. *Institutes*, 3.7.5.
21. *Institutes*, 3.7.6.
22. John Calvin, comm. on Luke 10:30–31, in *CNTC*, 3:38.
23. Rossetti, "Who Shall Deliver Me?," 238; see also Herman J. Selderhuis, *John Calvin: A Pilgrim's Life*, trans. Albert Gootjes (Downers Grove, IL: IVP Academic, 2009), 225–27.
24. *Institutes*, 3.7.9.

willing to bear adversity with patience, a theme that Calvin develops in the next chapter.

Cross Bearing

It is hard to know which would have astonished John Calvin more: the "health and wealth" heresy or its current popularity. His perspective on the Christian life was altogether more somber: "For whomever the Lord has adopted and deemed worthy of his fellowship ought to prepare themselves for a hard, toilsome and unquiet life, crammed with very many and various kinds of evil."[25] He is not writing out of an innate pessimism or as someone embittered by trouble but because he understands what following Christ involves. Jesus's life was dominated by the cross. From his birth it cast a shadow that deepened throughout his years on earth. He came to this world to die, to be proclaimed as "Christ crucified" (1 Cor. 1:23), and his followers can anticipate that as they walk in his steps, they will be "killed all the day long" (Rom. 8:36). "We must all be ready," Calvin says, "for our whole life to represent nothing but an image of death, until it produces death itself, even as the life of Christ is nothing but a prelude to death."[26] This taking up the cross is the external counterpart to inner self-denial—the surrender of the life accompanying and following that of the heart. While an intensely painful experience, it is at the same time profoundly beneficial and results in everlasting joy.

Calvin divides cross bearing into two categories. It refers first to the calamities that are the lot of all humanity—the inescapable hurts and griefs, heartbreaks and frustrations of life in a fallen world. Added to these are persecutions that Christians undergo because of their faith, so that believers can expect to suffer more, not less, than others. There is no need to devise artificial methods of suffering, seeking it out as in the penitential regimes of monasticism. It will come inevitably in the ordinary course of life, which is precisely where the Lord wants us to bear our cross, as did his Son. Every human is assigned a portion of suffering, but this is not a cross unless it is carried willingly:

---

25. *Institutes*, 3.8.1.
26. Calvin, comm. on Phil. 3:10, in *CNTC*, 11:276.

Though God lays both on good and bad men the burden of the cross, yet unless they willingly bend their shoulders to it, they are not said to bear the cross; for a wild and refractory horse cannot be said to admit his rider, though he carries him. The patience of the saints, therefore, consists in bearing willingly the cross which has been laid on them.[27]

This identification with Christ in his death is important not only as the path to life but also because it is immensely helpful in our sanctification. By itself, of course, suffering has no intrinsic ennobling power, for it can make men bitter and harden their hearts against God. But when the believer accepts it in faith, understanding that it is conforming him to the image of Christ, he is able to embrace it as a special favor from God:

> How much can it do to soften all the bitterness of the cross, that the more we are afflicted with adversities, the more surely our fellowship with Christ is confirmed! By communion with him the very sufferings themselves not only become blessed to us but also help much in promoting our salvation.[28]

What benefits, then, do we derive from cross bearing? It humbles us. When life is comfortable, we can become self-reliant and self-satisfied, arrogantly secure in our imagined strength and goodness. But troubles bring us low and deflate our unwarranted confidence. In sickness or bereavement, we find that our faith is weaker than we had thought and our strength small, and we cry desperately to God for help. David's experience becomes ours:

> As for me, I said in my prosperity,
>   "I shall never be moved."
> By your favor, O LORD,
>   you made my mountain stand strong;
> you hid your face;
>   I was dismayed.
>
> To you, O LORD, I cry,
>   and to the Lord I plead for mercy. (Ps. 30:6–8)

---

27. CR, 45:418–82, cited in John H. Leith, *John Calvin's Doctrine of the Christian Life* (Louisville: Westminster John Knox, 1989), 79.
28. *Institutes*, 3.8.1.

"Believers, warned, I say, by such proofs of their diseases, advance towards humility and so, sloughing off perverse confidence in the flesh, betake themselves to God's grace."[29]

It is only under the cross that we learn by experience how faithful God is and how ready to help his people in time of trouble. We may believe this in theory, but it is the actual receiving of his strength when we need it that confirms in our minds the worth of his promises. This strengthens our hope for the future and leads us to rest always on him alone. Calvin explains,

> And it is of no slight importance for you . . . to distrust yourself that you may transfer your trust to God; to rest with a trustful heart in God that, relying upon his help, you may persevere unconquered to the end; to take your stand in his grace that you may comprehend the truth of his promises; to have unquestioned certainty of his promises that your hope may thereby be strengthened.[30]

Another of the Lord's purposes in sending afflictions is to teach us to obey, for it is when our own wills are crossed that we discover how ready we are to follow his commands, just as Abraham's obedience was demonstrated when he was told to offer up Isaac. Trouble calls forth and develops latent graces of patience and submission. The cross is the necessary medicine for our ingrained pride and selfishness, administered according to our individual needs. Calvin explains,

> For not all of us suffer in equal degree from the same diseases, or, on that account, need the same harsh cure. . . . But since the heavenly physician treats some more gently but cleanses others by harsher remedies, while he wills to provide for the health of all, he yet leaves no one free and untouched, because he knows that all, to a man, are diseased.[31]

If we wander away from God, he may use suffering to bring us back to himself, chastening us as a father does his beloved children. We are

---

29. *Institutes*, 3.8.2.
30. *Institutes*, 3.8.3.
31. *Institutes*, 3.8.5.

to see his kindness in this, not complaining at the pain we experience but recognizing in it a token of his benevolence.

Cross bearing also involves persecution for the sake of righteousness, "a singular comfort. For it ought to occur to us how much honor God bestows upon us in thus furnishing us with the special badge of his soldiery."[32] All the faithful will be hated and injured by the world, and this should lead us to "rejoice and be glad, for your reward is great in heaven" (Matt. 5:12). This cross is peculiar to the Christian and should be borne cheerfully, since through it Christ wills to be glorified in us.

Yet Calvin's humanity and pastoral wisdom shine out when he explains that cheerfulness can coexist with anguish. The point of a cross is that it hurts terribly, and this is the paradox and glory of Christian suffering. He has no time for what he calls the "iron philosophy" of Stoicism. Our Lord himself shed tears over his own trials and over the misfortunes of others. He warned his disciples, "You will weep and lament, but the world will rejoice" (John 16:20), and he pronounced a blessing on those who mourn (cf. Matt. 5:4). As Calvin describes, "If all fear is branded as unbelief, how shall we account for that dread with which, we read, he was heavily stricken [Matt. 26:37; Mark 14:33]? If all sadness displeases us, how will it please us that he confesses his soul 'sorrowful even to death' [Matt. 26:38]?"[33]

This is sane and wonderfully tender pastoring. God's people have crosses to bear, but they are not asked to pretend that they enjoy them. We are not to be disappointed with ourselves when we find it difficult to endure. It is natural that there will be a conflict between our dread of pain and our acceptance of it as being part of God's purpose for us. A quiet confidence upholds us in the midst of apprehension, a gladness underneath our tears. Calvin elaborates,

> For the adversities themselves will have their own bitterness to gnaw at us; thus afflicted by disease, we shall both groan and be uneasy and pant after health; thus pressed by poverty, we shall be pricked by the arrows of care and sorrow; thus we shall be smitten by the pain of disgrace, contempt, injustice; thus at the funerals of our dear ones we shall weep the tears that are owed to our nature.

32. *Institutes*, 3.8.7.
33. *Institutes*, 3.8.9.

But the conclusion will always be: the Lord so willed, therefore let us follow his will.[34]

All that he does is for our benefit, so that we can carry our cross with thankfulness: "We are afflicted in every way, but not crushed; perplexed, but not driven to despair; persecuted, but not forsaken; struck down, but not destroyed; always carrying in the body the death of Jesus, so that the life of Jesus also may be manifested in our bodies" (2 Cor. 4:8–10). It is to this life, the crown beyond the cross, that Calvin turns next.

Meditation on the Future Life

"If anyone would come after me, let him deny himself and take up his cross and follow me," said Jesus (Matt. 16:24). Follow him where? To heaven. For his journey did not end at the cross. He was raised on the third day and later ascended into heaven, where he now sits at the right hand of God the Father. So following Christ inevitably leads to a future life in glory. Wilhelm Niesel explains, "The imitation of Jesus Christ implies a looking forward to the eternal consummation and the bearing of the cross implies the aspiration towards future blessedness."[35] It is not only the crucified but the ascended Christ whom we follow and to whom we are united and with whom our destiny is inextricably linked. As members of his body, what has already happened to him has happened to us, and in fellowship with him by the Spirit, "he is not only brought down to us on this earth, but our souls are also raised up to him so that we can participate here and now in his ascended life and glory."[36] This is what biblical theologians call "the presence of the future," the reality that we are even now participating in the life to come. The Latin *meditatio*, which in its English translation we understand as "calm contemplation," can also mean "preparation" and "practice," and all three senses are evident in Calvin's teaching, for by "meditation" he "did not mean otherworldly speculation but actual participation in a life of fellowship with God."[37]

---

34. *Institutes*, 3.8.10.
35. Niesel, *Theology of Calvin*, 149.
36. Ronald S. Wallace, *Calvin, Geneva and the Reformation: A Study of Calvin as Social Reformer, Churchman, Pastor, and Theologian* (Edinburgh: Scottish Academic Press, 1988), 198.
37. Leith, *Calvin's Doctrine of the Christian Life*, 160.

In T. H. L. Parker's words, "The believer thinks about the future life. More, he prepares for it. More, he practises it in this life."[38]

Preparation for our future life helps complete the disciplines of self-denial and cross bearing. By showing us the vanity of earthly things, it enables us to renounce self and liberates us from the grip this world holds us in.[39] It also makes suffering easier to bear when we reflect on what comes after it, just as our Lord endured the cross "for the joy that was set before him" (Heb. 12:2). And we experience the benefits not merely in one direction, for the afflictions of life in turn lead us to long more eagerly for the blessings of the world to come.

Such meditation, then, is not only natural in light of our destiny but also spiritually advantageous in the present. For this world exerts on us a magnetic attraction:

> Our minds, stunned by the empty dazzlement of riches, power, and honors, become so deadened that they can see no farther. The heart also, occupied with avarice, ambition, and lust, is so weighed down that it cannot rise up higher. In fine, the whole soul, enmeshed in the allurements of the flesh, seeks its happiness on earth.[40]

So God uses suffering to wean our affections from this world. Wars and tumults remind us that here there is no lasting peace. Economic hardship points to where true riches are to be found. Disappointments in our relationships keep us from seeking from other people what God alone can give. We need this discipline to keep us from being intoxicated by the present life, for since it has "much show of pleasantness, grace and sweetness wherewith to wheedle us, it is very much in our interest to be called away now and again so as not to be captivated by such panderings."[41] There is something incorrigibly earthy in us that makes it difficult to "seek the things that are above, where Christ is" (Col. 3:1). So the Lord teaches us by repeated and painful lessons that our treasure is in heaven: "If God has to instruct us, it is our duty, in turn, to listen to him calling us, shaking us out of our sluggishness,

---

38. T. H. L. Parker, *Calvin: An Introduction to His Thought* (London: Continuum, 1995), 92.
39. See François Wendel, *Calvin: Origins and Development of His Religious Thought*, trans. Philip Mairet (Glasgow: Collins, 1978), 252.
40. *Institutes*, 3.9.1.
41. *Institutes*, 3.9.2.

that, holding the world in contempt, we may strive with all our heart to meditate on the life to come."[42]

This "contempt" for the world is comparative only. We are to accept our present life with thankfulness, counting it among God's blessings, for to do otherwise would be ingratitude indeed. The daily benefits that he confers on us prove his loving fatherhood and whet our appetite for fuller revelations of his generosity. "Since, therefore, this life serves us in understanding God's goodness, should we despise it as if it had no grain of good in itself?"[43] It is in comparison with the life to come that this life is to be despised. "For, if heaven is our homeland, what else is the earth but our place of exile? If departure from the world is entry into life, what else is the world but a sepulcher?"[44] We are to hate it insofar as it holds us subject to sin but should be prepared to remain in it, like a sentry remaining faithfully at his post of duty, until it please the Lord to call us away.

Yet we know that to be with Christ is far better, and we should long for our full inheritance. Calvin is scornful of Christians who dread death, "gripped by such a fear . . . that they tremble at the least mention of it, as of something utterly dire and disastrous."[45] While such trepidation is understandable, our faith should be able to overcome it. If inanimate creation "waits with eager longing" for the consummation, how much more should we who will "obtain the freedom of the glory of the children of God" (Rom. 8:19, 21)? "Even though the blind and stupid desire of the flesh resists, let us not hesitate to await the Lord's coming, not only with longing, but also with groaning and sighs, as the happiest thing of all."[46]

To look forward to meeting our Lord in glory is infinitely comforting and enables us to endure with patience, and even with joy, the sufferings of the present age. Troubled though we may be by the wickedness and apparent prosperity of the ungodly, we can without difficulty endure such evils. For the day is soon coming when "the Lord will receive his faithful people into the peace of his kingdom, . . .

---

42. *Institutes*, 3.9.2.
43. *Institutes*, 3.9.3.
44. *Institutes*, 3.9.4.
45. *Institutes*, 3.9.5.
46. *Institutes*, 3.9.5.

will feed them with the unspeakable sweetness of his delights, will elevate them to his sublime fellowship—in fine, will deign to make them sharers in his happiness."[47] Without this assurance, we would either sink into despair or settle for the empty satisfactions of this world. But "if believers' eyes are turned to the power of the resurrection, in their hearts the cross of Christ will at last triumph over the devil, flesh, sin, and wicked men."[48]

The Present Life

Does God exist for our sake? The prevailing "spirituality" of our day suggests in a thousand ways that he does. Many of our contemporaries in the churches see God as a desirable extra, a useful resource in emergencies. They would never put it so crassly, of course. But popular books and preachers, not to say many prayers, of the early twenty-first century are in effect assuring us that he is mainly there to help us in times of difficulty, to enrich our lives in various ways, to be the great "Need Meeter." Authentic Christian spirituality, on the other hand, is diametrically opposed to such this-worldliness and maintains that life on earth is a preparation for heaven, which is our true home and the location of all that is ultimately important.

This certainly was Calvin's view. We are pilgrims in the world, following Christ to heaven, and so should see this life not as an end in itself but as a means to assist us on our journey to God: "If we must simply pass through this world, there is no doubt we ought to use its good things in so far as they help rather than hinder our course."[49] This perspective is why Calvin, rather than dealing first with the present life and then with the life to come, as we might have expected, reverses the order in this section. It also explains his change of tone. At the end of chapter 9, he sounds like the preacher in Ecclesiastes, crying, "Vanity of vanities! All is vanity" (1:1), as, from heaven's vantage point, he looks down on earth. Yet in this chapter we find him rejoicing in food and drink, in the scent of flowers, and in the beauty of ivory and gold. He is not contradicting himself but making

---

47. *Institutes*, 3.9.6.
48. *Institutes*, 3.9.6.
49. *Institutes*, 3.10.1.

a profound theological point, as summarized by Battles: "It is the hope of the life to come that gives meaning and purpose to the life which we presently live."[50] We can properly enjoy this world only when we have first learned to despise it in favor of our eternal inheritance. We do not appreciate its blessings as we should until we have reached the point where we are prepared to do without them.

The problem is not so much with the world as with ourselves, because we so easily slip away from a balanced use of its good things into either asceticism or license. The Scriptures do not restrict us, in our enjoyment of God's gifts, to the absolute minimum necessary for sustaining life. But most people then rush to the other extreme and lose themselves in self-indulgence. Calvin returns to this issue in his chapter on Christian freedom, where he makes some extremely perceptive comments on how this liberty can be abused:

> Christian freedom is, in all its parts, a spiritual thing. Its whole force consists in quieting frightened consciences before God—that are perhaps disturbed and troubled over forgiveness of sins, or anxious whether unfinished works, corrupted by the faults of the flesh, are pleasing to God, or tormented about the use of things indifferent. Accordingly, it is perversely interpreted both by those who allege it as an excuse for their desires that they may abuse God's good gifts to their own lust and by those who think that freedom does not exist unless it is used before men, and consequently, in using it have no regard for weaker brethren.[51]

While he agrees that specific and rigid rules for behavior are unwarranted, he insists on some general principles that are to govern our use of the blessings of this life.

The first and chief of these is that "the use of God's gifts is not wrongly directed when it is referred to that end to which the Author himself created and destined them for us, since he created them for our good and not for our ruin."[52] This section should be required reading for all who have accepted uncritically the slander that Calvin and his

---

50. Battles, *Interpreting John Calvin*, 299.
51. *Institutes*, 3.19.9.
52. *Institutes*, 3.10.2.

spiritual descendants were dour utilitarians, philistines with no appreciation of the finer things of life. Kenneth Hare's quip is representative of such caricature:

> The Puritan through Life's sweet garden goes
> To pluck the thorn and cast away the rose.
> And hopes to please, by his peculiar whim,
> The God who fashioned it and gave it him.[53]

Yet here we find Calvin discoursing enthusiastically, almost poetically, on the creation of trees that are "pleasant to the sight" as well as "good for food" (Gen. 2:9) and on "wine to gladden the heart of man" (Ps. 104:15):

> Has the Lord clothed the flowers with the great beauty that greets our eyes, the sweetness of smell that is wafted upon our nostrils, and yet will it be unlawful for our eyes to be affected by that beauty, or our sense of smell by the sweetness of that odor? What? Did he not so distinguish colors as to make some more lovely than others? What? Did he not endow gold and silver, ivory and marble, with a loveliness that renders them more precious than other metals or stones? Did he not, in short, render many things attractive to us, apart from their necessary use?[54]

Here is the basis for a Calvinist aesthetic, for a worldview that recognizes that "the earth is the LORD's and the fullness thereof" (Ps. 24:1). This is a man who truly believes and rejoices in the fact that God "richly provides us with everything to enjoy" (1 Tim. 6:17).[55] Calvin states, "Away, then, with that inhuman philosophy which, while conceding only a necessary use of creatures, not only malignantly deprives us of the lawful fruit of God's beneficence but cannot be practiced unless it robs a man of all his senses and degrades him to a block."[56]

This, however, is not the greater danger. Far more common is the temptation to give in to the desires of our fallen nature and become

---

53. A. Kenneth Hare, *The Raven and the Swallow* (Oxford: Holywell, 1908), 42.
54. *Institutes*, 3.10.2.
55. For more on this topic, see *Institutes*, 2.2.13–16, or, for example, Calvin's commentary on Gen. 4:20–21, where, from the abilities granted to the sons of the Cainite Lamech, he describes "the liberal arts and sciences" as "excellent gifts of the Spirit, diffused through the whole human race."
56. *Institutes*, 3.10.3.

addicted to worldly pleasure. A remedy against this is to remember always that the good things of life come from God and that we are to thank him for them and use them to his glory. We are abusing food and drink if we indulge in them to the extent that we are incapacitated for the duties of piety or our calling in life. We are misusing the gift of clothing "if with its elegance and glitter we prepare ourselves for shameless conduct."[57] We must "make no provision for the flesh, to gratify its desires" (Rom. 13:14). As we are seeing increasingly in the shallow materialism of our society, "many are so delighted with marble, gold, and pictures that they become marble, they turn, as it were, into metals and are like painted figures,"[58] for it is true of idols that "those who make them become like them" (Ps.115:8). John Leith explains that for Calvin, "the essence of life . . . inheres in fellowship with God. God's blessings of food and clothing are designed as aids to this fellowship. Intemperance transforms the means of fellowship into the end of life itself."[59]

Our use of the present life and its blessings is intimately connected with the immediately preceding topics. Self-denial and cross bearing train us to hold lightly the things of this world, as does meditation on the future life. All combine to help believers "deal with the world as though they had no dealings with it. For the present form of this world is passing away" (1 Cor. 7:31). Moderation is the key—"to indulge oneself as little as possible; but, on the contrary, with unflagging effort of mind to insist upon cutting off all show of superfluous wealth, not to mention licentiousness, and diligently to guard against turning helps into hindrances."[60] Calvin himself was a prime example of the lifestyle he recommended, for he lived simply and refused gifts, even when offered by the city government. Although large sums of money passed through his hands, particularly for needy refugees, his accounting was scrupulous and his whole estate at death amounted to the modest sum of less than 200 ecus.[61] When he urged those "who have narrow and

---

57. *Institutes*, 3.10.3.
58. *Institutes*, 3.10.3.
59. Leith, *Calvin's Doctrine of the Christian Life*, 153.
60. *Institutes*, 3.10.4.
61. Writing at the beginning of the twentieth century, Williston Walker suggested that Calvin's estate was "the equivalent in value perhaps from fifteen hundred to two thousand dollars, including the worth of his library." Walker, *John Calvin: The Organiser of Reformed Protestantism, 1509–1564* (New York: Putnam, 1906), 431.

slender resources . . . to go without things patiently,"[62] he was writing from experience.

Another principle to help us guard against worldliness is to remember that we are stewards, that all we have has been entrusted to us by the kindness of God and that we must one day render account to him. The Master before whom we must appear "has greatly commended abstinence, sobriety, frugality, and moderation, and has also abominated excess, pride, ostentation, and vanity."[63]

In a final section, Calvin calls us to look in all of life to the Lord's calling, which he describes as "in everything the beginning and foundation of well-doing."[64] "Each individual has his own kind of living assigned to him by the Lord as a sort of sentry post," Calvin says, "so that he may not heedlessly wander about throughout life. Now, so necessary is this distinction that all our actions are judged in his sight by it."[65] He is not recommending a static feudal society, with the lower orders condemned to "keep their place." Commenting on Paul's injunction that "each one should remain in the condition in which he was called" (1 Cor. 7:20), Calvin says, "It would be asking far too much, if a tailor were not permitted to learn another trade, or a merchant to change to farming. . . . He only wishes to correct the thoughtless eagerness which impels some to change their situation without any proper reason."[66] To know what God has called us to do in this world and then to do it will bring order, harmony, and contentment into our lives. This is the mighty Reformation doctrine of calling, later developed by the Puritans and their successors.[67] The theology that allowed no place for works whatever in respect of salvation was, paradoxically, to lead to the greatest outburst of good works the world has ever seen.

Calvin, characteristically, ends this section on the Christian life on a pastoral, encouraging note:

---

62. *Institutes*, 3.10.5.
63. *Institutes*, 3.10.5.
64. *Institutes*, 3.10.6.
65. *Institutes*, 3.10.6.
66. *CNTC*, 9:153.
67. See, for example, George Swinnock, *The Christian Man's Calling*, vols. 1–2 of *The Works of George Swinnock* (1868; repr., Edinburgh: Banner of Truth, 1992); Richard Baxter, *A Christian Directory*, 4 vols. (London, 1672–1673).

It will be no slight relief from cares, labors, troubles, and other burdens for a man to know that God is his guide in all these things. . . . Each man will bear and swallow the discomforts, vexations, weariness, and anxieties in his way of life, when he has been persuaded that the burden was laid upon him by God. From this will arise also a singular consolation: that no task will be so sordid and base, provided you obey your calling in it, that it will not shine and be reckoned very precious in God's sight.[68]

The Christian Life Today

John Calvin's teaching had a profound influence on the daily lives of future generations. Alexandre Ganoczy remarks, for example, that "Puritanism with its Calvinistic roots contributed . . . to the origin of what we characterize as North American civilization; and the Reformed churches of Europe produced social, cultural and economic elites everywhere."[69] Yet this distinctively Reformed or Calvinistic lifestyle has become a rare phenomenon in the early years of the twenty-first century, for modern Christians live in a way that Calvin would have found alien and disturbing. Their piety, ambitions, value systems, work habits, spending patterns, and leisure pursuits are far removed from those of sixteenth- and seventeenth-century believers. There has been a limited resurgence of interest in Calvinistic doctrine, particularly in the area of soteriology, but this has not so far been matched by any sustained endeavor to develop a contemporary Calvinistic way of life.

Is this because he was too much a man of his time? Was his view of the Christian life valid for his era but not deeply enough rooted in the eternal Scriptures to bear transplanting to a new and very different environment? Such is by no means the case. G. K. Chesterton violently disliked what he imagined Calvinism to be, and his genial little detective, Father Brown, can reliably be provoked to irritation by any mention of the theology or disciples of Geneva. But Chesterton might perhaps forgive a paraphrase of one of his most celebrated *bon mots*:

---

68. *Institutes*, 3.10.6.
69. Alexandre Ganoczy, "Calvin's Life," trans. David L. Foxgrover and James Schmitt, in *The Cambridge Companion to John Calvin*, ed. Donald K. McKim (Cambridge: Cambridge University Press, 2004), 24.

"The Calvinistic ideal has not been tried and found wanting; it has been found difficult and left untried." Calvin is neglected as a guide to daily living not because he is out of date but because our present generation is spiritually compromised. Believers are too weak, indolent, and in love with this world to welcome his bracing medicine. Yet the truth is that he is stunningly relevant for our present time, for he is strong where we are weak, and he sounds notes that we desperately need to hear. His teaching, if understood and followed, would produce a revolution in daily Christian living that could, under God, transform the Christian community and command attention for the gospel from blasé postmoderns who

> want to see as well as hear, to find authenticity in relationship as the precursor to hearing what is said. . . . What postmoderns want to see, and are entitled to see, is believing and being, talking and doing, all joined together in a seamless whole. This is the great challenge of the moment for the evangelical Church.[70]

What would the Christian life look like if shaped by this short section of the *Institutes*? It would be characterized by the following marks.

A Life Lived Consciously in Union with and Imitation of Christ

The key element of the Christian life is that it is precisely that—"Christian," that is, life "in Christ." We are not ordinary people, living more or less as others do, if rather more morally, but with an extra compartment for religion. Instead, we are extraordinary people, born again, new creations, living on this earth an existence created and sustained by supernatural power. To use Calvin's exultant phrase, "We are God's," and this should shape every moment and every activity. We need to learn to think theologically about ourselves, to realize what God's grace has done for us and in us and then to live out of that awareness. Paul's first imperative in Romans does not come until chapter 6, and it is directed not toward our behavior but toward our thinking: "So you also must consider yourselves dead to sin and alive

---

70. David F. Wells, *Above All Earthly Pow'rs: Christ in a Postmodern World* (Grand Rapids, MI: Eerdmans, 2005), 315.

to God in Christ Jesus" (Rom. 6:11). As D. Martyn Lloyd-Jones puts it, "The first thing that is absolutely essential to our being delivered from sin . . . is that we should realize the truth about ourselves."[71] Our primary need is to know who we are.

In particular, the Christian life is following Christ. Evangelicals have been so afraid of any suggestion of faith by works that they have tended to overlook the many Scriptures that speak of the Lord Jesus as our pattern, our example. But this is to distort his call to "follow me." He is, thank God, the Savior who delivers us from the wrath to come. But that salvation is worked out as we walk in his steps. We need to be imitators of Christ. This may indeed be one of the main contemporary barriers to the gospel. Too many of us just do not act like our Master.

A Life Set Free from the Idolatry of Self

Self is the idol of our age. It is cosseted by psychiatrists, worshiped as the source of true fulfillment. In David Wells's words, "The self is seen simply as having a potential that, though not unlimited, is nevertheless still vast and largely untapped. Deep within it are the springs from whence flow its own healing waters. This understanding of the self implies an unwavering faith in its capacities."[72] People, even in the churches, are self-absorbed, self-regarding members of the me generation, embracing "the notion that I am singularly important in the grand scheme of things; and consequently anyone who attempts to relativize me, my abilities, or my needs is blaspheming the god-like importance my narcissism leads me to ascribe to myself."[73] This poison seeps into our thinking in a thousand ways.

But we must set our faces against this idolatry and learn to regard self as our enemy. The gospel assures us that fulfillment is to be found in turning from self to God, in whom we live and move and have our being. To be liberated from destructive self-centeredness is to find our true selves in Christ. Self-denial is the path to life.

---

71. D. Martyn Lloyd-Jones, *Romans: Exposition of Chapter 6; The New Man* (London: Banner of Truth, 1972), 112.

72. David F. Wells, *Losing Our Virtue: Why the Church Must Recover Its Moral Vision* (Leicester, UK: Inter-Varsity Press, 1998), 122.

73. Carl R. Trueman, *Minority Report: Unpopular Thoughts on Everything from Ancient Christianity to Zen-Calvinism* (Fearn, Ross-shire, Scotland: Mentor, 2008), 160.

A Life Committed to the Service of Others

In a busy world, with multiple duties in family, work, and church, many believers have opted out of social or community involvement. Apart from giving to charity, we do little of a practical nature to help our fellow man. Our patron saints are too often the priest and the Levite on the road to Jericho, and we tend to leave the meeting of need to professionals or the state. It is a far cry from Calvin's Geneva, where the Reformer reorganized the education system, urged the magistrates to provide work for the unemployed, supported the new hospital in its care for the destitute and disabled, and helped administer poor relief. Calvinists everywhere were admired for their commitment to their communities and to practical expressions of charity. Leland Ryken records,

> The Anglican divine Lancelot Andrewes noted in 1588 that the Calvinist refugee churches in London were able "to do so much good as not one of their poor is seen to ask in the streets," and he regretted that "this city, the harborer and maintainer of them, should not be able to do the same good."[74]

When we take seriously Calvin's insistence that self-denial is demonstrated by love for our neighbor, we will reclaim those ministries of love and mercy for which the Christian church was once known. We will emerge from our comfortable neighborhoods and take up the costly, productive challenge of helping the needy. This will provide opportunities to speak of that love of Christ that we are in the process of demonstrating. The hurting and hopeless will not only see but also profit from our good works and may be brought to glorify our Father who is in heaven.

A Life That Is Realistic about This World and Oriented toward Heaven

It could be argued that Calvin's downbeat assessment of life in this world was colored by his own difficulties. That he was tormented with severe and multiple illnesses is well known, and his letter to the physicians of Montpellier in 1564, in which he describes some of his

---

74. Cited in Leland Ryken, *Worldly Saints: The Puritans as They Really Were* (Grand Rapids, MI: Zondervan, 1990), 177.

ailments, is painful reading.[75] The death of his infant son and then, after only nine years of marriage, of the wife whom he had grown to love, allied with a turbulent life of controversy, disappointments, threats of serious danger, and chronic overwork could all, it might be claimed, have led to an unwarranted pessimism about this earthly existence.

In fact, it is we in our comfortable Western society who are out of touch with reality. Our present lifestyle is comparatively and atypically luxurious and pain-free, which insulates us from some of "the sufferings of this present time" (Rom. 8:18) and creates false expectations of what we can expect from our existence in this world. To most of our fellow believers throughout history, and to many of our contemporaries in the faith, it is indeed a vale of tears. The better country shines brightly before them, and they are not terrified at the thought of death or tempted to want to linger on earth. Calvin's astringent assessment jolts us out of our intoxication with this life and its pleasures. Warned by him, we will not want to settle down. We will not become bitter or fall to pieces when calamity comes. It will be further proof that here we are strangers and pilgrims. The fascination with heaven and its glories, so tragically lacking in our Christian generation, will be fanned into flame within us, and we will live more joyfully and productively in its light.

A Life in Which Moderation Is the Path to Enjoyment

It is the lie of Satan, from Eden onward, that restraint is the enemy of fulfillment. Our age has bought the lie and believes that more is always better and that excess is the path to guaranteed satisfaction. The results are plain to see, from an epidemic of life-shortening obesity to the ecological crisis in which mankind is wasting and rapidly depleting the resources of the planet. In this, as in many areas, Calvin is amazingly contemporary:

> The custody of the garden was given in charge to Adam, to show that we possess the things which God has committed to our hands, on the condition, that being content with a frugal and moderate

---

75. *Letters of John Calvin: Selected from the Bonnet Edition with an Introductory Biographical Sketch* (Edinburgh: Banner of Truth, 1980), 242–44.

use of them, we should take care of what shall remain. Let him who possesses a field, so partake of its yearly fruits, that he may not suffer the ground to be injured by his negligence; but let him endeavour to hand it down to posterity as he received it, or even better cultivated.[76]

What impinges on us more immediately perhaps is our consumeristic society, the frenzy of buying and having that we can so easily be sucked into.

But Scripture warns us to "be on [our] guard against all covetousness, for one's life does not consist in the abundance of his possessions" (Luke 12:15). We need to be content with less, to follow a more basic lifestyle, practicing what we profess to believe about the comparative value of earthly and heavenly treasures. This will teach us again the enjoyment of simple things and enable us to point out to both our wealthy neighbors and our poverty-stricken neighbors that there is a better way. We may find that the witness of moderation will strike a surprising chord in the lemmings who are beginning to see the cliff edge approaching.

A Life That Is at the Same Time Heroic and Ordinary

Calvin's favorite metaphor for the Christian life is that of the soldier. He frequently uses the word "hero" and urges God's people to be filled with determination and fortitude. Leith explains, "Believers ought to be undaunted. . . . Faith animates us to strenuous action in the same way as unbelief manifests itself by cowardice or cessation of effort. Lack of the heroic quality leads to sin."[77] This is a necessary emphasis at a time when too many Christians have settled for private devotion, personal peace, and affluence. Our influence in the culture is waning largely because so many have fled the battlefield. We need again the iron in our blood that led our forefathers to take the claims of King Jesus into every area of life, no matter what the cost.

Yet this heroism is not divorced from but earthed and expressed in the everyday duties of life. It is touching and entirely typical that

---

76. John Calvin, comment on Gen. 2:15, in *A Commentary on Genesis*, trans. John King (London: Banner of Truth, 1965), 1:125.

77. Leith, *Calvin's Doctrine of the Christian Life*, 85–86.

the great Reformer, after his magnificent exposition of the heights and wonders of the Christian life, ends by assuring blue-collar workers, whose tasks may be considered "sordid and base," that to faithfully discharge their calling will make their work "shine and be reckoned very precious in God's sight."[78] This spirit is echoed in George Herbert's poem "The Elixir," in which he reflects on the search of the alchemists for the philosopher's stone that, they thought, could transmute base metals into gold:

> Teach me, my God and King
> In all things thee to see,
> And what I do in anything,
> To do it as for thee. . . .
>
> A servant with this clause
> Makes drudgery divine:
> Who sweeps a room as for thy laws,
> Makes that and th' action fine.
>
> This is the famous stone
> That turneth all to gold.[79]

It is usually in the ordinary, everyday things that we glorify God. On September 11, 2001, while hundreds of panic-stricken people were rushing out of that doomed building in New York, others were hurrying in the opposite direction, into the inferno of terror, flame, and death. Why? They were firemen, and this was what they had been trained to do. When asked about it afterward, one of them said simply, "We were just doing our jobs." Could there be any better ending for a Christian life than to be able to say to the Lord: "I glorified you on earth, having accomplished the work that you gave me to do" (John 17:4)? We, who are "in Christ," have the best of all precedents.

---

78. *Institutes*, 3.10.6.
79. George Herbert, "The Elixir," in *The Complete English Poems*, ed. John Tobin (New York: Penguin, 2004), 174.

15

Knowing God through Adversity

Derek W. H. Thomas

In the Book of Job is set forth a declaration of such sublimity as to humble our minds.

—John Calvin, *Institutes of the Christian Religion*

As yet, we know not what will be the event. But since it appears as though God would use your blood to sign his truth, there is nothing better than for you to prepare yourselves to that end, beseeching him so to subdue you to his good pleasure, that nothing may hinder you from following whithersoever he shall call. For you know, my brothers, that it behoves us to be thus mortified, in order to be offered to him in sacrifice.

—John Calvin, letter to the five prisoners of Lyons, May 15, 1553

The Pastoral Side of Calvin
The study of Calvin's sermons reveals a side of the Reformer that, while not essentially different from the *Institutes* or commentaries, shows his awareness of pastoral needs and issues.[1] In an illuminating

---

1. Portions of this chapter are adapted from Derek Thomas, *Calvin's Teaching on Job: Proclaiming the Incomprehensible God* (Fearn, Ross-shire, Scotland: Mentor, 2004). Used by permission of Christian Focus.

passage in his *Sermons on Job*, Calvin seems to be self-consciously aware of the importance of his task as a preacher to those in pain:

> For afflictions are as diseases: and if a physician uses one medicine for all diseases, what a thing will that be? Some disease is hot, and some is cold: some disease requires that a man should be kept dry, and some other that he should be refreshed with moisture: one disease will have a man kept close, and another will have him to go abroad. You see then that a physician shall kill his patients, if he have not a regard of their diseases: yea and it becomes him also to be acquainted with the complexions of patients. Even so ought we to consider of those whom God visits with afflictions.[2]

The sermons provide Calvin with a vehicle for expressing his theological convictions in a manner different from his more celebrated theological writings.[3] This chapter examines, as a case in point, Calvin's preaching on the book of Job.[4]

Historical Setting of Calvin's *Sermons on Job*

That Calvin should have turned to the book of Job in the years 1554–1555 is, in one sense at least, unsurprising.[5] Six months before

---

2. John Calvin, "Sermon 78" (Job 21:1–6), in *Sermons on Job*, 16th–17th Century Facsimile Editions (1574; repr., Edinburgh: Banner of Truth, 1993), 366.a.59. Sermons are cited by sermon number with the passage treated set in parentheses, and all come from this edition of Calvin's *Sermons on Job*. Spelling from these sermons has been modernized throughout this chapter.

3. On the printing of Calvin's sermons, see Jean-François Gilmont, *John Calvin and the Printed Book*, trans. Karin Maag, SCES 72 (Kirksville, MO: Truman State University Press, 2005). On Calvin's preaching, see B. G. Armstrong, "Exegetical and Theological Principles in Calvin's Preaching with Special Attention to His Sermons on the Psalms," in *Ordenlich und Fruchtbar: Festschrift für Willem van 't Spijker*, ed. Wilhelm Herman Neuser and Herman J. Selderhuis (Leiden: Groen en Zoon, 1997), 191–203; Richard Stauffer, *Dieu, la création et la providence dans le predication de Calvin* (Bern: Peter Lang, 1978); Stauffer, "L'homilétique de Calvin," in *Interprètes de la Bible: Études sur les réformateurs du XVIe siècle*, ThH 57 (Paris: Éditions Beauchesne, 1980), 167–81; T. H. L. Parker, *Oracles of God: An Introduction to the Preaching of John Calvin*, LEH (London: Lutterworth, 1947); Parker, *Calvin's Preaching* (Louisville: Westminster John Knox, 1992); Dawn DeVries, "Calvin's Preaching," in *The Cambridge Companion to John Calvin*, ed. Donald K. McKim (Cambridge: Cambridge University Press, 2004), 106–24; G. Sujin Pak, *The Judaizing Calvin: Sixteenth Century Debates over the Messianic Psalms*, OSHT (Oxford: Oxford University Press, 2010).

4. See also Paul Lobstein, "Les sermons de Calvin sur le livre de Job," in *Études sur la pensée et l'oeuvre de Calvin* (Neuilly: Editions de "La Cause," [1927?]), 51–67; Susan E. Schreiner, "Calvin as an Interpreter of Job," in *Calvin and the Bible*, ed. Donald K. McKim (Cambridge: Cambridge University Press, 2006), 53–84; Schreiner, *Where Shall Wisdom Be Found? Calvin's Exegesis of Job from Medieval and Modern Perspectives* (Chicago: University of Chicago Press, 1994); Schreiner, *The Theater of His Glory: Nature and the Natural Order in the Thought of John Calvin* (1991; repr., Grand Rapids, MI: Baker Academic, 1995); Thomas, *Calvin's Teaching on Job*.

5. The attempt to date precisely Calvin's sermons on Job is, according to T. H. L. Parker, "doomed to failure." *Calvin's Preaching*, 168. Parker reasons that if the sermons on Deuteronomy

the commencement of the Joban sermons, on August 13, 1553, Michael Servetus arrived in Geneva, making his way that afternoon to hear Calvin preach in Saint Pierre's Cathedral. Despite Calvin's protests for a more humane method than burning, the eventual decision of October 25, 1553, by the Venerable Company of Pastors of Geneva to have Servetus executed as a heretic was to bring down on the Reformer a torrent of criticism. In the years leading up to the Servetus affair, Calvin's enemies had been looking for opportunities to criticize him. Writing to Bullinger in September 1553, some seven months after the commencement of the sermons on Job, Calvin recounted how the Servetus issue still troubled his relationship with the city council:

> Indeed they cause you this trouble, despite our remonstrances; but they have reached such a pitch of folly and madness, that they regard with suspicion whatever we say to them. So much so, that were I to allege that it is clear at mid-day, they would forthwith begin to doubt of it.[6]

In the previous year, 1552, the rise of the Libertines and the general opposition to Calvin had made it impossible for him to leave the city for a month. Tensions in the city were at such levels that Calvin felt unable to attend the wedding of his friend Christopher Fabri. The Reformer eventually left Geneva only because he heard that Guillaume Farel was dying.[7]

In 1553 the issue of ecclesiastical discipline, thought to have been decided in the *Ecclesiastical Ordinances* of 1541, was challenged by the Small Council. In the February elections of 1552, Calvin's long-standing opponent Ami Perrin was elected as first syndic. Pierre Tissot, Perrin's brother-in-law, became the city's lieutenant. The "Perrinist" party (otherwise known as the Libertines) sought to challenge the agreed-on policy regarding ecclesiastical discipline, insisting that prior

---

(which immediately followed the Job sermons) began on Wednesday, March 20, 1555, the last sermon of Job must have been on the previous Friday or Saturday, March 15 or 16, 1555. Working backward, and assuming that Calvin followed his usual plan of preaching each weekday of every other week plus preaching once on the Wednesday of the light week, this dates the beginning of the 159 Job sermons on February 26, 1554. See Parker, *Calvin's Preaching*, 169.

6. Calvin to Heinrich Bullinger, September 7, 1553, in *Tracts and Letters*, 5:427.

7. In the event, of course, Farel did not die but recovered sufficiently to marry a woman considerably younger than himself and, in the end, outlive Calvin himself.

to the Easter Communion of 1553, they be sent a list of all those currently excommunicated together with a list of reasons. The challenge to Calvin was incontrovertible. On February 15, 1553, Calvin wrote to the persecuted French believers on his need of being "tamed" by such trials:

> It is very difficult for me not to boil over when someone gets impassioned. Yet so far no one has ever heard me shouting. But I lack the chief thing of all, and that is being trained by these scourges of the Lord in true humility. And therefore it is all the more necessary that I should be tamed by the free rebukes of my brethren.[8]

By Monday, July 24, 1553, the Genevan Reformer asked to be allowed to resign. The request was denied.

Matters worsened in September; the case of Philibert Berthelier's request to be absolved by the Small Council instead of by the Consistory highlighted the distance between the state and church.[9] By Sunday, September 3, 1553, following a warning for the excommunicated not to present themselves at the Lord's Supper, Calvin evidently thought this might be his last sermon in Geneva. He preached on the farewell address of Paul to the elders at Ephesus (Acts 20:13–38). During the administration of the sacrament, the armed Libertines present made a gesture as though they might seize the sacrament forcibly. Calvin spread his arms over the Table and defied them, and they left.[10] However, Calvin was not dismissed, as he had feared. Berthelier's case dragged on throughout the following year, eventually being settled in the Consistory's favor in January 1555.

In addition, Calvin's health was a matter of great concern. In 1563–1564, Calvin could write to his physicians in Montpellier in considerable detail about the "ulcer in the haemorrhoid veins," "nephritis," and the passing of stones "so big that it tore the urinary

---

8. The translation is Parker's. T. H. L. Parker, *John Calvin: A Biography* (Philadelphia: Westminster, 1975), 115. The letter is not included in the Beveridge and Bonnet edition of Calvin's letters.

9. Philibert Berthelier was part of a group of interrelated families in Geneva who called themselves *les enfants de Genève*. Berthelier himself was a coarse man who along with others had tried, by exaggerated fits of coughing, to prevent Calvin from preaching.

10. See the account in Theodore Beza [Bèze], *The Life of John Calvin*, trans. Henry Beveridge (a translation of Beza's second *Life of Calvin* in 1844), reprinted with minor alterations in *BTM* 227/228, August/September 1982, 41.

canal."[11] But even in 1553, Calvin's sermon delivery was said to be asthmatic and painful. Job would seem to have been an obvious choice for Calvin to preach through.

Earlier that summer, perhaps recalling the very issues in Job, Calvin wrote (not for the first time) to five French prisoners in Lyons. After exhorting them to faith and constancy in their trials, Calvin mused on the apparent injustice of their condition:

> It is strange, indeed, to human reason, that the children of God should be so surfeited with afflictions, while the wicked disport themselves in delights; but even more so, that the slaves of Satan should tread us under foot, as we say, and triumph over us. However, we have wherewith to comfort ourselves in all our miseries, looking for that happy issue which is promised to us, that he will not only deliver us by his angels, but will himself wipe away the tears from our eyes.[12]

Geneva, too, was in turmoil. Support for Calvin was minimal. Reforming the city was costly. Calvin was ridiculed.[13] In conditions of injustice and civil strife, Job seemed an appropriate book to turn to for guidance.[14]

Ambrose, Augustine, and Aquinas on Job

There was historical precedent in turning to Job for a series of sermons: among the great works on Job were those by Ambrose, Augustine, Gregory the Great, Hilary of Poitiers, Jerome, and Thomas Aquinas. Was Calvin influenced by any of these former exegetes? What is immediately apparent in the *Sermons on Job* is their dissimilarity to the great works on Job that preceded them. Gregory, for example, had written thirty-five books filling six volumes on Job, outlining the traditional literal, allegorical, and moral senses of each line. As

---

11. *CO*, 20:253. On Calvin's medical history, see J. Wilkinson, "The Medical History of John Calvin," *PRCPE* 22, no. 3 (1992): 368–83.

12. Calvin to the prisoners of Lyons, July 7, 1553, in *Tracts and Letters*, 5:413.

13. Beza records that it was fairly common for dogs to be named Calvin, sometimes shortened to Cain. Calvin was also hissed at and booed in the streets. Some, including Philibert Berthelier, deliberately coughed through his sermons, passing wind or belching when Calvin complained. Theodore Beza, *Life of John Calvin*, trans. Henry Beveridge, in *Tracts and Letters*, 1:lii.

14. See William G. Naphy, *Calvin and the Consolidation of the Genevan Reformation* (Manchester, UK: Manchester University Press, 1994), 157–59.

a sixth-century Christian, Gregory had viewed the Old Testament allegorically and typologically, each verse of Job alluding to Christ in some way. Calvin, on the other hand, as we shall see, was careful and reticent in his use of typology and critical of the use of allegory.

For Calvin, Job was a book first and foremost about God.[15] Its accents were essentially theological in nature. In that sense, Calvin had not turned to Job because of its obvious themes of suffering and trial—Calvin did not believe the book of Job contained solutions to these great moral dilemmas of the universe. Rather, he sought to turn the congregation in Geneva, and his own soul, to the reality of God's sovereignty and power in the contingencies of seemingly disordered life. Nowhere is this power more radically shown than in Calvin's opening words to the Joban series of sermons: "The thing that we have briefly to bear in mind in this story, is, that God hath such a sovereignty over his creatures, as he may dispose of them at his pleasure."[16]

The sermons were recorded by the professional stenographer Denis Raguenier, who had been employed as such starting September 29, 1549. The *Sermons on Job* were first published in French in 1563, during Calvin's lifetime. This was the period of the outbreak of the first of the French Wars of Religion, following the Massacre of Vassy in 1562. Perhaps not incidentally, a second edition appeared in French in 1569, after the Reformer's death, at the point when the Huguenot cause looked bleak during the second civil war. A third French edition appeared at the beginning of the seventeenth century (1611), following the assassination of King Henry IV and during the persecution that came in its wake. A German translation was made in 1587–1588, followed by a Latin translation in 1593.[17] Before that, however, an English translation was made by Arthur Golding (ca. 1536–ca. 1605) in 1574, about a decade after its initial publication in French.[18] Given

---

15. It would seem fitting, following the attacks on Calvin by Albert Pighius in 1542 and more recently by Jerome Bolsec in 1551, that Calvin should take up a systematic exposition of a work of Scripture largely dominated by the doctrine of providence.

16. Calvin, "Sermon 1" (Job 1:1), l.a.28.

17. A separate German translation of the concluding prayers in the Job sermons was also made and published in 1592.

18. Arthur Golding was responsible for a number of other English translations of Calvin's sermon series, including those on Galatians (1574), Ephesians (1576), and Deuteronomy (1583). T. H. L. Parker says of him, "Golding writes a strong, energetic prose, keeping close enough to the

the popularity of Calvin's *Sermons on Job*—four English editions were published in the first ten years following Golding's translation, far outstripping the popularity of the English edition of the *Institutes*—it is difficult to understand Calvin's initial reluctance to seeing their publication. We know of no plans by the Reformer to write a commentary on Job, for example. But part of the popularity of the *Sermons on Job*, no doubt, lay in the fact that Calvin's preaching made little reference to Geneva itself. Concerned as Calvin was with the exposition of the text, the relevance of these sermons became immediately applicable wherever they were read.

Calvin's Analysis of the Argument of Job

A problem arises for any interpreter of the book of Job: how to maintain consistently Job's integrity. The issue is exacerbated by the fact that testimony to his righteousness is given both by the author of Job (Job 1:1) and by God himself as bookends to the work (1:8; 42:8).[19] That Job was not sinless is a point Calvin stresses in the exegesis of the book, but Job had "a good case":

---

original to do justice to Calvin's own style." *Calvin's Preaching*, 72–73. Born in London, Golding is said to have been educated at Queen's College, Cambridge, but his name is not found in the college register. In 1549 he was in the service of Edward Seymour, Duke of Somerset and Lord Protector of England. Among his accomplishments was the translation of Ovid's *Metamorphoses* in April 1567 (said to have been known to William Shakespeare) and Seneca's *De Beneficiis* in 1577–1578. Said to have Puritan sympathies, Golding concentrated on the translation of works by Calvin and Beza. Among his patrons were Sir William Cecil; Sir Christopher Hatton; Robert Dudley, Earl of Leicester; Robert Devereux, Earl of Essex; Sir William Mildmay; Lord Cobham; and the Earl of Huntingdon. He was a member of the Elizabethan Society of Antiquaries, founded by Archbishop Matthew Parker in 1572. His sole original publication was *A Discourse upon the Earthquake that hapned throughe this realme of Englande, and other places of Christendom, the first of Aprill 1580* . . . , in which he alluded to the judgment of God on the godlessness of the age. His translation of Calvin's *Sermons on Job*, *Sermons of M. John Calvin upon the Booke of Job*, was first published in London in 1574 and dedicated in December 1573 to Robert, Earl of Essex—at least according to the *Dictionary of National Biography*. However, according to David Henry Stam, it was dedicated to Robert Dudley, Earl of Leicester, which is probably the correct view. David Henry Stam, "England's Calvin: A Study of the Publication of John Calvin's Works in Tudor England" (PhD diss., Northwestern University, 1978), 113. Reprints followed in 1579, 1580, and 1584. For further details, see *Dictionary of National Biography*, ed. Sir Leslie Stephen and Sir Sidney Lee (Oxford: Oxford University Press, 1967–1968), 8:75–77. Two different editions of Golding's translation of Job's sermons were printed by Henry Binnemars for Lucas Harrison and George Bishop in 1574, perhaps because the company required a printer to keep a book in print and available for sale if he desired to maintain his copyright. No more than 1,250 copies of a work could be printed from any one typesetting, a rule that ensured the continuation of labor for the company. The two editions are in quite distinct typesettings. The edition consulted in this chapter was George Bishop's. See Stam, "England's Calvin," 21, 101.

19. "There was no hypocrisy nor dissimulation, nor any doubleness of heart in him." Calvin, "Sermon 1" (Job 1:1), 3.a.67. Cf. Job "was as a mirror of patience." Calvin, "Sermon 28" (Job 7:7–15), 130.b.18.

But herewithall we have further to mark, that in all this disputation, Job maintains a good case, and contrariwise his adversaries maintain an evil case. And yet it is more, that Job maintaining a good quarrel, did handle it ill, and that the other setting forth an unjust matter, did convey it well. The understanding of this, will be as a key to open unto us this whole book.[20]

How, then, can the righteousness of God be sustained in the face of such testimony? The issue depends on the integrity of Job's claim to "innocence," but Calvin is ambivalent about this claim. In the opening sermon, he gives eloquent testimony to Job's godliness:

It is said, that he was a sound man. This word sound in the Scripture is taken for a plainness, when there is no point to feigning, counterfeiting, or hypocrisy in a man, but that he shows himself the same outwardly that he is inwardly, and specially when he hath no starting holes to shift himself from God, but lays open his heart, and all his thoughts and affections, so as he desires nothing but to consecrate and dedicate himself wholly unto God. The said word hath also been translated perfect, as well by the Greeks and the Latins. But forasmuch as the word perfect hath afterward been misconstrued: it is much better for us to use the word sound. For many ignorant persons, not knowing how the said perfection is to be taken, have thought thus: Behold here is a man that is called perfect, and therefore it follows, that it is possible for us to have perfection in ourselves, even during the time we walk in this present life. But they deface the grace of God, whereof we have need continually. For even they that have lived most uprightly, must have recourse to God's mercy: and except their sins be forgiven them, and that uphold them, they must all perish.[21]

Throughout his exegesis, Calvin upholds this defense of Job's character, against the view taken by Job's counselors, who maintain that

---

20. Calvin, "Sermon 1" (Job 1:1), 1.b.34.

21. Calvin, "Sermon 1" (Job 1:1), 3.a.40. Rejecting "perfect" for "sound" in his comments on Job 1:1, Calvin adds, "So then, although that they which have used the word perfect, have meant well: yet notwithstanding for as much as there have been some that have wrested it to a contrary sense, (as I have said) let us keep still the word Sound. Then look upon Job, who is called Sound. And how so? It is because there was no hypocrisy nor dissimulation, nor any doubleness of heart in him." Calvin, "Sermon 1" (Job 1:1), 3.a.62.

Job's suffering is due to sin on his part. A case can thus be made for "innocent suffering."

Since Job has "a good case," the immediate cause of Job's suffering must not be seen as retribution for personal guilt on Job's part. Taking up Job's protest in Job 9, Calvin remarks,

> Thus you see what Job meant by saying that he was wounded without cause: that is to wit, as if a man should have demanded of him, do you know any evident cause in yourself why God punishes you? I see none. For Job was handled after a strange fashion. . . . Job therefore saw not to what end God did this: there was no reason in it, as to his knowledge. That is true: for he speaks not in hypocrisy.[22]

The theology of instant retribution, therefore, is an inappropriate measurement of suffering. It is the canon of Job's friends to be sure, but it is one that Calvin consistently repudiates.

Interpreting the Hand of God

For Calvin, the book of Job is about the doctrine of providence. Early in his expositions of Job, he remarks, "Nothing happened without his providence."[23] Whereas in the *Institutes* Calvin could concern himself with the profound issues of the relationship of divine providence and sin, Calvin's overriding concern in the Job sermons is that we "learn from," "profit from," and "apply" God's providence.[24] Sometimes, he compares man to beasts, unable to discern the hand of God in all things.[25] Consequently, it is possible to "misread" providence. Equally, Calvin insists that afflictions do no good unless God works in our hearts by the Holy Spirit.[26] That is why Job needed wisdom to discern the misplaced counsel that he received from his friends suggesting that his afflictions were judgments from God. Calvin complains at one

---

22. Calvin, "Sermon 35" (Job 9:16–22), 163.b.13.
23. Calvin, "Sermon 5" (Job 1:9–12), 23.b.14.
24. See, e.g., Calvin, "Sermon 3" (Job 1:5), 12.a.57; "Sermon 17" (Job 4:20–5:2), 78.b.38; "Sermon 20" (Job 5:11–16), 88.b.66.
25. See, e.g., Calvin, "Sermon 40" (Job 10:16–17), 189.a.16; "Sermon 112" (Job 31:5–8), 529.a.36.
26. "For it is not enough for God to strike us with his hand, except he touch us within also by his holy spirit." Calvin, "Sermon 21" (Job 5:17–18), 94.b.36.

point that "Job turns God's providence quite upside down, and that instead of comforting and cheering himself therewith, he would fain that God were far off."[27] Similarly, Calvin bristles at Bildad's simplistic and monothematic interpretation of God's works of providence, insisting as he does that Job's suffering is a judgment from God.[28] A measure of discernment is necessary, Calvin insists, in order to interpret God's providence correctly.[29]

While Calvin is consistently critical of the advice of Bildad, Eliphaz, and Zophar, he is untiringly supportive of the contribution of Elihu. According to Susan Schreiner, "There are few people in the Bible Calvin admires more than Elihu."[30]

In particular, Elihu sees adversity as educative rather than necessarily retributive.[31] Adversity is often pedagogic, for "sometimes it is his will to try the obedience of good men."[32] Commenting on Job 36:6–14 and drawing on Elihu's distinctive contribution therein, Calvin brings to the surface the various pedagogic inferences of suffering. Thus, affliction serves several ends: it is "the true school mistress to bring men to repentance"; it weans us from dependence on the things of this world.[33] Significantly, afflictions are by God's appointment; they are God's "archers," his artillery.[34] Afflictions are a part of God's "double means" whereby he humbles us (the other means being his word).[35] Applications of this nature underline the importance of Elihu for Calvin. They form the basis on which Calvin understands the entire book of Job and the lessons that are to be learned throughout the book.

---

27. Calvin, "Sermon 29" (Job 7:16–21), 133.b.66.

28. Calvin, "Sermon 67" (Job 18:1–11), 315.a.10.

29. "For the holy Scripture puts a difference between the outward things that are done, and the purpose of God which is not known but to the faithful, which lift up themselves above their own reason and above all their natural wits. For we shall never attain to the knowledge of God's Majesty [*cognoissance de la maiesté de Dieu*], except we be carried up above all our own ability." Calvin, "Sermon 5" (Job 1:9–12), 23.b.19; *CO*, 33:80.

30. Schreiner, *Where Shall Wisdom Be Found?*, 131. Schreiner adds that whereas Aquinas believed that Elihu "abused" Job's words, "Calvin disagrees; in his view, Elihu was right" (133).

31. Cf. "He teaches us to receive his grace, sometimes by the chastisements which he gives us, and sometimes by afflictions and great stripes of his rods. And if he see that we be dull and slow, he strikes the harder, so as we are compelled to come unto him, because we be utterly quelled and can hold out no longer." Calvin, "Sermon 128" (Job 33:29–34:3), 601.a.45.

32. Calvin, "Sermon 121" (Job 32:11–22), 569.b.57.

33. Calvin, "Sermon 140" (Job 36:6–14), 658.b.9, 658.b.54.

34. Calvin, "Sermon 5" (Job 1:9–12), 21.a.28, 21.a.42; "Sermon 27" (Job 7:1–6), 124.b.13; "Sermon 63" (Job 16:10–17), 295.b.65, 296.a.8; "Sermon 71" (Job 19:17–25), 331.a.1; "Sermon 150" (Job 38:18–32), 704.b.62.

35. Calvin, "Sermon 140" (Job 36:6–14), 660.b.32.

Echoing the opening lines of the *Institutes*, Calvin states that af-flictions help us in knowing God and knowing ourselves.[36] Though Calvin accepts Job's innocence to a degree, he is not averse to the sug-gestion that our sins well deserve afflictions. Thus, afflictions show us our sins and cause us to flee in repentance.[37] But in the main, Calvin is concerned in Job to allude to other features of afflictions, lessons that emerge from the mysterious and unexplained occurrence of di-verse providences. Hence, while afflictions are "blessed," "good," and for our "profit," we are not always "privy to their purpose."[38] They therefore should humble us and cause us to be more reverent before God.[39] Afflictions also drive us to desire more of God's help, provok-ing us to return to him by drawing us to him and thereby taming us.[40] Furthermore, Calvin insists that the afflictions of the godly last only for a time and that God afflicts the believer no more than he can bear.[41]

In addition, Calvin adds that such providences are unavoidable.[42] They "light upon" everyone at God's "good pleasure."[43] None are too "insignificant" to avoid God's attention. Trials are periods of peculiar temptation that require God to "moderate our afflictions."[44] Not that everyone experiences equal measures of trial; there are degrees of suf-fering.[45] Not everyone is afflicted alike.[46]

Trials, then, are to be welcomed by God's children as a privi-lege.[47] There is a reason for suffering; providence is intelligent and purposive. The distribution of trials is not whimsical or arbitrary.

---

36. Calvin, "Sermon 20" (Job 5:11–16), 88.b.55; "nous cognoistre afin," CO, 33:246.

37. Calvin, "Sermon 21" (Job 5:17–18), 95.a.67; "Sermon 64" (Job 16:18–22), 300.a.63; "Sermon 140" (Job 36:6–14), 658.a.48; "Sermon 142" (Job 36:20–24), 667.a.37.

38. Calvin, "Sermon 18" (Job 5:3–7), 81.a.17; "Sermon 5" (Job 1:9–12), 21.b.37; "Sermon 159" (Job 42:9–17), 749.a.19; "Sermon 21" (Job 5:17–18), 96.a.2; "Sermon 128" (Job 33:29–34:3), 602.a.10; "Sermon 132" (Job 18:21–26), 623.b.14; "Sermon 158" (Job 42:6–8), 743.b.27.

39. Calvin, "Sermon 121" (Job 32:11–22), 569.b.29; "pour les humilier," CO, 35:29; see also "Sermon 7" (Job 1:20–22), 30.a.20.

40. Calvin, "Sermon 20" (Job 5:11–16), 88.a.59, 92.a.63; "Sermon 21" (Job 5:17–18), 94.a.52; "Sermon 38" (Job 10:1–6), 179.b.23; "Sermon 141" (Job 36:15–19), 662.a.47.

41. Calvin, "Sermon 5 (Job 1:9–11), 22.b.56; "Sermon 21" (Job 5:17–18), 97.b.14.

42. "It is impossible that God's children should live in this world and not be in many perils continually." Calvin, "Sermon 20" (Job 5:11–16), 89.b.14.

43. "Afflictions light upon all men without exception." Calvin, "Sermon 21" (Job 5:17–18), 94.b.3. "Our afflictions befall us not without his good pleasure." "Sermon 27" (Job 7:1–6), 124.b.12.

44. Calvin, "Sermon 67" (Job 18:1–11), 315.b.58.

45. Calvin, "Sermon 23" (Job 6:1–9), 105.a.11.

46. Calvin, "Sermon 6" (Job 1:13–19), 24.b.30.

47. Calvin, "Sermon 21" (Job 5:17–18), 95.a.34.

The purpose of the trial may be hidden to us but not to God.[48] God has "another will which may be compared to a deep abyss."[49] In this respect, God's providences are essentially incomprehensible to us. There are "secret and incomprehensible judgments."[50] There are "high mysteries," which are "above our ordinary capacity."[51] In our comprehension of certain providences, we ought to be content to limit ourselves to that which God has revealed about them.[52] The information necessary to decipher certain providences is withheld at God's behest.[53] Consequently, we ought not to fret about the means of our deliverances. It is this perception—that a fatherly hand guides our lives, even as the source of trials—that makes it possible for the believer to view all affliction as a joy rather than a sorrow. We are not to judge God harshly just because we fail to see the reason that lies behind certain providences.

Providence and Sin

While it is true that there is an aspect to providence that ever remains a mystery to us, Calvin would have us learn that some providences are meant to be clear in their instructive qualities. For example, Calvin, speaking in general terms and not necessarily about Job, alludes to the "two purposes" that afflictions serve: first, to mortify visible sins; second, to bring to the surface those sins that are not immediately apparent.[54] Thus, providence ought to cultivate self-examination.[55] It facilitates the conviction of known sin and the drawing out of otherwise-hidden vices within us.[56] This explains why, for Calvin, providence is to be praised. Providence is proof of God's interest in us. "And so," Calvin writes, "the great-

---

48. "My comfort is to pray God to give me eyes, not only to behold present things, but also to know those things by faith which are hidden from me as now." Calvin, "Sermon 27" (Job 7:1–6), 126.b.11.

49. *Institutes*, 1.17.2.

50. Calvin, "Sermon 30" (Job 8:1–6), 138.b.18.

51. Calvin, "Sermon 147" (Job 38:1–4), 692.a.26; "Sermon 40" (Job 10:16–17), 188.a.51.

52. Calvin, "Sermon 17" (Job 4:20–5:2), 78.b.38.

53. "He teaches us that which he knows to be expedient for us at this time." Calvin, "Sermon 82" (Job 21:22–34), 384.b.35.

54. Calvin, "Sermon 5" (Job 1:9–12), 20.a.7.

55. "But every man must enter into himself, and examine his own state and life: and when we find any fault in ourselves, we must condemn it." Calvin, "Sermon 18" (Job 5:3–7), 80.a.39.

56. Calvin, "Sermon 29" (Job 7:16–21), 136.b.10; 136.a.68.

est mishap that can light upon us, is when God suffers us to welter in our own wickedness."[57] However, Calvin insists that blessing is not automatically derived from providence; some do not profit by affliction.[58] Some, despite the variety of providences, still reveal a scant knowledge of their sinfulness. But others are deeply affected by a sight of their sins.[59] For Calvin, such conviction of God's wrath against our sins is the greatest of all afflictions.[60] There are "secret sins" that continue to lurk within the heart that providence ought to bring to the surface so that we might acknowledge them.[61]

Dark providences, or trials, no matter how great their intensity, do not sanctify by any power inherent within them.[62] It is possible to disdain trials and thereby despise "the chastening hand" of God.[63] In this way, men are like anvils: "The beating upon them is not able to change their nature, for we see how they beat back blows again."[64] Thus, trials may "blind" us and make us incoherent.[65] Trials are profitable only for those who are exercised to piety as a result of them. Unless the Holy Spirit works in us, trials will only harden and destroy.[66]

All this calls forth our submission to God's providence.[67] Calvin is fond of using the expression "We play the horses that are broken loose" to convey the notion of an unwillingness to yield to God's

---

57. Calvin, "Sermon 21" (Job 5:17–18), 95.b.26.

58. "We see then before our eyes, that many men are the more unhappy for being chastised at God's hand, because they profit not in his school, nor yet take any good by his corrections." Calvin, "Sermon 21" (Job 5:17–18), 95.a.29.

59. "For whosoever is touched rightly and to the quick, shall feel himself as it were in hell when he bethinketh him of his sins, and specially if God summon him before his seat, and make him feel how guilty he is." Calvin, "Sermon 38" (Job 10:1–6), 175.b.25.

60. Calvin, "Sermon 41" (Job 10:18–22), 193.a.3.

61. Referring to Ps. 19:13 and to the use of "secret sins," Calvin comments, "For it behooves us to know our sins, or else we cannot confess them to be sins. . . . God sees more clearly than we do." Calvin, "Sermon 23" (Job 6:1–9), 153.b.51.

62. "Afflictions cannot always tame and subdue men." Calvin, "Sermon 90" (Job 23:13–17), 425.a.30.

63. For Calvin's use of Heb. 12 and the warning given about "the root of bitterness" that can sometimes accompany trials, see Calvin, "Sermon 21" (Job 5:17–18), 96.a.45.

64. Calvin, "Sermon 21" (Job 5:17–18), 94.b.41.

65. "Whenever we have any trouble, straightaway without regarding what it is, our eyes are dazzled at it, so as we cannot discern between red and green, but we babble out this and that to no purpose." Calvin, "Sermon 24" (Job 6:8–14), 111.b.29.

66. "Till God has touched us with his holy spirit, it is impossible that his chastisements should serve to bring us back to repentance, but rather they shall make us to wax worse, and worse." Calvin, "Sermon 21" (Job 5:17–18), 94.b.54.

67. "So long as men are forepossessed with pride, so as they ween themselves worth anything, you shall see them so locked up [*enserrez*] as the grace of God can never enter into them." Calvin, "Sermon 28" (Job 7:7–15), 129.b.44; CO, 33:351.

rule.[68] We are to "honor" God's judgments and not fight against them even when they are incomprehensible to us.[69] Trials of this kind are meant to wean us from our dependence on all but God himself;[70] they serve the goal of consecration.

Meekness

For Calvin, meekness is an essential quality of every Christian.[71] What is meekness? It is that teachable spirit that receives what God says to us.[72] Trials ought to cultivate sincerity and openness before God.[73] Thus, for Calvin, all religion is summarized by the fear of God.[74]

Understanding Job as a model, Calvin differentiates godly fear from servile fear.[75] Godly fear, Calvin suggests, is a response to the goodness of God as much as it is to his majesty.[76] Fear and awe are the response of the soul to God's omniscience, steadfastness, and power.[77] Does this mean that we ought never to be afraid of God? No, for Calvin, such would border on presumption. The judgments of God are meant to make those afraid who have cause to be afraid.[78] Such godly fear explains Job's initial response to the trial.[79] The judgments of God should provoke in the godly a similar response.[80] Contempla-

---

68. Calvin, "Sermon 36" (Job 9:23–28), 167.b.4.

69. Calvin, "Sermon 30" (Job 8:1–6), 138.b.18.

70. Calvin, "Sermon 125" (Job 33:18–25), 588.a.54.

71. "If we will be God's children, we must have the spirit of meekness [*mansuetude*]." Calvin, "Sermon 26" (Job 6:24–30), 118.a.42; CO, 33:320.

72. "To have a meek mind [*esprit debonnaire*]" is for Calvin "to receive what is said unto us." Calvin, "Sermon 26" (Job 6:24–30), 118.b.52; CO, 33:322. Cf. "Would we then show how we profit in God's word? It behooves us above all things to have a meek and gentle spirit [*esprit debonnaire et paisible*]." Calvin, "Sermon 128" (Job 33:29–34:3), 603.a.57; CO, 35:122.

73. Calvin, "Sermon 35" (Job 9:16–22), 160.b.67.

74. "Thus you see, how that under this fearing of God, here is comprehended all religion: that is to wit, all the service and honor which the creatures owe unto their God." Calvin, "Sermon 10" (Job 2:11–13), 4.b.45.

75. "We have to understand that it is not a slavish fear (as men term it:) but it is so termed in respect of the honor which we owe him." Calvin, "Sermon 1" (Job 1:1), 4.b.31.

76. "To fear God it behooves us to be sure of his goodness." Calvin, "Sermon 103" (Job 28:10–28), 486.a.35.

77. Calvin, "Sermon 29" (Job 7:16–21), 136.a.39, 136.a.60; "Sermon 148" (Job 38:4–11), 695.a.68; "Sermon 88" (Job 33:1–7), 415.b.7.

78. "That in considering God's judgments, we must look higher than our own wits can reach unto: for that is the cause why we fear not God so much as we ought to do. Yet notwithstanding we diminish not his power, in not fearing the highness that is in him, which ought to make us afraid." Calvin, "Sermon 142" (Job 36:20–24), 666.a.52.

79. "If we be given to the fear of God, we shall have a firm and well settled state." Calvin, "Sermon 17" (Job 4:20–5:2), 77.a.27.

80. "Therefore when God doth so show us his judgments, let us quake at them, and let us stand in fear and awe of him, submitting ourselves wholly to that which he says and utters." Calvin, "Sermon 18" (Job 5:3–7), 83.b.30.

tion of providence ought to induce awe in our hearts toward God[81] and a sympathy toward others in adversity.[82] Such fear involves having a right understanding of God and his works, a mind and heart not given over to speculation. Godly fear reveres Scripture and desires to profit from it.[83] Such godly fear in response to God's providences ought, writes Calvin, to "shut our mouths," cause us to renounce ourselves, prevent us from presumption, "overboldness," and "vanity."[84] It should result in true joy, "the true mark whereby to discern God's flock from all the wild beasts that range abroad."[85] Adversity, in particular, is suited to the cultivation of the fear of God since it underlines our frailty and insecurity apart from God's fatherly hand upon us.[86] Nor is this godly fear known by any, save those who are in Christ.[87]

Patience

Another consequence of the sometimes dark and mysterious providences of God is to teach us patience. Without it, no service can please God.[88] In "Sermon 7," Calvin gives an interesting definition of *patience*. Insisting that it does not mean insensitivity to pain, he goes on to amplify the term to mean "when they can modestly moderate themselves, and hold such a measure, as they cease not to glorify God in the midst of all their miseries."[89] Calvin accepts that Job was a patient man, but he cautions on the misuse of James's commendation.[90]

---

81. Calvin, "Sermon 19" (Job 5:8–10), 86.a.39.

82. "That such as have no pity upon the poor wretched creatures which are in adversity, have given over the fear of God. . . . That to prove ourselves to have the fear of God, it behooves us to labor to do good to the afflicted . . . we must be softened by the sight of every one that is in distress." Calvin, "Sermon 25" (Job 6:15–23), 113.b.22, 113.b.50.

83. Calvin, "Sermon 103" (Job 28:10–28), 485.6.35.

84. Calvin, "Sermon 37" (Job 9:29–35), 173.b.25; cf. "Sermon 138" (Job 35:12–15), 649.a.21, 649.a.65; "Sermon 148" (Job 38:4–11), 697.b.24; "Sermon 103" (Job 28:10–28), 487.b.60; "Sermon 150" (Job 38:18–32), 706.b.44; "Sermon 102" (Job 38:10–28), 480.b.41.

85. Calvin, "Sermon 103" (Job 28:10–28), 487.a.35, 487.a.20.

86. Calvin, "Sermon 141" (Job 36:15–19), 663.b.14.

87. "The fear of God will never be in us, till we be come to the point that we spoke of which is, that we know God's mercy as it is offered us in our Lord Jesus Christ: Namely that we be drawn unto him by his goodness, where through he allures us, and that we have the boldness to call upon him as our father, so as we return unto him even when we be utterly dismayed." Calvin, "Sermon 103" (Job 28:10–28), 487.a.54.

88. "If we be not patient when God scourges us, all the service that we do unto him will be no great matter." Calvin, "Sermon 5" (Job 1:9–12), 20.a.62.

89. Calvin, "Sermon 7" (Job 1:20–22), 29.a.14.

90. Commenting on the commendation of Job in James 5:11, Calvin remarks, "If, however, it be asked, Why does the Apostle so much commend the patience of Job, as he had displayed many signs of impatience, being carried away by a hasty spirit? To this I reply, that though he sometimes failed through the infirmity of the flesh, or murmured within himself, yet he ever surrendered

Job was deeply troubled by his "passions" during the course of his trial, thereby causing him at times to become impatient.[91] Impatience is more than a dislike of adversity; it is a passionate and willful opposition.[92] Impatience manifests itself in striving against God and finding fault with him, in making ourselves "equal" with God, "as when we be so mad as to run rushing against him."[93] Citing Elihu favorably, Calvin insists that impatience gains us nothing and that those who exercise it are "stark fools."[94] Furthermore, unrepentant impatience will add to the rigor of our final judgment.[95]

Prayer

It is hardly surprising that Calvin makes mention of prayer several times in his *Sermons on Job*. Trials force us to cry unto God.[96] Prayer, then, is an expression of our utter dependence on God: it is a corollary of providence.[97] Prayer is also expressive of our communion and "closeness" to God, a response to the revelation of fatherly goodness to us.[98] Thus, for Calvin, the Christian life is prayer; it is the greatest privilege we know.[99] Prayer expresses the (subjective) act of believing and the (objective) focus of what we believe. It is an expression of our belief in God's sovereignty. The need for prayer is our frailty; our tendency to collapse under pressure calls from us a cry for help from God.[100] In this

---

himself to God, and was ever willing to be restrained and ruled by him. Though, then, his patience was somewhat deficient, it is yet deservedly commended." *Comm.*, 22:351–52.

91. "True it is that he was not utterly destitute of patience: but he ceased not to be tormented with horrible passions." Calvin, "Sermon 30" (Job 8:1–6), 138.b.68. Calvin admits that the best are impatient in some way. "Sermon 123" (Job 33:8–14), 580.a.30.

92. "It is not simply a grief conceived of the misliking of our adversities when we be weary of them: but it is an excessive heartburning or stomaching against them, when we cannot submit ourselves simply unto God to dispose of us at his pleasure." Calvin, "Sermon 67" (Job 18:1–11), 314.a.20.

93. Calvin, "Sermon 153" (Job 39:22–35), 719.a.42.

94. Calvin, "Sermon 146" (Job 37:14–24), 687.b.62; "Sermon 152" (Job 39:22–35), 721.a.24.

95. "Therefore let us learn that whensoever we lift up our neb [*le bec*, i.e., 'beak' or 'snout'] against God, we shall win nothing by it, but our words shall flip into the air, and vanish away as smoke. Nevertheless let us mark by the way, that our words shall not fall to the ground, but must be registered to our great and horrible confusion. Then if our pride be such as we dare murmur against God: such blasphemousness must needs come to a reckoning, and not scape unpunished." Calvin, "Sermon 146" (Job 37:14–24), 688.a.18; CO, 35:348–49.

96. Calvin, "Sermon 19" (Job 5:8–10), 88.b.50.

97. Calvin, "Sermon 4" (Job 1:6–8), 18.a.51.

98. Calvin, "Sermon 126" (Job 33:29), 595.b.48.

99. "The greatest honor that God requires at our hands, is that we should call upon him in all our adversities." Calvin, "Sermon 70" (Job 19:13–16), 327.b.36.

100. Thus, in the opening sermon, Calvin can say, "Seeing then that we be so easily carried away: we ought the rather to pray unto God, that when we have a good case, he himself will vouchsafe to guide us in all singleness by his holy spirit." Calvin, "Sermon 1" (Job 1:1), 2.a.19.

way, adversity encourages us to pray when, perhaps, we have neglected prayer.[101] Interestingly, Calvin reiterates in the *Sermons on Job* something that he made explicit in the final edition of the *Institutes*: that prayer be made according to the tenor of the covenant of grace.[102] So Calvin can insist that "we request nothing which is not agreeable to his will."[103] In this way, Calvin links prayer with God's promises.[104] Thus, Calvin is scathing toward those who subject God to their own demands, whatever they may be.[105]

As to the manner of prayer, Calvin again insists on sincerity: "Let us rather lay open our hearts before God . . . so as we have nothing wrapped up in them."[106] Prayer is thus part of a spiritual battle, one in which we need the assistance of the Holy Spirit to enable us to persevere in prayer[107] and to keep us from stumbling.[108] In this way, prayer is a microcosm of the Christian life. In the same way, as we struggle with adversity in life, so we struggle with it in prayer. What seems to be "unanswered" prayer calls forth from us both patience[109] and perseverance.[110] In this way, prayer is a means of grace in adversity.

Self-Denial

Trials, the onset of dark providences, may bring out the worst in us. They manipulate the affections in a way that is inappropriate. Our affections, therefore, need to be tamed.[111] According to Calvin, the

---

101. Calvin, "Sermon 126" (Job 33:29), 595.b.47.

102. "To pray rightly is a rare gift [*Unde sequitur singulare esse recte orandi donum*]." *Institutes*, 3.20.5; CO, 2:629.

103. Calvin, "Sermon 24" (Job 6:8–14), 108.b.17.

104. "Let us be well advised that we be sober minded when we fall in hand with praying unto God, and that we have well considered aforehand what things God promises and permits." Calvin, "Sermon 24" (Job 6:8–14), 109.a.1.

105. "Behold (say I) an untolerable [*sic*] presumptuousness, when a mortal man will bear such sway, as God must be subject to his demands." Calvin, "Sermon 24" (Job 6:8–14), 108.b.50.

106. Calvin, "Sermon 24" (Job 6:8–14), 109.a.18. "We must not come unto God with our head upright, nor be so bold as to make so far account of him, that he should do whatsoever we have conceived in our brain." "Sermon 24" (Job 6:8–14), 109.a.28.

107. "Spiritual battles, praying God to strengthen us, for we see how all man's strength fails in that behalf, so as we shall be quickly overwhelmed if we be not propped up from above." Calvin, "Sermon 41" (Job 10:18–22), 193.a.20.

108. Calvin, "Sermon 141" (Job 36:15–19), 663.b.14.

109. Calvin, "Sermon 70" (Job 19:13–16), 327.a.32. Cf. "Sermon 18" (Job 5:3–7), 80.a.63.

110. Calvin, "Sermon 99" (Job 27:8–12), 466.a.11. Cf. "Sermon 109" (Job 30:11–21), 515.b.57.

111. "We have not utterly renounced ourselves [*tout renoncé à nous-memes*]. He that hath not yet learned to tame his affections and to subdue his will to the sensing of God, notwithstanding

godly must respond to providence by learning self-denial. The proper response to cross bearing is a true repentance.[112] In the person of Job, then, we have both a positive and negative model: positive, in that Job appears to Calvin again and again to be a model of the pious life; but negatively, too, in that Job's excessive "passions" sometimes got the better of him.[113] We need to learn to put "both feet upon our affections" lest we be guilty of an intemperate response to providence.[114] Our affections blind us;[115] they rob us of our understanding;[116] they make us ungovernable.[117] A due sense of God's majesty and greatness should encourage us to temper our response.[118] Calvin calls on us to "mistrust" our affections,[119] even to repress them.[120] We are to learn to mistrust ourselves.[121] In an illuminating pastoral insight, Calvin remarks, "If he give his excessive passions head, the same must needs rebound back upon himself or against himself."[122] In this way, Calvin treats Job's lapses into melancholy, as expressions of "the passions of the flesh."[123]

The Spiritual Battle

The *Sermons on Job* provides Calvin with an opportunity to speak with great clarity as to the nature of providence that believers like Job can expect in this world. Thus, God may treat us "roughly," as certain physicians might in order to cure us from some ill.[124] It may

---

that it be hard for him to do: knows not yet in good earnest what it is to live well and faithfully." Calvin, "Sermon 66" (Job 17:6–16), 309.b.55; cf. CO, 33:382.

112. Calvin, "Sermon 31" (Job 8:7–13), 142.a.25.

113. Calvin, "Sermon 29" (Job 7:16–21), 135.b.17.

114. Calvin, "Sermon 111" (Job 31:1–4), 523.b.15. Cf. "bridle our affections," "Sermon 112" (Job 31:5–8), 529.b.21.

115. Calvin, "Sermon 12" (Job 3:11–19), 54.a.45.

116. The French is "parlé sans y penser." Calvin, "Sermon 51" (Job 13:16–22), 241.a.40; CO, 33:641.

117. Calvin speaks of our affections "boiling up" [*bouillantes*]. "Sermon 11" (Job 3:2–10), 51.b.29; CO, 33:149. "We be so heady [*violents*] in our affections, we cannot judge God's works with a settled mind [*sens rassis*]." "Sermon 56" (Job 14:16–22), 261.b.40; CO, 33:695.

118. "All our over great and excessive affections, all our murmurings [*nos affections trop grandes et excessives*], and all other such like things: proceed of this, that we know not what God is, and that we spoil him of his Majesty, asmuch as lies in us." Calvin, "Sermon 123" (Job 33:8–14), 581.a.47; CO, 35:61.

119. The French is "qu'il y a lors des bouffees plus que vehementes en nous." Calvin, "Sermon 136" (Job 35:1–7), 640.a.21, 58; CO, 35:221.

120. Calvin, "Sermon 65" (Job 17:1–5), 305.b.18.

121. Calvin, "Sermon 110" (Job 30:21–31), 518.b.28.

122. Calvin, "Sermon 38" (Job 10:1–6), 176.b.3.

123. Calvin, "Sermon 29" (Job 7:16–21), 134.b.47.

124. Calvin, "Sermon 21" (Job 5:17–18), 96.a.63.

appear as though God picks us up and throws us down again.[125] God may "dispose of his creatures at his own pleasure."[126] Calvin is careful not to suggest that Job is being punished for his sins, thereby falling into the trap of his counselors, who seem only to possess an "instant retribution" theology of suffering. Nevertheless, he does allow for general comments about chastisement throughout the sermons.[127] Such chastisement is painful. God's wrath kindles our sins like tinder.[128] God need but raise his hand, and we would all perish.[129] That is why providence ought to teach us to be humble before God, recognizing that apart from his grace and mercy, we would all know greater affliction than we do.[130] God does not cease to love us even when he afflicts us.[131] In the midst of affliction, he makes us taste his goodness.[132]

Painful experiences of providence have a bearing on our relationship to others, Calvin suggests. We may learn to profit from affliction by learning sensitivity to others who likewise experience trials.[133] In this way, providence cultivates our experience of the communion of saints.[134]

We have already noticed that prayer is a microcosm of the Christian life, reflecting in its struggle the difficulties encountered with providence. Calvin elaborates in many of the Joban sermons on the nature of this struggle: the Christian life is meant to be a fight all the way. As we shall see, this idea harmonizes with Calvin's overall portrayal of the Christian life, particularly in his exegesis of Romans 6–8. In the *Sermons on Job*, Calvin faces this issue head-on. Sensitive to

---

125. "He lifts us up as if we were little kings, and . . . he seems to have a fatherly care of us, and to prefer us above all creatures: and afterward throws us down as men in the picture of the wheel of fortune." Calvin, "Sermon 29" (Job 7:19–21), 133.a.19.

126. Calvin, "Sermon 2" (Job 1:2–5), 7.a.44.

127. "We see how they that have some goodly outward show, become brutish: and therefore let us be sure that God visits us with his whips because of our sins." Calvin, "Sermon 17" (Job 4:20–5:2), 79.a.4.

128. Calvin, "Sermon 19" (Job 5:8–10), 84.a.20.

129. "For what would become of us, if God should stretch out his arm against us? Alas, what creature were able to stand before him? Verily he needs no more but to show one angry look, and behold all the world should perish." Calvin, "Sermon 21" (Job 5:17–18), 97.b.17.

130. Calvin, "Sermon 21" (Job 5:17–18), 97.b.41.

131. "God in afflicting us does not cease to love us." Calvin, "Sermon 30" (Job 8:1–6), 139.a.26.

132. "God scourges us, yet he ceases not to give us some taste of his goodness [*goust de sa bonté*]." Calvin, "Sermon 12" (Job 3:11–19), 57.a.33; CO, 33:164.

133. "God hath knit us in such ways together [*Dieu nous a tellement unis*]." Calvin, "Sermon 25" (Job 6:15–23), 113.a.39.

134. Calvin, "Sermon 73" (Job 20:1–7), 345.b.20.

Job's great loss, the emotional, psychological trauma he experienced, and his physical sickness, Calvin insists that none of these equal in intensity the spiritual struggle within Job's soul.[135] Prayer, then, prepares us for this battle.[136] The nature of the Christian life is a race requiring us to persevere with all diligence.[137] Calvin emphasizes the imagery of pilgrimage and conflict, the holy war in which the believer is inevitably engaged. In a remarkable passage in "Sermon 66," Calvin muses on the possibility of a quietist view of the Christian life:

> Were we as it were in a faire meadow, that we might run along the rivers side in the shadow, and that there might be nothing but pleasure and joy in all our whole life: who could vaunt that he had served God with good affection? But when God sends us things clean contrary to our desire, and that we must be fain one while to enter into a quagmire, another while to march upon rugged stones, and another while to be cumbered with briers and thorns: when we must be fain to meet with hedges and ditches and to leap over them, and when we shall have traveled a great while, it shall still seem that we have gone very little or nothing forward, and yet we see no end of our journey: behold, it is a troublesome temptation to us that covet to walk according to God's will. And why so? Because we have not utterly renounced ourselves. He hath not yet learned to tame his affections, and to subdue his will to the serving of God, notwithstanding that it be hard for him to do: knowing not yet in good earnest what it is to live well and faithfully. So the[n] let us practice that which is spoken here of holding on our ways, that is to say, of knowing that if we be desirous to rule our life according to God's law, the way is very difficult, and it will not be done without many lets and hindrances: and yet we must be firm and constant to hold on our way still.[138]

---

135. Thus in the opening sermon, Calvin can pinpoint the nature of the entire book of Job as a spiritual battle: "Surely these spiritual battles are far more harder to be borne, than all the mysteries and adversities that we can suffer by any persecution." Calvin, "Sermon 1" (Job 1:1), 1.b.26.

136. "And therefore let us prepare ourselves to such spiritual battles, praying God to strengthen us, for we see how all man's strength fails in that behalf, so as we shall be quickly overwhelmed if we be not propped up from above." Calvin, "Sermon 41" (Job 10:18–22), 193.a.19.

137. "According also as the Scripture exhorts us, showing us that this life here is but as a race, and therefore we may not go loiteringly, but every man must cheer up himself, and prick and spur forward himself." Calvin, "Sermon 17" (Job 4:20–5:2), 76.b.10.

138. Calvin, "Sermon 66" (Job 17:6–16), 309.b.39.

For Calvin, Job is proof that the experience of strife and opposition is not indicative of some spiritual malfunction of the lack of faith: suffering is to be expected; opposition is normative. We ought to "prepare ourselves for battle."[139]

The conflict is internal and subjective as well as external and objective. Internally, Satan knows the sin that lies within our hearts. He makes full use of it.[140] Thus, in the Joban sermons, Calvin sees affliction as a means of enabling mortification.[141] Satan does not understand that as believers we are no longer in bondage to the flesh or to him.[142] But since Job's suffering is not directly related to any indwelling sin as such[143]—Calvin's acceptance of Job's "good case"—the focus of opposition in Job is not so much the world or remaining corruption within Job's heart but Satanic intrusion. In the *Institutes*, Calvin comments that Satan seeks "to drive the saint to madness by despair."[144] Though Calvin insists that Satan is ultimately powerless,[145] what power he has, he has by virtue of God's decree[146] and permission.[147] The "Devils are God's hangmen";[148] Satan is the destroyer,[149] the hinderer,[150]

---

139. Calvin, "Sermon 22" (Job 5:19–27), 99.a.63; "apprester aux combats," CO, 33:272.

140. Calvin, "Sermon 5" (Job 1:9–12), 19.a.67.

141. See Calvin's use of the word "mortification" [*mortifie*] in "Sermon 5" (Job 1:9–12), 20.a.8; "Sermon 13" (Job 3:20–26), 58.a.18; "Sermon 158" (42:6–8), 744.b.49; and "Sermon 125" (Job 33:18–25), 588.a.52. Thus afflictions serve to "bridle our tongues" and hearts. "Sermon 28" (Job 7:7–15), 130.a.24. They also urge us to be better disposed to seek the heavenly life. "Sermon 159" (Job 42:9–17), 750.a.18.

142. "But in the meanwhile he had no understanding of God's grace, how strong and invincible the same is in us." Calvin, "Sermon 5" (Job 1:9–12), 21.a.52.

143. Job's covenant with God as to the use he made of his eyes provides Calvin with an interesting explanation of how Satan may employ our faculties for his ends: "Our eyes which were created to look upon God's works, to the end we might be taught to love, reverence and fear him; are become as it were the baudes [*maquereaux*, i.e., "pimp," or "brothel-keeper"] of Satan, and are as it were enticers, which come to beguile us and work our destruction." Calvin, "Sermon 112" (Job 31:5–8), 529.a.15.

144. *Institutes*, 1.18.1. Cf. "If the Devil may win that at our hands, he is well apayed: but if God wakens us, then doth the Devil labour to drive us to despair." Calvin, "Sermon 90" (Job 23:13–17), 425.a.13.

145. Calvin, "Sermon 4" (Job 1:6–8), 15.a.46.

146. Calvin, "Sermon 5" (Job 1:9–12), 21.a.68.

147. "The Devil is held short, and that howsoever he play the mad fiend against our salvation, yet can he do nothing further than is permitted him from above." Calvin, "Sermon 4" (Job 1:6–8), 16.a.47.

148. "The Devils are as it were God's hangmen to execute his judgments and the punishments which he will have done upon the wicked. Also they are as his rods whereby he chastises his children. To be short, it behooves the Devil to be the instrument of God's wrath, and to execute his will." Calvin, "Sermon 5" (Job 1:9–12), 22.a.20.

149. "The Devils are always busy to procure our destruction." Calvin, "Sermon 4" (Job 1:6–8), 17.a.33.

150. "And further, that for as much as we be continually beset with many stumbling blocks, and the Devil practices to thrust us out of the right way." Calvin, "Sermon 2" (Job 1:2–5), 5.a.61.

the devourer,[151] and the seducer.[152] With his wiles,[153] he accuses,[154] tempts,[155] and deceives—convincing us that he is our friend and ally and that God is our real enemy.[156] But the devil is our real enemy.[157] He may even drive us to despair.[158] Without God's continual supervision, Satan would overpower and destroy us.[159] But in all this, God overrules Satan's activity for our good, using the bitterness of providence as medicine for the cure of our souls.[160] In some, God permits Satan to wreak greater havoc than in others.[161] And in some, God allows Satan to do his worst, thus reminding us that, apart from God's grace, we are altogether without hope.[162]

Service

It is against such opposition that we are called on to live out our Christian lives. Nowhere is this call to Christian piety defined more succinctly than in "Sermon 66":

> Lo what the life of the faithful is in effect: that is to wit, that they shall never be without many temptations: and specially that we be subject to so many miseries during the time that we be in this earthly wayfaring, that such as endeavor to serve God best, cease not to be often overpressed with many inconveniences, and many afflictions. But what for that. When we be astonished (as it

---

151. "But behold, God tells us that Satan is like a roaring Lion which hath his throat ever open to swallow us up: and that we have no weapons to resist him, except he give us them." Calvin, "Sermon 4" (Job 1:6–8), 16.b.9.

152. "David then being one of God's children, was notwithstanding sometimes delivered into the power of Satan, to be beguiled by him." Calvin, "Sermon 5" (Job 1:9–12), 22.b.48.

153. "For the wiles are infinite which he forges in his shop: and therefore it behooves us the more to stand upon our guard." Calvin, "Sermon 4" (Job 1:6–8), 18.b.54. Cf. "The Devil puts a toy in our head." "Sermon 1" (Job 1:1), 1.b.19.

154. Cf. Calvin's comm. on Job 1:9 in "Sermon 5" (Job 1:9–12), 21.a.8, and on 2:4–5 in "Sermon 8" (Job 2:1–6), 36.a.36.

155. Calvin, "Sermon 4" (Job 1:6–8), 17.a.42.

156. "The Devils comes to put a toy in our head, that God is our deadly enemy." Calvin, "Sermon 4" (Job 1:6–8), 1.b.18.

157. "For he is our chief enemy whom we have chiefly to resist, that we may repulse all the practices and devices which he can attempt against us." Calvin, "Sermon 82" (Job 21:22–34), 385.b.6.

158. "One of Satan's policies is to drive us to despair." Calvin, "Sermon 35" (Job 9:16–22), 163.a.5. Note how Calvin counsels his hearers not to despair but to trust in God; see "Sermon 10" (Job 2:11–13), 46.b.52; "Sermon 128" (Job 33:29–34:3), 602.b.59.

159. "But if God once withdraw himself from us, or do but only slack his hand a little, by and by we shall be overcome by Satan." "Sermon 5" (Job 1:9–12), 23.b.47.

160. Calvin, "Sermon 5" (Job 1:9–12), 23.a.3.

161. "But also for that he gives Satan full power over them, and lets him have the bridle, to reign in such houses at his own pleasure." Calvin, "Sermon 18" (Job 5:3–7), 82.b.54.

162. Calvin, "Sermon 74" (Job 20:8–15), 348.a.54.

cannot be but we must think it strange at the first brunt), let us fight against such temptations, and let us hold on in the right way without starting out of it. And although we find much hardness in ourselves, let us pray God to give us such an invincible strength, as we may continue in his service even to the end, notwithstanding that Satan labour to thrust us out of it.[163]

Continuing "in his service" is something Calvin was desirous to preach to his congregation in Geneva. Surrounded as they were by many difficulties, the Genevans had friends beyond the city who were in greater distress and need. Calvin sought to encourage his listeners against the malaise of despair and dysfunctionalism. God orders his rule in such a way as to encourage new areas of service for us to perform.

For Calvin, God's providential ordering of trials is also a means of cultivating and encouraging usefulness in the kingdom. In the opening sermon on Job, Calvin sees in the patriarch a model of pious service rendered to God.[164] In that sense, Job exemplifies the role for which we were created.[165] Every detail of God's self-revelation to us is in order that we might know him and serve him better.[166] And our chief service? It is to praise God in every circumstance.[167]

Knowing God through Adversity

As Calvin alludes to these many pedagogic lessons of adversity, one appears to emerge again and again: through adversity, we come to know God better. Through adversity, we grow in our understanding and appreciation of God, expanding from a knowledge of God as Creator to a knowledge of God's goodness, greatness, wisdom, and love.[168] Of particular interest is the way Calvin draws attention to God's "fatherly" love in the midst of trials.[169] Adversity enables us to

---

163. Calvin, "Sermon 66" (Job 17:6–16), 310.b.7.
164. Calvin, "Sermon 1" (Job 1:1), 3.b.15.
165. Calvin, "Sermon 1" (Job 1:1), 4.b.25.
166. Calvin, "Sermon 30" (Job 8:1–6), 138.a.4.
167. Calvin, "Sermon 148" (Job 38:4–11), 696.a.29.
168. Calvin, "Sermon 4" (Job 1:6–8), 17.b.25. "Also it behooves us to acknowledge his dominion and superiority over us." "Sermon 1" (Job 1:1), 4.b.42; cf. "Sermon 128" (Job 33:29–34:3), 604.b.16; "Sermon 30" (Job 8:1–6), 138.a.4.
169. Calvin, "Sermon 17" (Job 4:20–5:2), 79.b.5.

appreciate the immensity and mystery of God—that he is beyond our grasp, hidden from us, and in many ways incomprehensible to us.[170] "It behooves us to humble ourselves," says Calvin, "and to wait till the day come that we may better conceive God's secrets which are incomprehensible to us at this day."[171]

We know him only "in part."[172] God often appears as though he hides his face from us.[173] Early in the exposition of Job, Calvin is drawn to the conclusion that "there is nothing better than to submit all things to God's majesty."[174] Similarly, Calvin begins a sermon on Job 13, reminding his hearers of the previous sermon, the essence of which was that "the Scripture shows us many things which our understanding cannot brooke."[175] Continuing in the same sermon, Calvin reminds them that God is of "another manner of one than they have imagined him to be: for they have not an eye to the infinite glory that is in him."[176] We do not have the mental capacity to grasp God adequately: God's judgments are "too deep a dungeon for us to go down into."[177] In summary, therefore, Calvin urges, "We must know the incomprehensible majesty of God."[178]

---

170. Calvin, "Sermon 19" (Job 5:8–10), 86.a.46; "Sermon 138" (Job 35:12–15), 648.b.65.
171. Calvin, "Sermon 5" (Job 1:9–12), 22.b.27.
172. Calvin, "Sermon 123" (33:8–14), 582.a.22.
173. "He hides his face from us, when he afflicts us, and when we know no reason why he works after that sort. Therefore when God holds us so in ignorance, it is a hiding of his face from us." Calvin, "Sermon 133" (Job 34:26–29), 629.a.28.
174. Calvin, "Sermon 7" (Job 1:20–22), 32.a.8.
175. Calvin, "Sermon 50" (Job 13:11–15), 232.a.28.
176. Calvin, "Sermon 50" (Job 13:11–15), 234.b.4.
177. Calvin, "Sermon 119" (Job 32:1–3), 561.b.38.
178. Calvin, "Sermon 33" (Job 9:1–6), 152.b.3.

16

Predestination

Paul Helm

Christ . . . is the mirror wherein we must, and without
self-deception may, contemplate our own election.

—John Calvin, *Institutes of the Christian Religion*

A Dreadful Idea?

In the popular mind, John Calvin is associated with *predestination*:
it is held that he invented the dreadful idea and that it dominates his
thought.[1] Both these claims are in fact false. It is more accurate to say
that Calvin inherited the idea, from Augustine and the Augustinian
tradition as it affected theologians such as Thomas Aquinas, Anselm
of Canterbury, and Martin Luther, and ultimately that he took it from
Paul. And the idea was far from dominating the rest of his thought. In
fact, in the *Institutes* it is much less prominent than it is, for example,
in Aquinas's *Summa Theologiae*. In fact, it appears almost as an after-
thought in book 3. It was certainly not a "central dogma" or an axiom

---

1. Portions of this chapter are adapted from Paul Helm, *Calvin: A Guide for the Perplexed*
(London, T&T Clark, 2008). Used by permission of Bloomsbury Publishing Plc.

from which Calvin attempted to derive the other aspects of Christian theology in the manner of a euclidean theorem.

The topic of predestination arises for discussion precisely because Calvin observes that not everyone receives God's saving grace: "The covenant of life is not preached equally among men."[2] And because Calvin holds that hearing about Christ is necessary to receiving him, it follows that the distribution of God's saving grace in Christ is uneven or unequal. The plain fact is that not everyone receives Christ, and this, together with the teaching of Scripture to that effect, leads Calvin to the conclusion that God's saving grace is not granted to the entire human race but that God has discretion regarding to whom he is merciful.

In this chapter, I primarily intend to offer an outline exposition of Calvin's view of predestination as it is found (mainly) in the *Institutes*. I shall also try to draw out two other themes connected with it. The first is to show how in Calvin's thought predestination and providence interlock. The second is to indicate how the theme of union with Christ, and in particular the twofold gift that Christ gives to his people, also intersects with Calvin's understanding of election, and with it, of predestination.

Predestination

At one point in his treatment of justification, Calvin writes as follows:

> Indeed, [Scripture] presents this order of justification: to begin with, God deigns to embrace the sinner with his pure and freely given goodness, finding nothing in him except his miserable condition to prompt Him to mercy, since he sees man utterly void and bare of good works; and so he seeks in himself the reason to benefit man. Then God touches the sinner with a sense of his goodness in order that he, despairing of his own works, may ground the whole of his salvation in God's mercy.[3]

Justification is not a reward for merit, nor do merits play any part in it. The same is true of sanctification, of *conversio*.

---

2. *Institutes*, 3.21.1.
3. *Institutes*, 3.11.16.

The bestowing of the twofold graces of Christ's work, however, is not random or haphazard. It has its reason in God. In granting his salvation, God "sees the cause of kindness in himself."[4] So if the kindness of God is the cause of salvation, and if not everyone enjoys this salvation, then it must be that God causes some to receive his grace and denies it to others. The idea that where the gospel goes is a matter of accident or that its effectiveness is due solely or crucially to the exercise of human free will is forcefully dismissed by Calvin—the first notion because, according to Calvin's understanding of divine providence, everything that happens is the result of the determining counsel of God; the second notion because man's will, his inner spirit or direction, is enslaved to sin and so cannot by itself choose to receive God's grace.

It is not even sufficient for such a change to take place that the grace of God should aid or encourage or woo a person. Something more powerful is needed, life from the dead, sight to the blind: the grace of God that is needed must be effectual; it must actually secure the conversion of the one to whom it comes. This is a key idea of the Reformation, and it is significant that both Calvin and Luther wrote books on the bondage of the will to sin. Because of the will's slavery to sin, God's grace has to be powerful enough to unshackle the sinner and free him. The grace must be "effectual grace," to use the phrase first coined, it seems, by Augustine.[5] That is, it must not merely make freedom from slavery possible, but it must actually free from slavery.

By using such language, the language of this powerful saving grace that is bestowed with discrimination, though not given according to anything in the recipient that deserves it, Calvin takes us "behind the scenes" to God's secret choice, to his election of the church and his predestining of them to enjoy all the blessings of Christ's atonement, chief among which are justification and sanctification, leading to their glorification. Grace here and glory hereafter. So God's grace has two aspects: it is the grace of an undeserved initiative, and it is the grace of liberating power.

In the *Institutes* Calvin says that predestination is "God's eternal decree, by which he determined with himself what he willed to become

---

4. *Institutes*, 3.11.16.

5. "It is true, therefore, that many are called but few chosen. Those are chosen who are effectually [*congruenter*] called." Augustine to Simplicianus, in *Augustine: Earlier Writings*, ed. and trans. John H. S. Burleigh, LCC 6 (London: SCM, 1953), 395.

of each man. For all are not created in equal condition; rather, eternal life is foreordained for some, eternal damnation for others."[6] It is important, however, to grasp that although Calvin (and the mainstream Christian tradition) is not universalistic, even if he were a universalist, a doctrine of election and predestination would still be required. For as he saw things, whether viewed in particularistic or universalistic terms, salvation is not automatic. It is never a human right. It is willed by God, who need not have willed it. It is an utterly gracious act. So, necessarily, God has to make a choice, the choice to bring such grace to men and women and to destine those whom he chooses to grace and provide salvation through Christ, whether those whom he chooses are in fact the entire human race or only a part of it.

Predestination is often used as loosely equivalent to *election* and to the destining of those elected to salvation. To think more precisely, however, predestination is the consequence of election, Calvin says. God chooses the church, his elect, by his pure grace and mercy and then predestines them to receive his grace and enjoy his glory through the means that he has provided. They are chosen "in Christ"; that is, in the eternal mind of God, they are to share in the destiny of Christ—in his death and resurrection, his ascension and glorification—and they share this because of Christ's work on their behalf. Christ is the "elect one," the chosen cornerstone.

God is the author of election and predestination, and since God is eternal, election and predestination are eternal as well. So each person is born already destined to life or to death. God's eternal predestining is experienced and effected in "real time," as God manifests his sovereign grace in a person's effectual call and all that follows this. Those not so predestined God mysteriously—that is, for reasons we cannot now comprehend—passes by.

This is so-called double predestination, the doctrine of predestination and reprobation, taught as clearly (if not more clearly) by (say) Aquinas as by Calvin.[7] But it is also important to note that Calvin does not use the term *double predestination* (though he is often said to),

---

6. *Institutes*, 3.21.5.
7. Thomas Aquinas, *Summa Theologiae*, ed. Thomas Gilby (Garden City, NY: Image Books, 1969), 1a.23.

nor does he *deduce* reprobation from election. He does not argue that because some are predestined to life, *therefore* some are predestined to death. Rather, he finds reprobation clearly taught in Scripture and credible for that reason. (Calvin did not think that one ought to believe only what is convenient or comfortable to believe or only what one can immediately fathom.)

There is good reason for not using the phrase *double predestination*, though Calvin does not tell us whether this was his reason for not using it. The reason is this: while the destiny of each person is fixed before he or she is born, and God withholds his grace from some, those who suffer the fate of the reprobate and are separated from the presence of God do so because of their sin, which God has chosen to permit and mysteriously decreed (in their case) not to pardon. In reprobation God passes them by, leaving them to the consequences of their own sin. Those who are elected, however, are elected not, in a parallel way, because of their merit but solely as a result of God's grace, coming to them in a way that is utterly undeserved. Predestination and reprobation issue equally from God's will. The ground of the ultimate destiny of the reprobate is sin; the ground of predestination to life is grace. The source of each is God's choice. But in one case the choice results in unpardoned sin, while in the other it results in pardon through the imputation of Christ's righteousness. In contrast, *double predestination* implies an exact symmetry between the mode of salvation and the mode of damnation, and that, according to Calvin, is an unscriptural idea.

"Besides," Calvin reasons, "their perdition depends upon the predestination of God in such a way that the cause and occasion of it are found in themselves."[8] Why then are those who are elected favored over those who are reprobated? "He who here seeks a deeper cause than God's secret and inscrutable plan will torment himself to no purpose."[9] Yet the God who reprobates is not God of "absolute might." For "the will of God is not only free of all fault but is the highest rule of perfection, and even the law of all laws."[10]

---

8. *Institutes*, 3.23.8.
9. *Institutes*, 3.24.12.
10. *Institutes*, 3.23.2.

Calvin also distinguishes between the election of the nation of Israel and that of individuals:

> Although it is now sufficiently clear that God by his secret plan freely chooses whom he pleases, rejecting others, still his free election has been only half explained until we come to individual persons, to whom God not only offers salvation but so assigns it that the certainty of its effect is not in suspense or doubt. These are reckoned among the unique offspring mentioned by Paul [Rom. 9:8; Gal. 3:16ff.]. The adoption was put in Abraham's hands. Nevertheless, because many of his descendants were cut off as rotten members, we must, in order that election may be effectual and truly enduring, ascend to the Head, in whom the Heavenly Father has gathered his elect together, and has joined them to himself by an indissoluble bond.[11]

The choice of Israel as that nation in whom all peoples of the world should be blessed does not of itself guarantee the eternal election of any child of Abraham, as is seen most vividly in the case of Jacob and Esau. Each was a descendant of Abraham, each was born in circumstances that were about as similar as it is possible to achieve, yet the younger was preferred to the elder, not simply chosen to perform a crucial historical role but chosen to eternal salvation just as surely as Esau was passed by.

Calvin makes clear that the issue Paul is dealing with when he discusses the cases of Jacob and Esau in Romans 9 is not merely the political or national role that each will play but their eternal destinies, the matter that gives Paul "great sorrow and unceasing anguish" (Rom. 9:2), as is underlined in Romans 9:11 and what follows. The point is worth emphasizing given the tendency of some to think of election in merely national or political terms.

Not only is God the author of predestination to grace and glory, then, but he is also the source of it. In fact, we need three concepts to articulate properly Calvin's view of predestination: *election, predestination,* and *foreknowledge.* But we must note what, according to Calvin, this term means as it applies to God. He is emphatic that

---

11. *Institutes,* 3.21.7.

those who are predestined do not depend on anything in them that God foreknows or that qualifies them to receive his mercy. As he puts it, commenting on Romans 8:29, the foreknowledge of God "is not a bare prescience . . . but the adoption by which he had always distinguished his children from the reprobate."[12]

This point is also worth emphasizing, for foreknowledge is what, conceptually speaking, binds election and predestination together. Foreknowledge is the knowledge that God has of his own will, of what he has decided, and, as a consequence, of what he will do or allow. It is his "mind." Part of his mind, understood in this sense, is his knowing choice of some and his bypassing of others. It is like the knowledge that I have that I am going to Skegness on holiday once I have decided to go there. As a result of this knowledge, I take active steps to get to Skegness at the correct time. So divine foreknowledge is determinative; it is not the knowledge that a mere observer gains.

That such foreknowledge is not merely the knowledge that a spectator has of the game or the play but is the expression of God's will or purpose becomes clear in Paul's use of it in Romans 11:2, "God has not rejected his people whom he foreknew." The people whom he foreknew are those whom in his eternal "mind" he elected. And once elected, always elected. So it is preposterous, Paul implies, that God should reject those whom he has an eternal mind to save, those whom he foreknew. Having chosen them, he is "minded" to save them, and his foreknowledge of them ensures that all the means are made available to effect this salvation. Commenting on Romans 11:2, Calvin says,

> By the verb *foreknow* is not to be understood a foresight, I know not what, by which God foresees what sort of being any one will be, but that good pleasure, according to which he has chosen those as sons to himself, who, being not yet born, could not have procured for themselves his favor.[13]

If such foreknowledge concerns the "mind" of God, then election is part of it; it is that aspect of his mind that decides what he is minded

---

12. *Comm.*, on Rom. 8:29.
13. *Comm.*, on Rom. 11:2.

to do in respect of human salvation. It is not election based on fore-knowledge in the sense of what God knows as a result of inspecting his creation or of eternally foreknowing what people yet unborn will make of their various opportunities; it is determinative. What, then, is predestination? It is the actual willing of God, the bringing to pass in real time of God's eternal foreknowledge that he has of those whom he has eternally elected, his chosen people. As the apostles Paul and Peter state, "For those whom he foreknew he also predestined" (Rom. 8:29), "according to the foreknowledge of God the Father" (1 Pet. 1:2).

Unconditional election, the nature of God's foreknowledge, and the predestination that follows from it raise obvious objections. The election of some and the passing by of others seem quite unfair. And the basis on which the election is grounded seems arbitrary, since it cannot be for merit in the ones chosen or indeed for anything that would predispose God to favor them. How does Calvin answer these points?

It is important to understand that Calvin is not a philosopher, handling inert data, concepts, and arguments and trying to formulate a watertight system. He is confronted by the announcement of the will of the sovereign Creator and Redeemer. Whatever may be said to reduce the starkness of unconditional election, it is ultimately a matter of the character of God's purpose. Reasoning backward to answer the question "Why these and not those?" is not stopped by brute empirical fact or by the operation of luck or chance or fate, but it ends at the righteous will of God. Calvin states,

> For God's will is so much the highest rule of righteousness that whatever he wills, by the very fact that he wills it, must be considered righteous. When, therefore, one asks why God has so done, we must reply: because he has willed it. But if you proceed further to ask why he so willed, you are seeking something greater and higher than God's will. . . . And we do not advocate the fiction of "absolute might"; because this is profane, it ought rightly to be hateful to us. We fancy no lawless god who is a law unto himself. . . . The will of God is not only free of all fault but is the highest rule of perfection, and even the law of all laws.[14]

---

14. *Institutes*, 3.23.2.

That is one response: God's will is righteous but inscrutable: "We must always at last return to the sole decision of God's will, the cause of which is hidden in him."[15] But of course, this is not an answer to the objection. It simply locates the place where the answer is to be found. Calvin is content with this, as his mentor Paul was, respecting as he always does the Creator-creature distinction and refusing to speculate about why God decrees as he does.

But there is a second question. Why, if some are chosen to eternal life, do others perish? Why not universalism? Calvin's answer to this question is to argue that God does not owe anything to any person and so has no obligation to treat everyone equally:

> As all of us are vitiated by sin, we can only be odious to God, and that not from tyrannical cruelty but by the fairest reckoning of justice. But if all whom the Lord predestines to death are by condition of nature subject to the judgment of death, of what injustice toward themselves may they complain? . . . How perverse is their disposition to protest is apparent from the fact that they deliberately suppress the cause of condemnation, which they are compelled to recognize in themselves, in order to free themselves by blaming God.[16]

But once again, we must note that what Calvin says does not amount to an explanation. If a person were to prefer to give something to one beggar and not to another, when he has sufficient means for both, it is hardly a satisfactory explanation to be told that each were equally undeserving. Why then did he not give to both? Perhaps the person was offering his largesse purely arbitrarily. Or perhaps he took a liking to one over the other. Calvin refuses to take either of these options, though critics of Calvin have frequently imputed to him the first, the idea of a purely whimsical God. Rather, he simply draws a veil over the character of the divine choice, taking his cue from Paul in Romans 9:19–20 and 11:33–34: "Whenever then we enter on a discourse respecting the eternal counsels of God, let a bridle be always set to our thoughts and tongue, so that after having spoken soberly

---

15. *Institutes*, 3.23.4.
16. *Institutes*, 3.23.3.

and within the limits of God's word, our reasoning may at last end in admiration."[17] Calvin's approach is guarded: he affirms predestination, yet unwilling to speculate about it, he stays within the contours of what is revealed.

To summarize, Calvin's attitude to these problems is in a sense religious, not philosophical. In our effort to discover the rationale for God's action, we come to the limits of human comprehension. We can note certain features of God's action, but ultimately we must recognize his sovereignty and especially his righteousness and must reverence both. So Calvin is circumspect and careful in the way he approaches the "secret" purposes of God. But he is not embarrassed. He thinks that the teaching of predestination has positive value. It underlines the freeness of God's grace and humbles the believer, while at the same time making him confident about the future.

Providence

As we shall see, for Calvin, predestination and providence are not easily separable, as if predestination has to do with God's grace and providence with "nature," and as if the doctrine of providence is a piece of natural theology and predestination a case of revealed theology. For Calvin, predestination, the outworking in time of God's eternal election, is an aspect of divine providence.[18]

So for Calvin, predestination is an aspect of providence. According to him, God not only created the universe, he also rules or governs every aspect of it, including evil events and actions. And he rules the created order teleologically, purposively, in order to accomplish a certain end or ends. What happens is not "blind," as in "blind fate," but is the outcome of the wisdom and goodness of God. Neither are those events that are evil and that apparently thwart his will just bad luck, ruled by fortune; they are in fact made to serve his will. God "willingly

---

17. *Comm.*, on Rom. 11.33.

18. The fact that Calvin treats providence and predestination in different places in the 1559 *Institutes* ought not to mislead us. Providence as he treats it in the *Institutes* is intertwined with the destiny of the church. I believe that he separated them, bringing providence forward to book 1, to minimize the potential for confusing free will as human choice, which is involved with providence, and free will as a well-motivated choice of the good, which is the result of predestination. I have tried to show this in "Calvin, the 'Two Issues,' and the Structure of the *Institutes*," *CTJ* 42, no. 2 (2007): 341–48.

permits" evil, and so all actions, including evil actions, are decreed by him. As that providence was supremely at work in the death of Jesus (Acts 2:23; 4:28), so the will of God is enmeshed in everyday events, including political and religious machinations. The language of "willing permission," which Calvin borrowed from Augustine, is meant to show that God decrees the evil but not in the sense that he is himself morally culpable. It is true that in some sense God wills the evil; it forms a part of his decree of all that comes to pass. Yet he does not will it as evil, but he has a righteous purpose in all that he decrees. He does not exercise merely a general providential supervision. Calvin thought that the idea of a mere general supervision, besides being unscriptural, came dangerously near to the idle deity of the Epicureans. God's providence is thus all-embracing. Calvin states, "But anyone who has been taught by Christ's lips that all the hairs of his head are numbered [Matt. 10:30] will look farther afield for a cause, and will consider that all events are governed by God's secret plan."[19]

In defending such a comprehensive account of providence, Calvin was not introducing a novelty into the Christian faith, even though his account of providence is perhaps unmatched in its clarity and trenchancy. His view was simply the standard Christian view. Aquinas, for example, affirms that everything is subject to divine providence:

> Now the causality of God, who is the first efficient cause, covers all existing things, immortal and mortal alike, and not only their specific principles but also the source of their singularity. Hence everything that is real in any way whatsoever is bound to be directed by God to an end; as the Apostle remarks, *The things that are of God are well-ordered* [Rom. 13:1]. Since his Providence is naught else than the idea whereby all things are planned to an end, as we have said, we conclude quite strictly that all things in so far as they are real come under divine Providence.[20]

For Calvin, predestination is that aspect of God's governance of all things that concern the destiny of the elect and of the reprobate. Even

---

19. *Institutes*, 1.16.2.
20. Aquinas, *Summa Theologiae*, 1a.22.2.

when he separated providence from predestination in his ordering of material in the *Institutes*, the examples he uses in discussing how providence works are often drawn from the affairs of the church, both from the Old Testament and New Testament. For Calvin claims that all events are governed by God's secret plan, especially those that concern his church, and that nothing takes place without his deliberation. The reason why providence is integrated into Calvin's thought about predestination is that God has a special providential care for his church, and in any case it is only the believer who can make the proper use of the doctrine of providence, as we shall shortly see. Predestination, then, is implied not only by the doctrine of providence itself but also by the proper use of that doctrine. Calvin states,

> Whence Christ, when he declared that not even a tiny sparrow of little worth falls to earth without the Father's will [Matt. 10:29], immediately applies it in this way; that since we are of greater value than sparrows, we ought to realize that God watches over us with all the closer care [Matt. 10:31]; and he extends it so far that we may trust that the hairs of our head are numbered. What else can we wish for ourselves, if not even one hair can fall from our head without his will? I speak not only concerning mankind; but, because God has chosen the church to be his dwelling place, there is no doubt that he shows by singular proofs his fatherly care in ruling it.[21]

It is a linchpin of Calvin's account of the relation of providence and evil that there is "diversity of purpose" in providence; in the one event, a human agent, Satan, and the Lord may each have different purposes. He works this out in some detail from the case of Job:

> How may we attribute this same work to God, to Satan, and to man as author, without either excusing Satan as associated with God, or making God the author of evil? Easily, if we consider first the end, and then the manner, of acting. The Lord's purpose is to exercise the patience of His servants by calamity; Satan endeavors to drive him to desperation; the Chaldeans strive to acquire gain from another's property contrary to law and right. So great is the

---

21. *Institutes*, 1.17.6.

diversity of purpose that already strongly marks the deed. There is no less difference in the manner. The Lord permits Satan to afflict His servant; He hands the Chaldeans over to be impelled by Satan, having chosen them as His ministers for this task. Satan with his poison darts arouses the wicked minds of the Chaldeans to execute the evil deed. They dash madly into injustice, and they render all their members guilty and befoul them by the crime. Satan is properly said, therefore, to act in the reprobate over whom he exercises his reign, that is, the reign of wickedness. God is also said to act in His own manner, in that Satan himself, since he is the instrument of God's wrath, bends himself hither and thither at His beck and command to execute His just judgments.[22]

Furthermore, "the several kinds of things are moved by a secret impulse of nature," though Calvin emphasizes that God is the origin and the immediate Sustainer of all that is.

While God is the first cause and the upholder of all that he has created, and his governance of the universe is neither enclosed "within the stream of nature" nor borne along by a "universal law of nature" (as the Stoics held), nevertheless, different kinds of secondary causes operate in the creation.[23] Calvin is not an occasionalist; he does not think that there is only one causal agent in the entire universe, God, and that all other so-called causes are simply constant conjunctions of events. Nor does this emphasis on sovereignty indicate a mechanistic outlook, because, as we have noted, divine providence is a teleological arrangement for Calvin. So there is an enormous difference between providence and either fatalism or physical determinism. The natural ends of the various orders of creation may be thought of as subordinated to the ultimate divine end. Calvin attempts carefully to balance an emphasis on divine sovereignty with a recognition of the efficacy of secondary causes of various kinds.

Christ as the Mirror of Election

We may now consider our topic from another perspective. Since Calvin holds that not everyone is elected by God to salvation and so

---

22. *Institutes*, 2.4.2.
23. *Institutes*, 1.16.3.

predestined by him to grace and glory, the question arises, How may a person know whether he is among the chosen? Calvin's answer is that the grounds of such assurance are conceptually connected with what the people of God are predestined to enjoy.

In a classic passage in the *Institutes*, Calvin asserts that Jesus Christ is the mirror of our election. Calvin explicitly guards himself against the charge that the particularism of eternal election ought to lead us to be uncertain and to speculate as to whether we are among the elect. To avoid self-deception, we must reason from our communion with Christ:

> But if we have been chosen in him, we shall not find assurance of our election in ourselves; and not even in God the Father, if we conceive him as severed from his Son. Christ, then, is the mirror wherein we must, and without self-deception may, contemplate our own election. For since it is into his body the Father has destined those to be engrafted whom he has willed from eternity to be his own, that he may hold as sons all whom he acknowledges to be among his members, we have a sufficiently clear and firm testimony that we have been inscribed in the book of life, if we are in communion with Christ.[24]

Two matters are noteworthy in Calvin's treatment of Christ as the mirror of election. First, the emphasis on being in communion with Christ, and second, Calvin's understanding of a person's union with Christ. A person is in communion with Christ when he is united to Christ in his death and resurrection. Calvin emphasizes that Christ is God the Father's twofold gift to us.

But what did Christ in fact merit for us? What are these maximally beneficial gifts that God the Father provides for us through the work of God the Son? The answer to these questions takes us to the heart of Calvin's understanding of how Christ benefits us, his understanding of Christ's "double grace," justification and sanctification.

For from Christ we receive a double gift. Calvin's basic thought, as he moves from considering the work of Christ to how that work is applied to us and affects us, is that by the unspeakable mercy of God, we

---

24. *Institutes*, 3.24.5.

are united to Christ, and from that one "mystical" union, two distinct but inseparable benefits flow. He has a favorite illustration to help us. He says that Christ is like the sun, from which we receive both light and heat. Light is not heat, and heat is not light, but each comes from the same source and is inseparable from the other. Likewise, justification (the reckoning of a person righteous in God's sight) is not sanctification (the renewing of a person's character by Christ's indwelling Spirit), and sanctification is not justification, but each of these comes from the one Christ as by God's grace we are united to him. Calvin explains,

> These benefits are joined together by an everlasting and indissoluble bond, so that those whom he illumines by his wisdom, he redeems; those whom he redeems, he justifies; those whom he justifies, he sanctifies. But, since the question concerns only righteousness and sanctification, let us dwell upon these. Although we may distinguish them, Christ contains both of them inseparably in himself. Do you wish, then, to attain righteousness in Christ? You must first possess Christ; but you cannot possess him without being made partaker in his sanctification, because he cannot be divided into pieces [1 Cor. 1:13].[25]

It is important to grasp that for Calvin, this union with Christ does not depend on anything we do or have, not even on our faith. We are "chose[n] in him before the foundation of the world" (Eph. 1:4). In fulfillment of this election, God graciously gives Christ to us to be grasped by faith. Faith (another gift of God) is our response to the announcement of the gospel; it is not what procures the gift in the first place. For the gift springs from "this unique life which the Son of God inspires in his own so that they become one with him."[26]

Calvin here refines Luther's view of justification by faith alone through the "alien" righteousness of Christ. Calvin's doctrine of "double grace" breaks apart the medieval idea that justification is moral renewal. No, says Calvin, following Paul, justification is the declaring of a person to be righteous, and this is appropriated by faith alone, as the righteousness of Christ is imputed to the believer. But there is moral

---

25. *Institutes*, 3.16.1.
26. *Institutes*, 3.1.2.

renewal, and it is inseparable from justification. For inseparably accompanying justification, as the second aspect of Christ's "donation," is sanctification. Both justification and sanctification are the gifts of grace. They are not to be separated, but they are not to be confused, as the medieval church confused them, with (Calvin believed) ultimately disastrous consequences.

It is this twin gift of Christ to us that fills the "mirror." If a person sees in his life the twin inseparable graces, justification and sanctification, then he can have confidence about his election. So, Calvin notes, we have communion with Christ when we have "put on" Christ, when we live because he lives, when we are in union with him, united in his death and resurrection. That is the gift of sanctification, but justification is first of all: "The Heavenly Father will count as his sons all those who have received him in faith."[27]

In interpreting Calvin, the influential twentieth-century theologian Karl Barth seemed to think that his use of the idea of a "mirror" was simply a strategy, a pastoral rule for changing the subject from the *decretum absolutum* to Christ.[28] But this is not so. According to Calvin, God's decree to save some particular person cannot now be separated from all the means that he has also decreed to bring that person to his final destiny. Perhaps God could have decreed another set of means. For example, perhaps he could have decreed that upon being converted, a person would be immediately translated to heaven, thus avoiding a long and often wearisome earthly pilgrimage. So we can only find the certainty of our election in Christ. He is the mirror of election; that is, it is a person's relation to Christ, or rather the evidence of that relation, that gives her the only possible grounds to be assured that she is indeed a Christian. She has no other means open to her, least of all the means of having direct access to God's mind to discern whom he has eternally elected. Calvin's point is a logical one, and thus a point of principle. It is not merely pragmatic or pedagogic.

This is one answer to those troubled by the thought that predestination makes us helpless. The chief thing, for Calvin, is that a person

---

27. *Institutes*, 3.24.5.
28. Karl Barth, *Church Dogmatics*, trans. G. W. Bromiley, ed. G. W. Bromiley and T. F. Torrance (Edinburgh: T&T Clark, 1956), 2.2.63.

should be in communion with Christ. If a person comes to Christ, enjoying his twofold grace, then in Calvin's view, that person is entitled to draw the inference that he is elected. Not otherwise.

Second, he treats this matter as an aspect of God's providence. If Christ is proclaimed and we learn about him, this is providential. If as part of learning about Christ and the way of salvation, we learn that the gift of God's grace in Christ comes to a person as a result of an eternal election, how shall we respond? We might be tempted to try to discover whether we are elect by directly inquiring of God. If the answer is yes, then we can rest content. If no, then we are thrown into utter despair. But is this the way to go? Calvin's answer is this: as a prudent man observes the connection between means and ends, and adopts means appropriate to his ends, so we must, to gain the knowledge of election, look for evidence of what, in God's purposes, election leads to:

> For even though faith in election prompts us to call upon God, still, when we frame our prayers, it would be preposterous to thrust this upon God or to bargain upon this condition: "O Lord, if I have been chosen, hear me." For it is his will that we be content with his promises, and not inquire elsewhere whether he will be disposed to hear us. This prudence will free us from many traps if we know how to apply to a right use what has been rightly written.[29]

The Uses of Predestination

Is predestination a "dreadful" idea? Calvin did not think so. He thought, following Augustine, that we have no business being silent about the doctrine of predestination, as if it is a shameful thing, something that will cause alarm and despondency.

We have noted more than once that Calvin's view of predestination is strongly connected with his view of providence. God's providence over his creation is *particular*—"meticulous," as it is sometimes called—reaching to every detail, and it is *secret*. In general, God does not disclose to us what he will do in advance or why he will do it. So

---

29. *Institutes*, 3.24.5.

what Calvin says about "fatherly providence" will help us fill out the ways in which predestination is meant to have a practical function.

Take, for example, all the sorrows and evils that befall the Christian. Calvin says that they are, paradoxically perhaps, part of God's fatherly care of him. Providence is not simply divine government that conserves the creation, in all its detail, in existence, but it is also purposive. God in his sovereign mercy predestines his saints to glory, and his providential control of their lives is a means to that end. The bad things that happen to good people, then, are a part of God's heavenly wisdom, preparing them for their heavenly home. There is a strong element of otherworldliness about Calvin's spirituality.

Someone who believes that nothing happens by chance but that everything comes from the hand of God will come to regard what befalls him or her differently from someone who thinks that evils may happen for no reason at all or that how things turn out is a matter of luck or that one's destiny is written in the stars or that one makes one's own future. Yet Calvin brings out this value in sometimes surprising ways.

For example, one might think that his view of predestination ought to make us lazy. If God has ordained all the details of our lives, including whether we enjoy his salvation, what is there for us to do? We might think that Calvin's attitude would be something like this: *If God is going to favor us, then he is going to favor us. If he is going to bring evil, then he is going to bring evil. Either way, there is nothing to be done.* But this is not what he says. For instance, he thinks that we ought to have a very different attitude toward the past than we have toward the future:

> The Lord has inspired in men the arts of taking counsel and caution, by which to comply with his providence in the preservation of life itself. Just as, on the contrary, by neglect and slothfulness they bring upon themselves the ills that he has laid upon them. How does it happen that a provident man, while he takes care of himself, also disentangles himself from threatening evils, but a foolish man perishes from his own unconsidered rashness, unless folly and prudence are instruments of the divine dispensation in both cases. For this reason, God pleased to hide all future events from us, in order that we should resist them as doubtful, and not

cease to oppose them with ready remedies, until they are either overcome or pass beyond all care.[30]

As we have noted, there is a general, divinely ordained connection between means and ends, and the prudent person will respect this. We have already seen this in Calvin's treatment of Christ as the mirror of election. If you want to be sure of your election and so of ultimate glory, you must examine whether you have communion with Christ. Similarly, if you want to arrive safely at the other side of the road, then it is well to take care in crossing it. You may get safely across if you are careless, and you may perish even though you are careful. But in general there is a connection between preparing and succeeding. And there is an infallible connection between election and being in communion with Christ.

But further than this, and very surprisingly, Calvin says that we ought to think about the future as if God's decree, his providential rule, does *not* extend to it:

> Wherefore, with reference to the time future, since the events of things are, as yet, hidden and unknown, everyone ought to be as intent upon the performance of his duty as if nothing whatever had been decreed concerning the issue in each particular case. Or (to speak more properly) every man ought so to hope for success in all things which he undertakes at the command of God, as to be freely prepared to reconcile every contingency with the sure and certain Providence of God.[31]

Note here the references to duty and to the command of God. In the *Institutes* Calvin puts the point slightly differently:

> Therefore I shall put it this way: however all things may be ordained by God's purpose and sure distribution, for us they are fortuitous. Not that we think that fortune rules the world and men, tumbling all things at random up and down, for it is fitting that this folly be absent from the Christian's breast! But

---

30. *Institutes*, 1.17.4.
31. John Calvin, *A Defence of the Secret Providence of God*, in *Calvin's Calvinism*, trans. Henry Cole (1558; repr., London: Sovereign Grace Union, 1927), 236.

since the order, reason, end, and necessity of those things which happen for the most part lie hidden in God's purpose, and are not apprehended by human opinion, those things, which it is certain take place by God's will, are in a sense fortuitous. For they bear on the face of them no other appearance, whether they are considered in their own nature or weighed according to our knowledge and judgment.[32]

To make sense of what Calvin is claiming here, it is necessary to understand that he may use the phrase "the will of God" to refer both to the *command* of God, that which sets out our duty, and to the *decree* of God, his plan, which is mostly hidden from us. If our future is hidden from us, how should we live? Calvin's answer is this: as far as possible, by making the revealed will of God our guide and by leaving the outcome to his wisdom and goodness.

Perhaps it is in relation to the evils of life that Calvin's view of God's sovereign purposes in our lives (not a view that he invented, of course, but the regular doctrine of the Christian church that he adopted) is most distinctive, as in this eloquent passage:

> But we must so cherish moderation that we do not try to make God render account to us, but so reverence his secret judgments as to consider his will the truly just cause of all things. When dense clouds darken the sky, and a violent tempest arises, because a gloomy mist is cast over our eyes, thunder strikes our ears and all our senses are benumbed with fright, everything seems to us to be confused and mixed up; but all the while a constant quiet and serenity ever remain in heaven. So must we infer that, while the disturbances of the world deprive us of judgment, God out of the pure light of his justice and wisdom tempers and directs these very movements in the best-conceived order to a right end.[33]

God's judgments are hidden, and there is frequently a dislocation or mismatch between what we see happening and what God's purpose is in what we see. We may see confusion, but we should not conclude from the appearance of things that this is how they really are. Besides

---

32. *Institutes*, 1.16.9.
33. *Institutes*, 1.17.1.

encouraging moderation, such a view of God and of his purposes, properly internalized, promotes humility, adoration, soberness, trust in God, gratitude for favorable outcomes, patience in adversity, "incredible freedom from worry about the future," submission to God, confidence in him, relief, freedom from anxiety, fearlessness, comfort, and assurance.[34]

One might even say that people who believe this and who act consistently on it will have a different kind of religion from those who believe that sometimes events are out of God's control or take him by surprise or who believe that God is frequently having to abandon plan A and adopt plan B instead. If we believe that God exists to maximize the area of our comfort zone or to provide health, wealth, or success of some kind, and that he is duty bound to provide us with a life that has a beginning, a middle, and a happy ending, then we shall have a different religion from if we believe that God our Father is working all things, including evils and losses of various kinds, for our good, where this good is not to be understood in terms of present and immediate gratification but conformity to the image of Christ. It is part of such a view that we should defer to God's will, like Paul in the experience of his thorn in the flesh, and be made to see that his grace is sufficient for us—his strength is made perfect in weakness (cf. 2 Cor. 12:7–10).

Calvin firmly held that our life here is preparatory for our life hereafter, and one way that he motivates his readers to virtue is by encouraging them to have regard for the life to come. He devotes a separate section to this matter in his account of the life of a Christian man in the *Institutes*. In a way that is largely foreign to modern Christian spirituality, Calvin believes that the ills of this life should prompt us to hope for the life to come, not of course to prompt us to project a life to come out of thin air, in the sense proposed by Ludwig Feuerbach and Karl Marx, but to intensify hope for what the Christian is convinced on good grounds is to come. "The mind is never seriously aroused to desire and ponder the life to come," Calvin says, "unless it be previously imbued with contempt for the present life"—this is part of "the discipline of the cross."[35] Because the present life has "many

---

34. *Institutes*, 1.17.2–11.
35. *Institutes*, 3.9.1.

allurements," our captivation to it must be broken: "What, then, I beg of you, would happen if we enjoyed here an enduring round of wealth and happiness, since we cannot, even with evil continually goading us, be sufficiently awakened to weigh the misery of this life?"[36]

Without question, the matters we have been touching on are both difficult to follow and difficult to swallow. Calvin does not deny this. But as the last phase of our discussion has shown, he nevertheless has a very practical view of how these abstruse matters are to work themselves out. Predestination is not simply a theological conundrum, something for the professionals. The fact of predestination is not to be a source of speculation but to encourage us to be sure of our relation to Christ, the mirror of election. Calvin's teaching on God's grace in Christ and his providential governing of all events is intended to enrich and to give character to our lives. The fact of *God's* providence over all things is to energize us to use the means he has provided for the present and to do our best to prepare for the future, while leaving the outcome in his hands.

---

36. *Institutes*, 3.9.2.

17

The Church as Mother

John W. Tweeddale

God has filled my mind with zeal to spread his Kingdom and to further the public good. I am duly clear in my own conscience, and have God and the angels to witness, that since I undertook the office of a teacher in the church, I have had no other purpose than to benefit the church.

—John Calvin, *Institutes of the Christian Religion*

Calvin's Ecclesiological Legacy

John Calvin was a churchman. He ministered to the church. He sought to reform the church. And he wrote about the church. That much is undisputed.[1] But not everyone agrees that Calvin made a significant

---

1. Two studies support this claim. Frederik A. V. Harms states that while the doctrine of the church is not "the sole organizing principle that unites all of Calvin's theology, the promotion of the church's restoration and ongoing reformation is the main purpose behind all his labors." Harms, *In God's Custody: The Church, a History of Divine Protection; A Study of John Calvin's Ecclesiology Based on His Commentary on the Minor Prophets*, RHT 12 (Göttingen: Vandenhoeck & Ruprecht, 2010), 12. Benjamin C. Milner, however, overstates the role of the church in his argument for the "absolute correlation of the Spirit and the Word" as the unifying principle in Calvin's theology. See Milner, *Calvin's Doctrine of the Church*, SHCT 5 (Leiden: Brill, 1970), 4–5, 190–96.

contribution to a theology of the church. While recognizing that he saw the church as "the crucial arena for the reformation," William Bouwsma argues that Calvin "gave little attention to the church as a subject of theological reflection."[2] He states that Calvin's chief concern focused on practical matters relating to the visible church, where attention was mostly given to "ecclesiastical organization and practice rather than ecclesiology."[3] In contrast, Elsie Anne McKee claims that "the doctrine of the church is arguably Calvin's most creative contribution to historical theology."[4] Like Bouwsma, McKee demonstrates that Calvin's pastoral ministry concentrated on the visible church in Geneva. She nuances her argument, however, to show the "subtle yet ingenious" way Calvin links together the invisible and visible church in pastoral ministry and worship.[5]

These two assessments of Calvin's theology reflect a tension in scholarship on how best to understand his ecclesiology. Yosep Kim makes the case that scholars on Calvin's doctrine of the church fall into two broad categories. Some emphasize "the theological implications of Calvin's ecclesiological ideas" by focusing primarily on "the spiritual identity of the Church as the fellowship of Christians." Other scholars "examine the practical aspects of the visible Church in Calvin's ecclesiology" by concentrating on "the functional identity of the Church as the agent of God's grace for believers."[6] Part of the

---

2. William J. Bouwsma, *John Calvin: A Sixteenth-Century Portrait* (New York: Oxford University Press, 1988), 214. For a critique of Bouwsma, see Richard A. Muller, *The Unaccommodated Calvin: Studies in the Foundation of a Theological Tradition*, OSHT (New York: Oxford University Press, 2000), 10, 79–81; Eva-Maria Faber, "Mutual Connectedness as a Gift and a Task: On John Calvin's Understanding of the Church," in *John Calvin's Impact on Church and Society, 1509–2009*, ed. Martin Ernst Hirzel and Martin Sallmann (Grand Rapids, MI: Eerdmans, 2009), 123.

3. Bouwsma, *John Calvin*, 214.

4. Elsie Anne McKee, *The Pastoral Ministry and Worship in Calvin's Geneva*, THR 556 (Geneva: Librairie Droz, 2016), 17; cf. McKee, *John Calvin on the Diaconate and Liturgical Almsgiving*, THR 197 (Geneva: Librairie Droz, 1984); McKee, *Elders and the Plural Ministry: The Role of Exegetical History in Illuminating John Calvin's Theology* (Geneva: Librairie Droz, 1988).

5. McKee, *Pastoral Ministry and Worship*, 17–18, 31–38.

6. Yosep Kim, *The Identity and the Life of the Church: John Calvin's Ecclesiology in the Perspective of His Anthropology* (Eugene, OR: Pickwick, 2014), 2. Milner's book *Calvin's Doctrine of the Church* is an example of older research that focused primarily on "the theological implications" of Calvin's ecclesiology, while the work represented by Robert M. Kingdon et al., eds., *Registers of the Consistory of Geneva in the Time of Calvin*, vol. 1, *1542–1544* (Grand Rapids, MI: Eerdmans, 2000), illustrates more recent research that has analyzed "the practical aspects" of Calvin's ecclesiology as it was developed in his pastoral ministry in Geneva. Kim argues that Bouwsma's 1988 biography signals a shift in Calvin studies toward more historical, as opposed to theological, evaluations of his ecclesiology. Herman Selderhuis makes a similar claim by noting that current research on Calvin's ecclesiology, represented in Kingdon and others, has focused

difficulty with interpreting Calvin on this issue arises from his speaking of the church in more than one way. As Kim explains, Calvin sees the church as having a "twofold identity": "its spiritual identity as the body of Christ and its functional identity as the mother of all believers."[7] Keeping this spiritual and functional distinction in view is important for reading Calvin on the church.

The clearest summary of Calvin's doctrine of the church may be found in book 4 of the *Institutes*. He outlines the topics he intends to expound in a single sentence: "Our plan of instruction now requires us to discuss the church, its government, orders, and powers; then the sacraments; and lastly, the civil order."[8] While this statement previews the themes covered in book 4, it hardly does justice to the scope of the final book of the *Institutes*. Book 4 is the largest and most unwieldy of the four books that make up Calvin's tome. Although scholars disagree on how he organized book 4, there is general consensus that it represents a high point in Calvin's reflections on the church. François Wendel suggests that the emphasis of book 4 is "altogether centred in the problem of the Church"; by that he means that Calvin's main concern in the fourth book is to develop a cohesive theology of the church that accounts for the various topics outlined in his "plan of instruction."[9] Kim further observes that book 4 represents "the most mature and organised presentation of Calvin's ecclesiology" and exhibits "no drastic change or revision" from earlier editions of the *Institutes*.[10] For the purpose of this chapter, we use the opening four sections of the first chapter in book 4 as a case study to evaluate Calvin's ecclesiology. This portion is especially important not only because it provides a window

---

on "the more organizational aspects of the church, such as church discipline, church offices, the church-state relation and the unity of the church." See Selderhuis, "Church on Stage: Calvin's Dynamic Ecclesiology," in *Calvin and the Church: Papers Presented at the 13th Colloquium of the Calvin Studies Society, May 24–26, 2001*, ed. David Foxgrover (Grand Rapids, MI: Calvin Studies Society, 2002). On the reception of Calvin's ecclesiology, see Eduardus Van der Borght, "Calvin's Ecclesiology Revisited: Seven Trends in the Research of Calvin's Ecclesiology," in *John Calvin's Ecclesiology: Ecumenical Perspectives*, ed. Gerard Mannion and Eduardus Van der Borght (London: T&T Clark, 2011), 220–31.

7. Kim, *Identity and Life*, 1.

8. *Institutes*, 4.1.1.

9. François Wendel, *Calvin: Origins and Development of His Religious Thought*, trans. Philip Mairet (London: Collins, 1963), 291.

10. Kim, *Identity and Life*, 12. For an overview of the development of "Calvin's creative teaching on the church" in the various editions of the *Institutes*, see McKee, *Pastoral Ministry and Worship*, 18.

into the rest of book 4 but also because it encapsulates his well-known description of the church as mother. The use of this metaphor helped Calvin construct an ecclesiology that was biblically, theologically, historically, and practically informed, as well as cast a vision for reforming the church that addressed both its spiritual and functional dimensions.

Mother Church

Calvin's discussion on the church in book 4 of the *Institutes* flows from his treatment of the Christian life in book 3. The link between these two books is important. Broadly speaking, they consider the work of Christ in relation to individuals (book 3) and the church (book 4). Calvin opens book 4 by stating, "As explained in the previous book [i.e., book 3], it is by the faith in the gospel that Christ becomes ours and we are made partakers of the salvation and eternal blessedness brought by him."[11] In other words, Calvin emphasizes the primacy of faith in Christ for salvation. But this does not mean that the church is unimportant. Due to our "ignorance," "sloth," "weakness," and "fickleness of disposition," Calvin insists that "we need outward helps to beget and increase faith within us."[12] From the outset of book 4, Calvin conceives of the church in terms of God's accommodation to human frailty.[13] To strengthen our faith through the preaching of the gospel and the administration of the sacraments, God "deposited" these helps in the church.[14] For this reason, the church is vital for knowing God in Christ. This is why Calvin titles book 4 "The External Means or Aims by Which God Invites Us into the Society of Christ and Holds Us Therein."[15] This emphasis on the divinely appointed ways that God serves his people through his word reflects a common theme in the Reformation.

For example, Peter Martyr Vermigli, whose *Common Places* was edited to reflect the structure of Calvin's *Institutes* (1559), gave con-

---

11. *Institutes*, 4.1.1.
12. *Institutes*, 4.1.1.
13. On the relationship between accommodation and ecclesiology, see Kim, *Identity and Life*, 115–16; for the standard treatment on Calvin's teaching on accommodation, see Jon Balserak, *Divinity Compromised: A Study of Divine Accommodation in the Thought of John Calvin*, SEMRR 5 (Dordrecht: Springer, 2006).
14. *Institutes*, 4.1.1.
15. The Latin reads, "De externis mediis vel adminiculis quibus Deus in Christi societatem nos invitat et in ea retinent." CO 2:745.

siderable thought to the "outward meanes which God uses for the salvation of his people, and the preservation of man's societie."[16] Reformers like Calvin and Vermigli believed that God gave to the church external means like preaching, baptism, and the Lord's Supper to summon and sustain his people in union and communion with Christ.

Calvin's teaching on the external means connects his doctrine of the church to his doctrines of God and Christ. Through these divinely ordained means, Calvin argues that God accommodates himself "to our capacity" so that we might "draw near to him."[17] He does so by instituting "shepherds and teachers" (Eph. 4:11) who are charged to expound Scripture and administer the sacraments in accordance with the delegated authority given to them to care for Christ's church. As Calvin explains in his commentary on Ephesians 4:11, these external means represent God's design to govern the church in Christ. He states,

> The external ministry of the word is also commended, on account of the advantages which it yields. Certain men appointed to that office, are employed in preaching the gospel. This is the arrangement by which the Lord is pleased to govern his church, to maintain its existence, and ultimately to secure its highest perfection.[18]

For Calvin, Elsie Anne McKee contends, "Eph. 4:11–12 was perhaps *the* critical text for the biblical doctrine of ministry."[19] One reason for the importance of this biblical text is the connection it makes between the authority of Christ as head of the church and the work of those who minister in his name. By framing his discussion on pastoral ministry in terms of God's accommodation to the needs of his people

---

16. Peter Martyr Vermigli, *The Common Places of Peter Martyr*, trans. Anthony Marten (London, 1583), 4.1.1; cf. Richard A. Muller, *Christ and the Decree: Christology and Predestination in Reformed Theology from Calvin to Perkins*, SHT 2 (Grand Rapids, MI: Baker Academic, 2008), 57–58; Jason Zuidema, *Peter Martyr Vermigli (1499–1562) and the Outward Instruments of Divine Grace* (Göttingen: Vandenhoeck & Ruprecht, 2008).

17. *Institutes*, 4.1.1.

18. *Comm.*, on Eph. 4:11; see the same line of reasoning in his sermons on Eph. 4:11–12 and 4:11–14, in *John Calvin's Sermons on Ephesians* (Edinburgh: Banner of Truth, 1998), 361–89.

19. McKee, *Pastoral Ministry and Worship*, 155, italics original. She helpfully traces Calvin's thought on this text through his commentary, sermons, and the various editions of the *Institutes*. On the role of exegesis as it relates to Calvin's *Institutes* and his commentaries, see McKee, "Calvin's Teaching on the Elder Illuminated by Exegetical History," in *John Calvin and the Church: A Prism of Reform*, ed. Timothy George (Louisville: Westminster John Knox, 1990), 147; cf. Muller, *Unaccommodated Calvin*, 118–39.

and Christ's authority over the church, Calvin grounds ecclesiastical practice in doctrinal categories.

This leads Calvin to reflect on the role of the church in the Christian life. He states,

> I shall start, then, with the church, into whose bosom God is pleased to gather his sons, not only that they may be nourished by her help and ministry as long as they are infants and children, but also that they may be guided by her motherly care until they mature and at last reach the goal of faith.[20]

By drawing on this maternal metaphor, Calvin emphasizes the indispensable role that the church plays in gathering, nourishing, guiding, and maturing Christians in holiness, which for Calvin is the "goal of faith."[21] The church, in short, is essential for the well-being of the Christian. Furthermore, to be united to Christ by faith entails being joined together with his church. You cannot have one without the other. In this sense, Calvin applies the words of Jesus on marriage to the church, "For what God has joined together, it is not lawful to put asunder" (cf. Mark 10:9).[22] The notion of a churchless Christian runs contrary to the teaching of Scripture. In both the Old and the New Testament, an inseparable bond joins God and his people.

Calvin's teaching on the church as mother is captured in his axiom "For those to whom he is Father the church may also be mother."[23] This principle was not original with Calvin. He echoes the early church father Cyprian, who famously stated, "He cannot have God as a father who does not have the Church as a mother."[24] The maternal description of the church is also found in Augustine, who, in his *Commentary on the Psalms*, draws attention to the familial love that exists between God and the church:

---

20. *Institutes*, 4.1.1.
21. See *Institutes*, 4.1.17; cf. *Comm.*, on Eph. 5:25–27.
22. *Institutes*, 4.1.1.
23. *Institutes*, 4.1.1. The Latin reads,". . . quibus ipse est pater, ecclesia etiam mater sit." *CO* 2:746.
24. Cyprian, *The Unity of the Church*, in *Saint Cyprian: Treatises*, trans. and ed. Roy J. Deferrari, FC 36 (New York: Fathers of the Church, 1958), 100. The Latin reads, "Habere jam non potest Deum Patrem qui Ecclesiam non habet matrem." *De unitate Ecclesiæ*, in *Patrologiae Cursus Completus, Series Latina*, ed. Jacques-Paul Migne (Paris, 1844–1864), 4:519.

Let us love the Lord our God, and let us love his Church: him as our Father, her as our Mother; him as Lord and her as his handmaiden, for we are his handmaiden's children. But this marriage is cemented by intense charity. . . . Dearly beloved, hold fast to both. Be united, all of you, in this. Hold fast to God, your Father, and to the Church, your Mother.[25]

While Cyprian and Augustine use the metaphor of mother to stress the unity of the universal church in Christ, Calvin applies this principle more specifically to the work of the visible church. Rooted in a local church, Christians grow through the ministry of the word of God. This subtle shift can also be seen in Luther, who, in his Large Catechism, describes the Christian church as "the mother that begets and bears every Christian through the word of God." Luther's point is that the Holy Spirit uses divinely appointed "ways and means" in the church to help Christians advance in holiness. More specifically, the Spirit "illumines and inflames hearts" through the ministry of the word so that Christians will "grasp and accept it, cling to it, and persevere in it."[26] Although Reformers such as Luther and Calvin self-consciously aligned themselves with early church fathers like Cyprian and Augustine, they refined inherited ways of describing the church as mother to articulate a vision for reforming local churches according to the ordained means of grace revealed in Scripture.

Some evangelicals today may stumble over Calvin's words in this passage. Yet it is important to note that Calvin introduces the concept of the church as mother in the context of a polemic against the Roman Catholic Church. One of his stated goals in book 4 is "to call back godly readers from those corruptions by which Satan, in the papacy, has polluted everything God has appointed for our salvation."[27] This anti–Roman Catholic polemic was a common feature among the Reformers in their efforts to articulate a more biblically faithful ecclesiology. Heinrich Bullinger, for example, starkly declares that

---

25. Augustine, *Expositions of the Psalms*, vol. 4, *73–98*, trans. Maria Boulding, pt. 3, vol. 18 in *The Works of Saint Augustine: A Translation for the 21st Century* (Hyde Park, NY: New City Press, 2002), 302; cf. Migne, *Patrologiae Cursus Completus, Series Latina*, 37:1140.
26. Martin Luther, *Large Catechism*, in *The Annotated Luther*, vol. 2, *Word and Faith*, ed. Kirsi I. Stjerna (Minneapolis: Fortress, 2015), 360–61.
27. *Institutes*, 4.1.1.

the church of Rome "is not the holy mother church, she is not an uncorrupted matron and virgin. . . . Our holy mother, the church, is an undefiled virgin, hearing only the voice or doctrine of her only well-beloved husband, placing all the means of life and salvation in him alone."[28] Readers should also keep in mind that Calvin's reference to the "motherly care" of the church comes on the heels of his argument for the primacy of *sola fide* in book 3. When Calvin describes the church as mother, we should neither conflate his teaching with the Roman Catholic doctrine of the church nor think that his ecclesiology jeopardizes the principle of justification by faith alone. Even in the opening section of book 4, we discover several features of Calvin's theology of the church. In particular, his use of the metaphor of mother to depict the visible church emerges out of his concern to safeguard the Reformation's teaching on the gospel, confront the ecclesiastical corruption he encountered in the Roman Catholic Church, extend the arguments of the church fathers in more concrete ways that reflect his commitment to the authority of Scripture, and feature how God accommodates to the needs of his people by using outward and ordinary means to grow the church in Christ.

The Creed and the Church

In the next section, Calvin considers what it means to confess the words from the Apostles' Creed, "I believe . . . the holy catholic church." At first glance, the connection to his previous section on the church as mother may not be obvious. But the creedal formula allows Calvin to lay the groundwork for the rest of book 4. He states, "The article in the Creed in which we profess to 'believe the church' refers not only to the visible church (our present topic) but also to all God's elect, in whose number are also included the dead."[29] Calvin uses the creed to introduce a central component to his theology of the church, namely, the distinction between the visible and the invisible church.

The paradigm of the invisible and visible church should not be understood as suggesting that there are two entirely different churches

---

28. Heinrich Bullinger, *The Decades of Henry Bullinger: The Fifth Decade*, trans. H. I., ed. Thomas Harding (Cambridge: Cambridge University Press, 1852), 92. Bullinger outlines five biblical metaphors for the church in this sermon: house, kingdom, sheepfold, vine, and mother.
29. *Institutes*, 4.1.2.

but one church seen from two vantage points. The term *invisible church* is a slight misnomer in that it is invisible to us but not to God. It represents the universal church as God sees it. Calvin states,

> Sometimes by the term "church" [Scripture] means that which is actually in God's presence, into which no persons are received but those who are children of God by sanctification of the Holy Spirit. . . . The church includes not only the saints presently living on earth, but all the elect from the beginning of the world.[30]

The *visible church* denotes "the whole multitude of men spread over the earth who profess to worship one God and Christ."[31] It is seen wherever the word of God is faithfully proclaimed and the sacraments of baptism and the Lord's Supper are faithfully administered. Yet "in this church are mingled many hypocrites who have nothing of Christ but the name and outward appearance."[32] The visible church contains those who profess faith in Christ, which recognizes that not everyone who professes faith actually possesses it, while the invisible church encompasses only the elect.[33]

Calvin introduces the distinction between the invisible and visible church in relation to the Apostles' Creed in order to encourage those who may be disaffected by what they see in local churches. He states, "The word 'believe' is used because often no other distinction can be made between God's children and the ungodly, between his own flock and wild beasts."[34] By making this distinction, Calvin offers a framework for harmonizing the ecclesiastical dissonance that many Christians experience when attempting to reconcile what Scripture

---

30. *Institutes*, 4.1.7.

31. *Institutes*, 4.1.7.

32. *Institutes*, 4.1.7.

33. Scholars have tended to overemphasize the place of Calvin's doctrine of election in his ecclesiology. E.g., Marijn de Kroon, *The Honour of God and Human Salvation: A Contribution to an Understanding of Calvin's Theology according to His "Institutes,"* trans. John Vriend and Lyle D. Bierma (Edinburgh: T&T Clark, 2001), 147; Georg Plasger, "Ecclesiology," trans. Randi H. Lundell, in *The Calvin Handbook*, ed. Herman J. Selderhuis (Grand Rapids, MI: Eerdmans, 2009), 323; David N. Wiley, "The Church as the Elect in the Theology of Calvin," in George, *John Calvin and the Church*, 96. While election is undoubtedly an important component of Calvin's ecclesiology, other teachings such as divine accommodation, the headship of Christ, the ministry of the Holy Spirit, and the authority of Scripture are also formative for his ecclesiology. A better perspective is to view Calvin's ecclesiology as a multifaceted theological construction that defies one-dimensional programmatic evaluations.

34. *Institutes*, 4.1.2.

teaches about the invisible church with what they have witnessed in the visible church. For this reason, Calvin squabbles with those who insert the preposition *in* into the phrase "I believe the holy catholic church." He marshals arguments from Augustine and perhaps Rufinus in their respective expositions of the Apostles' Creed to show that "in early times it was accepted as beyond controversy that people should say, 'I believe the church,' not '*in* the church.'"[35] Calvin maintains that the preposition *in* is best reserved for faith in the triune God. This is why we confess in the creed, "I believe in God the Father . . . in Jesus Christ, his only Son, our Lord . . . in the Holy Spirit." Calvin insists that we believe *in* the triune God, because "our trust rests in him."[36] But the same cannot be said of the church. Our faith resides not in the church but in God.

The visible church exists amid opposition. Although "the Devil moves every stone to destroy Christ's grace" and "God's enemies" rage against the church, Calvin assures his readers that "it cannot be extinguished."[37] Such confidence in the church's future stems from its spiritual identity as the elect of God.[38] "But because a small contemptible number are hidden in a huge multitude and a few grains of wheat are covered by a pile of chaff," Calvin explains, "we must leave to God alone the knowledge of his church, whose foundation is his secret election."[39] While Christians at times may be discouraged by the apparent lack of true believers in the visible church, they should avoid speculating about the total number of God's elect. Commenting on 2 Timothy 2:19, Calvin states, "We must not judge . . . whether the number of the elect is great or small; for what God hath sealed he wishes to be, in some respect, shut up from us. Besides, if it is the prerogative of God to *know who are his*, we need not wonder if a great number of them are often unknown to

35. *Institutes*, 4.1.2. Calvin refers to one who "bears Cyprian's name." McNeill identifies this pseudo-Cyprian as Rufinus. See *Institutes*, 2:1013n5; cf. Augustine, *Treatise on Faith and the Creed*, in *Nicene and Post-Nicene Fathers of the Christian Church*, 1st ser., ed. Philip Schaff (1886–1890; repr., Grand Rapids, MI: Eerdmans, 1956), 3:331; Rufinus, *A Commentary on the Apostles' Creed*, in *Nicene and Post-Nicene Fathers of the Christian Church*, 2nd ser., ed. Philip Schaff and Henry Wace (1890–1900; repr., Grand Rapids, MI: Eerdmans, 1987), 3:557. On Calvin's use of the church fathers, see Anthony N. S. Lane, *John Calvin: Student of the Church Fathers* (Edinburgh: T&T Clark, 1999).

36. *Institutes*, 4.1.2.

37. *Institutes*, 4.1.2.

38. For more discussion on how the doctrine of election serves as a comfort for the church, see Wiley, "Church as the Elect," 112–13; cf. Kim, *Identity and Life*, 133.

39. *Institutes*, 4.1.2.

us."[40] Rather than conjecture about who is part of the invisible church, Christians should take comfort in knowing that God has ordained the work of the visible church to draw the elect to Christ. Through the means of preaching God's word, the Holy Spirit issues the "inner call" to God's elect.[41] Elsewhere in the *Institutes*, Calvin explains the relationship between preaching and the inner call of the Holy Spirit. He states, "The very nature and dispensation of the call . . . consists not only in the preaching of the Word but also in the illumination of the Spirit. . . . This inner call, then, is a pledge of salvation that cannot deceive us."[42] The "outward Word" is like a "pipe" through which God's "secret grace [flows] to us."[43] In Calvin's ecclesiology, the doctrine of election has a pastoral benefit in giving confidence to God's people to rely on the outward means of the word of God, knowing that the Holy Spirit will use it to bring the elect to Christ.

As the elect of God, the church belongs to Christ. For Calvin, the doctrine of election is closely related to the topics of Christology and ecclesiology. He states, "It is not sufficient . . . for us to comprehend . . . the multitude of the elect, unless we consider the unity of the church as that into which we are convinced we have been truly engrafted." The goal of election is to draw God's people into fellowship with Christ and one another. He continues, "For no hope of future inheritance remains to us unless we have been united with all other members under Christ, our Head."[44] Since there is only one Christ, there can be only one true church. This is why the church is called "catholic," or "universal." The doctrine of the church represents the application of the work of Christ on behalf of the elect. Building on several Pauline texts in Romans, 1 Corinthians, and Ephesians, Calvin underscores the connection between Christ as the head and the church as the body: "But all the elect are so united in Christ that as they are dependent on one Head, they also grow together into one body, being joined and knit together as are the limbs of a body."[45] The

---

40. *Comm.*, on 2 Tim. 2:19, italics original; cf. *Institutes*, 4.1.2.
41. *Institutes*, 4.1.2.
42. *Institutes*, 3.24.2.
43. *Institutes*, 3.24.3.
44. *Institutes*, 4.1.2.
45. *Institutes*, 4.1.2. Cf. *Comm.*, on Rom. 12:4–8; 1 Cor. 10:17; 12:12–13, 14–27; Eph. 1:22–23; 4:16.

church of Jesus Christ has been made "truly one." Therefore, those who are united to Christ must "live together in one faith, hope, and love, and in the same Spirit of God." But even more, the inner calling that comes to the elect by the Holy Spirit through the outward word of God means that God's chosen people have been called not only to enter "into the same inheritance of eternal life but also to participate in one God and Christ."[46]

Calvin's use of the Apostles' Creed gives him a platform to introduce his teaching on the invisible and visible church. One of the reasons he does so is to urge Christians not to lose hope in the work of the church, even if they are disappointed by what they see in the church. Based on the teaching of Scripture as summarized in the creed, we believe the visible church is God's plan to redeem the elect. "Although the melancholy desolation which confronts us on every side may cry that no remnant of the church is left," Calvin notes, "let us know that Christ's death is fruitful, and that God miraculously keeps his church as in hiding places."[47] From our perspective, the church often experiences heartache, persecution, and even heresy.[48] But we do not see everything God is doing to secure the salvation of the elect in Christ as the Spirit works through the preaching of the word and the ministry of the visible church.

The Communion of the Saints

Calvin continues his discussion on the church and the Apostles' Creed by considering the phrase "I believe . . . the communion of saints." He acknowledges that this clause is "generally omitted by the ancients." Yet its value should not be overlooked since "it very well expresses what the church is."[49] This article of faith speaks to how we should relate to others who profess faith in Christ. Calvin explains that it "applies to some extent to the outward church, in that each of us

---

46. *Institutes*, 4.1.2.
47. *Institutes*, 4.1.2.
48. Related to this point, Amy Plantinga Pauw has written a helpful discussion on Calvin's understanding of the church's failings and sinfulness. She observes, "The perception of scandalous failings in the established church significantly shaped Reformed ecclesiology from the beginning. . . . Reformed ecclesiology affirms the church's peccability." Pauw, "Practical Ecclesiology in John Calvin and Jonathan Edwards," in *John Calvin's American Legacy*, ed. Thomas J. Davis (Oxford: Oxford University Press, 2010), 94.
49. *Institutes*, 4.1.3.

should keep in brotherly agreement with all God's children, should yield to the church the authority it deserves, in short, should act as one flock."[50] Belief in the communion of the saints should inform how we care for one another.

The expression "communion of the saints" provides an essential category for how the church should function as the "the society of Christ." Calvin states, "It is as if one said that the saints are gathered into the society of Christ on the principle that whatever benefits God confers upon them, they should in turn share with one another."[51] Affirmation of the communion of the saints neither negates "the diversity of graces" that are gifted to Christians by the Holy Spirit nor implies that an individual must forfeit "his private possessions." Rather, following the example of early Christians in Acts 4:32, a community of believers should have "one heart and soul." In expounding this passage in his commentary, Calvin argues that "where faith beareth the chief sway," it knits the hearts and wills of God's people together.[52] As the society of Christ, we are to treat fellow Christians in ways that reflect how God treats us in Christ. For additional support, Calvin builds on Paul's exhortation to the Ephesians to be "one body and one Spirit," just as they "were called to the one hope" (Eph. 4:4). Calvin's line of reasoning is as stunning as it is straightforward. He forcefully states,

> We ought to be united, not in part only, but in body and soul. . . . We are called to one inheritance and one life; and hence it follows, that we cannot obtain eternal life without living in mutual harmony in this world. One Divine invitation being addressed to all, they ought to be united in the same profession of faith, and to render every kind of assistance to each other. Oh, were this thought deeply impressed upon our minds, that we are subject to a law which no more permits the children of God to differ among themselves than the kingdom of heaven to be divided, how earnestly should we cultivate brotherly kindness! How should we dread every kind of animosity, if we duly reflected that all who separate

---

50. *Institutes*, 4.1.3. Cf. Calvin, *Reply to Sadoleto*, in *Theological Treatises*, 231.
51. *Institutes*, 4.1.3.
52. *Comm.*, on Acts 4:32; cf. *Institutes*, 4.1.3.

us from brethren, estrange us from the kingdom of God! And yet, strangely enough, while we forget the duties which brethren owe to each other, we go on boasting that we are the sons of God. Let us learn from Paul, that none are at all fit for that inheritance who are not one body and one spirit.[53]

The principle of the communion of the saints flows from the doctrine of union with Christ. If Christians are "truly convinced" that "God is the common Father of all and Christ the common Head," then they must be united in brotherly love and share the benefits God has given them with one another.[54] Calvin's development of the communion of the saints in relation to union with Christ shares commonalities with the ecclesiology of Martin Bucer. A colleague and mentor of Calvin's in Strasbourg, Bucer envisioned the local church as the ministry of the ongoing work of Christ through his Spirit and word. At the beginning of his *Concerning the True Care of Souls*, Bucer states, "The church of Christ is the assembly and fellowship of those who are gathered from the world and united in Christ our Lord through his Spirit and word, to be a body and members of one another, each having his office and work for the general good of the whole body and all its members."[55] For Calvin and Bucer, the visible church is a tangible picture of the fellowship believers have with Christ and one another.

The creedal declaration of the communion of the saints should strengthen the resolve of Christians to support the visible church. Calvin gives three reasons why "the church could neither totter nor fail" even if "the whole fabric of the world were overthrown."[56] First, the work of the visible church "cannot waver or fail" since it is the means God has chosen to bring the elect to saving faith in Christ. Second, the church's security rests in the surety of Christ.

---

53. *Comm.*, on Eph. 4:4; cf. *Institutes*, 4.1.3.
54. *Institutes*, 4.1.3.
55. Martin Bucer, *Concerning the True Care of Souls*, trans. Peter Beale (Edinburgh: Banner of Truth, 2009), 1. On Bucer's role in the development of Calvin's doctrine of the church, see Alexandre Ganoczy, *The Young Calvin*, trans. David Foxgrover and Wade Provo (Edinburgh: T&T Clark, 1987), 159–62; Bruce Gordon, *Calvin* (New Haven, CT: Yale University Press, 2009), 82–102; cf. Willem van 't Spijker, *The Ecclesiastical Offices in the Thought of Martin Bucer*, trans. John Vriend and Lyle D. Bierma, SMRT 57 (Leiden: Brill, 1996), 357–66.
56. *Institutes*, 4.1.3.

Since the church has been "joined to the steadfastness of Christ," he "will no more allow his believers to be estranged from him than that his members be rent and torn asunder."[57] Third, Calvin draws on several Old Testament texts, such as Psalm 46:5; Joel 2:32; and Obadiah 17, to remind his readers that the promises of God guarantee the ultimate success of the church.[58] Calvin believes that the creedal formulation of the communion of the saints provides "a wealth of comfort" for Christians. But that does not mean the visible church will always be marked by unity on this side of eternity. This tenet "belongs to the realm of faith."[59] It is intended to remind Christians to trust in the triune God to build the church. The doctrine of the communion of the saints establishes "certainty in our hearts that all those who, by the kindness of God the Father, through the working of the Holy Spirit, have entered into fellowship with Christ, are set apart as God's property and personal possession; and that when we are of their number we share that great grace."[60] As Calvin uses the creed to sketch the core principles of his theology of the church, he interweaves doctrinal categories with pastoral concerns in order to highlight the way God "invites us into the society of Christ and holds us therein."

The Visible Church

Having outlined the creedal shape of his ecclesiology, Calvin returns to considering the church as mother. He states, "But because it is now our intention to discuss the visible church, let us learn even from the simple title 'mother' how useful, indeed how necessary, it is that we should know her."[61] The metaphor of mother is used by Calvin to describe the work of the visible church in caring for the people of God. He states, "For there is no other way to enter into life unless this mother conceive us in her womb, give us birth, nourish us at her breast, and lastly, unless she keep us under her care and guidance until, putting off mortal flesh, we become like the

---

57. *Institutes*, 4.1.3.
58. Cf. *Comm.*, on Ps. 46:5; Joel 2:32; Obad. 17; cf. *Institutes*, 4.1.3.
59. *Institutes*, 4.1.3.
60. *Institutes*, 4.1.3.
61. *Institutes*, 4.1.4.

angels."[62] The basic point is that the visible church is indispensable
in the Christian life. But to understand more clearly in what sense
the visible church serves in a motherly role for believers, we need to
examine two well-known passages in Calvin's commentaries.

First, in his exposition of Galatians 4:26, Calvin argues that the
church "as the mother of believers" is the place God has ordained for
Christians to mature in the faith. He states, "It is only through the
instrumentality of the Church that we are 'born of God,' (1 John 3:9)
and brought up through the various stages of children and youth, till
we arrive at manhood."[63] Commenting on 1 Timothy 3:15, Calvin
illustrates the value of the church by comparing it to a home. He explains, "To express it in a more homely manner, is not the Church the
mother of all believers? Does she not regenerate them by the word of
God, educate and nourish them through their whole life, strengthen,
and bring them at length to absolute perfection?" Through the agency
of the church, God "employs pastors" to minister word and sacrament
to his people for the duration of their lives.[64] Ultimately, to reject the
support of the church as mother is to refuse to have God as Father. As
Calvin states, "And certainly he who refuses to be a son of the Church
in vain desires to have God as his Father. . . . This designation, 'the
mother of us all,' reflects the highest credit and the highest honor on
the Church."[65] The reason why Calvin emphasizes the maternal metaphor is because he believes the visible church is the Christian's earthly
home, wherein God uses his ordained servants to educate and nourish
his people through his word.

Second, in his exposition of Ephesians 4:12, Calvin argues that
the church is a function of the ongoing ministry of Christ. He states,
"If the edification of the church proceeds from Christ alone, he has
surely a right to prescribe in what manner it shall be edified. But Paul
expressly states, that, according to the command of Christ, no real
union or perfection is attained, but by the outward preaching." Since
Christ has authority over the church, he has prescribed the outward

---

62. *Institutes*, 4.1.4.
63. *Comm.*, on Gal. 4:26.
64. *Comm.*, on 1 Tim. 3:15.
65. *Comm.*, on Gal. 4:26. On the role of God as Father, see Herman J. Selderhuis, *Calvin's Theology of the Psalms*, TSRPRT (Grand Rapids, MI: Baker Academic, 2007).

preaching of the word of God to be the means to save his people. To accomplish this, Christ by his Spirit sets apart qualified men to preach the word. Calvin continues, "We must allow ourselves to be ruled and taught by men. This is the universal rule, which extends equally to the highest and to the lowest. The church is the common mother of all the godly, which bears, nourishes, and brings up children to God, kings and peasants alike; and this is done by the ministry." Those who neglect the church make themselves to be "wiser than Christ," since they disregard the means Christ has given them for knowing him by his Spirit through his word.[66]

By stressing the maternal role of the church, Calvin uses a biblical image to feature the way God governs and grows his people through his word. This description allows Calvin to articulate the functional role of the visible church in the life of believers.[67] Calvin cites a series of Old Testament prophetic texts to argue that "away from her [the church's] bosom one cannot hope for any forgiveness of sins or any salvation."[68] The point is not that the church saves but that the church is the place where God's ordained means of grace—the preaching of the word and the sacraments of baptism and the Lord's Supper—are found. Calvin understands that the Spirit of God does not invite men and women into the society of Christ apart from these divinely appointed means. As McKee explains, the visible church "is God's chosen instrument for the gospel to be offered to human beings, so anyone who departs from that proclamation is leaving the means which God ordained for salvation."[69] In the visible church, God accommodates to the weaknesses of his people who need their faith strengthened. Shifting the image from home life to the school room, Calvin states, "Our weakness does not allow us to be dismissed from her [the church's] school until we have been pupils all our lives."[70] Apart from the visible church, there is no ordinary way for someone to know the salvation God provides in Christ. For Calvin, "God's fatherly favor and the especial witness of spiritual life are limited to his flock, so that it is

66. *Comm.*, on Eph. 4:12; cf. *Institutes*, 4.1.4.
67. See Kim, *Identity and Life*, 99–125.
68. *Institutes*, 4.1.4.
69. McKee, *Pastoral Ministry and Worship*, 32.
70. *Institutes*, 4.1.4.

always disastrous to leave the church."[71] The point is that Christians never outgrow their need for the motherly care of the church.

Conclusion

Calvin's discussion of the church as mother was a way for him to describe the work of the visible church. As I. John Hesselink observes, "Calvin's high doctrine of the church . . . laid great stress on the authority and indispensability of the visible, earthly church."[72] Throughout his ministry, Calvin stressed the importance of the local church. In Bruce Gordon's words, Calvin was "a man of the Church"; his "genius was to discover the Church, and teach what it was to be part of that body if one lived in a besieged city, under a capricious Tudor monarch or as a refugee facing persecution and exile."[73] Calvin's brilliance is reflected in his ability to cast a vision for reformation through the visible church. Contrary to the suggestion that Calvin's organizational framework for reforming the churches in Geneva was devoid of theological reflection, his ecclesiastical agenda set forth in the *Institutes* weaves together biblical, theological, historical, and practical arguments that inform his doctrine of the church. As Kim contends, "Calvin always tries to discuss his idea of the Church from a theological perspective."[74]

Drawing from the creedal tradition and the history of exegesis, Calvin used theological interpretations of biblical texts to address the practical needs of sixteenth-century churches.[75] In describing the church as mother, Calvin refined the arguments of church fathers, promoted the Reformation's doctrine of salvation, developed a theological framework for his doctrine of the church, and encouraged fellow Christians not to forsake the means of grace that God had given in the ministry of the visible church.

---

71. *Institutes*, 4.1.4.
72. I. John Hesselink, *Calvin's First Catechism: A Commentary*, with the 1538 catechism trans. Ford Lewis Battles, CSRT (Louisville: Westminster John Knox, 1997), 155.
73. Gordon, *Calvin*, viii.
74. Kim, *Identity and Life*, 10.
75. See McKee, "Teaching on the Elder," 147. On Calvin as a practical Reformer, see Benjamin B. Warfield, "Calvin and the Reformation," in *Selected Shorter Writings of Benjamin B. Warfield*, ed. John E. Meeter (Phillipsburg, NJ: Presbyterian and Reformed, 1970), 1:403; Pauw, "Practical Ecclesiology," 92–93.

18

The Sacraments

Keith A. Mathison

It seems to me that a simple and proper definition would be to say that [a sacrament] is an outward sign by which the Lord seals on our consciences the promises of his good will toward us in order to sustain the weakness of our faith.

—John Calvin, *Institutes of the Christian Religion*

A Misunderstood Doctrine?

In the five hundred years since the birth of John Calvin, students of his writings have yet to reach complete consensus on the meaning of his doctrine of the sacraments. Even in his day, readers reached opposite conclusions. The Zurich Reformer Heinrich Bullinger told Calvin that his views on the Lord's Supper were indistinguishable from those of the Lutherans. The Lutherans, on the other hand, could see no difference between Calvin and the Zwinglians.[1] Among Reformed theologians, some have rejected Calvin's doctrine as incoherent, while others

---

1. B. A. Gerrish, *Grace and Gratitude: The Eucharistic Theology of John Calvin* (Minneapolis: Fortress, 1993), 3.

have judged it to be consistent and biblical.[2] We may choose either to accept or reject Calvin's doctrine, but before we decide whether Calvin was correct, we must first have some understanding of what he actually taught.

Historical Context

In 1520, Martin Luther published *The Babylonian Captivity of the Church*, criticizing the Roman Catholic doctrine of the sacraments.[3] This book focused on three particular errors of the Roman church's eucharistic doctrine and practice: First, the cup was withheld from the laity, and they received only the bread. Second, Rome taught the doctrine of transubstantiation, saying that at the moment of consecration, the substance of the bread and wine is changed into the substance of the body and blood of Christ. Third, Rome taught that the Mass is a propitiatory sacrifice for sins.

The Reformers agreed in their rejection of Rome's understanding of the Mass as a sacrifice and in their criticism of Rome's withholding of the cup. They also agreed in their rejection of transubstantiation, but they could not agree on the proper explanation of Christ's presence in the Supper.[4] Luther continued to maintain the idea that the body and blood of Christ were somehow really present. He proposed a real but illocal presence of Christ in the bread and wine.[5] In Zurich, Huldrych Zwingli rejected Luther's formulation of the doctrine, arguing that the only kind of presence that could be predicated of a true human body, such as Christ's, was local, or circumscriptive, presence. Zwingli proposed a more symbolic doctrine. He denied that the bread

---

2. See Ralph Cunnington, "Calvin's Doctrine of the Lord's Supper: A Blot upon His Labors as a Public Instructor?," *WTJ* 73, no. 2 (2011): 215–36.

3. Martin Luther, *The Babylonian Captivity of the Church*, in *Luther's Works*, vol. 36, *Word and Sacrament II*, ed. Abdel Ross Wentz (Philadelphia: Fortress, 1959), 3–126. For a more thorough overview of the immediate historical context, including discussions of Cornelius Hoen, Andreas Karlstadt, and others, see Keith A. Mathison, "The Lord's Supper," in *Reformation Theology: A Systematic Summary*, ed. Matthew Barrett (Wheaton, IL: Crossway, 2017), 643–73.

4. The medieval scholastics distinguished among several types of presence: local, or circumscriptive, presence is the mode of presence characteristic of finite physical things; illocal, or definitive, presence is a type of spiritual presence characteristic of finite spiritual beings, such as angels; repletive presence is a type of presence characteristic of an infinite spiritual being and is properly predicated only of God. For a fuller explanation of these terms, see Richard A. Muller, *Dictionary of Latin and Greek Theological Terms: Drawn Principally from Protestant Scholastic Theology* (Grand Rapids, MI: Baker, 1985), 239–43.

5. See, for example, his 1528 *Confession concerning Christ's Supper*, in *Luther's Works*, vol. 37, *Word and Sacrament III*, ed. Robert H. Fischer (Philadelphia: Muhlenberg, 1961), 214–17.

and wine were the body and blood of Christ and claimed that the Supper was simply a commemoration of Christ's death.[6]

The disagreement between Luther, Zwingli, and others, led to an ongoing and increasingly bitter debate among Protestants over the meaning of the Supper. Sadly, an early attempt to resolve the issues at the 1529 Colloquy of Marburg failed.[7] The ongoing debate among German and Swiss Protestants over the meaning of the Supper seriously hampered efforts toward a consolidated Reformation.[8] Among those who attempted to find a way to bring the two sides together were Martin Bucer and, later, John Calvin.[9]

The Lord's Supper was not the only subject of controversy at this time. Anabaptists were raising serious questions about baptism, denying the legitimacy of Roman Catholic baptism and, more seriously, denying the appropriateness of infant baptism. The birthplace of the Anabaptist movement is sometimes traced to Zurich, and the presence of Anabaptists in the cities that had accepted evangelical doctrine often caused uncomfortable difficulties for the Reformers.[10] Disputes between the magisterial Reformers and more radical Reformers, such as the Anabaptists, would continue throughout Calvin's lifetime and beyond.[11]

Doctrinal Development (1536–1564)

Before looking at Calvin's teaching on the sacraments, we must determine whether it is necessary to speak of Calvin's *doctrines* of the sacraments. The question whether Calvin's doctrine of the sacraments, and particularly his doctrine of the Lord's Supper, substantially changed

6. Zwingli's most important book on the Supper and the one that most clearly outlines his view is his *Friendly Exegesis, That Is, Exposition of the Matter of the Eucharist to Martin Luther.* An English translation is available in Huldrych Zwingli, *Writings*, vol. 2, *In Search of True Religion: Reformation, Pastoral and Eucharistic Writings*, trans. H. Wayne Pipkin (Allison Park, PA: Pickwick, 1984), 233–369; see also W. P. Stephens, *The Theology of Huldrych Zwingli* (Oxford: Clarendon, 1986), 184.

7. For a history of the Colloquy of Marburg, see Hermann Sasse, *This Is My Body: Luther's Contention for the Real Presence in the Sacrament of the Altar* (Minneapolis: Augsburg, 1959), 187–294.

8. Bruce Gordon, *Calvin* (New Haven, CT: Yale University Press, 2009), 53.

9. Gordon, *Calvin*, 161–64.

10. See, for example, Zwingli's attempts in his *Fidei Expositio* (1531) to dissociate his reform efforts from those of the Anabaptists.

11. Willem Balke, *Calvin and the Anabaptist Radicals*, trans. William Heynen (Grand Rapids, MI: Eerdmans, 1981).

over time has become the subject of renewed scholarly interest. Some Calvin scholars of previous generations claimed that Calvin's doctrine remained essentially unchanged over the course of his career.[12] Based on their study of Calvin's writings, Thomas Davis and others disagree.[13]

Davis argues that there is evidence of substantial "change and development" in Calvin's doctrine of the Lord's Supper between the first edition of his *Institutes* in 1536 and the time of his death in 1564.[14] Davis does demonstrate observable change, but most of it occurs before 1541, when Calvin leaves Strasbourg and returns to Geneva. As Davis explains, "The foundations, then, of Calvin's eucharistic theology are in place at the end of the Strasbourg period."[15] He adds,

> What remains is for Calvin to implement his eucharistic theology as he serves as pastor in the city of Geneva; to fine-tune his concept of eucharistic instrumentality in his biblical commentaries as it relates to how God has always used secondary instruments to reveal knowledge of himself to his people; and finally, to refine his notion of how Christ communicates his body and blood to the believer as he engages Westphal in debate.[16]

There is implementation, fine-tuning, and refinement of his doctrine between 1541 and 1564, and this may be loosely termed "development," but implementation, fine-tuning, and refinement are not the same as substantial "change" to the key elements of the doctrine.

Wim Janse agrees with Davis that Calvin's doctrine of the Supper underwent significant development.[17] According to Janse, Calvin's eucharistic views display "Zwinglianizing (1536–1537), Lutheranizing (1537–1548), and again spiritualizing tendencies (1549–

---

12. See, for example, Kilian McDonnell, *John Calvin, the Church, and the Eucharist* (Princeton, NJ: Princeton University Press, 1967), 3; J. K. S. Reid, "General Introduction," in *Theological Treatises*, 13.

13. Thomas Davis, *The Clearest Promises of God: The Development of Calvin's Eucharistic Teaching* (New York: AMS Press, 1995).

14. Davis, *Clearest Promises*, 6.

15. Davis, *Clearest Promises*, 128.

16. Davis, *Clearest Promises*, 129.

17. Wim Janse, "The Sacraments," in *The Calvin Handbook*, ed. Herman J. Selderhuis (Grand Rapids, MI: Eerdmans, 2009), 344.

1550s)."[18] Janse argues that Calvin's shifting tendencies may have been determined by his confidence in the possibility of forming a consensus with the Lutherans at any given point in time. According to Janse, when Calvin considered such a consensus attainable, he formulated his doctrine as closely to that of the Lutherans as possible.[19]

Of course, it is neither helpful nor historically accurate to claim that Calvin's doctrine of the sacraments sprang, like Athena from the head of Zeus, fully grown. His lifelong studies and his frequent interactions with friends and foes alike helped him hone his ideas. This does not mean, however, that his core ideas were in constant flux. As Henri Blocher indicates in his critique of the development thesis, one can find so-called "Zwinglian," "Lutheran," and "spiritual" language throughout Calvin's career.[20] When all the evidence is examined, it indicates that by 1541, at the very latest, Calvin's doctrine of the sacraments was basically settled.[21]

What we find from 1541 forward is simply further explanation and clarification, not substantive change. This should not be surprising considering the subject matter. It is worth observing what Calvin says about the difficulty he experienced in attempting to verbalize his doctrine: "My mind can think beyond what my tongue can utter."[22] He had the basic ideas in mind by 1541, but he was continually trying to express them more clearly. Clarification, rather than revision, more accurately expresses what was occurring between 1541 and 1564.

Possible Influences on Calvin's Doctrine

Granted that Calvin's earliest writings (between 1536 and 1541) reveal a developing doctrine of the sacraments, it is necessary to explore, however briefly, some of the possible influences on his thinking during this time. In the years before 1536, when he came to Geneva, Calvin read widely. By this time, he was already very well read in the early

---

18. Wim Janse, "Calvin's Eucharistic Theology: Three Dogma-Historical Observations," in *Calvinus Sacrarum Literarum Interpres: Papers of the International Congress on Calvin Research*, ed. Herman J. Selderhuis, RHT 5 (Göttingen: Vandenhoeck & Ruprecht, 2008), 39.

19. Janse, "Calvin's Eucharistic Theology," 40.

20. Henri A. G. Blocher, "Calvin on the Lord's Supper: Revisiting an Intriguing Diversity, Part 1," *WTJ* 76, no. 1 (2014): 61–65.

21. For the argument that Calvin's doctrine was settled by 1536, see Charles Partee, *The Theology of John Calvin* (Louisville: Westminster John Knox, 2008), 277.

22. *Institutes*, 4.17.7.

church fathers.[23] He had a particular respect for the biblical exegesis of John Chrysostom and the theology of Augustine.[24] Augustine's explanation of the relationship between signs and the things signified, for example, would be key to Calvin's formulation of his own doctrine of the sacraments.[25]

Calvin was also familiar with many of the writings and confessions of the first generation of Reformers. He was acquainted with the works of Zwingli and Luther, although he could read only those works of Luther that were available in Latin.[26] He had probably already read the first edition of Philipp Melanchthon's *Loci Communes*, published in 1521.[27] Calvin was also likely familiar with the most important Protestant confessions written in the first decades of the Reformation: the Augsburg Confession (1530), the Tetrapolitan Confession (1530), the First Confession of Basel (1534), and the First Helvetic Confession (1536).

When Calvin came to Geneva in the late summer of 1536, the city had been officially evangelical for only a few months. The city had adopted the Reformation faith officially in May 1536.[28] During his brief first stay in Geneva, Calvin worked closely with Guillaume Farel, whose understanding of the sacraments was basically Zwinglian.[29] Given Farel's influence in the reformation of Geneva, it is hardly surprising that Calvin's writings from the earliest part of this period contain some Zwinglian emphases.

Calvin and Farel were forced to leave Geneva around Easter of 1538, and Calvin eventually settled in Strasbourg. There he came under the influence of Martin Bucer, another experienced Reformer

23. Anthony N. S. Lane, *John Calvin: Student of the Church Fathers* (Edinburgh: T&T Clark, 1999), 47.

24. Lane, *John Calvin*, 38–39.

25. Joseph Fitzer, "The Augustinian Roots of Calvin's Eucharistic Thought," in *Articles on Calvin and Calvinism*, ed. Richard C. Gamble, vol. 10, *Calvin's Ecclesiology: Sacraments and Deacons* (New York: Garland, 1992); see also Christopher Elwood, *The Body Broken: The Calvinist Doctrine of the Eucharist and the Symbolization of Power in Sixteenth-Century France*, OSHT (New York: Oxford University Press, 1999), 62–63.

26. Sasse, *This Is My Body*, 321.

27. He had certainly read Melanchthon's work by the time he wrote the 1539 edition of his *Institutes*. See Richard A. Muller, *The Unaccommodated Calvin: Studies in the Foundation of a Theological Tradition*, OSHT (New York: Oxford University Press, 2000), 125–28.

28. Gordon, *Calvin*, 70.

29. See "Guillaume Farel's Summary (1529)," in James T. Dennison, *Reformed Confessions of the 16th and 17th Centuries in English Translation* (Grand Rapids, MI: Reformation Heritage Books, 2008–2014), 1:51–111.

some twenty years his senior. As Bruce Gordon observes, "The Zwinglian influences detectable in the 1536 *Institutes* evaporated during Calvin's stay in Strasbourg between 1538 and 1541."[30] There are at least two possible reasons for this: first, Bucer's impact on Calvin, and second, the confessional context of Strasbourg.

Bucer's influence on Calvin is almost universally acknowledged. The historian Wilhelm Pauck puts it this way: "The type of church which we call Calvinistic or Reformed is really a gift of Martin Bucer to the world through the work of his strong and brilliant executive, John Calvin."[31] Bucer's understanding of the sacraments had undergone development, but by 1528, he had settled into his own view, which was "favorable to Luther without really being Lutheran."[32] Bucer was tireless in his attempts to find a formulation of the doctrine of the sacraments that would unite the Lutherans and the Zwinglians.[33] In this endeavor, he would be followed by Calvin.[34]

The confessional context of Strasbourg also likely influenced Calvin. In 1530, Strasbourg had accepted the Tetrapolitan Confession, written by Bucer and Wolfgang Capito. In 1531, when Strasbourg joined the Schmalkaldic League, the city signed the Lutheran Augsburg Confession without abandoning the Tetrapolitan Confession. Both confessions were officially held until 1536, when the Wittenberg Concord was concluded.[35] From that point forward, the official confession of Strasbourg was the Augsburg Confession. This was the confessional context when Calvin arrived in Strasbourg in September 1538 to minister to the French refugees.[36] As with the other ministers in the city, Calvin could not teach anything contrary to the official confession. He and Bucer were likely able to work in this confessional

---

30. Gordon, *Calvin*, 167.

31. Quoted in Steven Ozment, *The Age of Reform, 1250–1550: An Intellectual and Religious History of Late Medieval and Reformation Europe* (New Haven, CT: Yale University Press, 1980), 363. See also François Wendel, *Calvin: Origins and Development of His Religious Thought*, trans. Philip Mairet (Durham: Labyrinth, 1963), 332.

32. McDonnell, *John Calvin*, 75–76.

33. Martin Greschat, *Martin Bucer: A Reformer and His Times*, trans. Stephen E. Buckwalter (Louisville: Westminster John Knox, 2004), 70.

34. David C. Steinmetz, *Calvin in Context* (New York: Oxford University Press, 1995), 172; see also Joseph N. Tylenda, "The Ecumenical Intention of Calvin's Early Eucharistic Teaching," in *Reformatio Perennis: Essays on Calvin and the Reformation in Honor of Ford Lewis Battles*, ed. B. A. Gerrish, Pittsburgh Theological Monograph Series 32 (Pittsburgh: Pickwick, 1981), 27–28.

35. Gordon, *Calvin*, 85.

36. W. Nijenhuis, *Ecclesia Reformata: Studies on the Reformation* (Leiden: Brill, 1972), 112.

context because the language of the Augsburg Confession was vague enough to allow them to teach with clear consciences.

Calvin returned to Geneva in September 1541. By this time, his own sacramental views were settled, but he continued to clarify and elaborate on his views for the rest of his life. Of crucial importance in the elaboration of Calvin's views during these years was the second sacramental controversy between the Reformed churches and the Lutherans. This controversy was ignited after Calvin and Bullinger worked out a consensus statement on the Lord's Supper in 1549, known as the Consensus Tigurinus.[37] A polemical war of words began between Calvin and other Reformed leaders on the one side and Lutherans such as Joachim Westphal and Tilemann Heshusius on the other.[38] This controversy consumed a significant amount of Calvin's time and energy, but it helped him clarify his sacramental views.

Union with Christ

Calvin's teaching on the sacraments must be placed within its proper context in his larger theological system. Thus, a word is necessary concerning Calvin's doctrine of union with Christ. As Joel Beeke has explained, Calvin "could scarcely speak of any doctrine apart from union and communion with Christ."[39] Philip Ryken notes that union with Christ was "one of the controlling principles of his soteriology, or doctrine of salvation."[40] This is evident in the 1559 edition of his *Institutes*, where Calvin begins book 3 by saying, "First, we must understand that as long as Christ remains outside of us, and we are

37. See Paul Rorem, *Calvin and Bullinger on the Lord's Supper* (Nottingham, UK: Grove Books, 1989); Rorem, "The Consensus Tigurinus (1549): Did Calvin Compromise?," in *Calvinus Sacrae Scripturae Professor: Calvin as Confessor of Holy Scriptures*, ed. Wilhelm H. Neuser (Grand Rapids, MI: Eerdmans, 1994), 72–90. The Consensus Tigurinus was a compromise statement that represented Bullinger's views much more so than it did Calvin's; see Wendel, *Calvin*, 330; Davis, *Clearest Promises*, 30, 56; Gordon, *Calvin*, 179.

38. See Joseph N. Tylenda, "The Calvin-Westphal Exchange: The Genesis of Calvin's Treatises against Westphal," *CTJ* 9, no. 2 (1974): 182–209. See also Wim Janse, "Joachim Westphal's Sacramentology," *LQ* 22, no. 2 (2008): 137–60.

39. Joel R. Beeke, "Appropriating Salvation: The Spirit, Faith and Assurance, and Repentance (3.1–3, 6–10)," in *A Theological Guide to Calvin's "Institutes": Essays and Analysis*, ed. David W. Hall and Peter A. Lillback, Calvin 500 Series (Phillipsburg, NJ: P&R, 2008), 273.

40. Philip Graham Ryken, "The Believer's Union with Christ," in *John Calvin: A Heart for Devotion, Doctrine, and Doxology*, ed. Burk Parsons (Lake Mary, FL: Reformation Trust, 2008), 193.

separated from him, all that he has suffered and done for the salvation of the human race remains useless and of no value for us."[41]

Calvin's doctrine of union with Christ is particularly important for understanding his doctrine of the sacraments. It is necessary for grasping his doctrine of baptism, and as Wayne Spear observes, "It is at the heart of the meaning of the Lord's Supper."[42] In order to understand Calvin's doctrine of union with Christ, it is helpful to consider his continually repeated idea that God is the source of all life. Calvin teaches that "our only and eternal God is the spring and fountain of all life."[43] The problem facing humanity now is that union with God and thus participation in eternal life were lost by Adam as a result of his sin.[44] As Calvin explains, "Since he [man] was alienated from God by sin, he was likewise excluded from the communion of all the goods which can not be had anywhere except in Him."[45]

Although believers who lived before the coming of Christ enjoyed "a real participation in God,"[46] after the incarnation, union with God takes place by means of union with Christ. Calvin conceives of three types of union with Christ. This threefold union can be discerned throughout Calvin's writings, but it is most clearly set forth in his 1555 correspondence with Peter Martyr Vermigli. Vermigli initiated the correspondence, writing to Calvin on March 8, 1555, and to Theodore Beza around the same time.[47] Vermigli shared his view of the threefold

---

41. *Institutes*, 3.1.1. On the relationship between Calvin's doctrine of union with Christ and his doctrines of justification and sanctification, see Cornelis P. Venema, *Accepted and Renewed in Christ: The "Twofold Grace of God" and the Interpretation of Calvin's Theology*, RHT 2 (Göttingen: Vandenhoeck & Ruprecht, 2007); Venema, "Union with Christ, the 'Twofold Grace of God,' and the 'Order of Salvation' in Calvin's Theology," in *Calvin for Today*, ed. Joel R. Beeke (Grand Rapids, MI: Reformation Heritage Books, 2009), 91–113.

42. Wayne R. Spear, "The Nature of the Lord's Supper according to Calvin and the Westminster Assembly," in *The Westminster Confession into the 21st Century: Essays in Remembrance of the 350th Anniversary of the Westminster Assembly*, ed. Ligon Duncan (Fearn, Ross-shire, Scotland: Mentor, 2009), 3:361.

43. "Calvin's Catechism (1537)," in Dennison, *Reformed Confessions*, 1:356.

44. *Institutes*, 2.1.6.

45. John Calvin, *Institutes of the Christian Religion: 1541 French Edition*, trans. Elsie Anne McKee (Grand Rapids, MI: Eerdmans, 2009), 50.

46. *Institutes*, 2.10.7.

47. An English translation of the letter to Beza is found in Peter Martyr Vermigli, *Life, Letters, and Sermons*, ed. and trans. John Patrick Donnelly, vol. 5 of *Peter Martyr Library*, ed. John Patrick Donnelly and Joseph C. McLelland, SCES 42 (Kirksville, MO: Thomas Jefferson University Press, 1999), 134–37. An English translation of the March 8 letter to Calvin is found in George Cornelius Gorham, *Gleanings of a Few Scattered Ears* (London: Bell and Daldy, 1857), 340–44.

union with Christ and asked for Calvin's thoughts. Calvin responded on August 8, 1555.[48]

In his response, Calvin describes what Duncan Rankin terms an incarnational union, a mystical union, and a spiritual union.[49] Rankin helpfully summarizes the meaning of each of these:

> The hypostatic union and resultant incarnational communion involve the man Jesus, who in his humanity is a man just like other men, sin excepted. Mystic communion is a definitive sacred ingrafting into the life of Jesus Christ by the action of the Holy Spirit upon faith. Spiritual communion is the progressive enjoyment of the Spirit and blessings of Christ's life that flow from mystic union.[50]

If we keep these three kinds of union and communion in mind, some of Calvin's more perplexing statements regarding the sacraments become clearer.

In his correspondence with Vermigli, Calvin mentions Christ's incarnational union with humanity only in passing. It is "that communication which the Son of God hath with our nature, by assuming our flesh that he might become our brother."[51] As Rankin observes, the incarnational union is the union of the eternal Word with the humanity that believers share with every other person.[52] This incarnational union is necessary because the fall had separated humanity from God.[53] The common theme that one finds in Calvin from 1536 to 1559 is that the Son became what we are in order to impart to us what is his.[54]

Regarding Christ's mystical union with believers, Calvin writes, "At the same time that we receive Christ by faith, as he offers himself in the gospel, we are made truly members of him, and life flows unto

---

48. An English translation of the relevant portion of this letter is found in Theodore Beza, *The Life of John Calvin*, trans. Francis Sibson (Philadelphia: J. Whetham, 1836), 309–11.

49. W. Duncan Rankin, "Calvin's Correspondence on Our Threefold Union with Christ," in *The Hope Fulfilled: Essays in Honor of O. Palmer Robertson*, ed. Robert L. Penny (Phillipsburg, NJ: P&R, 2008), 250.

50. Rankin, "Calvin's Correspondence," 250.

51. John Calvin to Peter Martyr, August 8, 1555, in Beza, *Life*, 309.

52. Rankin, "Calvin's Correspondence," 234.

53. *Institutes* (1541), 222–23.

54. *Institutes* (1541), 223; cf. *Institutes*, 2.12.2.

us from him as *a capite, from the head*."[55] The incarnational union makes possible the mystical union of Christ with believers, but the mystical union is "a definitive event in the lives of the elect."[56] It involves believers only. Calvin emphasizes the importance of this union throughout his career. In his 1537 catechism, Calvin writes, "Christ, therefore, makes us thus participants in himself in order that we, who are in ourselves sinners, may be, through Christ's righteousness, considered just before the throne of God."[57] This union is necessary because in ourselves we do not possess eternal life. The source of life is God, and this life flows to us from Christ. In his 1553 commentary on John 6:35, Calvin explains, "Our souls do not *live* by an intrinsic power, so to speak, that is, by a power which they have naturally in themselves, but borrow *life* from Christ."[58]

Calvin's descriptions of mystical union with Christ can begin to help us understand one of Calvin's most misunderstood phrases, namely, "the life-giving flesh of Christ."[59] Calvin explains what he means by this phrase in his commentary on John 6:51:

> For as the eternal Word of God is the fountain of *life*, (John i.4,) so his flesh, as a channel, conveys to us that *life* which dwells intrinsically, as we say, in his Divinity. And in this sense it is called life-giving, because it conveys to us that life which it borrows from another quarter.[60]

Once we have noted Calvin's distinction between Christ's body and the divine life that it mediates to us by virtue of our mystical union, we must also observe that the two are inseparable. According to Calvin, the body and the benefits of Christ must be distinguished, but they cannot be separated. At the beginning of book 3 of the 1559 *Institutes*, he reminds his readers, "All that [Christ] possesses is nothing to us

---

55. Calvin to Peter Martyr, August 8, 1555, 309, italics original.
56. Rankin, "Calvin's Correspondence," 245.
57. "Calvin's Catechism (1537)," in Dennison, *Reformed Confessions*, 1:368. Calvin teaches that both justification and sanctification are benefits of our union with Christ (e.g., *Institutes* [1541], 318), but he does not make union with Christ the ground of our justification. The ground of our justification is the imputed righteousness of Christ (e.g., *Institutes*, 3.11.2). In this connection, it is also helpful to read Calvin's refutation of Osiander's doctrine; see *Institutes*, 3.11.5–12.
58. *Comm.*, 17:250.
59. Partee, *Theology of John Calvin*, 275–76.
60. *Comm.*, on John 6:51 (17:262).

until we grow into one body with him."[61] In the following chapter, the point is made even more clearly: "For we await salvation from him not because he appears to us afar off, but because he makes us, ingrafted into his body, participants *not only in all his benefits but also in himself.*"[62]

Finally, regarding Christ's ongoing spiritual union with believers, Calvin explains that it is "the effect and fruit" of the mystical union.[63] "For after Christ, by the internal operation of the Spirit, has subdued and united us to himself in his body, he continues to us a second operation of the Spirit, by which he enriches us with his gifts."[64] We have seen that mystical union is a definitive event, but as Rankin explains, "Spiritual communion is an ongoing, progressive relation."[65] This communion can grow and be strengthened over the course of the believer's life. As Calvin expresses it, "the life of Christ increases" in believers.[66] It is this union that Calvin explicitly associates with the Supper.[67] He does not associate this spiritual nourishment and strengthening, however, exclusively with the Supper. He attributes the same benefit to the gospel, to the word of God.[68]

It may help to summarize all that we have said about Calvin's doctrine of union with Christ by pointing out an analogy he frequently uses to illustrate his basic idea. As we have seen, Calvin describes God as "the spring and fountain of all life."[69] Christ, as the second person of the Trinity, shares in this life, and by virtue of his incarnation, he becomes, as it were, a fountain. Calvin explains, "Christ's flesh is like a fountain, since it receives the life flowing down from the divinity in order to transfer it to us."[70] Finally, "the bond of this joining is the Holy Spirit, by whom we are united together, and He is like a canal or channel by which all that Christ is and possesses comes down to us."[71] Comparing life to water, then,

61. *Institutes*, 3.1.1.
62. *Institutes*, 3.2.24, italics added.
63. Calvin to Peter Martyr, August 8, 1555, 310.
64. Calvin to Peter Martyr, August 8, 1555, 310.
65. Rankin, "Calvin's Correspondence," 245.
66. Calvin to Peter Martyr, August 8, 1555, 311.
67. Calvin to Peter Martyr, August 8, 1555, 311.
68. Gerrish, *Grace and Gratitude*, 128.
69. "Calvin's Catechism (1537)," in Dennison, *Reformed Confessions*, 1:356.
70. *Institutes* (1541), 555; cf. *Comm.*, on John 6:11; Rom. 1:3.
71. *Institutes* (1541), 556.

Calvin says that God is the source, or wellspring; the incarnate Christ is the fountain bringing the "water" to the surface and making it accessible; and the Holy Spirit is the channel connecting the fountain to us over any distance.

The Sacraments

Book 4 of the 1559 edition of the *Institutes* opens with the following words:

> As explained in the previous book, it is by the [*sic*] faith in the gospel that Christ becomes ours and we are made partakers of the salvation and eternal blessedness brought by him. Since, however, in our ignorance and sloth (to which I add fickleness of disposition) we need outward helps to beget and increase faith within us, and advance it to its goal, God has also added these aids that he may provide for our weakness.[72]

Among those outward helps discussed in book 4 are the sacraments. As Robert Godfrey notes, "For Calvin the sacraments were one of the most important helps or aids that the Spirit of God uses for his people in their weakness (4.1.1)."[73]

Calvin's basic definition of the sacraments remained consistent throughout his career. In the 1559 edition of the *Institutes*, Calvin writes, "It seems to me that a simple and proper definition would be to say that it is an outward sign by which the Lord seals on our consciences the promises of his good will toward us in order to sustain the weakness of our faith."[74] He continues several paragraphs later: "A sacrament is never without a preceding promise but is joined to it as a sort of appendix, with the purpose of confirming and sealing the promise itself, and of making it more evident to us and in a sense ratifying it."[75]

The first thing we note in this definition is that the sacraments are said to be "signs." According to Calvin, it is important to distinguish

---

72. *Institutes*, 4.1.1.
73. W. Robert Godfrey, "Calvin, Worship, and the Sacraments (4.13–19)," in Hall and Lillback, *Theological Guide to Calvin's "Institutes,"* 372.
74. *Institutes*, 4.14.1.
75. *Institutes*, 4.14.3; cf. *Institutes* (1536), 87.

the sign from that which it signifies.[76] A failure to distinguish the two inevitably leads people to attribute to the sign that which properly belongs only to the reality that it signifies or to attribute to the human minister that which properly belongs only to God. At the same time, although the sign must be distinguished from that which it signifies, it cannot be separated from it (assuming proper reception by faith). In Calvin's words, the sign and the reality "are neither disjoined nor separated."[77] A failure to join the two inevitably leads people to view the signs as empty figures.

Calvin's understanding of the relationship between the sacraments and union with Christ is evident when he says that the purpose of the sacraments "is to bring us to communion with Christ."[78] Responding to Lutheran criticisms of his doctrine, Calvin adds,

> If it is on the dignity of the sacraments that their heart is set, what better fitted to display it than to call them helps and means by which we are either ingrafted into the body of Christ, or being ingrafted, are drawn closer and closer, until he makes us altogether one with himself in the heavenly life?[79]

In other words, Calvin associates the sacraments with mystical union and spiritual union.

Calvin's language can cause some confusion if we do not recall what he has said about the relationship between signs and the things they signify (distinct but not separate). This relation allows him, in some contexts, to attribute (using metonymy) the effect of the thing signified to the outward sign. In his commentary on Romans 6:3, he explains that this is how Paul often speaks to believers: "Paul, according to his usual manner, where he speaks of the faithful, connects the reality and the effect with the outward sign; for we know that whatever the Lord offers us by the visible symbol is confirmed and ratified by their faith."[80]

To understand what Calvin is saying, it is also necessary to examine Calvin's description of the sacraments as instruments.[81] The idea that

---

76. *Institutes*, 4.14.15.
77. John Calvin, "Mutual Consent in Regard to the Sacraments," in *Tracts and Letters*, 2:224.
78. "Mutual Consent," in *Tracts and Letters*, 2:222.
79. "Mutual Consent," in *Tracts and Letters*, 2:222–23.
80. *Comm.*, on Rom. 6:4 (19:221).
81. Elwood, *Body Broken*, 70–71.

the sacraments are instruments is found throughout Calvin's writings. In his *Commentary on Romans*, for example, Calvin says that God has designed the sacraments "to be instruments (*instrumenta*) of his grace."[82] In his 1547 response to the Council of Trent, he more specifically describes the sacraments as "instrumental causes" (although not in the sense that Rome uses that phrase).[83] By the time of his 1559 *Institutes*, he is still referring to the sacraments as means and instruments.[84]

As instrumental causes, the sacraments have no inherent power of causality.[85] An instrumental cause is a type of secondary cause that is used by a primary cause to bring about some effect.[86] The sacraments, then, do not work *ex opere operato* ("by the work performed") as Rome claims.[87] Calvin explains, "It is not at all by the material of water, and bread and wine that we obtain possession of Christ and his spiritual gifts."[88] The primary cause is God. In the sacraments, "God alone properly acts."[89] Calvin elaborates, "Thus, in Baptism, God washes us by the blood of his Son, and regenerates us by his Spirit; in the Supper he feeds us with the flesh and blood of Christ."[90] In other places, such as his commentary on John 1:26, Calvin refers to Christ as the one who performs what the signs figuratively represent.[91] He also emphasizes the necessity of the Holy Spirit's work.[92] He is the one "who brings the graces of God."[93] And, as Calvin explains, the Holy Spirit is given by God only to his own.[94]

Calvin's basic definition of the sacraments also emphasizes that they aim to increase or support existing faith: "As our faith is slight and feeble unless it be propped up on all sides and sustained by every means, it trembles, wavers, totters, and at last gives way."[95] One

---

82. *Comm.*, on Rom. 4:11 (19:164).
83. John Calvin, *Acts of the Council of Trent, with the Antidote*, in *Tracts and Letters*, 3:174. Calvin explicitly denies that baptism is the instrumental cause of justification. *Antidote*, in *Tracts and Letters*, 3:116–17.
84. *Institutes*, 4.14.12.
85. *Institutes*, 4.14.17; see also McDonnell, *John Calvin*, 167.
86. Muller, *Dictionary*, 61–64.
87. *Institutes*, 4.14.14.
88. "Mutual Consent," in *Tracts and Letters*, 2:228.
89. *Antidote*, in *Tracts and Letters*, 3:176.
90. *Antidote*, in *Tracts and Letters*, 3:176.
91. *Comm.*, on John 1:26.
92. *Institutes*, 4.14.9–10.
93. *Institutes* (1536), 92.
94. *Institutes* (1541), 504.
95. *Institutes*, 4.14.3.

implication of this is that the sacraments attest to already-existing redemption. Calvin uses the same language in 1536 and in 1559 to testify to this fact: "For baptism attests to us that we have been cleansed and washed; the eucharistic Supper, that we have been redeemed. In water, washing is represented; in blood, satisfaction."[96]

The fact that the sacraments attest to an existing redemption helps us understand Calvin's emphatic insistence on the necessity of faith to receive what is promised in the sacraments. In this regard, the sacraments are identical to the word. Both must be received by faith:

> It is therefore certain that the Lord offers us mercy and the pledge of his grace both in his Sacred Word and in his sacraments. But it is understood only by those who take Word and sacraments with sure faith, just as Christ is offered and held forth by the Father to all unto salvation, yet not all acknowledge and receive him. In one place Augustine, meaning to convey this, said that the efficacy of the Word is brought to light in the sacrament, not because it is spoken, but because it is believed.[97]

When the word is preached or the sacraments are given to an unbeliever, it is like speaking to the deaf or giving food to a corpse. When there is faith, however, and the Holy Spirit is working, "God accomplishes within what the minister represents and attests by outward action."[98]

Faith is necessary to receive what is promised in the sacraments just as it is necessary to receive what is promised in the word because the sacraments have the same office as the word, namely, "to offer and set forth Christ to us, and in him the treasures of heavenly grace."[99] It is in this sense that the sacraments are, as Augustine described them, "visible words."[100] The sacrament "represents God's promises as painted in a picture and sets them before our sight, portrayed graphically and in the manner of images."[101] We might say that the sacraments are sign language for the spiritually hearing-impaired.

---

96. *Institutes*, 4.14.22; cf. *Institutes* (1536), 94.
97. *Institutes*, 4.14.7.
98. *Institutes*, 4.14.17.
99. *Institutes* (1536), 91.
100. *Institutes*, 4.14.6.
101. *Institutes*, 4.14.6.

There is not a complete parallel, however, between the word and the sacraments. The word can be proclaimed without the sacrament, but the sacrament cannot even exist without the word. As we have already seen, the sacrament never lacks a preceding promise. As Calvin explains, "The sacrament requires preaching to beget faith."[102] The sacraments require the preceding promise because they are "seals" of those promises. Seals are meaningless if there is nothing to seal. Although the word can be given without the sacraments, this should not be misunderstood to mean that the sacraments are superfluous. Their sealing function is important.[103] In his 1545 catechism, Calvin emphasizes this point, saying that the person who voluntarily abstains from using them because he thinks he has no need of them "condemns Jesus Christ, rejects His grace, and quenches His Holy Spirit."[104]

Baptism

According to Calvin, baptism was given to us by God "first to serve our faith before him; secondly, to serve our confession before men."[105] In connection with the first purpose, there are three things baptism does to serve our faith before God, three promises given in the visible word of baptism. They are remission and purification of our sins, mortification of the flesh, and union with Christ, that we might share in his blessings.[106]

The first thing that baptism signifies, the first thing it promises as a visible word appended to the preached word, is the remission and purification of sins. If this is the first way that baptism "serves our faith," it necessarily presupposes faith. In his 1541 *Institutes*, Calvin explains that baptism "is intended by God to be a sign and mark of our purification, or, to explain it better, He sends baptism to us as a message by which He declares, confirms, and assures us that all our sins *have been* remitted, covered, abolished, and wiped out."[107]

---

102. *Institutes*, 4.14.4.
103. *Institutes*, 4.14.5.
104. "Calvin's Catechism (1545)," in Dennison, *Reformed Confessions*, 1:511.
105. *Institutes* (1536), 94; see also "Calvin's Catechism (1537)," in Dennison, *Reformed Confessions*, 1:386.
106. *Institutes* (1536), 94–98.
107. *Institutes* (1541), 510, italics added; cf. *Institutes*, 4.15.1.

Calvin makes it abundantly clear that the water of baptism has no inherent power to purify, cleanse, or remit sins.[108] Baptism does not effect these things. It is the blood of Christ alone that cleanses and purifies.[109] We receive such benefits by faith alone. The cleansing of our bodies with water is a visible image of the cleansing of our souls by the blood of Christ. Calvin explains, "Baptism does not promise us any other purification than being sprinkled with the blood of Christ, which is shown in an image by the water, because of the likeness between Christ's blood and washing and cleaning with water."[110]

The second and third ways that baptism serves our faith are associated with our mystical and spiritual union with Christ. Baptism serves our faith by showing us "our death (mortification) in Jesus Christ and also our new life in Him."[111] Calvin compares this to an engrafted branch drawing nourishment from the root:

> As a graft draws its substance and nourishment from the root into which it has been inserted, so those who receive baptism with the proper faith will truly feel the efficacy of Jesus Christ's death in the mortification of their flesh, and likewise of His resurrection in their vivification of spirit.[112]

The third way that baptism serves our faith is "its testimony to us that we are not only engrafted into the death and life of Christ, but so united and joined to Christ himself that we become sharers in all his blessings."[113] Baptism certifies that "we are so united to Him that He makes us participants of all His goods."[114] Calvin has a particularly helpful explanation of this point in his commentary on 1 Corinthians 12:13:

> He speaks, however, of the baptism of believers, which is efficacious through the grace of the Spirit, for, in the case of many, baptism is merely in the letter—the symbol without the reality;

---

108. *Institutes*, 4.15.2.
109. *Institutes* (1541), 511.
110. *Institutes* (1541), 511.
111. *Institutes* (1541), 512.
112. *Institutes* (1541); cf. *Institutes*, 4.15.5.
113. *Institutes* (1536), 98.
114. *Institutes* (1541), 512.

but believers, along with the sacrament, receive the reality. Hence, with respect to God, this invariably holds good—that baptism is an engrafting into the body of Christ, for God in that ordinance does not represent anything but what he is prepared to accomplish, provided we are on our part capable of it.[115]

Calvin did not change this doctrine at any point in his career. Even in the 1559 edition of the *Institutes*, he teaches that baptism testifies that "we are not only engrafted into the death and life of Christ, but so united to Christ himself that we become sharers in all his blessings."[116]

We have seen that Calvin describes the sacraments as instruments, but how does he apply this idea to baptism specifically? In his 1536 edition of the *Institutes*, Calvin denies that baptism is an instrument, affirming only that it is a representative sign.[117] In later writings, however, Calvin consistently affirms the instrumental nature of baptism. In his *Acts of the Council of Trent, with the Antidote*, for example, he refers to baptism as "the ordinary instrument of God in washing and renewing us."[118] Since baptism is the instrument of God, Calvin argues that we must receive baptism "as from the hand of God."[119]

Calvin explains all this in some detail in his commentary on Acts 22:16. There he affirms that God alone cleanses us from sin and that there is no material cause other than the blood of Christ. The formal cause is the Holy Spirit, but "there is an inferior instrument, and that is the preaching of the word and baptism itself."[120] The sign of baptism is conjoined with the reality (the promise) where there is faith, and in such cases, "we are said to receive and obtain what we believe we are given by God, whether we begin then first to recognize it or whether, having known it before, we come to have a more certain possession of it."[121]

In other words, in some cases a person may place saving faith in God's word days, months, or years before he or she receives the seal of that promise in baptism. It is also possible that a person may place

115. *Comm.*, on 1 Cor. 12:13 (20:406).
116. *Institutes*, 4.15.6.
117. *Institutes* (1536), 98–99.
118. *Antidote*, in *Tracts and Letters*, 3:180.
119. *Institutes* (1541), 516.
120. *Comm.*, on Acts 22:16 (19:303).
121. *Institutes* (1541), 517.

saving faith in the promise of God's word as that promise is being sealed by the visible word in baptism. Calvin thus speaks of baptism as the seal of a promise that either has already been believed or is being believed. In his defense of infant baptism, he speaks, as discussed further below, of the sacrament as sealing a promise that may be believed long after the sign is given to the child. In every case, the signified reality is only received when there is faith.

Since such language in Calvin's work is sometimes taken out of context, it must be remembered that Calvin emphatically asserts that grace is neither tied to nor enclosed within the sacrament of baptism.[122] Nor does the human administrator of baptism accomplish the spiritual effects. When it is said of baptism, Calvin explains,

> that it is the laver of regeneration, (Titus iii. 5) a washing away of sins, the fellowship of death, and burying with Christ, (Rom. vi. 4) and a grafting into the body of Christ, it is not declared what man, being the minister of the outward sign, doth; but rather what Christ doth, who only giveth force and efficacy unto the signs.[123]

Or to put it more succinctly, "Man is merely the hand; it is Christ alone who truly and properly baptizes."[124]

According to Calvin's basic definition, baptism not only serves our faith before God in the three ways we have described, but it also serves our confession before men. This aspect of Calvin's doctrine also remains constant over the course of his career. What he teaches in 1536 is essentially the same as what he teaches in 1559: "Baptism serves our confession before men. Indeed, it is the mark by which we publicly profess that we wish to be reckoned God's people; by which we testify that we agree in worshiping the same God, in one religion with all Christians; by which finally we openly affirm our faith."[125]

Given what we have said about Calvin's doctrine of baptism, this question remains: How did he defend the practice of baptizing the infant children of believers? Calvin based his argument on a particular

---

122. *Institutes* (1541), 516.
123. *Comm.*, on Acts 1:5 (18:41).
124. *Antidote*, in *Tracts and Letters*, 3:180.
125. *Institutes*, 4.15.13.

understanding of the relationship between the old and new covenants. As Hughes Oliphant Old explains, "It is the argument from covenant theology which forms the basis of Calvin's position."[126] The covenant, Calvin argues, "applies no less today to the children of Christians than under the Old Testament it pertained to the infants of the Jews."[127] The covenant promise is made to believers *and their seed.* Thus, the baptism of the children of Christians "ratifies the covenant made with them by the Lord."[128]

Because the children of Christians belong to the covenant community, they are to receive the covenant sign of baptism, just as male children in the old covenant community received the sign of circumcision. The analogic relationship between circumcision and baptism, therefore, becomes central to Calvin's argument for the practice.[129] Both circumcision and baptism, according to Calvin, signify the same reality: the promise of forgiveness of sins and mortification of the flesh. They differ in externals only.[130]

What then of the necessity of faith? Calvin's view on this question shows signs of development. In 1536, Calvin proposed that infants possess faith in common with adults.[131] Later, Calvin would reject the idea of infant faith and emphasize that the promise made in baptism remains firm from the time it is made onward.[132] This means that the promise may be received by faith long after the administration of baptism. Calvin writes, "Infants are baptized into future repentance and faith, and even though these have not yet been formed in them, the seed of both lies hidden within them by the secret working of the Spirit."[133] Calvin does not fully answer all the questions his doctrine of infant baptism raises.[134] But the basic idea is clear enough: Infants are baptized to seal the covenant promise made to them. At whatever

---

126. Hughes Oliphant Old, *The Shaping of the Reformed Baptismal Rite in the Sixteenth Century* (Grand Rapids, MI: Eerdmans, 1992), 141.

127. *Institutes*, 4.16.5.

128. *Institutes*, 4.16.21.

129. *Institutes*, 4.16.3; see Egil Grislis, "Calvin's Doctrine of Baptism," *CH* 31, no. 1 (1962): 51.

130. *Institutes*, 4.16.3–4.

131. *Institutes* (1536), 101–2.

132. *Institutes* (1541), 518; *Institutes*, 4.15.17.

133. *Institutes*, 4.16.20.

134. See Grislis, "Calvin's Doctrine of Baptism"; Gerrish, *Grace and Gratitude*, 117–19; John W. Riggs, *Baptism in the Reformed Tradition: A Historical and Practical Theology*, CSRT (Louisville: Westminster John Knox, 2002), 69.

point in time they exercise saving faith, they receive what was promised in baptism and are engrafted into Christ.

The Lord's Supper

Calvin rejected the distinctives of the Roman Catholic doctrine of the Lord's Supper: transubstantiation, the sacrifice of the Mass, the withdrawal of the cup, and the adoration of the host. He also took issue with certain aspects of the doctrine found in the formulations of earlier Reformers such as Luther and Zwingli. His own attempt to express the biblical doctrine of the Supper, however, did not win universal consent either. His doctrine can be difficult to understand at times not only because he wrote so much about it in so many different contexts but also because of the number of careful distinctions that he always assumes but does not always make explicit every time he writes on the subject.

Most interpreters of Calvin recognize that union with Christ is central to his doctrine of the Supper.[135] Many, however, do not clearly distinguish between mystical union and spiritual union. We recall that Calvin associates the Supper specifically with spiritual union, a progressive strengthening or nourishing of the life of Christ in believers that is theirs as a fruit and effect of the mystical union. The mystical union with Christ, however, is necessary because only those who have "partaken of his flesh and blood may at the same time enjoy participation in life."[136]

This idea of strengthening or nourishment ties directly into one of the stated uses of the Lord's Supper. According to Calvin, the purpose of the Lord's Supper is found in the words "given for you" and "shed for you." He explains,

> The present distribution of the body and blood of the Lord would not greatly benefit us unless they had once for all been given for our redemption and salvation. They are therefore represented

---

135. See, for example, Gerrish, *Grace and Gratitude*, 133; John D. Nicholls, "Union with Christ: John Calvin on the Lord's Supper," in *Union and Communion, 1529–1979* (London: Westminster Conference, 1979), 36; Davis, *Clearest Promises*, 56–57; Janse, "Calvin's Eucharistic Theology," 43; Spear, "Nature of the Lord's Supper," 361.

136. *Institutes*, 4.17.9.

under bread and wine so that we may learn not only that they are ours, but that they are as life and food for us.[137]

This is the first use of the Supper.[138]

This idea of spiritual nourishment recurs frequently in Calvin's writings on the Supper. Just as bread and wine nourish our bodies, the flesh and blood of Christ nourish our souls.[139] Grasping this aspect of Calvin's doctrine helps us understand what he says about the "bread of life" discourse in John 6 and its relation to the Lord's Supper. According to Calvin, John 6 is not "about" the Lord's Supper, but John 6 and the Supper are both about the same thing. In fact, what is taught in John 6 is the promise that is sealed in the Lord's Supper.[140] The Supper seals the promise that Christ is the bread of life.[141]

What is the relationship, then, between the signs of bread and wine and the body and blood of Christ? According to Calvin, when Christ said, "This is my body," he was speaking figuratively.[142] The expression is an example of metonymy, in which the name of the reality is given to the sign.[143] Thus, the sign is distinguished from the reality it signifies. But it is also a sign that "exhibits" the reality, a sign "by which the reality is presented to us."[144] This is possible because the reality, although distinct from the sign, is connected with the sign. Calvin writes, "It is regarded by me as beyond all controversy, that the reality is here conjoined with the sign."[145] Calvin's use of the Chalcedonian "distinction without separation" concept allows him to steer a careful course between the pure symbolism of Zwingli and the sacramental realism of Luther.[146]

Calvin's view of the relation between the sign and the thing signified is reflected in his view of the parallelism between the earthly sacramental action and the corresponding heavenly action. As Calvin

---

137. *Institutes* (1536), 103.

138. *Institutes* (1541), 548.

139. *Institutes*, 4.17.3.

140. *Comm.*, on John 6:54; *Institutes*, 4.17.1; 4.17.4; 4.17.14.

141. *Institutes*, 4.17.1; 4.17.4; 4.17.14.

142. See *Institutes*, 4.17.20–25.

143. John Calvin, "Second Defence of the Sacraments in Answer to Westphal," in *Tracts and Letters*, 2:301.

144. *Comm.*, on 1 Cor. 11:24 (20:377); cf. *Institutes* (1541), 552.

145. *Comm.*, on 1 Cor. 11:24 (20:378).

146. Janse, "Calvin's Eucharistic Theology," 38.

explains, "Now if it is true that the visible sign is offered to us to seal the gift of the invisible thing, we must have this indubitable confidence that, in taking the sign of the body, we likewise receive the body."[147] In fact, "whatever the minister pronounces with his lips according to the word of God and figures by a sign, Christ inwardly performs."[148] The Lord's Supper, then, is "to the true worshipper of God a heavenly action, or a kind of vehicle which carries them above the world."[149]

Given Calvin's assertion that believers receive the body of Christ in the Supper and that we are nourished by partaking of it, three additional questions must be answered for us to grasp his doctrine: (1) Do we actually partake of Christ's *body*? (2) What does it mean to *partake*? (3) *How* do we partake? It is particularly important to distinguish the first two questions. A failure to observe the difference between *what* we "eat" and the *act* of "eating" has led to no little confusion in attempts to explain Calvin's doctrine of the Supper.

Regarding the first question, Calvin teaches that believers do partake of Christ's body. This is found repeatedly in all Calvin's writings on the subject. He says, for example, "To have our life in Christ our souls should be fed on his body and his blood, as their proper food."[150] Again, our "souls feed on *his flesh and blood*."[151] Those who receive the promise by faith "are actually made partakers of his flesh and blood."[152] We partake not only of his divine nature but also of his body.[153] We partake of the actual body of Christ because it is the actual body of Christ with which we are united by faith. As Calvin explains, "Those who are united by faith, so as to be his members, eat his body truly or in reality."[154] Christ, then, is the object of our union and thus the object of our partaking.

We also participate in Christ's benefits by virtue of our participation with him. We cannot have his benefits unless we have him. As Calvin ex-

---

147. *Institutes* (1541), 557.

148. "Second Defence," in *Tracts and Letters*, 2:310; cf. "Mutual Consent," in *Tracts and Letters*, 2:237–38.

149. John Calvin, "True Partaking of the Flesh and Blood of Christ," in *Tracts and Letters*, 2:519.

150. John Calvin, *Short Treatise on the Supper of Our Lord*, in *Theological Treatises*, 147.

151. *Comm.*, on John 6:54 (17:265).

152. *Comm.*, on Matt. 26:26 (17:209).

153. *Institutes* (1541), 554; *Institutes*, 4.17.7.

154. "True Partaking," in *Tracts and Letters*, 2:522.

plains in his 1540 *Short Treatise on the Supper of Our Lord* (published in 1541), "We must conclude that two things are presented to us in the Supper: Jesus Christ as source and substance of all good; and second, the fruit and efficacy of his death and passion."[155] Fifteen years later, defending his views against the Lutheran Westphal, his views remained the same: "Christ is truly offered to us by the sacraments, in order that being made partakers of him, we may obtain possession of all his blessings; in short, in order that he may live in us and we in him."[156]

Although there is a real communion with the body of Christ, there is no local (or "real") presence of the body in the Supper. Calvin distinguishes the two, saying, "Though I have classed among opinions to be rejected the idea that the body of Christ is really and substantially present in the Supper, this is not at all repugnant to a true and real communion."[157] Calvin denies the local presence of Christ in the elements because he believes such a presence is impossible for a true human body such as belongs to Christ.[158] Such a local presence is unnecessary in any case because the Holy Spirit is able to unite things separated by space.[159]

The second question we must answer regards the meaning of the act of partaking. What does it mean "to partake" or "to eat"? Calvin says that "we eat [Christ's] flesh, when, by means of it, we receive life."[160] At this point it is important to note the distinction Calvin draws between union with Christ and transfusion of his life. The transfusion of life depends on union with Christ and cannot be separated from it, but the two ideas are distinct. Calvin explains:

> If Christ is our head, and dwells in us, he communicates to us his life; and we have nothing to hope from until we are united to his body. The whole reality of the sacred Supper consists in this— Christ, by ingrafting us into his body, not only makes us partakers of his body and blood, but infuses into us the life whose fullness resides in himself: for his flesh is not eaten for any other end than to give us life.[161]

---

155. *Short Treatise*, 146.
156. "Second Defence," in *Tracts and Letters*, 2:274.
157. "Second Defence," in *Tracts and Letters*, 281.
158. *Institutes*, 4.17.29.
159. *Institutes*, 4.17.10.
160. *Comm.*, on Matt. 26:26 (17:210).
161. John Calvin, "Last Admonition to Joachim Westphal," in *Tracts and Letters*, 2:377.

The Supper, then, is associated with the spiritual union because by means of it, believers who are already engrafted into Christ "may grow more and more together with him, until he perfectly joins us with him in the heavenly life."[162]

As Calvin explains, life is "infused into us *from* the substance of Christ's flesh," to which we are united.[163] Calvin is clear that what is infused is Christ's life, not the substance of his body itself. There is no transfusion or mingling of any material substance.[164] When we understand this distinction that Calvin draws between union with Christ and transfusion of his life, we understand how he can deny the charge of virtualism.

Both Tilemann Heshusius and Frederick Staphylus charged Calvin with teaching that believers partake only of Christ's life, or virtue. Calvin denied the charge.[165] According to Calvin, we actually partake of the body of Christ. We are in union with him, not merely with his life. However, to partake of his body (i.e., to "eat" it) is to receive life from it. We partake of (i.e., receive life from) the actual body of Christ by virtue of our union with him.[166]

Our third question involves the mode of eating. *How* do we receive life from the actual body of Christ? Calvin teaches that we partake of Christ's body only by faith.[167] He rejects the Zwinglian idea that eating is equivalent to faith. Eating is not identical to faith; it is the effect of faith.[168] Calvin also calls the mode of eating "spiritual," not because believers partake only of Christ's divine nature but because the Holy Spirit transfuses life into us from Christ's flesh.[169] Calvin also rejects the Lutheran doctrine of oral partaking in which the true body is received with the mouth by both believers and unbelievers.[170] Because partaking is by faith, only believers partake of the body of Christ. The body and blood are offered to all but received only by believers.[171]

---

162. *Institutes*, 4.17.33.
163. "Second Defence," in *Tracts and Letters*, 2:277, italics added; cf. "Last Admonition," in *Tracts and Letters*, 2:416; "True Partaking," in *Tracts and Letters*, 2:502.
164. *Institutes*, 4.17.32.
165. "True Partaking," in *Tracts and Letters*, 2:501–2, 518.
166. To see what Calvin is *not* teaching here, see his refutation of Osiander in *Institutes*, 3.11.5–12.
167. *Institutes* (1541), 553.
168. *Comm.*, on John 6:35.
169. "Second Defence," in *Tracts and Letters*, 2:282–83.
170. "Last Admonition," in *Tracts and Letters*, 2:402.
171. *Comm.*, on 1 Cor. 11:27.

The second use of the Lord's Supper is "to exercise us in the re-membrance of Christ's death."[172] This is done in order that we might confess before men "that the death of Christ is our life."[173] The third use of the Supper is to "quicken and inspire us both to purity and holiness of life, and to love, peace, and concord."[174] In this sense, the Lord's Supper is rightly called the "bond of love."[175]

In terms of the church's practice, the first point that must be made is that the sacrament cannot stand apart from the word. The prom-ise must be declared in order to be sealed.[176] Second, because it is a means by which Christ nourishes us spiritually, the Supper is to be observed frequently. From 1536 on, Calvin never stopped arguing that the Supper should be observed *at least* once a week.[177] Third, Paul's admonition in 1 Corinthians 11:28 means that among partici-pants, self-examination is required before partaking of the Supper.[178] This does not mean that perfection is required, because the Supper is intended to be medicine for the sick.[179] The need for self-examination *does* mean that children are not to be admitted to the Supper until they have received by faith the promise given in their baptism.[180] The need for self-examination does not absolve ministers of their duty to guard the Table and excommunicate unrepentant sinners.[181]

In opposition to Roman Catholic worship practices, Calvin advo-cated a simple liturgy. In his 1542 "Form of Administering the Sacra-ments," Calvin recommends that following the sermon, the eucharistic liturgy should proceed as follows:

- the words of institution
- the excommunication of all notorious sinners
- a call to self-examination
- an invitation to the Table

---

172. *Institutes* (1536), 109.
173. *Institutes* (1536), 109.
174. *Institutes*, 4.17.38.
175. *Institutes*, 4.17.38.
176. *Institutes*, 4.17.39.
177. *Institutes* (1536), 113, italics added; cf. *Institutes*, 4.17.43.
178. *Short Treatise*, 152.
179. *Institutes*, 4.17.42.
180. *Institutes*, 4.16.30.
181. John Calvin, "Articles concerning the Organization of the Church and of Worship at Geneva," in *Theological Treatises*, 50.

- assurance for the spiritually weak
- the promise of true partaking of Christ's body and blood
- a call to gratitude for the goodness of our Savior
- a call to raise our hearts and minds on high in worship of our sovereign God[182]

Conclusion

If John Calvin was convinced of anything, it was that his doctrine of the sacraments was perfectly clear. If students of Calvin are convinced of anything, it is that his self-assessment was a little off the mark. Certain aspects of his doctrine can be difficult to comprehend. Many of the main points, however, can be discerned. Consensus regarding his meaning on every detail may not be reached anytime soon, but continued reflection is worthwhile. As Calvin might say, we study this subject in such depth not because the sacraments are an end unto themselves but because they direct our eyes to the promises of our Savior and Lord Jesus Christ, whose body and blood were given for us for the forgiveness of our sins.

---

182. John Calvin, "Form of Administering the Sacraments," in *Tracts and Letters*, 2:119–22.

19

God's Preservation of His Saints

Robert A. Peterson

And they shall never perish. It is the incomparable fruit of faith that Christ bids us be sure and untroubled when we are brought by faith into His fold. But we must also see what basis this assurance rests on. It is that He will be the faithful guardian of our salvation, for He says that it is in His hand. And as if this were not enough, He says that they will be safely protected by His Father's power. This is a remarkable passage, teaching us that the salvation of all the elect is as certain as God's power is invincible. And Christ was not just tossing this Word thoughtlessly into the air, but giving a promise which should remain deeply fixed in their minds. Therefore, we infer that Christ's saying indicates that the elect are firmly certain of their salvation.

—John Calvin, *Commentary on the Gospel according to St. John*

Assurance and Preservation

I have taught a course on the life and thought of John Calvin more than half a dozen times over the years. Each time students unfamiliar with his famous theology book, *Institutes of the Christian Religion,* respond in the same way—with amazement. They are amazed at how pastoral and edifying Calvin's theology is. But not all agree with this assessment of Calvin's teaching. Referring to Calvin and his theological heirs, philosopher of religion Jerry Walls writes, "Calvinist believers who struggle with their assurance can never know with certainty that they are one of the elect."[1] Contrary to this contention, Calvin had a robust doctrine of assurance and expected those to whom he ministered to know that they were both elect and saved.

The assurance of salvation is built on the fact that God not only saves his people but also keeps them saved to the end. This work of divine keeping is sometimes called *the perseverance of the saints*. But that term is also used to refer to their continuing to believe the gospel. Thus both God's keeping of us and our keeping on are referred to by the term *the perseverance of the saints*. To avoid confusion and in the interest of clarity, I refer to God's keeping the saints saved as his *preservation* of them. With its outline drawn from the *Institutes*, this chapter

- shows that Calvin teaches preservation;
- distinguishes his view from that of Roman Catholicism;
- considers his terms for preservation;
- shows the broad biblical basis for his belief;
- summarizes his theology of preservation; and
- recaps his pastoral applications of the doctrine.

Calvin Teaches That God Preserves His Saints

Although Calvin teaches preservation in many places in the *Institutes*, it is surprising to find that the main concentration of this teaching—in 3.24.6—is relatively brief, consisting of only five pages. Nevertheless, there Calvin clearly affirms his belief in preservation:

The fact that, as we said, the firmness of our election is joined to our calling is another means of establishing our assurance. For those whom Christ has illumined with the knowledge of his name and has introduced into the bosom of his church, he is said to receive into his care and keeping. All whom he received, the Fa-

---

1. Jerry L. Walls and Joseph R. Dongell, *Why I Am Not a Calvinist* (Downers Grove, IL: InterVarsity Press, 2004), 192.

ther is said to have entrusted and committed to him to keep unto eternal life.[2]

God assures us, Calvin explains, by linking his choice of us ("our election") with his bringing us to himself ("our calling"). Those whom God chooses, he effectively summons to himself in the gospel. The ones whom Christ illumines spiritually and receives into his church, he loves and keeps saved. All this is the Father's will. After mentioning that believers sometimes suffer from the spiritual disease of anxiety about their future destination, Calvin, as physician of the soul, offers the cure—heavy doses of Holy Scripture:

> But Christ has freed us from this anxiety, for these promises surely apply to the future: "All that the Father gives me will come to me; and him who will come to me I will not cast out" [John 6:37]. Likewise, "This is the will of him who sent me, the Father, that I should lose nothing of all that he has given me but should raise it up again at the last day." [John 6:39; cf. Vg.] Again: "My sheep hear my voice . . . and they follow me. I know them, and I give them eternal life, and they shall never perish, and no one shall snatch them out of my hand. My Father, who has given them to me, is greater than all, and no one can snatch them out of my Father's hand." [John 10:27–29 p.] . . . And here is why Paul magnificently lords it over life and death, things present and to come [Rom. 8:38]. . . . Elsewhere, Paul says the same thing: "He who has begun a good work in you will bring it to completion at the day of Jesus Christ" [Phil. 1:6].[3]

Notice Calvin's heavy reliance on the word of God to prove that God preserves his saints. This is characteristic of Calvin's teaching. Accordingly, after beginning with his *Institutes*, I use Calvin's commentaries on various books of Scripture to survey the contours of his teaching on preservation.

Calvin Opposes Rome's View of Preservation and Assurance

Calvin's affirmation of preservation comes into clearer focus when contrasted with the medieval Roman Catholic view. This view taught

2. *Institutes*, 3.24.6.
3. *Institutes*, 3.24.6.

that regular believers were not expected to enjoy assurance of salvation but that assurance was available only to saints by a special revelation from God. Calvin takes strong exception to this view, which
he labels "the scholastic dogma of the uncertainty of salvation,"[4] because, in his eyes, it is destructive of saving faith:

> This passage [Rom. 8:38–39] clearly contradicts the schoolmen
> [i.e., medieval Catholic theologians], who foolishly maintain that
> no one is certain of final perseverance, except by the favour of a
> special revelation, and this, they hold, is very rare. Such a dogma
> wholly destroys faith, and faith is certainly nothing if it does not
> extend to death and beyond. On the contrary, however, we are to
> have confidence that He who has begun a good work in us, will
> accomplish it until the day of the Lord Jesus.[5]

In Calvin's estimation, Rome's view breeds doubt and uncertainty.
Peter, to the contrary, grants believers assurance of salvation and rests
that assurance on a faith supported by the power of God:

> Blessed be the God and Father of our Lord Jesus Christ! According
> to his great mercy, he has caused us to be born again to a living
> hope through the resurrection of Jesus Christ from the dead, to an
> inheritance that is imperishable, undefiled, and unfading, kept in
> heaven for you, who by God's power are being guarded through
> faith for a salvation ready to be revealed in the last time. (1 Pet.
> 1:3–5)

Calvin sets Peter's words in opposition to Rome's:

> We see indeed that under the Papacy a diabolical opinion prevails
> that our final perseverance is doubtful because we are uncertain
> whether tomorrow we shall be in the same state of grace. But Peter
> does not leave us in suspense like this. He maintains that we stand
> by the power of God, in case any doubt arising from a conscious-
> ness of our own infirmity should disquiet us. However weak we
> may be, our salvation is not uncertain, because it is sustained by
> God's power. As, then, we are sustained by faith, so faith itself

---

4. Calvin, comm. on Rom. 8:34, in *CNTC*, 8:186.
5. Calvin, comm. on Rom. 8:38, in *CNTC*, 8:189.

receives its stability from God's power. Hence its security is not only for the present, but also for the future.[6]

Calvin Uses Various Terms for Preservation

Calvin employs various expressions to describe God's keeping of his people for final salvation. Although he does not seem to have used the term common today—*eternal security*—Calvin comes close when he speaks of "this great security which dares to triumph over the devil, death, sin and the gates of hell."[7] He speaks of Christ's keeping his sheep safe as his "preserving their salvation."[8] His most common term for preservation is the historical designation *perseverance*, used by Augustine before him, for example. Calvin speaks of "the certain hope of final perseverance,"[9] "the gift of perseverance,"[10] or simply "perseverance."[11] He uses other terms as well, writing of "the certainty of their salvation"[12] and "security . . . for the future."[13]

The variety and frequency of Calvin's usage of preservation terminology highlights the importance that he attaches to this doctrine for the Christian life. Listen as he extols its practical benefit:

> In short, when the Christian looks at himself, he can only have grounds for anxiety, indeed despair, but because he is called into fellowship with Christ, he can think of himself, in so far as assurance of salvation is concerned, in no other way than as a member of Christ, thus making all the blessings of Christ his own. In this way, he will lay hold of the certain hope of final perseverance (as it is called), if he looks upon himself as a member of Christ, who cannot possibly fail.[14]

Calvin Bases His Belief in Preservation on Many Passages

In *Institutes* 3.24.6, Calvin cites several biblical passages that in his estimation teach preservation, including Psalm 138:8; John 6:37, 39; 10:27–29;

---

6. Calvin, comm. on 1 Pet. 1:5, in *CNTC*, 12:233.
7. Calvin, comm. on Rom. 8:34, in *CNTC*, 8:185–86.
8. *Institutes*, 3.22.7.
9. Calvin, comm. on 1 Cor. 1:9, in *CNTC*, 9:24; cf. comm. on Rom. 8:38, in *CNTC*, 8:189.
10. *Institutes*, 3.24.6.
11. Calvin, comm. on 1 John 2:19, in *CNTC*, 5:258; *Institutes*, 3.24.6.
12. Calvin, comm. on Rom. 8:33, in *CNTC*, 8:184.
13. Calvin, comm. on 1 Pet. 1:5, in *CNTC*, 12:233.
14. Calvin, comm. on 1 Cor. 1:9, in *CNTC*, 9:24.

17:6, 12; Romans 8:30, 38–39; Ephesians 1:13–14; Philippians 1:6; and 1 John 2:19. Here we consider most of these passages and others that expand on his succinct discussion of preservation in the *Institutes*.

Psalm 73:24

> You guide me with your counsel,
> and afterward you will receive me to glory.

This verse contains one of the clearest promises of eternal life to be found in the entire Old Testament. Calvin sees it as assuring believers of future eternal glory with God because of his relentless grace:

> As the verbs are put in the future tense, the natural meaning, in my opinion, is, that the Psalmist assured himself that the Lord, since by his leading he had now brought him back into the right way, would continue henceforth to guide him, until at length he received him into His glorious presence in heaven. We know that it is David's usual way, when he gives thanks to God, to look forward with confidence to the future. Accordingly, after having acknowledged his own infirmities, he celebrated the grace of God, the aid and comfort of which he had experienced. . . . David then assures himself of eternal glory, through the free and unmerited favour of God.[15]

Psalm 138:7–8

> Though I walk in the midst of trouble,
> you preserve my life;
> you stretch out your hand against the wrath of my enemies,
> and your right hand delivers me.
> The Lord will fulfill his purpose for me;
> your steadfast love, O Lord, endures forever.
> Do not forsake the work of your hands.

Calvin understands David's words of comfort to saints in trouble as bearing witness to God's preserving his people for final salvation. Calvin sees great pastoral benefit in the psalmist's testimony to God's constancy and dependability:

---

15. *Comm.*, on Ps. 73:24.

David concludes with the best reason, from the eternity of the Divine goodness, that the salvation granted him would be of no limited and merely evanescent character. This he confirms still farther by what he adds, that it is impossible God should leave his work, as men may do, in an imperfect or unfinished state through lassitude or disgust. . . . What is the cause of that anxiety and fear which are felt by the godly, but the consciousness of their own weakness and entire dependence upon God? At the same time they rely with full certainty upon the grace of God. . . . The use to be made of the doctrine is, to remember, when we fall or are disposed to waver in our minds, that since God has wrought the beginning of our salvation in us, he will carry it forward to its termination.[16]

John 6:37–39

All that the Father gives me will come to me, and whoever comes to me I will never cast out. For I have come down from heaven, not to do my own will but the will of him who sent me. And this is the will of him who sent me, that I should lose nothing of all that he has given me, but raise it up on the last day.

Based on this passage, Calvin teaches that Christians are safe because of the work of the Trinity on their behalf. The Father and the Spirit cooperate for our salvation: "Again, we deduce that God works in His elect by such an efficacy of the Spirit that none of them falls away [6:37]."[17] The Son faithfully executes the Father's orders, including keeping believers: "But the Son's only purpose is to fulfil His Father's commands. Consequently, He will never turn away those sent by His Father [6:38]."[18]

In addition, Calvin grounds our preservation in God's sovereign purpose: "Christ declares that He has been manifested to the world to confirm what the Father has decreed on our salvation by actually effecting it. . . . He now declares that the Father's purpose is that believers may find salvation secured in Christ [6:38–39]."[19]

With memorable words, Calvin also bases our safety in Christ on his immutable promise:

---

16. *Comm.*, on Ps. 138:8.
17. Calvin, comm. on John 6:37, in *CNTC*, 4:160–61.
18. Calvin, comm. on John 6:38, in *CNTC*, 4:161.
19. Calvin, comm. on John 6:38–39, in *CNTC*, 4:161.

I should lose nothing. That is, "I should not let it be taken from me, or perish." By this He means that He is not the guardian of our salvation for a day or two, but that He will care for it to the end, and bring us, so to say, from the starting point to the finishing post. This is why he mentions the final resurrection. . . . Let it, therefore, be fixed firmly in our minds that Christ has stretched out His hand to us and will not desert us in mid-course, but we may rely on His leading and boldly dare to raise our eyes to the last day.[20]

John 10:28–29

I give them eternal life, and they will never perish, and no one will snatch them out of my hand. My Father, who has given them to me, is greater than all, and no one is able to snatch them out of the Father's hand.

Commenting on this text, Calvin assures believers of ultimate redemption based on Christ's faithfulness: "It is the incomparable fruit of faith that Christ bids us be sure and untroubled when we are brought by faith into His fold. But we must also see what basis this assurance rests on. It is that He will be the faithful guardian of our salvation, for He says that it is *in His hand.*"[21]

Another basis of assurance that Calvin finds in John 10 is Jesus's gracious promise. He writes, "And Christ was not just tossing this Word thoughtlessly into the air, but giving a promise which should remain deeply fixed in their minds. Therefore . . . Christ's saying indicates that the elect are firmly certain of their salvation."[22]

But neither Christ's faithfulness nor his promise is the basis of preservation that Calvin most accentuates in this passage. Rather, repeatedly, he underscores God the Father's almighty power:

We are surrounded by powerful enemies, and so great is our weakness that we are not far from death every moment. But He who keeps what we have committed unto Him is *greater* and more

---

20. Calvin, comm. on John 6:39, in *CNTC*, 4:161. Italics within quotations are original.
21. Calvin, comm. on John 10:28, in *CNTC*, 4:273.
22. Calvin, comm. on John 10:28, in *CNTC*, 4:273.

powerful *than all*; and so we have nothing to be afraid of, as if our life were in danger.

In short, our salvation is certain because it is in the hand of God. Our faith is weak, and we are given to wavering; but God has taken us in His hand and is powerful enough to scatter with a breath all the efforts of our enemies.

And no one is able to snatch them out of the Father's hand. . . . For from the invincible power of God, Christ deduces that the salvation of the godly is not exposed to their enemies' desires, because God, who has taken them under the protection of His hand, would first have to be overcome.[23]

John 17:12–13, 15, 17

While I was with them, I kept them in your name, which you have given me. I have guarded them, and not one of them has been lost except the son of destruction, that the Scripture might be fulfilled. But now I am coming to you, and these things I speak in the world, that they may have my joy fulfilled in themselves. . . . I do not ask that you take them out of the world, but that you keep them from the evil one. . . . Sanctify them in the truth; your word is truth.

Calvin sees numerous proofs of God's preservation of his people in Jesus's famous prayer. First, he mentions the Father's power: "Christ says that He kept them in the Father's name. . . . He means, therefore, that it would be inconsistent if they should now perish; as if by His departure God's power were extinguished or dead."[24]

Second, Calvin points to Christ's keeping believers safe. While he was with the disciples, he kept them in his role as mediator on earth. Since his ascension, however, "He tells the disciples to raise their minds direct to heaven as soon as they begin to be deprived of the outward help. From this we conclude that Christ keeps believers today no less than before, but in a different way, because divine majesty is displayed openly in Him."[25]

---

23. Calvin, comm. on John 10:28–29, in *CNTC*, 4:273.
24. Calvin, comm. on John 17:12, in *CNTC*, 5:142.
25. Calvin, comm. on John 17:12, in *CNTC*, 5:142–43.

Third, according to Calvin, our preservation in John 17 is due to the Father's grace:

> He teaches what the safety of the godly consists in. It is not that they are free from all vexations and cultivate ease and pleasure, but that in the midst of danger they remain safe by God's help. . . . In short, He does not promise His disciples the grace of the Father to relieve them of all anxiety and toil, but to furnish them with unconquerable strength against their adversaries. . . . For He wishes them to fight, but does not allow them to be mortally wounded. . . .
>
> God renews us by His Spirit, and confirms in us the grace of renewal and continues it to the end.[26]

Romans 5:6, 8–10

> For while we were still weak, at the right time Christ died for the ungodly. . . . But God shows his love for us in that while we were still sinners, Christ died for us. Since, therefore, we have now been justified by his blood, much more shall we be saved by him from the wrath of God. For if while we were enemies we were reconciled to God by the death of his Son, much more, now that we are reconciled, shall we be saved by his life.

Sensitive as he is to literary devices, Calvin correctly sees that Paul employs the Jewish argument "from the greater to the lesser" to make a strong case for preservation. Paul argues this way twice, once in terms of justification and once in terms of reconciliation. The former argument goes like this: if when we were condemned sinners Christ died to justify us, now that we have been justified he surely will save us from the coming wrath. The latter argument runs as follows: if when we were alienated from God we were reconciled to him by Christ's death, now that we have been reconciled he surely will keep us saved until the end by Christ's resurrection.

Calvin combines Paul's two arguments:

> The present argument proceeds from the greater to the less. . . .
> "If Christ," he says, "had mercy on the ungodly, if He reconciled

---

26. Calvin, comm. on John 17:15, 17, in *CNTC*, 5:144–45.

His enemies to the Father, and accomplished this by virtue of His death, He will now much more easily save them when they are justified, and keep in His grace those whom He has restored to grace, especially since the efficacy of His life is now added to His death."[27]

Because Christ purchased salvation for us, a salvation that not only saves us but keeps us saved, he has showered us with his grace that ever increases and banishes fear from our hearts, as Calvin eloquently declares:

> It would not have been enough for Christ to have once procured salvation for us, were He not to maintain it safe and secure to the end. This is what the apostle now asserts, declaring that we have no need to fear that Christ will terminate the bestowal of His grace upon us before we have come to our appointed end. Such is our condition since He has reconciled us to the Father, that He purposes to extend His grace to us more effectively, and to increase it day by day.[28]

The sum of the matter, then, for Calvin the theologian and pastor, is that believers in Christ have abundant cause for assurance of salvation. He states, "We have, therefore, ample proof to strengthen our minds with confidence in our salvation."[29]

Romans 8:30–39

> And those whom he predestined he also called, and those whom he called he also justified, and those whom he justified he also glorified.
>
> What then shall we say to these things? If God is for us, who can be against us? He who did not spare his own Son but gave him up for us all, how will he not also with him graciously give us all things? Who shall bring any charge against God's elect? It is God who justifies. Who is to condemn? Christ Jesus is the one who died—more than that, who was raised—who is at the right hand of

---

27. Calvin, comm. on Rom. 5:6, in *CNTC*, 8:108.
28. Calvin, comm. on Rom. 5:8–9, in *CNTC*, 8:109–10.
29. Calvin, comm. on Rom. 5:10, in *CNTC*, 8:110.

God, who indeed is interceding for us. Who shall separate us from the love of Christ? Shall tribulation, or distress, or persecution, or famine, or nakedness, or danger, or sword? As it is written,

"For your sake we are being killed all the day long;
we are regarded as sheep to be slaughtered."

No, in all these things we are more than conquerors through him who loved us. For I am sure that neither death nor life, nor angels nor rulers, nor things present nor things to come, nor powers, nor height nor depth, nor anything else in all creation, will be able to separate us from the love of God in Christ Jesus our Lord.

This is the single most powerful preservation passage in all Scripture, because it is an extended passage and its main theme is preservation. Paul marshals argument after argument to prove that God's people are safe in his sovereignty, fatherly favor, justice, and love.[30] In Romans 8:29–30, Paul teaches that by God's sovereign power, believers have been foreknown, predestined, called, justified, and glorified. Of course, our glorification is still future, but it is so certain that Paul expresses it in the past tense. Calvin comments, "Although glorification has as yet been exhibited only in our Head, yet because we now perceive in Him the inheritance of eternal life, His glory brings to us such assurance of our own glory, that our hope may justly be compared to a present possession."[31]

Commenting on Paul's words "What then shall we say?" (8:31), Calvin focuses on "the fatherly favour of God," which is one of his ways of signifying God's grace:

He teaches us by these words that the invincible courage which overcomes all temptations resides in the fatherly favour of God. . . . Paul bids the saints lay hold on the fatherly love of God before all things, so that, by relying on this shield, they may confidently triumph over all evil. It is a bronze wall for us that when God is favourable to us we shall be secure against all danger. Paul, however,

---

30. For an exposition of Paul's argument, see Robert A. Peterson, "'Though All Hell Should Endeavor to Shake': God's Preservation of His Saints," *Presb* 17, no. 1 (1991): 40–57.
31. Calvin, comm. on Rom. 8:30, in *CNTC*, 8:182.

does not mean that we shall have no opposition, but he promises us victory over every kind of enemy.[32]

Furthermore, when the apostle declares, "If God is for us, who can be against us?" (8:31), Calvin correctly points readers to meditate on God's almighty power as the source of believers' preservation: "There is no power under heaven or above it which can resist the arm of God. If, therefore, we have Him as our defender, we need fear no harm whatever. That man alone displays true confidence in God who is content with His protection, and has no fear sufficient to make him despair."[33]

In light of Paul's words "He who did not spare his own Son but gave him up for us all, how will he not also with him graciously give us all things?" (8:32), Calvin extols Christ as "a pledge of God's boundless love towards us." Indeed, he is the supreme pledge thereof:

> It is a notable and shining proof of His inestimable love that the Father did not hesitate to bestow His Son for our salvation. Paul therefore draws his argument from the greater to the less—since He had nothing dearer, more precious, or more excellent than His Son, He will neglect nothing which He foresees will be profitable to us.[34]

Paul next argues for preservation based on God's justice: "Who shall bring any charge against God's elect? It is God who justifies." Calvin explains,

> Seeing, therefore, that it is He who justifies us, there is no place for accusation. . . . Paul . . . wished to arm the sons of God from top to bottom with the confidence which wards off anxieties and fears. . . . God will not admit any accusation against us, because He has absolved us from all blame. . . . No adversary, therefore, can shake, much less destroy, our salvation.[35]

Calvin powerfully interprets Paul's words "Who is to condemn?":

> Christ is the One who once suffered the punishment due to us, and thereby professed that He took our place in order to deliver us.

---

32. Calvin, comm. on Rom. 8:31, in *CNTC*, 8:183.
33. Calvin, comm. on Rom. 8:31, in *CNTC*, 8:183.
34. Calvin, comm. on Rom. 8:32, in *CNTC*, 8:184.
35. Calvin, comm. on Rom. 8:33, in *CNTC*, 8:184–85.

Anyone, therefore, who desires to condemn us after this must kill Christ Himself again. But Christ has not only died, He has also come forth as conqueror of death, and triumphed over its power by His resurrection.[36]

Having summarized Paul's case for preservation based on God's sovereignty, fatherly favor, and justice, Calvin turns to the apostle's argument from God's love, "Who shall separate us from the love of Christ?" (8:35). Calvin writes,

God, who once in His love embraced us, never ceases to care for us. . . . As clouds, though they obscure the clear view of the sun, do not wholly deprive us of its light, so in our adversity God sends us the rays of His grace through the darkness, lest any temptation should overwhelm us with despair. . . .

The assurance of this, fixed deep in our hearts, will always draw us from hell to the light of life, and will be of sufficient strength to support us.[37]

Paul famously wrote that nothing is "able to separate us from the love of God in Christ Jesus our Lord" (8:39). Calvin's response is eloquent: "To confirm us more strongly in the things which we experience, Paul now bursts into hyperbole. Should anything in life or death, he says, seem able to tear us away from God, it will not do so. Indeed, the very angels themselves, were they to attempt to overthrow this foundation, will do us no harm."[38]

1 Corinthians 1:7–9

. . . as you wait for the revealing of our Lord Jesus Christ, who will sustain you to the end, guiltless in the day of our Lord Jesus Christ. God is faithful, by whom you were called into the fellowship of his Son, Jesus Christ our Lord.

Sincere Christians sometimes think that because ultimate salvation is future, this prevents us from having assurance now. Calvin challenges this line of reasoning:

---

36. Calvin, comm. on Rom. 8:34, in *CNTC*, 8:185.
37. Calvin, comm. on Rom. 8:35, 37, in *CNTC*, 8:188.
38. Calvin, comm. on Rom. 8:38, in *CNTC*, 8:188–89.

It is as if he [Paul in 1 Cor. 1:8] said, "Even if you are in a state of suspense because you are expecting a salvation that has still to come, you ought to be certain, nevertheless, that the Lord will never give you up, but, on the contrary, that He will increase what He has begun in you, so that when that day will come, in which all must appear before the judgement seat of Christ (II Cor. 5.10) we may then be found blameless."[39]

Calvin analyzes Paul's presentation of preservation here and summarizes it in two points. First, God's faithfulness assures believers of final salvation: "God is unwavering in His purpose. Since that is so, He does not, therefore, make fun of us in calling us, but He will maintain His work for ever."[40]

Second, preservation is based on God's promise to maintain our union with Christ:

The Corinthians cannot be thrown aside, because they were once called by the Lord "into fellowship with Christ." . . . For the whole purpose of the Gospel is that Christ be made ours, and that we be ingrafted into His body. . . . Because he is called into fellowship with Christ, he can think of himself, in so far as assurance of salvation is concerned, in no other way than as a member of Christ. . . . In this way, he will lay hold of the certain hope of final perseverance . . . if he looks upon himself as a member of Christ, who cannot possibly fail.[41]

Ephesians 1:13–14

In him you also, when you heard the word of truth, the gospel of your salvation, and believed in him, were sealed with the promised Holy Spirit, who is the guarantee of our inheritance until we acquire possession of it, to the praise of his glory.

Not only are the Father and Son involved in keeping the saints saved, but the Holy Spirit has roles to play as well—he is God's seal and earnest guaranteeing our salvation—as Calvin indicates in his exposition of this text:

---

39. Calvin, comm. on 1 Cor. 1:8, in *CNTC*, 9:22.
40. Calvin, comm. on 1 Cor. 1:8, in *CNTC*, 9:23.
41. Calvin, comm. on 1 Cor. 1:8, in *CNTC*, 9:23–24.

It is as if [Paul] said, "Having called the Gospel the Word of truth, I will not prove it by the authority of men; for you have the Author Himself, the Spirit of God, who seals the truth of it in your hearts." . . . This office Paul ascribes to the Holy Spirit. . . . The true conviction that believers have of the Word of God, of their own salvation, and of all religion, does not spring from the feeling of the flesh, or from human and philosophical arguments, but from the sealing of the Spirit, who makes their consciences more certain and removes all doubt.

Thus, when we have received the Spirit of God, we have God's promises confirmed to us, and we are not afraid that He will retract. . . . The Spirit, then, is the earnest of our inheritance, that is, of eternal life, unto redemption, that is, until the day of complete redemption comes.[42]

Ephesians 4:30

And do not grieve the Holy Spirit of God, by whom you were sealed for the day of redemption.

Calvin's comments on this verse are short and sweet: "For the Spirit of God is like a seal, by which we are distinguished from the reprobate, and which is impressed on our hearts that we may be assured of the grace of adoption. He adds, '*Unto the day of redemption*,' that is, till God conducts us into the possession of the promised inheritance."[43] Christians are safe in the keeping of the Father, Son, and Holy Spirit, and the triune God wants us to know it.

Philippians 1:6

And I am sure of this, that he who began a good work in you will bring it to completion at the day of Jesus Christ.

Despite the fact that Calvin is sometimes depicted as dour, joy has a place in his life and writing, as is shown by his comments on this verse: "Paul's confidence in them for the future furnishes an additional reason for joy." But what is the source of the apostle's confidence for

---

42. Calvin, comm. on Eph. 1:13–14, in *CNTC*, 11:131–32.
43. Calvin, comm. on Eph. 4:30, in *CNTC*, 11:194.

the Philippians' final salvation? Calvin has a ready response: "Paul assuredly did not derive this confidence from the steadfastness or excellence of men, but simply from the fact that God had declared His love to the Philippians."[44] God's promises in his word give his people strong confidence that he will preserve them.

Calvin encourages his readers that believers are to "exercise themselves in constant meditation upon the benefits of God, that they may encourage and confirm hope for the future, and always ponder in their mind this syllogism."[45] The Reformer then offers a formal argument with a conclusion based on premises:

> God does not forsake the work which His own hands have begun,
> as the Prophet bears witness. (Ps. 138.8; Isa. 64.8)
> We are the work of His hands.
> Therefore He will complete what He has begun in us.[46]

Calvin clarifies a possible misunderstanding: "When I say we are the work of His hands, I do not refer only to creation, but to the calling by which we are adopted as His sons."[47]

1 Thessalonians 5:23–24

> Now may the God of peace himself sanctify you completely, and may your whole spirit and soul and body be kept blameless at the coming of our Lord Jesus Christ. He who calls you is faithful; he will surely do it.

Sanctification is initial, progressive, and final. It is initial when God sets sinners apart from sin and to himself by constituting them his saints (1 Cor. 1:2; 2 Thess. 2:13). Progressive sanctification involves our ongoing growth in holiness (1 Thess. 4:3–6). It also is final. First Thessalonians 5:23–24 is Paul's powerful promise of final and complete sanctification for all believers in Christ (see also Eph. 5:25–27). Calvin captures the connection in Paul's thought between 1 Thessalonians 5:23 and 5:24:

---

44. Calvin, comm. on Phil. 1:6, in *CNTC*, 11:228–29.
45. Calvin, comm. on Phil. 1:6, in *CNTC*, 11:229.
46. Calvin, comm. on Phil. 1:6, in *CNTC*, 11:229.
47. Calvin, comm. on Phil. 1:6, in *CNTC*, 11:229.

Faithful is he that calleth you. As he has declared in his prayer the extent of his regard for the well-being of the Thessalonians, so now he confirms them in their assurance of the divine grace. . . . When the Lord has once adopted us as His children, we are to hope that His grace will be continued to us. He does not promise that He will be our Father for one day only, but adopts us on condition that He is to cherish us ever afterwards. Our calling should therefore be to us evidence of eternal grace, for He will not leave the work of His hands incomplete.[48]

Hebrews 6:13–20

For when God made a promise to Abraham, since he had no one greater by whom to swear, he swore by himself, saying, "Surely I will bless you and multiply you." And thus Abraham, having patiently waited, obtained the promise. For people swear by something greater than themselves, and in all their disputes an oath is final for confirmation. So when God desired to show more convincingly to the heirs of the promise the unchangeable character of his purpose, he guaranteed it with an oath, so that by two unchangeable things, in which it is impossible for God to lie, we who have fled for refuge might have strong encouragement to hold fast to the hope set before us. We have this as a sure and steadfast anchor of the soul, a hope that enters into the inner place behind the curtain, where Jesus has gone as a forerunner on our behalf.

It is common knowledge that Hebrews 6:1–12 is one of the strongest warning passages in all Scripture. It is not as well known that Hebrews 6:13–20, following on the heels of this famous passage, is a strong preservation passage. Calvin understands this well. He draws the link between God's faithfulness and the certainty of his promises: "God's name is not expressly used here, but is to be understood, because unless He fulfils his promises, He is shown to be unfaithful."[49]

Commenting on Hebrews 6:17, Calvin praises how far our gracious Father condescends to assure his people of his promise to preserve them:

---

48. Calvin, comm. on 1 Thess. 5:24, in *CNTC*, 8:381.
49. Calvin, comm. on Heb. 6:13, in *CNTC*, 12:82.

See how tenderly God indulges our slowness, as a good Father should. He sees that we will not be satisfied simply with His Word and therefore to impress it more fully on our hearts He adds His oath. This makes it clear how important it is for us for this certainty of His goodness towards us to be manifest, so that there is no further occasion for hesitation or fear. . . . Certainty of salvation is therefore a necessary thing and in order to secure it God who forbids rash swearing has deigned to take His oath.[50]

Calvin is arrested by the comparison in 6:19–20 between our faith, which rests on God's word, and an anchor: "We have this as a sure and steadfast anchor of the soul, a hope that enters into the inner place behind the curtain, where Jesus has gone as a forerunner on our behalf." He continues,

But just as an anchor is let down through the midst of the water to a dark, hidden place, and while it remains there it holds the ship that is exposed to the waves safely in its station so that it is not swept away, so our hope is fixed on the unseen God. . . . That is why he says that the anchor is *sure and steadfast*. It is possible for an anchor to be torn or for a cable to break or a ship to be broken in pieces by the violence of the waves. That happens on the sea. But the power of God to support us is quite different, as is also the strength of hope and the firmness of His Word.[51]

The writer to the Hebrews mixes nautical and priestly metaphors to good effect when he speaks of "a sure and steadfast anchor of the soul, a hope that enters into the inner place behind the curtain, where Jesus has gone as a forerunner on our behalf" (6:19–20). Calvin underlines the assurance that these words bring believers:

The apostle is therefore right when he states that our High Priest has entered heaven, because He has done so not only for Himself, but also for us. There is therefore no cause to fear that the door of heaven may be shut to our faith, since it never is disjoined from

---

50. Calvin, comm. on Heb. 6:17, in *CNTC*, 12:84. See also Calvin, comm. on Heb. 6:18, *CNTC*, 12:85.

51. Calvin, comm. on Heb. 6:19, in *CNTC*, 12:86.

Christ. Because it is for us to follow Christ who goes before us, He is called our Fore-runner.[52]

Hebrews 7:25–27

Consequently, he is able to save to the uttermost those who draw near to God through him, since he always lives to make intercession for them.

For it was indeed fitting that we should have such a high priest, holy, innocent, unstained, separated from sinners, and exalted above the heavens. He has no need, like those high priests, to offer sacrifices daily, first for his own sins and then for those of the people, since he did this once for all when he offered up himself.

Christians often understand the importance of Christ's death for their salvation better than they understand the importance of his resurrection for the same. The writer to the Hebrews lays proper emphasis on both Christ's crucifixion and resurrection, as the quotation above shows. Because Jesus is alive, he remains a priest forever. Calvin succinctly draws out the importance of this reality for our deliverance: "The fruit of eternal priesthood is our salvation, if we gather this fruit by faith, as we should."[53]

Christ as high priest and mediator far surpasses his Old Testament counterparts. As Calvin says,

Although the high priest carried the names of the twelve tribes on his shoulders and their symbols on his breast, yet he alone went into the sanctuary while the people stood in the courtyard. But now that we rely on Christ as Mediator, we enter by faith right into heaven, because there is no longer any veil to obstruct us. God appears to us openly, and invites us lovingly to meet Him face to face.[54]

Because the crucified one is the risen one, we are safe in his care. Because our mediator and great high priest's sacrifice is perfect, God

---

52. Calvin, comm. on Heb. 6:19, in *CNTC*, 12:87.
53. Calvin, comm. on Heb. 7:25, in *CNTC*, 12:101.
54. Calvin, comm. on Heb. 7:25, in *CNTC*, 12:101.

is satisfied, and we are forgiven forever. Calvin writes, "His sacrifice was such that its once-for-all oblation sufficed to the end of the world. He offered Himself."[55] And because he makes ongoing intercession on our behalf in the Father's presence, Calvin explains, he maintains our salvation: "It belongs to a priest to intercede, in order that the people may find favour with God. Christ is continually doing this because He rose from the dead for this purpose. He justifies His rightful Name of Priest by His continual task of intercession."[56]

1 Peter 1:3–5

Blessed be the God and Father of our Lord Jesus Christ! According to his great mercy, he has caused us to be born again to a living hope through the resurrection of Jesus Christ from the dead, to an inheritance that is imperishable, undefiled, and unfading, kept in heaven for you, who by God's power are being guarded through faith for a salvation ready to be revealed in the last time.

As is not uncommon in Scripture, Peter bases our salvation on Christ's death and resurrection. And he attributes our preservation for the present and the future to God's power, as Calvin observes: "However weak we may be, our salvation is not uncertain, because it is sustained by God's power. As, then, we are sustained by faith, so faith itself receives its stability from God's power. Hence its security is not only for the present, but also for the future."[57]

1 John 2:19

They went out from us, but they were not of us; for if they had been of us, they would have continued with us. But they went out, that it might become plain that they all are not of us.

John warns of deniers of the Father and the Son who infiltrated the churches, failed to persuade them of error, and then left. Although they remained in the church for a time, they did not really belong to

---

55. Calvin, comm. on Heb. 7:27, in *CNTC*, 12:103.
56. Calvin, comm. on Heb. 7:25, in *CNTC*, 12:101.
57. Calvin, comm. on 1 Pet. 1:5, in *CNTC*, 12:233.

Christ. If they had belonged to him, they would not have forsaken the fellowship of believers. Now, having left, they have revealed their true colors. They are "antichrists," as John calls them (2:18, 22). Calvin agrees with this interpretation: "[John] says plainly that those who fell away had never been members of the Church."[58] But why do the people of God not fall away too? Calvin answers that they are kept by the faithful Holy Spirit, whose calling of them to faith in Christ confirms their election by God for salvation:

> It is impossible for them [true believers] to be alienated from the Church. For the seal which God engraves on their consciences by His Spirit cannot be obliterated. The incorruptible seed which has struck root cannot be pulled up or destroyed. He is not speaking here of men's constancy but of God's, whose election must be confirmed. Wherefore he has good reason to say that, where God's calling is effectual, perseverance will be certain. In short, he means that those who fall away have never been thoroughly imbued with the knowledge of Christ but only had a slight and passing taste of it.[59]

1 John 5:18

> We know that everyone who has been born of God does not keep on sinning, but he who was born of God protects him, and the evil one does not touch him.

Here modern translations offer a different rendering than Calvin. The ESV, for example, reads, "He who was born of God [i.e., Christ] protects him [i.e., the believer]." Calvin translates, "*Whosoever is begotten of God* [a reference to believers] *keepeth himself*." I believe that Calvin errs here, but his explanation is still worthy of quotation as a testimony to his belief in preservation: "[John] transfers to us what belongs to God. For were any of us the keeper of his own salvation, it would be a wretched protection. . . . Therefore, believers keep themselves from sin inasmuch as they are kept by God."[60]

---

58. Calvin, comm. on 1 John 2:19, in *CNTC*, 5:257.
59. Calvin, comm. on 1 John 2:19, in *CNTC*, 5:257–58.
60. Calvin, comm. on 1 John 5:18, in *CNTC*, 5:312.

Conclusion on Biblical Material

We have surveyed seventeen passages from Calvin's biblical commentaries, in which he taught God's preservation of his saints. We could have examined more passages, but these are more than sufficient to show that Calvin teaches preservation not only in *Institutes* 3.24.6 but abundantly in his commentaries as well.

A Theological Summary of Calvin's Case for Preservation

Believers Are Preserved by the Working of the Trinity

Calvin's case for preservation is broadly based, resting on the sure foundation of the working of the Father, Son, and Holy Spirit. The Father loves us and will never stop doing so: "He does not promise that He will be our Father for one day only, but adopts us on condition that He is to cherish us ever afterwards."[61] When the gracious Father, therefore, brings us into his family, we have "evidence of eternal grace," for he who saved us once freely by his grace, "will not leave the work of His hands."[62]

The Son of God also loves us and keeps us: "Christ is the One who once suffered the punishment due to us. . . . Anyone, therefore, who desires to condemn us after this must kill Christ Himself again."[63] The risen, victorious Christ is no longer subject to death. As a result, we are safe in his care. Furthermore, he is no longer on earth but appears in God's presence in heaven on our behalf: "But now that we rely on Christ as Mediator, we enter by faith right into heaven. . . . God appears to us openly, and invites us lovingly to meet Him face to face."[64]

The Holy Spirit also preserves God's children, so that their eternal redemption is assured: "Thus, when we have received the Spirit of God, we have God's promises confirmed to us."[65] Calvin continues, "The Spirit, then, is the earnest of our inheritance, that is, of eternal life . . . until the day of complete redemption comes."[66] Once God

---

61. Calvin, comm. on 1 Thess. 5:24, in *CNTC*, 8:381.
62. Calvin, comm. on 1 Thess. 5:24, in *CNTC*, 8:381.
63. Calvin, comm. on Rom. 8:34, in *CNTC*, 8:185.
64. Calvin, comm. on Heb. 7:25, in *CNTC*, 12:101.
65. Calvin, comm. on Eph. 1:13, in *CNTC*, 11:132.
66. Calvin, comm. on Eph. 1:14, in *CNTC*, 11:132.

has saved his people, they are as secure in his grace as the seal of his Spirit is invincible: "It is impossible for them to be alienated from the Church. For the seal which God engraves on their consciences by His Spirit cannot be obliterated."[67]

Believers Are Preserved by God's Attributes

The truth that the Trinity works to keep us saved prompts a question: What attributes of God are most evident in our preservation? Calvin cites three: God's grace, power, and faithfulness.

Our preservation depends on God's grace, and Calvin connects that grace to each person of the Godhead. In the *Institutes*, he teaches that the people whom Christ brings into his church, "he is said to receive into his *care and keeping*, . . . *into his care and protection*."[68] Here Christ's love is the basis for our preservation. The Holy Spirit also plays an important role because "the Spirit of God is like a seal . . . which is impressed on our hearts that we may be assured of the grace of adoption."[69] Of course, the Reformer also hails the great love of God the Father. It is due to the Father's help that "in the midst of danger they remain safe." He lauds "the grace of the Father" that grants them "unconquerable strength against their adversaries."[70]

Our preservation also depends on God's power, as Calvin makes plain: "Our salvation is not uncertain, because it is sustained by God's power."[71] Elsewhere he assures us that "the salvation of all the elect is as certain as God's power is invincible."[72]

Predictably, Calvin ascribes this keeping power to each of the three persons of the Trinity: "*No one is able to snatch them out of the Father's hand.* . . . From the invincible power of God, Christ deduces that the salvation of the godly" cannot be overthrown, "because God, who has taken them under the protection of His hand, would first have to be overcome."[73]

---

67. Calvin, comm. on 1 John 2:19, in *CNTC*, 5:257–58.
68. *Institutes*, 3.24.6, italics added.
69. Calvin, comm. on Eph. 4:30, in *CNTC*, 11:194.
70. Calvin, comm. on John 17:25, in *CNTC*, 5:145.
71. Calvin, comm. on 1 Pet. 1:5, in *CNTC*, 12:233.
72. Calvin, comm. on John 10:28, in *CNTC*, 4:273.
73. Calvin, comm. on John 10:28–29, in *CNTC*, 4:273.

In the *Institutes*, he also credits preservation to the Son: "Christ does not allow any of those whom he has once for all engrafted into his body to perish [John 10:28]; for in preserving their salvation he will perform what he has promised—namely, he will show forth *God's power, which 'is greater than all'* [John 10:29]."[74]

The Spirit's power keeps us, too, because "the seal which God engraves on their consciences by His Spirit cannot be obliterated. The incorruptible seed which has struck root cannot be pulled up or destroyed." As a result, "perseverance will be certain."[75]

Our preservation also depends on God's faithfulness, which Calvin also ascribes to the Father, Son, and Holy Spirit. The Father's faithfulness undergirds our salvation: "God [the Father] is unwavering in His purpose. Since that is so, He does not, therefore, make fun of us in calling us, but He will maintain His work for ever."[76] Christ's faithfulness preserves us too: "Christ bids us be sure and untroubled when we are brought by faith into His fold. . . . He will be the faithful guardian of our salvation."[77] And the Spirit is faithful to keep us, for when God seals our minds "by His Spirit," he is speaking "not . . . of men's constancy but of God's."[78]

A Pastoral Summary of Calvin's Case for Preservation

Calvin teaches that great practical benefits accrue to those who know and love the Lord. His various pastoral applications of God's preservation of his saints are all variations on one theme: confidence. Preservation confirms to us God's eternal grace, frees us from worry, strengthens our faith, proves that he continues to love us, and assures us of final salvation.

God's Preservation Confirms That We Are the Objects of His Eternal Grace

While meditating on God's faithfulness, Calvin rejoices in his promise of "eternal grace." He writes, "He does not promise that He will be

---

74. *Institutes*, 3.22.7, italics added.
75. Calvin, comm. on 1 John 2:19, in *CNTC*, 5:257–58.
76. Calvin, comm. on 1 Cor. 1:8, in *CNTC*, 9:23.
77. Calvin, comm. on John 10:28, *CNTC*, 4:273.
78. Calvin, comm. on 1 John 2:19, in *CNTC*, 5:257–58.

our Father for one day only, but adopts us on condition that He is to cherish us ever afterwards." When God effectively calls us to himself through the gospel, this should "be to us evidence of eternal grace, for He will not leave the work of His hands incomplete."[79]

God's Preservation Erases Doubts and Frees Us from Anxiety

All believers are at times assailed by doubts. In the *Institutes*, Calvin the pastor insists that Christ's preservation meets that need: "If we still doubt whether we have been received by Christ into his care and protection, he meets that doubt when he willingly offers himself as shepherd, and declares that we shall be numbered among his flock if we hear his voice [John 10:3]."[80]

All believers also at times suffer anxiety concerning the future. Here, too, Christ is a faithful Savior who frees his people from anxiety's grip: "Anxiety about our future state steals in. . . . But Christ has freed us from this anxiety, for these promises surely apply to the future."[81] What are "these promises" that Calvin cites? They are some of the very preservation passages that he comments on and that we cited earlier in this essay: Psalm 138:8; John 6:37–39; 10:28–30; Romans 8:38–39; Philippians 1:6; and 1 John 2:19.

God's Preservation Strengthens Our Weak Faith

By God's grace believers keep on believing, but every one of us knows the experience of failing in faith, of not believing as strongly as we would like. Calvin applies God's preservation to this need:

> In short, our salvation is certain because it is in the hand of God. Our faith is weak, and we are given to wavering; but God has taken us in His hand and is powerful enough to scatter with a breath all the efforts of our enemies. It is very important for us to look at this, so that fear of temptations may not dismay us.[82]

Or as Calvin succinctly says in another place, "We have, therefore, ample proof to strengthen our minds with confidence in our salvation."[83]

---

79. Calvin, comm. on 1 Thess. 5:24, in *CNTC*, 8:381.
80. *Institutes*, 3.24.6.
81. *Institutes*, 3.24.6.
82. Calvin, comm. on John 10:28–29, in *CNTC*, 4:273.
83. Calvin, comm. on Rom. 5:10, in *CNTC*, 8:110.

God's Preservation Proves That He Continues to Love Us

We stand in constant need of assurance that God loves us. And that great assurance is exactly what God gives us: "It is a notable and shining proof of His inestimable love that the Father did not hesitate to bestow His Son for our salvation." God could give no greater pledge of his love than this, "since He had nothing dearer, more precious, or more excellent than His Son." Indeed, Christ is "a pledge of God's boundless love towards us."[84] Can we be certain that God will continue to love us? Calvin answers affirmatively: "We must stand firm in the belief that God, who once in His love embraced us, never ceases to care for us."[85]

God's Preservation Assures Us of Final Salvation

While commenting on 1 Peter 1:5, Calvin teaches that God wants believers to have confidence of final salvation because, though they are very weak in themselves, they are upheld by God's mighty power:

> *We are kept by the power of God.* We must note the connexion in his saying that we are kept while in the world, and at the same time our inheritance is reserved in heaven. Otherwise the thought would immediately creep in, "What help is it to us that our salvation is laid up in heaven, when we are tossed here and there in this world as in a stormy sea? What help is it to us that our salvation is secured in a quiet harbour, when we are driven to and fro among a thousand ship-wrecks?" The apostle, therefore, anticipates objections of this kind, when he shows that though we are exposed to dangers in the world we are yet kept by faith, and that though we are thus near to death we are yet safe under the guardianship of faith. As faith itself through the infirmity of the flesh often quails, we would always be anxious about the morrow, if the Lord did not help us.
>
> We see indeed that under the Papacy a diabolical opinion prevails that our final perseverance is doubtful because we are uncertain whether tomorrow we shall be in the same state of grace. But Peter does not leave us in suspense like this. He maintains that we

---

84. Calvin, comm. on Rom. 8:32, in *CNTC*, 8:184.
85. Calvin, comm. on Rom. 8:35, in *CNTC*, 8:186.

stand by the power of God, in case any doubt arising from a consciousness of our own infirmity should disquiet us. However weak we may be, our salvation is not uncertain, because it is sustained by God's power. As, then, we are sustained by faith, so faith itself receives its stability from God's power. Hence its security is not only for the present, but also for the future.[86]

86. Calvin, comm. on 1 Pet. 1:5, in *CNTC*, 12:233.

20

The Last Things

Cornelis P. Venema

Now we know that outside Christ there is nothing but confusion in the world. And although Christ had already begun to set up the kingdom of God, it was His death that was the true beginning of a properly-ordered state and the complete restoration of the world.

—John Calvin, *Commentary on the Gospel according to St. John*

The Last Things according to Calvin

During the course of church history, certain doctrines have captured the attention of the church in different periods of time.[1] The Reformation focused on the church's understanding of the gospel, particularly the justification of sinners before God. The church of the sixteenth century was largely occupied with the question of Luther: How can I—a sinner who deserves judgment—find acceptance with God? This was not the exclusive concern of Luther and the Lutheran wing of the Reformation,

---

1. Portions of this chapter are adapted from Cornelis P. Venema, "Calvin's Doctrine of the Last Things: The Resurrection of the Body and the Life Everlasting (3.25 et al.)," in *A Theological Guide to Calvin's "Institutes,"* ed. David W. Hall and Peter A. Lillback (Phillipsburg, NJ: P&R, 2008), 441–67. Used by permission of P&R Publishing.

as is evident from Calvin's assertion in the *Institutes* that the doctrine of justification is the "main hinge on which religion turns."[2]

The Reformation's focus on justification should not negate the importance of other biblical teachings to its understanding of the gospel. The subject of this chapter, Calvin's eschatology (or doctrine of the last things), is a case in point. Calvin's relatively brief treatment of this doctrine in his best-known work, the *Institutes*, might suggest that it is an insignificant aspect of his theology, but this is not so. Calvin's theology should be measured not simply from the content of his *Institutes*, which he describes as a "handbook" to his commentaries. His theology can be fully appreciated only through carefully considering the entire body of his theological writings, especially his lifetime labor in biblical commentary and interpretation. Even if some features of biblical eschatology may seem to be given short shrift in the *Institutes*, Calvin extensively addresses the full range of eschatological topics in his commentaries and theological writings.

Consequently, this summary of Calvin's eschatology is not limited to his *Institutes*. Calvin directly addresses the topic of eschatology in a short chapter in the *Institutes* (3.25), which is of particular importance. But it is not by itself a sufficient measure of Calvin's treatment of the "last things." Consistent with Calvin's own understanding of the relationship between his biblical commentaries and the *Institutes*, this summary also considers the most important evidence from his exegetical and theological writings. To ensure a comprehensive treatment of Calvin's eschatology, this summary follows the traditional sequence of topics in the locus concerning eschatology: it first examines individual eschatology, or the intermediate state, and then examines several aspects of general eschatology, including the "signs of the times" and Christ's second advent, the antichrist, the millennium, the resurrection of the body, and the life everlasting and consummation of all things.[3]

---

2. *Institutes*, 3.11.1.

3. Among the sources on Calvin's eschatology in English, the following are especially helpful: Heinrich Quistorp, *Calvin's Doctrine of the Last Things*, trans. Harold Knight (London: Lutterworth, 1955); T. F. Torrance, "The Eschatology of Hope: John Calvin," chap. 4 in *Kingdom and Church: A Study in the Theology of the Reformation* (Edinburgh: Oliver & Boyd, 1956); David E. Holwerda, "Eschatology and History: A Look at Calvin's Eschatological Vision," in *Exploring the Heritage of John Calvin*, ed. David E. Holwerda (Grand Rapids, MI: Baker, 1976), 110–39; François Wendel, *Calvin: Origins and Development of His Religious Thought*, trans. Philip Mairet (1963; repr., Grand Rapids, MI: Baker, 1997), 284–90.

General Features of Calvin's Eschatology

Before considering Calvin's treatment of these eschatological topics, it is necessary to note several general features of Calvin's theology of particular importance to interpreting his eschatology. In his approach to the subject of the last things, Calvin exhibits the same reluctance to speculate beyond the boundaries of Scripture that is a mark of his theology in general. He also exercises great care to interpret the Scriptures in a way that honors their unity and focuses on the person and work of Christ. These characteristics of Calvin's method result in his comments on eschatology being restrained, devoid of the excessive curiosity often present in the eschatological views of his contemporaries as well as of many present-day theologians. It would also be a mistake to restrict consideration of his eschatology to the coming of Christ at the end of the age. Since Calvin emphasizes that Christ's end-time work has already commenced in the present age of the gospel's preaching through the church, it is necessary to note aspects of Calvin's "inaugurated" or "realized" eschatology. For Calvin, the future work of Christ at his second advent will complete the redemptive work he has already begun in believers by his Spirit through the word of the gospel.

The Knowledge of God through Revelation

At the outset of his summary of the Christian faith in the *Institutes*, Calvin observes that nearly all Christian wisdom consists in the knowledge of God and of ourselves. In his *Institutes*, Calvin sets forth in a comprehensive manner what we know about this on the basis of God's word. For Calvin, the knowledge of God and ourselves, which constitutes the subject matter of all Christian theology, may be drawn only from God's self-disclosure in his revelation. Consequently, Calvin's theology is a theology of the word of God, basing its claims on God's revelation in Scripture. This means that the subject of eschatology, as far as Calvin treats it in his writings, can be based only on a proper interpretation of what the word of God teaches about the future.

There are at least three important characteristics of Calvin's understanding of the knowledge of God and ourselves.[4] The first is Calvin's

---

4. For studies of Calvin's doctrine of the knowledge of God, see Edward A. Dowey Jr., *The Knowledge of God in Calvin's Theology*, 3rd ed. (Grand Rapids, MI: Eerdmans, 1994); T. H. L.

insistence that *this knowledge derives exclusively from the word of God*. We know God and ourselves, according to Calvin, only insofar as God makes himself known to us by "accommodating" himself to human capacity.[5] Because Calvin insists that the knowledge of God and ourselves derives from God's revelation through the word, he emphatically rejects any theology that oversteps the boundaries of God's own witness concerning himself. A second characteristic of Calvin's understanding of this knowledge is his insistence that *our knowledge of God relates to his works in relation to us*. Unlike the more speculative method of some scholastic theologians of his time, Calvin focuses in the *Institutes* on the "near and familiar" manner in which God communicates himself to us as our Creator and Redeemer.[6] The third characteristic of Calvin's understanding is that the knowledge of God is more than mere cognitive or intellectual apprehension of God's revelation. *Since the knowledge of God is intimately joined to the knowledge of ourselves, it transforms our lives.* To know God properly produces heartfelt trust and reverence toward him. Calvin often points to the inseparable connection between the knowledge of God and true piety. In the second chapter of the first book of the *Institutes*, he writes,

> Now, the knowledge of God, as I understand it, is that by which we not only conceive that there is a God but also grasp what befits us and is proper to his glory, in fine, what is to our advantage to know of him. Indeed, we shall not say that, properly speaking, God is known where there is no religion or piety.[7]

Calvin's approach to the knowledge of God and ourselves is particularly evident in his treatment of eschatological topics. Rather than engage in speculation or indulge in idle curiosity about the future,

---

Parker, *Calvin's Doctrine of the Knowledge of God* (Grand Rapids, MI: Eerdmans, 1959); Benjamin B. Warfield, "Calvin's Doctrine of the Knowledge of God," in *Calvin and Calvinism* (New York: Oxford University Press, 1931), 29–130.

5. *Institutes*, 1.13.1.
6. *Institutes*, 1.5.9.
7. *Institutes*, 1.2.1. Cf. *Institutes*, 1.2.2, where Calvin provides a representative definition of piety: "I call 'piety' [*pietas*] that reverence joined with love of God which the knowledge of his benefits induces. For until men recognize that they owe everything to God, that they are nourished by his fatherly care, that he is the Author of their every good, that they should seek nothing beyond him—they will never yield him willing service."

Calvin is careful to safeguard the boundaries of scriptural teaching in this area. Throughout the history of the church, the topics of eschatology have often tempted theologians to assert more than is biblically warranted. In Calvin's reflection on eschatological subjects, however, there is a striking reserve and caution. Even a brief perusal of book 3, chapter 25, of Calvin's *Institutes* is sufficient to impress the reader with his reluctance to say more than the Scriptures say on such matters. In this chapter and elsewhere, Calvin often speaks critically of those who exceed the boundaries of biblical revelation by speculating about the future state of the individual believer or the precise nature of the final state. He resists the kinds of questions that often occupied the attention of medieval theologians. Calvin is always keenly interested in the way the knowledge of the future shapes the piety and life of believers. Rather than satisfying a merely intellectual interest in the last things, Calvin's eschatology invariably focuses on the way such knowledge transforms the lives of believers as they live in hopeful expectation of the fulfillment of God's promises in Christ.

The Interpretation of Biblical Prophecy

One of the most important challenges that the doctrine of the last things poses for a Christian theologian is the proper interpretation of biblical prophecy. In eschatological debates during the last century or more, this challenge has often been linked to the view represented in the Scofield Reference Bible—dispensational premillennialism. Though it would be anachronistic to suggest that Calvin's handling of biblical prophecy explicitly answers the approach associated with dispensationalism, his interpretation of biblical prophecy provides an outstanding model that has much to contribute to modern debates. Unlike the tendency of dispensational theology, Calvin interprets all biblical prophecy from the conviction that God's purposes for his people find their realization in Christ, the head of the church, and that the church is a body of believers composed of all the elect, Jew and Gentile alike. For Calvin, it is simply impossible to view God's purposes for Israel and the church as separate or to interpret the promises to Israel in any other way than in terms of their fulfillment in the gathering of the church by the Spirit and word of Christ.

The best way to ascertain Calvin's approach to the interpretation of biblical prophecy is to examine his commentaries, especially his treatment of the Old Testament Prophetic Books. In these commentaries, Calvin offers an extensive interpretation of how Old Testament prophets prepared the way for the coming of Christ in the fullness of time. In Calvin's understanding of the history of redemption in the Old Testament, the Lord was preparing his people for the coming of Christ and the eventual consummation of his saving work in the new heavens and earth. The "gospel," which Calvin defines as the gracious promise of reconciliation through the work of Christ, was previously proclaimed under the "law" and has now been fulfilled in the first advent of Jesus Christ. Though the Old Testament promises were expressed in the language of types and shadows, Calvin interprets these promises in New Testament terms. As examples, the promised "land" of the old covenant represents the future inheritance of a new heavens and earth; the "temple" foreshadows Christ and his church, and ultimately the new creation where God will dwell forever in the midst of his people; the kingship of David anticipates the eternal kingship of his promised Son.[8] For Calvin, the work of the triune God as Creator and Redeemer finds its historical fulfillment in the coming of Jesus Christ, who is the focus of Scripture from Genesis to Revelation.[9]

A fine illustration of Calvin's treatment of biblical prophecy can be seen in his commentary on the Old Testament book of Daniel. Several features of Calvin's *Commentary on Daniel* are especially noteworthy. First, in this commentary (particularly the section on Dan. 2:44–46), Calvin frequently criticizes exegetes, including Jewish commentators, who entertain curious questions that exceed the limits of responsible interpretation. When interpreting Daniel, it is important to resist the attraction of imaginative exegesis. Second, Calvin links the prophecies of Daniel regarding the future coming of God's kingdom with the events at the time of Christ's first advent. Calvin's basic hermeneutical commitment to a Christological reading of the Scriptures is clearly evident throughout his exposition of the book. God's purposes in

---

8. *Institutes*, 2.10–11.
9. *Institutes*, 3.2.6; 3.2.29.

history for the redemption of his people and the establishment of his kingdom are fulfilled in the person and work of Christ. And third, Calvin frequently argues that the fulfillment of Daniel's prophecies (and those found in Matt. 24:1–34) will not be confined to the events of Christ's first coming.[10] The future unfolding of God's purposes in Christ, revealed in Daniel's prophecies, includes the entire period between the first and second advents of Christ. What begins at Christ's first coming is brought to completion only at his second coming. The fullness of the kingdom, which commenced at Christ's first coming, will be realized only through the administration of the gospel. The kingdom purposes of God, though already realized in some measure through the ministry of Christ and his church, will ultimately be fulfilled only at the last day.

It has been suggested that Calvin's aversion to eschatological speculation accounts for his failure to write a commentary on Revelation. In his dissertation on Calvin's eschatology, Andrew Martin Davis ascribes Calvin's neglect of Revelation to his distaste for speculation and maintains that this was a deliberate omission on his part.[11] T. H. L. Parker, who devotes some attention to this question, suggests that Calvin's failure to write a commentary on the book of Revelation stemmed from his conviction that "apocalyptic is foreign to the New Testament's complete revelation of Christ." Parker adds that it is simply a piece of scholarly "gossip" to claim that Calvin regarded Revelation as an obscure book whose interpretation was uncertain.[12]

Perhaps the likeliest explanation for Calvin's omission of a commentary on Revelation is that he was unable to complete all his commentaries before his death. Noting that Calvin wrote commentaries on a number of Old Testament apocalyptic writings—including Ezekiel and Daniel—which significantly influenced Revelation, Eric De Boer has offered the hypothesis that Calvin was preparing to write

---

10. Cf. Calvin, comm. on Matt. 24:1–34, in *CNTC*, 3:73–99. In his handling of this difficult passage, Calvin allows that the prophecy of Daniel concerning the temple's destruction in Jerusalem may be fulfilled on several occasions, and he describes events that are "typical" of the entire interadvental period between Christ's first and second advents.

11. Andrew Martin Davis, "A New Assessment of John Calvin's Eschatology" (PhD diss., Southern Baptist Theological Seminary, 1998), 174–81.

12. T. H. L. Parker, *Calvin's New Testament Commentaries* (Grand Rapids, MI: Eerdmans, 1971), 78.

a commentary on Revelation but was never able to realize this intention.[13] According to De Boer, Calvin may have broken off his exposition of the New Testament books later in his life and devoted his
attention to the Prophetic Books of the Old Testament in order to prepare for his anticipated exposition of Revelation, the only prophetic
book in the New Testament.

Of all the hypotheses regarding the omission of a commentary on
Revelation in Calvin's corpus, De Boer's seems the most plausible.
Though it is true, as noted, that Calvin was averse to eschatological
speculation, this aversion was not directed against the advisability
of interpreting apocalyptic portions of Scripture. Unlike some modern students of the Bible, Calvin draws no sharp distinction between
prophetic and apocalyptic books. Calvin's convictions regarding the
canonicity of the book of Revelation and his substantial commentaries
on many of the Old Testament prophecies suggest a belief that a commentary on the book of Revelation would have been desirable, were
there opportunity to write one. Furthermore, Calvin's commentaries
on those Old Testament books that form an important background for
the interpretation of Revelation—especially Daniel—contain sufficient
clues to anticipate what would likely have been Calvin's approach.
Calvin's aversion to speculation was always directed against theologies
that exceeded the boundaries of scriptural revelation, not against the
proper interpretation of Scripture itself.

Elements of "Inaugurated Eschatology" in Calvin's Teaching

In modern discussion of biblical eschatology, a distinction is often
drawn between "inaugurated" and "future" eschatology. This distinction emphasizes that the first advent of Christ marks the fulfillment of
the Old Testament promises and commences the final period in history,
during which God will realize his saving purposes in Christ. "Inaugurated eschatology" refers to what might be called "the presence of the
future," which has already begun with the coming of Christ. "Future
eschatology" refers to the consummation of all God's saving purposes

---

13. Eric A. De Boer, "The Book of Revelation in Calvin's Geneva," in *Calvin's Books: Festschrift for Peter De Klerk on the Occasion of His Seventieth Birthday*, ed. Wilhelm H. Neuser,
Herman J. Selderhuis, and Willem van 't Spijker (Heerenveen: Uitgeverij J. J. Groen en Zoon,
1997), 40.

in Christ that will only take place at his second advent. Though this language is not Calvin's, it captures an important feature of biblical eschatology that is clearly present in Calvin's theology.

An important theme in Calvin's understanding of the Christian life is that of "meditation on the future life."[14] In Calvin's understanding of the Christian life, set forth at length in chapters 6–10 of book 3 of the *Institutes* (popularly published as the *Golden Booklet of the True Christian Life*), Calvin describes the life of the Christian as an "imitation" of Christ. Believers whom the Spirit unites to Christ by faith are called, in conformity to Christ, to deny themselves and bear their cross. In his description of what such self-denial and cross bearing require, Calvin emphasizes that the whole Christian life is governed by an eschatological hope for the life to come. As believers experience the struggles that characterize life in this world, they are sustained by an eager anticipation of the life to come. So eager is this anticipation that Calvin speaks of how it produces a kind of "contempt for the present life."[15]

Some students of Calvin's theology object to Calvin's use of this language and conclude that he is commending otherworldly asceticism. Martin Schultze, for example, ascribes a dominating place in Calvin's theology to this theme. According to Schultze, Calvin's theology reflects an eschatology that is uninterested in the transformation of life in this world.[16] There are several problems with this criticism of Calvin's view. First, it is claimed that Calvin derives this emphasis from nonbiblical sources, such as humanism and ancient Greek philosophy. Calvin, however, describes the believer's meditation on the future life in distinctly Christological terms as an implication of what it means to live in conformity to Christ.[17] Second, Calvin balances his emphasis on "contempt for the world" with an emphasis on the proper "use"

---

14. *Institutes*, 3.9.1–6.

15. *Institutes*, 3.9.1.

16. Martin Schultze, *Meditatio futurae vitae: Ihr Begriff und ihre herrschende Stellung im System Calvins* (Leipzig, 1901). Quistorp offers a cogent refutation of Schultze's interpretation. *Calvin's Doctrine*, 51–54.

17. Holwerda notes that the phrase "contempt for the world" did not originate with Calvin but is borrowed from the devotional literature of his time, the classic example of which is Thomas à Kempis's *On the Imitation of Christ and Contempt for the World*. Whereas à Kempis's use of the phrase calls for withdrawal from worldly engagements, Calvin's use of it calls for seeking a new form of life in the world in union with Christ. Holwerda, "Eschatology and History," 118–19.

of this life and its helps.[18] For Calvin, contempt for the world is only
to the extent that it has been negatively corrupted through human
sinfulness and disobedience. It is certainly not contempt for the world
as God created it or as the Spirit of Christ is renewing it. For this reason, Calvin speaks of how the believer should receive all God's good
gifts with gratitude and use them in the service of God and others.
Third, the criticism of this theme in Calvin often fails to distinguish
between an eschatological orientation that is world denying and one
that is governed by the theme of union with Christ. It is particularly
significant that Calvin parallels meditation on the future life with
what he terms in *Institutes* 3.25 "meditation on the resurrection of
Christ." The whole of the Christian life is imbued with the theme of
hope. This hope is not for the ultimate release of the Christian from
life in the body but for the renewal of life—even the resurrection of
the body—in the life to come.

In addition to Calvin's emphasis on the future orientation of the
believer's life, he describes the believer's saving union with Christ in
a way that is thoroughly future oriented. Calvin notes, in a remarkable phrase, that believers always embrace Christ "clad in his own
promises."[19] Even though believers already enjoy salvation through
union with Christ in a way that surpasses what believers knew in the
old covenant, they continue to look forward to the fullness of salvation in the future. The saving benefits of the believer's union with
Christ through the ministry of the Spirit carry the promise of a glorious future when the work of Christ's Spirit in believers is completely
accomplished.

Accordingly, when Calvin describes the saving benefits of this
union in book 3 of the *Institutes*, he speaks of the "twofold grace"
of justification and sanctification. Each of these dimensions of Calvin's Christology has far-reaching implications for the doctrine of
the last things.

Through union with Christ, believers enjoy by faith the grace of
free justification, which anticipates God's final verdict. Justification
in Calvin's conception is a thoroughly eschatological benefit; it an-

---

18. *Institutes*, 3.10.
19. *Institutes*, 2.9.3.

ticipates the judgment of the last day and assures the believer that there is no longer any prospect of condemnation. By virtue of Christ's atoning death and resurrection, believers enjoy a present declaration of free acceptance with God, which will be publicly confirmed at the last judgment.

Those who are joined to Christ by faith simultaneously enjoy the working of the Spirit in sanctification. The regeneration of believers in union with Christ means, for Calvin, that the image of God is being restored in them. Unlike free justification, which is a definitive declaration of right standing with God, sanctification is a work of the Spirit that will perfectly conform believers to Christ in the final state of glorification. The goal of redemption is the full conformity of believers to Christ in indefectible holiness. This goal is not yet fulfilled, but its firstfruits are evident in the lives of all true believers who share in Christ's victory over the power of sin and death.

Calvin's understanding of the gospel benefits of free justification and sanctification in union with Christ through faith gives his theology a strongly eschatological complexion. The future has already commenced for the believer, who is already now freely justified and sanctified. But it has not yet reached its fulfillment, when the work of Christ is perfected in all those who belong to him by faith.

The Location of Eschatology in Calvin's Institutes

Before turning to a summary of Calvin's future eschatology, it is necessary to consider briefly where he locates his treatment of the doctrine of the last things in the *Institutes*. The primary place where Calvin discusses the doctrine of the last things is in chapter 25 of book 3. A review of the various editions of the *Institutes* shows that this chapter was completely rewritten and significantly enlarged in the 1559, or final, Latin edition. Only a small fragment of the chapter stems from the first edition of 1536. Beginning with the 1539 edition and in all later editions of the *Institutes*, Calvin treats the topics of the resurrection and the life everlasting at the close of his exposition of the Christian faith, which is based on the summary provided in the Apostles' Creed. Prior to the final Latin edition of 1559 and the French edition of 1560, the earlier editions of the *Institutes* follow a structure that roughly parallels the classical plan of Christian catechisms: the Decalogue, the Apostles' Creed, the Lord's Prayer, and the sacraments. The present form of chapter 25 is found only in the two final editions of the *Institutes*. This final version of the chapter substantially expands Calvin's comments in earlier editions and is located not in a section on the Christian faith as summarized in the Apostles' Creed but in book 3, which bears the title "The Way in Which We Receive the Grace of Christ: What Benefits Come to Us from It, and What Effects Follow."

Though there has been considerable debate regarding the structure of Calvin's *Institutes*, the arrangement of material seems to be governed by at least three broad considerations: the distinction between the "twofold knowledge of God" as Creator (book 1) and Redeemer (books 2–4); the Trinitarian arrangement of the articles of the Apostles' Creed (book 1: God the Father; book 2: God the Son; books 3–4: God the Holy Spirit); and the influence of Calvin's commentaries, particularly his *Commentary on Romans*.[20] None of these considerations can explain all Calvin's decisions regarding where to address a common topic of Christian theology. However, they do give us a sense for the overall structure of Calvin's theology as it is summarized in his *Institutes*, and they help us understand the interpretive context for Calvin's exposition. Though Calvin discusses the last two articles of the creed in chapter 25, at the end of book 3, before taking up the topic of the church in book 4 (reversing the sequence of the creed's final articles), he clearly understands the topics he considers in book 3 to anticipate the doctrine of the church. Only within the society of the church does Christ unite believers to himself by his Spirit and word and grant them full participation in all the saving benefits of his mediation.

It is not difficult to discern the significance of this location for Calvin's treatment of the resurrection of the body and the life everlasting. The redemptive work of Christ as mediator is imparted to believers by the ministry of the Holy Spirit, who unites believers to Christ and

---

20. Richard A. Muller suggests that the structure of Calvin's *Institutes* reflects a variety of factors, including Philipp Melanchthon's *Loci Communes*, which follows the outline of Paul's letter to the Romans, and Calvin's exegetical commentaries. *The Unaccommodated Calvin: Studies in the Foundation of a Theological Tradition*, OSHT (New York: Oxford University Press, 2000), 118–39.

grants them all the benefits of redemption. Through union with Christ, believers enjoy a double benefit: free justification or acceptance with God and the renewal of their lives in conformity to the image of God. The purpose of God the Father in redemption is to restore believers to acceptance, and to conform them to the image of Christ in true knowledge, righteousness, and holiness. The work of the triune Creator and Redeemer aims to bring to glory those who are united to Christ and to restore the brokenness and disorder of sin in human life. Calvin's treatment of the resurrection of the body and the life everlasting represents, accordingly, the goal of the believer's union with Christ. In union with Christ, believers are justified, sanctified, and ultimately glorified. Considering the location of chapter 25 in the *Institutes*, it might well be titled "The Believer's Glorification in Union with Christ." The glorification of believers concludes the gracious work of God that has already begun through faith-union with Christ. The "already" of gospel blessings in the present carries with it, according to Calvin, the sure promise of the "not yet" of the full disclosure and realization of these blessings in the life to come.

Future Individual Eschatology: The Intermediate State

In traditional discussions of eschatology, it is customary to divide future eschatology into two parts. The first part focuses on individual eschatology, especially what is commonly termed the "intermediate state." The intermediate state refers to what becomes of believers between their death and their resurrection. The second part focuses on general eschatology, namely, what will occur in the period prior to Christ's second advent and in conjunction with the final judgment. The remainder of this treatment of Calvin's eschatology summarizes his teaching in these areas, particularly his discussion of these topics in *Institutes* 3.25.

In the course of Calvin's discussion of the resurrection of the body in *Institutes* 3.25, he takes up the topic of the intermediate state in connection with two errors that are taught by those whom Calvin calls "perversely curious men."[21] The first of these errors is the claim that

---

21. *Institutes*, 3.25.6.

the soul of man dies with the body or falls asleep during the intermediate state, only to be resurrected at the last day. The second is the claim that the resurrection bodies of believers are radically new, not renewed and glorified bodies.

Calvin begins his comment on the error of those who deny an intermediate state by noting that he has earlier addressed the subject of the distinction between the soul and the body in his treatment of the doctrine of creation.[22] Though he does not explicitly refer to his early treatise *Psychopannychia*, which constitutes a more extensive refutation of the doctrine of "soul sleep," he offers a short summary of its argument.[23] Those who deny an intermediate state, teaching that the soul dies with the body or falls asleep prior to the resurrection, fail to distinguish between the soul and the body and deny the truth that the soul is "that part of us in which the divine especially shines, and in which there are such clear tokens of immortality."[24] They also fail to acknowledge the clear scriptural teaching of a conscious intermediate state in which believers enjoy communion with Christ in the period between death and resurrection.[25] Admittedly, we are not free to speculate about the nature of the soul's intermediate state, as some have done in the history of Christian theology. But we must affirm what the Scriptures teach without inquiring "too curiously" beyond its boundaries.[26]

Among students of Calvin's eschatology, some allege that his view of the intermediate state betrays an unbiblical overemphasis on individual, in distinction from cosmic, eschatology. Since Calvin's conception of the intermediate state depends on his doctrine of the "immortality of the soul," Calvin's eschatology at this juncture is said to owe as much to the influence of Greek philosophy as to biblical

---

22. See *Institutes*, 1.5.5; 1.15.
23. For a critical edition of this work, which was published first in 1542 and then in a revised edition in 1545, see John Calvin, *Psychopannychia*, ed. Walther Zimmerli (Leipzig: A Deichertsche Verlagsbuchhandlung, 1932). An English translation by Henry Beveridge is provided in *Tracts and Treatises*, 3:413–90.
24. *Institutes*, 3.25.6.
25. Calvin's understanding of the intermediate state excludes the Roman Catholic dogma of purgatory. According to Calvin, the dogma of purgatory has no scriptural warrant and belies the believer's union with Christ, whose atoning death fully satisfies the eternal and temporal penalty of the sins of his people. For Calvin's evaluation of this dogma, see *Institutes*, 3.5.6–10; *Canons and Decrees of the Council of Trent, with the Antidote*, in *Tracts and Treatises*, 3:160–61.
26. *Institutes*, 3.25.6.

revelation—or even more so. Despite Calvin's insistence that Christian theology must avoid speculation and remain within the limits of scriptural revelation, his doctrine of the intermediate state departs from his own strictures regarding how a true knowledge of God and ourselves is to be achieved. Rather than echoing the scriptural emphasis on the resurrection of the body as the primary promise for the believer's future in union with Christ, Calvin is criticized for placing an undue emphasis on the immortality of the soul and disparaging the body as a kind of "prison house" of the soul.

An examination of Calvin's teaching in the area of anthropology confirms that he does insist on a sharp distinction between the soul and the body, and he ascribes a kind of preeminence to the soul.[27] When Calvin treats the subject of human nature as it was created by God, he notes that "man consists of a soul and a body" and defines the soul as "an immortal, yet created essence."[28] The soul is said to indwell the body as a kind of "house," and death is described as release of the soul from the "prison house of the body."[29] While Calvin acknowledges that all man's faculties and gifts, both of the soul and of the body, belong to man's creaturely integrity as God first created him, he also maintains that the soul is the "principal" part of the human constitution and the "proper seat" of the image of God.[30] He even acknowledges that, with respect to our understanding of the soul, Plato alone among the philosophers had a keen understanding of its "immortal substance."[31] In his treatment of the intermediate state, Calvin appeals to the distinction between the soul and the body to undergird his opposition to the "soul sleep" and mortalism views that were taught in the history of the church and by some of his contemporaries. Death brings about a separation between the body and the soul, and the soul of the believer continues to enjoy conscious fellowship with Christ until the general resurrection at the last day.

---

27. For a general discussion of Calvin's teaching regarding the soul, see Quistorp, *Calvin's Doctrine*, 55–107.

28. *Institutes*, 1.15.2.

29. *Institutes*, 1.15.2. Calvin uses the language of the body as a "prison house" in his *Psychopannychia*: "If the body is the prison of the soul, if the earthly habitation is a kind of fetters, what is the state of the soul when set free from this prison, when loosed from these fetters?" In *Tracts and Treatises*, 3:443.

30. *Institutes*, 1.15.3.

31. *Institutes*, 1.15.6.

Though there may be some incidental, unbiblical notes in Calvin's treatment of the distinction between the soul and the body, critics of Calvin's view need to put in proper perspective his understanding of this distinction. Calvin's distinction between the body and the soul is one that is expressly drawn in the Scriptures, and it is to the Scriptures that Calvin ultimately appeals in arguing for a conscious intermediate state. An important part of Calvin's argument is that the doctrines of "soul sleep" and mortalism are in conflict with the scriptural assurances that even death cannot separate believers from Christ. Calvin's disparaging use of the language of the body as a kind of "prison house" for the soul is mitigated by a number of clear themes in his theology. The whole of man's constitution in the state of integrity—soul and body—owes its existence to God's work of creation. For Calvin, this is a basic assumption that undergirds the biblical hope for the resurrection of the body. In his affirmation of the resurrection of the body, Calvin carefully distinguishes between sin and its consequences, which are accidental features of man's nature, and the original goodness of man's creatureliness, which will be restored—even surpassed—in the future state of glory. Calvin's eschatology includes a clear affirmation of the renewal and restoration of the fullness of the believer's creaturely constitution, body and soul. Therefore, it is incorrect to argue that Calvin's teaching regarding the intermediate state commits him to an individualistic eschatology that terminates upon the soul's communion with Christ and largely overlooks the biblical themes of the resurrection of the body and the renewal of the created cosmos.

Calvin's response to the second of these errors—that the bodies of the saints are altogether new and not the glorified form of their present bodies—is drawn largely from his letter to Laelius Socinus written in June 1549. This error, reminiscent of the ancient error of the Manichaeans, who disparaged the body and earthly existence, fails to acknowledge that believers—as members of Christ—will enjoy the same resurrection and glorification he enjoyed. The resurrection of the body does not promise the bestowal of another body but rather the renewal and glorification of the present body. In an important statement, which provides a general principle regarding the relation between creation and redemption, Calvin notes that "if death, which takes its origin from the fall of man, is accidental, the restoration which Christ has brought belongs to that self-same body which began to be mortal."[32] The corruption and weakness of the flesh is an adventitious or accidental quality that does not belong intrinsically to the body as God first created it.[33] Redemption restores what sin has corrupted and deformed, but it does not displace what God created good. Consequently, Calvin insists that there is a continuity between the present body and the resurrected body, though he simultaneously insists on the discontinuity that is due to the glorification of the believer's body in union with Christ.

Future General Eschatology

Those who criticize Calvin's eschatology as too "individualistic" tend to neglect the broader themes of his general eschatology. In his treatment of the last things in *Institutes* 3.25, Calvin clearly places the promise of the future in Christ in a broader framework than individual eschatology alone. He gives particular attention to the resurrection of the body and in this context also addresses the final state that awaits believers and unbelievers. Calvin's handling of these topics illustrates not only the breadth of his eschatology but also the comprehensive scope of God's saving work in Christ, which will ultimately issue in nothing less than the restoration of all things.

The "Signs of the Times" and Christ's Second Advent

Before turning to Calvin's understanding of the resurrection of the body and the restoration of all things in the final state, it is necessary to note how Calvin views the course of history prior to the return of Christ. Consistent with the pattern of traditional Christianity, Calvin teaches that the second advent of Christ is the great future event that will mark the conclusion of God's redemptive work in history. Though Calvin vigorously opposes any attempt to date the time of Christ's return, he does discuss how history will unfold in the period between Christ's first and second coming.

---

32. *Institutes*, 3.25.7.
33. See *Institutes*, 3.28.8: "As to substance . . . we shall be raised again in the same flesh we now bear, but . . . the quality will be different."

Calvin's understanding of the character of interadvental history is illustrated by his treatment of biblical passages that speak of the so-called signs of the times. In his handling of these passages, Calvin consistently rejects any attempt to determine the time of Christ's return. In his extensive comments on Matthew 24, which describes the events that will occur in conjunction with the destruction of the temple in Jerusalem and prior to Christ's coming, Calvin follows the pattern identified in his interpretation of the biblical prophecy of Daniel. According to Calvin, Christ's words in this passage describe not only events that coincide with his first coming, including the destruction of the temple, but also the entire period from the time of his first coming until the end of the present age. The interpretation of Christ's words in this passage requires an acknowledgment that its prophecy will be fulfilled at earlier and later points in the course of redemptive history.

In his opening comments on Matthew 24, Calvin notes that the disciples' response to Christ's prophecy of the destruction of the temple in Jerusalem reveals that "they link the coming of Christ and the end of the world with the overthrow of the temple as inseparable events: and they understand the end of the world to mean the restoration of all things so that nothing may be lacking to complete the happiness of the godly."[34] The disciples' questions about the destruction of the temple and the consummation of the age illustrate that they confused the "completeness of Christ's kingdom with its beginning."[35] Christian believers, who recognize in Christ's coming the beginning of the fulfillment of God's promises under the law, know that Christ's kingdom is a "spiritual" kingdom and that it will come only by way of the preaching of the gospel to the nations over an extended period of time. All the signs that Christ enumerates in the opening verses of this passage—wars and rumors of wars, pestilences, famines, earthquakes—will characterize the entire period of history between the time of Christ's first and second advent. Calvin interprets Christ's discourse in Matthew 24, therefore, at least in its first part (24:3–14) to offer a portrait of the struggle that will occur between his kingdom and the kingdom of Satan until he returns at the end of the age. Meanwhile, as

---

34. Calvin, comm. on Matt. 24:3, in *CNTC*, 3:75.
35. Calvin, comm. on Matt. 24:3, in *CNTC*, 3:76.

the gospel is preached to the nations, the church will undergo "a long and sad epic of woes," which will test the allegiance of believers and their steadfastness in obedience to Christ.[36] Though Christ prepares his disciples in this part of the discourse for the tribulation that the church will have to endure until the end of the age, he distinguishes between the impending destruction of the temple in Jerusalem, which occurred in AD 70, and the lengthy period of the church's testing that will endure until he comes at a time that no one may determine.

While Calvin interprets the first part of the discourse in Matthew 24 as a description of the entire interadvental period, he interprets the second part of the discourse—24:15–28—as a prophecy of the imminent destruction of the temple in Jerusalem. Though Calvin does not use the terms, his interpretation of Matthew 24 includes "futurist" and "preterist" elements. Since Christ disconnects the events of the temple's destruction in AD 70 and the consummation of the age at his second coming, Calvin regards some of the discourse to describe the entire period of history during which the gospel is being preached to the nations and some to predict the event of the temple's destruction under Titus and his legions in AD 70. Calvin also observes that in this section of Matthew 24, Christ appeals to the prophecy of Daniel regarding the "abomination of desolation." For Calvin, Daniel's prophecy was first fulfilled in Antiochus IV Epiphanes's desecration of the temple in Jerusalem in 168 BC, but it will receive further fulfillment in the impending destruction of the temple in AD 70. The earlier destruction of the temple by Antiochus was, in this respect, a "type" of the subsequent destruction of the temple by Titus.

Calvin's interpretation of the next, and most difficult, part of the discourse, Matthew 24:29–36, illustrates his Christological interpretation of biblical prophecy. Though a number of interpreters appeal to the language of 24:34—"Truly, I say to you, this generation will not pass away until all these things take place"—to maintain that all the events described in the discourse to this point were predicted to occur during the lifetime of Jesus's contemporaries, Calvin takes a more nuanced approach. In Calvin's reading of these verses, the events that were to occur at the destruction of the temple in Jerusalem are

---

36. Calvin, comm. on Matt. 24:14, in *CNTC*, 3:83.

"typical" of the present age and will recur throughout subsequent history until the great event of Christ's coming at the end of the age. The language that Christ employs to describe his coming requires, according to Calvin, understanding it as a description of the great day of the Lord at the consummation of the present period of history. When Christ says that "all these things [will] take place" during the time of the generation to whom he first spoke the words of Matthew 24, he means to refer to those events that are associated with the destruction of the temple. Throughout the discourse, however, and again in 24:36, which declares that "concerning that day and hour no one knows, not even the angels of heaven, nor the Son, but the Father only," Christ is also responding to that part of the disciples' question relating to the consummation of the age. Here Christ teaches, according to Calvin, that the present period of history will be a protracted one, during which the gospel of Christ's kingdom will be preached to the whole world. Though no one is able to know the day or the hour of Christ's coming, his return is certain and will mark the end of the church's tribulation during this present age. To use modern terms, Calvin is neither a "postmillennialist" nor a "full preterist" in his treatment of the "signs of the times." It would be more correct to describe him as "eclectic," acknowledging past, present, and future dimensions to these signs.

The Antichrist

Calvin's understanding of the "signs of the times" provides an appropriate setting for a brief comment on a well-known aspect of Calvin's eschatology: the coming of the "antichrist." An especially important passage for Calvin's interpretation of Christ's coming and the events that will precede it is 2 Thessalonians 2. In his exposition of this passage, which speaks of a future period of apostasy and lawlessness as well as the appearance of the "man of lawlessness" (2:3), Calvin places it in the broad context of the conflict in history between the kingdom of Christ and the kingdom of the "antichrist." Though he refuses to use this passage as a basis for determining a timetable regarding future events, Calvin regards its depiction of apostasy and the emergence of the antichrist as a description of a falling away that will occur among the people of God, the church, prior to the return of Christ. Unlike many of his medieval predecessors, Calvin does not identify "that which restrains" such apostasy with the Roman Empire. Rather, he identifies the present restraint of apostasy and lawlessness with the work of Christ through the preaching of his word in the power of the Holy Spirit.

One feature of his interpretation of this passage is well known and of particular significance: his identification of the "man of lawlessness" with the papacy.[37] According to Calvin, this mysterious figure represents the spirit of opposition to Christ's kingdom and gospel that has come to expression in the papacy. Although Calvin shared this view with many of his Reformation contemporaries, he stopped short of identifying this mysterious figure with any particular pope or using it to ascertain whether the return of Christ was imminent at the time of the Reformation. Even the language in this passage regarding Christ's return may not be restricted to his second advent, since "Paul does not think that Christ will accomplish this in a single moment."[38]

The Millennium

One of the more controversial topics in Christian eschatology is the subject of the millennium, the one-thousand-year period of Christ's reign with his saints described in Revelation 20:1–6. Since Calvin never wrote a commentary on the book of Revelation, his view of the millennium needs to be gleaned from occasional references throughout his writings. Calvin does, however, comment on the subject of the millennium in *Institutes* 3.25. There he refers to the millennium in his consideration of several errors pertaining to the doctrine of the resurrection.

It is noteworthy that Calvin regards *chiliasm*, which limits the reign of Christ on earth to a future period of one thousand years, to be a serious error.[39] In his refutation of this particular error, Calvin notes that it has been present throughout the history of the church from the

---

37. Calvin, comm. on 2 Thess. 2:3, in *CNTC*, 8:399. For a summary of Calvin's argument for identifying the antichrist with the institution of the papacy, see *Institutes*, 4.7.

38. Calvin, comm. on 2 Thess. 2:8, in *CNTC*, 8:404.

39. *Institutes*, 3.25.5. For general treatments of Calvin's criticism of chiliasm, see Quistorp, *Calvin's Doctrine*, 158–62; Davis, "New Assessment," 240–47.

time of the apostles. The appeal to Revelation 20 on the part of the chiliasts is only a "pretext," however, since the language of "one thousand" does not "apply to the eternal blessedness of the church but only to the various disturbances that awaited the church, while still toiling on earth."[40] The principal objection that Calvin raises to the teaching of chiliasm is that it limits the "inheritance of the life to come" in the kingdom of God to a period of one thousand years. Such a restriction in the temporal duration and blessedness of Christ's future kingdom casts "reproach upon Christ" and fails utterly to do justice to the biblical teaching regarding the perpetuity of Christ's kingdom in its consummation.[41] Among contemporary advocates of such chiliasm in Calvin's day, some deny the doctrine of eternal punishment of the wicked, arguing that such punishment would be excessive when compared to the temporal nature of human sin. In his refutation of this objection, Calvin notes that it fails to reckon with the truth of God's majesty and justice, which are too little esteemed.[42]

The pattern of interpretation that marks Calvin's comments on the book of Daniel is evident in the way he treats the topic of the millennium. Calvin rejects chiliasm, or the teaching of a future one-thousand-year reign of Christ on the earth, as a childish "fiction" hardly requiring refutation.[43] In Calvin's eschatology, the idea of a future reign of Christ on the earth militates against some of the most fundamental features of his understanding of the kingdom of God and the realization of that kingdom in the course of redemptive history. The kingdom of God is not simply a future period but a present reality that commenced with the first advent of Christ—itself a fulfillment of a long period of "preparation" under the administration of the old

---

40. *Institutes*, 3.25.5.

41. *Institutes*, 3.25.5.

42. *Institutes*, 3.25.5. Among his contemporaries, a number of Anabaptists may have taught the views Calvin is here condemning, for example, Hans Denck, Balthasar Hubmaier, Sebastian Franck, and Melchior Hoffman.

43. For a similar assessment, cf. Calvin, comm. on Dan. 7:27. In his rejection of chiliasm, Calvin regards it as a peculiar "Jewish" heresy. This opinion was generally shared by the other Reformers, including Heinrich Bullinger, who, in the Second Helvetic Confession 11.14, wrote, "We further condemn Jewish dreams that there will be a golden age on earth before the Day of Judgment, and that the pious, having subdued all their godless enemies, will possess all the kingdoms of the earth." Calvin's opposition to chiliasm places him in a long tradition of interpretation of Revelation, which was represented among the church fathers by Tyconius and Augustine. For a treatment of the influence of Augustine and Tyconius on Calvin's interpretation of Rev. 20, see Davis, "New Assessment," 28–57.

covenant. This kingdom, which not only spans the period between the first and second advents of Christ but also includes the glorious future of consummate blessedness, cannot be restricted in temporal duration to a period of one thousand years. Furthermore, this kingdom is a "spiritual" kingdom whose coming and ultimate realization will transpire through the proclamation of the gospel of Christ and the work of the Holy Spirit. Though Calvin does not identify the kingdom exclusively with the church, he insists that the church is the principal instrument that Christ uses to effect God's purposes for redemption. Since the ultimate achievement of God's redemptive purposes entails no less than the renewal and renovation of the whole created order, Calvin regards chiliasm in all its forms to be subeschatological. Such a one-thousand-year reign of Christ would represent a kind of "in-between kingdom" that fails to acknowledge the reality of Christ's present kingship or the perfected glory of the future consummation of the kingdom.

The Resurrection of the Body

The primary focus of Calvin's treatment of eschatology in *Institutes* 3.25 is on the resurrection of the body. Calvin begins by noting the importance of the hope of the resurrection for the entirety of the Christian life. Echoing themes that he emphasized in his treatise on the Christian life (in *Institutes* 3.6–10) and his prior description of redemption through union with Christ, Calvin insists that believers must always cling to Christ in hope. The expectation of believers for the fullness of redemption in union with Christ will not be fulfilled in this life and world. Rather, believers must walk with their "minds lifted up to heaven," pressing onward toward the hope of their calling in Christ. Employing language reminiscent of his description of the Christian pilgrimage as a "meditation upon the future life," Calvin notes that "he alone has fully profited in the gospel who has accustomed himself to continual meditation upon the blessed resurrection." Even though Plato enjoys the distinction of having recognized that "man's highest good . . . is union with God," none of the ancient philosophers understood that the achievement of this good depends on the "sacred bond" of union with Christ. Only in Christ, whose resurrection from the dead is "already completed," do believers have the promise of the fullness of redemption. The life of the Christian is one of hope, a continual anticipation of the day of Christ's coming when Christ's work already begun in the believer will reach "its completion."[44]

In the remainder of his treatment of the resurrection of the body, Calvin appeals to two grounds for the believer's confidence and hope. The first is Christ's resurrection, which constitutes a type of the believer's resurrection. The second is the power of God. Because many philosophers had no knowledge of Christ, they were able to teach the immortality of the soul but were unable to affirm the resurrection of the flesh. On the principle that believers through union with Christ have a full participation in all that is his, we may be confident that the Holy Spirit will "quicken" believers in union with him.[45] Even though the prospect of the believer's resurrection in union with Christ exceeds the ordinary "course of nature," it does not exceed the greatness and power of God, who is able to grant life from the dead and ensure the believer's inheritance in Christ.

Calvin begins and ends his consideration of various objections to the doctrine of the resurrection by noting that a denial of the resurrection is common within paganism—and even at times among the people of God (cf. the Sadducees). This denial, however, is refuted by the ancient practice of burial, which is before the eyes of all men a kind of "earnest of new life."[46] The meticulous care that is devoted to the preparation of bodies for burial is a testimony to the expectation of resurrection and new life. Indeed, the etymology of the word *cemetery* suggests that it is a "sleeping place," which is a kind of anteroom for the body as believers await the resurrection of the last day.

In a brief concluding section of this part of *Institutes* 3.25, Calvin addresses a question that often arises in discussions of the resurrection of believers: What about the resurrection of the ungodly? To speak of the resurrection of believers and unbelievers, Calvin observes, seems to suggest that the resurrection is a sort of common benefit of Christ's work that accrues to both. In his reply to this question, Calvin argues that there is a radical difference between these resurrections. The res-

---

44. *Institutes*, 3.25.2.
45. *Institutes*, 3.25.3.
46. *Institutes*, 3.25.5.

urrection of the ungodly is not, strictly speaking, a benefit of Christ's redemptive mediation. It is rather a "resurrection of judgment," which manifests the power, justice, and prerogatives of Christ as the one whom the Father has appointed as the Judge of all flesh.[47] This resurrection is an "incidental resurrection of the wicked, in which they will be unwillingly haled before the judgment seat of Christ."[48] Most often, however, when the Scriptures speak of the resurrection, they mean to refer to the heavenly glory that will properly belong to those who are members of Christ. Since Christ came "properly not for the destruction of the world but for its salvation," this is the chief emphasis to be found in the word of God.[49]

The Life Everlasting and the Consummation of All Things

Calvin's concluding observations on the life everlasting in *Institutes* 3.25 emphasizes the fruitlessness of undue speculation about the final state. Calvin affirms that the final state will be one "filled with splendor, joy, happiness, and glory."[50] But he insists that these things are so far removed from our present perception as to remain largely hidden from us. Believers will enjoy the most intimate communion with God, which is the highest blessedness and joy. Yet Calvin strongly cautions his reader to "keep sobriety, lest forgetful of our limitations we should soar aloft with the greater boldness, and be overcome by the brightness of the heavenly glory."[51] In this connection, Calvin indirectly criticizes the discussions among many medieval theologians that amount to little more than "dangerous speculations" that exceed the limits of God's word.[52]

One question that he does acknowledge to be legitimate regards diversity of rewards in the kingdom of God. In addition to the gift of eternal life, which will be the common inheritance of all believers, God will variously distribute particular gifts to his servants to acknowledge their service in his name. In a final section on the future of the reprobate, Calvin exhibits similar restraint. Though we must

---

47. *Institutes*, 3.25.9.
48. *Institutes*, 3.25.9.
49. *Institutes*, 3.25.9.
50. *Institutes*, 3.25.10.
51. *Institutes*, 3.25.10.
52. *Institutes*, 3.25.10.

affirm the scriptural teaching of the doctrine of eternal punishment, we must also recognize that the biblical descriptions of hell use "physical metaphors" that should not be pressed unduly. The focus of our understanding, so far as the doctrine of hell is concerned, should be on what it means to be "cut off from all fellowship with God."[53]

With these comments on the final state of believers and unbelievers, Calvin concludes his treatment of the last things in his *Institutes*. We would be remiss, however, not to add a few comments on Calvin's broader conception of the final state and the consummation of all things. Recent students of Calvin's theology sometimes refer to what is termed the "extra" dimension of Calvin's theology.[54] This language means to call attention to the way Calvin distinguishes between Christ's work as mediator of creation and his work as mediator of redemption. Contrary to the neoorthodox interpretation that governed Calvin studies in the early and mid-twentieth century, more recent studies of Calvin's theology have noted the importance of Calvin's distinction between the knowledge of God as Creator and that of God as Redeemer. The presupposition for Calvin's treatment of redemption in Christ is the biblical doctrine of the creation and ordering of all things by the Word and Spirit of God. According to Calvin, the knowledge of God as Redeemer can be understood only within the framework of the doctrine of creation. The eternal Son through whom all things were made is the one through whom all things are being redeemed. Redemption, accordingly, amounts to nothing less than the restoration of all things to proper order through the mediation of Christ and the work of his Spirit.

Because Christ is the mediator of creation and redemption, Calvin views the first advent of Christ as a decisive moment in the realization of God's redemptive purposes. With Christ's coming, the promises of the old covenant are being fulfilled, and the purpose of God to renew all things has commenced. In describing the significance of Christ's coming and his saving work, Calvin is fond of speaking of

---

53. *Institutes*, 3.25.12.
54. See Heiko A. Oberman, "The 'Extra' Dimension in the Theology of Calvin," *JEH* 21, no. 1 (1970): 43–64. By the "extra" dimension of Calvin's theology, Oberman means to refer to the "mutuality" and "discontinuity" (48) between the created order and redemption in the work and purposes of God.

the comprehensive purpose of God as a "restoration" of all things to "proper order." In his commentary on John 13:31, Calvin offers a comprehensive statement of the purpose of Christ's advent and crucifixion:

> For in the cross of Christ, as in a splendid theatre, the incomparable goodness of God is set before the whole world. The glory of God shines, indeed, in all creatures on high and below, but never more brightly than in the cross, in which there was a wonderful change of things—the condemnation of all men was manifested, sin blotted out, salvation restored to men; in short, the whole world was renewed and all things restored to order.[55]

Calvin uses similar language in his comments on John 12:31:

> The word *judgment* is taken as "reformation" by some and "condemnation" by others. I agree rather with the former, who expound it that the world must be restored to due order. For the Hebrew word *mishpat* which is translated as *judgment* means a well-ordered constitution. Now we know that outside Christ there is nothing but confusion in the world. And although Christ had already begun to set up the kingdom of God, it was His death that was the true beginning of a properly-ordered state and the complete restoration of the world.[56]

In these and similar statements, Calvin clearly views the work of Christ as issuing in nothing less than the renovation of the whole creation, a reversal of the consequence of human sin and disobedience. In his "threefold office" as prophet, priest, and king, Christ reveals the fullness of the word of God, reconciles a new humanity to God, and by means of the "scepter of his kingdom," subdues all things to new obedience.[57] Calvin's conception of the person and work of Christ, accordingly, represents a compelling eschatological vision in which the whole course of history is brought to its appointed end—the renewal of the fallen creation in service to the triune God.

---

55. Calvin, comm. on John 13:31, in *CNTC*, 5:68.
56. Calvin, comm. on John 12:31, in *CNTC*, 5:42. See also comm. on Isa. 65:25, in *Calvin's Commentary*, 8:405–6; comm. on 2 Thess. 1:5, in *CNTC*, 8:388–90.
57. Calvin, comm. on Hos. 1:11.

Conclusion

Even though this summary of Calvin's eschatology has touched on a wide diversity of topics, it remains in some respects only an overview of Calvin's understanding of the last things. There are three features of Calvin's view that are of special significance in considering his eschatology and its contribution to the church's present understanding of the last things.

First, Calvin's most important contribution to the church's contemporary reflection on the doctrine of the last things lies in his approach to the interpretation of biblical revelation. Unlike the highly sensational and often speculative approach of many in the history of the church, especially in the last century, Calvin carefully seeks to stay within the boundaries of the Scriptures. He consistently refuses to attempt dating the time of Christ's return. Though the sixteenth-century Reformation witnessed a number of apocalyptic movements and predictions of the imminent return of Christ, Calvin avoids every form of excessive curiosity about the future. Only God knows the future, and he has been pleased to make known the main lines of what will transpire prior to Christ's return. In Calvin's handling of eschatology, he exhibits an extraordinary reserve, which stands as a model for believers today. What the Spirit of Christ has revealed to the church must be affirmed by faith, but we must respect the limits of what the Spirit has chosen to leave unrevealed.

Second, in the area of eschatology, Calvin's focus is always on the person and work of Christ. In his interpretation of biblical prophecy, Calvin reads the Old Testament as a history of the Lord's covenantal favor toward his people. This history points to and finds its focus in the coming of Christ in the fullness of time. Christ is the key who unlocks the Scriptures' meaning—past, present, and future. With the coming of Christ in the fullness of time, all the promises of the old covenant are fulfilled. And yet what God has commenced to do in Christ to establish his everlasting kingdom is itself a pledge of what remains. Believers embrace Christ, as Calvin so beautifully expresses it, "clad in his own promises."[58] The great benefits of salvation through union

---

58. *Institutes*, 2.9.3.

with Christ—free justification before God and the sanctification of the Holy Spirit—are promissory of the believer's future glorification. Through faith alone, believers have the forgiveness of sins through Christ and know that "there is therefore now no condemnation for those who are in Christ Jesus" (Rom. 8:1). The future verdict, which will be publicly revealed in the day of judgment, is already sealed to the believer. Furthermore, the Spirit of Christ has begun the work of regeneration or sanctification, which involves the restoration of believers in the image of God and in conformity to Christ in true knowledge, righteousness, and holiness. Though believers are not perfected in this life, they eagerly anticipate the completion of this work of God's grace in them by the Spirit. The future of the believer in union with Christ is bright with promise and expectation. The Christ-centeredness of Calvin's eschatology is also evident in the way he emphasizes the theme of "meditation on the future life." The life of the believer is a pilgrimage that will lead to the promised land of rest in Christ in the final state of glory. Through faith-union with Christ, all the benefits of redemption are secure—not only free acceptance and renewal by the Spirit of Christ but also the resurrection of the body and the renewal of all things.

And third, contrary to the claims of some students of Calvin's theology, the scope of Calvin's view of the future is as wide as creation and as long as the panorama of history from creation to consummation. It is of no small importance to Calvin's eschatology that he insists on a "twofold knowledge of God" that encompasses creation and redemption. The ultimate goal of all history and the saving work of the mediator, Jesus Christ, who is also the mediator of creation, is to restore all things "to proper order."[59] All things are of, from, and unto the praise of God the Father, the Son, and the Holy Spirit. This great theme of *soli Deo Gloria* governs Calvin's theology generally and his eschatology particularly. When the great saving purposes of God in Christ are consummated, according to Calvin, the company of all the elect will be gathered before the presence of God. They will be gathered in the context of the coming of a new heavens and earth, wherein righteousness dwells. The wicked and persistently unbelieving

---

59. Calvin, comm. on Isa. 35:1.

will be cut off from God's blessed presence. The righteous, who have clung to Christ by faith, will enjoy the blessedness of unbroken fellowship with God. Heaven and earth will be reconciled. Sin and its consequences will be utterly eradicated. All things will be made new.

Though Calvin's eschatology may require refinement here or there, it expresses some of the most basic themes of the historic, orthodox Christian faith. For this reason, in this area, as well as in so many others, Calvin remains a reliable interpreter of the Scriptures for the benefit of the church of Jesus Christ.

Afterword

R. C. Sproul

John Calvin was a Gulliver in the land of Lilliputians, a titan in the midst of dwarfs. He stands head and shoulders above the rank and file of theologians, scholars, and biblical experts down through the ages. He abides in the elite company of men like Saint Augustine, Thomas Aquinas, Martin Luther, and Jonathan Edwards. As Aristotle received the epithet "the philosopher," so Calvin received a similar sobriquet from Philipp Melanchthon, who referred to Calvin simply as "the theologian."

When we examine the lives and work of the great theologians of Christian history, we notice a certain sameness in the emphasis they bring in their teaching. They were all driven to their knees with a sense of wondrous awe for the majesty of God. Yet they expressed themselves in different ways with different styles and aptitudes. Augustine was a genius with respect to a philosophical understanding of theology, and he probed the depths of the metaphysical basis for the Christian faith. Thomas Aquinas shared that philosophical bent but was more concerned with bringing to pass a systematic summary of the whole scope of Christian doctrine. Luther was a man of profound insight; he was neither a philosopher nor a systematician but rather one who seized on world-changing vignettes of insight. But John Calvin stands alone in church history as the master of systematizing biblical truth with doctrine. He was driven by a desire to interpret all the details of biblical revelation. Rarely, if ever, have we found a systematic theologian so well versed in the data of Sacred Scripture as we find in Calvin. Able to quote lengthy passages of the Bible with one breath, followed by a considerable recitation by memory from the writings of Saint Augustine, Calvin mixed his mastery of linguistics with his heart set on fire by the word of God.

Calvin's place in history is not without irony. It is interesting that as he completed his theological studies at the University of Paris, Ignatius of Loyola began his education at the university. Who would imagine that these two individuals would become representatives for two traditions engaged in one of the most important theological clashes to mark all church history—the clash of Reformation thought with that of Roman Catholic thought as developed by Loyola in his formation of the Society of Jesus, known for producing the most prodigious scholars of the Roman Catholic Church. Whereas most theologians have the initials PhD or ThD after their name, those who were schooled in the society founded by Loyola have the letters SJ appended to their names, indicating their membership in the Jesuit order.

In the Reformation itself, it was Luther who was the pioneer in the efforts to recover the doctrine of justification by faith alone. That doctrine was obscured in medieval theology, and the gospel itself was plunged into darkness. Calvin shared the zeal of Luther for that central doctrine of the faith, calling it the "hinge on which religion turns." Calvin's grand passion, however, went beyond his commitment to the doctrine of justification by faith alone to a captivating zeal to guard the church against the encroachment of idolatry in manifold forms. It was Calvin who said that by nature, we as fallen human beings are *fabricum idolarum*, or "idol factories." Our propensity to exchange the truth of God for a lie and serve the creature rather than the Creator has turned us into veritable idol factories, in which we mass-produce these hellish substitutes for the glory of God. Calvin desired to remove all vestiges of idolatry from the practice of the church. By his own admission, he called for a strict limitation of certain elements of worship that in and of themselves weren't necessarily idolatrous. But because they had been so often associated with practices that did degenerate into idolatry, Calvin thought it necessary to make worship simple and free from any hint of liturgy that might bring in its wake a renewed commitment to idolatrous practices and set misguiding examples for future generations.

His own passion for preaching and teaching saw him in indefatigable energy mounting the platform to preach and to teach a multitude of times each week in Geneva. The academy he founded there was an institution that would enrich the life of the church for generations to come, as such successors to Calvin as Theodore Beza and Francis Turretin further refined the specifics of Calvin's teaching. Geneva became a refuge for those who were persecuted throughout Europe. Those fleeing from Queen Mary Tudor's persecution in England came to Geneva, where they, under Calvin's tutelage, accomplished the translation of the Bible into English with study notes. This was the Geneva Bible, which was the dominant English Bible for a hundred years. It was the Bible of Shakespeare and the Bible the Pilgrims brought to the shores of America. Among those refugees studying at the feet of Calvin was an ex–galley slave by the name of John Knox, who took the teaching he learned there back to his native Scotland, where he was used of God to pioneer the Scottish Reformation.

Looking at Calvin's role in church history, we notice that no theologian seems to be so vilified, so hated, so caricatured as John Calvin. Because of people's basic indisposition to the doctrines of grace in general and the doctrine of predestination in particular, Calvin is regarded as the dour, mean-spirited creator of the concept of the horrible decrees of election and reprobation. The irony is that there's nothing in Calvin on these doctrines that was not first in Luther, nothing in Luther's doctrine of election that was not first in Augustine, nothing in Augustine's teaching on the matter that was not first in Paul, and, of course, nothing in Paul's teaching on the doctrines of grace that was not first expounded by the Lord Jesus himself. Lutherans modified the doctrines of Luther after his death, but these modifications did not affect the Swiss arm of the Reformation, and Calvin's teaching became seen as the only branch of Christendom that taught these great doctrines.

The general ignorance that the church suffers from in church history has cost the church an accurate appreciation for how God used this man of Geneva. Would that the preachers of our day might learn from Calvin in his biblical exposition and in his passion for biblical truth, that the church could once again experience the breakthrough of a modern Reformation. In our day, as it did in antiquity, and again in the sixteenth century, the church stands between Migdol and the sea. Behind us, pursuing us to the death, are the chariots of Pharaoh, hostile to the things of God, motivated to destroy them from the earth. In front of us stands the impassable sea. We need a Moses. We need a Calvin, who in this generation will raise his arms to the heavens, so that the Lord God Almighty will open the seas afresh that the people of God may pass through on dry ground into safety. Our debt to John Calvin is considerable. We must be mindful of his work, as God continues to use Calvin's teaching to lead the church to truth and out of the abyss of error.

Appendix

Reading Calvin and His Interpreters

John W. Tweeddale

Reading Calvin is a joy. But knowing where to start can be overwhelming. Every year, a steady stream of new articles, chapters, books, and dissertations on Calvin feeds into an existing ocean of popular and scholarly resources on the sixteenth-century Reformer. A simple way to appreciate the vast amount of available material is to skim the annual Calvin bibliography in the November edition of the *Calvin Theological Journal*. The past twenty years of bibliographies compiled by Paul Fields, among other pertinent resources, can be found on the H. Henry Meeter Center website, hosted by Calvin College and Calvin Theological Seminary. These bibliographies are invaluable for anyone wanting to know more about Calvin.

While research on Calvin is important, there is no substitute for reading Calvin himself. To modify C. S. Lewis's dictum in his essay on old books, it is easier to read Calvin than about Calvin. As Lewis contends, "First-hand knowledge is not only more worth acquiring than second-hand knowledge but is usually much easier and more delightful to acquire."[1] In the hopes of encouraging firsthand knowledge

---

1. C. S. Lewis, introduction to *St. Athanasius on the Incarnation*, trans. a religious of C.S.M.V. (London: A. R. Mowbray, 1953), 3.

of Calvin, at least in English translations of his works, here are several suggestions for getting started.

Calvin's Writings

The best place to begin is John Calvin, *A Little Book on the Christian Life*, translated by Aaron Clay Denlinger and Burk Parsons (Orlando, FL: Reformation Trust, 2017). Taken from book 3 of the final and definitive Latin edition of the *Institutes of the Christian Religion* (1559), this new translation of Calvin's *Golden Booklet* serves as an accessible entry point into his most well-known theological treatise. For those wanting to tackle the entire work, the two-volume *Institutes of the Christian Religion*, edited by John T. McNeill, translated by Ford Lewis Battles (Philadelphia: Westminster, 1960), is not perfect but remains the standard English translation of Calvin's "sum of piety." At a pace of four to five pages a day, someone could read the complete tome in one year.

Calvin's classic book went through a total of five editions throughout his lifetime (1536, 1539, 1543, 1550, 1559). For those interested in the development of Calvin's theology, the first edition of his work, *Institutes of the Christian Religion* (1536 ed.), translated and edited by Ford Lewis Battles (Grand Rapids, MI: Eerdmans, 1986), offers a fascinating glimpse into the early years of his ministry. Calvin, however, was much more than a man of one book. The *Institutes*, no matter what edition or translation you read, is best experienced in the context of his biblical and exegetical writings.

In the span of five straightforward expositions, totaling just under a hundred pages, Calvin's *Sermons on the Beatitudes*, translated by Robert White (Edinburgh: Banner of Truth, 2006), encapsulate the biblical clarity and pastoral warmth of his preaching. The short prayers at the end of his sermons are worth the price of the volume. A more substantial example of his preaching can be found in his densely packed but justly praised *Sermons on the Epistle to the Ephesians* (Edinburgh: Banner of Truth, 1973), which runs to forty-eight sermons. Reading his sermons underscores the basic point that Calvin was first and foremost a minister of the gospel, whose chief calling was to care for his congregation in Geneva.

Perhaps the easiest way to access Calvin is through his commentaries. His exegetical method is marked by "brevity and simplicity."[2] As a result, he tends to focus on the exposition of Scripture, without usually getting bogged down in other details. While modern editions exist, the nineteenth-century collection of Calvin's commentaries published by the Calvin Theological Society are available in several print, electronic, and online formats and are perfectly fine for dipping into his exegetical thoughts on most, if not all, biblical books. For those who prefer a more bite-size approach, *Heart Aflame: Daily Readings from Calvin on the Psalms* (Phillipsburg, NJ: P&R, 1999) provides page-long selections from Calvin's beloved *Commentary on the Psalms* for every day of the year.

Calvin's pastoral and theological writings illustrate the breadth of his ministry. A smattering of his works can be read in the useful but dated *Calvin: Theological Treatises*, translated by J. K. S. Reid (Philadelphia: Westminster, 1954). This work is especially valuable in gathering together a cross section of creedal and catechetical texts relating to Calvin's ecclesiology. For example, it includes Calvin's *Reply to Sadoleto* and *The Necessity of Reforming the Church*, both of which capture the thrust of his vision for the Reformation and can be easily read in a sitting or two. Still the best place to access his occasional writings is the handsomely reprinted seven-volume *Tracts and Letters of John Calvin*, edited by Henry Beveridge and Jules Bonnet, translated by Henry Beveridge, Jules Bonnet, David Constable, and Marcus Robert Gilchrist (Edinburgh: Banner of Truth, 2009), which brings together the nineteenth-century collections of his works by the Calvin Translation Society (vols. 1–3) and of his letters by the Presbyterian Board of Publication (vols. 4–7). These works can also be found in numerous places online. Calvin's letters in particular help reveal the man behind the theologian and are well worth the time and effort. For two superb examples of Calvin's polemical and doctrinal writings, with modern translations, see *The Bondage and Liberation of the Will: A Defence of the Orthodox Doctrine of Human Choice against Pighius,*

---

2. Richard C. Gamble, "*Brevitas et facilitas*: Toward an Understanding of Calvin's Hermeneutic," *WTJ* 47 (1985): 1–17; Gamble, "Exposition and Method in Calvin," *WTJ* 49 (1987): 153–65; cf. Richard A. Muller, *The Unaccommodated Calvin: Studies in the Foundation of a Theological Tradition*, OSHT (New York: Oxford University Press, 2000), 236n94.

edited by A. N. S. Lane, translated by G. I. Davies, Texts and Studies in Reformation and Post-Reformation Thought 2 (Grand Rapids, MI: Baker, 1996), and *The Secret Providence of God*, edited by Paul Helm, translated by Keith Goad (Wheaton, IL: Crossway, 2010).

As can be seen, Calvin was more than the author of the *Institutes*. He was a pastor, scholar, commentator, polemicist, correspondent, and reformer. So when you read him, read across his literary corpus. Study the *Institutes*, then cross-reference a passage in his commentaries, work through a sermon, track down his treatises, and don't forget his letters. While the works listed in this section are among the most popular of Calvin's writings available in English, there are many more, some translated and others still in Latin and French, to explore. For a near-comprehensive overview of Calvin's works, see the standard reference by Wulfert de Greef, *The Writings of John Calvin: An Introductory Guide*, translated by Lyle D. Bierma, expanded edition (Louisville: Westminster John Knox, 2008).

Calvin's Life and Theology

The best way to read any text is in context. Reading Calvin is no different. The books listed below should help readers better understand the various historical, political, and theological contexts that shaped Calvin's life and theology.

For biographies, Theodore Beza's *The Life of John Calvin*, found in volume 1 of *Tracts and Letters*, is an appreciative tribute to his mentor and a pleasure to read. T. H. L. Parker's *John Calvin: A Biography* (Philadelphia: Westminster, 1975) has aged fairly well and remains the best of the twentieth-century biographies. The most accessible account is W. Robert Godfrey's *John Calvin: Pilgrim and Pastor* (Wheaton, IL: Crossway, 2009); it is without question the best place to start. Next, Herman J. Selderhuis's *John Calvin: A Pilgrim's Life*, translated by Albert Gootjes (Downers Grove, IL: IVP Academic, 2009), offers a lucid and enjoyable narrative of Calvin the man that nicely features his correspondence and writings. Finally, Bruce Gordon's *Calvin* (New Haven, CT: Yale University Press, 2009) gives readers a better understanding not only of Calvin but also of the world he inhabited. It rightly holds pride of place as the definitive biography on Calvin.

For those wanting a study guide as they work through the *Institutes*, four books stand out for drawing the reader into the text. The value of these companions is that they are intended to be read alongside the *Institutes*. Ford Lewis Battles's thorough *Analysis of the "Institutes of the Christian Religion" of John Calvin* (1980; repr., Phillipsburg, NJ: P&R, 2001) provides the most detailed outline of the *Institutes* and is especially valuable for tracing Calvin's line of argument. Anthony N. S. Lane's *A Reader's Guide to Calvin's "Institutes"* (Grand Rapids, MI: Baker Academic, 2009) excels at highlighting the key points of Calvin's work in a concise format and is most useful as a quick reference. J. Mark Beach's *Piety's Wisdom: A Summary of Calvin's "Institutes" with Study Questions* (Grand Rapids, MI: Reformation Heritage Books, 2010) provides the best section-by-section summaries of the *Institutes*, as well as thoughtful questions that are ideal for group discussion. And David B. Calhoun's *Knowing God and Ourselves: Reading Calvin's "Institutes" Devotionally* (Edinburgh: Banner of Truth, 2016) is a carefully crafted devotional that uses the *Institutes* to open not only the rest of Calvin's writings but, more importantly, the text of Scripture.

Regarding Calvin's theology, older scholarship tended to read him through the lens of the *Institutes*. At the top of the list are François Wendel's *Calvin: Origins and Development of His Religious Thought*, translated by Philip Mairet (New York: Harper & Row, 1963), and T. H. L. Parker's *Calvin: An Introduction to His Thought* (Louisville: Westminster John Knox, 1995). More recently, David W. Hall and Peter A. Lillback have gathered an impressive list of Reformed pastors and theologians to provide *A Theological Guide to Calvin's "Institutes": Essays and Analysis*, Calvin 500 Series (Phillipsburg, NJ: P&R, 2008); this book is the best of the wide-ranging eight-part Calvin 500 Series edited by Hall. And Bruce Gordon has traced the history and reception of Calvin's masterpiece from its first publication to the present day in *John Calvin's "Institutes of the Christian Religion": A Biography*, Lives of Great Religious Books (Princeton, NJ: Princeton University Press, 2016).

Moving beyond the *Institutes*, Michael Horton's *Calvin on the Christian Life: Glorifying and Enjoying God Forever*, Theologians on the Christian Life (Wheaton, IL: Crossway, 2014), is an excellent and readable introduction to the Reformer that sets his understanding of piety within his overall theology. Herman J. Selderhuis's *Calvin's Theology of the Psalms*, Texts and Studies in Reformation and Post-Reformation Thought (Grand Rapids, MI: Baker Academic, 2007), concentrates on Calvin's *Commentary on the Psalms* to show how his doctrine of God informs his exegetical, doctrinal, and experiential formulations. For more advanced studies, Richard A. Muller challenges prevailing readings of Calvin by situating him in his intellectual contexts in *The Unaccommodated Calvin: Studies in the Foundation of a Theological Tradition*, Oxford Studies in Historical Theology (Oxford: Oxford University Press, 2000). Paul Helm analyzes the philosophical underpinnings of Calvin's theology in *John Calvin's Ideas* (Oxford: Oxford University Press, 2004) and *Calvin at the Centre* (Oxford: Oxford University Press, 2010). Jon Balserak probes Calvin's self-understanding as a prophet in *John Calvin as Sixteenth-Century Prophet* (Oxford: Oxford University Press, 2014). And Scott M. Manetsch uncovers the extraordinary network of pastors that Calvin helped organize in *Calvin's Company of Pastors: Pastoral Care and the Emerging Reformed Church, 1536–1609* (Oxford: Oxford University Press, 2013). While these works are geared toward academic audiences, they are worth the investment for those wanting to know more about Calvin than what was covered in this book.

If you are new to scholarly research on Calvin, perusing *The Cambridge Companion to John Calvin*, edited by Donald K. McKim (Cambridge: Cambridge University Press, 2004), *The Calvin Handbook*, edited by Herman J. Selderhuis (Grand Rapids, MI: Eerdmans, 2009), and the published proceedings of the Calvin Studies Society will quickly get you up to speed. Furthermore, the footnotes in the chapters of this volume should give you plenty of additional resources to investigate as you continue reading Calvin and his interpreters.

Contributors

Joel R. Beeke (PhD, Westminster Theological Seminary) is president and professor of systematic theology and homiletics at Puritan Reformed Theological Seminary. He is author of *Debated Issues in Sovereign Predestination: Early Lutheran Predestination, Calvinian Reprobation, and Variations in Genevan Lapsarianism* (Vandenhoeck & Ruprecht, 2017) and *Reformed Preaching* (Crossway, 2018).

David B. Calhoun (PhD, Princeton Theological Seminary) is professor emeritus of church history at Covenant Theological Seminary. He is author of the two-volume *Princeton Seminary* (Banner of Truth, 1994) and *Knowing God and Ourselves: Reading Calvin's "Institutes" Devotionally* (Banner of Truth, 2016).

Edward Donnelly (DD, Geneva College) is retired pastor of Trinity Reformed Presbyterian Church in Newtownabbey, Northern Ireland, and professor emeritus of New Testament at Reformed Theological College, Belfast, Northern Ireland. He is author of *Peter: Eyewitness of His Majesty* (Banner of Truth, 1998) and *Biblical Teaching on the Doctrines of Heaven and Hell* (Banner of Truth, 2001).

J. V. Fesko (PhD, University of Aberdeen) is professor of systematic and historical theology at Reformed Theological Seminary, Jackson. He is author of *Beyond Calvin: Union with Christ and Justification in Early Modern Reformed Theology (1517–1700)* (Vandenhoeck & Ruprecht, 2012) and *Theology of the Westminster Standards: Historical Context and Theological Insights* (Crossway, 2014).

W. Robert Godfrey (PhD, Stanford University) is chairman of Ligonier Ministries, a Ligonier Ministries teaching fellow, and president emeritus and professor emeritus of church history at Westminster Seminary California. He is author of *John Calvin: Pilgrim and Pastor* (Crossway, 2009) and *Learning to Love the Psalms* (Reformation Trust, 2017).

Michael A. G. Haykin (ThD, University of Toronto) is professor of church history and biblical spirituality at the Southern Baptist Theological Seminary and director of the Andrew Fuller Center for Baptist Studies. He is coauthor (with C. Jeffrey Robinson Sr.) of *To the Ends of the Earth: Calvin's Missional Vision and Legacy* (Crossway, 2014) and author of *The Missionary Fellowship of William Carey* (Reformation Trust, 2018).

Paul Helm (MA, Oxford University) was professor of the history and philosophy of religion at King's College, London, from 1993–2000. He is author of *Calvin: A Guide for the Perplexed* (T&T Clark, 2008) and *Calvin at the Centre* (Oxford University Press, 2010).

Douglas F. Kelly (PhD, University of Edinburgh) is professor emeritus of theology at Reformed Theological Seminary. He is translator of John Calvin's *Sermons on 2 Samuel: Chapters 1–13* (Banner of Truth, 1992) and author of a multivolume *Systematic Theology* (Christian Focus, 2014).

Steven J. Lawson (DMin, Reformed Theological Seminary) is founder and president of OnePassion Ministries and a Ligonier Ministries teaching fellow. He is author of *The Expository Genius of John Calvin* (Reformation Trust, 2007) and *John Knox: Fearless Faith* (Christian Focus, 2014).

Keith A. Mathison (PhD, Whitefield Theological Seminary) is professor of systematic theology at Reformation Bible College. He is author of *Given for You: Reclaiming Calvin's Doctrine of the Lord's Supper* (P&R, 2002) and *The Lord's Supper: Answers to Common Questions* (Orlando, FL: Reformation Trust, 2019).

Stephen J. Nichols (PhD, Westminster Theological Seminary) is president of Reformation Bible College, chief academic officer of Ligonier Ministries, and a Ligonier Ministries teaching fellow. He is author of *The Reformation: How a Monk and a Mallet Changed the World* (Crossway, 2007) and *Reformation ABCs: The People, Places, and Things of the Reformation—from A to Z* (Crossway, 2017).

K. Scott Oliphint (PhD, Westminster Theological Seminary) is dean of faculty and professor of apologetics and systematic theology at Westminster Theological Seminary. He is coeditor (with William Edgar) of the two-volume *Christian Apologetics Past and Present: A Primary Source Reader* (Crossway, 2009–2011) and author of *Covenantal Apologetics: Principles and Practice in Defense of Our Faith* (Crossway, 2013).

Burk Parsons (DMin, Reformed Theological Seminary) is senior pastor of Saint Andrew's Chapel in Sanford, Florida; a Ligonier Ministries teaching fellow; chief publishing officer for Ligonier Ministries; and editor of *Tabletalk* magazine. He is editor of *John Calvin: A Heart for Devotion, Doctrine, and Doxology* (Reformation Trust, 2008) and cotranslator and coeditor (with Aaron Clay Denlinger) of John Calvin, *A Little Book on the Christian Life* (Reformation Trust, 2017).

Robert A. Peterson (PhD, Drew University) is a writer and theologian. He taught for many years at various theological seminaries. He is author of *Calvin and the Atonement* (Mentor, 2009) and *Salvation Applied by the Spirit: Union with Christ* (Crossway, 2015).

R. C. Sproul (Drs, Free University of Amsterdam) was founder of Ligonier Ministries. He was also founding pastor of Saint Andrews Chapel in Sanford, Florida; first president of Reformation Bible College; and executive editor of *Tabletalk* magazine. He coedited (with Stephen J. Nichols) *The Legacy of Luther* (Reformation Trust, 2016) and authored *The Consequences of Ideas: Understanding the Concepts That Shaped Our World* (Crossway, 2018).

Derek W. H. Thomas (PhD, University of Wales) is senior minister of First Presbyterian Church in Columbia, South Carolina; Chancellor's

Professor of Systematic and Pastoral Theology at Reformed Theological Seminary; and a Ligonier Ministries teaching fellow. He is author of *Calvin's Teaching on Job: Proclaiming the Incomprehensible God* (Mentor, 2004) and *Strength for the Weary* (Reformation Trust, 2018).

John W. Tweeddale (PhD, University of Edinburgh) is academic dean and professor of theology at Reformation Bible College. He served as an assistant editor of the *Reformation Study Bible* (Reformation Trust, 2015) and is author of *John Owen and Hebrews: The Foundation of Biblical Interpretation* (T&T Clark, 2019).

Cornelis P. Venema (PhD, Princeton Theological Seminary) is president and professor of doctrinal studies at Mid-America Reformed Seminary. He is author of *Accepted and Renewed in Christ: The "Twofold Grace of God" and the Interpretation of Calvin's Theology* (Vandenhoeck & Ruprecht, 2007) and *Christ and Covenant Theology: Essays on Election, Republication, and the Covenants* (P&R, 2017).

Guy Prentiss Waters (PhD, Duke University) is James M. Baird Jr. Professor of New Testament at Reformed Theological Seminary in Jackson, Mississippi. He is author of *Justification and the New Perspectives on Paul* (P&R, 2004) and *The Life and Theology of Paul* (Reformation Trust, 2017).

Paul Wells (ThD, Free University of Amsterdam) is professor emeritus of systematic theology at the Faculté Jean Calvin, Aix-en-Provence, France, and editor in chief of *Unio cum Christo*. He is cotranslator (with Marie de Védrines) of Calvin's *Institutes* in modern French, *Institution de la religion chrétienne* (Excelsis/Kerygma, 2009), and author of *Taking the Bible at Its Word* (Christian Focus, 2013).

General Index

abortion, 113
Abraham, obedience of, 408
Abrahamic covenant, 333
Academy of Geneva, 116, 577
accommodation, 237–38, 239, 240
  and ecclesiology, 474–75, 487
Adam
  and the law, 311–15
  sin of, 312–13
ad fontes, 29, 180
adoption, 390
adultery, 111–12
adversity, knowing God through, 447–48
afflictions, 276, 408, 433–35, 445
Alciati, Andrea, 27
"alien" righteousness of Christ, 463
allegorical interpretation, 182, 430
almsgiving, and the Lord's Supper, 67
"already" and "not yet," 103, 557
Ambrose, 253, 429
Ameaux, Benoyte (or Benoite Amyaulx),
  114–15
Anabaptists, 87, 308, 378n45, 566n42
  on the Holy Spirit, 380
  on infant baptism, 491
  rebuked in Calvin's sermons, 192
  on soul sleep, 21
analogy of faith, 183
Andrewes, Lancelot, 421
angels, 346
anger management, 117–18
Angoulême, 36
Anselm, 354, 449
antichrist, 538, 564–65
antinomianism, 220n67, 333
Antiochus IV Epiphanes, 563
anxiety, 542
Apostles' Creed, 111, 112, 121–22, 203,
  205, 215n46, 229n13, 478–82, 556

application, in Calvin's sermons, 169–70,
  190–93
application of redemption, 389–92
Arianism, 47
Aristotle, 245n56, 257, 575
art and artists, 269–70
"Articles concerning the Organization
  of the Church and of Worship at
  Geneva," 48–49
asceticism, 402, 404, 414, 553
assurance, 389–92, 517–18, 543–44
astronomy, 261
atonement, 354–55, 356
Augsburg Confession (1530), 494, 495
Augsburg Interim, 136
Augustine, 91, 150, 216, 331, 352, 380,
  429, 575
  on the church, 476–77, 480
  on election, 577
  on grace, 451
  influence on Calvin, 176
  on perseverance, 521
  on predestination, 449, 465
  on sacraments as visible words, 504
  on sign and thing signified, 494
  on will of God, 459

Babylonian Captivity of the Church (Luther),
  190
Balserak, Jon, 584
baptism, 505–10
  as confession before men, 508
  instrumental nature of, 507
  and purification of sins, 505–6
  as visible word, 505, 508
Barth, Karl, 200, 213, 218n56, 236n31,
  243n51, 309, 353n66, 377, 464
Basel, 37–38, 43, 52–53, 204, 209

Scripture Index

Biblical references in a note that mark merely a location in one of Calvin's commentaries have been omitted from the Scripture index.